ART DECO 1910–1939

Exhibition
Catalogue

ART DECO 1910–1939

Edited by Charlotte Benton, Tim Benton and Ghislaine Wood

V&A Publications

First published by V&A Publications, 2003

V&A Publications
160 Brompton Road
London SW3 1HW

Designed by Janet James

V&A photography by Christine Smith, Mike Kitcatt
and Richard Davis, V&A Photographic Studio

ISBN 1 85177 387 8

A catalogue record for this book is available from
the British Library

Printed and bound in Italy by LEGO SpA

FRONT AND BACK JACKET ILLUSTRATIONS:
Gordon Miller Buehrig, Auburn 851 'Boat Tail' Speedster.
American, 1935. Private collection.

FRONTISPIECE:
Paul Colin, *Josephine Baker*. Plate from Paul Colin, *Le
tumulte noir*, Paris, 1927. Colour pochoir. NAL. ©ADAGP,
Paris and DACS, London 2002.

PART 1 OPENER:
Detail of Edgar Brandt, *Oasis*, screen. See plate 33.1.

PART 2 OPENER:
Lacquer samples. Lacquer on wood. Japanese, c.1850-75.
Acquired from Siegfried Bing in 1875. V&A: 1100-1875.

PART 3 OPENER:
Detail from Jean Dupas, *Les Perruches*. See plate 12.14.

PART 4 OPENER:
Detail of Maurice Marinot, vase. See plate 18.3.

PART 5 OPENER:
Detail of Egmont Arens and Theodore C. Brookhart,
'Streamliner' meat slicer. See plate 34.4.

V&A Publications
160 Brompton Road
London SW3 1HW
www.vam.ac.uk

Contents

Sponsor's Foreword

Ernst & Young is delighted to sponsor *Art Deco 1910-1939*.

This is the eighth major sponsorship that Ernst & Young has been associated with since we began our arts sponsorship programme in 1994. It is our first at the V&A, and its prized reputation as the greatest museum of applied and decorative arts in the world makes it a highly suitable partner for us. The diversity of its collections and its role as an educator and inspirer is unsurpassed and we are proud to work with it on such an outstanding exhibition as *Art Deco*.

Art Deco was a style for the bold, the innovative and for the entrepreneurs of the changing world. As one of the world's largest business advisors, we pursue the same principles of vision and innovation for our clients. Like Art Deco, we aim to be a progressive force in the modern world.

We also welcome this opportunity to make a contribution to cultural life.

We hope you enjoy this book and that it provides a beautiful reminder of this groundbreaking exhibition.

Nick Land

Chairman, Ernst & Young

⧓ ERNST & YOUNG

List of Contributors

Paul Atterbury is a specialist in nineteenth- and twentieth-century art and design with an interest in the history of technology. He was curator of *The Victorian Vision: Inventing New Britain* (2001) and contributor to the accompanying book. He is also the author of *Victorians at Home and Abroad* (2001).

Jeremy Aynsley is Head of the School of Humanities at the Royal College of Art, where he teaches on the V&A/RCA History of Design programme. Recent publications include *Graphic Design in Germany, 1890-1945* (2000) and *A Century of Graphic Design* (2001). His current research concerns magazines and interior design in Europe and America, 1890-1930.

Oriana Baddeley is Research and Postgraduate Programme Director, Camberwell College of Arts, the London Institute. Her doctoral subject formed the basis for her contribution to the 1992 Hayward Gallery exhibition and catalogue *The Art of Ancient Mexico* (1992), and she has written extensively on contemporary Latin American art.

Charlotte Benton is an independent architecture and design historian. She was a founding editor of the *Journal of Design History*. Her main research interests are in French design of c.1918-55 and the work of architects and designers who fled Nazism. Her publications include *A Different World? Emigré Architects in Britain, 1928-1958* (1995). She is the editor of *Figuration/Abstraction: Public Sculpture in Europe, 1945-68* (2003).

Tim Benton is Professor of Art History at the Open University. He has co-curated a number of exhibitions, including *Thirties: British Art and Design before the War* (1979), *Le Corbusier, Architect of the Century* (1987) and *Art and Power* (1996). Recent publications include 'Humanism and Fascism', in *Comparative Criticism* (2001) and 'La Maison de week-end dans le paysage parisien', in *Le Corbusier et Paris* (2001).

Rafael Cardoso is a writer and Assistant Professor in the Department of Art and Design at the Pontificia Universidade Católica in Rio de Janeiro, Brazil. He is co-editor of *Art and the Academy in the Nineteenth Century* (2000) and author of *Uma introdução à história do design* (2000).

David Crowley is a historian working at the Royal College of Art, London. His specialist interest is in the cultural history of Central Europe in the nineteenth and twentieth centuries. He is the author of *Nationalism and Nation State: Design in Poland from the Vernacular Revival to the International Style* (1992) and is currently writing a book on the history of Warsaw.

Penelope Curtis is the Curator of the Henry Moore Institute in Leeds, where she directs a programme interrogating historic and contemporary definitions of sculpture. She is the author of *Sculpture, 1900-1945* (1999), has written on twentieth-century British and European sculptors and monuments, and has curated a range of exhibitions, often in collaboration with contemporary artists.

Christopher Frayling is Rector of the Royal College of Art, Chairman of the Design Council, the longest-serving Trustee of the V&A, and an award-winning broadcaster on radio and television. He has written thirteen books on design, film and popular culture, including *The Face of Tutankhamun* (1992).

Tag Gronberg is Head of the School of History of Art, Film and Visual Media at Birkbeck College, London University. She is the author of *Designs on Modernity: Exhibiting the City in 1920s Paris* (1998) and has published extensively on 1920s French art, architecture and design. She has contributed to *Art History*, *The Journal of Design History* and *The Oxford Art Journal*. Her next book is on late nineteenth- and early twentieth-century Viennese art and visual culture.

Jennifer Hawkins Opie is Chief Curator of Ceramics and Glass at the V&A Museum. She specializes in ceramics and glass of the nineteenth and twentieth centuries and the present day. She has been responsible for many exhibitions, including *Scandinavia: Ceramics & Glass in the Twentieth*

Century (1989). She also contributed the section on Helsinki and Finnish Jugend to the exhibition book *Art Nouveau 1890-1914* (2000).

Mark Haworth-Booth joined the V&A in 1970 and in 1977 was appointed Curator of Photographs in the Prints, Drawings and Paintings Collection. He has curated many exhibitions and his numerous publications include *E. McKnight Kauffer: A Designer and his Public* (1979).

Juliette Hibou is Assistant Curator of *Art Deco 1910-1939*. Her area of research is French furniture. She contributed to the forthcoming catalogue of the V&A's French furniture collection and is a member of the V&A Research Department. She is also London correspondent for the art magazine *L'Estampille-L'Objet d'art*.

Anna Jackson is a Curator in the V&A's Asian Department. Her research interests include the cultural relationship between East Asia and the West in the nineteenth and early twentieth centuries. She has contributed essays to *Art Nouveau 1890-1914* (2000) and *The Victorian Vision: Inventing New Britain* (2001). She is also responsible for the Museum's collection of Japanese textiles. Her other publications include *Japanese Country Textiles* (1997) and *Japanese Textiles in the Victoria and Albert Museum* (2000). She is also the author of *The V&A Guide to Period Styles: 400 Years of British Art and Design* (2002).

Amin Jaffer is a Curator in the V&A's Asian Department. He is an expert on furniture and interiors in colonial India and is a regular lecturer and contributor to periodicals on this subject. He is the author of *Furniture from British India and Ceylon* (2001) and *Luxury Goods from India: The Art of the Indian Cabinet-Maker* (2002).

Wendy Kaplan is Department Head and Curator of Decorative Arts at the Los Angeles County Museum of Art. She is author, co-author or editor of many books on nineteenth- and twentieth-century design, including *'The Art that is Life': The Arts and Crafts*

Movement in America (1987); *The Arts and Crafts Movement* (1991); *Designing Modernity: The Arts of Reform and Persuasion* (1995); *Charles Rennie Mackintosh* (1996); *Leading 'The Simple Life': The Arts and Crafts Movement in Britain* (1999).

Stéphane Laurent is Assistant Professor at the Université de Paris I Panthéon-Sorbonne, where he is responsible for the History of Design and the Decorative Arts. He is the author of several works in this area, including *L'Art utile: Les écoles d'arts appliqués sous le Second-Empire et la Troisième République* (1998); *L'Ecole Boulle* (1998); *Chronologie du design* (1999); *Bernard Buffet, le peintre crucifié* (2000). He contributes to several art magazines and is currently editing a publication on the Ecole Nationale Supérieure des Arts Décoratifs, founded in Paris in 1765.

Reino Liefkes is Senior Curator of Ceramics and Glass at the V&A Museum. Born and educated in the Netherlands, he specializes in European glass from the Renaissance to the present day. He was a driving force behind the V&A Glass Gallery and his publications include *Glass* (1997). He also contributed to *Murano '900: vetri e vetrai* (1996) and *Elegant Eating: Four Hundred Years of Dining in Style* (2002).

Nicolas P. Maffei completed his PhD, 'Designing the Image of the Practical Visionary: Norman Bel Geddes, 1893-1958' at the Royal College of Art in 2001. He is currently Senior Lecturer in Critical Studies at the Norwich School of Art and Design. He has lectured widely on the history of design and his publications include the special issue of the *Journal of Design History* on 'Technology and the Body' (Winter 2001).

Arthur Marwick set up the History Department at the newly-founded Open University in 1969 and, in 1993, the Sixties Research Group, of which he remains Co-Director despite his retirement in 2001. His books include *Beauty in History: Society, Politics and Personal Appearance since 1500* (1988), *The New Nature of History: Knowledge, Evidence, Language* (2001) and *The Arts in the West since 1945* (2002).

Jeffrey L. Meikle is Professor of American Studies and Art History at the University of Texas at Austin. He has published *Twentieth Century Limited: Industrial Design in America, 1925-1939* (1979) and *American Plastic: A Cultural History* (1995), which received the Dexter Prize from the Society for the History of Technology.

Valerie Mendes is a fashion historian. She began her career at Manchester University's Whitworth Art Gallery. She was head of the V&A's Textiles and Dress Department from 1990 to 2001 and is now an honorary V&A Research Fellow. She has curated numerous exhibitions and published widely on fashion and textiles. Her books include *The Victoria and Albert Museum's Textile Collection: British Textiles from 1900 to 1937* (1992); *Modern Fashion in Detail* (with Claire Wilcox, 1998); *Black in Fashion* (1999).

Christopher Menz is Senior Curator, Decorative Arts (International) at the National Gallery of Victoria, Melbourne. He worked at the National Gallery of Australia, Canberra (1985-9) and was Curator of European and Australian Decorative Arts at the Art Gallery of South Australia, Adelaide (1989-2001). His major exhibitions include *Morris & Company* (1994), *Regency* (1998) and the Australian component of *Australia + Germany: International Craft Triennale* (2000). He is the author of *Australian Decorative Arts, 1820s–1990s* (1996).

Gillian Naylor is former Professor in the History of Design at the Royal College of Art. She has published books on the Arts and Crafts movement, Hector Guimard, the Bauhaus and William Morris, as well as many articles on nineteenth- and twentieth-century design. Her publications include: *The Arts and Crafts Movement: A Study of its Sources, Ideals and Influence on Design Theory* (1971, 1990); *The Bauhaus Reassessed: Sources and Design Theory* (1985); *William Morris by Himself: Designs and Writings* (1988).

Clare Phillips is a Curator in the V&A's Metalwork, Silver and Jewellery Department. She has a particular interest in twentieth-century and contemporary jewellery. Her publications include *Jewelry: From Antiquity to the Present* (1996) and *Jewels and Jewellery* (2000). She was also a contributor to the V&A's major exhibition and book *Art Nouveau 1890-1914* (2000).

Annemarie Riding is Assistant Curator in the National Art Library at the V&A. In 1994 she helped mount an exhibition of contemporary designer bookbinders, *Cover Story: A New Look at Bookbinding*, held at the Crawford Arts Centre, St Andrews.

Rowan Watson is Head of Collection Development in the National Art Library at the V&A. He teaches on the MA course in the History of the Book at the Institute of English Studies, School of Advanced Study, University of London. Among his recent publications is 'Bing, Art Nouveau and the Book in the Late Nineteenth Century', *Apollo* (May 2000).

Ghislaine Wood is Curator of *Art Deco 1910-1939* and co-curated the major exhibition *Art Nouveau 1890–1914* held at the V&A in 2000. She contributed to the accompanying book and is author of *Art Nouveau and the Erotic* (2000) and *Essential Art Deco* (2003). She is a member of the V&A's Research Department.

Jonathan M. Woodham is Professor of Design History at the University of Brighton, where he is also Director of the Design History Research Centre. He has written many articles and books on various aspects of design history, including *Twentieth Century Design* (1997). He is a member of several journal editorial boards including those of the *Journal of Design History* and *Design Issues*.

Acknowledgements

Three years in the making, the *Art Deco* exhibition and publication could not have happened without the support of a vast number of people.

Ernst & Young have made the exhibition possible through their generous support and we would especially like to thank them for their involvement.

There are very few museums world-wide that could undertake a project on this scale and the success of *Art Deco* is testament to the breath and depth of expertise in all departments of the V&A. We are grateful to all our colleagues within the Museum. There are several people who deserve special mention. Juliette Hibou, the Assistant Curator and Tina Manoli, the Exhibition Co-ordinator, have worked tirelessly to make the book and exhibition what they are and we are deeply indebted to them for their dedication. Special thanks to the contributors to book, many of whom advised on the selection of works for the exhibition. They are named overleaf. Anna Jackson, Amin Jaffer, Jennifer Opie and Reino Liefkes have given invaluable advice and been a tremendous support throughout the project.

Many international scholars, curators, private collectors and advisors have generously given their time and helped with research. We are extremely grateful for the assistance of Stephane-Jacques Addade, Victor and Greta Arwas, John P. Axelrod, Jeff Bacon, Sylvia Barisione, Stella Beddoe, Oliver Bernard, Ken Bolan, Andrew Bolton, Jean-Marcel Camard, Andrew Crisford, William Crouse, Lydia Cresswell Jones, Benoist Drut, Sharada Dwivedi, Ralph Esmerian, Marion Faisal, Jeannine Falino, Matteo Fochessati, Gianni Franzone, Adriana Friedman, Audrey Friedman, Barry Friedman, Sonja Ganne, Dr Gerhath, Irena Goldschneider, Edgar Harden, Jana Hornekova, Graham Hutt, John Jesse, Ian Jenkins, HH The Maharaja of Jodhpur, Stewart Johnson, Tess Johnston, Conor Jordan, Shibata Jun'ichi, Mori Junko, Saitō Keisuke, Peter Kaellgren, Dr Kelly, Arto Keshinian, Marianne Lamonaca, Daphne Lingdon, Nancy McClelland, Mark Macdonald, Takanami Machiko, Duncan McLaren, Tsuchida Maki, Claire Marc, Félix Marchilac, Tim Martin, Okabe Masayuki, David Mirvish, Steen Nottelmann, Eric Nussbaum, Alexander Payne, Charles Pineless, Penny Proddow, Lars Rachen, Michael and Steven Rich, John Robbins, Xavier Roberts, Joel Rosenkrantz, Jeffrey Salmon, Li Kong San, Gad Sassower, Edouard Sébline, Deborah Shinn, Nigel Strudwick, Vivienne Tam, Zhou Zhi Tsong, Jacques de Vos, John Waddell, Gerard Widdershoven, Mitchell J. Wolfson, James Zemaitis.

We are indebted to the private lenders to the exhibition (some have been mentioned and many wish to remain anonymous), and to the many curators and specialists from lending institutions who also kindly gave of their time and knowledge.

For the book, special thanks to the V&A Publications team Mary Butler, Ariane Bankes, Monica Woods, Nina Jacobson, Geoff Barlow, Clare Davis, Claire Sawford and Victoria Standing; to Lucy Trench for her meticulous editing, to Janet James for the beautiful book design and to Robin Lambert for translation.

The book would be a shadow of itself without the consistently high standards of the V&A Photographic Studio, thanks to Christine Smith, Mike Kitcatt, and Richard Davis.

Numerous volunteers and interns have worked on the book, providing assistance with research and bibliographies. We would particularly like to thank Roxanne Peters, Leslie Freudenheim, Geraldine James, Sarah Gaskin and Rachel Woods.

Albert Neher has shouldered an enormous responsibility for the management of conservation, including the ambitious restoration of the Foyer of the Strand Palace Hotel and the determination of the V&A Technical Services department has seen these projects through. From Exhibitions, Press, Marketing, Design, Development and Research thanks to Linda Lloyd Jones, Jane Drew, Julie Taylor, Anna Fletcher, Debra Isaac, Patricia O'Connor, Gareth Harris, Jane Rosier, Moira Gemmill, Alice Cooper, Will Bryant, Carolyn Sargentson, Jane Pavitt, Malcolm Baker and Karen Livingstone. All have had tremendous faith. We are also grateful to Casson Mann and GTF for their inspired exhibition design and graphics.

Finally, special thanks to Paul Greenhalgh whose initial idea it was to do the show and who has been a constant source of encouragement.

Charlotte Benton
Tim Benton
Ghislaine Wood

PART **1**

Introduction

1 The Style and the Age

Charlotte Benton and Tim Benton

Art Deco is the name given to the 'modern', but not Modernist, twentieth-century style that came to worldwide prominence in the inter-war years and left its mark on nearly every visual medium, from fine art, architecture and interior design, to fashion and textiles, film and photography (plate 1.1).[1]

The period was one of dramatic technological change, social upheaval and political and economic crises, of bewildering contrasts and apocalyptic visions.[2] From the 'Roaring Twenties' to the Depression, the inexorable spread of capitalism was mirrored by that of Fascist and Communist totalitarian regimes, while remorseless globalization was accompanied by isolationist nationalism. At the same time, the spread of mass-produced consumer goods, accompanied by the perfection of promotional methods to generate demand, prioritized visual appeal in the seduction of the would-be consumer. From the nouveau riche 'flapper' decorating her Parisian apartment to the struggling farmer in the American Midwest leafing through mail order catalogues for new equipment, hope lay in novelty. Never was fantasy so functionally necessary for survival, whether to industry or the individual.

Part of the fascination of the style lies precisely in its confrontation of new values with old, and in the hint of fragility and tragedy that often lurks behind its glitter – themes evocatively portrayed in F. Scott Fitzgerald's novel, *The Great Gatsby* (1925).[3] And, as revolutions in transportation and communication opened up the world, not only to the wealthy traveller but also to the reader of popular magazines or the cinema-goer in Bombay or Budapest, Manhattan or Morecambe, Shanghai or Singapore, the forms of this dream coalesced in Art Deco.

John and Ruth Vassos trenchantly identified both the dream's fundamental frivolity and the ruthless commercial interests that fed it:

> Feed the eye, stimulate the imagination, tickle the appetite of the mob with pictures of pretty girls. With pictures of legs … Weeklies, monthlies, dailies; newspapers, news reels; from the pulpit, from the press, from the editorial pages, from the radio; don't

leave a surface untouched … impress the client – million dollar budgets, human interest, sales pressure, psychology of the consumer, consumer demand. An edifice reaching to the skies, and built on BUNK.[4]

At the same time, their own publications and designs – like those of other Deco designers – contributed to the fragile 'edifice' whose foundations were laid by the powerful confluence of commerce and desire (plate 1.2). It was symptomatic of this context that Art Deco taste was communicated as much by transitory effects – in the 'wave of brilliant colour' of the new shop window displays, or in fashion and advertising – as by more durable means. The phenomenon was well expressed by the American critic Edwin Avery Park writing in 1927, 'The new spirit in design is creeping in about the edges. It fastens first upon objects of a transitory and frivolous nature.'[5]

1.1 Tamara de Lempicka (born in Poland), *Jeune fille en vert*. Oil on panel. Around 1927. Centre Georges Pompidou, Paris. MNAM. © Photo: CNAC/MNAM – Dist. RMN. © ADAGP, Paris and DACS, London.

1.2 John Vassos, *The Department Store*. Illustration from Ruth Vassos, *Contempo*, New York, 1929. NAL.

1.3 Paul Manship, *The Flight of Europa*. Bronze. American, 1925. Collection Lionel and Geraldine Sterling. Photo courtesy of Conner · Rosenkranz, New York.

1.4 Jacques-Emile Ruhlmann, corner cabinet. Lacquered rosewood, ivory and rare woods. French, 1916. Gift of Sydney and Frances Lewis. Virginia Museum of Fine Arts, Richmond. Photo: Katherine Wetzel. © ADAGP, Paris and DACS, London 2002.

Given that contemporaries themselves associated 'the new spirit in design' with the fleeting, the frivolous and the nakedly commercial, it is perhaps not surprising that some later commentators have doubted whether Art Deco was a style at all: 'The critical re-evaluation of which Art Deco today is the object cannot deny that it consists more of a taste than a style, and this is also responsible for the slippery way it resists theoretical categorization.'[6] On the other hand, Art Deco's first chronicler, Bevis Hillier, confidently asserted, 'With justice … we can describe it as the last of the total styles.'[7] Yet despite – and perhaps even because of – this lack of consensus a vast literature has grown up around the far from transitory legacy of this 'new spirit'.[8] Furthermore, the term 'Art Deco' not only has currency among specialists and enthusiasts but, unusually for a style label, it has resonance for a

large lay public. Many people correctly associate the label with the inter-war years and can name examples of Deco designers such as René Lalique or Clarice Cliff.

Not only does the style label exist and have meaning(s), but also it has been attached, cumulatively, to a large and heterogeneous body of artefacts whose sole common denominator seems to lie in their contradictory characteristics. They include works inspired by, but not copied from, historic western high styles or vernacular traditions, *and* those inspired by 'exotic', non-western traditions; works inspired by cultures of the far distant past *and* those inspired by contemporary avant-garde art (plate 1.3); works that are meticulously handcrafted, made of rare and luxurious materials, intended for an elite, *and* mass-produced designs, made in new, low-cost materials, aimed at the popular market (plates 1.4 and 1.5); works that embrace naturalistic, geometric or abstract surface decoration, *and* those that have no surface decoration but whose forms are

1.5 René Lalique, box and cover. Bakelite. French, c.1935. V&A: C.15-1981. © ADAGP, Paris and DACS, London 2002.

1.6 Walter Gilbert, frieze panel. Cast and painted aluminium. Made by the Bromsgrove Guild, for the Derry & Toms building, London. British, 1933. V&A: M.262-1984.

themselves decorative (plates 1.6 and 1.7). And so on. Not for nothing did Martin Greif observe, 'I suspect that the term "Art Deco" should really be "Art Decos" (accent on the plural) and that the term embraces at least ten to fifteen mutually exclusive "styles", each of which (if we take the trouble to observe them carefully) can be separated from the others.'[9] And little wonder that some have drawn the conclusion that Art Deco has neither stylistic nor methodological coherence. As Greif put it: 'We have allowed the term to embrace virtually everything that was produced between the two world wars, from the finest French furniture of Pierre Legrain to the tubes of Tangee lipstick purchased at the local five and dime … surely there's a world of difference.'[10]

For others, however, Art Deco's very eclecticism has been part of its compelling charm and attraction: 'Art deco was not … really a "style" in the traditional sense, but a curiously wonderful mixture of several contemporary styles with traditional and popular undercurrents. It is art deco's unusual position – somewhere between the high styles of the avant-garde and a fully-fledged conservative attitude – that makes it fascinating.'[11] And some have seen the 'curiously wonderful mixture' embraced by the term 'Art Deco' as an invigorating challenge:

> …the term has caught on. It has a certain 'snap' and an energy that is compelling. A … critical issue is not to define [it] so closely that we close the door on our own interest, but to recognise that we are really interested in studying all forms from the inter-war years – high art and popular … If we can use the term Art Deco not to designate a specific style, but rather that it is inclusive and connotes the tremendous fertility of ideas, culture and design beginning in the early twentieth century and reaching a peak in the 1920s and 1930s, we will better serve our own purpose.[12]

The philosopher Ludwig Wittgenstein offers a useful analogy for unravelling Art Deco in his concept of a 'family of resemblances' to explain the word 'games'.[13] Wittgenstein understood the meaning of words as 'a complicated network of similarities, overlapping and criss-crossing'.[14] He pointed out that the word 'game' covers a range of usages that include contradictions (some games have rules, some don't, some involve winning and losing, some don't) and that the very range of these meanings makes the word richer and more useful. Similarly, we might argue that the words 'Art Deco' are richer and more interesting for embracing apparently irreconcilable works, such as an exquisite, hand-crafted cabinet by Jacques-Emile Ruhlmann and an industrially moulded Bakelite radio (see plate 10.3).[15] Visitors to the first major international manifestation of Art Deco, the *Exposition internationale des arts décoratifs et industriels modernes* held in Paris in 1925 (hereafter referred to as the Paris 1925 Exhibition), would have understood precisely what Wittgenstein was getting at. To present-day eyes, the polarities and dissonances that have troubled many later commentators were readily visible in the exhibition displays (see plates 6.15, 12.5, 15.14 and 16.9). Yet contemporaries were struck by their similarities and sense of unity: 'All the works of art collected here show a family resemblance which cannot fail to be noticed by even the least prepared [visitors].'[16]

Using such perceptions as clues, we can try to identify some of the features that link the apparently antithetical works ascribed to Art Deco. They often refer to historic styles, whether western or non-western, but are not literally dependent on them, though they are often respectful of them. They are often influenced by avant-garde art and design yet, unlike these, they make no claim to being disinterested and are, in fact, thoroughly contingent and engaged with the commercial world. But whether inspired by traditional or by avant-garde sources, they have a tendency to simplified form and an absence of three-dimensional, applied ornament. They are 'decorative' even when they do not employ ornament; and they frequently stress 'surface' zvalues or effects. They are often novel or innovative – but not radical or revolutionary. They frequently employ new technologies, even when their forms and methods also reference tradition. They often refer, overtly or symbolically, to 'modern' themes, such as youth, liberated sexuality and aspects of contemporary mechanical culture, through a recurrent visual repertoire of frozen fountains, sunbursts and zigzags, and references to electrification, mechanization and transportation. Although it is clear that a strict formalist template is inadequate to interpret the phenomenon, Art Deco artefacts can be seen to employ common elements in their visual language, as well as common themes.

Like most styles, Art Deco was named long after its demise. Although the architect Le Corbusier employed the headline '1925 Expo: Arts Déco' for a series of articles on the decorative arts published in 1925 in his journal *L'Esprit nouveau*, his use of the diminutive for 'decorative arts' was intended to mock their practice, not to identify a style.[17] The first use of the phrase 'Art Déco' as a style label occurred in France in 1966, in an exhibition titled *Les années '25': Art Déco/Bauhaus/Stijl/Esprit Nouveau* and its accompanying catalogue. Here the term was used to distinguish French decorative arts of the 1910s and 1920s from those contemporary strands of Modernist design represented by the Bauhaus, De Stijl and the group around *L'Esprit nouveau*.[18] Reviews of the exhibition gave the phrase some currency outside France, but it was not until two

1.7 Jean Puiforcat, clock. Nickel-plated bronze and white marble. French, 1932. Primavera Gallery, New York.

years later that the words 'Art Deco' were explicitly used to identify a style, when Bevis Hillier published his book *Art Deco of the 20s and 30s*.[19] Hillier gave cogent reasons for selecting the label and defined Art Deco as:

> an assertively modern style, developing in the 1920s and reaching its high point in the 1930s ... a classical style in that, like neo-classicism but unlike Rococo or Art Nouveau, it ran to symmetry rather than asymmetry, and to the rectilinear rather than the curvilinear; it responded to the demands of the machine and of new materials ... [and] the requirements of mass production.[20]

Three years later, he refined this definition, identifying two main strands:

> the feminine, somewhat conservative style of 1925, chic, elegant, depending on exquisite craftsmanship and harking back to the eighteenth century; and the masculine reaction of the thirties, with its machine-age symbolism and use of new materials like chrome and plastics in place of the old beaux-arts materials such as ebony and ivory...[21]

Between them, the 1966 exhibition and Hillier's texts established the key – if contradictory – characteristics, as well as the chronological parameters (c.1910-39), of Art Deco.

Early authors followed Hillier in identifying the style with a trend in the French decorative arts that was expressed most clearly at the Paris 1925 Exhibition. Some of these, including Martin Battersby, insisted that the term Art Deco properly applied only to the historicizing variant of this trend – or 'modernized traditional', as we have called it elsewhere in this book – which was largely eclipsed after 1925 by the spread of the non-historicist variant – or 'decorative Modernism', as we have sometimes called it here.[22] But, whereas the identification of Art Deco with French luxury production of the 1910s and 1920s has been sustained by several French writers,[23] most

1.8 Ocean Drive, Miami Beach.

Photo: Tim Benton.

later authors, especially Americans, acknowledge the significance of this work to the evolution of the style, but follow Hillier in attaching the term to a much wider range of productions. Typically, they include both luxury and popular goods, from the whole inter-war period, and from countries other than France. These critics see the style as following a trajectory from 'rich Parisian beginnings – pure, high-style Art Déco – to … jazzy, Streamline Moderne American offshoots'.[24]

Architecture is often central to this more inclusive view of Art Deco, which was given a boost by the conservation movement that emerged in America in the 1970s and focused on the rehabilitation of popular buildings of the 1920s and 1930s. Cinemas, theatres, skyscrapers and many public works buildings of this era, which had been all but ignored in the three decades following the Second World War, were now seen to embody core American values.[25] The numerous Art Deco societies that sprang up in major American cities at this time became powerhouses for the promotion of the style in the United States.[26] And, as popular publications and exhibitions raised public awareness of Art Deco, the label came to be applied to an increasingly vast cultural terrain, both in America and elsewhere.[27] It was used to designate anything with a 'period' feel that looked 'modern',[28] to appeal to a nostalgia for the frivolity and stylishness of the era, and to be associated with the lifestyle values of fashionable figures of the period, such as Josephine Baker, Cecil Beaton and Noël Coward.

Before going further, we must ask how and why 'Art Deco' as a style label came to be invented in the mid- to late 1960s. Hillier was writing soon after an interest in the decorative arts of the inter-war period had begun to gain currency among private collectors, dealers, museum curators, graphic designers and television and film directors. By this time, the Art Nouveau revival had consumed itself and was, anyway, *vieux jeu* to the increasingly style conscious youth of the day. Fashion pundits began to predict that the next trend would be based on the Twenties

and Thirties, and new galleries sprang up, or existing ones were converted, to cater to, and stimulate, the new taste. Soon museum curators began to dust down long neglected groups of objects acquired during the 1920s and 1930s or chase after new acquisitions to reflect the developing interest.[29] At the same time, surviving patrons and Deco designers were rediscovered and fêted; and leading auction houses began to realize vast prices for quality pieces from the estates of such collectors and designers.[30] By the early 1970s the Art Deco phenomenon had well and truly taken off. And, in 1971, when a 'gargantuan' exhibition, *The World of Art Deco* – with over 4,000 objects – was shown at the Minneapolis Institute of Arts, its catalogue was designed in a neo-Deco style.[31] Mirroring the commercial origins of the style, the study of Art Deco had become inextricably bound up with its merchandizing. For some, this rapid commodification of Art Deco was thoroughly distasteful and marked it out definitively as a child of its time.[32]

In Europe and America the late 1960s was a period of rapid social and cultural change, with growing scepticism of establishment values, the emergence of the anti-Vietnam War protest movement, the cult of youth – conspicuously represented by the success of pop groups like the Beatles and the Rolling Stones – and the rise of the 'counter-culture'. Neo-Deco graphic design captured the mood. In these and subsequent years many of the intellectual orthodoxies of the post-war period would be challenged. In architecture and design, and in their respective histories, criticisms of Modernism began to be voiced, targeting its perceived formalist aridity and progressive loss of social idealism. These criticisms, together with the emergence of what would come to be designated 'Post-modernism',[33] helped nourish an appreciation of Art Deco's formal richness, variety and inventiveness, as well as its popular associations. Some of the most ardent supporters of the re-evaluation of Art Deco in America were the architects Denise Scott Brown and Robert Venturi, who were early champions of the

conservation of Art Deco buildings in New York and Miami Beach (plate 1.8).[34] David Gebhard has nicely captured the complementary relationship between Modernist and Art Deco taste:

> During the decades of the 1940s through the 1960s no aspect of architecture was held more in disdain than that of the Art Deco of the 1920s and 1930s. Art Deco, the popularised modern of those decades, was either ignored by our major architects and writers, or it was dismissed as an unfortunate, obviously misguided effort: the sooner forgotten the better. Those who exposed [sic] high art modernism during the thirty years from 1940 to 1970 condemned the Art Deco [sic] for preserving too many traditional architectural values, for being too concerned with the decorative arts and popular symbolism, and for being too compromising in its acceptance of the imagery of high art modern architecture of the twenties and thirties. All of these accusations against the Art Deco were true – the difference today is that we are inclined to feel that all of these qualities which were looked on so disdainfully were, in fact, assets, not defects.[35]

In Britain and elsewhere, the New Left, now critical of Modernism, contributed a theoretical underpinning to the new celebration of popular culture, notably through its re-presentation of texts on mass culture from the inter-war years by members of the Frankfurt School, such as Theodor Adorno and Walter Benjamin.[36] Nourished by such trends, design history emerged as a discrete discipline in the 1970s, questioning the dominant Modernist accounts of inter-war design, rejecting Modernism's narrow 'canon' and substituting approaches that, in legitimating the study of popular artefacts, offered support in principle to the academic study of Deco. And in America, the spread of American studies and material culture studies provided a solid base for the study of popular visual culture.[37]

Despite the development of an auspicious framework for the serious study of Art Deco in its popular incarnation, surprisingly few scholars gave extended attention to the style in their own publications.[38] One who did was Gebhard, whose study of the Californian Moderne defined distinct tendencies within Art Deco and located these in a meaningful and consistent critical terminology derived from the period.[39] Gebhard designated as 'Moderne' those works that represented an important strand in American inter-war architecture and displayed elements of Modernism but would be rejected by 'serious' Modernist architects (or architectural historians). He also used the term 'Streamline Moderne' to differentiate modern commercial and entertainment buildings from those of 'avant-garde' (or 'dyed-in-the-wool') Modernists.[40] He distinguished both from the 'Zigzag Moderne' of the 1920s, which was influenced by the Paris 1925 Exhibition, and from the 'WPA Moderne' of American public buildings of the New Deal era.[41] Although Gebhard himself was reluctant to use the term Art Deco, other authors began to employ a similar terminology to characterize distinct tendencies within the style. In the inter-war

years, the terms 'Moderne' and 'modernistic' had often been used disparagingly, to denote 'false' modernity, or 'imitation' Modernism. Now, however, they came to be used in a positive sense, particularly by American authors, to identify popular inter-war expressions of modernity in architecture and design, of the type that stands somewhere between Modernism and the various expressions of classicism current in the period.[42]

Knowledge and judgment must play a part in establishing the boundaries of what is and is not Deco, as well as in attributing works to particular categories of Deco. Such judgments depend on deciding what role intention plays, and whether the sources or precedents referenced in the design have been sufficiently transformed by new materials, new formal ideas and new techniques of production to

1.9 Le Corbusier (Charles-Edouard Jeanneret), Pierre Jeanneret, Charlotte Perriand, chaise-longue. Chrome-plated tubular steel, painted sheet steel, rubber and leather upholstery. Made by Gebrüder Thonet. 1928-9. V&A: W.11-1989. © FLC/ADAGP, Paris and DACS, London 2002.

1.10 Berthold Lubetkin, Highpoint One, Highgate, London. 1935-6. Photo: Tim Benton.

achieve a synthesis of a type to justify the label Art Deco. In the case of architecture, 'WPA Moderne', 'stripped classical' or 'modernized classical' Art Deco buildings typically incorporate Deco ornamental features and decorative details but also frankly express their modern steel or concrete structure in large expanses of plain wall surfaces and large windows. But the issue of intention is complex. Art Deco as we have characterized it so far, including 'decorative Modernism', can be distinguished from Modernism by the latter's stated aims, which were utopian and emancipatory.[43] And yet works that have been generally accepted as Modernist are frequently included in books on Art Deco, or employed in other media to connote Art Deco attributes. As an example, Highpoint One, a Modernist apartment block in Highgate, London, was designed in 1935-6 by the Georgian-born architect Berthold Lubetkin.

Its vestibule – with glazed bricks, cream-painted surfaces and terrazzo planters – has featured in many soft focus filmic recreations of Thirties England, in which it is read as a stylish Art Deco interior (plate 1.10). Yet although the vestibule's visual attributes match the stereotype of Deco, the architect's intentions were very different; it was designed as a 'social condenser', intended to instil a sense of collective (as opposed to individual) identity in the apartments' inhabitants.[44] Other Modernist designs have also lent themselves to similar interpretations. The well known chaise-longue by Le Corbusier, Pierre Jeanneret and Charlotte Perriand (1928), with its chromed tubular steel frame, its sensuous, anthropomorphic curves and its luxurious cowhide covering, can be seen as Art Deco, though it was intended by its creators as a rationalist design capable of mass production (plate 1.9).[45]

In part, these contradictory readings result from the way works were seen at the time.[46] But they also result from present-day debates over the necessity and value of considering questions of intention and conditions of production in interpreting works of art and design.[47] In one view, knowledge of the original conditions of production and intention is irrelevant to understanding, which can interpret the work of the past as it chooses. The opposite view holds, however, that richness, complexity and depth of understanding are lost unless the voice of the author and an awareness of time, place and cultural resonance are incorporated within the processes of reinterpretation that necessarily take place as succeeding generations consume the productions of the past.

Where, then, do this book and its related exhibition stand and what is their particular contribution? They assume that Art Deco is properly applied, as a style label, to a 'family' of works from the 1910s and the inter-war years whose purpose was decorative. The approach, therefore, is inclusive as to form, medium and place, presenting a rich and varied mix of fine and decorative arts, architecture, sculpture, fashion, film, photography and industrial design from all over the world. The genie long ago escaped from the bottle and it no longer makes sense to deny the use of the term Art Deco to works that have been identified as such in countless magazines, books and exhibitions. The formal and typological diversity of the style is considered a positive quality, rather than an indication of its ideologically inconsistent nature, and one that presents an intriguing challenge. In this perspective, Hillier's belief that it is 'wise to use one name – Art Deco', and his view of the underlying 'continuity and essential unity' of the style, has seemed preferable to Greif's plural 'Art Decos', or Gebhard's various categories of 'Moderne', however locally useful these distinctions might be.

Often seen as a reaction against Art Nouveau and the Secession style, Art Deco is considered here as, in many respects, their successor. The formal legacy of the earlier style, principally transmitted by the cubic forms and flat, geometricized or abstract ornament employed by Viennese and other designers in the early 1900s (see plate 10.2),[48] is readily visible in Art Deco, but so, too, is the fascination with stylized naturalistic decoration.[49] The interest in the 'exotic' to be found in Art Nouveau is also a significant constituent of Art Deco.[50] Furthermore, correspondences between Art Nouveau and Art Deco can be glimpsed in less tangible qualities. The 'varied visions' characteristic of the earlier style are defining features of Art Deco; and, like Art Nouveau, Art Deco

has proved a 'multi-facetted, complex phenomenon that defied – then and now – any attempt to reduce it to singular meanings and moments'.[51]

Like Art Nouveau, Art Deco – as well as its contemporary and rival, Modernism – was a response to, and nurtured by, the new technologies, social change and initiatives towards cultural modernization of its age. Like Art Nouveau, too, Art Deco fused ideas of the 'universal' with the 'local', though it significantly extended the boundaries of the former with its borrowings from the far distant past and from far-flung cultures. In contrast to Art Nouveau, Art Deco was not permeated by a belief in the redemptive value of art; nevertheless it was, to a large extent, premised on the notion that modern artistic ideas could be used to palliate – even 'streamline' – the interface between the consumer and the workings of the market-place. It was a pragmatic style rather than a utopian one – in the sense in which the work of the designers of the Arts and Crafts movement, Art Nouveau and Modernism was utopian. And yet, in a period in which notions of 'the collective' came increasingly to be associated with totalitarian regimes, Art Deco's address to the 'individualism' of desire– however illusory we can see this to have been, in an age when mass production and the techniques of manipulating consumer desire were significantly extended – could be seen to stand for democratic values.

The first section of this book addresses the strikingly various sources on which Art Deco drew, ranging from the artefacts of ancient and distant cultures – such as those of Egypt and Africa – via the historic high styles and vernacular traditions of nineteenth-century Europe, to contemporary European avant-garde art. This bewildering variety of sources, and the apparent insouciance with which many Art Deco designers raided them for purely novel effects, has tended to confirm perceptions of the style as lacking coherence. And yet, as these essays collectively demonstrate, there was a consistent underlying impulse to these activities. Like their Modernist colleagues, Art Deco designers were acutely conscious of those features of the early twentieth-century world that qualitatively and quantitatively distinguished it from earlier periods. And they became increasingly aware that the conventions of western post-Renaissance visual culture could not be infinitely 'modernized' and meaningfully reconciled with the new products and typologies of an increasingly mechanized and mass culture. In looking to 'exotic' and ancient cultures, or the 'new vision' of contemporary avant-garde art, Art Deco designers were able to find forms and motifs

with which to renew their decorative vocabulary. As importantly, however, they were able to find the means of liberating themselves, of thinking 'outside the box', in order to respond to the new design problems with which they were daily confronted. Furthermore, these ancient and otherwise distant sources proved to have associations that perfectly meshed with the popular tastes of the period for youthful energy, glamour, luxury and the hint of danger. Contemporary perceptions of astonishing congruencies between the ancient and the modern worlds, as of East and West, go some way to explaining the otherwise puzzling phenomenon of the huge popular interest that attended some of the discoveries of the arcane worlds of archaeology and anthropology of the era.

As a coda to this first section, the distinctive 'language' – or 'languages' – of Art Deco are explored in essays that, respectively, focus on the recurrent iconographical and decorative repertoire of the style and on one of its most distinctive 'dialects', that of 'the exotic'. Both essays show how the distinctive themes, images and associations of early European Art Deco, developed mainly in the context of elite consumption, had resonance for a much wider spectrum of contemporary society and in very different contexts. They also show that although Art Deco took on new, local, inflections as it spread, and was sometimes radically transformed, many of its central themes and motifs transcended geographical and cultural boundaries and ethnic differences.

The second section focuses on France. The rise of the style is seen as a response to challenges – increasingly frequent from the mid-nineteenth century onwards – to French authority in matters of style, taste and quality of production, as a result of which France's once world-beating luxury industries had lost their competitive edge. The key strategies that the French adopted to counter this state of affairs, culminating in the Paris 1925 Exhibition, are identified. These included efforts to 'construct' a 'modern' style through the reworking of national traditions; the provision of better infrastructural support; and a selective emphasis on the promotion of those categories of production – notably fashion and film – that could be associated with both 'Frenchness' and 'modernity'.[52] Also underlined here is the significance of new techniques of merchandizing, represented to great effect in the 1925 Exhibition by the jewel-like vitrines of luxury goods boutiques and by the pavilions of the leading French department stores.

The third section explores Art Deco in many of the European countries that participated in the 1925

Exhibition, as well as in different genres. The essays on countries show that similar processes of modernization occurred Europe-wide, though at varying speeds and inflected by nationally or regionally distinct debates, practices and tastes. The modernization of historic high styles – often those with specifically national and bourgeois associations – was also a common feature (plate 1.11). Contemporary social themes found their way alike into Italian ceramic design, the figurative decoration of Scandinavian glassware and the mannered stylizations of porcelain figurines for German and Austrian manufacturers. The 'exotic', too, was a recurrent theme, whether in designs for metalwork, furniture or silk batik wall hangings in the Netherlands, or in Austrian textiles (see plates 7.4 and 15.15). And the influence of avant-garde art, seen from an early date in Czechoslovak ceramics and furnishings and in Italian textiles (see plates 16.3 and 19.1), also appeared in German ceramic

and metalwork designs and in Scandinavian work (see plates 15.4 and 17.8). In most of these countries, too, the modernization of the stylized, abstract (or abstracted) motifs of 'popular' vernacular traditions also contributed significantly to early Deco, particularly in Central Europe and Scandinavia (see plates 16.7, 16.9 and 17.11). Britain, however, appears to stand slightly apart from the countries of continental Europe. Here the Arts and Crafts ethic retained a strong influence and when the modernistic strand of Deco began to influence commercial production in the late 1920s and early 1930s it met with fierce criticism. To present-day eyes, however, the type of mass-produced ceramics that then attracted criticism now appear as thoroughly authentic expressions of the style. Furthermore, in the hands of architects and designers such as Raymond McGrath, Oliver Bernard, Oliver Hill, Edward McKnight Kauffer and Syrie Maugham, or in the cinema designs of the Odeon chain, Art Deco in Britain

found undeniably stylish and convincing expression in both up-market and more popular contexts.

The essays on genres address Art Deco in architecture, fashion, jewellery, photography, graphics, bookbinding and book jackets. From these it is clear that the characteristics of Art Deco may be configured differently and given different emphases in different genres, and also that the style may be constituted as much by an attitude, a look, an approach, or a context as by definable formal features. And yet, there are many common characteristics. An interest in the use of colour for striking decorative effect can be found in the bold detailing of New York skyscrapers as well as in the bright colours or dramatic monochromes used by Parisian couturières or high-class jewellers. Exotic themes and motifs are often found – as in the Egyptian references that appeared not only in fashion but also in graphics, architecture and bookbindings. The influence of avant-garde art can also be seen in

1.11 Josef Hoffmann, bowl.
Gilded metal. Austrian, c.1924.
V&A: M.41-1972.

architectural decoration, in the backdrops and raking angles employed by photographers, in the motifs used to decorate fine bindings, in poster designs, and in the 'collage' techniques employed by couturiers.

In several genres, luxury materials expressive of the surface glitter and hedonistic tastes of the age were used – in fine bookbindings, for example, or in jewellery that employed rare and brilliant oriental stones in dramatic new settings. New materials, expressive of new technologies, were increasingly used for both practical purposes and their inherent decorative qualities in Art Deco buildings. Other kinds of new – or 'alternative' – materials were used to achieve bold new effects of colour or scale in jewellery. And the fascination of the age with the qualities of materials is also seen in new photographic processes, such as solarization, and in the portrayal of the metallic glitter or shiny smoothness of contemporary couture fabrics in fashion photography (see plates 23.16 and 25.10).

There was also the fascination of that other rapidly developing new 'material' – artificial light – that was present everywhere. It is to be seen not only in photographs on the theme of electricity, or in the dramatic raking light effects used in fashion and advertising photography, but also in the widespread use of artificial lighting for the purposes of publicity and display, and in architecture (plate 1.12).

From around 1925, there was an increasing tendency for the style so far largely associated with luxury production and the individual client to be adapted to mass production and a popular market. And Art Deco was rapidly adopted by genres (such as advertising graphics and film) and typologies (such as the cinema) that were themselves identified with a mass audience. By the mid-1920s, too, a hint of streamlining had appeared in European Deco. It could be seen not only in the abstracted, shiny forms of the 'new mannequin'[53] but also in the clothes associated with the *garçonne* look and in the new types of jewellery that developed in response to these new, contoured fashions in dress and hairstyling (see plate 24.9). Streamlined forms also began to be represented in other genres, such as photography; and, by the early 1930s, streamlined forms – rather than decorative detail – increasingly defined the architectural expression of Art Deco (see plate 22.5).

Many of the essays on genres indicate that, from the mid-1920s, Art Deco was an increasingly worldwide phenomenon. They touch on the mechanisms by which the style was transmitted and identify some of the transformations it underwent in

the process. The essays in the fourth section survey more systematically Art Deco's spread to countries, regions and continents far distant from its place(s) of origin. They are introduced by essays on those key elements of contemporary culture – transport and Hollywood film – that were powerfully suggestive of the telescoping of geographical distance and cultural difference. Their own design was influenced by Art Deco; they stood for the twin poles of Art Deco's association with both elite *and* mass culture; and they themselves became a powerful means of the transmission of the style.

In devoting substantial space to Art Deco in America, we have followed the conventional view that it was here that Art Deco made the widest popular impact and saw its most significant transformation. There are other reasons for this emphasis, however. During the inter-war years, America came to

1.12 Ernest Wamsley Lewis, detail of the circle lighting, New Victoria theatre, London. 1930. © English Heritage, NMR.

represent 'the prototype of modernity' for peoples all over the world. It also came to be seen, both by many of those countries still under the sway of European imperial powers – yet beginning to nurture ambitions for independence – and by those already liberated from colonialism, as *the* exemplar of a former European colony that had begun to develop a distinctive independent culture while also emerging as a world power. Many of these countries and regions now looked to America as well as Europe for symbols of modernity with which to express their own cultural and economic aspirations, finding them as much in the iconic imagery of Manhattan as in Paris couture (plate 1.13).

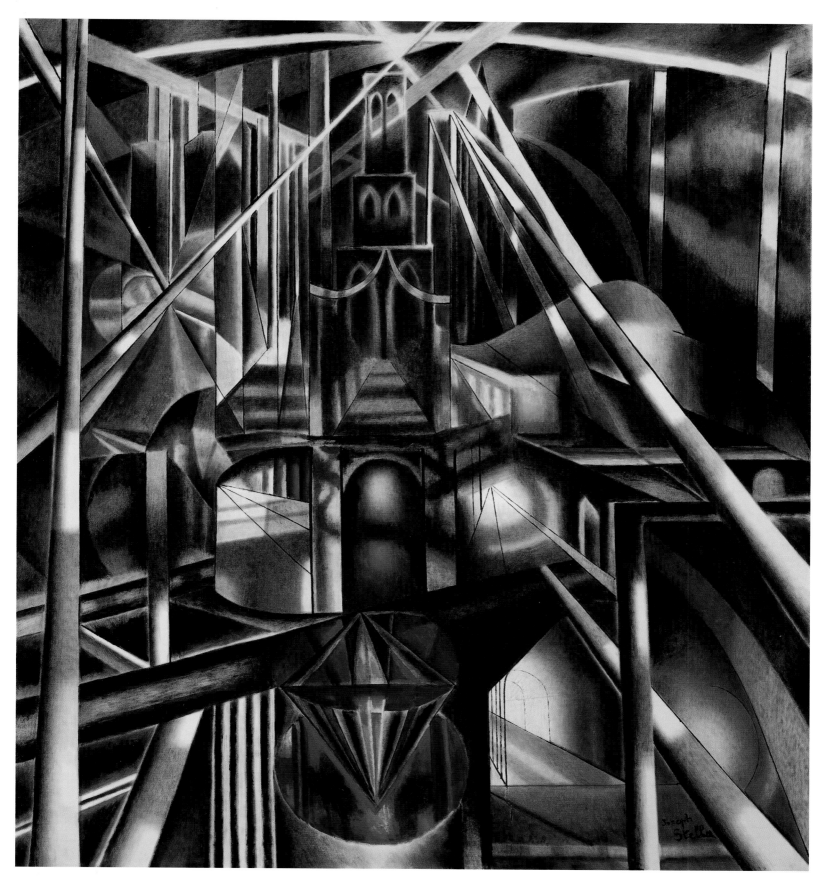

1.13 Joseph Stella, *Old Brooklyn Bridge*. Oil on canvas. American, *c*.1941. Gift of Susan Morse Hilles in memory of Paul Hellmuth.

Museum of Fine Arts, Boston.

Latin America and China migrant architects, artists and designers – American as well as European – played a significant role in its spread. And everywhere the style was also transmitted through the medium of Hollywood film.

In the first instance, the spread of Art Deco was often associated with European or Europeanized elites. This was the case in Latin America; in India, where the style was associated both with princely patrons and with an outward-looking urban business elite; in Shanghai, where it was associated with the activities of the Anglo-American business community; and in South Africa, where it came to represent the developing industrial interests of the white elite. In Japan it came to be associated with a particularly Japanese view of modernity. And yet, especially through the cinema (as represented by the combination of cinema buildings, films, promotional posters and fanzines), Art Deco also increasingly reached popular audiences and penetrated beyond major urban centres. It was seen as a means to 'modernize main street' in small towns all over Depression America; its forms and decoration were to be found in buildings for the poor (as well as the rich) in Latin America; and its familiar motifs – such as the stylized sunburst – penetrated to remote villages in India.

There were several predisposing factors for Art Deco's global spread. One of the strongest was its association of 'modernity' with cosmopolitanism and high fashion, as well as with commerce and new technologies. Another was its emphasis on the decorative, especially in countries or regions with strong decorative traditions. In these contexts it often proved more 'user friendly' than its austere, anti-decorative cousin – Modernism. Its individualist – rather than collectivist – emphasis, as well as its associations with commerce and communications, made it attractive not only in America but also in Japan, where modernization was closely associated with a new sense of individualism. The style's formal eclecticism and lack of prescriptive theory also allowed it to accommodate a wide range of local and regional traditions and practices without losing its essential character. So, while Art Deco's distinctive repertoire of frozen fountains, stylized floral and animal decoration, zigzag motifs and sunbursts, found its way all over the world, these motifs could easily be substituted or supplemented – and

The means by which the style was transmitted were several. The Paris 1925 Exhibition was widely reported by official delegations and the foreign press – both popular and specialist;[54] in addition, albums of high quality photographs and pochoir prints, some devoted to the exhibition, others focusing on particular *métiers*, were circulated widely.[55] Travelling exhibitions of French decorative arts were sent abroad. Many foreign artists, architects and designers became familiar with the new tendencies at first hand, through visiting the exhibition or through studies or travel in Europe. Wealthy clients – whether

from America, India or Japan – could (and did) buy or commission work direct from Paris. And department stores, as well as new boutiques and specialist galleries, were quick to promote the style. Several French designers were hired as consultants, by foreign concerns, particularly in America. Although they were not always successful in translating their ideas to new contexts, they pointed the way for local designers to adapt the style. Emigration was another important factor. Successive waves of European designers settled in America and contributed to the development of Art Deco, while in Australia, India,

1.15 Suzuki Hyōsaku II, chest. Lacquer on wood. Japanese, 1937. Municipal Museum, Kyoto.

1.16 Cigarette lighter. Chromium-plated steel and white plastic. American, c.1925. Made by the Art Metal Works Inc. for Ronson, Newark. V&A: Circ.266-1971.

'naturalized' – by similarly stylized abstract and naturalistic motifs with local or regional meanings, ancient and modern.

In America, the vocabulary of Deco was at first 'naturalized' through references to the imagery and culture of the modern metropolis – in the use of skyscraper forms and motifs, and in angular decoration suggestive of the syncopated rhythms of jazz. In Australia and New Zealand, native flora and fauna and Aboriginal and Maori motifs made an appearance. In Latin America, the abstract, geometric forms of European Deco, sometimes themselves inspired by the culture of the region, were exchanged for similar motifs with local resonance, drawn from indigenous native culture. In India, Art Deco was used both to modernize local or regional decorative conventions and, in its streamlined form, to express a sense of international modernity (plate 1.14). And in Japan an awareness of the powerful influence of the orient on recent European styles eased Art Deco's translation into an authentically modern 'national' style (plate 1.15). In America, a second phase of naturalization occurred in the Depression years, with the widespread application of streamlining, not only to means of transportation, where it had – at least notionally –

a scientific rationale, but also to architecture and the design of a wide range of consumer goods (plate 1.16). In the context of styling, streamlining allowed designers to reinvent the decorative without recourse to ornament.

As Art Deco spread, it became associated with many of the genres and typologies already familiar from its European incarnation – notably graphics, fashion and textiles, new types of consumer goods and the architecture of commerce and pleasure. But the distinct modernizing agendas of different countries and regions gave it new types of meanings. In several countries it came to be associated with 'official' culture. In Europe – with the exception of France – this had rarely been the case.

Art Deco is a complex style, but as this book shows, it is by no means resistant to conventional methods of categorization and interpretation, despite the difficulties posed by its formal eclecticism and the variety of genres it encompassed. The problems of overlap between Art Deco and Modernism and Art Deco and other contemporary styles are not altogether resolved here. But they were not resolved by contemporaries either, as is strikingly demonstrated in the interiors commissioned by the Maharaja of Indore for his palace, Manik Bagh,

where 'decorative Modernist' designs sat cheek by jowl with what we may now have to learn to call 'Modernist decorative' designs.[56] What we hope to have done, however, is to provide a study that takes Art Deco seriously across the spectrum of its lifespan and stylistic forms, and offers some signposts to ways of understanding both the variety and the unity of this complex phenomenon. In claiming this as a serious enterprise, however, it should be emphasized that – almost uniquely among art historical styles – some of Art Deco's most persistent meanings are to be found in fantasy and fun.

2 The Great War, Mass Society and 'Modernity'

Arthur Marwick

There are no closed periods in history, but the period between the two wars, 1918-39, the period of Art Deco, is as nearly self-contained, as nearly defined by certain distinctive, and in some ways unique, characteristics as any. The precise effects of the horrific and all-pervasive experiences of the First World War, in all its ramifications (revolution, unprecedented regimentation on the home fronts, a sense of indebtedness to the ordinary men who fought and the ordinary women who kept domestic life going) are much argued over by historians. Indisputably, there were many continuities with the pre-war years; equally indisputably it was impossible to escape the many, and often contradictory, legacies of the war. In high political circles and among the general population there was determination that such slaughter should not happen again, and optimism that a better world could be constructed. Yet, there was also a sense of deep foreboding as the international economic crisis at the end of the 1920s was followed by a succession of international geopolitical and military crises.

The other great legacy of the war was the sense of a break with the past, a break into the world of 'modernity'. 'Modernization' is the rather vague term used to encompass what are held to be the key developments in modern societies, which will be discussed in this essay. As important as the actual changes which transformed these societies was the way they were perceived and by whom. The period between the two world wars can legitimately be described as the first, and indeed classic, era of 'mass society' (plate 2.1); from now on, public opinion – the opinion of the mass consumer – was to be as important in forming taste as the preferences of the elite. We need also to take into account the effects of the great scientific discoveries of the later nineteenth century and the early twentieth century, which overthrew many of the older certainties about the nature of the universe; nor should we neglect the influence of actual political and social events. The modern world could connote the taming of natural forces and unprecedented advances in the amenities

of life; it could also connote the deplorable living conditions that accompanied urbanization, unimaginative standardization, the inanities of mass consumption and mass entertainment, the brutalities of colonial wars, and the unimaginable slaughter of the First World War. In the elite arts, rejoicing in the new was often not very far from despondency and foreboding.

However, there can be no doubt as to the all-pervasiveness, across classes and across nations, of the sense of 'modernity', many hating it, most (particularly among 'the masses') loving it. 'Modernity' meant being in touch with the future – before 1914 the standard belief of the thoughtful was in no more than 'progress'; it connoted, as a wealth of private letters and popular newspapers demonstrates, a whole new world. In it the dominant factors were: democracy (even if only a reality in Western and Northern Europe, America and the white Dominions); new cityscapes; fast transport; new roles for women; and a 'new spirit' (with mechanization and big business harnessing both art and science to the aspirations of the 'common man'). A cartoon in the *Glasgow Evening Times* of 19 September 1927 entitled 'Peeps into the Wonderful Future' featured a North American cityscape, a mad scientist, a sky full of aircraft, an electric railway, and a plethora of advertisements for cosmetics and domestic conveniences.[1] In short, it captured the essence of 'modernity', of which Art Deco is a central facet.

Whatever the actual realities within the Soviet Union, Nazi Germany, Fascist Italy, other Fascist and semi-Fascist countries and the liberal democracies (the leading ones being the United States, the United Kingdom, France, Germany prior to the advent of Hitler in 1933), all governments – even that of Japan, still an archaic empire in so many ways – claimed to be acting in the interests of 'the common man'.[2] There had been scattered legislation with regard to franchise and welfare reforms from the late nineteenth century onwards, particularly in Germany, Austria and Britain, but there is a notable concentration in the years immediately following the

2.1 John Gutmann, *Elevator Garage, Chicago*. Gelatin silver print. American, 1936. Ford Motor Company Collection. Gift of Ford Motor Company and John C. Waddell, 1987. The Metropolitan Museum of Art, New York.

war and, in regard to social welfare, steady enactments throughout the subsequent twenty years. Britain in 1918 granted the vote to all adult males (two-fifths of them had been without it in 1914) and, with a small property qualification, to all women over 30; this led the way without difficulty to all women over 21 getting the vote in 1928. In America, where adult males had the vote, though with severe discrimination against blacks, votes for (in effect, white) women became law in 1919. In France, where adult men already had the vote, the attempt by the National Assembly to extend the vote on the same terms to women was thrown out by the Senate, where the anti-clerical majority feared that women would be ruled by their priests. The same process took place in Italy – with or without votes, newly confident women, in their leg-displaying apparel, were a much-noted phenomenon on the social scene. Japan in 1918 increased its electorate from one million to three million and elected its first commoner to the prime ministership. For the rest of the period it was ruled by aristocrats, but one of them, an admirer of Britain, introduced universal male suffrage in 1925. Desperate to appear modern, the dictators of Brazil (in 1932) and Turkey (in 1934) granted universal suffrage to women.

The Russian, the Austro-Hungarian, the German empires all collapsed under the pressures of war. The new Weimar Republic in Germany was in many ways a model liberal democracy, dominated by the Social Democrats. The Weimar constitution itself guaranteed rights to employment, health, education and housing. Unfortunately, Germany was soon afflicted by rampant inflation and massive unemployment. The Soviet Union, in theory, had the most comprehensive social provisions, crèches, schools, paid holidays, employment rights for women. But in practice the government, and its secret police, was waging an internal war against many of its own citizens. In Austria, the Social Democrats carried through much progressive legislation, but were subject to heavy resistance, sometimes in the form of military action, from traditionalist forces.

In the newer countries, with the exception of Czechoslovakia, there was scarcely the will, let alone the resources, to implement welfare policies. This was largely true, too, of Italy where the disruptions of war had been severe. The claim of Mussolini when he seized power in 1922 was that he was introducing a form of government much superior to ineffectual democracy, one which would deliver to the people what they deserved. The same claim was made by Hitler when he took power in 1933, perfectly legally since the Nazis were the majority

2.2 Irene Fawkes, jacket for
BBC Year Book, London.
Colour lineblock. British, 1930.
V&A: AAD 1995/8/8.

party, though with only one third of the vote. In both countries, of course, brutal suppression of all opposition soon followed.

For France, the destruction and loss of life caused by the war was disastrous; though bad enough, it was considerably less for Britain. Thus the welfare legislation in Britain was both more thorough and more effectively put into operation. In France, a law of 23 April 1919 granted the 8-hour day and 48-hour week; but it was frequently not implemented. There were various other laws on different aspects of social welfare. Then in April 1936 came the election for the first time in France of a genuinely left-leaning government, the (note the title) Popular Front government of Léon Blum. But it was short-lived and France sank into a period of confusion and intensified civic violence under a right-wing government, which in 1938 followed the Fascist and Nazi example by commandeering French radio.

A crucial element in the advent of 'modern', 'mass' society was the way in which technology was exploited, particularly in the development of mass communications. Because of the use of aircraft, mainly for reconnaissance purposes, during the war, there was a high demand for the production of radio valves: to use up the huge capacity, civilian radio companies were rapidly set up in the post-war years. Film, exploited for national propagandist purposes, gained in prestige among middle-class and respectable upper-working-class audiences; at the same time, only American studios could afford to

devote resources to entertainment films and thus came very near to eclipsing the individual European film industries. It is often said that the phenomenal success of silent film as an international medium of communication was due to the fact that it did not depend upon spoken language. There is obviously truth in this, but enormous significance does attach to the advent, at the end of the 1920s, of sound films which more forcefully established fashions, set agendas and reinforced the position of America as both the prototype of everything modern (particularly for non-European countries), and yet a place in many ways different and, at first, distant from Europe.

Mass-circulation newspapers already existed in the main western countries before the First World War; but the war was certainly an important factor in the development of the newspaper-reading habit in the emergent countries of Eastern Europe. Advertising, in the press but also on hoardings, was a prominent feature of pre-war societies in the West. But harnessed to national purposes during the war, it moved into a new dimension after the conflict, aided by considerable expansion in specialist agencies. In America, radio, more than anything else, was a medium for commercial advertising. Britain led the way in setting up an autonomous government corporation with an improving mission and no advertisements, the BBC (plate 2.2). The other European countries followed, rather imperfectly. State corporations were very much used for government propaganda, while private, highly commercialized companies also existed.

Meanwhile, international communications and trade were creating the potential for economic and cultural globalization, but this was by no means a simple process. In all countries the era up until the First World War was one of rising prices which meant expansion and optimism for everyone save workers unable to secure wage rises. In Britain, Germany, Italy and the Eastern European countries, that boom collapsed shortly after the end of the war. In France and America however, it continued: in America until the stock market crash of 1929, in France a couple of years longer. The international economy presented a paradoxical picture. As a result of the war, there was devastation in Europe, but more players, with greater productive capacity, around the world. This meant more trading opportunities, but more deliberately created barriers to trade.

Other key areas of technological development were: the production and utilization of electric power; the manufacture of plastics, man-made fibres and pharmaceuticals; further refinements of the internal combustion engine, for both land and air transport; the use of advanced building techniques for the ever-higher skyscrapers. The pacesetter in this new technology-based economic expansion, obviously, was America, where, also, new methods of business management were most vigorously pursued. The needs of advertisers to find a powerful expressive language of persuasion, which would appeal to a wide buying public and operate at the scale of the cityscape as well as in the media, fuelled the spread of Art Deco in Europe and America.

Another feature of urban life was the transition from private enjoyment for the affluent family to mass leisure activities for the ordinary man and ordinary woman. Perhaps the most potent symbol of this was the construction everywhere of large-scale dance halls whose only entry requirement was the modest price of admission. These, along with cinemas, sprang up everywhere: palaces of democracy and of dreams, they were built in a style to match and given names like Palais de Danse and Alhambra (see plate 3.7). Then there were the international exhibitions themselves. Not all of their buildings were necessarily temporary: some exhibition halls, very definitely intending to retain a mass clientele, remained, as of course did the football stadium built to accompany the 1924 *British Empire Exhibition* at Wembley. We should note also the expansion of spectator sports, the popularity of tennis, walking, cycling, the attempts of governments to popularize physical jerks (plate 2.3).

2.3 Tom Purvis, *Harrogate: The British Spa*, poster. Colour lithograph. British, c.1928. V&A: E.566-1928.

CHEMIN DE FER DU NORD

NEDERLANDSCHE SPOORWEGEN

SOCIÉTÉ NATIONALE DES CHEMINS DE FER BELGES

ÉTOILE DU NORD
DU DEJEUNER PULLMAN AU DINER
PARIS — BRUXELLES — AMSTERDAM
COMPAGNIE DES WAGONS-LITS

2.4 Cassandre (Adolphe Mouron), *Etoile du Nord*, poster. Colour lithograph. French, 1927. V&A: E.224-1935.

The burgeoning light industries produced a whole range of new or improved domestic appliances – from telephones to wireless sets, phonographs and electric irons. These required custom-built factories, and if the factories were to be located in residential areas, they had to have a certain stylishness, in line with the surrounding houses (see plate 22.14). Then there were the artefacts of the transport revolution, themselves often influenced by the new technological shibboleth of streamlining: aeroplanes, seaplanes, ships, record-seeking locomotives; trains for the expanding metros, subways, tubes and U-bahns (with, often, various kinds of station furniture); buses, trams, trolley-buses. New transport systems called forth new posters (plate 2.4).

In America industrial output nearly doubled between 1922 and 1929, and the gross national product rose by 40%. By 1928 real wages were one third higher than in 1914. Within industry there was a heavy emphasis on standardization, division of labour, mass production and mergers. During the 1920s, 8,000 mergers took place, so by 1930 the 200 largest non-financial corporations owned almost one half of the corporate wealth.[3] To be sustained, mass production needed mass consumption, and mass consumption needed mass advertising: by 1927 the nation's advertising bill had doubled since 1920 to $1.5 billion.[4] For consumer goods, washing machines, refrigerators, vacuum cleaners, radio sets, phonographs, cars, purchasing by installments became common. Chainstores, A. & P. Rexall and Woolworth's, catered to the desire for the minor appurtenances of life. The advent of mail order companies, led by Sears, Roebuck, entailed the production of catalogues which by their very nature placed a great emphasis on the image of the product.

The American census of 1920 showed that 51.4% of the population of 106 million lived in communities of 2,500 or more, scarcely a potent indication of urbanization. More important, one in four Americans lived in the 68 cities of 100,000 or more. During the 1920s, getting on for 20 million more people moved into the cities. The phenomenon of continuing and accelerating urbanization, and especially the growth of suburbs, in Europe as well as in America, is very important in regard to lifestyles and consumer choices. But particularly important when it comes to matters of fashions and avant-garde styles is the emergence of certain metropolises (not necessarily capitals), each usually having particular districts where the intellectuals and their places of entertainment were to be found. In Europe, the new metropolis of greatest importance was Berlin, now a centre of outrage to the stiff Prussians who had once dominated it. Paris, and particularly the districts of Montparnasse and Montmartre, had been well established before the war, with artistic figures of all nationalities (including American, Japanese, Romanian) all partially lured by Paris's reputation for sexual daring, unacceptable in the European empires or in the great peripheral countries. In the United States, New York was establishing itself in the 1920s as an exciting metropolis, with its bohemian quarter, Greenwich Village, and its enticing black quarter, Harlem. Many parts of the world looked to American cities as models of modernization.

American cities were rendered distinctive through their skyscrapers. By the end of the nineteenth century, Manhattan Island, the heart of New York City, had already been completely built over. The main reason for the appearance of the first skyscrapers, which took place from the late 1880s, was obvious enough: in boom times land values rose sharply. This provided a strong motivation for the building of skyscrapers in all the main cities, but in addition the skyscraper became a symbol of civic pride, in effect, an essential adjunct of any city worthy of the name. By 1929, America had 377 buildings of 20 storeys or more. Advances in technology were most notably exploited in Manhattan, where for a time the tallest building was the one designed to publicize one of the big three motor corporations; the Chrysler building (1928) remained the most impressive example of Art Deco applied to a skyscraper (plate 2.5). However, in 1931 the top prize for height passed to the Empire State building, 380 metres (1,248 feet) high, with 184,000 square metres (2 million square feet) of office space. In all countries, new buildings of massive size were required to accommodate the commercial and industrial conglomerates and their servants, the broadcasting and film production companies, the advertising agencies.

2.5 William Van Alen, Chrysler building, New York. 1927-30. © Photo: Romilly Lockyer/Getty Images/The Image Bank.

As in commercial life, so in morals, America was both exemplar and exception. It was partly because of the very considerable influence exerted by socially conscious women's groups that a reform which – outside of Australia, New Zealand and parts of Wales and Scotland – would not have been considered such anywhere else, was implemented. By the Volstead Act of January 1920, the following words became the core of the eighteenth amendment to the American constitution: 'After one year from the ratification of this article, the manufacture, sale, or transportation of intoxicating liquors within … the United States … for beverage purposes is hereby prohibited.' Apart from the upper-class women who led the movement, this legislation had the support of the rural middle class of commercial farmers and the urban middle class of small businessmen and white-collar workers. It could therefore be described as a 'people's measure'. Yet, in spite of prohibition, the glamour of liquor and the high life as presented in films created a widespread vogue for cocktail cabinets (plate 2.6).

In Europe there was a tradition of strong centralized government. In America there was widespread hostility not just to strong central government but to individual states passing social legislation. When America's first post-war president, Warren Harding, declared, 'We want less government in business and more business in government',[5] he was not just speaking as the representative of a wealthy minority (which he undoubtedly was), but expressing a popular philosophy. The invocation of 'the people' in the much-quoted statement of his successor, Calvin Coolidge, is genuinely significant: 'the chief business of the American people is business'.[6] In fact, the powers of central government increased considerably in the United States, just as they did in Europe, though little was done to promote social welfare or social cohesion. During the war there was a massive black migration to the north and west. Living standards rose for black industrial workers, but so also did racial tensions. The violently racist Ku Klux Klan was revived in 1915 and was responsible for a vicious and lasting campaign against blacks, and also Jews and Catholics. A leading Klansman, Hiram Wesley, saw himself as the spokesman for the common (racially pure) man, rather as Hitler did, calling for 'a return of power into the hands of the everyday, not highly cultured, not overtly intellectualized, but entirely unspoilt and not de-Americanized, average citizen of the old stock'. The individual states did raise the school-leaving age to sixteen or eighteen, and many sponsored higher education institutions. The national illiteracy rate, 11% in 1900 was down to 4.3% in 1930; the

2.6 Maurice Adams, cocktail cabinet. Ebonized mahogany, rustless metal casing and chromium mounts. British, 1933. V&A: W.96-1978.

2.7 *Footlight Parade*, directed by Lloyd Bacon, choreographed by Busby Berkeley. Photofest. © (1933) Turner Entertainment Co. An AOL Time Warner Co. All Rights Reserved.

number of students in higher education had risen from under a quarter of a million to rather over a million.[7] And reasonable education formed a good environment for innovative design.

In conditions of growing prosperity for the majority, policies of support for business enterprise rather than social welfare seemed self-justifying. The situation was changed by the appalling Depression that followed upon 'black Thursday', the stock market crash of 24 October 1929. Unemployment came to be in America, as it was in Europe practically throughout the entire inter-war period, *the* social problem of the age, and one which could not simply be dismissed as an inevitable part of the normal working of the economic system. Contrary to myth, the incumbent Republican president, Herbert Hoover, was profoundly affected, and he encouraged energetic public works and loans programmes. However, when 20,000 unemployed and near-starving war veterans camped out in Washington, they were violently expelled, two of them being killed. The dreadful scenes were there for everyone to see on the newsreels, the first example of the mass media affecting an election. Meantime, Franklin D. Roosevelt, as governor of New York, had introduced unemployment benefits there, a measure that was shortly followed by the state of Wisconsin (January 1932). Roosevelt was the Democratic candidate in the 1932 election: he was a master of cosy, yet vigorous, radio chats and furnished a second example of the political influence of the mass media. He polled 57% of the votes.

Roosevelt's New Deal involved a frenzy of legislation. Some of it was trivial, some of it ill-judged, some of it quickly abandoned. But there was a kind of multiplier effect: for every family that actually benefited, there were several others who felt a confidence that something positive was being done. Probably the most useful measure was going off the gold standard, a defiance of traditional economic orthodoxy that was repeated in all the western countries (most of whom had only managed to struggle back onto the gold standard a few years before). Business innovation did continue, mass marketing expanded, oil strikes brought surprising pockets of prosperity. Talking films were mostly (though not entirely) cheerful and escapist: there were the spectacular musicals of Busby Berkeley and Frank Capra's fables of the decent, and ultimately victorious, small-town American (plate 2.7). While Europe struggled to recover from Depression, the twin growth areas of consumerism and mass advertising settled more and more in America and the wider world.

Turning to the situation elsewhere, it is clear that the international economy had become fully established in the nineteenth century with Britain its major operator and principal beneficiary, though this position was severely challenged by America and Germany even before 1914. The war disrupted the delicate international trading mechanism, leading in turn to conditions of depression and unemployment. Many countries deliberately tried to protect their own industries, and thus obstructed international trade. Australia, New Zealand and Canada, taken for granted as integral components of the British Empire, had suffered appalling losses in the war. After it, they looked more and more towards the United States. But the war had also brought America into Europe, and for all sorts of reasons, despite American political isolation, the circulation of ideas and customs between America and Europe accelerated in the inter-war years. The world, in a not inaccurate cliché, was being pulled closer together through improved communications, from submarine cables to air transport. Most notable, and allied to the popularity of dancing during and after the war, was the spread of the quintessential black American music, jazz (plate 2.8).

While the North American economy drew itself out of recession, the European empires (notably the French and the British) experienced a last great colonial age, in which ideas and artefacts were greatly influenced by imperial pride and colonial possessions. By the mid-1930s, 30% of all French foreign trade was with her colonies; by 1939 the French Empire accounted for 45% of all French overseas investment, compared with 9% in 1914.[8] One agency for (allegedly) fostering internationalism, while at the same time indulging national pride and displaying the richness and variety of colonial possessions, was the international exhibition. In the seventy years between 1851 and 1916 there were 59 genuinely international exhibitions, and in the twenty-one years between 1918 and 1939, twenty. The inter-war period is thus as much a period of international exhibitions as was the second half of the nineteenth century. This certainly distinguishes it from the period after 1945 when the number of exhibitions fell greatly. In 1922 the French held the *Exposition coloniale nationale* (purely French and not classified as international) at Marseilles. Britain then had the *British Empire Exhibition* at Wembley, in 1924/5. There were further colonial exhibitions in 1924 at Strasbourg and 1930 in Antwerp. Also in 1930 the centennial of the French conquest of Algeria was celebrated in elaborate festivals in both Algeria and France. From 6 May to 15 November 1931 the *Exposition coloniale internationale* was held in Paris. It was publicized as 'Le Tour du Monde en un Jour', though the tour notably avoided the British Empire. Without doubt, the French organizers were keen to assert the importance of co-operation among the colonizing powers in establishing and maintaining what they saw as a beneficial colonial world order; and to stress the West's responsibility to continue colonization and the good works it entailed. Before these, however, the French had held the most famous of these international exhibitions, the *Exposition internationale des arts décoratifs et industriels modernes* of 1925. This brought together what was thought to be the best and most representative of contemporary work from both inside and outside the colonial empires, and provided – retrospectively – the label 'Art Deco' for the style embodied in these works.

2.8 Jan Matulka (born in Czechoslovakia), *Musical Instruments*. Oil on canvas. American, c.1927. Collection John P. Axelrod, Boston, MA. Courtesy Museum of Fine Arts, Boston.

PART 2

Sources and Iconography

3 Egyptomania

Christopher Frayling

In the 12-volume *Encyclopédie des arts décoratifs et industriels modernes*, issued to coincide with the Paris 1925 Exhibition, the influence of ancient Egypt on contemporary design was scarcely mentioned. The introductory volume went out of its way to dismiss 'archeological reconstruction, so dear to the nineteenth century ... as misleading in "definitive" works as in ephemeral theatre designs'. As well as this, it consistently criticized the thesis that 'new forms of décor are only ancient forms revived'.[1] This chimed with the overall aim of the exhibition which, in the words of its *Information for Exhibitors*, was to display 'works combining new inspiration with real originality': reproductions, imitations and counterfeits of ancient styles were strictly prohibited.[2] Archeological discoveries, and *décorateurs* travelling to exotic places, might be a stimulus to mid-1920s design (plate 3.1); but the transformation of historical sources had to be self-evident to the viewer.

Volume IV of the *Encyclopédie*, dealing with furniture and 'colonial art', was a little less defensive about the question of ancient influences. It sought to explain the recent vogue for exoticism with reference to easier tourism and cheaper travel: 'Colonial tourism allows artists, helped these days by travel grants, to extend their visual researches. Others, even more numerous, have dreamed after reading books. It would be rash to underestimate the powerful influence of exoticism on actual creators.'[3] But still no mention of Egypt. This may well have been because of the exhibition's emphasis on France and French colonial territories. To the organizers, the Nile style now belonged to antiquarianism, plus the fact that the show had originally been planned before the First World War, when Egyptian archeological discoveries were yet to hit the headlines.

Whatever the motivation of the organizers, the illustrations that accompanied their texts contained plenty of visual evidence that French *décorateurs* had indeed been inspired by ancient Egypt, as well as by many other ancient cultures. This can be seen in a glass table-sculpture by René Lalique, which resembled a wall relief in a Pharaonic tomb; a forged iron grille with a lotus flower motif; a stained-glass design by the Mauméjean brothers depicting *Le Luxe* as a riot of pyramid shapes, ancient jewels and stepped ziggurats; scarab and cobra bracelets; and a *Vision d'Orient* in the stage design section which consisted of an ancient Egyptian temple with the figures of chorus girls carefully arranged in geometric poses on the steps.[4]

Such images made reference to Egyptian motifs, but in doing so designers also abstracted from them – often turning them into triangles and other geometric shapes, as in *Le Luxe*. They also combined them with elements from other sources: Egyptian and Mayan, for example, are sometimes difficult to distinguish. To designers of the 1920s this visual language probably had less to do with the cultural specificity of 'ancient forms' such as Egyptian, Mycenean, Chinese and Mayan, than with geometry. It represented the absorption of Modernism – in the form of basic geometric shapes, speed lines and assorted flat patterns – into the vocabulary of the decorative arts. This was done in ways that would 'go' with contemporary luxury interiors and complement both the construction and style of luxury architecture, making the style a decorative idiom for modern life.

A report sponsored by the British Department of Overseas Trade – to assess the overall economic importance of the exhibition, and any lessons arising from the lukewarm reaction to the national pavilion, which had been assembled quickly and on the cheap – huffed and puffed about 'the overwhelming predominance of France' and about the fact that the only African exhibits were from French provinces or protectorates.[5] It concluded that 'recent archeological and historical discoveries' had been influential on some exhibits, but only mentioned 'the discovery of the pottery of the Chinese Han Dynasty' and 'recent Mycenean discoveries'.[6] Still there was no mention of ancient Egypt – particularly surprising given the fact that one of the greatest archeological discoveries of all time had occurred just three years before, with a cast of leading players who were all British.

3.1 Cartier, Egyptian sarcophagus vanity case. Gold, platinum, carved bone, sapphires, emeralds, diamonds, onyxes and enamel; interior with folding mirror, tortoiseshell comb, lipstick holder and cigarette compartment. French, 1925. Cartier Collection, Geneva. Photo: Nick Welsh. © Cartier.

resembled 'the property-room of an opera of a vanished civilisation'. When Harry Burton, the British photographer seconded to the dig from the Metropolitan Museum's Egyptian expedition, produced his classic images of the tomb's excavation, they often resembled dramatic stills from a movie studio: in 1924, Burton was to visit Hollywood for advice on lighting (plate 3.2).[8] Readers of official accounts in the newspapers viewed the clearing of the tomb through these images: in black and white in the London *Times*, and in colour in the *Illustrated London News*.

The presentation to a non-specialized public of the countless 'wonderful things' as they emerged into the sunlight of the valley was to lead to a major cultural phenomenon, or, to use a 1920s word, a 'craze'. Tutmania (which the *Daily Express* in the autumn of 1922 preferred to call 'Tutankamen Ltd') was probably the most significant peacetime mass media event, up to then, of the twentieth century. It became a news phenomenon in itself, even after the initial excitement at the find had been exhausted.

On 4 November 1922, the archeologist Howard Carter had uncovered the first stone step leading down to the tomb of the boy-pharaoh Tutankhamun (who died in 1323 BC) in the Valley of the Kings near Luxor.[7] Three weeks later, accompanied by the sponsor of the expedition Lord Carnarvon, Carter made a small breach in the upper left-hand corner of the sealed doorway leading into the tomb and caught his first flickering glimpse of the 'wonderful things' piled up inside. Something of a film buff as well as a gifted draughtsman, Carter described the most famous moment in the history of archeology in cinematic terms. As his eyes gradually grew accustomed to the light in the total immersion of the tomb, the 'details of the room within', his flickering candle and the blurred image of gold suddenly came into focus as if on a stage, or through a camera lens, or on the screen of a cinema. For a second, Carter thought he was looking at wall paintings; then, as he adjusted focus, he realized they were three-dimensional things – 'everywhere the glint of gold'. The sight, he wrote in his notebook that same night,

3.2 Harry Burton, the treasury of Tutankhamun's tomb. Gelatin silver print. October 1926. Photograph for the Egyptian Expedition. The Metropolitan Museum of Art, New York.

3.3 Binding for Anatole France, *Balthasar*, Paris, 1926. Dark red calf with inlay of calf and niger of various colours; gilt and blind tooling. French, 1926. NAL.

The craze touched every aspect of design, from the 'Tutankamen Rag', played by the jazz orchestra in the ballroom of the Winter Palace Hotel, Luxor, to the latest lines in Egyptian-inspired garments, furniture, interior designs, bookbindings and fashion accessories in London, Paris, Berlin and New York (plate 3.3). Smart young women such as Lady Elizabeth Bowes-Lyon (later the Queen Mother) simply had to include a Tut-inspired outfit embroidered with ancient motifs in their honeymoon trousseaus. The craze inspired the design of everything from shop window displays to factories.

In Paris, Pierre Cartier predicted on 8 February 1923 that 'the discovery of the tomb will bring in some sweeping changes in fashion in jewellery'. His most spectacular piece of Tutmania was an Egyptian temple gate clock, made by Maurice Couet in 1927 and based on an engraving of the gate of Khons in the Napoleonic *Description de l'Egypte*,[9] with Tut-inspired incisions around the edges (plate 3.4). Other design drawings for related pieces of jewellery, with family resemblances to the clock, have survived.[10] Van Cleef & Arpels competed with brooches and bracelets depicting vultures, Anubis dogs, baboons and assorted scenes from the 'Egypt of the Pharaohs' using sapphires, rubies, emeralds and onyx; Leon Bakst unveiled his 'Isis' collection; Jean Dunand designed lacquered neck pieces with brightly coloured geometrical motifs; a perfume from Ramsès of Cairo called 'Secret de Sphinx' came on the market; and the *Folies Bergère* popularized the Egyptian-style ostrich-feather fan (based on that in box 272, according to Howard Carter's careful documentation) in a titillating tableau called 'Pleasures of the Nile'.[11]

3.4 Cartier, Egyptian temple gate clock. Gold, silver gilt, mother-of-pearl, coral, enamel, lapis lazuli, cornelian and emeralds. French, 1927. Cartier Collection, Geneva. Photo: Nick Welsh. © Cartier.

3.5 Sequin jacket with Egyptian motifs. Hand-beaded lurex. Probably French, c.1922-9. V&A: T.91-1999.

The *New York Times* on 7 February 1923 reported that 'businessmen all over the world are pleading for Tut-Ankh-Amen designs for gloves, sandals and fabrics'. A fortnight later, the headline was 'Egypt Dominates Fashion Show Here – Designs Copied From Luxor Pictures Decorate Many Suit Models – Prize Wrap Has Hathor – Tomb Vogue Will Prolong Bobbed Hair'. The Egyptian trend was 'on' before the discovery, said the report, but now it had become a fashion – a fashion for new styles of garments (with low waists, wraps around the hips, and fabrics falling to the ankles), and a fashion for Egyptian colour combinations and motifs (plate 3.5 and see plate 23.14). Then, hot on the heels of the Hathor wrap, the Luxor gown and even the Carnarvon frock, it was the turn of the pharaoh's sandals, which 'May Set New Style'. Soon patent lawyers were asking the $64,000 question: 'Who owns the name of Tut-Ankh-Amen?' Apparently, claims for the exclusive commercial use of 'Tut, Tut-tut and Two-Tank and other variations' had been filed all over the place. Even the word *ushabti* had become a brand name for

a type of tiny doll patterned after the many small wooden *shabti* figures (intended to do manual work on the pharaoh's behalf in the afterlife) found in the tomb's antechamber. Another company went for the name 'Tutankham' – a cunning mixture of Tut and Omar Khayyam – instead. The message was clear. Tutankhamun had become a brand.[12]

This was not the first time that couturiers had turned to Egypt. Indeed, some Parisian designers were claiming that they had foreseen the trend of 1923 one whole season before the Tutankhamun publicity; which was why 'all the excitement about Madame Tutankhamen's frocks leaves Paris the least little bit indifferent', as an American *Vogue* editorial on 1 April pointed out: 'But she doesn't mind admitting that it is also due in part to the royal resurrection itself, for Paris dearly loves a keen interest in its clothes. Pleating was never better – and that's Egyptian. Tiered skirts are seen – and they are Egyptian too.'[13]

By mid-July 1923 *Vogue* was already cautioning that 'so much attention has been drawn to Egypt's

influence on our frocks that the mode is becoming self-conscious about it'. *Becoming*? As fashion historian Micki Forman has suggested, the mode had been self-conscious from the word go.[14]

Meanwhile, in England the *Daily Express* of 9 March 1923 was breathlessly announcing, 'The Tutankhamen hat has arrived.' It could be viewed at Liberty's in Regent Street, where 'old Egyptian patterns borrowed from the British Museum have been adapted to headgear'. Four pictures of models wearing variations on the hat – 'as Pharaoh wore them?' – were printed side by side with pictures of the bridesmaids chosen for Lady Elizabeth Bowes-Lyon's wedding to the Duke of York, which was to take place on 26 April. At the same time, the *Illustrated London News* observed – in an article printed opposite a full-page picture of the royal wedding cake – 'Egyptian and modern styles share the honours where bridal gowns are concerned this spring'. The *Daily Mail*, meanwhile, predicted that summer fashions including 'bathing dresses' would follow the same trend.[15]

3.6 Jean Dunand, *La Pêche*. Coloured and moulded gold lacquer panel. Reduced-scale version of the mural in the *Normandie* smoking room. French, 1935. Private collection. © ADAGP, Paris and DACS, London 2002.

As James Stevens Curl rightly observes in his study of the Egyptian Revival:

> The furnishings and other contents of the pharaoh's mausoleum were of such superlative design and quality that they became models almost overnight, and not only for rare artefacts. Modern publicity ensured a widespread following for the Nile style. Fashionable ladies wore Egyptianizing 'Cleopatra' earrings, while their aspiring sisters contented themselves with less perfect jewellery ...[16]

Howard Carter wrote of the 'decisive moment' on 26 November 1922 when he saw 'everywhere the glint of gold'. This opulence was first reflected, remarkably quickly as we have seen, in the fashions of spring 1923. The influence on interiors took longer. One of the most striking examples was in the design of some of the interiors of the *Normandie*, launched in 1935 as the largest and most powerful ocean liner yet constructed for the transatlantic run. Parisian couturiers and the organizers of the 1925 Exhibition may have downplayed the Egyptian discoveries, but the key *décorateurs* of the *Normandie* had no such inhibitions. The first class *fumoir* was surrounded by five huge gilded lacquer panels designed by Jean Dunand and covered in Egyptian-style bas-reliefs. One of Dunand's finest relief panels, 'La pêche', also appeared in a reduced version: it depicted ancient fishermen harpooning and netting fish from reed Nile boats (plate 3.6). The designer acknowledged that 'these panels are expressly intended to seem abundant and high flown'.[17]

A whole social world away from luxury liners, the discovery of the tomb of Tutankhamun took the Egyptian style to the high street for the very first time. In the process, it retained some of the connotations of wealth, exoticism, sensuality, mystery and even a touch of the Old Testament. In Britain, mass-produced accessories and ornaments made of Bakelite and plastic, with hieroglyphics, winged discs, scarab beetles, obelisks, nude goddesses and assorted stepped forms, appeared in the shops next to Tut-related tins, cigarette packets, ashtrays and other ephemera. In 1924 Huntley & Palmer issued a biscuit tin in the shape of a funeral urn, with ancient Egyptians bearing gifts all around the base, and big golden rings as handles. Luxor toilet requisites ('preferred by fastidious women') launched a new advertising slogan: 'Have you, too, discovered Luxor?' Cinemas, such as – in the London area alone – the Kensington (1926), the Carlton, Upton Park (1929), the Luxor, Twickenham (1929), the Astoria, Streatham (1930) and the Carlton, Essex Road (1930), were built with temple façades, lotus-topped columns or 'daring Egyptian decorative schemes' within (plate 3.7).

The boy-pharaoh seemed – across the spectrum of visual culture – to be both ancient and modern at the same time. Ancient, in the obvious sense that – in the words of The Times leader of 16 February – 'five hundred years later did Homer sing ... at the first glimmering of European civilization'. Modern, in the sense that he died so young (between seventeen and twenty years old, Carter eventually estimated, like all those young soldiers in the trenches of Flanders) and, by a very 1920s telescoping of time, was an incarnation of the very essence of Modernism. The New York Times, under the headline 'Like Casualties from the Trenches', reported on 10 February 1923: 'As the objects have been brought

out, spectators have remarked that from the manner in which they were bandaged and transported with almost tender care on the stretcher-like trays, they reminded one of casualties being brought out of the trenches or casualty clearing stations.' The Manchester Guardian quoted photographer Harry Burton as saying that Tutankhamun must have been a dapper figure, as well as an outdoorsy young ruler and soldier, 'a man of fashion, scrupulously exact in the fit and hang of his garments'.[18] Tut was young, he was hip, and he evidently liked to surround himself with the latest luxury items: his funerary arrangements were like being buried with a favourite Type 35 2-litre Bugatti racer.

Avant-garde artist Wyndham Lewis celebrated this paradox by naming his pet dog 'Tut'. He also wrote provocative articles about the connections between modern art and the research conducted by G. Elliot Smith into ancient funeral ceremonies and mummification. Fernand Léger turned his attention from machines to pyramids and tomb paintings. René Clair (with Man Ray and Marcel Duchamp) included a camel in a sequence showing a Parisian funeral cortège as part of the film Entr'acte (1925). And the sculptor Alberto Giacometti, with his brother Diego, made a plaster table lamp (with the light concealed in the central vase) directly based on the lotus-like calcite lamp found in the burial chamber. The painter C. R. Nevinson supported the idea of a delegation of avant-garde artists and art critics visiting Luxor, to 'appraise the importance' of the artefacts to the modern world. The significance of pre-perspective and the flat depiction of the figure would be high on the agenda. Critic Clive Bell disagreed: 'I do not regard the art of the Tutankhamen period as at all of first-rate importance', he commented in an interview.[19]

Robert Graves and Alan Hodge, in their book The

Long Weekend, evoked the impact of these 'wonderful things' on London society by stressing 'the modernist spirit':

The discovery ... was given typical Twentyish publicity. Ancient Egypt became the vogue – in March 1923 the veteran Professor Flinders Petrie lectured on Egypt to an entranced Mayfair gathering. Replicas of the jewellery found in the Tomb, and hieroglyphic embroideries copied from its walls were worn on dresses ... Even the new model Singer sewing machine of that year went Pharaonic [actually it predated 1923], and it was seriously proposed that the Underground extension from Morden to Edgware, then under construction, should be called Tutancamden, because it passed through Tooting and Camden Town.

Graves and Hodge wondered why the 'interesting, ancient and beautiful discoveries' made at the same time by the archeologist Sir Leonard Woolley at Ur of the Chaldes in Mesopotamia (today's Iraq) did not capture the public imagination to the same extent. 'The fact was that Tutankhamen, who had succeeded his revolutionary father-in-law the Pharaoh Akhenaton, seemed somehow to embody the modernist spirit: whereas the Mesopotamians were boringly ancient.' One of the explanations for the special popular interest, they concluded, was the glint of gold.[20]

Evelyn Waugh agreed, and deplored the trivializing effects of Tutmania in one of his travel essays called 'Labels' (1929), compiled after visits to Bodell's Hotel in Port Said and the Mena House Hotel in Cairo: 'The romantic circumstances of the Tutankhamen discovery were so vulgarized in the popular press that one unconsciously came to regard it less as an artistic event than some deed of national prowess – a speed record broken, or a birth in the Royal Family.'[21]

3.7 George Cole, Carlton cinema,

Essex Road, London. 1930.

© Crown Copyright. NMR.

A few years earlier in Hollywood, Cecil B. De Mille had begun preparing his epic version of *The Ten Commandments* for Paramount Studios. De Mille was convinced that a mixture of religious epic, special effects, a parallel 'story of sin' set in the present day (which would, in fact, take up the lion's share of screen time), and Victorian morality contrasted with fashionably Egyptian opulence would ensure a mass audience. He ordered the Cairo offices of the Lasky Company to get hold of written and visual material on the discovery, and took a lot of persuading not to make King Tut (rather than Ramses II) the pharaoh who chased the Israelites out of Egypt. The film opened in December 1923; it cost $1.5 million and grossed $4 million. De Mille was to return to an ancient Egyptian theme in 1934 with *Cleopatra*, which owed less to Victorian paintings and more to contemporary decorative arts (plate 3.9). Visually to link a story that actually happened between 51 and 30 BC to one that happened over 1,200 years earlier, it began and ended with the great stones of a royal tomb opening and closing.[22]

In the Valley itself, Howard Carter and his team of archeologists found the 'world-wide publicity', with its attendant hordes of bored, hot and frustrated journalists and tourists, to be a huge irritation. When later asked what he thought of all the fuss about King Tut, Carter would testily reply 'the answer is spherical and in the plural'.[23] And yet, some of the most enduring monuments to Tutmania were singularly appropriate responses to the discovery, whatever Carter might say: in Paris, the Art Deco jewellery and pieces of furniture that are preserved in various collections; in Berlin, the sequence from Fritz Lang's film masterpiece *Metropolis* (planned 1924, released 1926), where the robot Maria – representing woman as a pleasure machine in the society of the future – performs an erotic, Deco-style Egyptian dance to amuse the dinner-jacketed guests in a city night-club (plate 3.8); in Moscow, the mummified corpse of the revolutionary leader Lenin, who died in January 1924 and was preserved with an embalming fluid, said to have been based on one 'used by the ancient Egyptians', so he could be worshipped forever – as the last pharaoh – in his glass-covered sarcophagus within a stone mausoleum at the foot of the Kremlin wall; in New York, the skyscraping and chrome-spangled Chrysler building, designed by William Van Alen and constructed in 1928-30, with its references to the Luxor temple amid the hubcap friezes, stainless steel gargoyles and brickwork wheels on the outside,

stylized lotus-flowers on the elevator doors inside, and pyramidal windows everywhere – a mixture of the luxury of ancient Egypt and the mechanical precision of the motor car; in London, the flamboyant frontage of the Hoover factory on the Great West Road designed by Wallis, Gilbert & Partners in 1930 – of which J. B. Priestley famously wrote three years later 'Being new it did not look English' (see plate 22.14).[24]

From the strictly 'historical' point of view, the discovery of the tomb of Tutankhamun added very little to the sum of knowledge about ancient Egypt. The tomb contained no written documents, which disappointed the philologists of the Egyptological establishment. 'What have we found out?', wrote Carter. 'Remarkably little when you come right down to it.' But, as philologist Alan Gardiner concluded, there was no doubt whatsoever about the visual significance of the find: 'as a revelation of the *artistic* achievement of the period, the discovery was quite unparalleled. Nothing like it had been discovered before.'[25] One reason why news of the discovery so rapidly turned into news of all sorts of other things was that there was so little textual 'history' to write about: another history, a design history, emerged to take its place.

3.8 *Metropolis*, directed by Fritz Lang, 1926. BFI Stills, Posters and Designs. Courtesy of Transit Film GmbH.

3.9 Claudette Colbert wearing Egyptian head-dress, bracelet and ring, in *Cleopatra*, directed by Cecil B. De Mille, 1934. BFI Stills, Posters and Designs. Courtesy of Universal Studios Licensing LLLP.

4 Deco Sculpture and Archaism

Penelope Curtis

Not all Deco sculpture is 'archaic', and not all 'archaic' sculpture is Deco. The influence of the archaic was widespread and certainly preceded Art Deco. Many visual artists, including those who had studied the classical canon in the cast galleries of their art schools, were influenced by a wave of new archeological discoveries,[1] and inspired to look beyond the corpus of Hellenistic sculpture (or Roman copies) to their 'archaic' predecessors. Such traits can be seen in the first decade of the century in the work of Antoine Bourdelle, Paul Manship, Georg Kolbe and even of a so-called 'Classicist' such as Aristide Maillol (plates 4.2 and 4.3).

By the time we enter the Deco period properly speaking (that is to say by the 1920s), we find many artists using archaic sculpture to simplify their figurative modelling – from so-called 'figurative' artists such as Ludwig Kasper or Hermann Blumenthal, on the one hand, to so-called 'abstract' artists such as Henry Moore on the other. Yet, their work is far too severe to fit into the Art Deco category. Indeed, the simplification provoked by the archaic tended, on occasion, towards an almost 'ugly' aesthetic that would seem to counter everything represented by Art Deco.

So why have the two been linked together? In many countries, in the first two decades of the century, the news of archeological discoveries was either absolutely current, or was filtering through by means of museum displays and illustrated literature (see Chapters 3 and 5). In any case, a new awareness of ancient sculpture was, naturally, especially meaningful for sculptors. Whether Egyptian, Etruscan or Cretan, the increasing range of alternative norms of figuration deeply affected a period when figuration was still central to practice.

4.2 Paul Manship, *Europa and the Bull*. Bronze. American, 1924. Collection John P. Axelrod, Boston, MA.

4.1 Carl Milles, *Dancing Maenad*. Bronze. Swedish, 1912. Carl Milles Museum, Stockholm. © DACS 2002.

But though we might term Moore's interest in the Mayan, or Epstein's in the African, 'archaic', we do not. Instead, these interests have traditionally been termed 'primitive', or more recently, 'non-western'. The reason, I think, for their not being seen as part of the archaizing tendency is closely connected to Art Deco. The archaic influence in sculpture has been most widely linked to the decorative and linear forms of Art Deco and, consequently, often appears in relief form (plate 4.1). The Art Deco composition is very often slightly contorted so as to fit into a frame, as if the image were a woodcut, rather than freely modelled in the round. In fact, in many ways Art Deco style is rather closer to sources that are not so readily grouped under the 'archaic' label (which we would understand as pre-classical) – Indian, for example – which have a greater voluptuousness and virtuosity of design.

The archaic was largely discovered in ancient sites, in carving, in stone. It was, ipso facto, a decorative style in that it was found on and within architecture. While the modern archaic was to be found on the façades of buildings, by no means all relief sculpture in the first two decades of the century was both archaic and Deco. Bourdelle's series of tympanum carvings of 1910-13 for the Théâtre des Champs Elysées in Paris (designed by the architect Auguste Perret) was among the most influential relief works of the period (plate 4.3). This work, I would argue, is 'archaic' but not Deco, whereas another contemporary relief – Joseph Bernard's *La Danse* – which later featured, in four differently enlarged versions, at the Paris 1925 Exhibition, could be Deco because it was not archaic (see plate 12.2). Bourdelle's reliefs represented a 'classical' subject – Apollo and the Muses – but in such anti-classical form that they provoked considerable controversy. They avoided being subsumed as decorative art precisely because of their ungainliness; they were blunt-cut, angular, crudely modelled and somewhat

4.4 Raoul-Eugène Lamourdedieu, lamp stand. Silver-plated bronze, marble and glass. French, c.1930. V&A: Circ.197-1972.

contorted. The comparatively fluid grace of Bernard's treatment made it more suitable for the Art Deco environment, not least because of the repeatability and adaptability of the extended motif.

Bourdelle's important collaboration with Perret was a linear style, appropriate to the latter's concrete architecture in its slightly blunt muscularity, with unconventional massing and detailing. By the 1920s, however, the 'archaic' was becoming increasingly easy on the eye, streamlined to take account of mass production, and closely associated with the market for decorative goods for 'modern living'. The use of the lithe 'modern' female, strutting or prancing on her tip-toes, seems to have its roots in an archaic-modern style which precedes Art Deco, with an alternative source in the growing sculptural enthusiasm for modern dance in the years around 1914 (and itself an archaizing interest) (plate 4.4).[2] Bourdelle's fascination with Isadora Duncan (who inspired the Champs-Elysées frieze) was shared by many sculptors in Europe and America who were interested in her unconventional (un-pretty) postures and movements. The long career of the Swedish academician Carl Milles, largely devoted to producing aerial and axial figures, must also have fed into the popularization of the moving, airborne figure. One might well see Milles's decorative figures and

4.3 Antoine Bourdelle, *La Danse, Isadora Duncan et Nijinsky.* Plaster. French, 1910-13. Study for a relief for the Théâtre des Champs Elysées, Paris. Musée Bourdelle, Paris. © PMVP. Photo: Briant/Ladet. © ADAGP, Paris and DACS, London 2002.

4.5 Jacques Lipchitz (born in Lithuania), *Woman with Gazelles*. Bronze, edition of 7. 1911. © Estate of Jacques Lipchitz. Courtesy Marlborough Gallery, New York.

fountain ensembles as the highbrow version of the energetic dynamism so characteristic of Art Deco at all levels. Although Milles's repertoire of classical subjects is largely standard, their arrangements are increasingly jazzy, especially after his removal to America in 1930.

Archaic–modern sculpture has a symmetrical and linear tendency (stemming, I suggest, from its association with the architectural relief). This was transferred into set groups or tableaux, which, though nominally three-dimensional, are primarily pictorial and work especially well as decorative punctuation marks or screens. Notable examples emanated from three very different sculptors working in different countries: Italy, France and America. Libero

4.6 Paul Manship, *Dancer and Gazelles*. Bronze. American, 1916. Francis Lathrop Bequest Fund. The Metropolitan Museum of Art, New York. Photo: Jerry L. Thompson.

4.7 Gio Ponti, 'La conversazione classica', vase. Porcelain. Italian, 1927. Made by Richard-Ginori. The Mitchell Wolfson Jr Collection. The Wolfsonian-Florida International University, Miami Beach, Florida. Photo: Silvia Ross.

Andreotti's *Diana and Actaeon* (1913-14) is remarkably close to *Woman with Gazelles* by Jacques Lipchitz (1911) and *Dancer and Gazelles* by Paul Manship (1916) (plates 4.5 and 4.6).[3] In an inverse manner to bozzetti or maquettes, these large, full-scale sculptures suggest themselves as diminutive and infinitely repeatable. They represent a number of characteristics of Art Deco sculpture. They would work just as well as a design for a bookplate as for a sculpture in the gallery. Although they represent movement, the movement is contained. The sculpture is rhythmic rather than dynamic, and the rhythm folds back in on itself, rather than creating any kind of sculptural tension.

This kind of 'designed sculpture' was progressively downgraded in status until it was literally no more than a beautiful pattern, wrought in iron, to adorn villas such as the Courtaulds' Eltham Palace at Greenwich, London, or the Serralves in Porto, which both had Art Deco interiors showcasing leading European craftsmen and artists. This is decorative sculpture. Its roots may lie in Andreotti's interest in the Quattrocento, or in Manship's enthusiasm for Assyrian and Indian sculpture, but it has moved a long way from academia. The works are objects of

desire, not only for the elite who patronized the exclusive Parisian salons or for the Côte d'Azur villas of the educated patron, but also for the many who wished to furnish their new apartments in a manner that spoke of the twentieth century. Such images preceded the seemingly inexhaustible supply of dynamic female (and male) figurines that were made by artists such as Demêtre Chiparus, Ferdinand Preiss and Pierre Le Faguys and marketed by commercial *maisons d'édition* (plate 4.8).[4] In deriving their models from the contemporary and actual stars of sport and dance, their creators followed a trend already set by more serious artists, such as Georg Kolbe, who had represented Nijinsky in a syncopated pose even before the Jazz Age.

In acknowledging the growth of a 'modern' sculpture that was also small-scale (which in the work of sculptors such as François Pompon, Rembrandt Bugatti and John Skeaping helped to re-invigorate and transform the nineteenth-century *animalier* tradition), we move some distance from archaism (see plates 12.11 and 21.7). The Depression stimulated artists to find alternative ways of working, and there are many examples of successful partnerships with enterprising companies (such as Wedgwood, Royal Doulton or Richard-Ginori) to produce 'modern' items within a largely conventional language of decorative ceramic ware. The designs produced by the architect Gio Ponti (frequently in collaboration with the sculptor Andreotti) for Ginori are perhaps an unusually intellectual example of such a collaboration (plate 4.7).[5] Ponti inserted classical motifs into a chic contemporary context, but even if his delightful designs seem apolitical, his project has to be understood in the context of the right-wing reclamation of the Mediterranean at this time (especially in Italy). Etruscan types were used for various political purposes, but indicate a consistent concern for an 'indigenous' Italian classicism. Ponti wished to assert an everyday classicism, using Etruscan, Pompeian and Ostian references to assert the domestic lineage.

The chic of Art Deco sculpture – its clean and streamlined forms, its use of lustrous and often shiny materials – may have roots in the work of the pre-war avant-garde (Boccioni and Brancusi, for example, see plates 9.4 and 34.8), but chic is not in any serious sense an attribute of the archaic. And if we were to examine Brancusi's forms (which undoubtedly were debased into popular decorative sculpture) we would find them in folk and primitive art rather than in the archaic. Art Deco sculpture celebrates modern pleasures and provides them with

a superficial classical pedigree. It can readily be associated with certain places (the cinema, the ocean liner, the luxury villa), with certain materials (new synthetic plastics, chrome, brass and colonial woods) and with certain themes (the classical myth, the Mediterranean), but to what extent is it archaic? To my mind there is something of a mismatch here. Art Deco sculpture is rarely part of the more serious formal investigation that marks the use of the archaic at this time. This search was less commonly conducted in luscious or exotic materials, and less commonly associated with primarily attractive results. The use of the archaic to give a more austerely constructed form, with a taut inner construction and a less highly modelled surface (as seen, for example, in the work of Georg Kolbe or Gerhard Marcks in Germany, Carl Burckhardt in Switzerland, Charles Despiau in France, or J. Havard Thomas in England), needs to be distinguished from the less searching use of the 'archaic' in some Art Deco sculpture. In the latter category surely belong English sculptors such as Gilbert Bayes, Walter Gilbert and even Sargeant Jagger, who are often neglected because they do not fit in the usual categories of British sculpture. In fact, their very decorativeness makes them more European, and 'archaic' in the Art Deco sense.[6]

That sculpture was exhibited at the Paris 1925 Exhibition is certainly no guarantee of its 'Deco' quality. Jan Štursa's *Victory* (1921) shows his personal affiliation to Rodin and derives from a *retardataire* commission.[7] How elastic is the 'Art Deco' term? Should it be used for works made well after 1925? The sculptural programme of New York's Rockefeller Center (1931-9) can be seen as an Art Deco project par excellence, and indeed many of the sculptors involved were immigrants with a European training (see plates 22.11 and 22.12). Its concern was to achieve a modern 'unity of the arts', absorbing motifs from classical mythology within a bold modern idiom derived as much from the billboard as from the Beaux-Arts.[8] But would we be right to see the 1937 *Exposition internationale des arts et des techniques* in Paris as effectively embracing its 1925 predecessor? I think not. The classicism portrayed in the 1937 commissions, notably in the Palais de Tokyo complex, is a much more grounded, rounded and (one might say) classical figuration. The *Apollo* by Despiau intended for this exhibition (but not finished in time) is neither archaic, nor Deco. With 1937 we confront a serious return to a non-archaic classicism which alerts us to the very different European climate of the 1930s.

4.8 Demêtre Chiparus (Romanian),
Les Girls. Bronze and ivory.
Around 1930. Private collection.

5 Ancient Mexican Sources of Art Deco

Oriana Baddeley

In Larry Cohen's 1982 film *Q: The Winged Serpent*[1] the ancient Mexican god Quetzalcoatl is resurrected, by a deranged curator from the Metropolitan Museum, to terrorize New York from a nest within the pinnacle of the Chrysler building (plate 5.1).[2] While most other elements of this tongue in cheek horror movie are manifestly ridiculous there is a strange appropriateness in the juxtaposition between the architecture of this iconic building and the iconography of Aztec religion. The association of the architectural aesthetics of Art Deco New York with the culture of ancient Mexico is not merely a Post-modernist irony. As early as 1931 the New York papers could introduce an article on Diego Rivera under the heading 'Mexican Artist Calls Manhattan Towers Offspring of Old Yucatan Temples'[3] and expect a sense of recognition from a popular audience. The block-like mass, ziggurat forms and patterns of Manhattan's skyline, or the jutting eagles of the Chrysler building, evoked rather than replicated the militaristic decorations of Aztec temple design. However, there was a brash assertion of power and extravagance in their design, a shared fascination with geometric form, which carried a resonance of the lost civilizations of Mesoamerica (plate 5.2).

These geometric forms and patterns, seen as intrinsic characteristics of the art of ancient Mexico, found new life in the architecture and design of the 1920s and 1930s, primarily through their introduction into the architectural languages of North America. This was not a learned reworking of the visual culture of past civilizations, and it frequently lacked authenticity. Instead, the introduction of ancient Mexico to the conceptual framework of western designers stems from a wider aspiration, to escape from the constraints of the classical European tradition and to contravene the accepted rules of proportion and articulation. Ancient Greece and Rome were replaced by their perceived opposites, ancient cultures outside of the European norms. In this context, the accuracy of historical or geographic quotation was not important since the priority was to achieve a novel, exotic effect (plate 5.3).

The tendency that is found in the formal languages of Art Deco to make dislocated reference to ancient cultures is a commonly recognized characteristic of the style, frequently referred to in passing as if too obvious to need explanation. Often the historical sources are used eclectically, in an undiscriminating

raid on the pattern books of the past. Egyptian, Japanese, Islamic, Celtic or Mesoamerican motifs appear to co-exist in the artistic vocabulary of the designer, giving the impression of an unspecified historicism. The self-consciousness of the appropriation of ancient design motifs appears to diminish the need for explanation or exploration of meaning, the act of reference becomes self justifying.

This promiscuousness was perhaps not surprising, given that the term 'Mesoamerican' was used to describe all the ancient cultures of modern day Mexico and Central America – encompassing a multiplicity of cultural forms – and given Art Deco's birth amid the assertive nationalisms of the World Fairs.[4] In fact, many of the elements of ancient American design that appealed to the exponents of Art Deco can be traced to the impact of works such as Antonio Peñafiel's 'Aztec Palace' at the 1889 Paris World Fair[5] or Edward H. Thompson's models of Maya architecture for the 1893 Chicago *Columbian Exhibition* (plates 5.4 and 5.5). These two nineteenth-century manifestations of the introduction of Mesoamerican motifs within the context of contemporary design exemplified a duality

5.3 Lydia Bush-Brown Head, 'Temple of the Mayan Indians'. Silk. American, 1926. Gift of Mrs Francis Head. Cooper-Hewitt, National Design Museum, Smithsonian Institution.

of approach that was to remain central to the popularization of ancient Mexico in the 1920s and 1930s. The 'Aztec Palace' was the most expensive and largest display Mexico had ever put on at a World Fair. In its design Peñafiel attempted a complex synthesis of ancient Mexican motifs and symbolism within a context of 'modern' European taste. Token gestures were made to the Aztec aesthetic but the pavilion functioned primarily as a symbol of a new, independent, modern and cosmopolitan Mexico. The symbols of the pre-Conquest past were represented via the formal languages of Europe.[6] The severe geometries of Aztec sculpture were softened and transformed into classically proportioned figural representations, more palatable to a Parisian audience. The patterning and decorative detail retained a greater authenticity but brought together temporally distant source material into an amalgam of styles. The 'Aztec Palace'

5.4 Antonio Peñafiel, 'Aztec Palace' for the Mexican pavilion at the 1889 Paris World Fair. Larson Collection, California State University, Fresno.

presented a synthetic Mexico by dissolving identity into easily reproducible forms and filtering out the perceived impurities. By contrast, the models of the Maya temples at Uxmal and Labna shown at the Chicago Exhibition attempted to give as accurate as possible a reconstruction of the Yucatec ruins. Their creator was the archeologist and American Consul to Mexico, Edward H. Thompson. His presentation appeared under the mantle of scientific enquiry not nationalist rhetoric, part of an attempt to illustrate the progressive stages of formal development within the diversity of 'exotic' architecture.[7] Mayan architecture appeared at the Chicago Exhibition as exemplary of a specific stage of aesthetic development rather than as a symbol of post-colonial identity. It was shown in all its reconstructed glory, the repeating patterns of stonework emphasizing the complexity of the exterior façades – interior space became an irrelevance. The shared characteristics

of such geographically remote civilizations as Mesoamerica and Japan could be noted at the exhibition and added to the storehouse of architectural knowledge available to the contemporary practitioner. This vision of decorated surface and interlocking form was to serve as the initial inspiration for Frank Lloyd Wright's abiding interest in ancient American architecture.[8] To some extent, however, the models of the Maya temples of the Yucatan appeared as dislocated from historical

reality as the 'Aztec Palace'; they floated into the western imagination as pristine and deserted utopias divorced from any understanding of cultural context.

Through these hybrid and often fantastical works the architectural detail of ancient Mexico entered the repertoire of ornamentation available to early twentieth-century western architects and designers and their audiences. Few of the artists and designers who used these stereotyped stylistic references had first hand knowledge of the places and objects they

5.5 Edward H. Thompson, replica of Mayan nunnery temple at Uxmal. *Chicago, Columbian Exhibition Album*, New York, 1893. Cooper-Hewitt, National Design Museum, Smithsonian Institution.

5.6 Robert Stacy-Judd, Aztec
Hotel, Monrovia, California.
1925. Francis Onderdonk,
The Ferro-Concrete Style,
New York, 1928. NAL.

were visually quoting. Like a game of 'Chinese whispers', shapes, designs and iconographic details were passed from building to building, object to object; Mesopotamian could be merged with Mayan with little pedantry as to the accuracy of the visual reference. In fact, the very purpose of the activity was to assert a set of shared characteristics across time and space. The works of Robert Stacy-Judd, such as his 1925 Aztec Hotel in Monrovia, include specific references to Maya architecture but also use decorative detail that refers more generally to Mesoamerican culture (plate 5.6).[9] The decorative detail 'explains' itself, as in the great exuberance of 'exotic' cultural references in the cinema architecture of the Twenties and Thirties. The famous 1927 Mayan Theatre in Los Angeles, designed by Morgan, Walls & Clements, manifests perfectly this aspect of the Art Deco appropriation of archaic design motifs (plate 5.7). The elaborate façade, interior murals and decorations pay lip service to its nomenclature but show little regard for consistency of derivation.

Elements from widely disparate historical and geographic locations are amalgamated into a hybrid style as distant from any notion of an original as Disney's *Aladdin* is from *Arabian Nights*. However, it is arguable that this spirit of fantasy is appropriate to both the form and function of the building and it is, in a sense, irrelevant that the architects have subverted the norms of an archaic aesthetic. The patterning of the façade evokes textile design, but more Peruvian than Mayan, a reflection of the general tendency to amalgamate the ancient cultures of America into an amorphous whole. By using elements from the temporally diverse indigenous cultures of South, Central and North America, a surface appearance of the 'Indian Americas' was created.[10] In the slightly later building of 1929 for the Sampson Rubber and Tire Company, by the same team, the amalgamation of styles incorporating both Old and New World sources is equally evident, despite the acknowledged inspiration of the Temple of Khorsabad.

While recognizing this deliberately homogenizing aspect of Art Deco's approach to Mesoamerican sources, it is also necessary to challenge the presumed randomness of the choice of inspiration. In the Americas the nineteenth century had witnessed a growing need to lay claim to an ancient past that symbolized difference from that of Europe in various ways. In the newly independent states of Latin America the particular derivation of the historical reference often carried enormous symbolic meaning (see Chapter 37), while in the United States an amorphous vision of indigenous American culture was increasingly called upon to exemplify national identity.[11]

In this frame of meaning, while developmental models such as those of the Chicago Exhibition – based on a nineteenth-century classification of cultural achievement, in which cultures occupied specific positions within a hierarchy of development from barbarism to civilization – were significant, so too were other sources. The search for ancient roots found its most obvious source of visual material in the representations of Maya architecture, which in the early twentieth century could boast by far the greatest number of scholarly publications illustrating both ruined remains and artists' reconstructions of temple complexes.[12] From the late eighteenth century on, the North American and European imagination had been captured by the exploration of the mysterious temple cities of the Maya. In the mid nineteenth century the Maya civilization was popularized further by the bestselling books of John L. Stephens and his artist companion Frederick Catherwood.[13] In the later part of the nineteenth century, following the success of Stephens and Catherwood, a series of well-received publications focused on the Maya as the high civilization of the Americas. Through these publications Maya art and architecture was rediscovered by foreign audiences and perceived as somehow distant from the violent excesses associated with the Aztecs. The emphasis on a figurative style of representation, the complexity of the hieroglyphic script and the romance of the 'lost' ruins in the jungle all compounded this vision of the Maya as a people disconnected from the barbaric and savage natives described by Spanish conquerors. By contrast, as late as the first years of the twentieth century Aztec/Central Mexican sculpture was seen as artefact not art because of its contravention of the norms of classical aesthetics. Maya carving, however, with its flowing organic lines and emphasis on the human form was taken far more seriously as an art form. By 1913, not only was Maya art acknowledged as existing in its own right, it was also deemed by

Herbert Spinden in his *Study of Maya Art* to be of greater artistic merit than the art of Egypt.[14] By 1914 the Carnegie Institute had begun archeological work in the region, under the direction of Sylvanus Griswold Morley, that was to be enormously influential in promoting an interest in Maya culture.[15] The Yucatan became the primary location of the 'mysterious past of the Americas', so much so, that in the early Twenties the *New York Times* sponsored an archeological expedition by the Peabody Museum[16] to explore the then remote eastern coast around Cancun.

The use of the term 'Mesoamerican' had also papered over a major divide within ancient American studies between Maya and Highland Mexican. By the 1920s, at the height of interest in Maya culture in the United States, the stark division between Maya/civilized, Aztec/barbaric began to blur. Manuel Gamio's explorations of the great city of Teotihuacan[17] revealed an older, grander civilization in highland Mexico. The writers and artists of the Mexican Revolution (1910-19) glorified the cultures of central Mexico, seeing the Aztecs as a symbol of the oppressed and colonized, not as barbaric savages. Key figures in the reappropriation of the Aztec past linked the aesthetic of the new machine age to that of ancient Mexico. Diego Rivera, for example, abandoned Cubism and experimented with ancient Teotihuacan mural techniques, while Edward Weston photographed the stark contours of its architecture. D. H. Lawrence and other visiting artists and writers picnicked in its ruins.[18] The Aztec past of post-revolutionary Mexican rhetoric was a golden era cruelly destroyed by European conquest, its roots stretching back to ancient times. The traditional distaste for the stark, geometric aesthetic of central Mexico was inverted to become a recognition of its abstract purity of form. Admiration for the elaborate detailing of Maya architectural decoration was replaced by a liking for the less cluttered, simpler

5.7 Morgan, Walls & Clements, Mayan Theatre, Los Angeles. Bas-relief façade with Mayan figures by Francisco Cornejo. 1927. Photo: John Margolies/Esto.

5.8 Auguste Lazo (Mexican), tile with
Mayan motifs. Stoneware. Made by
American Encaustic Tiling Co. 1928.
Collection John P. Axelrod, Boston, MA.
Courtesy Museum of Fine Arts, Boston.

5.9 Frank Lloyd Wright, Hollyhock House, Los Angeles. 1921. Photo: Nathalie Tepper/Arcaid.

5.10 Miller & Pflueger, Dental and Medical building, San Francisco. 1929.
Photo courtesy of Harsch Investments Properties.

outlines of the northerly cultures. The characteristics of the 'civilized' Maya began to look a little outdated – swept away by the assertive centralizing power of the Aztec imperial style. This shift of emphasis was even reflected in the archeological work of the Carnegie Institute project, which revealed a new hybrid form of ancient Mexican architecture through its excavations at the Yucatec city of Chichen Itza, with its clearly Toltec-influenced sculptural decorations.

In the historiography of Mesoamerican studies[19] the championing of either side of this divide provoked enormous partisanship, reflecting both the Mexican state's view of Mexico's heritage and the predilections of the international archeologist. While most scholars and archeologists were forced to recognize the close links between the two regions, they seldom strayed too far from specialization within one camp or the other. However, whether 'Mayanist' or 'Mexicanist', few authors challenged the notion of the Maya as the 'high culture' of Mesoamerica when basing such judgements on aesthetic criteria.

These changing interests and associations were reflected in the work of contemporary American and Latin American architects and designers seeking to express a cultural identity independent of European models. For these, the associated meanings of the design source within a wider cultural framework were frequently an intrinsic part of its appeal. In California, Frank Lloyd Wright's designs for private dwellings, the Millard, Freeman, Storer, Ennis and Hollyhock houses (1921-4) (plate 5.9), played with decorative themes from the Yucatec sites, casting them in concrete blocks – a style also used by his son Lloyd in the 1926 Sowden House. Possibly the greatest example of the Mayan revival of the 1920s was Miller & Pflueger's Dental and Medical building at 450 Sutter St in San Francisco (plate 5.10). The combination of complexity of decoration and simplicity of form, presented so clearly by Thompson in the Chicago Exhibition, offered a style indicative of both civilization and modern exoticism. The young architect combined a steel frame structure with terracotta tile decoration in Mayan style. While the lobby and the windows are elaborately ornamented, the massive exterior is uncompromisingly geometric. The building represented the 'new modern world' in its structure, and yet laid claim to its alternative heritage in its decoration. Pflueger's interest in a Pan-American aesthetic encompassed the contemporary as well as the ancient past of Mexico and he was crucially involved in inviting Diego Rivera to the United States to paint a mural at the Pacific Stock Exchange in 1931.[20]

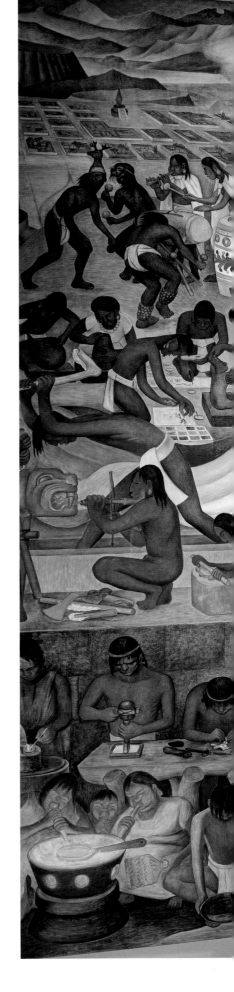

5.11 Manuel Amabilis, Mexican pavilion for the 1929 *Ibero-American Fair*, Seville. Collection Loïc Menanteau.

5.12 Diego Rivera, *Elements from the Past and Present*, panel B from *Pan American Unity*. 1940. City College of San Francisco. Originally painted and installed in the Palace of Fine and Decorative Arts at the 1939-40 *Golden Gate International Exhibition*. © City College of San Francisco.

At the same time, the shift of emphasis from the 'civilized' Maya to the assertive Aztec imperial style was manifested in Manuel Amabilis's compromise design for the Mexican pavilion at the 1929 Seville *Ibero-American Fair* (plate 5.11).[21] The pavilion was in the newly fashionable Maya–Toltec style and self-consciously incorporated modern constructional elements, aiming to create a synthesis of Mayan/Mexican, past/present that would represent the values of the new revolutionary Mexico. The sculptural decorations by Leopoldo Tomassi featured variations on the theme of the plumed serpent columns of Chichen Itza. The Maya–Toltec style offered a pre-Hispanic model of the way in which hybrid architectural forms could be unified, reflecting the interests of contemporary designers in a homogeneous ancient Mexican tradition.

The imagery of the deity Quetzalcoatl (variously translated as plumed serpent, feathered serpent, flying serpent), which was primarily associated with Teotihuacan, Toltec and Aztec iconography, in conjunction with the recognizable Mayan architectural ornament, also appealed to popular audiences. The Amabilis pavilion managed simultaneously to represent the specifics of the past and suggest the contemporary relevance of the ancient Mexican forms. The theme of unity was completed at Seville by the dominating central panel of eagle, serpent and cactus above the door. While the image was the recognizable representation of the Mexican state, it was also the insignia of the Aztec capital Tenochtitlan, reborn in colonial times as Mexico City. The changing tastes of international audiences in relation to decorative ornament in the early part of the twentieth century was clearly reflected in the shift of interest from Maya to Mexican cultural forms. The ornate intricacy of Mayan decoration gave way to the simpler, geometric mass of the central Mexican aesthetic, just as the move from the surface-obsessed Twenties to the shape-obsessed Thirties occurred.

In 1939, as war broke out in Europe, Timothy Pflueger invited Rivera back to San Francisco to participate in the *Golden Gate International Exhibition*. The original aim had been to have a two-year show of Old Masters, but the worried owners recalled their works after only one year leaving a large gap in the programme. Instead of the cream of the European heritage, Pflueger arranged for Rivera to become a living exhibit painting the largest of his murals in the United States. The title of the five-panelled work was *Pan American Unity* (plate 5.12). Panel B has the subheading *Elements from the Past and Present*. In the centre of the panel a Mexican peasant sculptor carves a massive feathered serpent. Rising from behind this image is Pflueger's Sutter St building. As with the Chrysler building at the beginning of this discussion the juxtaposition is appropriate. What better to represent the paradox of aspirations implicit in the revival of the ancient American past than the bird that slithers, the reptile that flies.

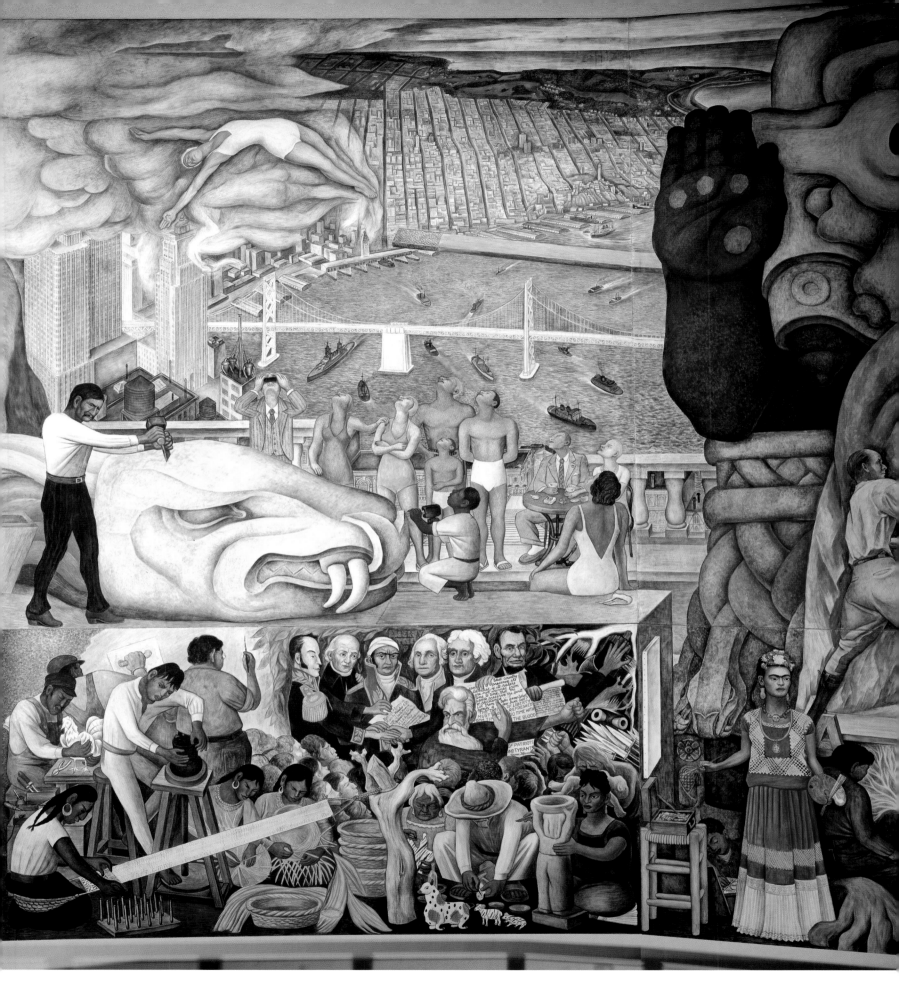

6 Inspiration from the East

Anna Jackson

Many artists and art historians of today ... proclaim that European art is dead and the maxim 'ex oriente lux' is to be most rigorously applied to our aesthetic culture, if it is to be saved from destruction.

Thus wrote Bengt de Törne in the first edition of the journal *Apollo* in June 1925. He felt the influence to be of grave concern, however, for the 'oriental manifesto is exceedingly dangerous ... all our admiration for oriental or any exotic art, however intense and enthusiastic, should help us find our own occidental soul, instead of losing it'.[1] While some may have viewed the impact of East Asia on western culture in the early decades of the twentieth century with alarm rather than enthusiasm, there is no doubt that the arts of Japan and China were important ingredients in the eclectic mix that informed the style and spirit of Art Deco.

Asian art had provided an inspiration to European artists and designers ever since trade between East and West was established in the sixteenth century. In the second half of the nineteenth century, when Japan burst upon the cultural scene following the 'opening' of the country to foreign trade and diplomacy, this influence became a dominant feature in the emergence of new artistic styles.[2] Japan had a particularly profound influence on Art Nouveau artists, designers and craftsmen who discovered in its art sophisticated aesthetic precedents that seemed simultaneously traditional and modern, exotic and, above all, decorative.[3] The simplification of pictorial space, the accentuation and interpenetration of pattern and ground, and the use of dramatic lines, bold, flat colours and geometric and stylized natural forms were all lessons drawn from East Asia that Art Deco absorbed through Art Nouveau. While it was generally the essence, rather than the specifics, of Asian patterns and structures that proved inspirational, particular Japanese and Chinese shapes and motifs were a feature of much Art Deco design (plates 6.1 and 6.2). Above all, however, it was the materials and techniques of East Asian art that proved most influential in the evolution of the style.

In the first decades of the twentieth century the development of international travel networks brought Asia closer to Europe, while numerous publications and exhibitions made its art available to an ever-growing audience. Dealers such as Yamanaka & Co., operating mainly in Britain and America, and C. T. Loo, based in his red pagoda in Paris, supplied Asian art to numerous private and public collections.[4] The art of Japan still had strong appeal, but there was a major shift of interest towards China. In 1911 Guillaume Apollinaire declared his belief that 'Chinese art – powerful, noble and sweeping – might well inherit the admiration that has hitherto been reserved for the Japanese, who, aping the great art of China, have produced only a dwarf.'[5] Certainly in

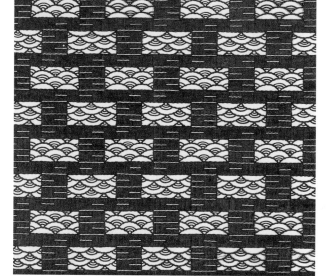

6.1 Detail from imperial dragon robe. Embroidered silk. Chinese, 19th century. V&A: T.199-1948.

6.2 Stencil for use in textile dyeing. Paper. Japanese, late 19th century. V&A: D.1163 and 1195-1891.

the years after the First World War the number of
books and articles written about Chinese art far
exceeded that written about Japan.[6] There were
various reasons for this: Japan was no longer much
of a mystery and its art had ceased to be a novelty;
excavations in China brought the art of early periods
to the attention of the West for the first time;[7] and,
most importantly, certain types of Chinese art were
attributed a particular cultural significance, a subject
that will be explored in more detail later in this essay.
In all, it was 'hard to recall so fundamental a
revolution in the opinions of the world of arts as the
marked change of attitudes towards Chinese art
among the leaders of artistic thought'.[8] A number
of important exhibitions of Chinese art took place
in Europe and America in the period, culminating in
1935 in the *International Exhibition of Chinese Art*
held at Burlington House in London, which featured
over 3,000 exhibits dating from the Neolithic period
to the eighteenth century.

Art Deco designers were drawn to various aspects
of Chinese art and design. The powerful, mysterious
motifs on ancient Shang and Zhou dynasty bronzes,
the elegant shapes and monochrome glazes of Sung
and Yuan dynasty ceramics, the simple lines of
Ming and Qing dynasty hardwood furniture and the
geometric forms and motifs common to much
Chinese decorative art and architecture, all provided
inspiration.[9] Interest in China was also aroused by
the work of the Russian émigré artist Alexandre
Iacovleff, who became famous in Paris in the 1920s
for his striking paintings and drawings of East Asia,
particularly the Chinese theatre (plate 6.3). Iacovleff
later accompanied the two momentous expeditions
led by Georges-Marie Haardt and financed by André
Citroën (see Chapter 11), the second of which, the
Croisière Jaune (1931-2), made the overland journey
across Asia from the Mediterranean to the East
China Sea.

The influence of Japan, and more especially China,
was evident in many aspects of Art Deco design.
In fashion the impact of Asia was apparent in the
abandonment of tightly corseted, highly structured
garments in favour of less tailored lengths of fabric
that wrapped or draped the body. In the 1920s this
was seen in evening coats that enveloped the wearer
and in the cylindrical line of the archetypal 'flapper'
dress, in which the flattened forms and straight
seams of Asian garments found their most visible
manifestation. The Japanese kimono was the most
obvious source for such styles, but the advent of
rounded necklines and tubular sleeves revealed the
influence of Chinese garments.[10] Many fashion plates
of the period were reminiscent of Japanese prints of

6.3 General Ma-Soo in *The Retreat of Kiai-Ting*.
Illustration from Chu-Chia-Chein and Alexandre Iacovleff,
The Chinese Theatre, London, 1922. NAL.

beautiful women, but the settings were often more
Chinese-inspired (plate 6.4). The patterns on clothes
were also more Chinese than Japanese in style.
Dragons chased around the waistband of one of the
gowns Paquin created for the 1925 Exhibition, while
the sequin and diamanté cloud-like motifs on the
rest of the garment echoed those found on Chinese
robes (plates 6.1 and 6.5).

Similar elements were seen in Art Deco jewellery.
Several of Cartier's cigarette and vanity cases derived

from Japanese inrō,[11] but on the whole the Chinese
influence on jewellery was far more apparent.
This was seen in the predominance of stylized and
geometric motifs, the popularity of tasselled
pendants (see plate 24.16) and, most importantly,
in the use of materials. Cartier often used lacquer
inlaid with mother-of-pearl taken from Chinese bowls,
trays or tables.[12] However, the material most
favoured for the creation of modern, colourful and
exotic jewellery was jade. 'Jade is all the rage at
present', declared one journal in 1922. 'It owes its
popularity, no doubt, both to its romantic association
with the gorgeous East and prehistoric art, and to
the beauty of its delicate colour.'[13]

6.4 Georges Lepape, 'La belle dame sans merci', evening gown by Worth. *La Gazette du bon ton*, Paris, 1921. NAL. ©ADAPG, Paris and DACS, London 2002.

6.5 Jeanne Paquin, 'Chimère', evening gown. Beaded silk. French, 1925. V&A: T.50-1948.

6.7 Boucheron, circular brooch. Jade, carved lapis lazuli and platinum. French, c.1925. Mauboussin, two bracelets. Gold, set with carved jade, lapis or coral. French, c.1927. Anon. bracelet. Carved jade, with coral set with diamonds on platinum. French, c.1925. Collection Victor and Gretha Arwas, London.

Jade is worked in various parts of the world, but is associated primarily with China, where it has been used since before 5000 BC.[14] Jade is to China what gold and precious gems are to the West. It is valued for both its physical and metaphorical attributes, a famous passage attributed to Confucius expressing the virtues believed to be embodied by the qualities of the stone:

> Anciently superior men found the likeness of all excellent qualities in jade. Soft, smooth and glossy, it appeared to them like benevolence; fine, compact and strong, like intelligence ... bright as a brilliant rainbow, like heaven; exquisite and mysterious ... like the earth ... esteemed by all under the sky, like the path of truth and beauty.[15]

The term jade is used to describe a variety of coloured stones, the most valuable of which are nephrite and jadeite which, though sharing similar qualities, are quite different in chemical composition and crystalline structure. Both stones come in a variety of colours, the most common of which are white and green. The main source of nephrite was the north-western province of Xinjiang, while jadeite was imported into China from Burma (plate 6.6).

6.6 Box, plate, marriage token and plaque. Jade. Chinese, 18th century. V&A: C.1929-1910; 1345-1882; C.1913-1910; C.1926-1910.

6.8 Edmond Dulac, 'Cathay Lounge' on the *Empress of Britain*, Canadian Pacific Company. 1931. Reproduced from Frank O. Braynard and William H. Miller, *Fifty Famous Liners*, Cambridge, 1982.

The majority of jade pieces used by Art Deco jewellers such as Cartier and Mauboussin were taken from Qing dynasty belt hooks, plaques and clasps (plate 6.7). Jade was also cut in China specifically for Deco jewellery.[16] Other jewellery, such as the corsage ornament exhibited by Boucheron at the 1925 Exhibition, incorporated pieces worked by western lapidaries from jadeite newly mined in Burma (see plate 24.5).[17] Much of the appeal of jade lay in its most characteristic colour. 'Jade green' became an Art Deco favourite and was replicated in materials such as opaque glass and Bakelite (see plate 33.7).

This taste for the East can been seen in the pages of many fashion magazines, not only in the clothes and jewellery featured but also in advertisements for evening bags in Chinese brocade or with Chinese-inspired clasps, perfumes with names such as 'Le jade' and 'Shanghai', and small ornamental Buddha figurines. Chinese-style interiors were also much in vogue. A 'Boudoir de Style Chinois' was created by the Mercier Frères in 1921 and Pierre Chareau's 'Petit Salon Chinois' was one of the great successes of 1924.[18] Perhaps the most famous of such interiors was the 'Cathay Lounge' on the *Empress of Britain*, the great ocean liner of the Canadian Pacific Company (plate 6.8). The ornamental fretwork, pale gold ceiling, columns faced with black glass and lacquered vermilion and ebony furniture were all designed by Edmond Dulac.[19]

Hollywood was also seduced by the lure of the East. Mysterious and exotic, Asia promised adventure, opulence and eroticism. One of the most famous films of the period was *Shanghai Express* directed by Josef Von Sternberg in 1932.[20] The story takes place in that most modern of settings, a train, and appealed to an audience intoxicated with a vision of contemporary China as a place of warlords, prostitutes, glamour and sin. It starred Warner Orland, a Swedish actor of Mongolian ancestry, Californian-born Chinese actress Anna May Wong and that ultimate female icon of the 1930s, Marlene Dietrich.

In *Shanghai Express* modern China was a place of danger as well as excitement. In *Flash Gordon*, a low-budget science fiction film series, China represented not just a contemporary danger but a future threat. The original comic strip from which the films were adapted had been noted for its Art Deco design, and the screen sets also combined oriental elements and Deco styling to create a fantasy world. Here China was personified as the evil genius Ming the Merciless, emperor of the planet Mongo, who threatens to destroy the earth.[21] This character was a successor to one of the most famous fictive villains of the period, Dr Fu Manchu, the creation of author Sax Rohmer.

6.9 Boris Karloff as Fu Manchu, in *The Mask of Fu Manchu*, directed by Charles Brabin, with art direction by Cedric Gibbons, 1932. Courtesy Ronald Grant Archive.

This sinister Chinaman, bent on world domination and the destruction of the West, is described as 'tall, lean and feline, high-shouldered with a brow like Shakespeare and a face like Satan, a close-shaven skull, and long, magnetic eyes of a true green cat. Invest him with all the cunning of an entire Eastern race, accumulated in one giant intellect ... and you have a mental picture of Dr. Fu Manchu, the yellow peril incarnate.'[22] Fu Manchu was also portrayed on screen, first by Warner Orland – who then went on to play a far less threatening Asian in the Charlie Chan films – and most famously by Boris Karloff in 1932 (plate 6.9). Although the stuff of escapist fantasy, the books and films appeared at a time when the menace of the 'yellow races' was being much debated. The fear that hordes of Asians, mysterious and cunning, were threatening to overrun the white race was fuelled by Japan's expansionist policies and China's political instability and growing Communist movement (see Chapter 35). 'Eight hundred million Asiatics', warned one journal, 'are struggling against the supremacy of the white race and growing Bolshevism is fanning the flame. All our civilisation is at stake.'[23]

While China of the present might have been feared, China of the past, and particularly Chinese art of the past, posed no such problems. Iacovleff's interest in the Chinese theatre, for example, was based on its links to 'noble traditions of past dynasties'. 'We are transported back', he declared, 'to the earliest times and see China as painted by Marco Polo.'[24] The Croisière Jaune traced the supposed route of the famous Italian traveller and, although Iacovleff's paintings and drawings were of contemporary China, the images of people such as Mongolian tribesmen implied an ancient, unchanging world. Similarly the fascination for jade was the stone's link to a mysterious, 'prehistoric' past. While the jade pieces incorporated into jewellery were no more than a few hundred years old, they were still from a vanished empire, material relics now owned and refigured by the West.

6.10 'Cabinet de l'Orient' in the studio of Jacques Doucet at Neuilly. *L'Illustration*, 1930. British Library.

that 'modern furniture in our houses would not be understandable in its search for noble simplicity and rare materials, if it were not linked to Chinese models'.[25] These models were old ones, however, the subject of the article being archaic Chinese bronzes. Early Chinese art was seen to embody a particular 'vitality' missing from the later, highly decorative, works that had appealed to the previous generation of western collectors. This shift of taste derived from the ideas of the French philosopher Henri Bergson, which were being cited in advanced aesthetic circles of the time.[26] In Britain, for example, they informed Roger Fry's enthusiasm for non-European culture. Fry was particularly drawn to Chinese art and in 1925 he edited a special *Burlington Magazine* issue on the subject.[27] In his *Last Lectures* he referred to a Zhou dynasty (1050-221 BC) bronze wine vessel owned by George Eumorfopoulos, one of the most significant collectors of the period, as a 'masterpiece of design' (plate 6.11). The object embodied the qualities of refinement and abstraction Fry valued in modern art. 'We no longer feel inclined to talk of barbarism', he wrote, 'rather of a naïve sensibility heightened by conscious aesthetic purpose.'[28]

In the inter-war period early China was one of a number of 'exotic' cultures – its 'otherness' defined more by remoteness of time than place – that came to be linked with concepts of the modern (see Chapter 11). This relationship between exoticism and modernity was clearly articulated in the collections, and the environments created to house them, of the Parisian couturier Jacques Doucet. His patronage of avant-garde painters and Art Deco designers was intrinsically related to his collecting of non-western art. His studio in Neuilly, created in 1925, included Chinese and African works and contemporary designs inspired by such sources. The sequence of three rooms culminated in the 'Cabinet de l'Orient' (plate 6.10). Although none of the Chinese objects shown on display in the room appear to be of any great age, they do reveal the prevailing interest in less highly finished and decorated forms.[29]

6.11 Wine vessel (*you*). Bronze. Chinese, Western Zhou dynasty, 11th-10th century BC. V&A: M.6-1935.

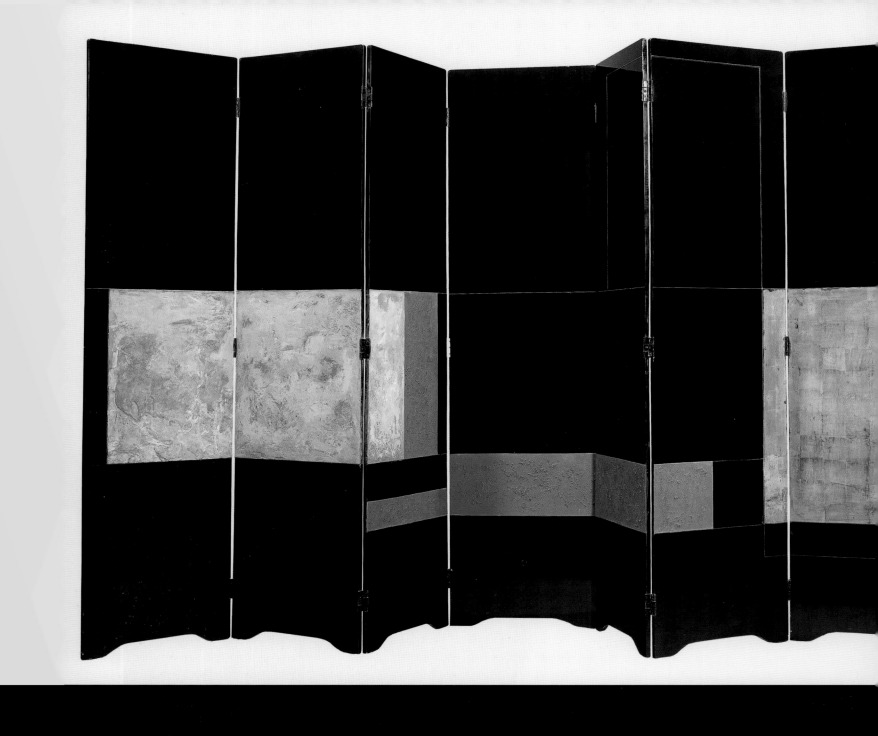

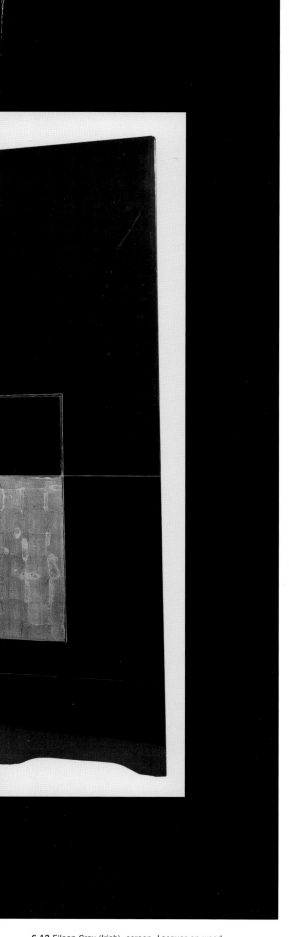

6.13 Panels from a shrine. Black and gold lacquer on wood.
Japanese, 19th century. V&A: W1-1913.

6.12 Eileen Gray (Irish), screen. Lacquer on wood.
Around 1928. V&A: W.40-1977.

In the centre of Doucet's 'Cabinet de l'Orient', on a Chinese carpet originally created to wrap around a pillar in a Buddhist temple, sits Eileen Gray's 'Lotus' table. This is one of a number of pieces of lacquer furniture Doucet commissioned from the artist after seeing her work displayed at the *Salon des artistes décorateurs* in 1913. The table takes up the theme of one of Gray's exhibits of 1913, *Om mani Padme Hum*, a deep blue lacquer panel with allegorical figures and a mother-of-pearl lotus.[30] Its symbolism and title, based on a Buddhist mantra, would not have been lost on a collector of Asian art such as Doucet. Doucet also bought a four-panel screen entitled *Le destin*. On this and other screens designed by Gray the large, undecorated areas of pure luxurious lustre are evidence of Gray's mastery of lacquer, the production of which had hitherto been the preserve of Asian craftsmen (plate 6.12).[31]

Lacquer is the sap of a tree native to East Asia.[32] After various refining processes to remove excess water and impurities it becomes a colourless, viscous liquid that hardens when exposed to oxygen under hot and humid conditions. It is applied in very thin layers to a base, often of wood. Each layer must be left to harden for a couple of days and then ground and polished smooth before the next layer is applied. Twenty or more layers are needed to obtain the desired results. The lacquer can be coloured and precious metals and other materials can be used to create decorative effects. Patterning can also be achieved through incising or carving into the lacquer surface. Lacquer was employed as an artistic medium in both China and Japan, but it was Japanese lacquerwork that particularly drew the attention of Eileen Gray and other Art Deco artists and craftsmen. They were attracted not only by the craft of its production, but also by the richness, depth and sensuality of its surfaces (plate 6.13).

Gray worked for a lacquer restorer in London before moving to Paris in 1906, where she met the

Japanese lacquer craftsman Sugawara Seizō,[33] who had settled in the city after coming to France for the *Exposition universelle* (World Fair) of 1900. The two artists embarked on a collaboration that was to last for forty years. Under Sugawara's tutelage Gray gained proficiency in lacquer and began to produce screens, furniture and small items such as bowls and plates (plate 6.14). She experimented with colours and textures and variations of traditional Japanese inlays such as metal dusts, sheets and foil, crushed eggshell and mother-of-pearl. She also used innovative materials such as sand and gravel. The strict environmental conditions needed to produce lacquer were first achieved by Gray in her bathroom, but in 1910 she set up a special workshop for herself and Sugawara.[34]

In 1912 the designer Jean Dunand also took lessons from Sugawara and he spent the following years experimenting with the lacquer process. In 1919 he started to use geometric patterns created from various coloured lacquers to decorate his metal pieces and in 1921 he exhibited his first large lacquer panel. While Gray's work became increasingly abstract, Dunand's employed both figurative and abstract decoration, often devised in collaboration with other artists. His output was prodigious. He produced screens, wall panels, furniture, portraits, vases, vanity cases, jewellery, boxes and bookbindings, as well as designing interiors for ships, private clients and special exhibitions (see plate 3.6). For the 1925 Exhibition Dunand created a smoking room panelled in black, red and silver lacquer, with furniture also in black lacquer with silver decoration (plate 6.15). The room was designed to be Japanese in feeling, both in its use of materials and colours and in its articulation of space. Although small, it was one of the most successful installations of the exhibition. 'The overall impression was truly of exceptional quality', wrote Henri Clouzot, 'everyone could … congratulate Jean Dunand on having been able to extract the secret of these beautiful lacquers from oriental artists and on having been able to apply that secret so felicitously to our modern western civilization.'[35]

Although lacquer is most commonly applied to wood, and most characteristically produces a smooth, shiny finish, Dunand used it to create a variety of surfaces and applied it to materials such as metal, leather and textiles to achieve different effects and textures. Other designers also experimented with lacquer. Elizabeth Eyre de Lanux, for example, used a method called *lacque arrachée* to create furniture with matt surfaces that appeared rough yet remained incredibly smooth to the touch.[36] Lacquer could also

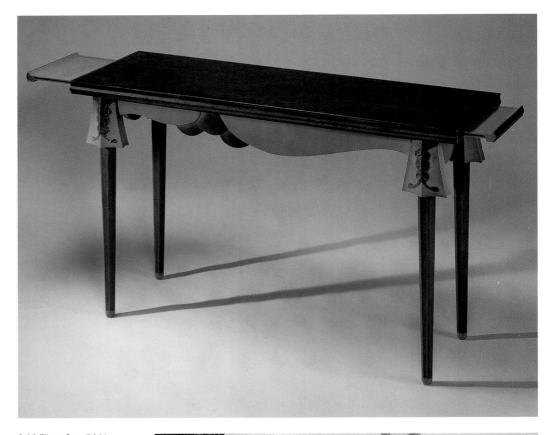

6.14 Eileen Gray (Irish), console table. Lacquered wood. Around 1918-20. Collection Jacques de Vos, Paris.

6.15 Jean Dunand, smoking room of the 'Pavillon d'une Ambassade Française' at the Paris 1925 Exhibition. Jean Saudé, *Une Ambassade française*, Paris, 1925. NAL. © ADAGP, Paris and DACS, London 2002.

be used to create a unified finish. In his smoking room of 1925, for example, Dunand used it to disguise the structural elements, such as the joints and dovetails, of his furniture. This ability to provide a continuous, smooth, strong surface made lacquer ideal for such purposes and allowed for the streamlined and contoured effects seen in much Art Deco furniture and furnishings. On a smaller scale it was also used as a setting for jewellery. Interest in the technical possibilities afforded by lacquer had been aroused during the First World War when Indo-Chinese workers were employed to lacquer the propellers of French air force planes, the finish proving to be a far more effective protector and preserver than varnish. These craftsmen subsequently found outlets for their lacquering skills in the artistic ateliers of Sugawara, Dunand and many leading jewellers.

As lacquer became 'not a fashion, but a passion'[37] some of Sugawara's fellow countrymen were inspired to come to Europe. Hamanaka Katsu, who arrived in Paris in about 1924 and subsequently exhibited at various salons, worked in collaboration with designers such as Ruhlmann. In 1935 he produced lacquer panels for the great ocean liner *Normandie* which boasted the most stunning Art Deco interiors, including Dunand's monumental decorative wall panels in the smoking room. The pioneering Japanese lacquer artist Yamazaki Kakutarō also visited France to study European techniques and became acquainted with Dunand and others (plate 6.16).

The interest in lacquer was part of a widespread taste for sumptuous surfaces and striking effects. Through its innovative use Art Deco designers absorbed and transformed a centuries-old East Asian artistic medium into the essence of modernity. However, the time and skill needed to work in lacquer meant that while 'it was new, distinctly novel', it was also 'oh so very, very expensive'.[38] In the 1930s the scientific development of synthetic 'lacquer' paints which could be sprayed on under industrial conditions meant that the luxurious effects of lacquer could be simulated by less costly means. Thus the appeal and influence of East Asia expanded from the taste of an elite few to become a crucial component in the popular consumption of the glamour, sensuality and exoticism of the Art Deco style.

6.16 Yamazaki Kakutarō, jewellery box.
Lacquer on wood. Japanese, 1934.
Kyoto Municipal Museum.

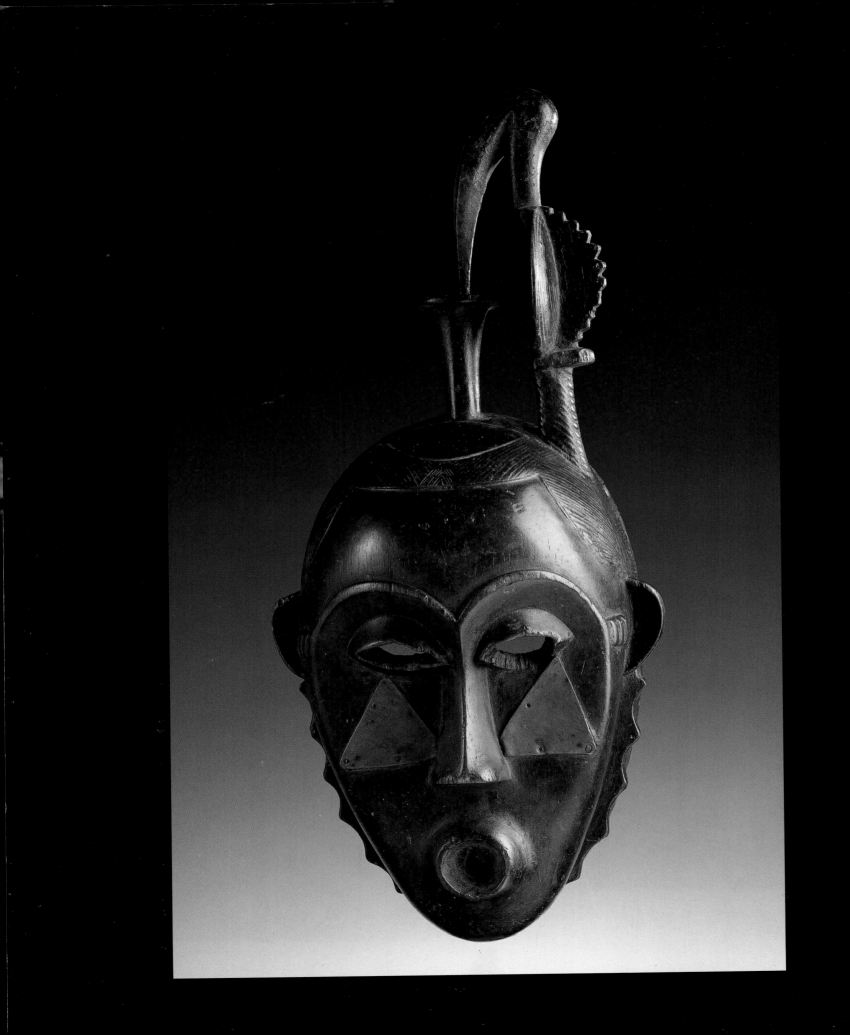

7 Collecting and Constructing Africa

Ghislaine Wood

> The interest of these fetishes lies essentially in their plastic form, even though they are sometimes made of precious materials. This form is always powerful, very far removed from our conceptions and yet capable of nourishing the inspiration of artists.[1]
> *Guillaume Apollinaire*

Art Deco drew on a range of archaic and 'exotic' sources but none gave the style its distinctive flavour more than Africa. For over twenty years, the rage for things African gripped artists and designers in Europe and America. Spawned by a heterogeneous group of specialists and enthusiasts, including artists, designers, writers, ethnographers, museum curators and early anthropologists, 'collecting Africa' became a passion for many and ultimately led to a fundamental change in western aesthetics. Picasso's infamous encounter with 'fetishes' at the Paris Trocadéro in 1907 represents a pivotal moment in the history of modern art. However, the influence of African art went far beyond the birth of Cubism and a new conception of pictorial space. Art Deco introduced geometric, abstracted patterns into numerous inter-war homes, thus bringing the 'primitive' into the realm of modern mass culture. From zebra skin covered chairs to Bakelite bangles, 'Africa' became the height of fashion. It was not just the formal, stylistic elements of African textiles, jewellery or sculpture that appealed; so, too, did the romanticized concept of a wild, tribal world, ordered by ancient mystery and ritual. For the fashionable, as for the avant-garde, this world seemed to provide a wellspring of primal creativity capable of injecting new life into jaded western traditions. As the collector and critic Paul Guillaume made clear, the desire for Africa went well beyond the body and the home: 'the mind of the modern man and woman must be Negro'.[2]

The route by which African art came to inspire Art Deco design is complex and largely dependant upon a changing conception of African material culture in Europe and America during the early years of the twentieth century. As a result, the aesthetic qualities

of a range of African artefacts, in particular sculpture and textiles, came to be widely appreciated. In 1912, the poet and critic Guillaume Apollinaire observed that 'a few art lovers like M. Guillaume ... have started to collect sculptures and all the works of art in general of those African and Oceanic peoples who are usually called savages'.[3] His observation reflects a sensitivity to the formal characteristics of tribal art that did not exist in the late nineteenth century or the early years of the twentieth century, when, furthermore, little distinction was made between the art of different regions within Africa, or that of other areas of the world, such as Oceania. Nor was it perceived as art but rather as ethnography with early collections, such as those of the Musée d'Ethnographie established in Paris in 1882, treating such objects less as explicitly cultural art forms than as ethnographic curios. The lack of aesthetic value assigned to such collections in the early years of the century is borne out by Picasso's recollection of the damp, dusty and 'disgusting' conditions in which they were housed in the Trocadéro: 'All alone in that awful museum, with masks, dolls made by the redskins, dusty manikins, Les Demoiselles d'Avignon must have come to me that very day, but not at all because of the forms; because it was my first exorcism painting.'[4] In 1912 Apollinaire was to make the case for a re-evaluation of the material: 'The Trocadéro is in urgent need of reform. Objects of a principally artistic nature should be separated from the ethnography and placed in another museum.'[5] Similar criticisms could have been made of the presentation of the many other public collections of tribal art that had been formed by the early years of the century, including those in museums in Moscow, Leipzig, London, Berlin, Oslo, Leiden and Copenhagen.

The years just prior to the First World War saw a reappraisal of African sculpture that went far beyond the boundaries of France. In a number of early publications a more considered approach began to emerge, while exhibitions including, or wholly dedicated to, African art took place in several cities.

7.1 Bird mask. Wood. Yaouré, Baoulé, Ivory Coast, early 20th century. Formerly in the collection of Paul Guillaume. Musée des Arts d'Afrique et d'Océanie, Paris.
© RMN – Photo: Labat/CFAO.

Through these, many artists and designers came for the first time into contact with African sculpture and were able to appreciate it as art. In 1911 in Budapest, for example, the *Kelley Kiàllitàs* (Oriental Exhibition) held in the House of Artists under the directorship of József Rippl-Rónai was possibly the first to exhibit African tribal objects alongside art from other non-western countries, including Persia, Japan, China, Tibet, Cambodia and India. Sixteen Oceanic and African sculptures were lent from the collections of the writer and journalist Miklos Vitez and, significantly for the development of Art Deco, from the designer Lajos Kozma (see Chapter 16). In Prague the Skupina Výtvarných Umělců (Group of Plastic Artists), which included the Cubists Otto Gutfreund and Josef Čapek, exhibited and published African sculpture as early as 1913. The impetus for this interest seems to have come from Paris; an article in *Umělecký Měsíčník* in June 1913 on Gutfreund's Cubist sculpture published images of African works belonging to the contemporary art dealer Daniel-Henry Kahnweiler and the leading dealer in African art, Joseph Brummer; and many artists in the group had close ties with Paris. A leading figure, the Czech art historian and collector Vincenc Kramář, bought works by Picasso and Braque from Kahnweiler, while artists such as Josef Chochol and Vlastislav Hofman openly acknowledged the influence of tribal art. Hofman wrote in 1913, 'We know the art of the primitive nations, the manifestation of a youthful, thirsty organism, a strong and simple expression ... New art uses the most conspicuous and expressive means, thus formally also the most abstract.'[6]

In Germany the artist August Macke published an article on African masks in the Blaue Reiter almanac in 1914, and in 1915 Carl Einstein's seminal work *Negerplastik* was published in Leipzig. Einstein's close involvement with avant-garde artists in both Germany and France gave him a unique insight into the relevance of African sculpture for the development of modern art, as did his friendships with Kahnweiler and Brummer. *Negerplastik*, sumptuously illustrated with a large number of African works, gave serious consideration to the plastic qualities of African art and became a vital source for artists and designers. Fernand Léger's designs for sets and costumes of the Ballet Suédois production of *La Création du monde* were based, in part, on illustrations from the book. Directed by Rolf de Maré, written by Blaise Cendrars, with choreography by Jean Borlin and music by Darius Milhaud, this production was one of the first to use African folklore, dance and design as source

material. It opened to great acclaim at the Théâtre des Champs Elysées in Paris in 1923. Its overt celebration of a specifically African creation myth can be seen as part of a growing emphasis by European artists and designers on the rejuvenating qualities of African art.

In America one of the most important promoters of African art, the Mexican illustrator Marius de Zayas, organized a groundbreaking exhibition for Alfred Stieglitz at the 291 Gallery in New York in 1914. The exhibition, designed by Edward Steichen, displayed African sculptures – many belonging to Paul Guillaume – alongside modern art. From its opening in 1905, 291 had become an important meeting place and focal point for New York's avant-garde and many designers and artists, including the photographer Man Ray, visited the exhibition. In 1916 de Zayas published *African Negro Art and its Influence on Modern Art*, which also had a widespread influence on the reception of African art in the United States.

The impetus for much that happened in the postwar years in the world of African art came from the extraordinary energy of one man – Paul Guillaume. His almost missionary fervour to elevate the status of tribal art contributed to the widespread vogue for *l'art nègre* in France in the 1920s. The most prestigious Parisian art dealer and collector between the wars, with extremely successful galleries first in the Rue de Miromesnil and then from 1916 in the Avenue de Villiers, Guillaume became the centre of a progressive, fashionable set. As a result, collecting African art became *de rigueur*. For many of his clients, the modern interior was not complete without African sculpture (see Chapter 11). His close collaboration with the respected critic and poet Guillaume Apollinaire lent credence to his project and a clear rhetoric to his publications. In 1919 Guillaume organized the *Première Exposition d'art nègre et d'Océanie*, which although not the first, was the most extensive exhibition of its kind to date. It included works both from his own and from other important private collections, including those of Jacques Doucet, André Level, Georges Menier and Maurice Vlaminck (plate 7.1). The exhibition catalogue makes Guillaume's proselytizing mission clear, 'the time has now come ... to show to a wider public an important selection of these strange artefacts. The figurative works have religious meaning. Art for art's sake is unknown to primitives.'[7] With a flair for publicity unmatched by other dealers, Guillaume organized a 'Fête Nègre' to promote the exhibition which, like the 'Negro Soirées' organized by Tristan Tzara at the Cabaret Voltaire in Zurich,

featured African-inspired dance. However, unlike the Dada events, the Fête was attended by the rich and fashionable and was reported in the society pages of newspapers and fashion magazines. A great success, it reinforced the association of African art with high fashion.

1919 also saw the publication of *L'Art nègre et l'art d'Océanie* by Henri Clouzot and André Level, the most prolific writers on tribal art of the period. Illustrated with works from the British Museum, the Trocadéro and Picasso's collection, it proposed that an aesthetic impetus governed the creation of tribal works. The authors did not, however, advocate that tribal artists had a parity of intellect with minds of the 'civilized' world; in fact, they had 'physiologically inferior cerebral development.'[8] As Jean-Louis Paudrat has observed, this attitude 'is representative of the thinking of a period in which the stakes of colonization often made it impossible to extend cultural relativism, reserved for artefacts alone, to other facets of society'.[9]

Even so, a gradual shift in the perception of ethnologists of tribal peoples and societies did occur during the 1920s. Level and Clouzot's judgments on the mental capacities of tribal people were vehemently countered in such works as *Primitive Art* published in 1927 by the German-American ethnologist Franz Boas. Stating in his preface, 'some theorists assume a mental equipment of primitive man distinct from that of civilized man. I have never seen a person in primitive life to whom this theory would apply', he went on:

> Anyone who has lived with primitive tribes, who has shared their joys and sorrows, their privations and their luxuries, who sees in them not solely subjects of study to be examined like a cell under the microscope, but feeling and thinking human beings, will agree that there is no such thing as a 'primitive mind', a 'magical' or 'prelogical' way of thinking, but that each individual in 'primitive' society is a man, a woman, a child of the same kind, of the same way of thinking, feeling and acting as man, woman or child in our own society.[10]

This shift in the perception of Africans, in part a product of the vogue for *l'art nègre* and in part the cause of it, had far-reaching consequences. The black-American writer and early leader of the

7.2 Textile. Raffia. Kuba, Democratic Republic of the Congo (formerly Zaire), early 20th century. Musée des Arts d'Afrique et d'Océanie, Paris. © RMN – Photo: H. Lewandowski.

negritude movement W. E. B. Du Bois first learnt of the traditions of his African ancestors from Boas. He recalled his reaction to a speech given by Boas at Atlanta University: 'he recounted the history of black kingdoms south of the Sahara for a thousand years. I was too astonished to speak. All of this I had never heard and I came then and afterwards to realize how the silence and neglect of science can let truth utterly disappear or even be unconsciously distorted.'[11]

The widespread diffusion and re-evaluation of African art in contemporary books, magazines, exhibitions and public and private collections, by theoreticians from various disciplines as well as dealers and collectors, gradually brought about a fundamental change, not only in attitudes towards African art but also towards Africans themselves. As a result, African art was rapidly adopted by designers searching for new sources with which to renew their decorative vocabulary.

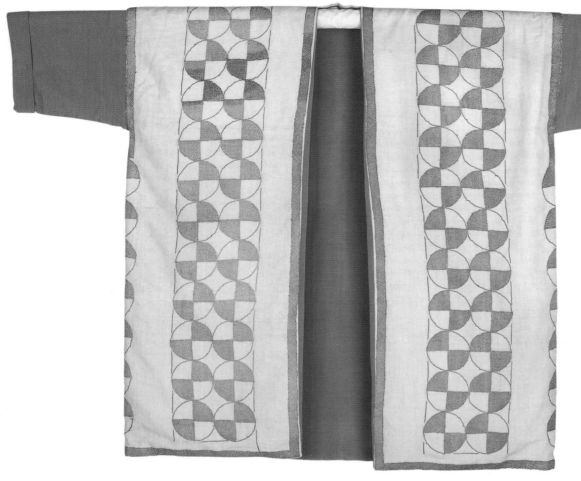

7.3 Myrbor, coat. Wool with gold thread embroidery. French, c.1925. V&A: T.221-1967.

The most pervasive influence of African art on Art Deco design was in the use of bold abstract, or geometric patterns. Derived mainly from Kuba textiles, shields and sculpture from the Gabon, Dahomey, Belgian Congo, Ivory Coast and Ghana, such patterns were applied to everything from textiles and wallpapers, to ceramics and jewellery (plate 7.2). Avant-garde artists, including Sonia Delaunay, were among the first to realize the potential of this new decorative language for design (see Chapter 9). However, they were quickly followed by designers working in all fields. The fashion house Myrbor, set up by Marie Cuttoli, not only embraced the new decorative language of African art but also sought African craft skills. Establishing an embroidery and tapestry workshop in Algeria, Marie Cuttoli produced haute couture designs that utilized native craft traditions. Many Myrbor designs included fine embroidery. A coat designed around 1925 derived not only its form from the T-shape gown worn all over North and West Africa, but also its decoration. Covered with quartered circles embroidered in silk, the design adapted a common Quranic symbol which

was used throughout Islamic North and West Africa (plate 7.3).

The use of geometric patterns derived from African sources was most common in Art Deco textile and wallpaper designs. The often subtle colours of the natural dyes used in African textiles were frequently substituted with bright, bold synthetic hues. However some Deco textiles were consciously Africanizing in their use of a muted organic colour range. Several designs by Camille Birke and Maria Likarz for the Wiener Werkstätte were available in a limited brown, orange and black colour range suggestive of West African textiles (plate 7.4). They were also given exotic names such as 'Guinea', 'Batavia', 'Montezuma', 'Lhasa', 'Basra', 'Mauritius' and 'Mombasa'. Camille Birke's abstract 'Tahiti' design was used to decorate the walls of the furniture section at the Paris 1925 Exhibition.

7.4 Maria Likarz, Ebro, fabric sample. Block-printed on silk. Austrian, 1926. Wiener Werkstätte. MAK, Vienna.

Ceramic design also reflected the passion for geometric pattern. The British firm of Carter & Co. had produced African-inspired designs as early as 1914. Following the lead of James Radley Young, Truda Carter began to experiment with Africanizing ornament from the mid-1920's (plate 7.5). Carter had lived with her husband, the ceramic designer John Adams, in South Africa from 1914, before returning to form the partnership of Carter, Stabler & Adams in 1921 (see Chapter 39). Directly inspired by African patterns, a characteristic example of her work is a vase of around 1930 decorated with bands of bold zigzags and stylized flowers. It uses the natural, earthy colours of African art rather than the bright palette popular in modernistic ceramics of the period. Similar tendencies can be seen in the work of a leading French ceramic artist, René Buthaud, who created some of the most striking French Art Deco ceramics (plate 7.7). Like many other artists and designers of this period, Buthaud avidly collected African art. Based in Bordeaux, then an important French port, he was able to acquire pieces brought back from French colonies in West Africa. He acknowledged the importance of African art for his own designs, which often combined simple forms with African-inspired patterns or figurative motifs. A range of works created for the 1931 *Exposition coloniale internationale* in Paris, and inspired by his collection, broke away from the use of geometric pattern. Instead, it developed an iconography of African figures, often accompanied by animals or set in tropical vegetation, and depicted in a restrained palette of black, brown, brick red and dark green.

The Deco designer to develop one of most subtle and sophisticated approaches to the use of geometric pattern was the Swiss-born Jean Dunand. Elegant, abstract patterns were applied to everything from lacquer furniture to jewellery. Dunand's work was sought after by the most fashionable clients of the day, and his commissions spanned the decoration of ocean liners, such as the *Normandie*, as well as the design of the African-inspired bangles worn by Josephine Baker and the designer Mme Agnès (plate 7.6). Like Buthaud, Dunand also developed stylized representations of the African figure in his work. A chair designed by Dunand and

7.5 Truda Carter, vase. Stoneware. British, c.1930. Made by Stabler & Adams, painted by Ruth Pavely. V&A: Circ.326-1976.

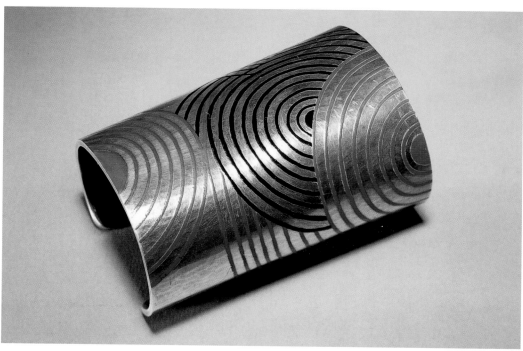

7.6 Jean Dunand, bracelet. Silver and enamel. French, 1927. Formerly in the collection of Mme Agnès. Collection Zoya Gerhath. © ADAGP, Paris and DACS, London 2002.

7.8 Chair. Wood. Tchokwe, Angola.

Musée des Arts d'Afrique et d'Océanie, Paris.

© RMN – Photo: J.G. Berizzi.

7.9 Jean Dunand and Jean Lambert-Rucki, chair.

Wood. French, 1924. Private collection, Paris.

© ADAGP, Paris and DACS, London 2002.

Jean Lambert-Rucki, with sculpted, figural legs and a zigzag, carved and decorated back, is based on a West African Tchokwe chair from the Congo or Angola (plate 7.9). Tchokwe chairs were themselves adapted in the seventeenth century from European models (plate 7.8). Their construction, with four legs, upright back and leather covered seat, set them apart from traditional African chairs. Their iconography of carved figures facing each had clear symbolic meaning, reinforcing the position of the tribal chief. By contrast, the appropriation of forms in the Dunand/Lambert-Rucki chair, without regard for meaning, is typical of the way Deco designers pillaged African art for its forms and patterns alone.

Pierre Legrain, studying African works in the collections of his patrons, the milliner Jeanne Tachard and the fashion designer Jacques Doucet, produced some of the most original Africanizing Art Deco designs. For Doucet's apartment in the Avenue du Bois in Paris and studio in Rue St James at Neuilly, Legrain designed a number of African-inspired stools and low tables. Due to its special role within tribal societies, seating furniture was comparatively rare in early collections of African art,

7.7 René Buthaud, vase. Stoneware.

French, c.1920. V&A: C.292-1987.

so Legrain sometimes adapted the forms of other African objects, such as small wooden neck rests, to create models for furniture. However, he closely followed a number of original African models for seats, adapting them to contemporary taste through the use of rich finishes in veneer or lacquer. Typical of this approach is his design for a stool for Doucet (plate 7.10). It resembles a Bondjos stool from Zaire, an example of which was in the Trocadéro collections from early in the century and which Legrain may well have seen (plate 7.11). However, he modified the brass studded geometric pattern of the African original; in his own design the surface of the stool is carved with a chevron pattern suggestive of the model but treated with a rich red and gold lacquer. The roughness of the original has been replaced with the conspicuously luxurious finish characteristic of much French Deco design. This kind of deliberate contrast between the 'primitive' and the 'modern' is also found in one of Legrain's most remarkable designs, a low table made for Pierre Meyer which combines a rectangular top and base with chamfered edges of the same proportions (plate 7.12). The two elements are separated by supports comprising square columns with ovoid discs, their perfect symmetry emphasized by the extraordinary use of materials. Snakeskin sheathes the top and the supports while the base and discs are veneered in nickel plate. A 'barbaric' severity of form is here combined with the modern taste for luxury materials and glamorous surface effects.

7.10 Pierre Legrain, stool. Lacquered wood, horn and gilding. French, c.1923. Sydney and Frances Lewis Endowment Fund. Virginia Museum of Fine Arts, Richmond. Photo: Ron Jennings.

7.11 Stool. Wood and brass. Bondjos, Democratic Republic of Congo (formerly Zaire). Musée des Arts d'Afrique et d'Océanie, Paris. © RMN.

7.12 Pierre Legrain, 'Python', table. Wood, plated nickel and snakeskin. French, c.1928. Designed for Pierre Meyer. Galerie Jacques de Vos, Paris.

The cost of such immensely rich and exotic materials could be prohibitive. Even the most affluent of clients occasionally baulked at the expense, the Vicomte de Noaïlles stating in a telegram to Legrain, 'I consider the cost of upholstering the stool truly impossible ... Piece must be completed but only hope for a drop in the price of fur or you find other more economical material.'[12] Nevertheless, the use of exotic animal skins and woods continued through much of the 1920s, and was part of the wider tendency within Art Deco. Alongside real and faux animal skins of all species – most commonly zebra, leopard, polar bear, crocodile and snake – sharkskin (or galuchat) became hugely popular. Often bleached and dyed to subtle, pale colours, sharkskin was frequently used for small personal objects such as cigarette boxes, make-up compacts or bookbindings. Some French designers, including André Groult, Clément Mère and Clément Rousseau, developed sophisticated techniques that incorporated sharkskin marquetry in their furniture designs (see plate 12.7). Rousseau took the technique to its pinnacle, combining sharkskin with ivory and exotic woods to create a complex, decorative marquetry unparalleled since the eighteenth century.

France's extensive African and Asian colonies provided a rich source for exotic materials. Increasingly, the promotion of tropical woods became the focus of French state agencies. At the 1931 Colonial Exhibition, a pavilion dedicated to colonial woods not only provided educational information on production and harvesting but also extolled the aesthetic qualities and different uses to which such materials could be put. Palm wood, palisander, macassar ebony, amaranth, amboyna and rosewood were among the most popular woods used in the French Art Deco furniture industry. Designers such as Jacques-Emile Ruhlmann used their extraordinary grains, often combining them with ivory – and occasionally dyed tortoiseshell – to explore new techniques of inlay and veneer.

The promotion of materials from the Empire in a period of fierce colonial competition was not a new strategy within the decorative arts. Belgium had aggressively promoted the use of ivory from the Belgian Congo from the late 1880s and continued to do so through the 1920s and 1930s. The Brussels silversmiths Philippe and Marcel Wolfers, famous for their flamboyant Art Nouveau designs, later produced sophisticated Art Deco objects incorporating ivory (plate 7.13).

The vogue for things African influenced nearly every aspect of Art Deco style – its decoration, forms, materials and techniques. African art inspired a renewal of decoration, providing an ancient guide towards modernity. Its geometric patterns and apparently spontaneous forms could be readily adapted to the contemporary need to respond in new ways to the challenges of modern urban life. Paul Guillaume acknowledged its importance for avant-garde art:

> before 1905 art in France and indeed in all Europe, was menaced by extinction. Five years later, the enthusiasm, the joy of the painters, their fever of excitement, made it apparent that a new renaissance had taken place. Not less evident was it that the honour of this renaissance belonged to Negro art ... one may almost say that there was a form of feeling, architecture of thought, a subtle expression of the most profound forces of life, which have been extracted from negro civilization.[13]

But W. E. B. Du Bois brilliantly summed up the wider contemporary passion for Africa and the articulating tensions between culture and nature, civilization and the primitive when he wrote in 1926, 'the Congo is flooding the Acropolis'.[14]

7.13 Philippe Wolfers, 'Gioconda', tea service. Silver and ivory. Belgian, 1925. Museum voor Siebekunst, Ghent. Courtesy of Studio Clarehout © DACS, 2002.

8 National Traditions

Juliette Hibou

The artist today no longer disdains the antique. He simply knows how to see it in a modern way, to make allusions, discreet quotes, highly modified borrowings that take the form of a homage. Thus, instead of going against tradition, our modern art easily ties in with it, adjusts it to itself.[1]

Although Art Deco was considered a new, modern style in 1925, it owed much to a variety of historical styles. It arose from a period of foreign competition and political conflict in which nationalism encouraged a return to tradition. In France modernized historical styles were used to symbolize a resumption of order. Also, many designers chose to emphasize their Frenchness by invoking the styles and the modes of production of past eras in which French decorative arts had been dominant. They drew inspiration from the Louis styles, the Directoire and Empire styles and the more bourgeois styles of the nineteenth century: Restauration, Louis-Philippe and Second Empire (plate 8.1). The German-speaking countries, too, looked to their national Baroque and Rococo traditions and, more importantly, to the Biedermeier style – another expression of bourgeois taste – for the roots of a new style. In their search for a contemporary national style, many countries, particularly those of Northern and Central Europe, but also France and Italy, turned to their folk culture to provide a rich source both for decorative patterns and for forms, techniques and materials. This eclecticism may seem contradictory when we consider that one of the reasons Art Deco was created was to counter the historicism of the preceding century and the perceived eclecticism of Art Nouveau.

In France another important impetus for the growth of Art Deco in the early twentieth century was the growing aesthetic and commercial success of Germany, which rapidly became a cause for alarm in France. By the 1910s German power was seen as a real threat to France, to both its economy and its national prestige. This concern was exacerbated after the important applied arts exhibition in Munich in

1908,[2] where the excellence of German craftsmanship and organization was revealed and assessed against the French exhibits. The exhibition was described in France as an 'artistic and commercial Sedan'.[3]

Two years later the 'Munich Decorators' were invited by Frantz Jourdain, founder and director of the *Salon d'automne* and a member of the French delegation to the Munich exhibition, to exhibit in the 1910 *Salon d'automne*. Their designs astonished the Parisians. Inspired in great part by the Biedermeier style, the German interiors demonstrated a sobriety, urbanity and unity of style that the French had not anticipated (plate 8.2). Each room was conceived under the supervision of a single architect, resulting in a harmonious effect that was lacking in the French displays. These new designs were greeted with a mixture of awe at the Germans' accomplishment and technical perfection, and hostile criticism of their aesthetic. Undisguised jealousy of the remarkable organization of the German displays was clear in many articles by French critics. M. P. Verneuil, for example, criticized the lack of national originality in the German designs. He wrote, 'I see the mark of many direct influences: the Biedermeier–Louis-Philippe style, the Second Empire and the English styles can be easily spotted. And the main impression is that of a Louis-Philippe style but heavier, enriched and Germanized.'[4]

It was, however, the medley of bold colours, unusual to French eyes, that attracted the attention of many critics. In 1915 Frédéric Masson described the 'Munichois' style as:

A style in which everything is violent, shocking, burning, in which the tones explode one against another, the crudest and most intense that one could imagine. That's the Munich style. And one sees greens whose acidity turns the stomach, crossed with lilac stripes that accompany a blood-red line; and what yellows! And what pinks![5]

French artists responded in the 1912 *Salon des artistes décorateurs*, whose exhibits showed that they had intensified their efforts to cultivate a modern

8.1 Atelier Français, interior for the 1913 *Salon d'automne*. *Art et décoration*, January 1914. NAL.

style. Their declared aim to put an end to Art Nouveau and create a new French national style was demonstrated in the selection policy. Prefiguring the regulations for the Paris 1925 Exhibition, this stated that 'Only those works will be accepted which are works of applied art, and which are clearly decorative in their composition, interpretation or destination. The works must demonstrate new tendencies; copies and imitations of past styles will be rigorously excluded.'[6]

However, it was also the radical originality of Art Nouveau that was perceived, by some, as a cause of its decline. André Vera believed it was Art Nouveau's 'clear rupture with tradition' that made it 'not sympathetic to the vast majority of the public'.[7] For him, a valid modern style should be imbued with meanings and symbols reflecting a national, cultural renaissance. Tradition, he believed, should not be rejected but built upon: 'No modernity without tradition … and no tradition without modernity.'[8] The 1912, 1913 and 1914 Paris salons[9] reflected the new importance given to the legacy of national styles. Paul Follot, Paul Iribe, Maurice Dufrène, André Groult, André Mare and Louis Süe all developed a new decorative idiom which echoed French tradition (plate 8.1). Revealingly, by the 1920s, the adjective 'modern' was rejected by this new generation of artists: they preferred to be regarded as 'contemporary'.[10] With a preference for simple, classical designs, they drew on the Neo-classicism of Louis XVI, the more severe Directoire and Empire styles, the Restauration style and the Louis-Philippe style.

Alongside their call for a new aesthetic to uphold French traditions of style and craftsmanship, these designers were united in their rejection of the slavish imitation of past styles and reviled the historicist craftsmen who carried on working in the Louis styles purely for economic reasons: 'The Faubourg Saint Antoine is totally insensitive to our aesthetic preachings; it does not care to see our country failing in its secular mission of being a pioneer in art: if it is not moved, it will continue to produce its counterfeits of revival furniture, for as long as revival furniture reigns in the homes of the powerful.'[11] This did not preclude the integration of historical pieces within the modern interior, however. Many designers were keen to create a style that would allow earlier works of art to be displayed alongside modern ones, something that the Art Nouveau commitment to the total artistic interior, or *Gesamtkunstwerk*, had failed to achieve. Some even actively collected works from earlier periods. André Groult was initially an antique dealer, specializing in eighteenth-century French decorative arts. As a designer he was one of the first

8.2 Theodor Veil, reception room for the 1910 *Salon d'automne*. *L'Art décoratif*, 1910. NAL.

8.3 Paul Follot, carpet. Wool. French, 1919-20. Made by D.I.M. V&A: T.77-1982.

8.4 Paul Follot, dressing table and chair. Carved, gilt and lacquered wood and portor marble. French, 1919-20. Musée d'Art Moderne de la Ville de Paris. © PMVP. Photo: Pierrain.

to adopt the new style and openly drew inspiration from works in his collection. His 'Chambre de Madame', in the 'Ambassade Française' at the 1925 Exhibition, was directly inspired by a traditional boudoir (see plate 12.5). Empire in its clear, simple form, it also owes a debt to the Louis XV style in spirit, the curvaceous lines of its furniture and the pastel colours suggesting elegance and intimacy. The couturier Jacques Doucet was also a great collector of fine eighteenth-century French decorative arts. He followed a similar, though more radical path when, in 1912, he decided to sell his historic collection and promote contemporary art and design. Another fashion leader, the society portrait painter and dandy Bernard Boutet de Monvel, was fascinated by a later period – the nineteenth century. In 1906 he

published a series of etchings representing the 'élégances d'autrefois', elegant men and women of the Empire, Directoire, Restauration and Second Empire periods. Importantly, he was one of the first to start collecting the decorative arts of this era and his collection may well have exerted considerable influence in fashionable circles.

Among the range of French historical styles that Art Deco drew on, the Louis XVI style (c.1760-95), with its Neo-classical ornaments and forms, was the first to influence designers. Paul Follot frequently used eighteenth-century shapes combined with luxurious materials and traditional techniques. A dressing table and chair shown at the 1920 *Salon des artistes décorateurs* is a striking example of the adaptation of this style (plate 8.4). Its ornament and materials characterize the first phase of Art Deco. The ornament is derived from the Louis XVI style, but the floral decorations are treated two-dimensionally and symmetrically; they are organized

densely in inverted cornucopias, juxtaposed with a geometric trellis. The result is a geometric, Cubist version of the naturalistic flowers and stems often encountered in Art Nouveau. The 'Cubist rose' was to become one of the emblems of the new style (see plate 14.10). Unlike its Louis XVI forbear, too, the ornament in Follot's desk has a structural function rather than a purely decorative existence since it supports the mirror. The materials are luxurious and carefully chosen, especially the marble with its golden veins in harmony with the gilt wood, and the techniques are those of traditional French *ébénisterie*. The ensemble is a unique, luxurious piece, within the French tradition, but undeniably modern.

The Directoire (1795-1804), Empire (1804-15) and Restauration (1815-30) styles, with their simple lines, warm wood veneers and sparse decoration were also much in favour. One of the most successful Art Deco designers, Jacques-Emile

Ruhlmann, became famous for his modernization of some of these earlier styles. His dressing table reinterprets a Restauration type from the 1820s with a rotating mirror and lyre-shaped base (plate 8.5). The outstanding aristocratic prototype for this was the famous *toilette* of the Duchesse du Berry.[12] The Ruhlmann table clearly demonstrates its lineage from this type characteristic of the 1820s in its shape, overall proportions and use of precious dark wood veneers (plate 8.6). Similarly, the armchair in his 'Grand Salon de l'Hôtel d'un Collectionneur' at the 1925 Exhibition was inspired by an Empire chair at Fontainebleau.[13] Ruhlmann confessed his debt to traditional styles but stressed the need to take into account contemporary circumstances, saying that 'Indeed, most of my works are of classical inspiration. And I often happen to take my students to Versailles. Naturally, it is not to incite them to copy antiques. One ought only to find inspiration in them, adapt them to our time.'[14] His free interpretations of his prototypes were modern in taking into account the element of comfort, putting the accent on pure and often orthogonal lines, and using few, often geometric, ornaments.

8.5 Dressing table. Mahogany veneer and white marble top. French, c.1825. V&A: W.17-1987.

8.7 Catalogue, *Grands Magasins du Louvre*, Paris, 1924, 'Meubles de salon styles Directoire et Empire' and 'Meubles modernes'. Bibliothèque Nationale de France, Paris.

8.6 Jacques-Emile Ruhlmann, dressing table. Oak with amaranth and mahogany veneer; ebony and ivory inlays; silver bronze mirror frame and fittings; mirrored glass. French, 1925. V&A: W.14-1980.

It was not only the most recognized designers at the luxury end of the market who turned to the past for inspiration. The leading department stores, which promoted and commercialized Art Deco alongside revival styles, were committed to a fundamentally traditional aesthetic conception of modern decorative arts. Pages from a catalogue of the Grands Magasins du Louvre show reproduction Empire-style furniture, still in demand, to be a close cousin of the modernistic pieces illustrated on the opposite page (plate 8.7).

The modernization of tradition was not limited to the furniture and interior design industry. In fashion, Paul Poiret captured the spirit of his time, reflecting the emergence of the new woman. His Empire-inspired dresses liberated women from confining structure and paid homage to the *élégante* of the Napoleonic era. The 'Joséphine' or '1811' designs are striking examples.[15] An energetic promoter of his work, Poiret had many of his designs illustrated. *Les Robes de Paul Poiret* of 1908, by Poiret's student Paul Iribe, demonstrates that the Directoire and Empire periods inspired not only the dresses, but also the whole conception of modern fashion and the interior (plate 8.8).

The Louis-Philippe style (1830-48), however, characterized by bourgeois, comfortable and simple interiors, became perhaps the greatest source of inspiration for French Art Deco designers. André Vera summarized the importance of this style:

> As far as furniture is concerned, we won't seek advice from the English nor the Dutch, but we shall pursue the French tradition, so that this new style will be a natural successor to the last traditional style we have, the Louis-Philippe style. As the Louis-Philippe style is not very far from us yet, and as it was developed under a *bourgeois* monarchy, its aim was to satisfy not only requirements but also customs that differ from ours less than those of any earlier times.[16]

Especially after the First World War, there was a rebirth of interest in this style as well as in the Second Empire – a more *tapissier* but quintessentially bourgeois style. Several exhibitions on these periods were shown, including *Le Décor de la vie sous le Second Empire* at the Musée des Arts Décoratifs (1922), *L'Art et la vie sous Louis-Philippe, 1830-1848* at the Hôtel Jean Carpentier (1926) and *Louis-Philippe et Napoléon III* at the Château de Fontainebleau (1928). Also, a number of books and articles, both scholarly and popular, on eighteenth- and nineteenth-century French decorative arts were published. The designers most influenced by the Louis-Philippe style were probably Louis Süe and

8.8 Paul Iribe, plate from *Les Robes de Paul Poiret racontées par Paul Iribe*, Paris, 1908. Pochoir colour print. NAL.

André Mare. In their marquetry, textile and wallpaper designs they gave its floral motifs a modern reinterpretation. Léon Moussinac saw in their designs 'a wish to return to a constructive logic that does not hide its sympathies for the work of 1840, to a means of examining the structure and architecture of a flower rather than its expression'.[17] André Groult's stylized floral ornaments and wallpapers, the woven textiles created for Ruhlmann's interiors and many of the patterns created by Edouard Bénédictus also find their roots in the self-assured classicism of the Louis-Philippe era. The use of contrasting, audacious hues by Bénédictus and a great many other Art Deco designers became a way to modernize traditional forms and motifs, though this was sometimes controversial and criticized as a 'German' influence.

It was not only the French who looked to their national traditions to create a new style. In nearly every European country tradition was used as a basis for a modern national style. In the German-speaking countries the Empire and Biedermeier periods exerted a considerable influence. The Wiener Werkstätte in Austria, founded in 1903 by Josef Hoffmann and Koloman Moser, had created a vocabulary of modern, geometric decoration, influenced by the English Arts and Crafts Movement and the art of Charles Rennie Mackintosh. This constituted a link between forward-looking ideas of the nineteenth century and developments in the early twentieth century. Increasingly, however, the Werkstätte designers drew on national sources of inspiration including the national Rococo, Empire and Biedermeier styles. In Germany, some members of the Deutscher Werkbund also investigated the use of national styles. Alongside former Art Nouveau designers were others for whom historical continuity was an important consideration. For them, a revival in art seemed possible only by reference to the past, particularly to the uncluttered forms and simple colours of the early nineteenth century.

Biedermeier (*c.* 1815-35) was essentially an urban style, modest and neo-classical, aimed at the bourgeoisie. It was characterized by solid forms, rich materials and sparse ornamentation (plate 8.9). Reviled during the second half of the nineteenth century, the style was rediscovered by designers and craftsmen early in the twentieth century. Important books were published during the 1910s by Joseph Folnesics, August Schestag, Joseph August Lux, Adolf Rosenberg and Max von Boehm, the first historians of the style. Paul Schultze-Naumburg advocated the Biedermeier style as a model of simple elegance, adaptable to modern conditions. For Josef Hoffmann, the 'Biedermeier time' was also 'the last period as we saw it, to offer a valid expression of art'.[18] And as early as 1905, Bruno Paul confessed his debt to the Empire and Biedermeier styles. A chair designed by Paul at that time, with the openwork pattern of its back and light satinwood veneer, is clearly indebted to Biedermeier (plate 8.10).[19] At the third German exhibition of arts and crafts in Dresden in 1906,[20] this new neo-classicism led the way; it was even more evident at the exhibition held in Cologne in 1914,[21] which showed the development of the ornamentation associated with Biedermeier furniture and furnishings. Bruno Paul, Peter Behrens, Adalbert Niemeyer, Albin Müller and Karl Bertsch were all experimenting with this style, leading Paul Schultze-Naumburg to write,

> When, in connection with the acceptance of tradition, I recommended relying on forms whose essence was most related to our own era, the early nineteenth century was quite naturally uppermost in my mind. For this was the epoch closest to us in time which brought forth forms redolent of a new, comprehensively educated bourgeoisie.[22]

It was not a return to the Biedermeier that he recommended, but that the style be taken as a point of departure and adapted and developed to meet the requirements of the day.

The Baroque and Rococo, popular in Jugendstil, continued to exert an influence. Dagobert Peche, designer for the Wiener Werkstätte from 1915 until his death in 1923, often found inspiration in the Austrian variants of these traditions, while also incorporating details from contemporary designs he had seen abroad. While in Paris in 1912 he studied the first Art Deco trends. Peche's highly decorative and expressionistic style represents the height of Art Deco in Austria and demonstrates the anti-rationalist strain that increasingly characterized the Wiener Werkstätte output in the post-war years. The design of much Austrian metalwork relied heavily on historical forms, using facetted, curved, neo-Baroque

8.9 Desk. Cherry wood and black-stained oak, with tin insets and green lacquer. Austrian, c.1825. MAK, Vienna.

8.10 Bruno Paul, chair. Beech frame, satinwood veneer inlaid with oak, raw silk upholstery. German, 1905. V&A: W.26-1990.

shapes with Mannerist floral ornaments for spouts and handles, as well as traditional techniques and precious materials such as silver, ivory and ebony. Otto Prutscher's silver tea service professes his debt to national traditions while being modern in its stylized lines (plate 8.11). Also working in an eighteenth-century mannerist spirit were German ceramic manufacturers like the Staatliche Porzellan-Manufaktur, Meissen and Rosenthal. Reinventing themselves, they employed sculptors to modernize traditional porcelain figurines and clocks. Although very much in the tradition of the eighteenth-century Rococo figurine, these works were modernized through the stylization of their lines, the elongation of their figures and the creation of new subjects (see Chapter 15).

This strategy of modernizing historical motifs and forms was also applied to the use of folk art. The Wiener Werkstätte and some German designers incorporated folk influences into their work. For some, such as Theodor Fischer and Richard

Riemerschmid, the sense of continuity that regional craft traditions inspired was important. However, there were other reasons for the adoption of the vernacular by Art Deco designers. Folk art encompassed the idea of a pre-industrialized art predicated on traditions of handcraft practice. It also represented the living idea of a nation-community, but perhaps most importantly, it had a direct visual and aesthetic appeal. The exploitation of folk art can be seen as another example of a decorative response to modernity. Its polychrome, simple, stylized, often geometric patterns, and the traditional techniques and materials, were central to the investigations of Art Deco designers.

French Art Deco designers also had recourse to a romanticized version of folk art, reviving regional traditions. In the *Salon d'automne* of 1912 Louis Süe and Paul Huillard presented an interior inspired by eighteenth-century Provençal traditions, its furniture shaped after garden furniture. The seats and sofa exemplified this return to regional tradition,

while the bright colours and decorative pattern of the basket of flowers were derived from the rustic style first introduced by Marie-Antoinette at the Trianon.[23] The 'modern art' departments of the French department stores also offered folk-inspired objects, which were produced in regional workshops. Primavera, at the Grands Magasins du Printemps, explained in its 1923 catalogue how the French provinces had been toured in search of traditional potters and weavers. The resulting bold, naïve patterns and forms on offer were described as being designed in harmony with modern interiors. The picturesque *toiles de Jouy*, much in favour during the late eighteenth and early nineteenth centuries, came back into fashion during the early twentieth century when many exhibitions and publications on the theme were produced. The repetition of little pictures representing pleasing bucolic or gallant scenes, such as hunts, walks in the countryside, and shepherds and shepherdesses were emulated in the textile designs of artists like Raoul Dufy. In designs for

8.11 Otto Prutscher, tea and coffee service. Silver and ivory. Austrian, c.1920. V&A: M.38-1970.

Bianchini-Férier, such as 'La chasse', 'La danse', 'L'escarpolette', 'Les Tuileries', 'Longchamp', 'Bagatelle' and 'La moisson',[24] he imitated the repetitive compositions and bucolic spirit but transposed the subjects and style into modern times (plate 8.14). While Dufy played with an aristocratic notion of the peasant and created sophisticated modern designs, Paul Poiret's Atelier Martine, created in 1912, consciously attempted to capture the naïve. Attended by working-class children, who were encouraged to develop spontaneous ideas, free of inhibiting formal training, the Atelier produced bold, brightly coloured patterns close in spirit to the idea of folk art shaped by artists (see plate 10.9).

Alongside these experiments with style, renewed interest in authentic folk techniques developed. Victor Lhuer, who worked as a designer for Paul Poiret as well as for the fur designer, A la Reine d'Angleterre, decided after the war to make his own fabrics according to traditional techniques. He set up a workshop in Boulevard Raspail, next to the fashionable Hôtel Lutétia, where some of his elegant foreign clientele, mostly Americans, stayed. He also collected documents on folk dress, from Brittany and the Bourbonnais in France,[25] but also from Italy, Spain and especially Romania, where he had been born and spent his early childhood. His designs for tunic dresses, sometimes elaborately draped, in rich, supple silks, are ornamented with geometric, highly colourful patterns drawn from his knowledge of traditional folk art but geometricized to reflect the new tastes. This sophisticated 'naïve' style was extremely successful among his international clientele (plate 8.12).[26]

By the 1930s the return to French traditions, in terms of patterns, materials and techniques, had become a question of patriotism and national identity. The trend reached its apogee in the *Salon des artistes décorateurs* of 1935 in designs dubbed by the press 'modernized tradition' or 'rustic modern'. The 'Rendez-vous des pêcheurs' by Jacques-Emile Ruhlmann, 1932, demonstrates this marked change in style. Ruhlmann's habitual sense of elegance and simplicity was here combined with a new interest in rusticity and the picturesque.

In Eastern and Northern European countries, the inspiration of folk art played an even more crucial role in Art Deco. At the end of the nineteenth century, the Arts and Crafts and Art Nouveau designers had embraced the vernacular in the belief that the essence of the national culture was present in its seemingly untouched traditions. These were then explored and redefined to build a sense of nationhood. This was particularly true of 'new'

8.12 Victor Lhuer, dress. Silk. French, c.1925-30. Private collection, Paris. Photo: Louis Gonzales.

8.13 Melkiorre Melis, vase. Earthenware, painted in enamels. Italian, c.1923. The Mitchell Wolfson Jr Collection. The Wolfsonian-Florida International University, Miami Beach, Florida. Photo: Silvia Ross.

countries or those long dominated by large powers – like Norway, Finland, Sweden, Poland, Hungary, Czechoslovakia and Yugoslavia. They developed the idea that the vernacular past held the key to what it meant to be 'Czech' or 'Finnish', and thus to the future. Their designs during the Art Deco period have to be understood in the context of these nationalist developments and attendant political meanings (see Chapters 16 and 17).

In turning to popular, folk patterns and colours, Art Deco artists and craftsmen also encouraged the use of local materials and traditional techniques. Lacemaking, for example, was revived in Czechoslovakia by modern designers such as Emilie Paličková-Mildeová who received a Grand Prix at the Paris 1925 Exhibition for her 'Little Sun'. Her designs show traditional, floral patterns and depict rural types wearing simple, folk dress, but they are treated in a modernized and stylized manner. In Poland, various societies and artists' colonies, such as the Kilim Polsky, were founded with the aim of modernizing and reviving the art of the *kilim*.[27] The traditional *kilim* with its bold, geometric patterns was readily adaptable to the modern taste for abstract decoration. Examples can be drawn from all over Europe, from Bohemia to Sweden (see plates 16.7 and 17.11) or Sardinia, where artists built upon their folk heritage to create a modern and national repertoire of forms, patterns and colours (plate 8.13).

Art Deco was not a modern form of historicism but, particularly in its early phase and until about 1925, it was certainly fired by the need to inscribe its creations within the continuity of the historic and national styles. Art Nouveau, in trying to use the past in its more 'bizarre' products while claiming to be completely new, failed to achieve this.[28] In that respect, Art Deco is a self-conscious, discerning eclecticism. In a period that increasingly saw Modernist propaganda for the rejection of historical styles, to make way for the advent of a modern style fully adapted to contemporary needs, there was also a strong reassertion of continuity with the past. This was achieved through the use of traditional and national styles and the modernization of traditional techniques and modes of production.

8.14 Raoul Dufy, *La danse*. Printed linen furnishing fabric. French, c.1925. Made by Bianchini-Férier. V&A: Circ.113-1939. © ADAGP, Paris and DACS, London 2002.

9 Avant-Garde Sources

Charlotte Benton and Tim Benton

The Exposition marks the coming of age of a new décor … as inevitable a manifestation of the forces of evolution as modern art … passing through the Porte d'Honneur one comes … upon a cubist dream city … its cubist shapes and futurist colors … looking like nothing so much as a Picasso abstraction… [1]

To many visitors to the Paris 1925 Exhibition, the first major international manifestation of Art Deco, the overwhelming impression was of a material world which, though it still retained numerous residual reminders of tradition, had been transformed. This transformation had been effected less by the introduction of new materials and processes (though there were plenty of examples of both) than by the new visual language, colour and iconography of early twentieth-century avant-garde art. Fauvism, Cubism, Expressionism, Futurism, De Stijl and Constructivism – frequently bundled together by contemporaries under the label 'Cubism' – had, by the mid-1920s, made an impact on all the decorative arts media, from bookbinding and silversmithing, via graphics and fashion, to photography and film (plate 9.1). And this impact was not limited to Moderne or 'decorative Modernist' designs; it also affected the work of more traditional practitioners and would impinge on that of the new breed of stylists and industrial designers who emerged in early 1930s America (plate 9.2).

In many ways this is surprising. Throughout the 1910s and 1920s first-hand knowledge of avant-garde art was confined to a small number of dealers, collectors, museum curators and other enthusiasts. Outside these circles such art was often viewed, at best, as cranky or alien; at worst, it was seen (and sometimes intended) as threateningly subversive of established traditions and values – whether social or cultural – and attracted hostile criticism and even outright abuse.[2] Furthermore, most avant-garde artists insisted on the autonomy of the work of art and firmly rejected any decorative intentions. And yet, by the late 1920s and early 1930s an increasingly wide public was familiar with the language of such art as applied in the popular media, fashion and quotidian domestic goods. You did not

9.1 Jean Goulden, clock. Silvered bronze with enamel. French, 1928. Collection Stephen E. Kelly. © Christie's Images Ltd 1999. © ADAGP, Paris and DACS, London 2002.

9.2 Walter Dorwin Teague, three Beau Brownie cameras. American, 1930-33. Royal Photographic Society Picture Library.

9.3 Fernand Léger, *Les disques dans la ville*. Oil on canvas. French, 1920. Centre Georges Pompidou, Paris. MNAM. Photo: CNAC/MNAM Dist. RMN. ©ADAGP, Paris and DACS, London 2002.

9.4 Umberto Boccioni, *Unique Forms of Continuity in Space*. Bronze. Italian, 1913 (cast 1972). Tate, London, 2002.

have to understand this art to appreciate its visual impact and meanings in an everyday context. Nor was it just its visual aspects that appealed to the wider public; the culture it represented was important too. This dual appeal can be readily seen in the graphic and poster designs of A. M. Cassandre and Edward McKnight Kauffer, who persuasively interpreted Cubist and Constructivist imagery for a general public (see plates 2.4, 20.7 and 29.1); in the work of photographers like Cecil Beaton and Man Ray, who introduced abstract and Surrealist images into their work (see plates 23.16 and 25.11); in mannequins designed by avant-garde artists like Alexander Archipenko and Salvador Dali, which contributed to the radical overhaul of shop window display that took place in the 1920s; and in European and American films by directors like Marcel L'Herbier and Jack Conway, who commissioned set and costume designs based on avant-garde art, or incorporated replicas of art works in their *mises en scène*, to connote a youthful, liberated and chic lifestyle (see plate 30.2).[3]

The reasons for this association between the decorative arts and a kind of art frequently claimed by its protagonists to be the antithesis of the decorative are several and complex, and only a few can be indicated here. One was that movements like Italian Futurism, which attempted to capture the sensation of the flux and increasingly rapid tempo of contemporary urban life, or the work of the painter Fernand Léger, which depicted in emblematic form the spread of mechanization that drove that increasingly rapid tempo, spoke to the experience of a wide public. Avant-garde art's formal indeterminacy on the one hand and its clarity on the other – represented by synthetic Cubist paintings or collages and Futurist sculpture, or by the synoptic representations of the contemporary urban environment to be found in paintings by Léger and Robert Delaunay – both caught the sense of flux and pace of the age and, simultaneously, suggested that they could be ordered or tamed (plates 9.3, 9.4, 9.5 and 9.6). Avant-garde art thus became synonymous with the idea of 'modernity' and what

9.5 Robert Delaunay, *Tour Eiffel*.
Oil on canvas. French, 1911.
Gift Solomon R. Guggenheim,
1937. Solomon R. Guggenheim
Museum. Photo: Sally Ritts.
© Solomon R. Guggenheim
Foundation, New York.
© L&M Services B. V. Amsterdam
20020704.

it meant to be 'modern', to which contemporaries the world over aspired, however different the local context or inflection.

Other reasons were to be found in social change. Increased opportunities for women to lead independent lives, whether in the workplace or socially, created wider aspirations to the kind of alternative lifestyle often associated with artists. And, in the 1920s, problems of overproduction and consumer resistance to tried and tested models increasingly encouraged manufacturers and retailers to adopt the idea of 'built-in obsolescence' and the practice of seasonal model changes, like the fashion industry, to stimulate demand. In this context, avant-garde art became just another 'source' to be raided and adapted – like the material culture of ancient Egypt or Mesoamerica – for its novelty and fashion value. Significantly, the couture industry, with its constant need for new designs was – with its associated textile manufacturers – an early enthusiast for the new imagery as well as a significant means of its wider diffusion, whether via dedicated fashion journals or the popular press.

Avant-garde artists and Deco designers often shared interests, patrons and friends. The Cubists' fascination with things African was shared by Eileen Gray, Pierre Legrain and Maria Likarz, among others (see Chapter 7 and plates 7.4 and 7.10).[4] The couturier Jacques Doucet was a keen collector of work by artists like Picasso, Jacques Lipchitz and Georges Braque as well as by decorative artists like Gray and Legrain (plate 9.7).[5] And the association between avant-garde art and Art Deco was also encouraged by decorative artists' ambitions. Pierre Legrain's selection of *de luxe* works by himself and other French decorative artists, published in a contemporary album, *Objets d'art*, indicates that

9.6 Albert Gleizes, *Brooklyn Bridge*. Oil and sand on cardboard. 148.1 x 120.4 cm. French, 1915. Mr and Mrs David Mirvish, Toronto. © ADAGP, Paris and DACS, London.
© Christie's Images Ltd 2002.

9.7 Jacques Lipchitz (born in Lithuania), fire surround. Limestone. French, c.1929. Formerly in the collection of Jacques Doucet. Museum of Fine Arts, Boston.

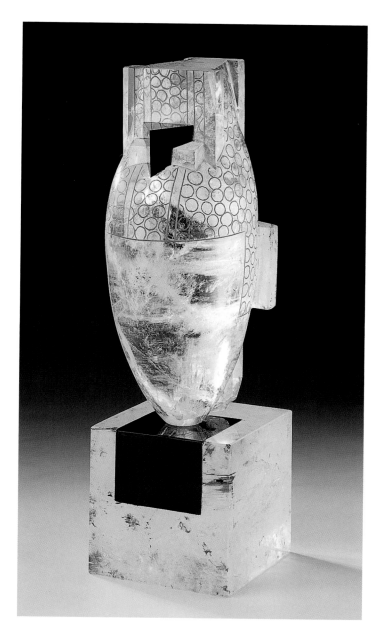

9.8 Josef Csaky (born in Hungary), sculpture of a head. Crystal and onyx. Around 1930. A wooden head was in the collection of Jacques Doucet. Private collection, Paris.

many of them wanted to be recognized as equal in stature to fine artists and to have their work valued accordingly (plate 9.8).[6] Similar tendencies could be found elsewhere, for example in the work of the Viennese metalsmith Franz Hagenauer, who specialized in decorative adaptations of the work of Brancusi and other abstract sculptors (see plate 15.9).[7] Equally, however, many designers working in more mundane materials, for mass production and the popular market, came to see forms and motifs derived from fine art as capable of bringing aesthetic value to even modest domestic environments, as well as giving value to their own practice.[8]

At the same time, avant-garde artists themselves took an interest in developments in decorative art. Fernand Léger was reportedly fascinated by the techniques of the couturière Madeleine Vionnet and used to visit her workshops to watch her at work.[9] Furthermore, several avant-garde artists themselves practised the decorative arts. In many respects this seems paradoxical, since they and contemporary art theorists often insisted on the absolute autonomy of both the fine artist and the work of art and firmly rejected the decorative. As Albert Gleizes and Jean Metzinger wrote, in their book *Du Cubisme*, published in 1912, 'Many consider that decorative preoccupations must govern the spirit of the new painters. Undoubtedly they are ignorant of the most obvious signs that make decorative work the antithesis of the picture.'[10] According to this reading, the only 'function' of the work of art was to engage the mind and arouse emotion through the effects of colour and form alone; the artwork was thus entirely independent of its context. By contrast, the applied or decorative arts were defined by the need to harmonize with their context. The idea that a work of art could be 'decorative', therefore, was anathema. Yet, despite such strictures, avant-garde artists turned to the decorative arts for a variety of reasons.

Many of those practising in the early decades of the century were imbued with the ethos of the Arts and Crafts and Art Nouveau movements, in which artists and architects had routinely designed domestic items and clothes for family and friends. Among these were the Russian-born artist Wassily Kandinsky who, in the early 1900s, designed decorative accessories, including wall hangings and handbags, in collaboration with his companion

9.9 Nikolai M. Suetin, writing set with inkpot. Porcelain, painted in enamels. Russian, c.1925. Made by the Lomonosov State porcelain factory, Leningrad. Bröhan-Museum, Berlin. Photo: Martin Adam. © DACS 2002.

Gabriele Münter; these seem to have been made for personal rather than commercial reasons. Similarly, the Cubist painter Juan Gris designed tapestry seat covers based on motifs from his paintings for a set of dining chairs owned by his dealer Daniel-Henri Kahnweiler.[11]

Other fine artists turned to design as a matter of political principle. In Italy, before the First World War, Filippo Tommaso Marinetti challenged Futurist artists to abandon their easels and actively engage in life. Although the first purpose of this engagement was to create havoc on the streets for political ends, some of the Futurists later set up craft workshops and worked in fashion illustration or advertising (see plate 19.6).[12] And in revolutionary Russia many artists joined the movement 'from the easel to the machine', in the belief that an autonomous art practice was inherently bourgeois and incapable of furthering the cause of the proletariat (plate 9.9).[13]

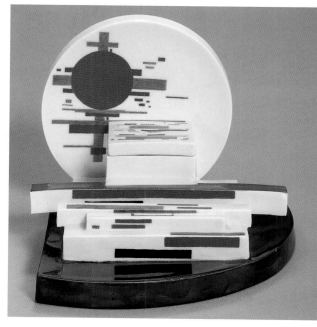

A belief in the interdependence and essential unity of the arts also played a part. In Holland, the highly theoretical and somewhat ascetic De Stijl group, which emerged in 1917, engaged with the design of furniture and interiors from the outset.[14] And yet the scheme for the Aubette cellar bar in Strasbourg by Theo van Doesburg and others shows that, even in De Stijl, the line between rigorous abstract art and purely decorative effects could be a fine one (plate 9.10). Similarly, in Germany, the Bauhaus, established in 1919 under Walter Gropius,[15] promoted cross-fertilization between fine art, crafts and industrial design. The forms and colours of fine artists associated with the Bauhaus were echoed in their colleagues' designs for textiles and other domestic wares.[16] Elsewhere, too, avant-garde artists – especially those familiar with European developments at first hand, like Lazar Segall in Brazil and Ruth Reeves in America – applied ideas first developed in their fine art practice to the decorative arts (plate 9.11).

Other considerations, too, prompted avant-garde artists' migration to decoration and design. Cubism's abandonment of the normative traditions of representation posed a dilemma for some moderately progressive artists. As Ami Chantre noted in 1913, 'too prudent to venture along the cubist road, which is rocky … [they] are renouncing painting … picking up the tools abandoned by the artisans in preference for machines, and in place of decorating our walls, they are furnishing our houses'.[17] Others turned to the decorative arts for purely pragmatic reasons, to support their own fine art practice or that of their partners. These included Raoul Dufy, who made bold fabric designs for the couturier Paul Poiret and the textile manufacturer Bianchini-Férier (see plates 8.14 and 10.7), as well as ceramic designs,[18] and the Ukrainian-born Sonia Delaunay, whose earliest designs were made for the Delaunays' Parisian apartment.[19] Delaunay translated the bright colours and often abstract forms of her own and Robert Delaunay's so-called 'simultaneous' paintings into designs for lampshades, textiles and clothes for themselves and their friends,[20] and made illustrations for the first 'simultaneous' book (plate 9.12 and see plate 13.10).[21] During the First World War, which the Delaunays spent in voluntary exile on the Iberian peninsula, her design activities expanded. Here, especially after 1917,[22] she designed clothes, accessories and occasional interiors for Madrid society figures; she also opened a shop, Casa Sonia, to sell her designs for the domestic interior.[23] Both Delaunays were also invited by the impresario Serge Diaghilev, then in Madrid, to design sets and costumes for the 1918 Ballets Russes production of *Cléopâtre*.[24] By the time they returned to France after the war, the impending Paris 1925 Exhibition had established a climate favourable to the expansion of design activities. A project to re-establish Casa Sonia in Nice fell through when its backers decided that her work was 'too modern',[25] but by 1923 Delaunay had sold more than 50 designs to a Lyon silk manufacturer. In the following year, she set up her own business with the couturier Jacques Heim, for which she designed dress fabrics, clothes and accessories, as well as rugs and other furnishing textiles.[26]

9.11 Ruth Reeves, 'Figures with Still Life', wall hanging. Block-printed cotton velvet. American, 1930. Made by W. & J. Sloane, New York. V&A: T.282-1932.

9.10 Theo van Doesburg (Christian Emil Kuepper), a floor plan for the Café Aubette, Strasbourg. Paper with ink, gouache and pencil. Dutch, 1926. Centre Georges Pompidou, Paris. MNAM. Photo: CNAC/MNAM – RMN. © ADAGP, Paris and DACS, London 2002.

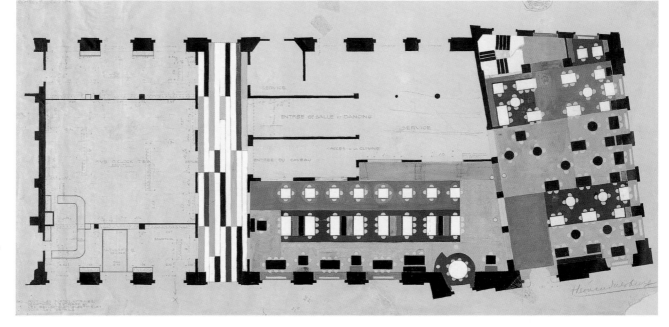

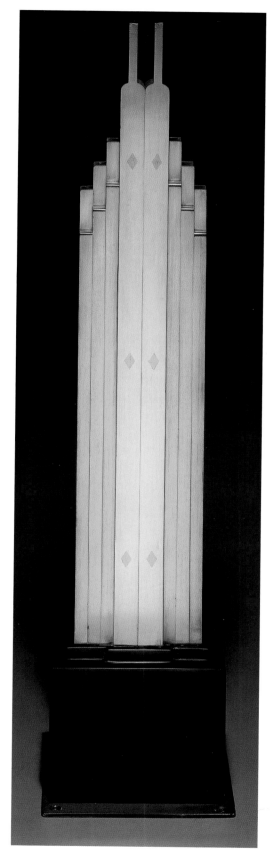

9.12 Sonia Delaunay (Russian), illustration for Blaise Cendrars, *La Prose du Transibérien et la petite Jehanne de France*, Paris, 1913. Watercolour. NAL: AM 1984-581. © L&M Services B. V. Amsterdam 20020704.

Besides avant-garde artists' direct ventures into decorative design, several contemporary artists gave a decorative inflection to the visual language of the avant-garde. These included the American sculptor John Storrs, who had lived in Paris, whose abstract sculptures and reliefs displayed a distinctively decorative character (plate 9.13).[27] All these examples belong, traditionally, to the history of Modernism rather than Art Deco. Yet they indicate that however puritanical avant-garde artists and theorists might be about the need to keep art divorced from function and decorative application, in practice there was a widespread interest in the overlap between the fine and decorative arts. As a result artists often broke their own rules. Furthermore, although their decorative designs were often made as one-offs, or in 'limited editions', principally intended for themselves or members of their immediate circle, they reached a wider audience and influenced commercial production. Kandinsky and Münter's decorative designs were exhibited at the Paris *Salon d'automne*. Giacomo Balla, Fortunato Depero and other Futurists wore their designs for 'aggressive', 'dynamic', 'activist' Futurist clothing in their provocative public performances in Italy and elsewhere. Designs by Depero, Enrico Prampolini and Balla were shown in the Italian exhibit at the Paris 1925 Exhibition (see Chapter 19), where they attracted favourable comment and prizes. And, by the early 1920s, Futurist imagery was directly associated with high fashion, through Ernesto Thayaht's designs for packaging for Madeleine Vionnet and his illustrations of her couture designs in journals such as the *Gazette du bon ton*. His adaptation of Futurist 'lines of force' to evoke the swirling movements of fashion models on a catwalk was influential for fashion graphics.[28] Clothes and furniture designed by the Russian Productivists, led by Alexander Rodchenko and Varvara Stepanova, were shown in the USSR exhibit at the 1925 Exhibition; if few visitors were impressed by their style and finish, they were nevertheless struck by avant-garde art's engagement with the everyday.[29] Sonia Delaunay's early designs received broader exposure through publication and their exhibition in Paris, Berlin (1914) and Stockholm (1916).[30] And her 'simultaneous' boutique, with Heim, at the Paris 1925 Exhibition brought her work to the attention of a larger and more varied audience (see plate 13.9).

9.13 John Storrs, *Forms in Space, Number 1*. Stainless steel and copper. American, *c*.1924. M. Francis Lathrop Fund, 1967. The Metropolitan Museum of Art, New York.

9.14 Raymond Duchamp-Villon, model for the Maison Cubiste. French, 1912. *L'Art décoratif*, February 1913. NAL.

As a result, she acquired several new clients, including the Dutch department store Metz & Co., Liberty of London and some American department stores; and she was invited to design costumes and sets for Marcel L'Herbier and René Le Somptier's films *Le Vertige* and *Le P'tit Parigot* (both 1926) – the earliest films to include Deco interiors and costumes – and an interior for the new Deco building for Bullocks' department store in Los Angeles (1928).[31]

The impact of such work on Art Deco designers was most visible in the 'decorative Modernist' and Moderne variants of Art Deco which, in the 1920s and 1930s, increasingly displaced the 'modernized tradition' of early Art Deco.[32] But the influence of avant-garde art on the latter was widely recognized from an early date; while it was often disparaged it was also welcomed by some. Louis Süe, a leading French protagonist of the modernization of national traditions, was surprisingly open to the lessons of Cubism, saying, 'I find cubism highly interesting … if we understand [it] as a reaction against the debaucheries, the orgies of impressionist colours, as a method, a discipline, a return to construction, to geometry … why not use what can serve us in it?'[33]

Süe's ideas were given practical form by his later collaborator, the fringe Cubist painter André Mare, in the so-called 'Maison Cubiste' exhibited at the Paris *Salon d'automne* in 1912.[34] Here Mare, who was also active as a designer and, like Süe, promoted the modernization of tradition (see Chapter 8), drew together the work of several artists associated with Cubism. The exhibit comprised a mocked-up façade designed by the sculptor Raymond Duchamp-Villon and an entrance hall, 'salon bourgeois' and bedroom (plate 9.14). The interiors were furnished to designs by Mare (furniture and wallpaper), Roger de la Fresnaye (clocks and fireplaces), Marie Laurencin (decorated mirrors), Maurice Marinot (glassware) and Jacques Villon (ceramics); they were hung with paintings by Albert Gleizes, de la Fresnaye, Laurencin, Fernand Léger and Jean Metzinger. Contemporary critics either ignored the exhibit or criticized it as 'decorative' and alien to the spirit of Cubism.[35] Yet, despite Cubism's clear influence on the façade of the 'Maison Cubiste', the interiors suggest that the intention was not to apply its visual language directly to the design of furnishings of the domestic environment. Mare's stated agenda was to 'make above all something very French, to remain within tradition', while at the same time returning to 'lines that are simple, pure, logical and even slightly cold' and to 'colours that are very fresh, very pure, very daring'.[36] The vision (or culture) of this new 'national' style was here co-opted to support the renovation of national traditions – a topical issue in the face of German competition and the international exhibition of modern decorative arts planned for Paris in 1915 (see Chapter 8).[37] In this context, the cubistic façade must be seen as a modern reinterpretation of the classic Parisian eighteenth-century *hôtel*; and the interiors as a demonstration of how the culture of Cubism could contribute to the modernization of the French bourgeois interior, with the successful integration of avant-garde works of art like Léger's *Passage à niveau*.

If the 'Maison Cubiste' did not represent a thoroughgoing application of Cubist forms and motifs to architecture and the decorative arts, this possibility was soon explored elsewhere. In Czechoslovakia, paradoxically again in the context of modernizing high national traditions, such as Baroque and Rococo, Cubist forms were applied, by Pavel Janák and others, to both the design of real buildings and the components of the interior (see Chapter 16).[38] Here and elsewhere, too, forms derived from Cubism were also employed in initiatives to revitalize regional vernacular traditions. In Poland, for example, the angular forms of Cubism were combined with forms and motifs derived from folk art, in architecture and designs for interiors (see plates 16.7 and 16.9).

There were other lessons to be learned from avant-garde art, too. Writing about the impact in France of Diaghilev's Ballets Russes, which first took Western Europe by storm in 1909, Lise-Léon Blum noted the contemporary fascination with the 'otherness' of avant-garde artistic ideas:

> Nothing is more completely foreign to our tradition than these violent clashes, these frenetic and intense dances, this instinctive candour, this limitless fantasy. The discordance is so brutal that one is astonished by the tenacious acclaim accorded these people here … The simple truth is that the Russians charm us because they trouble us…[39]

It was not just the rich, glowing colours of the sets and costumes designed by Léon Bakst, or the bright colours and 'naïve' patterns of designs based on folk art by the Rayonnist artists Mikhail Larionov and Natalia Goncharova, that appealed here, it was also their 'exoticism' (plates 9.15 and 9.16). Bakst's loose, free-flowing 'oriental' costumes were innovatory in the way they underlined the movement of the dancers' bodies, an effect that chimed with contemporary aspirations to less formal and more comfortable forms of dress, as well as greater opportunities to express sensuality. Their impact was rapidly visible in designs for dress and interiors by Paul Poiret and his Atelier Martine, which brought the sensuality of the harem into the everyday.[40]

Contemporary observers saw 'Cubism'[41] as directly responsible for the decline of applied three-dimensional decoration and its substitution by 'flat surfaces … [and] the quality of beauty in unadorned material'. The tendency to treat even tradition-derived naturalistic decorative motifs in a summary, angular manner which denied depth to the image was similarly ascribed to 'Cubism'.[42] Retrospectively, it is clear other contemporary cultural and material factors also played a part in bringing about such simplifications.[43] Furthermore, the impact of avant-garde art on Art Deco was not limited to simplification of form. It is also to be found in Deco designers' fascination with exotic and abstract patterns and effects of light and transparency, and in their willingness to experiment with collage and assemblage, introduce new typographic forms, use materials (old and new) in innovative ways and sometimes surprising combinations,[44] and employ both bold, bright colours and the muted browns and greys characteristic of Cubism. However, its most significant legacy is to be seen not in methods or formal quotations but in less tangible ways. The visual revolution set in process by Cubism and early abstract art brought about a 'Pictorial space ... [that had] lost its "inside" and become all "outside"', in other words that stressed the primacy of surface.[45] Ultimately, the fascination with surface effects (often sensual and brilliant) that links early and later manifestations of Art Deco – whatever the source of their formal inspiration and whether used in photography, film or the painstaking lacquer work of Jean Dunand, or in designs for mass production using new, synthetic materials (see plates 6.15 and 33.8) – derives from this source.

Deco designers' and avant-garde (or Modernist) artists' imaginations were nourished by many of the same sources. However, the former not only borrowed imagery that connoted modernity from the latter – whether from the literal mechanical references of Léger or the Constructivists, or from the more or less specific references to machines and speed of Futurism – they put in what the latter left out. Modernists like the painter Piet Mondrian and the architect Le Corbusier (who was also a painter) wrote with passion and understanding of

9.15 Léon Bakst (Russian), stage design for the Ballets Russes *Schéhérazade*. Gouache and watercolour with gold highlights on paper. 1911. Musée des Arts Décoratifs, Paris. Photo: Laurent Sully Jaulmes.

the excitement of modern urban life, the revolution in social customs and the miracles of modern transportation. But their paintings – autonomous and free of all contingencies – for the most part excluded any direct reference to these things. By contrast, Art Deco designers and architects filled their work with references to modernity – whether explicit images of skyscrapers, aeroplanes or trains, or more abstracted references to speed, mechanisation and flux (see plates 20.7 and 31.3).

They also translated into a decorative mode some of the more abstract ideas associated with avant-garde art. Contemporaries often interpreted Cubism in terms of a post-Euclidean geometry of space-time and acknowledged that the Futurist concept of modernity as a state of flux and dynamic energy derived from the writings of the French philosopher Henri Bergson. By the late 1920s it was a commonplace – even in more popular writing on the decorative arts – to see in any fragmentation of form, or fins or 'speed lines', the embodiment of the fourth dimension or 'dynamic' qualities. So, the stage was set for streamlining to develop as a quintessentially decorative, yet also abstract and functional, expression of modernity.

Art Deco was also permeated with theories of empathy and expressiveness derived from aesthetic theories that provided support for decorative abstraction. The key ideas of Wilhelm Worringer's *Abstraction and Empathy*,[46] first published in German in 1907, found their way into more general currency in Europe and America in the 1920s. Worringer took over the concept of 'empathy' (aesthetic pleasure as a pleasure in oneself, objectivized) from the philosopher and psychologist Theodor Lipps. He then juxtaposed it with a different form of aesthetic pleasure, that of abstract form and pattern – which Worringer saw as characteristic of primitive peoples faced with a terrifying world of contingencies. He also

quoted the philosopher Friedrich Schopenhauer to assert that modern life – with its bewildering changes and lack of firm religious convictions – had parallels with primitive cultures, and thus that abstract forms might palliate modern men and women's sense of alienation. From this he concluded that modern art would draw on the abstract decorative sensibilities of African and oriental cultures and that a synthesis of abstraction and empathy would evolve.

A later generation drew on such ideas to legitimize the work of the decorative artist and designer. As a result, in the writings of critics and historians of the 1920s and 1930s, such as Sheldon and Martha Cheney, the differences between a Brancusi sculpture and an industrial design would be collapsed; and the form of the former invoked to liberate the work of the designer of the latter from its otherwise entirely commercial constraints.[47] In this context, the independent artistic credentials of many designers would also be emphasized: 'Deskey and Dreyfuss, Geddes and Sakier, Lescaze and Kiesler, all speak the language of the Modern art studio, and all, to some degree, have practised in painting and sculpture.'[48]

Similarly, theories of abstract art were invoked to provide a justification for considering all artefacts, from fine art to mass-produced objects, in terms of their abstract form alone, in exhibitions such as *Form ohne Ornament*, shown in Stuttgart in 1924, and *Machine Art*, shown at the New York Museum of Modern Art (MOMA) in 1934 and their related publications.[49] MOMA's curators and others, like the British critic Herbert Read, insistently underlined the correspondences: 'the work of art is shown to be essentially formal; it is the shaping of material into forms which have a sensuous or intellectual appeal to the average human being'.[50] Paradoxically, therefore, it was at the most abstruse end of avant-garde art – abstraction – that the links between pure

and applied art, avant-garde art and Art Deco, were forged with most confidence.

Nevertheless, as a style that acknowledged the decorative and was increasingly dedicated to promotion and a mass audience, Art Deco was fated to incur the displeasure of most Modernists. Much Art Deco design ran counter to the influential views of the Austrian architect and theorist, Adolf Loos, which became a staple of Modernist theory and practice. In 1908 Loos had condemned the application of ornament to underlying forms, asserting that 'ornament is crime' and that the advance of civilization is marked by the progressive elimination of ornament.[51] Until the later 1920s Art Deco design was often both ornamental and decorative – qualities that distinguished it clearly from Modernism. Increasingly, however, through its appropriation of avant-garde imagery and discourse, Art Deco found ways both to accommodate and renew ornament and to maintain a sense of the decorative in forms that were, to all intents and purposes, unornamented (see plate 34.4). In doing so, it not only located itself at the centre of a wider spectrum of contemporary cultural expressions of 'modernity' but also increasingly impinged on Modernism's terrain. Not for nothing is that strand of American design that took its impetus from European Art Deco after 1925 known more familiarly to Americans as 'American Modern'.[52] Furthermore, in this simplified guise, that 'modernity … coloured by the pursuit of elegance and fashion'[53] would help pave the way for the worldwide acceptance of Modernism in the years following the Second World War. Finally, we might observe that the post-Cubist interaction between avant-garde fine art and the decorative arts was not all one way – 'the contemporary discourse of decoration' itself gained 'increasing purchase on the terms of new art' in the inter-war years.[54]

9.16 Pablo Picasso (Spanish), costume for the Chinese conjurer in the Massine Ballet *Parade*. Satin and silver cloth. Around 1917. Theatre Museum, London.
© Succession Picasso/DACS 2002.

MINISTÈRE DU COMMERCE ET DE L'INDUSTRIE

PARIS - 1925

EXPOSITION INTERNATIONALE DES ARTS DÉCORATIFS ET INDUSTRIELS MODERNES AVRIL - OCTOBRE

IMPRIMERIE DE VAUGIRARD _ PARIS

10 From Pattern to Abstraction

Jonathan M. Woodham

And so the basket and garland of flowers and fruits will become the mark of the new style, as in the eighteenth century, for instance, were the torch, the bow, the quiver and the arrows.[1]

André Vera's affirmation of 'le nouveau style' in an article of 1912 encapsulated many of the initial ornamental and decorative features of Art Deco. Vera saw this new style as evolving from the celebrated French design traditions of the past, reinvigorated by the use of stronger colours and stylized naturalistic decorative motifs. Much Deco design of the 1910s and 1920s was characterized by the use of figurative motifs such as flowers, plants and animals. By the later 1920s, however, there was increasing use, both in Europe and America, of abstract and geometric motifs, drawn from 'primitive', Cubist, Constructivist and other avant-garde sources (see Chapters 7 and 9). Although Modernism itself came to reject ornament, Art Deco drew freely on the visual repertoire of early Modernism to create a 'decorative machine aesthetic' more compatible with new materials and mass production technologies than a figurative aesthetic dependent on handcraft and the traditions of luxury goods.[2]

Robert Bonfils' poster for the Paris 1925 Exhibition provides a useful starting point to consider some of the key characteristics of Art Deco iconography and ornament (plate 10.1). Like many Deco designs it is strongly two-dimensional. The stylized basket of flat, abstracted flowers recalls not only motifs advocated by André Vera in 1912 but also Art Deco's roots in the Wiener Werkstätte (see Chapter 15).[3] Similarly stylized floral motifs could be seen in the work of many of Bonfils' French contemporaries, ranging from decorative inlays for cabinets by Jacques-Emile Ruhlmann and carpet designs by Paul Follot to decorative metalwork on the façades of 1920s Parisian shops (see plates 1.4 and 8.3).[4] The graceful central motif in Bonfils' poster, a female figure running alongside a leaping antelope, was a common contemporary symbol of speed in many designs for textiles, metalwork and ceramics in

Europe and the United States (see plate 21.6). However, there were also often abstract and technologically inspired representations of this theme. In Noel Fontaner's poster for the 1930 *International Automobil Ausstellung*, an abstracted profile head blends with a side view of the front of a speeding car, the wheel becoming 'the eye', the horizontal speed lines of the bonnet 'the hair'. In an American example, the Greyhound bus company's flying greyhound symbol was set against the long, horizontal 'speed whiskers' of the streamlined 'silverside' coaches designed by Raymond Loewy in 1940, combining traditional and contemporary metaphors of speed.

Several other distinctive features are also characteristic of Art Deco. The two small rectangles of three and four parallel lines used as decorative motifs by Bonfils recall similar devices employed by early Wiener Werkstätte designers, such as Otto

10.1 Robert Bonfils, poster for the Paris 1925 Exhibition. Colour woodblock. French, 1925. V&A: E.1200-1925.

10.2 Charles Rennie Mackintosh, smoker's cabinet. Ebonized wood with cedar wood veneer, inlaid with Erinoid. British, 1916. From Derngate, Northampton. V&A: Circ.856-1956.

10.3 Norman Bel Geddes,
'Patriot', radio. Catalin. American,
1940. Made by Emerson Radio
and Phonograph Corporation.
V&A: W.31-1992.

10.4 An executive of Sears, Roebuck
and Co. and Raymond Loewy standing
next to the Coldspot refrigerator.
1934. Laurence Loewy, Loewy Design.

Wagner.[5] Similar linear motifs were also used by
designers such as Charles Rennie Mackintosh, as in
his ebony and Erinoid clock (around 1917) for W. W.
Bassett-Lowke's house in Derngate, Northampton.
Here they ran in lines parallel to the square face,
linked to small inset rectangular shapes representing
the hours, each with a decorative pattern of dots,
one for each hour. A smoker's cabinet for Derngate
uses another common geometric motif to appear in
Art Deco, the chevron, here inlaid with yellow Erinoid
plastic (plate 10.2). Linear motifs were also widely
used in graphic design, anticipating features in
American streamlined designs, and were applied as
decorative details to static buildings or objects.

Representative of this widespread trend were the
lines running round Walter Dorwin Teague's Type C
Texaco petrol stations at canopy level (c.1934) and
those across the face of Norman Bel Geddes's
'Patriot' radio (1940) or down the centre of Raymond
Loewy designs for Coldspot refrigerators for Sears,
Roebuck (launched in 1935) (plates 10.3 and 10.4).
In Britain, a more straightforwardly decorative
application of such linear motifs was widely found,
as in the foyer of George Coles's Odeon Cinema in
Muswell Hill, London, of 1936.

A common feature in the Paris 1925 Exhibition
was the fountain motif. Its use ranged from the tops
of the pillars at the Porte d'Honneur to the two-
dimensional 'Jets d'eau' satin by Edouard Bénédictus
shown in the Ambassade Française (plate 10.5).
The motif was found across all decorative media,
from ceramics to textiles, jewellery to metalwork, as
well as in cinema design,[6] and was transmitted to
an international audience via Hollywood films. The
flowing curvilinear cascade motifs in the background

10.5 Edouard Bénédictus, 'Les jets d'eau', furnishing fabric. Jacquard woven cotton and viscose rayon. French, 1925. Musée de la Mode et du Textile, Paris. Photo: Laurent Sully Jaulmes.

10.6 *Our Blushing Brides*, designed by Cedric Gibbons and Merrill Pye. BFI Stills, Posters and Designs. © (1930) Turner Entertainment Co. An AOL Time Warner Co. All Rights Reserved.

grille in the fountain scene in Metro Goldwyn Mayer's *Our Blushing Brides* (1930) owe much to the iconography of Parisian precedents (plate 10.6). Similar devices were also frequently employed in architectural decoration.[7] The metal entrance screen of the Cheney Brothers store on Madison Avenue in New York City, by Ferrobrandt, Edgar Brandt's American distributor, featured fountain motifs. And even with the emergence of American consumer products, such as the 1933 Air-King radio by Harold Van Doren and John Gordon Rideout, memories of French Art Deco cascades can be seen in the parallel ribs and grooves running across the top and down the centre of the synthetic resin body (see plate 33.7).

Similarly, a geometrically abstracted sunburst motif was seen in many contexts. At the Paris 1925 Exhibition these included André Groult's cabinet (see plate 12.7), shown in the 'Ambassade Française', and Jacques Gruber's bronze and coloured glass panel over the entrance to Galeries Lafayette's La Maîtrise pavilion (see plate 14.6). There were several reasons for the popularity of this motif. The importance of sunlight and fresh air to health was widely promoted in this period, as many people moved from polluted city centres to healthier suburbs. Sunray lamps proliferated and the notion of sunbathing became increasingly popular. The sunburst, representing the moment of dawn, was also a metaphor for the future. Furthermore, because of its ready adaptability to mass production, it featured widely across all categories of everyday design, from cigarette boxes to textile designs and radio loudspeaker grilles. Like the fountain motif, it was taken up internationally. Sunray motifs were

115

10.7 Raoul Dufy, furnishing fabric. Printed linen. French, c.1920. Made by Bianchini-Férier. V&A: Misc.2:30-1934. © ADAGP, Paris and DACS, London 2002.

widely adopted in Britain in the 1930s, partly due to their fashionable associations with health but also in the context of the rapid growth of suburban housing. Simplified geometric rays emanating from a semi-circular sun were especially popular in designs for garden gates and fences, fireplaces and radio cabinets. The sunburst was also well suited to stained-glass windows for porches and doors in suburban houses. Domestic wares, not least ceramics, also provided opportunities for its proliferation. Eric Slater's 'Vogue' and 'Mode' shapes for his Shelley Potteries' tea services were often marketed with the 'Sunray' pattern in black, gold and orange and other striking colour combinations in the early 1930s (plate 10.8).[8]

The influence of the 'primitive' and the 'exotic' was an important factor in the evolution of Deco ornament (see Chapters 3, 5, 6 and 7). It stemmed from the growing interest in this area among collectors, artists, designers, museums and ethnographers in the early twentieth century, and several large exhibitions provided rich displays of visual source material. The simplified decorative forms provided both abstract and figurative motifs

that were particularly suitable for adaptation to graphics and the design of printed fabrics. Raoul Dufy worked closely with Paul Poiret's Atelier Martine and the Lyon textile firm Bianchini-Férier, for whom he produced fabric designs (plate 10.7). Many of the Atelier Martine's colourful, abstracted and rather two-dimensional floral forms drew on a local source of exotic inspiration – the zoological and botanical gardens of Paris; the designs were used for wallpapers, textiles, furniture, ceramics and interior design (plate 10.9).[9] Materials and exotic themes

10.8 Eric Slater, 'Vogue' dinner service with 'Sunray' pattern. Bone china, printed and painted in enamels. British, 1935. Made by Shelley Potteries Ltd. Geffrye Museum, London.

10.9 Atelier Martine, dress fabrics. Block-printed satin. French, 1919. For Paul Poiret. V&A: T.539, 540 and 541-1919. © ADAGP, Paris and DACS, London 2002.

associated with African colonies were found in many Deco artefacts, including lacquer screens by Jean Dunand depicting jungle scenes. A widespread fascination with exotic peoples, cultures and animals was also evident in designs for trademarks and in packaging for goods from exotic destinations – especially imported coffee, rum and liqueurs – with their decoratively abstracted, exotic imagery and flat, often stencil-like, forms (plate 10.10). Similarly, although Ivan da Silva Bruhns' geometric carpet designs were influenced by European avant-garde art, they also drew on the patterns of Berber rugs seen at exhibitions of Moroccan art in Paris (plate 10.11).

In Britain, imperial and colonial perspectives also afforded designers a rich source of inspiration.[10] Increasing focus on the Empire as a possible route for economic prosperity drew attention to the aesthetic possibilities offered to designers by the ethnic arts and crafts. Critic Amelia Defries wrote about ethnographic decoration and the industrial arts in the *Architectural Review* in 1924: 'we feel happy among the natural arts of mankind, as yet mercifully untouched by trade with the outside world. These are most valuable if we are to revive our aesthetic theory and base it on sound principles.'[11] Few designers responded directly to Defries's call, but increasing numbers of British designs drew inspiration from exotic sources. These included Oliver P. Bernard's ceramics with colourful, abstracted Middle-Eastern landscape scenes for a J. Lyons restaurant at the *British Empire Exhibition* at Wembley in 1924. And Egyptian precedents, boosted by the discovery of Tutankhamun's tomb in 1922 (and its replica displayed at Wembley), inspired a craze for neo-Egyptian ornament (see Chapter 3). Egyptiana was also widespread in the United States, though there was also a growing interest in geometrically inclined Aztec, Mayan and Native American sources (see Chapter 5).

Abstract geometric devices – such as chevrons, zigzags and broad bands of colour – were another important feature of Art Deco design. Such motifs were influenced by avant-garde fine art sources, including Cubism. They were typified by ceramics designed for Artěl by the Czech Cubist Pavel Janák; by Russian Constructivist textiles by Varvara Stepanova and packaging by Alexander Rodchenko in the 1920s; by 'simultaneous' textile designs by Sonia Delaunay; and even by the brightly coloured rectilinear blocks of colour found in Bauhaus tapestry designs (see plates 9.10 and 13.10). Such designs were readily compatible with mass production technologies and were often linked to new materials and finishes.

10.10 Edward McKnight Kauffer (American), *El Flamenco*, cotton-bale label. Colour lithograph. 1925-30. V&A: E.1094-1965.

The colourful phenolic resins of the 1920s, Monel metal trim, chromium plating and Vitrolite (available in a wide range of colours including robin blue, jade, tropic green, as well as number of marbled finishes) were particularly suited to abstract decorative effects and were widely used in everyday designs. In America, the White Tower Company hamburger chain, founded in 1926, commissioned designs for diners that used abstract geometric blocks of colour in the Deco style and later adopted the more streamlined forms and decorative motifs symbolic of the contemporary preoccupation with speed. Electricity, very much at the source of modern living and the emerging world of domestic appliances in the United States, was widely symbolized in decorative designs. These included Ruth Reeves's colourful 1930 'Electric' rug for W. & J. Sloane, where abstract motifs derived from lightning bolts were woven into the fabric, and Kodak's 'Coquette' outfit, where the camera and powder compact cases sported a fashionable silver lightning-bolt pattern and were available in at least three different colour-ways – lavender, green and blue.

Many designers explored the imagery of modern life and mechanization using an Art Deco aesthetic. Typical was A. M. Cassandre, whose striking posters for French railways captured the public's fascination with speed, new modes of travel and technological development (see plate 29.1). In the United States, designers were also inspired by such powerful symbols of modernity as skyscrapers, aeroplanes, electricity and the radio as they sought to find a truly American iconography rather than one derived from European precedent.[12] The transition from European influences towards a more thoroughbred American style can be seen in the shift away from the Cubist-influenced rendering in Ruth Reeves's 'Manhattan', a printed cotton textile for W. & J. Sloane of 1930 (see plate 31.8).[13] Reeves's design embraces a range of references to the American way of life (skyscrapers, power stations, aeroplanes, railway locomotives and telephone switchboards) but, like Clayton Knight's 'Manhattan' design for the Stehli Silks Corporation 1927 'Americana' print series, is rooted in French precedent. By contrast, drawing on the more abstract end of the Deco vocabulary, Abel Faidy produced 'skyscraper' inspired furniture designs for the Singleton apartment in Chicago in 1927, as did Kem Weber for the Barker Brothers store in Los Angeles. Paul Frankl also used stepped forms in a series of skyscraper bookcases in the late 1920s (see plate 31.7).[14] Although such stepped forms may refer to Viennese furniture from the turn of the century,[15] they are also testaments to the impact of the US zoning laws of 1916 (see Chapter 22). Skyscraper forms were also used in product design, as in the stepped form of the Air-King plastic radio cabinet (see plate 33.7).

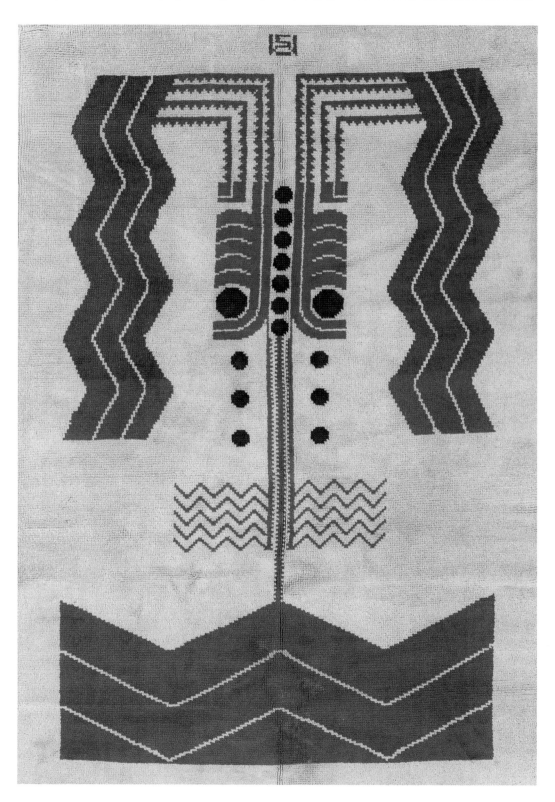

10.11 Ivan da Silva Bruhns,
carpet. Wool. French,
c.1930. Made by the
Savigny workshop. Galerie
Camoin Demachy, Paris.

10.13 Kem Weber (born in Germany), *Zephyr*, electric clock. Brass and Bakelite. American, *c*.1934. Made by Lawsin Time Inc. Gift of David Hanks. The Metropolitan Museum of Art, New York.

Other forms of mechanistic Deco imagery proliferated in the 1930s, reflecting public fascination with the symbolic expression of technological progress and the perceived need to bring about economic recovery through increased consumption. Such imagery was nowhere more apparent than at the 1939 World Fair in New York. Examples included Francis Keally and Leonard Dean's *Star Pylon*, representing the force of electricity in the Communications and Business Zone, and Ely Jacques Kahn and Muschenheim & Brounn's dramatic Transportation building, the entrance of which was based on the prows of two ocean liners.

Despite such shifts, traces of European influence remained. The jukebox, the archetypal embodiment of popular American material culture in the 1930s and 1940s, synthesized many aspects of modern American life, yet its apotheosis – the bestselling 1946 Wurlitzer Model 1015, designed by Paul Fuller – was also perhaps one of the most sensual and indulgent legacies of French Art Deco (plate 10.12).[16] Fuller's 17 jukebox designs (1935-48), with their vocabulary of brightly coloured plastic elements, geometric grilles, chromium-plated ornamentation and dramatic lighting, played a key role in Wurlitzer's success.

The public fascination with speed on land, sea and air gave rise to the phenomenon of streamlining, so

characteristic of American Art Deco. The aerodynamic, streamlined forms of the Chrysler Airflow automobile (1934), the Douglas DC3 airliner (1934) and Raymond Loewy's Pennsylvania Railroad 3768 locomotive of 1936 exerted a strong visual impact on all kinds of domestic products (see plate 34.6), in surface ornamentation emblematic of a speed-conscious, consumption-oriented age. Streamlined toasters, furniture, radios, clocks and tableware proliferated, often with the addition of horizontal decorative strips of chrome (or 'speed-whiskers') as found on contemporary trains and cars (plate 10.13). Streamlined elements may also be seen in architectural detailing, as in the entrance to the McGraw-Hill building, New York, by Raymond Hood and J. André Fouilhoux (1931) and the executive offices of the Johnson Wax Company, at Racine, Wisconsin (1936-9) by Frank Lloyd Wright (see plate 26.9). Significantly, Streamline Moderne in the United States was geared towards styling for obsolescence and increasing levels of consumption. By using decorative motifs drawn from the symbolism of rapidly changing contemporary technologies, products necessarily had a limited lifespan.

Many of the Art Deco motifs considered so far emerged at a time when the use of ornamentation and the decorative was being fiercely contested. The two-dimensionality of Art Deco had its roots in

nineteenth-century design reform debates, which focused on notions of 'authentic' and 'false' decoration. These debates gathered pace and intensity from the middle of the century onwards, when the designs of many textiles, wallpapers, carpets and other pattern-bearing surfaces were criticized for featuring realistic or three-dimensional floral motifs inappropriate for flat surfaces. Henry Cole's *Journal of Design* (1849-52), edited by educator and designer Richard Redgrave, carried many such critical discussions as well as more appropriately designed textile samples by designers such as Owen Jones, author of the highly influential *Grammar of Ornament* of 1856. There was considerable emphasis on abstractions from nature based on the principles of geometry as well as a concern for reproducibility. Something of the culture of the debate may be gleaned from Mr Crumpet's words to Mr Frippy about the 'Chamber of Horrors' in the Museum of Ornamental Art, in an essay in Charles Dickens's journal *Household Words*: 'the carpet in a room … is to be considered as a background. Imitations of fruit, shells, and hard substances in relief are improper. Treat the forms of flowers and leaves flatly, as ornaments, and not as imitations, if you please, but in the design painted upon a floor there must be nothing to contradict to the eye the necessary element of flatness'.[17]

10.12 Paul Fuller, jukebox, model 1015. American, 1946. Made by Wurlitzer. Courtesy of Deutsche Wurlitzer GmbH.

Such ideas continued to hold sway in progressive design circles in England and elsewhere in Europe in the early twentieth century. An articulate minority, particularly in Germany, argued for a style that would genuinely embrace the new century, a style that would include modern mass production technology, new materials, abstract forms and minimal applied decoration. Advocates of Modernism embraced aesthetic principles that prioritized form over decoration, using new materials in ways that were symbolically compatible with new modes of production and the modern age. As the Bauhaus-based artist Georg Muche wrote in 1926:

> The attempt to infiltrate the laws of design for industrial production with the findings of abstract art has led to the creation of a new style that rejects ornamentation as an old fashioned mode of expression of past craft cultures, but that nevertheless remains decorative … [The] fundamental laws of form … creatively investigated by means of abstract painting appear to have uncovered that these laws do not pertain just to the fine arts but are particularly significant in their general validity.[18]

Like their Modernist counterparts, Art Deco designers recognized 'authentic' rather than 'false' values in decoration and ornament. Many of the ornamental motifs associated with later Art Deco were symbolic of modern life but, with their far greater emphasis on colour, decoration and a sensual use of new materials, they were seen as decadent by advocates of Modernism and some other critics.

The immediate origins of the Modernist case for 'form without ornament' were to be found in the writings of the Austrian architect, designer and theorist Adolf Loos, who had attacked what he saw as the decadent decorative tendencies of the Wiener Werkstätte in his 1908 essay 'Ornament and Crime', which was first translated into French in 1913.[19] Loos believed that ornament was largely irrelevant in the modern world and that 'cultural revolution is equivalent to the removal of ornament from articles of everyday life'. Subsequently other Modernist voices were raised against the highly decorative nature of much contemporary design. In France, in his book L'Art décoratif d'aujourd'hui (1925), Le Corbusier paraphrased Loos's words in the maxim 'the more cultivated a people becomes, the more decoration disappears'. He also stated that 'the luxury object is well made, neat and clear, pure and healthy, and its bareness reveals the quality of its manufacture'.[20] Le Corbusier was not alone in reacting negatively to the decorative ostentation of the vast majority of the exhibits in the Paris 1925

Exhibition, and in 1929 he and other radical designers formed the Union des Artistes Modernes (UAM) to pursue their own artistic goals. In Germany too, in the 1920s, there was considerable discussion about the role of ornament and decoration. Modernist notions of a new design and new architecture were taken up by several German metropolitan authorities,[21] as well as being embodied in designs for buildings, interiors, furniture, equipment and graphics at the Bauhaus. The Deutscher Werkbund, a keen advocate of modernizing ideals before the First World War, also re-emerged as an important agency for aesthetic debate. In 1924 it mounted the exhibition Form ohne Ornament (Form without Ornament) in Stuttgart. Both handcrafted and industrially manufactured designs were displayed, addressing the theme from a range of perspectives. At this time of economic difficulty, ornament was seen as indulgent and unnecessary. Instead, standardized types and unornamented form, symbolizing both the machine age and continuity with the simplicity of form of many products of the pre-industrial era, were key considerations. Parallel notions underlay certain approaches in the United States, where there was concerted opposition in some quarters to the perceived indulgence of Art Deco, with its playful use of new materials and exploitation of abstract patterns and shapes as decorative motifs. The Museum of Modern Art (MOMA) in New York, established in 1929, promoted an emphatically Modernist aesthetic in exhibitions such as Machine Art (1934), curated by Philip Johnson. In his catalogue essay 'History of Machine Art', Johnson declared, 'The Paris Exposition of Decorative Arts of 1925, with its neo-classical trappings and bizarre ornament, made a strong impression on our designers. The problem in America has not been the conflict against a strong handicraft tradition but rather against a "Modernistic" French machine-age aesthetic.'[22] The Machine Art exhibition was a powerful Modernist statement, with its clean, undecorated, geometric industrial forms that employed modern materials and production technologies. Yet it attracted a significant level of critical and public support, partly because of the large number of American industrial products displayed. However, the European Modernist emphasis of MOMA's exhibits overall led to criticisms. The designer Russel Wright was particularly concerned that MOMA paid so little attention to contemporary American design achievements, whether skyscrapers, factory machinery, cocktail gadgets or streamlined refrigerators. He believed that there was a 'distinct American character of design

in all that is American'.[23] Although American Art Deco had initially embraced European aesthetic precedents, by then it possessed its own distinctive and indigenous qualities reflecting and symbolizing contemporary notions of glamour, consumerism, technological progress and speed.

A strong moral and even nationalistic tone pervaded British debates on Deco, with a number of critics seeing its bright, ephemeral styling as not only frivolous, but foreign. As Dorothy Todd and Raymond Mortimer commented on the Paris 1925 Exhibition: 'There were rooms for dancing, but none for reading, rooms for cocktails, but none for breakfast, rooms for undressing but none for sleeping. The decoration was modern, but it reflected unamiable aspects of modern life … it was the decoration of a civilisation without dignity, a civilisation ostentatious and capricious.'[24] Objectionable to many was the associated idea of 'jazz' styling with its brightly coloured, highly decorative patterns, a legacy of French practice in the mid-1920s. Typical of this genre were designs such as 'Excelsior', a geometrically patterned cotton and rayon textile (1928) for Warner & Sons by Albert Swindells, one of a number of the company's designers to visit the 1925 Exhibition. Other examples were Carlton Ware's 'Jazz' ginger jar produced in 1928 and Clarice Cliff's 'Diamonds' tea service (1929-30), a geometrically patterned, conical design in orange, yellow, black and blue (see plate 21.3). To advocates of the Modernist cause the word 'jazz' itself became a term of moral disapprobation. In his Enquiry into Industrial Art in England of 1937, Nikolaus Pevsner drew attention to the significance of 'jazz' fashions in carpet design. He wrote that in British carpets the 'oriental tradition was not inborn, and therefore too weak to resist the attack of post war jazz. Manufacturers accepted the fashion, shops were swamped, and the public followed without hesitation.'[25]

The contemporary allure of ornamentation and decoration is revealed in the thinking of Evelyn Waugh's fictitious interior decorator Mrs Beaver in A Handful of Dust (1934). Called in to refurbish a room in the Gothic Revival Hetton Abbey, she pronounced: 'the structure does limit one … you know, I think the only thing would be to disregard it altogether and find some treatment so definite that it carried the room, if you see what I mean … [Supposing] we covered the walls with white chromium plating and had natural sheepskin carpet.'[26] Mrs Beaver was the epitome of the real-life society interior decorator Syrie Maugham, widely known for her designs for all-white rooms (plate 10.14). Maugham also favoured the Moderne look, with its colourful abstract patterns, to enhance the decorative impact of her interiors and she commissioned striking rugs from designers such as Marion Dorn. The sensuality of Maugham's work was in stark contrast to the asceticism of the British Modernists, such as Wells Coates. However, despite the eloquent advocacy of the Modernist cause by writers such as Herbert Read in *Art and Industry* (1934), there was limited sympathy for any aesthetic that was resistant to ornament. In his 1935 essay on 'The Fitness of Ornament', H. S. Goodhart-Rendel, Vice-President of the Royal Institute of British Architects and Slade Professor of Fine Art, wrote of the contemporary tendency 'to allow art to shape an utensil but not to adorn it. Nevertheless signs are not wanting of a change towards greater toleration of ornament. The theoretic beauties of starkness are being banished to a yearly remoter ring of suburbs, while in art centres there are still gaieties to come.'[27]

Goodhart-Rendel's observation of a shift towards a 'greater toleration' of ornament went largely unheeded through the first few decades following the Second World War, when Modernism played a dominant role in historical accounts of architecture and design of the inter-war period. But the rise of Post-modernism led to a reappraisal of the role of ornament, colour and sensuality in art and design. This resulted in a fresh consideration of Art Deco as an alternative, important, readily intelligible and widely influential response to the challenge of modernity and the changing social, economic and cultural needs of a rapidly expanding consumer society in the inter-war years.

10.14 Syrie Maugham, all-white drawing room, with carpet by Marion Dorn. British, 1933. NAL.

11 The Exotic

Ghislaine Wood

As for reality we like it exotic

G. Bauer, 1925[1]

'Reality' for many people by the 1930s was permeated by the exotic. From the moment they switched on their mini ziggurat radios in the morning, to the moment they left their Egyptian-style cinemas at night, Art Deco exoticism surrounded them. Every aspect of modern living was given an exotic veneer, from the façades of factories and cinemas to the packaging of perfumes and chocolates. The ubiquitous iconography of tropical birds and animals, lush vegetation, sunbursts, dancing girls, lotuses, ogees and zigzags gave an exotic flourish to all kinds of design. Tropical woods and luxurious materials such as ebony, sharkskin and lacquer created sensual and glamorous surfaces in the modern home. Hollywood provided millions all over the world with extravagant spectacles, recreating Babylon in California and re-imagining Cleopatra as Claudette Colbert, while jazz embodied the rhythms of Africa. The exotic, a determining feature of Art Deco, was a vital component of modernity.

The term 'exotic' was commonly used in the first decades of the century but its meanings were manifold. It most frequently described 'primitive' or tribal artefacts but also referred to modern culture influenced by ancient, eastern or African art; it was applied to art, design, architecture, film, literature and people. Rarely used as a derogatory term, the 'exotic' suggested an exciting, sensual and decorative vision that carried the dynamics of nineteenth-century colonialism into a global future.[2] In this essay the term will loosely refer to the influence of non-western – particularly African – art forms on modern culture.

Exotic imagery and motifs were plundered from many cultures. Fuelled by the romance of recent archeological discoveries, the public imagination was fired by the ancient cultures of Egypt, Mesopotamia and Mesoamerica, whose veiled histories were open to endless fantasy and interpretation. The East, particularly the art of Japan and China, continued to

provide a rich source for style while the 'new' ancient world of Africa, at the forefront of public consciousness in a colonial age, became the exotic signifier of the modern *par excellence*. In those countries that were unimpeded by weighty national traditions the search for a modern iconography often turned inwards, towards 'native' sources. National flora and fauna replaced classical ornamentation in countries keen to assert their cultural independence. For example, motifs such as the moose and beaver in Canada or the goanna and koala in Australia answered a need for a national iconography, their appeal heightened by the lack of stylistic convention associated with their treatment (see plate 38.2). The art of indigenous peoples, from the Marajoara of Brazil to the Pueblo of New Mexico and Arizona or the Maori of New Zealand, crucially provided distinctive design languages that served both the need to assert national traditions and the desire for the exotic. In Mexico, for instance, increasing interest in folk traditions, fuelled 'by a great wave of nationalism [that] swept the country' after the Revolution, led to a re-evaluation of popular Mexican art. A major exhibition of the popular arts in Mexico City in 1920-21, organized by the Ministry of Commerce, Industry and Labour, was, according to Frances Toor writing in 1939, 'a revelation to the Mexicans themselves'. It became 'quite the mode among well-to-do Mexican families, especially those connected with the Government, to have a Mexican Room, decorated with Indian handcrafts'.[3] The novelty of the Mexican 'theme' room, where the inclusion of handcraft objects denoted the fashionable and the modern, is representative of just one aspect of the fascination with the exotic. Toor also acknowledged the role played by folk traditions in the creation of a national modern art:

it was a group of modern artists, whose work has made Mexican art world famous, who were responsible for the impulse given by the Government to the fine and popular arts. These artists, instead of looking abroad for subject matter and inspiration, found the real sources of their art in their own country.[4]

11.1 Alfred Janniot, *Tahiti*, sculptural decoration on the Musée des Colonies. Plate from Jean Charbonneaux, *Le Bas-relief du Musée des Colonies*, Paris, 1931. NAL.

While the exotic frequently served distinctly national, regional or racial needs, its use was always governed by one concept – renewal. In the words of a contemporary critic, describing the influence of African art, it was 'not a question of competing with the models of classical antiquity, but of renewing subjects and forms'.[5] Renewal was a distinguishing characteristic of Art Deco. Unlike the apostles of Modernism, Deco designers did not aim to re-

imagine the world following utopian models. For them, the exotic offered new ways of interpreting the contemporary world and was a means of rejuvenating design through a new decorative language. It could be safely appropriated and incorporated into existing cultural structures while simultaneously suggesting internationality and modernity. It promoted fantasies of erotic liberation, a legacy of its nineteenth-century heritage, and of an Ur existence, unadulterated by

industrialization. These fantasies evolved from their colonial incarnations to present a fractured image of modern desires and fears.

Perhaps the richest field for the study of the taste for the exotic is the vogue for *l'art nègre*. A phenomenon largely of the 1920s and seen in all the arts, it presents a fascinating picture of the shifting meanings and the disparate needs that exotic design served. It came to signify modernity in fashionable

11.2 Léon Jaussely and Albert
Laprade, Musée des Colonies for the
Paris 1931 Colonial Exhibition, Paris.
Gouache and wash on paper. French,
c.1931. Fonds Documentaire IFA.

Parisian interiors; in the frenetic world of the cabaret; in the monumental projects of colonial enterprise; and in the search for an African-American identity. These diverse cultural contexts will be the focus of this essay.

The exotic was appropriated by both individuals and the state. The most striking example of the latter was to be found at the 1931 *Exposition coloniale internationale* in Paris. Following important colonial exhibitions in Marseilles in 1906 and 1922 and Wembley in 1924, the 1931 exhibition, visited by over 33 million people, was prompted by the desire to stimulate markets at home and abroad and characterized by the attempt to fuse France with her colonies in the public imagination. The project for *La plus grande France* (Greater France) was two-fold. On the one hand, it was hoped that waning interest in France's colonial project could be stemmed through the promotion of a Greater France.[6] The official guide claimed 'our Africa, tightly bound to us now for both its defence and its prosperity, will become a magnificent and direct extension of our French humanity'.[7] On the other, it was believed that the colonies could revitalize all aspects of French culture and industry. The strategy adopted to promote Greater France and thereby colonial enterprise to a wider public was to stress the interdependence of France and her colonies. This was given a visual manifestation in the fusion of exotic imagery, forms and materials with modern, French Art Deco design. The design of many of the exhibition buildings, interiors and objects exemplified this strategy, but none better than the Musée des Colonies which, Hermann Lebovics has observed, literally 'wrapped native cultures within the high culture of European France'.[8]

Tensions surrounding the competition for the design of the building demonstrated the level of official concern over the choice of an appropriate architectural idiom. It was felt that the museum should 'transpose, in some way, the taste for exoticism without localizing its evocation'[9] and so present a vision of Greater France that was both modern and international. Léon Jaussely and Albert Laprade's spare, classicizing design with its elongated colonnade, partially veiling an enormous, 1,200 square metre (13,000 square foot) exotic bas-relief façade, managed to do both (plates 11.1 and 11.2). Described as 'a synthesis of the spirit of the primitive civilizations',[10] the building was modern and exotic. The bas-relief provided the exotic imagery

and performed the symbolic function of binding the colonies to France while simultaneously privileging the Metropole. Designed and executed by Alfred Janniot, an Art Deco sculptor with an acute awareness of the role of public sculpture,[11] the façade reliefs depicted 'the colonies' contribution to France'. With France at the centre, Africa and Oceania to the west and Asia and the American colonies to east, immense riches – in the form of raw materials and goods – were depicted flowing back to Paris through the industrial ports of France. The fecundity of the colonies was symbolized not only through the fleshy treatment of figures, animals and vegetation but also through the depiction of the colonies as a primitive realm entirely dependent upon the natural world. A 'great tapestry of stone',[12] the exotic was here made into pattern and used to explicitly convey the economic *raison d'être* of the colonies.

Like the exterior, the interior was conceived to represent the Asian colonies on the east and the African on the west, but the iconography of the exterior was reversed in the Salle des Fêtes, an enormous conference hall in the centre of the building. Here the contribution made by France to the colonies was depicted in fresco, with the personifications of Peace, Justice, Liberty, Science, Art, Commerce, Industry and Work shown dispensing 'civilization' to the colonized. Interestingly the *mission civilisatrice*, the historical justification for colonialism, is confined to the interior of the building, its insidious ideology of exploitation in the name of progress disguised but not discarded. Two oval rooms on either side of the Salle des Fêtes, furnished by Jacques-Emile Ruhlmann and Eugène Printz, were again dedicated to Africa and Asia. Their design schemes fused tropical woods, African and Asian imagery and contemporary, Art Deco design.[13] The decorative iconography of the interior was further reinforced by a series of monumental exotic paintings produced by Jean Dunand. Two canvases depicting the people of Africa and Asia lined the first floor vestibule to the library, the entrance of which was flanked by a pair of huge decorative vases (plates 11.3 and 11.4). The overall effect appropriately suggested an ancient temple entranceway where visitors were encouraged to marvel. Splendidly rich, modernizing decoration combined exotic imagery and materials to present a symbiotic relationship between France and her colonies – a relationship that was deemed vital to the progress of both.

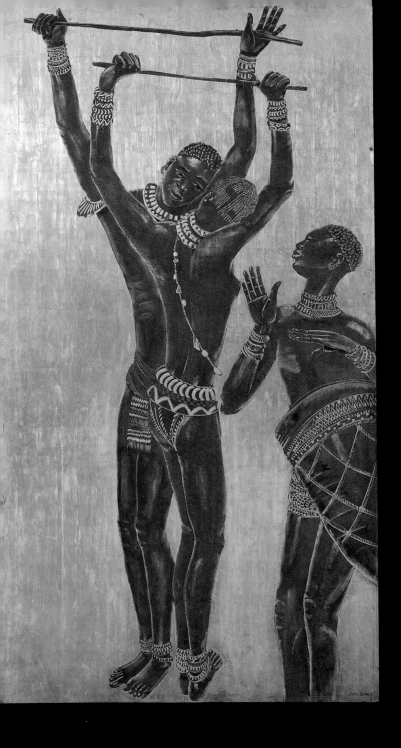

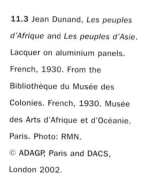

11.3 Jean Dunand, *Les peuples d'Afrique* and *Les peuples d'Asie*. Lacquer on aluminium panels. French, 1930. From the Bibliothèque du Musée des Colonies. French, 1930. Musée des Arts d'Afrique et d'Océanie, Paris. Photo: RMN. © ADAGP, Paris and DACS, London 2002.

11.4 Jean Dunand, pair of vases. Lacquered brass. French, *c.*1931. Musée d'Art Moderne de la Ville de Paris. © PMVP. Photo: Joffre. © ADAGP, Paris and DACS, London 2002.

Although the Colonial Exhibition was dominated by a 'panoply of exotic pavilions' devoted to the French colonies, other countries also participated. Buildings celebrating the colonial achievements of the Netherlands, Belgium, Brazil, Denmark, Portugal, Italy and the United States were erected, though notably absent were Germany and Britain.[14] Many participants used exotic imagery and spectacle, and none more effectively than Belgium, a country well practised in promoting its colonies.[15] The Belgian Congo pavilion, a monumental version of a western Nigerian palace, though not modernizing in its design provided a very modern experience. A display of gigantic spears flanked the entranceway to the pavilion, creating an awe-inspiring spectacle worthy of a Hollywood movie. Exotic spectacle was an important feature in other displays at the Colonial Exhibition and had been an established mode for exhibitions well before 1931. The main entrance at the *Exposition universelle* of 1900, the Porte Binet, had been an extravagance of eastern arches and minarets which, by night, were transformed into the shimmering illusion of an exotic palace. The illuminations at the Colonial Exhibition carefully created modern spectacle, while still emphasizing the exoticism and mystery of ancient cultures (plate 11.5).

If the national pavilions and the Musée des Colonies displays promoted an edifying and educative image of colonialism, the *industries de luxe* housed in the Palais de la Section Metropolitaine were devoted to the hardcore promotion of commerce. The Art Deco building, with its reinforced concrete tower 85 metres high (270 feet), represented the height of sophisticated metropolitan contemporary design, as did many of the new products on display. Numerous

companies were encouraged to participate and they developed new designs especially for the exhibition, applying exotic decoration to objects for markets at home and abroad. Indeed, much of the new design displayed at the exhibition represents the acutely commercial aspect of the vogue for *l'art nègre*. The firm of Louis Vuitton, whose pavilion was a synthesis of modernistic style and exotic decoration, created an overall design and marketing strategy to promote new products that was unique in its coherent use of the exotic. Matching crocodile travel cases and crystal toilet sets engraved with geometric patterns were displayed and photographed alongside African artefacts; invitations and posters depicted African sculptures rather than modern products (plate 11.6). It was through the association of the Vuitton brand with fashionable African art that the products attained glamour and desirability. The wealthy consumer could choose chic, exotic travel wares for a luxury cruise safe in the knowledge that they were the height of fashion (see plate 14.2).

The association of exotic high style with the *mission civilisatrice* had been indelibly forged with the highly publicized Croisière Noire trip across Africa in 1924-5. Organized by André Citroën and led by Georges-Marie Haardt and Louis Audouin-Dubreuil, the expedition was part scientific mission and part publicity stunt. Along with the Croisière Jaune of 1931-2 across Asia, it was important for the stimulation of popular interest in the exotic. The Croisière Noire was documented in film and photography, as well as in painting by the official expedition artist Alexandre Iacovleff. A major exhibition was then held in the Pavillon de Marsan in Paris in 1926 under the aegis of the Musée National d'Histoire Naturelle and the Société de Geographie de France.[16] Tremendously popular, its appeal was identified by Pierre Trévières: 'we know the undeniable influence that primitive peoples' original manifestations have on the current evolution of modern art. In our country, the precepts of *art nègre* creations have found defenders, adepts, apostles, fanatics. The Croisière Noire exhibition is from that point of view of major interest.'[17] An official film of the expedition was also widely distributed, the effect of which was to pit, in the public imagination, the full might of modern technology against a 'savage' world of impenetrable environments, wild animals and unknown peoples. Documented and framed for mass consumption by these flickering images, the modernity of the 'civilized' world was thrown into stark contrast against the 'primitivism' of the other. The inexorable progress of the modern world, metaphorically represented by the movement of

11.7 *La Croisière noire au Louvre*, exhibition poster. Colour lithograph. French, 1926. Musée des Arts d'Afrique et d'Océanie. © Photo: RMN – J. G. Berizzi.

this high-tech team across the continents, was contrasted with the unchanging, ahistorical tribal world. The result was to romanticize, for an urban public, all things African and to inextricably link the tribal with the modern. The connection was reinforced by the official poster and logo of the expedition, 'Femme mangbetou' (plate 11.7). Her hieratic pose, elongated head and elaborately constructed hair distilled much of what appealed most to public and artists alike. Set against a bold, abstract pattern, she symbolized the inherent decorative quality and spontaneous creativity of Africa. This colonial vision presented an icon for a new age. In the following years, the Mangbetou woman was restyled to sell a range of events, products and ideas, including the Pavillon des Tabacs at the 1931 Colonial Exhibition and the Black American magazine *Opportunity*.

11.8 Jacques-Emile Ruhlmann, the Parisian apartment of Georges-Marie Haardt. French *Vogue*, December 1927. NAL. © ADAGP, Paris and DACS, London 2002.

In December 1927 *Vogue* published an article entitled 'Le Cabinet de travail d'un grand voyageur'. It described the remodelling of Georges-Marie Haardt's Parisian apartment to display artefacts, trophies and paintings brought back from his historic trip. Designed by Ruhlmann in a spare, massive and masculine aesthetic, it further reinforced the association between French colonialism and urban sophistication (plate 11.8):

> Here everything is *art nègre* including seats and tables. Only the sofa is an exception; but again it is covered with neglectfully thrown panther skins. Kiti and logo stools, mangbetou tables, gris gris crouching on prismatic stands, fly-swatters, basketry with geometric decoration, everything contributes to an ensemble that is surprising because of its modern aspect, though the elements are all antique or exotic. Nothing could show better the influence of *art nègre* on contemporary taste.[18]

Written by the critic Jean Gallotti, the article reveals what was, by 1927, common thinking. African objects in themselves had come to represent the modern and were vital to the modern interior. This did not go unremarked:

> the feeling one experiences is in a way dual. The ceiling lamps in translucent glass, the central heating, the books displayed in a suspended bookcase, the carpet that covers the floor, all bear the marks of the most refined civilization; but on the other hand, the heavy ebony columns, the chairs that resemble elephants and the collections create a barbarian atmosphere.[19]

The use of African and other non-western art works to represent the modern is an integral aspect of the conception of the exotic Art Deco interior.

If Haardt's apartment represented a rather masculine fusion of the colonial and the exotic, other fashionable interiors evoked a feminized exotic. Many of the clients were fashion designers. The couturières Jeanne Lanvin and Suzanne Talbot (Mme Mathieu Lévy) both redesigned their homes along exotic lines

11.9 Armand Rateau, chaise-longue. Patinated bronze. French, 1920-22. For Jeanne Lanvin. Musée des Arts Décoratifs, Paris. Photo: Laurent Sully Jaulmes. © ADAGP, Paris and DACS, London 2002.

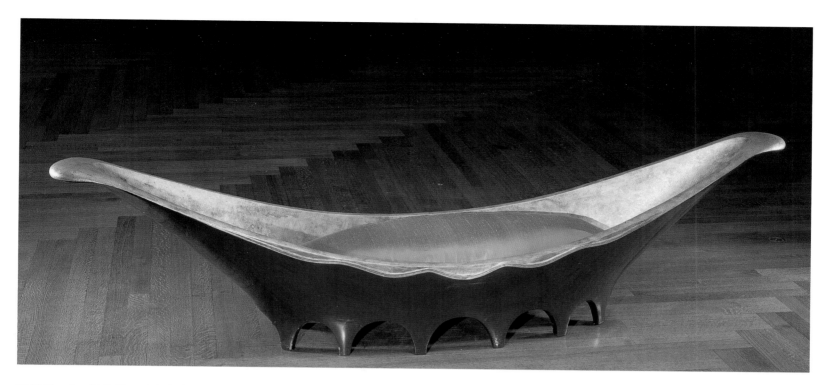

11.10 Eileen Gray (Irish), 'Pirogue', day bed. Lacquered wood with silver leaf. Around 1919-20. Gift of Sydney and Francis Lewis. Virginia Museum of Fine Arts, Richmond. Photo: Katherine Wetzel.

11.11 Eileen Gray (Irish), salon of the apartment of Suzanne Talbot, Rue de Lota, Paris. 1920. Eileen Gray Archives.

in the early 1920s. The design of Lanvin's *hôtel particulier* on the Rue Barbet-de-Jouy was conceived by Armand Rateau and represented a classicized exoticism derived from the imagery of the Ballets Russes. Like Edgar Brandt, Rateau often combined an unusual and highly skilled use of metal with exotic iconography. He was particularly fascinated by ancient bronze furniture and blended antique and oriental motifs to create deeply eclectic designs for metal furniture and fittings. The patinated bronze chaise-longue that he designed for Lanvin's terrace adopts an antique form but is supported by four stylized deer (plate 11.9). Suzanne Talbot's apartment on the Rue de Lota was redesigned by Eileen Gray, one of the most inventive Deco designers, whose work drew on many sources including classical, African and oriental (see Chapter 6). Her design for the Talbot apartment was innovative in its use of lacquer wall panels to create a dark, rich and sensual setting for the mix of lacquered furniture, African and ancient art with which the apartment was furnished. Like Ruhlmann, Gray designed the apartment to display a collection but unlike Ruhlmann she did not depend on a classical conception of space. Ruhlmann preserved the original proportions of the rooms in the Haardt apartment, using massive rosewood panelled columns to divide space, whereas Gray disguised

the original décor of the Talbot apartment with free-standing lacquer panels, textile wall coverings and false ceilings. Her modernizing intentions were further underlined by her use of abstract decoration and the sensual, allusive nature of lacquer. She exploited its dark, reflective surfaces, flecked with tarnished silver seams, to create a feminized, Symbolist environment. The Duchesse de Clermont-Tonnere directly equated the rich, atmospheric effects achieved through the use of lacquer within the interior with Symbolist painting.[20] Gray's 'Pirogue'

day bed, the form of which is derived from Polynesian and Micronesian dugout canoes but simultaneously suggests historical French models, is emblematic of her highly eclectic and often Symbolist conception of form and decoration at this time (plates 11.10 and 11.11).[21]

The design of Jacques Doucet's studio at Neuilly was perhaps the most important exotic Art Deco interior. A couturier and collector of modern and non-European art, Doucet's catholic taste was developed and guided by André Breton, a leading figure in Surrealism. His collection included works by Henri Rousseau, Pablo Picasso, Francis Picabia, Amadée Modigliani, Constantin Brancusi, Jacques Lipchitz, Josef Csaky, Pierre Legrain, Eileen Gray, Rose Adler, Marcel Coard, Etienne Cournault, Gustave Miklos and Jean Lambert-Rucki. The design of the studio, into which Doucet moved in 1928, just a year before his death, was the culmination of exoticizing tendencies that had increasingly dominated his commissions in the preceding years. The heart of the apartment was the 'Cabinet de l'Orient', which combined the display of avant-garde art and exotic Art Deco design with that of Chinese, Japanese, Native American and African art (see plate 6.10). Here again ancient or non-western objects came to represent the modern. Their value as a source for the renewal of style was highlighted and emphasized by their setting among exotic Art Deco furnishings and modern works that mimicked their forms. In fact, many of Doucet's Art Deco pieces imitated or were derived from an ancient or African original, and they often combined a distinctly new interest in the treatment of material, surface and finish with an ancient form or subject. It is unsurprising that Picasso's painting *Les Demoiselles d'Avignon*, a revolutionary new treatment of an old subject, had a prime position within the apartment. The juxtaposition of exotic materials, Africanized modern art and design, avant-garde art and non-European 'originals' within the Neuilly studio represents the archetypal transformation of the 'primitive' – both raw materials and culture – into the self-conscious modern urban environment. Eileen Gray's later description of Doucet's apartment as 'only a cluttered, slightly modernized version of the old, traditional eighteenth-century interior'[22] interestingly suggests the aristocratic tradition of building and framing a collection that Doucet emulated, but it denies the undoubtedly progressive stance this interior represented.

Several of Doucet's favourite designers, including Legrain, Csaky, Miklos and Lambert-Rucki, used African models to express modernity, but clearly depended upon their works being seen in the context of European avant-garde practice (see plate 9.8 and Chapter 9). These artists, like many, developed modes of representation derived from Cubism that made the exotic decorative. Their work, mediated by the fashion for *l'art nègre* and its corollary, the commercialization of all things from the colonies, made little or no distinction between modern, ancient or American 'African'. By contrast the San Francisco artist Sargent Johnson experimented with the forms of African art with the aim of creating a culturally conscious modern decorative style. Johnson, a black American, sought to develop 'a strictly Negro Art'. Its model, he explained, was 'not the culturally mixed Negro of the cities but the more primitive slave type as it existed … during the period of slave importation'.[23] Like many African-American artists he explored African art for forms, subjects and techniques that provided historical and racial resonance and meaning (plate 11.12). Grounded in the reality of the modern black American diaspora, rather than in the fantasy of colonial possession, the use of the exotic in America developed in dialectic tension to that of Europe.

Alain Locke, Professor of Philosophy at Harvard from 1924 and a leading figure in the New Negro movement and the Harlem Renaissance, urged African-Americans to look to their own heritage for the roots of a modern cultural expression,

> We must and ought to have a local school of Negro art, a local and racially representative tradition …
> It is not meant to dictate a style to the young Negro artist, but to point the lesson that contemporary European art has already learned – that any vital artistic expression of the Negro theme and subject in art must break through the stereotypes to a new style, a distinctive fresh technique, and some sort of characteristic idiom.[24]

11.12 Sargent Johnson, mask. Copper with ceramic inlay. American, c.1934. Collection John P. Axelrod, Boston, MA.

11.13 Aaron Douglas,
Aspects of Negro Life: Song of the Towers. Oil on canvas.
American, 1934.
Courtesy of Schomburg Center
for Research in Black Culture,
Art & Artifacts Division, the
New York Public Library, Astor,
Lenox & Tilden Foundation.

Many black American artists responded to this rallying-call. Aaron Douglas, Richmond Barthe and Sargent Johnson were among the first to explore African art as a source for a modern style. Aaron Douglas, the leading artist of the Harlem Renaissance, developed the most clearly Art Deco response. Arriving in New York in 1925, he studied mural painting with the German émigré artist and designer Winold Reiss and developed a decorative style that owed much to Art Deco, incorporating geometric pattern, Egyptian and African motifs, rays of light, exotic foliage and the ornamental treatment of figures and landscape. The adaptation of the 'Femme mangbetou' for the cover of the May 1927 issue of *Opportunity* demonstrates his awareness of contemporary European 'primitivist' tendencies. The image was no less exotic or extraordinary for black American audiences, but whereas in France the image represented 'colonial chic', here it signified the distinctly new sense of cultural consciousness associated with the philosophy of the New Negro movement.

Douglas's *Aspects of Negro Life* murals designed for the Countée Cullen branch of the New York Public Library in 1934 further promoted the notion of an ancient African-American lineage.[25] The subject of the series is the celebration of African-American culture, specifically music and dance, in the face of the hardships of the black diaspora. Designed in an exotic and decorative style, the last panel, *Song of the Towers*, climaxes with the creation of jazz (plate 11.13). Pictured among the skyscrapers, a man holds out a saxophone from which radiate rings of light and sound. An apocalyptic vision set in the city that gave birth to the Harlem Renaissance, the *Song of the Towers* embedded modern Black American culture in the urban metropolis. Douglas later explained the series in the following terms: 'at that time pleas could be heard on all sides for a visual pattern comparable to, or rather suggestive of, the uniqueness found in the gestures and bodily movements of the Negro dance, and the sounds and vocal patterns as found in Negro songs'.[26]

Jazz, in both Europe and America, was an integral component of the vogue for *l'art nègre*. Born of the fusion of European musical forms, complex West African rhythms and syncopation, American blues and ragtime, jazz came to simultaneously symbolize the exotic and modern urban living. The parallels between the complex patterns of jazz and the energetic geometric forms of Art Deco were clear, and as a result the style was often known as 'Jazz Moderne'. As a later musicologist wrote, 'it seems that the striking qualities of music of the blacks are found again in the ornamental arts, in the fine arts as well as in the arts that one terms applied; the same sense of symmetries, of oppositions, of repetitions and of accidents of rhythm'.[27] African music, like African sculpture, was perceived as contributing to a revival of western culture and the creation of modern identities, both African-American and white. The enormous impact of jazz on the development of popular culture did not go uncontested, however. In some quarters it was seen as a threat, as it crossed the boundaries of white and black culture and brought audiences together across the racial divide. Anne Shaw Faulkner writing in the *Ladies Home Journal* warned, 'Jazz originally was the accompaniment of the voodoo dancer, stimulating the half-crazed barbarian to the vilest deeds. The weird chant ... has also been employed by other barbaric people to stimulate brutality and sensuality. That it has a demoralizing effect upon the human brain has been demonstrated by many scientists.'[28] Most people ignored such views and flocked to the jazz clubs that opened in many cities.

11.15 Josephine Baker in her 'banana' skirt.
Gelatin silver print. Around 1926.
© Photo: Walery/Hulton Archive/Getty Images.

Many Harlem night-spots catered for mixed audiences, kept apart by segregation during the day. The Savoy Ballroom entertained a mixed crowd while the white-owned Cotton Club became the most fashionable night-club of the 1920s and the scene of a 'Nordic invasion'. The success of the Cotton Club depended, in large part, on the creation of an exotic fantasy realm. Decorated with palm trees, bongo drums and African inspired geometric pattern, every element of the entertainment was geared towards white audiences' expectations of the primitive. From the exotic floor shows to Duke Ellington's 'jungle style' compositions, the fantasy was complete. It was, though, a distinctly modern fantasy that desired a fusion of black and white.

The association of music, dance and *l'art nègre* with modernity was clearly visible in the work of black American performers outside the States. Many such artists, including Ada 'Bricktop' Smith, Sidney Bechet and Langston Hughes, hoping to escape segregation, moved to Paris in the 1920s. The singer and dancer Josephine Baker, more than any other, came to embody, for white audiences, both the 'exotic primitive' and the height of modernity. She first

11.14 Paul Colin, *Josephine Baker*, plate from Paul Colin, *Le Tumulte noir*, Paris, 1927. Colour pochoir. NAL.
© ADAGP, Paris and DACS, London 2002.

appeared in *La Revue nègre* in Paris in October 1925, where her 'Danse sauvage' enthralled and electrified audiences through its fusion of the primitive and the erotic. A jungle provided the setting for a scantily clad Baker to perform a frenzied, erotically charged sequence with her male co-star, Joe Alex. Janet Flanner, the American journalist, described her effect:

> She was an unforgettable ebony statue ... Whatever happened next was unimportant. The two specific elements had been established and were unforgettable – her magnificent dark body, a new model that to the French proved for the first time that black was beautiful, and the acute response of the white masculine public in the capital of hedonism of all Europe – Paris.[29]

André Levinson went further: 'The plastic sense of a race of sculptors came to life and the frenzy of African Eros swept over the audience. It was no longer a grotesque dancing girl that stood before them, but the black Venus that haunted Baudelaire.'[30] Baker's invented 'primitivism' had the effect of 'renewing' the erotic and re-framing it in modern performance. She became an icon overnight and one of the most frequently depicted stars of the time. Jean Dunand rendered her in lacquer, Alexander Calder captured her elasticity and electric energy in wire, Enrico Prampolini drew her as a dancing machine. She was photographed as wild animal and sophisticated diva. But perhaps the most archetypal images were created by Paul Colin in *Le Tumulte noir*, a collection of prints dedicated to Baker which satirically depicted the passion for *l'art nègre* and Baker as its 'primitive' epicentre (plate 11.14).

Baker's first performance at the *Folies Bergère* in 1926 used the familiar conceit of pitting modernity against the primitive. Devised by the artistic director Paul Derval, *La Folie du jour* focused on the ultra modern pastime of shopping. The show featured eight tableaux showcasing fashion and the Parisian shop window. While eight scantily dressed dancers were gradually clothed in luxurious outfits, Baker was gradually stripped. In a reverse striptease, the civilized world was once again contrasted with an imaginary primitive, and its artificiality found wanting in the face of the raw energy and sexuality of the exotic. With sets designed by the Mexican artist Miquel Covarrubias, it was in this production that Baker first wore her trademark 'banana' skirt (plate 11.15). The self-deprecating humour and irony of Baker's performance, particularly in the banana skirt, reveal the duality of her role as representative of both the primitive and the modern. It was through an appreciation of her performance that audiences

gauged their own modernity. Sieglinde Lemke has suggested that her dance proved a 'pas de trois' – a dance between mass culture, primitivism and Modernism.[31]

By the early 1930s the vogue for *l'art nègre* was beginning to wane. The brash commercialism of its swansong, the Colonial Exhibition, was epitomized in the organizers' attempt to cast the American Josephine Baker as the Queen of the French colonies – a role she refused to play. However, the draw of the fantasy exotic was no less powerful during the 1930s, though the passion for things African was replaced by a growing fascination with Native American and pre-Columbian art (plate 11.16).[32] André Breton described, in 1930, how 'the very particular interest that painters at the beginning of the twentieth century had for African Art' had shifted to 'American Art from before the conquest that along with Oceanic art, exercises an elective influence on artists'.[33] The Surrealists' interest in Mayan culture is testament to the continuing validity of the exotic for the rejuvenation of style and narrative. But for the mainstream culture that Art Deco represented the appeal of the exotic would diminish in the later 1930s as Nazi cultural politics created a fatal association between the primitive or the exotic and the degenerate.

11.16 Book cover. Jean Babelon, Georges Bataille and Alfred Métraux, *L'Art précolombien*, Paris, 1930. NAL.

PART 3

The Paris 1925 Exhibition

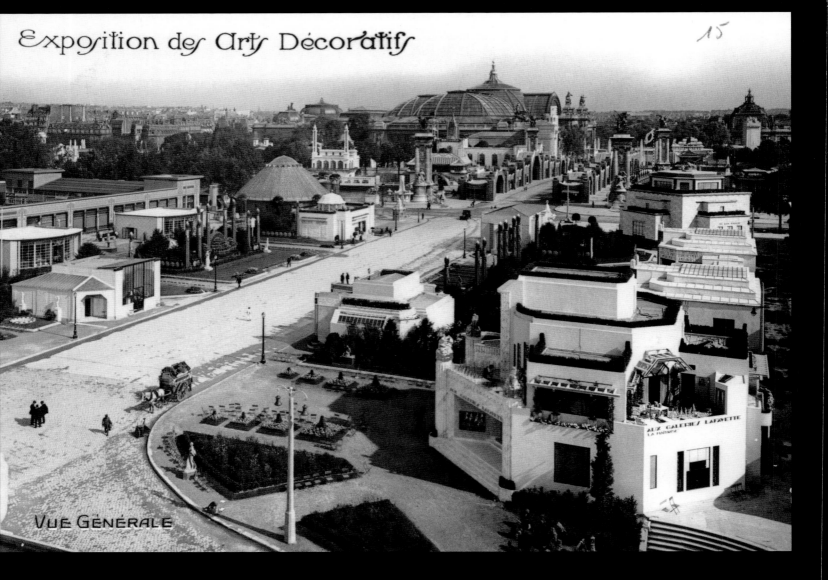

Exposition des Arts Décoratifs

15

Vue Générale

12 The International Exhibition

Charlotte Benton

There can be no risk of error in predicting that the art of 1925 is destined to take its place in due sequence with those named after the "three Louis"...[1]

For both contemporary and more recent commentators the Paris 1925 Exhibition has marked a defining moment in the evolution of what we now know as the Art Deco style, and a catalyst for its spread.[2] The 1925 Exhibition was not conceived as a World Fair like the Paris 1900 Exhibition but, like the 1902 Turin Exhibition,[3] was dedicated to 'modern' decorative arts. Unlike the latter, however, its main purpose was not to consolidate and encourage the spread of an international style but to reassert, in an international forum, France's authority as an arbiter of taste and producer of luxury goods, and Paris as the world centre of fashion. Although the exhibition succeeded in these aims in the short term, its luxury productions could have only a limited appeal – particularly after the 1929 Wall Street Crash – and the most visible marker of its success would be the spread, worldwide, of those aspects of its visual vocabulary that could be most readily adapted for more popular consumption.

The exhibition was shaped by France's ambitions in the years immediately after the First World War, but its origins lay in the early 1900s, when longstanding concerns about the 'crisis' of taste and quality of production in the decorative arts, and the consequences of these for national prestige and the economy, came to a head. At the beginning of the century French skills in the production of luxury goods were still unrivalled, as the radical Socialist politician Charles-Maurice Couyba pointed out: 'we are still the first when it comes to the production of luxury goods. No [other] country knows how to match a Majorelle or a Lalique for example.'[4] France still dominated home and foreign markets for such goods but, increasingly rapidly, both were being eroded and French goods copied, or imitated and adapted, for cheaper and more efficient methods of production elsewhere – as Couyba put it, 'foreigners commercialize our high priced models with an industriousness that endangers us more and more'.[5] At the same time, other countries had begun to produce new types of designs of good quality manufacture which could compete successfully with goods in 'the French taste', whatever their source of production.

Notable among these newly competitive producers was France's neighbour and old political enemy, Germany, which had seen a renaissance in its decorative arts in the years following the country's unification. This was largely due to initiatives that promoted the democratization of the arts as a means to achieve social and cultural unity and economic advance.[6] By the turn of the century, recognizing their significance to prestige and trade, Germany had begun to put substantial efforts into international exhibitions, rapidly achieving success in a field formerly dominated by France. Commenting on decorative arts at the Paris 1900 Exhibition, the French critic Charles Genuys observed that Germany had 'all of a sudden revealed itself as an artistic nation of the first order'.[7] And in 1904 Hermann Muthesius asserted that his country's exhibit at the St Louis Exhibition of that year showed that 'Germany [had] achieved a total indisputable applied art victory', which 'must necessarily arouse the idea in every visitor that today the centre of applied art development lies in Germany, perhaps in the same measure as it lay in France from the time of Louis XIV onward.'[8]

Muthesius was necessarily partisan; but his perceptions were shared by commentators of other nationalities.[9] Meanwhile, Germany had even encroached on France's 'home' territory. French observers noted a considerable increase in the number of 'German' and other foreign decorating firms and workshops in Paris; in 1910 the *Salon d'automne* hosted an exhibition of the work of the 'Munich Decorators', which, although it provoked hostile responses in the French press, achieved a considerable *succès d'estime* (see Chapters 8 and

12.1 Panoramic view of the Paris 1925 Exhibition, looking towards the Pont Alexandre III. Postcard. French, 1925. Private collection.

15); and, by 1913, the value of the German art industries' exports to the United States well outstripped that of their French counterparts.[10]

French decorative artists, critics and manufacturers were slow to respond to these challenges for several reasons. Chief among them was an unshakeable belief in the supremacy of French taste. This was bolstered by the inherited structure of the French decorative arts industries which, centred on small enterprises and independent workshops reliant on traditional handcraft skills, were ill equipped to foster innovatory design and produce reasonably priced quality goods. In addition, there was mutual hostility between decorative artists and manufacturers which inhibited collaboration between them; the dedicated infrastructure necessary to generate and co-ordinate initiatives was largely lacking; and, although the French made efforts to identify the reasons for their competitors' success, they were divided as how to respond. Xenophobic critics like Marius Vachon found ready support for their views on the need for retrenchment. Others acknowledged that a major cause of decline was the reliance of French decorative artists and manufacturers on the imitation of past styles. Among these was Siegfried Bing (a key figure in the rise of Art Nouveau in France) who, reporting on the vigour of contemporary developments in American decorative arts in 1895, regretted France's inability to recover the creative genius and innovatory approach on which its supremacy had been based.[11] These differences of view contributed, effectively, to the maintenance of the status quo. As a result, while its markets for luxury goods declined, France was unable to harness the purchasing power of the expanding middle class either at home or abroad.

During the early 1900s, however, the need to acknowledge the reasons for German success and adapt their lessons to French practice began to be more widely accepted, and in the years immediately preceding the First World War several changes occurred. Decorative artists now worked together more frequently to make their exhibition displays more coherent and effective; they also began to pay greater attention to designs for the middle-class market.[12] Already in 1907 Couyba, concerned that French decorative artists were 'so ingenious when it comes to the production of a unique piece', but not organized or equipped to produce 'current models in unlimited series', had suggested a well planned international exhibition of decorative art in his annual budget proposal to the Ministry of Fine Arts.[13] His project, rooted in 'art social' ideas, was intended to educate manufacturers and designers to new social

demands and means of production.[14] In 1909, a further proposal based on similar precepts was made by Roger Marx, who also suggested that past styles should be excluded 'except to the extent that they are rigorously adapted to the era in which they appear'.[15] A central theme of the 1925 Exhibition, 'modernity', was now established.[16] Two years later, a commission led by René Guilleré, a lawyer and President of the Société des Artistes-Décorateurs (SAD), was established to consider further the case for a major international exhibition. Guilleré acknowledged the need for French decorative artists and manufacturers to adopt new designs and production methods and was himself instrumental in advancing these through his connection with Primavera.[17] His commission's report emphasized the urgent need – in the face of the German 'threat' – to pursue the project. And, in 1912, the Chambre des Députés endorsed these recommendations, proposing that the exhibition be held in 1915.[18] Increasing international tensions ensured that the project was seen as essential to the national interest; yet, in February 1914, it was postponed, as a result of doubts about the ability of French designers and manufacturers to rise to the German challenge by 1915.[19]

During the war years the project was kept alive by French fears about Germany's post-war ambitions and a belief in the vital contribution the exhibition would make to France's recovery – as Henri Magne put it: 'Our country's prospects of a new era of prosperity depend on the exhibition's success.'[20] Several preparatory initiatives were also launched (see Chapter 14). Yet, although the project attracted public support, its 'modern' emphasis was contested, on the grounds that 'tout ce qui est nouveau est boche'.[21] Anti-modern sentiments were also encouraged by manufacturers of reproduction furniture, who had a vested interest in stemming consumer demand for new designs. And, towards the end of the war and in the years immediately following, such sentiments were sharpened by political events. The Russian Revolution, the establishment of 'soviets' – albeit short-lived – in Germany and Hungary, and labour unrest in France itself raised fears about the overthrow of the established order; 'modern' was now identified not only as 'boche' but 'Bolshevik'.[22]

In the reconstruction period, however, issues of 'modernity' and 'modernization' acquired more positive associations. France's need to rebuild its textile industries and revive steel production, along with the emergence of new consumer expectations, made industrial modernization more acceptable.[23]

In this context, France's economic dependence on its luxury industries was, arguably, diminished; nevertheless, they continued to be seen as central to short-term economic revival and to the pursuit of a 'politique de prestige'.[24] As the critic Yvanhoé Rambosson put it:

France owes it to herself to prove to the world that her artists, craftsmen and manufacturers have not lost their innovative ingenuity, the quality of balance and logic, especially allied to gifts of grace and fantasy, that have earned her, in the past, a universal sovereignty surer and more durable than that which flows from the power of arms.[25]

The luxury industries provided a quality 'marque' for French industry as a whole. Their revival represented a powerful symbol of the continuity of French cultural values and the recovery of material prosperity. These considerations, combined with the fear of renewed German 'economic aggression', ensured both the rapid resumption of preparations for the exhibition and a shift in its focus. The emphasis now moved definitively from 'art social' to luxury production, though officials emphasized that the proposed modes of display would allow objects to be seen in context.[26] At the same time, the regulations were revised to emphasize further the need for 'new inspiration' and 'real originality' in the selected exhibits, and renewed efforts were made to encourage French manufacturers to both embrace the 'modern' and collaborate with decorative artists (see Chapter 14).[27] Rescheduled for 1923, the exhibition was postponed once again, largely as a result of France's precarious economic circumstances, but it eventually opened in April 1925.

Post-war austerity, the state of international relations and widespread social tensions ensured that only around two dozen foreign countries agreed to participate, of which the majority were European.[28] Even among these there were significant absentees, including Germany and Norway; France alone was 'comprehensively represented' and its exhibits occupied some two-thirds of the total site.[29] The issue of German participation, first raised soon after the war, proved contentious – despite France's recent military victory. At issue were Germany's past aggression, its non-payment of war reparations and its stated ambitions to challenge French leadership in art and fashion.[30] Pascal Forthuny, a member of the exhibition committee, canvassed the views of leading politicians and figures in the arts and found opinions divided.[31] While some respondents opposed German participation, others saw it as essential – whether on political or artistic grounds. Among the latter were the decorative artists André Mare and Jacques-Emile Ruhlmann. The former's opinion was that 'it will show that our art is truly French ... and superior to theirs';[32] the latter stated that

> I am among those who want the 'combat' ... There is no doubt that our manufacturers and artists have much to learn ... from these formidable competitors ... [and] that their participation ... will make us try harder ... [and] that the contest will be stimulating, educative ... I am for the contest.[33]

In the event, an invitation was issued, but too late for Germany to assemble a coherent exhibit;[34] and the resulting absence of 'the most important centre of mid-European art influence caused an unfortunate void'.[35] The representation of non-European countries was sparse. The USA was offered a prime site but abstained in the belief that 'there was no modern design in America'[36] – a decision that was regretted by many American architects and designers as well as by Europeans aware of the USA's 'great contribution to recent architectural progress'.[37] Asia was patchily represented; Australasia and Latin America not at all; and the only African exhibits on show were those of French colonial possessions or protectorates,[38] though works of 'negro' inspiration were displayed in some of the other European pavilions.[39] Not surprisingly, the exhibition was considered 'mainly representative of modern European art'.[40]

In the years preceding the exhibition various sites had been proposed, some of which would have allowed the construction of permanent buildings.[41] With the definitive abandonment of an 'art social' perspective, however, and in line with the state's renewed 'politique de prestige', a site of some 23 hectares (55 acres) in the heart of Paris was designated, which was large enough for an important show yet small enough to impose rigorous selection.[42] The site was designed with its main axis running from the Porte d'Honneur – next to the Grand Palais – across the river to Les Invalides, with secondary axes along the Left and Right Banks. It incorporated two bridges – the Pont des Invalides and the Pont Alexandre III, the latter transformed for the purposes of the exhibition (plate 12.1). The most prestigious French pavilions occupied an area on the Left Bank bounded by the Place des Invalides, the Rue de Constantine and the river. The foreign pavilions and those of the French regions, press and colonies were sited on the Right Bank. In addition, the interiors of the Grand Palais (originally built for the 1900 Exhibition) were transformed, to host official receptions and present displays of French and foreign exhibits arranged under group classifications.[43]

The site's importance and its proximity to major cultural buildings precluded the construction of any permanent buildings and its selection was calculated to ensure that 'the very ephemerality of the event would suggest the cultural and economic power of a nation that could permit itself to construct a city within a city whose big and expensive pavilions would soon be torn down and forgotten'.[44] The architect Charles Plumet, a veteran of Art Nouveau, devised a unified 'plan d'ensemble' for the whole site, which regulated the location and 'footprints' of buildings, as well as their height and massing, and created vistas towards monuments in the surrounding city. Several of the buildings, despite their temporary purpose, were constructed in permanent materials – such as concrete and brick – but, for reasons of economy, most were constructed in timber and 'staff' (reinforced plaster). For the same reasons, some decorative details, such as the designs for wrought iron ornaments and crystal cupolas for the grand Porte d'Honneur by Edgar Brandt and René Lalique, had to be executed in plaster painted to represent iron and glass.

To counteract such visible markers of post-war stringency and suggest the image of luxury and glamour necessary to satisfy 'the craving for the spectacular and fantastic which was a natural product of the emotional strain of the war',[45] colour, novel surface decorations and scenographic effects were widely employed. A British observer noted that the ubiquitous plaster surfaces were 'finished in many new ways and often painted and picked out in silver and gold and bright colours'.[46] And the American critic Helen Appleton Read remarked that

> the first impression of the Exposition is startling. Passing through the silver obelisk-like towers of the *Porte d'Honneur* one comes at once upon a cubist dream city or the projection of a possible city in Mars, arisen over night in the heart of Paris, its unlikeness to any hitherto known architecture enhanced by its proximity to such traditional structures as the venerable grey façade of the Louvre, the tarnished grandeur of Les Invalides and the fast-mellowing floridity of the Grand Palais...[47]

Throughout this 'dream city' the pleasures of consumption were promoted by novel forms and sparkling surface effects, backed by the use of modern technology to enhance the sense of spectacle. As another American observer noted, 'everything on show was an appeal to our senses'.[48] The Pont Alexandre III was equipped with 'an elaborate arrangement of searchlights and waterworks ...[which] permits the illumination of the bridge at night and a cascade of colored water across the entire span of the bridge'.[49] The exhibition pavilions and their surroundings were made more alluring by night-time illumination, while major monuments visible from the exhibition grounds, such as Les Invalides and the Eiffel Tower, were illuminated to draw the surrounding city into the 'dream' (see plates 13.1 and 13.7).[50]

Within the main French section, pavilions and *galeries* were dedicated to the work of groups, leading designers, commercial concerns and particular manufacturers or *métiers* (plate 12.2).

12.2 Pierre Patout, 'Hôtel d'un Collectionneur' at the Paris 1925 Exhibition, with Joseph Bernard's sculptural frieze *La danse*.
Pierre Patout, *L'Architecture officielle et les pavillons: Exposition des arts décoratifs et industriels modernes*, Paris, 1925. NAL.

Here, the regulation of the buildings' overall design, their frequent planning around courtyards or gardens containing free-standing sculptures or fountains, the use of concrete or reinforced plaster painted in light colours to imitate concrete, and what the American critic W. Francklyn Paris dubbed an 'obsession of the geometrical, the massive, and the angular' resulted in a strong sense of unity.[51] Furthermore, the use of concrete and reinforced plaster not only encouraged a consistent simplification of architectural form, but also deterred the use of high-relief sculpted architectural decoration. Instead, decorative effects were frequently achieved by the addition of low-relief sculpted panels, motifs impressed directly into the plaster, mosaic details and grilles and panels of wrought iron in which 'new forms … were much in evidence' (see plates 14.4 and 14.5).[52] The consistency of effect was admired by many observers, though some regretted the absence of an identifiably 'French' character and thought the buildings marked by 'a far too conscious a striving after originality, novelty at any price … [which] deprives them of charm'.[53]

This conscious striving after novelty was also visible in the interiors. Helen Appleton Read considered that 'the exotic and the ultra are perhaps overstressed in the furniture and displays of interior decoration'. She went on to describe the 'sharkskin furniture, macabre bedroom schemes in violet blacks and blueish purples, jade and jewelled salons de

12.4 Pierre Chareau, 'Bibliothèque' in the 'Ambassade Française' at the Paris 1925 Exhibition. *Intérieurs en couleurs*, Paris, c.1926. NAL.

12.3 Henri Rapin, Pierre Selmersheim and others, 'Grand Salon' in the 'Ambassade Française' at the Paris 1925 Exhibition. Jean Saudé, *Une Ambassade française*, Paris, 1925. NAL.

bain, furniture representing negro sculpture, monkeyskin bedspreads and glass walls'.[54] Yet she and others also saw positive elements in such displays. W. Francklyn Paris noted that – despite their undoubted lavishness – French furnishings tended to be 'simple and costly, unadorned yet assertive' and that French decorative artists had

> while working individually and independently, arrived at a style which is homogeneous as well as characteristic, and which embodies the same principles [as the architecture] ... a certain masculinity, a soberness of ornamentation and a dependence upon effects produced by proportion and a richness of material rather than by elaborate carving or applied ornament.[55]

These tendencies were attributed to several factors, including post-war economic austerity, new materials and techniques,[56] the influence of 'Cubism'[57] and the 'functional' concerns of Modernist architects and designers. Yet if modernistic tendencies were conspicuous in the French section, so too was the grip of national traditions, albeit modernized. As an official British observer noted, 'The French ... found it difficult to eradicate the tradition which they have inherited. In 80 per cent of the French furniture shown, the work was characterized by sinuous lines and subtle curvature.'[58] Such tensions between modernity and tradition were prominent in the most celebrated French exhibits, including the SAD's 'Ambassade Française', Jacques-Emile Ruhlmann's 'Hôtel d'un Collectionneur' and the pavilions of the leading French department stores.

The SAD had been a moving spirit behind the original exhibition project but, as it developed, the society found itself rather sidelined.[59] It did, however, succeed in obtaining a state subsidy for its exhibit, based on a theme suggested by the Ministry of Fine Arts: 'The reception rooms and private apartments of a French embassy ... to be installed at an indefinite date in some unnamed foreign capital'.[60] In return for this subsidy, the state would acquire a number of important items from the exhibit for display in French embassies worldwide, and in museums and other official buildings in metropolitan France. The pavilion's architect was Charles Plumet and its interiors were designed by the society's members, working collaboratively. They included former 'young Turks' of Art Nouveau like Maurice Dufrène, Paul Follot and Pierre Selmersheim, as well as younger designers like Pierre Chareau, André Groult and René Herbst. More than thirty of them were involved in the design of the Grand Salon alone, to achieve what Gaston Varenne described as 'sumptuousness without a false note' (plate 12.3).[61] Sumptuousness was the common factor of all the interiors, whether they were 'modernized traditional' – like the Grand Salon – or 'decorative Modernist', like Pierre Chareau's 'Bibliothèque', with its Cubist-inspired desk and ingenious palmwood louvred cupola,[62] or Jean Dunand's black and silver lacquered 'Fumoir', with its uncluttered lines and brightly coloured cushion covers and screens inspired by African crafts and contemporary abstract art (see plates 6.15 and 12.4). In between were designs that combined

12.5 André Groult, 'Chambre de Madame' in the 'Ambassade Française' at the Paris 1925 Exhibition. *Intérieurs en couleurs*, Paris, 1926. NAL.

elements of both tendencies, such as André Groult's pastel-hued 'Chambre de Madame', with its voluptuous – almost anthropomorphic – sharkskin-clad furniture and sinuous lines, suggestive of both French tradition and Art Nouveau (plates 12.5, 12.6 and 12.7). To contemporary observers these formal nuances seemed to have been subsumed by the common observance of the conventions of luxury production, which resulted in a sense of 'variety without discord'.[63] The formal radicalism of Chareau and Dunand, which drew on Modernist sources, could be readily accommodated – and even admired – by French officials and critics. Yet, at the same time, avant-garde fine art was considered sufficiently contentious for the SAD to agree to the removal – for the purposes of the pavilion's official inauguration – of the painted panels by Fernand Léger and Robert Delaunay which hung in Rob Mallet-Stevens's entrance hall.[64] In the years that followed the exhibition, 'decorative Modernists' like Chareau and Dunand would become more assertive. This created tensions within the SAD which, in 1929, resulted in the formation of a breakaway group, the Union des Artistes Modernes, committed to representing modern artistic tendencies and opposed to the ambitions of the SAD's more conservative members to chase official commissions.[65]

In 1925 the 'modernized tradition' favoured by the veterans of Art Nouveau and younger 'nationalist' members of the SAD was still widespread. It characterized the most ambitious individual pavilion in the French section, the 'Hôtel d'un Collectionneur' by Jacques-Emile Ruhlmann, the most celebrated *maître-ébéniste* of the day.[66] He was often portrayed as an unrepentant elitist for his belief that 'New creations have never been made for the middle classes. They have always been made at the request of an elite which unsparingly gives artists the time and money needed for laborious research and perfect execution.'[67] But in practice Ruhlmann subscribed to the 'trickle down' theory. So, although he asserted that 'We must manufacture luxury furniture ... [for] it is the elite that launches fashion and determines the impetus', he also believed that 'it is by ricochet ... that the movement descends towards the masses'.[68] Ruhlmann was responsible for the overall design of the pavilion's interiors, which brought together work by several of his preferred associates, representing the spectrum of the *métiers* (plates 12.8 to 12.15).[69] With their sumptuous materials, meticulous craftsmanship and subtle play of decorative details, these interiors laid claim to high French traditions of design and production; and yet, as contemporaries were quick to observe, they

were unmistakeably 'modern'. Gaston Varenne considered the Grand Salon as perfectly calculated in colour and proportions and 'of such refinement and sobriety that he has succeeded in getting rid of all superfluous ornament',[70] and Helen Appleton Read noted 'rooms without corners, the doors and windows without trim, the cornices without ornament'.[71] Individual pieces also referenced modern tastes and practices in their iconography, materials or techniques.[72] Seen by millions, the pavilion confirmed Ruhlmann's reputation and brought his work to the attention of a rich clientele worldwide; it also came to be seen as paradigmatic of the exhibition's ambition to reassert the supremacy of French taste and skills in luxury production.

In this 'perfect consumer city' within a city,[73] pavilions like these were designed to market their luxury wares directly to wealthy clients; elsewhere in the French section similar strategies were followed. At every turn, visitors were offered opportunities for seduction by visual novelty and sumptuous materials – whether in the window displays and interiors of the Galerie des Boutiques on the Esplanade des Invalides and the boutiques on the Pont Alexandre III, or in the pavilions of the national manufactories and the modern decorative art studios of the leading French department stores.[74] These last were strategically sited to either side of the main axis, framing the entrance to France's prestige exhibits on the Esplanade des Invalides.[75] The stores' pavilions had many common features: they were of similar dimensions and massing and were symmetrically planned around prominent entrances (see plates 14.4 to 14.7). With extensively glazed exterior surfaces, they had good natural interior lighting by day and offered spectacular night-time effects. Other aspects of their design and detailing were also conceived to attract attention. The pavilion for La Maîtrise, by Joseph Hiriart, Georges Tribout and Georges Beau, was clad in white grained marble and sported a vast sunburst over its main entrance, made in coloured glass and gilded bronze; as a commentator aptly observed, 'a certain exterior magnificence is in order: it contributes to publicity'.[76] Internally, too, the pavilions followed a common programme – that of interiors and furnishings for a comfortably-off bourgeois family – and boasted impressive double height central spaces off which radiated smaller rooms. Despite these similarities, however, there were marked differences. All of the stores recognized the commercial value of a distinctive 'house style' for their studios' output, and this was clearly visible in the design of the interiors and furnishings, as well as in the publicity material

12.6 Marie Laurencin, *Portrait of a Woman*. Oil on canvas. French, 1925. Displayed in the 'Chambre de Madame' in the 'Ambassade Française' at the Paris 1925 Exhibition. Private collection. Courtesy of Thomas Gibson Fine Art Ltd, London. © ADAGP, Paris and DACS, London 2002.

12.7 André Groult, chiffonier. Mahogany, ivory and sharkskin. French, 1925. Displayed in the 'Chambre de Madame' in the 'Ambassade Française' at the Paris 1925 Exhibition. Musée des Arts Décoratifs, Paris. Photo: Laurent Sully Jaulmes. © ADAGP, Paris and DACS, London 2002.

(see plate 14.1). As a result, the work of Paul Follot and his colleagues at Pomone, aimed at a fairly conservative clientele, eschewed the direct imitation of past styles but was 'impregnated with the most traditional reminders', while the work of Djo-Bourgeois (Edouard-Joseph Bourgeois), Maurice Matet and colleagues for Studium Louvre represented 'a definite will to imagine the new', directed at a more adventurous – if similarly well heeled – clientele.[77]

The prominent role taken by the department stores in commissioning, having manufactured and marketing the kind of modern design we now know as Art Deco was not lost on the foreign retailers, designers and clients who visited the exhibition. As the British official observers Frank Warner and A. F. Kendrick noted, their pavilions 'did more, perhaps, than the classified displays of the different nations to enable an estimate to be formed of the degree to which the art of the present day is entitled to rank as a new style penetrating into all departments of artistic activity'.[78] Over the next few years, although manufacturers were mostly slow to respond to this 'new style', department stores the world over, 'ever alert for new and daring ideas', would play a leading role in promoting and diffusing it.[79] In the process, Art Deco would be naturalized and sometimes radically transformed.

12.10 Antoine Bourdelle, *Héraklès archer*. Bronze. French, cast 1909. Musée Bourdelle, Paris. Photo: Eric Emo. © ADAGP, Paris and DACS, London 2002.

12.8 Jacques-Emile Ruhlmann, 'Grand Salon' in the 'Hôtel d'un Collectionneur' at the Paris 1925 Exhibition. Maurice Dufrène, *Ensembles mobiliers: Exposition internationale, 1925*, Paris, 1925. NAL. © ADAGP, Paris and DACS, London 2002.

Grand Salon

12.9 Jacques-Emile Ruhlmann, Jean Dunand and Jean Lambert-Rucki, cabinet. Black lacquer with incised silver decoration. French, 1925. De Lorenzo, New York. Photo: Anthony Israel. © ADAGP, Paris and DACS, London 2002.

12.13 Stéphany for Jacques-Emile Ruhlmann, wall covering. Woven silk and cotton. French, 1925. Made by Cornille Frères. Musée Historique des Tissus de Lyon.

12.11 François Pompon, *Ours blanc*. Bronze. French, 1923-33. Musée d'Orsay. © Photo: RMN – A. Morin. © ADAGP, Paris and DACS, London 2002.

12.12 Jacques-Emile Ruhlmann, 'Araignée', table. Macassar ebony veneer. French, 1918-19. V&A: Circ.328-1967. © ADAGP, Paris and DACS, London 2002.

149

12.14 Jean Dupas, *Les Perruches*.

Oil on canvas. French, 1925.

Xavier Roberts Collection.

12.15 Jacques-Emile Ruhlmann, banquette. Private collection. A pair of armchairs. Private collection New York. Macassar ebony and bronze, with Aubusson tapestry by Emile Gaudissart. French, c.1925. Close variant of the suite made for the 'Grand Salon' of the 'Hôtel d'un Collectionneur'. Courtesy of Sotheby's London. © ADAGP, Paris and DACS, London 2002.

12.16 Armando Brasini, Italian pavilion at the Paris 1925 Exhibition. Adolphe Dervaux, *L'Architecture étrangère: Exposition des arts décoratifs et industriels modernes*, Paris, 1925. NAL.

12.17 Konstantin Stepanovic Melnikov, the USSR pavilion at the 1925 Paris Exhibition. Adolphe Dervaux, *L'Architecture étrangère: Exposition des arts décoratifs et industriels modernes*, Paris, 1925. NAL.

The foreign pavilions were more heterogeneous in style and materials than those in the main French section. And here, on occasion, the requirement for exhibits to be of 'modern inspiration' and 'real originality' was visibly tested, notably by Armando Brasini's grandiloquent, unremittingly historicist, Italian pavilion. Built in multi-coloured brick with travertine marble dressings and interiors clad in marble and ceramic, it was intended to suggest the permanency of the Fascist regime (plate 12.16). Neighbouring it, however, was Konstantin Melnikov's USSR pavilion, whose Constructivist design and red painted plywood construction was of indisputably 'modern inspiration', if similarly propagandist intentions (plate 12.17). Despite their heterogeneity, however, the foreign exhibits displayed similar generic tendencies to the French displays. Modernized, high-style 'national' traditions were identifiable in Aage Rafn's designs for the Danish pavilion (see plate 17.3), Gio Ponti's ceramics for Richard-Ginori in the Italian pavilion (see plate 19.2), Jaroslav Horejc's work for the Czechoslovak pavilion (see plate 18.6), Simon Gate's designs for the Swedish glassmakers Orrefors (see plate 17.6) and Josef Hoffmann's designs for the Austrian exhibit (plate 12.18 and see plate 1.11).

In many of the foreign exhibits – notably those of Central Europe, Scandinavia, the USSR and Asia – another type of 'national' tradition was prominent, in examples of contemporary 'peasant' or 'folk' art and designs influenced by these vernacular traditions. As a critic observed of the former, they 'presented the most striking examples of living immemorial tradition' while subverting the exhibition regulations since 'nothing could be more wanting in "modern inspiration" and the presence of "real originality"'.[80] And yet, in several of the exhibits, the relevance of such work to contemporary practice was clearly

demonstrated in designs of decidedly 'modern inspiration' which filtered folk traditions through the lens of contemporary avant-garde art and design. The most striking examples of these were to be found in the exhibits of those Central European countries recently liberated by the break up of the Austro-Hungarian Empire. Here vernacular traditions were self-consciously deployed to assert a new or restored national identity (see Chapter 16), as in František Kysela's tapestry designs for the Czechoslovak pavilion (see plate 16.4). Folk inspiration also pervaded the Austrian exhibit, of which René Chavance remarked that 'one perceives ... the profound mark of the milieu, of ethnic characteristics' in 'ceramics of popular inspiration ...

and leather bags ... made in a traditional way' produced by peasant industries' associations and decorative artists associated with the Wiener Werkstätte (see plate 15.6).[81] Distinctions between the prosaic and inventive uses of vernacular traditions were also to be found in the architectural design of the foreign pavilions. Gabriel Mourey regretted that the architect of the Greek pavilion seemed 'to have confined himself to collecting in his composition the most characteristic details of Greek peasant architecture', but found Józef Czajkowski's design for the Polish pavilion thoroughly invigorating (see plates 16.8 and 16.9).[82] Vernacular traditions were not absent from the French exhibits either, despite the impression of metropolitan sophistication

that permeated the main French section. Well aware of the need to address the concerns of conservative critics and regional interests, French officialdom fostered vernacular traditions and skills and regional identities, albeit encouraging their 'modernization' (see Chapter 14). Yet the majority of France's regional exhibits were placed on the same axis as the foreign pavilions, where their evidence of diversity could not impinge on the deliberately constructed homogeneity of the more prestigious French displays.

Like those in the main French section, the foreign exhibits displayed a tension between designs derived from national traditions and more explicitly Modernist work. Despite its historicist pavilion, the Italian exhibit included avant-garde designs by Fortunato

12.19 Josef Gočár and Jan Štursa,
Czech pavilion at the Paris 1925
Exhibition, with Otakar Švec's
Sunbeam Motorcycle. Adolphe Dervaux,
L'Architecture étrangère:
Exposition des arts décoratifs et
industriels modernes, Paris, 1925. NAL.

Depero and other Futurists (see plate 19.1), and the
Czechoslovak exhibit included photographs by
František Drtikol (see plate 25.4) and Otakar Švec's
sculpture *Sunbeam Motorcycle* (plate 12.19). Among
other foreign exhibits, 'the more extreme forms of
so-called "modernist" inspiration' were observed in
Latvian pottery strongly influenced by Russian 'ultra-
modernist' work, Dutch 'cubist' posters and Catalan
'cubist' jewellery.[83] Furthermore, regardless of
whether the exhibits drew on traditional or
'modernist' inspiration, contemporaries observed that
'almost everywhere the will to modernism dominates
the craftsmen', as evidenced by simplified forms
and 'an almost total suppression of ornament'.[84]

For various reasons, a number of well known
designers and manufacturers were absent from the

national displays. In the British exhibit, notable
examples were manufacturers of artificial silk, which
was 'conspicuous by its absence' though Britain then
held the world lead in its production.[85] In part, such
absences were accounted for by the caution of
national organizing committees in interpreting the
exhibition regulations and the high costs of space on
the exhibition site. But several manufacturers were
reluctant to exhibit because prohibitive customs
tariffs effectively denied them access to many of the
markets from which there might have been demand
as a result of exhibiting.

Assessing the exhibition's impact, the British
commentator H. P. Shapland took the view that 'It
may be stated at the outset ... that the French came
out of this competition very well indeed.'[86] In

logistical terms alone, the exhibition was a great success: between the end of April and the end of October 1925 some 16 million visitors passed through its gates. They included French and foreign tourists, journalists, official delegations, manufacturers and retailers, and artists, architects and designers; among them were many visitors from countries which – like the United States and Australia – were not represented in the displays. In aesthetic terms, too, the exhibition was widely seen as a success. Sir Hubert Llewellyn Smith, leader of the official British delegation, considered that 'as a display of originality and modern inspiration ... there can be no doubt that a triumphant success has been achieved. The whole Exhibition was permeated by the modern spirit, and ... yet the influence of tradition was still clearly recognizable.'[87]

Between 7,000 and 8, 000 prizes were awarded by the juries.[88] Llewellyn Smith and some others considered that these favoured works displaying 'the maximum of novelty' at the expense of 'most modern work in which the visible influence of tradition overshadowed that of novelty'.[89] In practice, however, the juries seem to have been even-handed and diplomatic in their awards – among the national exhibits, the folk-inspired Polish displays received the largest number of prizes.[90]

Despite its successes, the exhibition was not uncritically received. Ellow Hostache thought 'The entire Exposition ... a futile gesture ... a hopelessly lost opportunity for helpful accomplishment'.[91] Several French critics attacked the vast expenditure lavished on the project at a time of financial crisis, and they and some foreign observers regretted that the 'French and foreign decorators work only for a privileged class'.[92] Even those broadly in favour of the exhibition noted that it made a 'very serious omission' in throwing 'little or no light on the question of inexpensive design for working-class homes'.[93] Its critics included both those who regretted the loss of the 'art social' dimension of

the original project and those concerned with the interests of middle-class consumers impoverished by the First World War and its aftermath.[94] For the latter, Le Corbusier's austere 'Esprit Nouveau' pavilion – a prototype unit for a bourgeois apartment block or free-standing villa – and his book, *L'Art décoratif d'aujourd'hui* (1925) offered a compelling Modernist critique.[95] Other critics included representatives of the interests of American consumers and manufacturers, who highlighted the unsuitability of many of the exhibits to contemporary American lifestyles and mass production processes.[96]

Nonetheless, the exhibition was both a *succès d'estime* and a practical success for the French – at least in the short term.[97] It had a rapid and widespread impact outside France. For a time French decorators and decorative arts were much in demand: travelling exhibitions were shown in the United States and elsewhere; foreign department stores and small specialist boutiques or galleries imported exclusive lines by leading French designers; commissions and consultancies were offered to several designers by foreign private, institutional and corporate clients.[98] Yet France's backing of luxury production, combined with customs tariffs, limited the sales of original French work even before the Wall Street Crash wiped out the market for luxury goods. Furthermore, as in earlier periods, there was a rash of imitations of French designs from New York to Sydney, Rio de Janeiro to Shanghai. In the United States, outright plagiarism reached such proportions that the SAD refused to participate in the Chicago *Century of Progress* exhibition in 1933 in protest.[99] Europeans who saw the Paris 1925 Exhibition as 'essentially an exhibition of articles de luxe'[100] – especially those aware of Modernism's alternative agenda – saw little to learn in respect of designs suitable for modern production processes or the needs of less privileged consumers. Yet many of the jazzier, or 'decorative Modernist', forms and motifs of 1925 proved readily adaptable to new types of

product, new materials and machine production (see Chapters 10 and 33). Paradoxically, too, it was some of those with least direct connection with the decorative arts who were able to learn most from the exhibition, such as the hard-bitten motor manufacturers and marketing men of Detroit. They were acutely aware that Henry Ford's old adage 'any colour as long as it's black' had passed its 'sell by' date, of the growing influence of women in American automobile purchase and use, and of the rapidly developing science of consumer psychology. In response, they were quick to adapt the bright colours, bold textile designs and co-ordinated publicity seen in 1925 to the design and marketing of their very different products.

In 1924, Henri Magne had summed up French ambitions for the exhibition: 'An exhibition is not an end in itself: it is a point of departure. It is not enough that modern French art should triumph in 1925. It is essential that that triumph should continue.'[101] France did triumph in 1925, but its triumph was short-lived. The 1929 Wall Street Crash and ensuing Depression drastically reduced the market for luxury goods both at home and abroad; by 1930-1 some formerly highly successful French decorative artists sought to buy back examples of their work – to give it a scarcity value – and several were reduced to total penury. By this time the design initiative had passed elsewhere. As the official US Department of Commerce report on the 1925 exhibition had observed, 'The nation which most successfully rationalises the movement and brings its expression into terms acceptable and appropriate to modern living conditions and modern taste will possess a distinct advantage both as to its domestic and its foreign trade.'[102] In the early 1930s American commercial and design energies would be harnessed to convert Art Deco into 'terms acceptable and appropriate to modern living conditions and modern taste', allowing American manufacturers to find ways successfully to stimulate consumption (see Chapter 34).[103]

13 Paris 1925: Consuming Modernity

Tag Gronberg

'We have invited all nations', pronounced the *Catalogue général officiel* of the Paris 1925 Exhibition, but in fact the French section of this international exhibition took up approximately two-thirds of the 23-hectare (55-acre) site (see plate 12.1).[1] As with earlier Paris exhibitions, one of the prime functions of the *Exposition internationale des arts décoratifs et industriels modernes* was to define the identity and supremacy of French goods on the international market-place. What was distinctive in 1925 was not only the emphasis on the decorative arts identified as modern, but also the determination to display these in the context of consumption as opposed to production. Instead of confronting machine halls and technological exhibits, which had featured prominently in the French section of earlier exhibitions, such as that of 1889, visitors in 1925 were invited to stroll through streets of shops and around department store pavilions or to admire specially designed rooms for a French embassy. Certain displays, such as that for a French village, presented the continuity of traditional French values. But the mission in 1925, seven years after the end of the First World War, was heavily predicated on the future; exhibits of modern French decorative arts were to signal the post-war cultural and commercial renaissance of the nation.

How did this exhibition manifest a specifically French 1920s modernity? There were no soaring monuments to technology, such as the Eiffel Tower built in 1889, nor was it possible to erect bombastic modern 'palaces', such as the Grand and Petit Palais bequeathed by the 1900 *Exposition universelle* (World Fair). The Paris 1925 Exhibition was located on the same site as the 1900 Exhibition, in the centre of Paris, on the Right and Left banks of the Seine connected by the Pont Alexandre III. Unlike their predecessors in 1900, however, the organizers in 1925 were restricted to the construction of temporary buildings and gardens. The layout of the 1925 Exhibition made strategic use of its location in order to draw attention to the grandeur of Paris. Night and day, the exhibition presented Paris as the

city of spectacle. It showed off Paris in order that Paris could play its part in the exhibition's show-casing of French commodities. This was particularly evident from the vantage point of the Pont Alexandre III, at the heart of the exhibition. From here it was possible to enjoy dramatic views across the river towards that enduring symbol of the French capital, the Eiffel Tower (plates 13.1 and 13.2). (This particular *point de vue* was carefully recorded in the official report on the exhibition, the *Encyclopédie des arts décoratifs et industriels modernes au XXème siècle*.) A glittering, nocturnal version of *Paris ville lumière* was staged at and from the Pont Alexandre III: coloured lights illuminated the bridge as well as the fountains of water that spurted up from the Seine. Electric lights also transformed the Eiffel Tower, turning it into a giant advertisement for Citroën cars. In its updated and illuminated guise the Tower powerfully signified Paris and also the city's prestige. But the 1925 Exhibition also included rather different manifestations of modernity, for example the Pont Alexandre III itself, redesigned by Maurice Dufrène as a street of bijou small shops (plate 13.3). One review described the Pont Alexandre as the 'charnière' (hinge) of the exhibition.[2] This was partly a reference to its geographical location and the function of the bridge in connecting the two main exhibition sites, but Dufrène's *rue des boutiques* also acted as the hinge for particular conceptions of modernity. By 1925 the luxury boutique, characterized by its diminutive scale and the ephemerality of its fashionable goods, had become almost as important an icon of modernity as the Eiffel Tower.[3]

Despite potentially picturesque connotations (evoking medieval bridges laden with shops), the *rue des boutiques* on the Pont Alexandre III had more to do with notions of the modern city than with the nostalgia for a *vieux Paris* manifested by the display of that name at the 1900 Exhibition.[4] The idea of representing the contemporary city in terms of boutiques was not new. By 1925, the Parisian boutique was recognized not only as a means of

13.1 The Eiffel Tower illuminated by Citroën during the Paris 1925 Exhibition. Colour tinted photograph. French, 1925. Collection Tour Eiffel, Paris.

commerce (or exhibition display) but also as an important architectural component of town-planning. The 17th annual exhibition of the Paris *Salon d'automne* in 1924, for example, had included a city square comprised entirely of small shops as part of its 'Art Urbain' section.[5] Here, as elsewhere in Paris at this period, the boutique was presented as a manifestation of post-war reconstruction, an important means of restoring but also of renewing urban streets. Unlike vast department stores that housed a myriad of goods, boutiques were identified with more specialized and luxurious products, particularly those relating to the fashion and interior design industries. The design of boutiques, along with their carefully orchestrated window displays, were the object of much fascinated comment by arts journalists throughout the 1920s. The critic of the magazine *Beaux-Arts* reported on the 1925 Exhibition: 'the precious object, symbol of the merchandise on sale in the shop interior, is presented to the rapid glance of the passer-by. Boutiques too have been simplified. The commercial tabernacle with its isolated unique object has replaced the antique dealer's display.'[6] There was a growing interest in modern commercial façade architecture, but given the boutique's dramatic *vitrine* showcasing of the commodity, this form of urban renewal and modernization was associated as much with growing post-war luxury consumerism as with the efforts of particular designers or architects.[7]

Convenient, from the point of view of the promotional aspirations of the 1925 Exhibition, was the frequently reiterated identification of the luxury boutique as a specifically French, or rather, Parisian phenomenon. An essay on Parisian shop-fronts in the December 1919 issue of the post-war journal *La Renaissance de l'art français et des industries de luxe* proclaimed: 'Travellers are (for once) unanimously agreed that Paris, world capital, is the only city in the universe with luxury boutiques: they are a particularly Parisian speciality; neither Rome nor Brussels nor even London can compete.'[8] And indeed, visitors from abroad seemed in accord with such claims. The American Robert Forrest Wilson, in his book *Paris on Parade*, referred to the French capital as a 'gift and luxury shop', and Darcy Braddell penned an article for the British *Architectural Review* in praise of the 'little shops of Paris'.[9] There were significant gender implications in these characterizations of Paris as a world Mecca of luxury shops and shopping. Accounts such as those of Wilson and Braddell made it clear that their interest in this aspect of Paris was emphatically not from the point of view of the male shopper. Consumption in

13.2 The Eiffel Tower from the *rue des boutiques* in the Paris 1925 Exhibition. *Encyclopédie des arts décoratifs et industriels modernes au XXème siècle*, Paris, 1925. NAL.

13.3 The Pont Alexandre III with the *rue des boutiques* at the Paris 1925 Exhibition. Postcard. French, 1925. Private collection.

51. - EXPOSITION INTERNATIONALE DES ARTS DÉCORATIFS - PARIS 1925

VUE PANORAMIQUE DU PONT ALEXANDRE III   A. P

the shops of Paris was firmly and unequivocally defined as feminine. Wilson was quick to assert that 'it is, one must grant, primarily a woman's city we are observing. Paris's chief and most characteristic concern is with the outer adornment of women.'[10]

Notions of Paris as a woman's city played an important part in the identity and structure of the 1925 Exhibition. The *Encyclopédie* was happy to promote this image: 'Whereas men go to London for suits & shirts, women all dream of being dressed in Paris'[11] (plate 13.4). At the 1925 Exhibition those industries catering for the feminine toilette (what Wilson had referred to as 'the commerce of vanity') were prominently displayed. One of the five exhibition *groupes* was devoted to 'La Parure' and this in turn was subdivided into five *classes*: clothing, accessories, fashion, perfumes and jewellery. Although men's clothing was represented in the French section of the exhibition, the displays were predominantly of women's fashion, with an emphasis on the luxury end of the market and on expensive accessories. The exhibition's *Encyclopédie* emphasized the importance of the couture industries from the point of view of both national income and prestige, stressing that the 'art' of the couturier played an important role in the French balance of payment. Women's clothing was cited as a major export, totalling almost 2.5 billion francs in 1924.[12]

The exhibition's promotion of Paris as a 'woman's city' involved an emphasis on couture as a means of showcasing French artistic skills and 'genius'. The importance accorded to *la mode* related to claims that fashion was in some ways analogous to art itself. Fashion – the 'eighth art' as it was sometimes called – had appeared in the first post-war *Salon d'automne* in 1919 and then every year up until 1925. The status of couture, as of art, was sustained largely through the guarantee of its originality in the form of a signed 'name', as half-mockingly acknowledged by *Paris on Parade* in the chapter entitled 'Model by Pack-Ann':

Paris, to the average woman, means, primarily clothes. Clothes and style. The names and creations of Parisian clothes are familiar to her also. She knows about Worth and Lanvin and Paquin. In the fashion pages of magazines she has seen the names of Jenny and Vionnet. These are the names that thunder an imperious authority in America and throughout the rest of the world too.[13]

To devote a whole exhibition group to 'La Parure' involved not only the definition of couture as an *art décoratif* but also, more generally, a particular status for French *arts décoratifs modernes*. As a French guidebook to the 1925 Exhibition proclaimed:

13.4 Cover of *Paris: Arts décoratifs, 1925: Guide pratique du visiteur de Paris et de l'exposition*, Paris, 1925. NAL.

Is clothing – at least in its affiliation with the feminine toilet – a decorative art? It is, without a doubt, and the most venerable, that which leads all the others. It is also the art which relates most closely to modernity as it lives on surprise and novelty. In France, fashion is a major issue, a supremacy to which all our rivals must accede.[14] An identification with the production of haute couture was an important means of promoting Paris as the centre of modernity and consequently France as 'in advance' of other nations. Women's fashion defined the modern as the ephemeral, as the 'toujours du nouveau'.[15] Not only women's dress, but also everything to do with her toilette embodied this quality of the 'ever-new'. As the *Encyclopédie* commented: 'everyone finds it natural that fashion textiles should be designated by the term *nouveauté*'.[16] Thus Paris defined a modernity particularly in tune with modern consumerism, with its demands for novelty and change.

The *rue des boutiques* on the Pont Alexandre III was a glittering manifestation of this idea of Paris as world capital of luxury shopping. Overall co-ordination of the forty boutiques was the responsibility of Dufrène, but the various shop façades were individually designed by a distinguished group of architects and designers including Gabriel Guevrekian, Jacques-Emile Ruhlmann, René Herbst and Francis Jourdain. The 'street' comprised a virtual catalogue of both Parisian shop-front design and the *arts décoratifs* industries (plate 13.5). The upmarket fashion industries were extensively represented, in particular fur (Fourrures Blondell, Weil, Jungmann & Cie., T. Corby, Max, Revillon, Sonia Delaunay et

Heim, H. Vergne) and couture (Lina Mouton, Redfern); there were also displays of perfume, glass, precious metals, jewellery, interior design and furnishings. Whereas in 1889 the Eiffel Tower had allowed visitors to admire sweeping vistas of Haussmannized Paris, the *rue des boutiques* drew attention to the capital's areas of luxury shopping: around the Rue de la Paix (Delza jewellery) and the Place de la Madeleine (Fourrures Blondel); also those near the Champs-Elysées, such as the Rue Royale (A. A. Hébbard and Fourrures H. Vergne) and the Rue

13.5 Jacques-Emile Ruhlmann, Boutique des Fourrures Max at the Paris 1925 Exhibition. *Encyclopédie des arts décoratifs et industriels modernes au XXème siècle*, Paris, 1925. NAL. © ADAGP, Paris and DACS, London 2002.

13.6 Kees Van Dongen (Dutch), *Les arcades des Champs Elysées – Jardin des élégantes*, poster. Colour lithograph. 1927. V&A: E.507-1929. © ADAGP, Paris and DACS, London 2002.

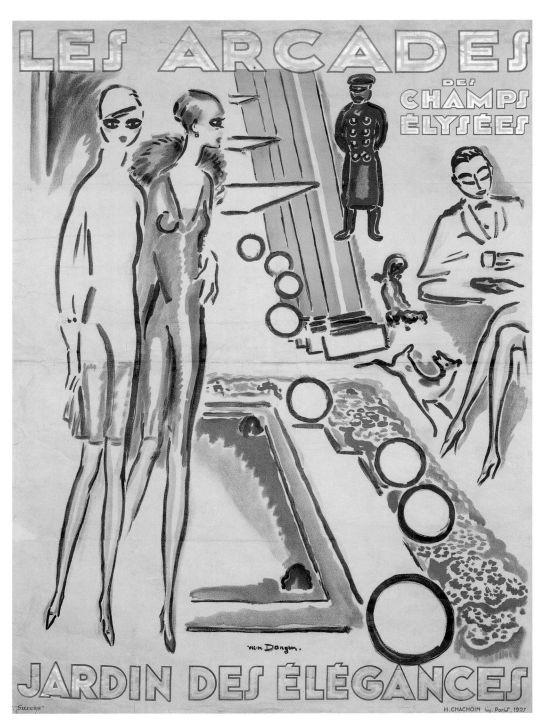

de la Boétie (Mme Pangon's Batik Français). The *Renaissance de l'art français et des industries de luxe* had proposed a similar cartography of the city as part of its campaign for a post-war renewal of Paris through its trade in luxury goods. In June 1923 the magazine focused on the exclusive areas around the Rue de la Paix and, a year later, on the streets near the Champs-Elysées (plate 13.6). *La Renaissance* proposed a distinctively feminine version of *urbanisme*: 'the dream of elegant [women] is presented as in a film which unrolls the panorama of shop-fronts on the Rue de la Paix, a paradise paved with diamonds, with shimmering textiles.'[17] The metaphor of a feminine dream as a panoramic sequence of boutiques was illustrated by photographs of the Rue de la Paix laid out as a continuous 'filmstrip' across the pages of the magazine.

In 1925 this cinematic unfolding was vividly realized in three-dimensional form along the *rue des boutiques*. The oneiric and film analogies were even more evident by night, when elaborate lighting and waterworks enhanced the dreamlike, fantasy aspects of the Pont Alexandre III. (The potency of this imagery is attested by a sequence of luridly tinted souvenir postcards depicting nocturnal views of the bridge (plate 13.7).) The exquisite presentation of a few choice luxury commodities in the modern boutique *vitrine* – dramatically staged and lit – was often described at the time as 'theatrical'. By the mid-1920s however, a comparison with cinema was in certain senses even more apt.[18] The 1925 Exhibition was the first French international exhibition to include film. As the *Encyclopédie* pointed out with relish, cinema (like photography) was a French invention. The promotion of cinema was one means of vaunting the modernity of French industrial and cultural production. The importance of the medium had been acknowledged by a series of exhibitions in Paris during the early 1920s. Like fashion (the 'eighth art') the 'seventh art', cinema, was incorporated into the post-war *Salons d'automne* (in the form of film showings), and in 1924 the Musée Galliéra showed an *Exposition de l'art dans le cinéma français*.[19] By this time, there were direct links between the *arts décoratifs* and French film production. Designers were now designing sets and costumes specifically for films. Indeed Marcel L'Herbier's 1924 *L'Inhumaine* has been described as a kind of dress rehearsal for the 1925 Exhibition; the film incorporated work by a whole range of artists, architects and designers who were to exhibit in 1925.[20] *L'Inhumaine* was evidence that, like the boutique, film could function as a showcase for modern French *arts décoratifs* (see plate 30.2).

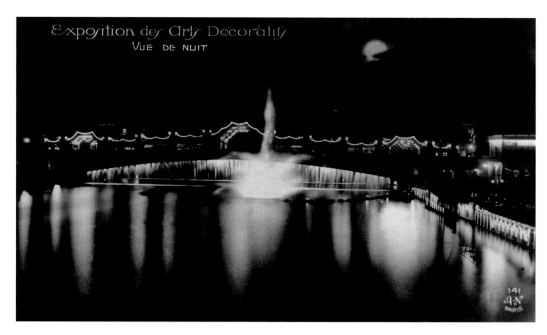

13.7 Night view of the Pont Alexandre III at the Paris 1925 Exhibition. Tinted postcard. French, 1925. Private collection.

There are further parallels to be drawn between the French boutique and cinema as manifestations and purveyors of 1920s modernity. At this date cinema was still (predominantly) a silent medium. The 1925 *Encyclopédie* stressed that by comparison with the theatre, film was a 'royaume du silence' and hence a more intrinsically visual experience.[21] A similar emphasis on muteness and visuality occurs in descriptions of the modern boutique. In a review of the boutiques displayed at the 1924 *Salon d'automne* a critic proclaimed: 'the boutiques of the past never had this ... silent countenance which is a product of modern urbanism'.[22] Here the display of individual (or very few) objects in the shop window was seen as 'silent' by comparison with the profusion (loquacity) of goods put on show in earlier periods. These ideas of a silent commerce were dramatically embodied by new types of window mannequin: 'mute' in their abstracted and non-realistic facial features, eye-catching as a result of their shiny and alluring surfaces.[23] It was argued that the pace of contemporary life had resulted in forms of selling that relied exclusively on the visual, as opposed to the more time-consuming sales patter and oral skills of shop personnel. Boutique windows, it would seem, were symptomatic of modernity in that they had transformed selling primarily into a matter of soliciting the gaze. One might compare this fascination with the isolation of individual commodities in the shop *vitrine* with the extensive writing at the period on the cinematic close-up. Both the boutique and the close-up were concerned, to borrow the words of the painter Fernand Léger,

with 'making images seen'.[24] A rather bizarre attempt to conjoin the impact of shop window and cinema screen is illustrated in a 1925 issue of the advertising journal *Vendre: Tout ce qui concerne la vente et la publicité*. This shows a novel means of selling: the *Ecran-Stop!* – a 'cinema' in a shop window.[25]

Anita Loos's 1925 comic novel, *Gentlemen Prefer Blondes: The Illuminating Diary of a Professional Lady*, gives us another, transatlantic take on notions of modernity construed in terms of Paris, women shoppers and, indeed, the cinema.[26] Lorelei Lee, the 'dumb blonde' protagonist and author of this *Illuminating Diary*, hails from Little Rock, Arkansas. The *Diary*, however tongue-in-cheek, is evidence of the fact that the 'dream' of Paris as a woman's city was not confined to France. Lorelei Lee's assessment that whereas 'London is Really Nothing', 'Paris is Devine [sic]' (titles to chapters three and four respectively) is based entirely on the possibilities for feminine expenditure afforded by the French capital. Lorelei keenly appreciates the 'authority of names' on which the Parisian luxury and beauty industries were based:

> And when a girl walks around and reads all of the signs with all of the famous historical names it really makes you hold your breath ... So when we stood at the corner of a place called the Place Vendôme, if you turn your back on a monument they have in the middle and look up, you can see none other than Coty's sign.[27]

Her enjoyment of the 'Eyefull' Tower is symptomatic of the fact that the visual enticements of Paris are directed at a specifically feminine audience; in Lorelei's own words: 'shopping really seems to be what Paris is principally for'.[28]

In *Gentlemen Prefer Blondes*, relationships with men are established primarily as a means of funding an 'educational' European Grand Tour of shopping excursions, a tour in which Paris forms the highlight. In a humorous context, the idea of an American shopping trip to Paris as 'educational' was long established.[29] To take one highly popular example: Charles Dana Gibson's bestselling folio album of illustrations, *The Education of Mr. Pipp* (published in 1899), includes scenes of Pipp's two glamorous daughters taking him to the Rue de la Paix in order to buy expensive jewellery and haute couture outfits. The caption reads: 'He has the opportunity of enlarging his horizon and of developing an interest in the real purpose of the trip.'[30] By 1925, the figure of the rapacious, out-of-control female shopper in Paris – along with her hapless and helpless male source of income – was familiar on both sides of the Atlantic, from serious fiction such as Emile Zola's 1883 novel *Bonheur des Dames* to Gibson's comical *Mr. Pipp*. The difference in the case of *Gentlemen Prefer Blondes* lay in the fact that its author was a woman who used the character of the female shopper in order to produce an explicitly feminine voice for the novel's protagonist. *Gentlemen Prefer Blondes* is an extremely funny novel; it is also very clever. Loos effectively shows up and mocks the stereotype of the woman shopper, partly through exaggeration, partly (the reader is led to suspect) because Loos finds it so easy inhabit the stereotype. At the same time the very fact of the book's sly wit undermines any idea of femininity as 'dumb'; this woman author is clearly neither mute nor stupid.

As the product of a woman writer, *Gentlemen Prefer Blondes* alerts us to an important aspect of early twentieth-century modernity: women's engagement with professional work. According to her autobiography, *A Girl like I*, Loos was born in California in 1893 and started writing film scripts at the age of twelve. She became a well known figure in the Hollywood film industry, writing scenarios for D. W. Griffith and Douglas Fairbanks. Although written over forty years after *Gentlemen Prefer Blondes*, it is notable that *A Girl like I* describes Loos's own career in film in terms reminiscent of her 1925 book. Indeed, Loos's autobiographical persona is strikingly similar to the dizzy flapper image of Lorelei Lee. The novel concludes with Lorelei marrying a rich husband as a means of embarking upon a career in the film industry. Her husband's money is to fund not only her stardom as a film actress, but also the scripts of a new gentleman friend. Lorelei's infatuation with cinema has (for the moment at least) displaced her lust for shopping; the final chapter of *Gentlemen Prefer Blondes* is entitled 'Brains are Really Everything'. In her autobiography, however, Loos goes one further, making no claims for her scriptwriting as intellectual work. She asserts that her writing was effortless and undertaken mainly to earn money in order to buy haute couture outfits by her favourite Parisian designers. Indeed, she seems to take as much pride in claiming that her newly bobbed hairdo influenced Parisian fashion as in her writing and achievements in the film industry.

This insistent emphasis on a consumerist femininity alongside reminiscences of a woman engaged in professional work relates in interesting ways to 1920s preoccupations with the *femme moderne*. As Mary Louise Roberts has argued in *Civilisation without Sexes*, the *femme moderne* was a product of the First World War.[31] Debates about the modern woman were one means of expressing anxieties about post-war social change, such as increasing consumerism and the instability of gender identities produced (in part) by the work and new professional opportunities now open to women. There were fears that with modernization both men and women had become unsexed. These anxieties are evident in the film and literature of the period. The female protagonist of the revealingly titled *L'Inhumaine* is a successful professional singer. It is the task of the film's narrative to transform this 'inhuman' (cold and heartless) character into a reassuringly feminine and loving woman. A similar process of refeminizing takes place in Victor Margueritte's bestselling novel *La Garçonne* (1922), in which the heroine runs an interior design shop. The *femme moderne* was thus a complex figure: threatening insofar as she signified destabilization and loss of established identities, tantalizing in her

13.8 Georges Lepape, cover for British *Vogue*, showing a model wearing a Sonia Delaunay 'simultaneous' dress, next to a 'simultaneous' car. January 1925. NAL. © ADAGP, Paris and DACS, London 2002.

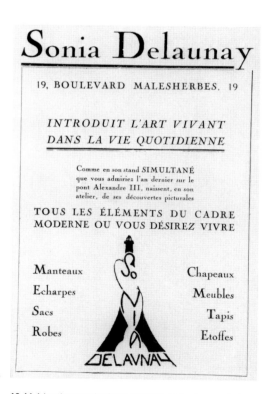

13.9 Sonia Delaunay's designs displayed in her Boutique Simultanée at the Paris 1925 Exhibition. René Herbst, *Devantures, vitrines, installations de magasins à l'Exposition internationale des arts décoratifs*, Paris, 1925. NAL. © L&M Services B. V. Amsterdam 20020402.

13.10 Sonia Delaunay (Russian), jacket. Cotton, wool and silk. 1924. Musée de la Mode et du Textile, Paris. Collection of the Union Française des Arts du Costume. Photo: Laurent Sully Jaulmes. © L&M Services B. V. Amsterdam 20020704.

promise of innovation and change. And above all, fashionable – during the 1920s there were any number of permutations on the 'boyish' *garçonne* look, characterized by cropped hair and short skirts.[32]

By 1925 therefore, the fascination with Paris as a 'woman's city' involved more than merely opportunities for luxury shopping. In its feminine guise 'Paris' signified a burgeoning consumerism that offered women new fantasies of freedom and liberation.[33] These fantasies were epitomized by images of the glamorous woman driver, the latest permutation on the theme of the fashionable female consumer.[34] But this version of Paris also designated a modernity in which, to a limited but growing extent, women appeared prominently as cultural producers.[35] There were clear indications of women's artistic production on the Pont Alexandre III with, for example, the boutiques displaying designs by Mme Pangon and Sonia Delaunay (plate 13.9). Delaunay's designs, characterized by bold geometrical patterns, were explicitly identified with the 1920s modern woman. Her stylish coats were bought by film actresses (such as Gloria Swanson) and by avant-garde artists and designers.[36] Photographs of models wearing Delaunay's fashions

in the 1925 Exhibition grounds show the quintessential *femme moderne*: the mannequins sport bobbed hair, cloche hats, short skirts – and a car decorated to match their chic outfit (plates 13.8 and 13.10, and see plate 23.3). Shortly after the exhibition, Delaunay went on to extend the range of her professional activities by producing fashion and textile designs for the cinema, for films about the fashionable lifestyle of the post-war nouveaux riches.[37] The success of Delaunay's designs is indicative of the importance of modernistic *art décoratif* as a means of representing the *femme moderne*, not only in her guise as updated *femme fatale* (the protagonist of so many popular 1920s films and novels) but also as the independent, professional woman. Delaunay's 1920s logo in which her name (Sonia) appears in the form of a curvaceous nude superimposed on a silhouette of the Eiffel Tower is a visually succinct and witty advertisement for her design practice (plate 13.11). It is also an acknowledgement of a modernity in which women's consumption and the possibilities for a feminine identity as professional practitioner not only coexisted but were in certain ways inextricably linked.[38]

Sonia Delaunay

19, BOULEVARD MALESHERBES, 19

INTRODUIT L'ART VIVANT DANS LA VIE QUOTIDIENNE

Comme en son stand SIMULTANÉ que vous admiriez l'an dernier sur le pont Alexandre III, naissent, en son atelier, de ses découvertes picturales

TOUS LES ÉLÉMENTS DU CADRE MODERNE OU VOUS DÉSIREZ VIVRE

Manteaux	Chapeaux
Echarpes	Meubles
Sacs	Tapis
Robes	Etoffes

13.11 Advertisement for Sonia Delaunay in *Programme de la Comédie des Champs-Elysées*, 1925-6. Bibliothèque Nationale de France, Paris. © L&M Services B. V. Amsterdam 20020704.

Boudoir par Gabriel Englinger
et Suzanne Guiguichon

Salle à manger par Maurice Du
frène

hall par Maurice Dufrène

architecture ~~ Décoration
meubles ~~ tapisserie ~ ride-
aux ~ voilages ~ tapis ~ tissu
soierie ~ coussins ~ broderies

Dentelles ~~ batik ~~ filets ~
papiers peints ~ céramique ~
peinture ~~ sculpture ~~ cris
tallerie ~~~ verrerie ~~~~~

lustre ~ luminaires ~~
ques ~ abat-jour ~ lampes
bronze, bimbloterie ~ ~
~ services de table ~~ nap

14 The Artist-Decorator

Stéphane Laurent

Art Deco came about in France as the result of a complex economic and cultural process with its roots in the nineteenth century. And, to some extent, it even seems to have been planned by a new pressure group: the artist-decorators.[1] With the rise of eclecticism, decoration and ornament had assumed greater importance in architecture during the nineteenth century. As a result, around 1875, a new term – the 'decorative arts' – was invented, and it had the effect of raising the status of this area of production.[2] At the same time, the authority of the architect, who had formerly controlled every detail of interior decoration, was challenged by a new figure: the artist-decorator. His origins are obscure: in earlier times he might have been an upholsterer, an interior decorator or a skilled craftsman but, as the nineteenth century reached its end, he began to assert himself as a master in his own right.

The upholsterer specialized in fabric coverings for furniture as well as in wall hangings and curtains. From the Second Empire (1851-70) onwards, his work became more prestigious because of the fashion for textiles that invaded the eclectic interiors. The upholsterer had to be a competent draughtsman and his control of the harmony of the ensemble, through his use of motifs and colours, eventually gave him total responsibility for the decoration of the interior. Gradually, the upholsterer replaced the architect in the domain of furnishing, co-ordinating the craftsmen who made the furniture, metalwork, ironwork, glass and ceramics.

Like the upholsterer, the industrial artist also aspired to social advancement. He originated as a skilled craftsman in one of the professions. In his workshop he was capable of producing both copies of traditional styles and objects designed by an architect or an artist. With the advance of democracy in France, training became available in the schools of applied arts, specially oriented to teach these craftsman drawing and composition and to give them a general education in the history of art and style. Museums and collections were also formed with the aim of educating such students. Instruction in

drawing for craftsmen had been available in France since the eighteenth century. However, the Great Exhibition of 1851 and the subsequent foundation of the South Kensington Schools and Museum prompted the establishment of new schools of art and design in France, as in Germany and elsewhere. The most famous of these were the Ecole Boulle and Ecole Estienne in Paris. This institutional support was originally intended to remedy the inadequate workshop apprenticeships that had evolved following the suppression of the guilds after the French Revolution.[3] These initiatives, which resulted from the rapidly increasing international competition for knowledge and commercial advantage, had an unexpected and unwelcome side effect, however. The industrial artists trained in the schools were rejected by the craftsmen in the workshops because they knew too much. Excluded from the traditional career-pattern, but well able to use their knowledge to exploit the rich field of the art professions, they gradually developed a new status, that of the artist-decorator. They exchanged blue collar for white collar and assumed a role that was much more attractive to them.

As the artist-decorators grew in confidence, they sought to establish an identity distinct from that of traditional craftsmen. As a result, they united to found the Société des Artistes Décorateurs (SAD) in 1901. Largely as a result of their efforts, legislation on artistic and industrial property rights was passed shortly afterwards. This defined the artist-decorators' right to be acknowledged as authors, a sign of the passionate quest for individuality and originality that characterized much artistic production in the first decade of the twentieth century.

Members of the SAD rapidly embraced the idea of a major international exhibition as a means of giving status to their production.[4] During the nineteenth century, governments had invested significant sums in World Fairs in order to promote trade and stimulate local industries.[5] From the 1860s onwards, French industrial artists began to take initiatives on their own behalf. Through the Union Centrale des

14.1 Advertising brochure for La Maîtrise, three interior views of the La Maîtrise pavilion at the Paris 1925 Exhibition. Bibliothèque Historique de la Ville de Paris.

Beaux-Arts Appliqués à l'Industrie, founded in 1864, they organized exhibitions in Paris. After a break during the 1870s, these exhibitions resumed under the Union's auspices.[6] Each took the theme of a single material (wood, metal, textiles and so on); however, they did not continue for long. At around the same time, after a half-century of growth, World Fairs arrived at saturation point: the exponential growth of knowledge and production made it impossible to show everything. The last exhibition of this type took place in Paris in 1900. In 1902, the *Prima esposizione internazionale d'arte decorative moderna* in Turin set a precedent for a new kind of international exhibition, devoted to the applied arts and focused on new design ideas.

Responding to these developments, French artist-decorators took up the campaign for a similar kind of exhibition, publicizing their ideas in the specialist press, which included a number of journals dedicated to the decorative arts, such as *Art et décoration*, *L'Art décoratif moderne* and the *Revue des arts décoratifs*. They already had experience of exhibiting, having shown their work in the decorative arts sections introduced in the annual exhibitions of the Société Nationale des Beaux-Arts, the Société des Artistes Français and, later, the *Salon d'automne*. Then, in

1904, they set up their own biennial exhibition at the SAD, where they exhibited art objects and furnishings. In 1911, the President of the SAD, the lawyer René Guilleré, submitted a report to the government on the desirability of an international exhibition of decorative arts in Paris. It was based on opportunist arguments about the need to counter 'the crisis' in the French art industries and to defend the French decorative arts.

Arguments of this kind had assumed a new vigour in France in the early twentieth century, with Germany's rise to economic power and its success in promoting German decorative arts in international exhibitions and markets (see Chapters 8 and 12). The influx of cheap German products of fairly modern appearance was seen as a threat to France's balance of trade. Anti-German feeling was still current after France's defeat in the Franco-Prussian War of 1870, and the subsequent loss of Alsace-Lorraine increased French animosity towards the Germans. Several formal inquiries were undertaken in an effort to understand the '*boche* system' and the reasons for German success. For example, the critic Marius Vachon compiled a report during the 1880s;[7] and later the sculptor François Rupert Carabin and even the young Charles-Edouard Jeanneret (later known as

Le Corbusier) were commissioned to make reports.[8] All underlined that the lead taken by the new nation was a result of German organization in creating efficient networks to link institutions, producers, designers and distributors.

The principle of the proposed international exhibition was approved in 1912; initially scheduled for 1915, its realization was postponed in 1914. During the First World War, however, the French government gave way to the artist-decorators' demands. The unprecedented spirit of national solidarity of these years allowed Albert Dalimier, Under-Secretary of State for the Fine Arts, to establish committees for the applied arts in 1916. These became active institutions of industrial-aesthetic propaganda. Among others, Louis Bonnier, Victor Prouvé, Emmanuel Pontrémoli and Hector Guimard chaired some of these committees; and Charles-Edouard Jeanneret was a member. A vast nationwide survey was undertaken to identify centres of decorative arts production. An 'offensive' was launched immediately after the end of the war, when the committees began – with varying degrees of success – the task of converting the least reluctant craftsmen to modern aesthetics. Regulations were also established for intending exhibitors. These were strict: no copies of historic models were to be allowed, only works of a modern character. This arbitrary regulation gave impetus to the emergence of the Art Deco style: through the establishment of a doctrinal aesthetic, the movement can be said to have been 'constructed'.

After 1917, two preparatory exhibitions of modern industrial art were organized at the Pavillon de Marsan in Paris. The regional committees also worked to promote the new aesthetic in the main provincial industrial centres, such as Rennes, Grenoble, Roubaix, Bordeaux and Nancy. Public awareness of the issues was promoted through lectures, competitions for students and continued training of the teaching staff in art schools. In 1921, Paul Steck, an academic Symbolist artist, who was also an inspector of the teaching of drawing, was

14.2 Louis Vuitton, travel case or *nécessaire Marthe Chenal*. French, exhibited at the Paris 1925 Exhibition. Musée Louis Vuitton, Asnières. © **LOUIS VUITTON MALLETIER**.

14.3 Marc Ducluzeaud and René Lalique, fountain in front of the Lalique pavilion at the Paris 1925 Exhibition. Pierre Patout, *L'Architecture officielle et les pavillons: Exposition des arts décoratifs et industriels modernes*, Paris, 1925. NAL. © ADAGP, Paris and DACS, London 2002.

made Inspector General of the Applied Arts, with the objective of co-ordinating action. Acting on behalf of Paul Léon, the Director of the Beaux-Arts, Steck became one of the *éminences grises* behind the 1925 Exhibition. The effects of these initiatives were piecemeal, however. Manufacturers who were confident of success with products in traditional styles were reluctant to exchange these for modern designs that did not have an assured market.

With the benefit of hindsight, it seems clear that a unique development occurred in France in the 1910s and early 1920s. Many factors contributed to the rise of Art Deco there. They included a reaction against Art Nouveau; an increasing complicity between critics, institutions and artist-decorators; responses to the challenge of German competition; and the solidarity of an enterprising younger generation which had been relatively untouched by the war.[9] By contrast, many of the foreign countries that were invited to participate in the 1925 Exhibition seem to have lagged behind in the development of the style.

Art Deco was immediately seen as a way of reinvigorating the French luxury goods industry. Indeed, the periodical *Renaissance de l'art français et des industries de luxe* was launched with precisely this objective in 1919. It was intended to promote the introduction of new forms in a traditional sector that had only reluctantly embraced Art Nouveau. There were precedents for this kind of initiative. The firms Gaston-Louis Vuitton and Bouilhet-Christofle had long been members of the official commissions on the decorative arts. They were particularly active in the Société de l'Encouragement de l'Art et l'Industrie (SEAI) and supported training for industrial artists. And since the nineteenth century all the leading French luxury goods firms had employed

artists and designers and promoted new designs, even if these were mostly limited to their exhibits in industrial and universal exhibitions (plate 14.2).

In the French sections of the 1925 Exhibition most exhibits were luxury goods. Firms such as Christofle for goldsmithing, Baccarat, Fauquez and Lalique for glass, and Fontaine for high-quality locks had their showcases on the Esplanade des Invalides. These mostly had specially designed pavilions conceived to complement their own new designs. Raoul Dufy's fabrics became famous in this way; and René Lalique's pavilion, with its monumental fountain, contributed to the fame and success of the Lalique firm (plate 14.3). However, firms that subsequently went out of business, like Fontaine, have largely been forgotten.

The site and construction costs of these pavilions seem to have been so high that some firms, such as Baccarat and Christofle, shared resources. Regional groups, probably following the advice of the regional committees, brought together local industries. Thus the pavilions of Lyon, Nancy and Saint-Etienne, and Roubaix and Tourcoing focused on textiles, Grenoble on glove making and Mulhouse on wallpaper. Here, once again, the initiative seems to have come from umbrella institutions rather than from the enterprises concerned. There were also initiatives to develop a bank of regional knowledge. The exhibition's impact on tourism was anticipated, as is shown by the example of the Alpes-Maritimes pavilion, and the City of Paris was well represented. A myriad of famous French firms also had stands in specialized sections of the exhibition, in the Grand Palais or in the boutiques on the Pont Alexandre III (see plate 13.3).

Until now, industrially produced Art Deco in France – being far removed from the prestige commissions given to artist-decorators by the bourgeoisie, the

business class, couturiers and theatrical stars – has been little studied. Some artist-decorators, such as Louis Süe and André Mare or André Fréchet, had designs for mass production in their portfolios, but chose to show unique objects – which were more prestigious – at the exhibition. A few, including Michel Dufet, were interested in design for mass production as the central aim of their work. However, Dufet was in Brazil in 1925, directing a firm making industrial furniture, and did not participate in the exhibition. Few businesses were convinced right from the start that they should participate in the exhibition. The art critic Marius Vachon, an early proponent of industrial art, led opposition to the Comité des Arts Appliqués, which he dubbed the 'Soviet of French industry' because of its aesthetic dogma. Only the Parisian industries were persuaded – though not without misgivings – to share the views of artist-decorators. Albert Goumain, for example, the President of the Fédération du Meuble, had difficulty convincing cabinetmakers to give up producing copies of former styles in favour of models designed by artist-decorators. Sculptors in wood complained about the scant attention paid to relief decoration in designs for Art Deco furniture. And although the 'industrial arts' were mentioned in the exhibition title, in practice they were only shown in an indirect manner: there were few examples of design for the new industries (such as transport). Those designs for a more popular market that were submitted were dispersed among the luxury goods and failed to attract attention. As a result, this aspect of the exhibition has been largely overlooked.

Among industrial and commercial exhibitors, the most enthusiastic and most important were the leading French department stores (plates 14.4, 14.5, 14.6 and 14.7). Since the *belle époque*, former students from the schools of applied arts, such as the professional school run by the Boulle furniture manufactory in Paris, had been recruited by these stores for their decoration departments. They designed an Art Nouveau pavilion for Printemps at the Paris 1900 Exhibition, at which Le Bon Marché and the Magasins du Louvre were also represented. Subsequently the stores established their own in-house studios which designed modern *objets d'art* and furnishings.

14.4 Henri Sauvage and Georges Vibo, Primavera pavilion for the Grands Magasins du Printemps at the Paris 1925 Exhibition. Pierre Patout, *L'Architecture officielle et les pavillons: Exposition internationale des arts décoratifs et industriels modernes*, Paris, 1925. NAL.

14.5 Louis Hippolyte Boileau, Pomone pavilion for Bon Marché at the Paris 1925 Exhibition. Pierre Patout, *L'Architecture officielle et les pavillons: Exposition internationale des arts décoratifs et industriels modernes*, Paris, 1925. NAL.

14.6 Joseph Hiriart, Georges Tribout and Georges Beau, La Maîtrise pavilion for Galeries Lafayette at the Paris 1925 Exhibition. Pierre Patout, *L'Architecture officielle et les pavillons: Exposition internationale des arts décoratifs et industriels modernes*, Paris, 1925. NAL.

14.7 Albert Laprade, Studium Louvre pavilion for the Grands Magasins du Louvre at the Paris 1925 Exhibition. Pierre Patout, *L'Architecture officielle et les pavillons: Exposition internationale des arts décoratifs et industriels modernes*, Paris, 1925. NAL.

14.8 Louis Süe and André Mare, Compagnie des Arts Français, chandelier. Glass. French, c.1924. V&A: C.146-1980.

14.9 Jean-Jacques Adnet, chandelier. French, c.1929. *Art et industrie*, January 1929. Bibliothèque Nationale de France, Paris. © ADAGP, Paris and DACS, London 2002.

The reasons for this development, which gave a new dimension to what had hitherto been an elitist movement in the decorative arts, need to be further researched.[10] Printemps was the first to take the initiative. The store had participated in the *Salon d'automne* in 1909 and, three years later, called in René Guilleré, who was by then well known, to take charge of a new design studio named Primavera. Guilleré had a legal background and was gifted in managing people, and it was probably he who convinced the director of Printemps of the need for a new department specializing in contemporary decoration, to match competition in the Parisian market from the German and Austrian Werkstätten.[11] The Primavera studio had a slow beginning: at first it only employed two artist-decorators but the number of staff quickly grew, with the recruitment of architects and craftsmen, and soon about 20 people were employed.

Primavera was the only design studio of its kind for nearly ten years. It was only after the First World War that other department stores decided to set up design studios, to profit from the craze for Art Deco in the wake of Primavera's success. Galeries Lafayette set up La Maîtrise in 1921; Bon Marché set up Pomone and the Magasins du Louvre set up Studium Louvre in the following year. In the absence of reliable figures it is difficult to estimate the extent

of their production. However, in March 1924, an advertisement by Primavera mentioned 9,327 models in its range, which indicates the success of its products. Although some of their designs belonged in the *de luxe* category, the design studios also used less costly materials with simplified but elegant forms to attract a less wealthy clientele. Only Paul Follot, the director of Pomone, was opposed in principle to the idea of mass production, fearing the effects of a decline in quality. He offered a fairly classical range of products to his clients, far removed from the more stripped down, modernistic style produced by Studium Louvre. The designs produced by the Maîtrise and Primavera studios offered a balance between these two extremes (plate 14.1). This diversity of production confirmed the heterogeneous character of Art Deco and undoubtedly suited the dynamics of the commercial market.[12]

The department stores assured the popularization of Art Deco by their sense of initiative and the links they established between art, mass communication, commerce and industry. In the early 1920s, Primavera had two factories belonging to Printemps. One was at Montreuil-sous-Bois and produced furniture, carpets, ironwork and 'staff' (reinforced plaster). The other was at Sainte-Radegonde, near Tours, and produced ceramics and objects in stone.

The Primavera design studio employed more than 300 craftsmen in Paris, in the provinces and in the colonies. As a result of this network, they could call on local expertise. This regional strategy was developed among craftsmen in the Nivernais and Berry regions, as well as Provence and Alsace, and culminated in the annual organization of a *petite foire* (small trade fair) by Printemps during the 1930s. Primavera's decentralized activities were in tune with contemporary aspirations towards regional expression in the decorative arts, a movement led by the critic Léandre Vaillat.[13]

Apart from the department stores, there were several other decorating studios in Paris. These were mostly run by furniture manufacturers, the traditional spearhead in the decorative arts. Meubles Artistiques Modernes (MAM) was founded in 1913 by Michel Dufet and produced furniture for the upper end of the luxury market. It managed to maintain production throughout the First World War and later worked with the painter Louis Bureau. The business was finally sold to the P. A. Dumas company, which continued to produce furniture until 1924, when it closed down. The Compagnie des Arts Français (CAF) was founded in 1919, under the directorship of Louis Süe and André Mare. They commissioned designs on a freelance basis from painters, sculptors and artist-decorators. The CAF was one of the few companies besides the department stores to produce designs in a variety of media. Besides furniture, it made glassware, fabrics, carpets and metalwork (plate 14.8). In 1928, the CAF was taken over by La Maîtrise, which appointed Jacques Adnet as director. He broke with the classicist Art Deco style of CAF and introduced a decorative Modernism (plate 14.9). In the same year, which seems to mark the end of the modernized traditional strand of Art Deco, Dufet took charge of the art workshop Le Sylve, which belonged to the shop Au Bûcheron. There too he imposed the same modernistic approach but, while he still produced luxury furniture, he also made cheap, good quality, mass-produced items.[14]

There was also another well-known design studio that had the same dual production policy: Décoration Intérieure Moderne (DIM), founded in 1914. It was directed by the cabinetmaker René Joubert and the theatrical designer Georges Nouveau, who was replaced in 1922 by Philippe Petit. The increasing overlap between Art Deco and Modernism seems to have posed few problems; and major projects were undertaken alongside the design and production of textiles, light fittings and furniture. This adaptability allowed collaboration between Art Deco enterprises and designers who are better known as Modernists, such as Jacques Le Chevallier and Jean Prouvé.

In extending the range of products on offer, the design studios had to employ designers and artist-decorators. Maurice Dufrène, who directed La Maîtrise, made its products synonymous with originality. Like the Behrens studio at AEG, the French design studios were a seedbed of talent. Some designers stayed long enough to gain considerable professional experience: these included Louis Sognot and Jean Burkhalter at Pomone, and Jacques Viénot – who later came to be considered as the founder of industrial design in France – at DIM. The style filtered down through designers during their training, and many subsequently set up their own design studios. Moreover, the department stores' design studios maintained close links with artist-decorators in other ways: they regularly showed in the exhibitions put on by the SAD and at the *Salon d'automne* and also placed advertisements in decorative arts journals, including *L'Esprit nouveau*.

Architecture apart, and despite its emphasis on luxury goods, the influence of the 1925 Exhibition in France can be measured as much in terms of the anonymous products of industry as in signed pieces. The domestic environment was modernized while its constitution was respected. The exhibition provided a large degree of inspiration for the models shown in the *Larousse ménager* (a household manual published in 1926 that had a wide circulation). And the Manufrance catalogue illustrated examples of Art Deco stoves, carpets and light fittings into the 1930s. The motif of the 'Cubist rose' was endlessly reproduced. It can be found, for example, on panels of enamelled ironware used in Alsatian kitchen equipment made by Godin (plate 14.10). Nevertheless, Art Deco designs were in the minority among the output of Godin and Manufrance, appearing as subsidiary sections in catalogues mainly presenting crude-looking objects best described as eclectic.

The overall impression given by the new *Salon des arts ménagers* (SAM), established in 1923 by Jules-Louis Breton, is similar. This Salon was first put on at the Champs-de-Mars and then at the Grand Palais in Paris, and was very successful. Around 100,000 visitors flocked to the early Salons, and their numbers grew over the years. The 1925 Exhibition had emphasized the progress made as a result of the introduction of gas, electricity and running water, through exhibits, illustrations and lectures, and the new Salon fulfilled the growing ambitions of the French public for domestic comfort and mechanical equipment. Its initiative was pursued by journals such as *Arts ménagers*, founded in 1927, and *Mon chez moi*, the publication of the Institut d'Organisation Ménagère founded by Paulette Bernège.[15]

Most of the objects shown in the early Salons were technical inventions that took no account of aesthetic considerations, and the contrast between the design of French goods and German and American goods soon became obvious. Only Calor took much care with the appearance of its electrical appliances, though some companies that had links with interior decoration, such as Lampe Berger, showed a sense of style in the design of their products. Similarly, manufacturers of Bakelite objects, such as the radio sets made by TSF (Téléphonie sans Fil), or products such as cigarette cases or boxes, took advantage of the new material to use modern shapes. However, it was undoubtedly in the rapidly developing field of visual communication that Art Deco found its greatest opportunities. Posters publicizing the products and many of the exhibition stands employed playful, naïve motifs and compositions, deliberately stylized and modernistic.

When the artist-decorators invented Art Nouveau at the end of the nineteenth century, they undoubtedly did not foresee that it would be a more ephemeral style than those of the Ancien Régime (such as Louis XIV or Louis XV). The reason for the style's short life is not difficult to identify: its apparent discontinuity with past styles and its stress on individualism. Ultimately Art Deco met a similar fate. It ended up being criticized for its heavy and rather aggressive forms. Increasingly, too, its forms converged with those of Modernism on the one hand and a twentieth-century form of stripped classicism on the other. As a style of compromise – even a 'constructed' style – Art Deco successfully established the artist-decorators' control over the French luxury goods industries, but this endeavour was short-lived. Its successful integration into the luxury domain made Art Deco a fashion that, for a short time, allowed the renewal of consumer products. Nevertheless, in opening the door to industrial aesthetics and design in France, it had a more lasting legacy.

14.10 Godin, stove, panel decorated with a 'Cubist rose'. Enamelled iron. *Catalogue Godin*, 1934.

PART 4

The Spread of Deco

15 Germany, Austria and the Netherlands

Reino Liefkes

Regional variants of Art Deco flourished in Germany, Austria and the Netherlands. In each of these countries, the development of new styles took place against a background of discussion about modern and historic styles, national identity and internationalism, folk art and exotic influences, crafts and mass production. As a consequence, despite the often widely different results, similar decorative tendencies based on conservative and popular responses to modernity can be observed. The Paris 1925 Exhibition provides a snapshot that enables us to compare tendencies in Austria and the Netherlands. Germany was invited to exhibit, in December 1924, but declined. Diplomatic relations with France were at an all-time low as a result of Germany's failure to pay war reparations, and it was too late to prepare a major display by April 1925, when the exhibition opened.[1]

Germany

Since the early years of the twentieth century, German architects and designers had been forging closer relationships with manufacturing industry, crafts workshops and retailers, in an effort to create a new style that was less individualist than Jugendstil and better suited to a modern, increasingly middle-class society. The Deutscher Werkbund, established in 1907 in Munich, brought together architects, designers and manufacturers with the aim of increasing the design quality of machine-produced goods. At the same time, artists and designers began to collaborate with small-scale, semi-industrialized workshops, benefiting from Germany's many skilled craftsmen. Some of the best known German designers of the Jugendstil period, such as Richard Riemerschmid and Bruno Paul, worked within such collaborative workshops to achieve a greatly simplified style suitable for standardization and machine production (see plate 8.10).[2]

The German government supported the development of the decorative arts as a source of national prestige and economic potential. Exhibitions of contemporary decorative arts were regularly shown abroad and in Germany itself. Also, a well organized teaching system was developed, which secured the influence of the best senior designers on younger generations. In 1901 Henry van de Velde became Director of the arts school in Weimar, where he soon founded a separate school of decorative arts. Riemerschmid became Director of the Kunstgewerbeschule (Decorative Arts School) in Munich in 1913, and after the First World War Bruno Paul became Director of the Vereinigte Staatsschulen für freie und angewandte Kunst (School for Fine and Applied Art) in Berlin. These initiatives paid off: by the years immediately preceding the First World War Germany had secured the position of the world's leading exporter of decorative arts.[3] The war, however, brought an abrupt end to this success. Germany was totally defeated, disillusioned and bankrupt. Industry now had little time for the Werkbund's aesthetic considerations, and when Walter Gropius combined van de Velde's two schools in Weimar to create the Bauhaus in 1919, its most radical ideas found their way into art education.

Histories of German design of the inter-war period have focused on the free utopian Modernism of the Weimar period – particularly as it was represented by the Bauhaus – and on the state-controlled absolutist art of the Nazi period.[4] Between these two extremes, however, there existed a group of designers firmly rooted in Germany's historic past who showed a clear historic inspiration, while being unmistakably modern in their use of standardized furniture types.[5] This style first emerged in the years immediately preceding the First World War and was represented by the work of a group of Munich designers associated with the Vereinigte Werkstätte für Kunst im Handwerk (United Workshops for Art in Handicraft). Their exhibit at the Paris *Salon d'automne* in 1910 made a deep impression on French critics and designers (see Chapter 8). Here interiors designed by Richard Riemerschmid, Théodor Veil, Adalbert Niemeyer, Paul Wenz, Richard Berndl and Karl Bertsch and others displayed an unmistakably historic inspiration; their use of simplified shapes, bold contrasting colours and careful overall co-ordination can be seen as proto-Art Deco (see plate 8.2).

This tendency continued after the war in several centres in Germany. One only has to glance through the pages of the influential magazine *Deutsche Kunst und Dekoration* to realize how widespread and influential it was throughout the inter-war years. Interiors by architects and designers such as F. A. Breuhaus, Bruno Paul, Karl Bertsch, Emil Fahrenkamp and Leo Nachtlicht show a similar restrained, simplified and modernized use of historical style and bourgeois formality, combined with surprisingly strong and vibrant colours. Compared to the Munich decorators' work in 1910, however, there is a more playful attitude towards historicism. The Biedermeier and Rococo styles provided the main sources of inspiration. German Art Deco designers, like those elsewhere, also drew on 'exotic' sources, but they chose a western historicist angle, focusing mainly on Rococo-style Chinoiserie. Although much of their ornamentation is used in a traditional way, it is distinctly modern in detail. A cabinet designed by Gerhard Schliepstein is typical in this respect (plate 15.1). Its red lacquer finish and overall shape are of obvious oriental inspiration, but its ornamental details are derived from Cubism.

15.2 Bruno Paul, 'Room for a Gentleman' at the 1928 *International Exhibition of Art in Industry* at Macy's, New York. *Die Kunst*, 1929. NAL.

15.3 Ludwig Gies, 'Jazzkapelle'. Porcelain. German, 1925. Staatliche Porzellan-Manufaktur. Bröhan-Museum, Berlin. Photo: Martin Adam. © DACS 2002.

In other designs for interiors, ornament was similarly added as a modernistic 'icing' to mirror and picture frames, to furniture and walls. The Munich sculptor Josef Wackerle designed striking plasterwork wall panels in a modernized 'Chinoiserie' style.[6] A more integrated example of orientalism is Bruno Paul's 'Room for a Gentleman', designed in 1925 and shown in the *International Exhibition of Art in Industry* at Macy's department store in New York in 1928. Its Japanese-inspired, screen-door type windows are in total harmony with the furnishings, creating a perfect Art Deco ensemble (plate 15.2).[7]

The commercial adoption of Art Deco within a more or less traditional framework is well illustrated by the porcelain industry. Germany had been the cradle of porcelain manufacture in Europe and had maintained a strong artistic tradition in this area as well as a strong international market position in the field of luxury tableware and decorative statuettes. As in the eighteenth century, sculptors received freelance design commissions, though some factories had their own, permanently employed modellers. In the 1920s they increasingly turned their attention to the design and production of decorative figurines whose stylization reflected a popular, commercial response to modernity.

Paul Scheurich was one of the most accomplished modellers working for Meissen. His subtly refined mannerist figures belong in the Rococo tradition while displaying an unmistakably contemporary personal touch.[8] Gerhard Schliepstein worked for the Staatliche Porzellan-Manufactur Berlin in 1924 and for Rosenthal in Dresden from 1925 until 1937. His figures and figure groups are more recognizably modern in their stylization.[9] With the figures left mostly white, the emphasis is on their elegant poses and elongated, flowing limbs, hands and feet. Most uncompromisingly modernistic are the works Ludwig Gies modelled for the Staatliche Porzellan-Manufactur. His 'Jazzkapelle' (Jazz Band) of 1925 and 'Mondschaf' (Moon Sheep) of 1926 are typical of his slightly disturbing expressionistic stylization (plate 15.3). Among others, the painter Ernst Böhm designed the décor of some vases for the Staatliche Porzellan-Manufactur, giving a modernizing gloss to work of Chinese inspiration.

Catering for a more popular market were the statuettes made by the Berlin firm of Preiss & Kassler (PK). Specializing in single female figures in carved ivory, bronze and mixed materials, this firm had already established its reputation before the war. When production resumed in 1919, its new Art Deco designs found a ready market in Germany as well as in Britain and elsewhere.[10]

Modernism became a major influence on German Art Deco in the second half of the 1920s. In metalwork, a trade based on strong local traditions of workshops and small factories working for the luxury market, designers were often willing to adopt an uncompromisingly contemporary stylization. The silverware of M. H. Wilkens & Söhne in Bremen, which embraced machine technology, included a number of elegant Art Deco designs.[11] Several independent silversmiths, like Emmy Roth in Berlin, started their own small workshops, while larger established firms also commissioned independent designers on an occasional basis.[12] The Berlin firm H. J. Wilm commissioned a design for a tea-set from Peter Behrens which combined classic lines with a luxurious finish, using smooth carved ivory for knobs and handles.[13]

Cheap pottery also played a role in the spread of Art Deco, with abstract, geometric patterns applied to simply-shaped objects for everyday use. Villeroy & Boch, based in Dresden between 1923 and 1935, and the Steingutfabrik Dresden, were particularly prolific, producing huge quantities of colourful and festive modern wares.[14] In a similar vein were Eva Stricker's playful geometric patterns and pottery shapes in designs for the Schramberg faience factory in the Schwarzwald (plate 15.4).[15]

After 1925, a more decorative and commercial version of mainstream Modernism became popular, especially for the design of cinemas, theatres and shops.[16] The firm Schwintzer & Graeff in Berlin produced elegant decorative chandeliers in chrome-plated metal, often incorporating tube lighting, for use in public buildings (plate 15.5). Ludwig Hohlwein, Germany's leading graphic artist, regularly adopted the Art Deco style for his persuasively modern commercial graphics.[17]

During the Nazi period the influence of Modernism ceased when the Nazis attacked it as 'Jewish-Bolshevik' and promoted traditionalist, nationalist designs for domestic use and neo-classicism in the public sphere. Their attitude to Art Deco seems to have been more ambivalent, perhaps because of its frequent use of national styles as a source.

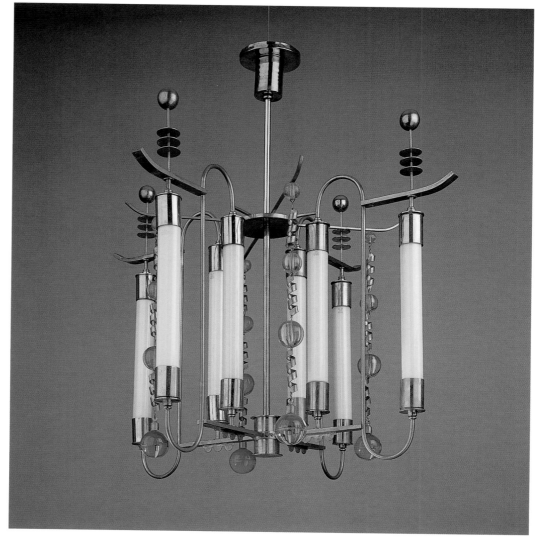

15.4 Eva Stricker, tea pot. Stoneware. German, c.1930. Schramberg faience factory. Bröhan-Museum, Berlin. Photo: Martin Adam.

15.5 Franz Haegele, chandelier. Glass and metal. German, 1930s. Schwintzer & Graeff. Bröhan-Museum, Berlin. Photo: Martin Adam.

Austria

Austria's contribution to the Paris 1925 Exhibition was on an enormous scale, in respect of both the size of its pavilion and the number of exhibits.[18] A republic only since the collapse of the monarchy in 1918, Austria was determined to present itself to the world in the grandest possible fashion, despite economic difficulties.

The Austrian exhibit consisted of a cluster of buildings including a main pavilion, designed by Josef Hoffmann, a tower, incorporating a gigantic organ, by Oskar Strnad, a Viennese café by Josef Frank and a 'Glashaus' (House of Glass) by Peter Behrens (see plate 12.18). Additional exhibits in the Grand Palais and on the Esplanade des Invalides represented the work of many Viennese workshops, design schools and decorative artists, as well as provincial ateliers. Special displays were dedicated to photography and architecture and to individual retailers and manufacturers.

Hoffmann was overall artistic director of the Austrian contribution, and his influence was evident on many levels. Apart from his responsibility for the architectural design, many of the exhibits were designed by his pupils from the Kunstgewerbeschule and from the Wiener Werkstätte. Hoffmann had been a founder of the Wiener Werkstätte in 1903 and his designs of that period had been characterized by geometric simplicity, elegance of form and simple, geometrical ornament. From about 1905 onwards, however, his work became less severe, as financial problems led the workshops to adopt a less uncompromising style. Although his designs were still characterized by simple shapes, he introduced more elaborate ornament in the form of stylized floral motifs inspired by local folk art.[19]

The Wiener Werkstätte became particularly well known for its colourful fabrics, with abstract geometric and stylized floral patterns. The French couturier Paul Poiret purchased a large number of these on his first visit to the workshops in 1911, and they had an immediate impact on his work and that of his workshop, the Atelier Martine. However, it would be wrong to see the Wiener Werkstätte solely as a source of inspiration for the creators of Art Deco in France. It also, to a large extent, defined Art Deco in Austria. Its increasingly decorative tendencies became more pronounced under the influence of Dagobert Peche, who inspired a move towards a much more painterly, playful and intuitive style.[20] Peche joined the workshops in 1915, having been a freelance designer for the textiles department since 1911. His early work had been strongly influenced by Hoffmann and Koloman Moser, but also had roots in the more decorative aspects of Art Nouveau and was inspired by ornament from the Renaissance, Baroque and Rococo periods.

Unlike most of his contemporaries, Peche saw ornament as the essence of the decorative arts. Ornament and surface treatment should not simply follow the shape of an object, nor be applied merely for the purposes of beautification: they should be integral to its shape and character. Peche's stylish playfulness and luxurious elegance were already apparent in a cabinet designed in 1913 (plate 15.7). Its overall shape and character recall Rococo cabinets with oriental-style lacquer and ormolu mounts, but its detailing is entirely original. The simple shape and straight fluting of the upper part of the lacquered body both contrast and blend with the giant gilt escutcheons in the shape of a bouquet of flowers that cover the cabinet's face in a seemingly random, diagonal pattern. Increasingly, Peche used ornament for its own sake in the design of purely decorative pieces, employing a wide variety of materials, ranging from paper and tin plate to silver gilt and ivory. A jewellery box of 1917 has a nominal practical function but this is overwhelmed by the flourish of ornament. The dream world of refined luxury that Peche sought to create found an instant rapport with wealthy, pleasure-seeking Viennese.

He provided the new bourgeoisie with a means of escape from the reality of political change and economic crisis into a lifestyle suggestive of bygone courtly splendour. Peche took the Werkstätte into the world of mundane luxury goods and high fashion. His overtly decorative work, with its original, modern interpretation of a historic past, is the earliest full-blown manifestation of Art Deco in Austria. Peche's influence on the Werkstätte was substantial: Hoffmann's designs in the 1910s and 1920s, especially for precious silver objects, retain a simple basic form but have a new decorative freedom and playfulness (see plate 1.11).

Hoffmann entrusted Peche with the organization and direction of a new department in 1915, the Künstlerwerkstätte – a series of spaces for the use of artists who were not officially part of the Wiener Werkstätte.[21] Peche ran these as a master-class, and designs deemed successful were sold through the Wiener Werkstätte shop. The workshops attracted almost exclusively female artists, many of whom had been Hoffmann's students at the Kunstgewerbeschule. One of the most talented was Christa Ehrlich, who became a junior assistant and worked in a wide variety of media including graphics, textiles, fashion, plasterwork and later also silver.[22] She decorated the interior of the 'Salle des Vitrines' in the Austrian pavilion at the 1925 Exhibition, whose walls were completely covered with glass-fronted showcases. The frames and glazing bars of the showcases and glass ceiling were hand-painted with floral, folk-art inspired patterns and motifs in white on a black ground. This gave the otherwise stark and regimented showcase a luxurious decorative finish comparable to the effect of oriental lacquer (plate 15.6). The showcases were filled with artefacts, many designed by members of the Wiener Werkstätte or their pupils. Hoffmann's pupils and the Künstlerwerkstätten were particularly well represented, especially with ceramics and textiles.

15.6 Interior view of the Austrian
pavilion at the Paris 1925 Exhibition.
Bildarchiv der Osterreichischen
National Bibliothek, Vienna.

15.7 Dagobert Peche, cabinet.
Ebonized tropical hardwood and
gilded wood. Austrian, 1913.
MAK, Vienna.

15.8 Charlotte Calm-Wierink, head of a girl. Earthenware, painted in enamels. Austrian, 1920-25. Wiener Werkstätte. V&A: C.185-1986.

The folk-art traditions that inspired Erlich's show-case decorations were echoed in the deliberately crude modelling of some of the ceramic figures and figure groups by Mathilde Flögl, Susi Singer and Vally Wieselthier, which drew on local folk pottery traditions. Wieselthier, Singer and others also made female figures and heads that elegantly stylized the archetypal female image of the 'Roaring Twenties' and are more sophisticated in their modelling (plate 15.8). Their elongated limbs, almond-shaped eyes and stylishly cropped hairstyles are all slightly at odds with the deliberately blotched and colourful painting, which gives them a spontaneous character, totally unlike the contemporary German porcelain figures designed by Schliepstein and others. A similar kind of stylization can be seen in the enamel-painted figures on glass by Lotte Fink for the Viennese glassmakers J. & L. Lobmeyr. The company was particularly renowned for its high-quality, wheel-engraved glass that built on the rich Central European tradition of the Baroque period. It produced contemporary

15.9 Franz Hagenauer, mirror.
Brass and mirrored glass. Austrian,
c.1925. Hagenauer workshops.
Bröhan-Museum, Berlin.
Photo: Martin Adam.

decorative designs by Wiener Werkstätte members and others, which were engraved by skilled craftsmen in the Lobmeyr workshop (see plate 18.6).[23]

Despite Austria's huge investment in the 1925 Exhibition and its acclaimed pavilion, the overall reception of its exhibit was relatively disappointing. Also, the displays provoked some fierce criticism on the home front:

> what we see now in the showcases is just the same as what we have been getting in the displays of the Wiener Werkstätte ... for more than a decade ... Unfortunately, nearly everything on show has as its objective the creation of luxury, a luxury that has become prohibitive and has long been superfluous, both to us and for those nations which understand our individuality.[24]

By the 1920s, the Wiener Werkstätte itself had lost some of its best designers and accepted too many second-rate assistants. The influence of Künstlerwerkstätten on the Werkstätte became increasingly strong and caused the quality of its output to become uneven, prompting the architect Adolf Loos to refer to the Werkstätte ironically as 'Wiener Weiberkunstgewerbe' (Viennese Women's Crafts).[25] Its patterned fabrics remained popular but, with the economic crisis of the late 1920s and early 1930s, the workshops found it increasingly difficult to compete in international or local markets. By the end of 1931 they had ceased to operate and the remaining stock was sold off by auction in the following year.

Although the Wiener Werkstätte dominated the decorative arts scene in Vienna, other workshops, artists and craftsmen in the city also made important individual contributions to Art Deco. The porcelain factory Augarten worked closely with Wiener Werkstätte designers. The firm of Friedrich Goldscheider produced earthenware figures in fashionable Twenties dress from 1923 onwards. The sculptural figures, lamps and mirror frames in wood, brass and bronze made by the Hagenauer workshop in Vienna show a decorative playfulness that is typical of Austrian Art Deco (plate 15.9).[26] Similar stylization can be found in the work of the Bimini workshop, founded by Fritz Lampl in 1923, whose lamp-worked glass animals and dancing or sporting figures had great popular appeal.[27]

The Netherlands

The Dutch selection committee for the 1925 Exhibition was dominated by the Amsterdam School, a group of architects centred on the Amsterdam based society Architectura et Amicitia.[28] In the 1910s and early 1920s this group developed a modern, theatrical and expressionist style which drew its inspiration from a wide variety of sources, including German Expressionism and oriental arts from Japan, China, Tibet and Dutch Indonesia, but also from natural phenomena such as seashells or crystals. Its most prolific members, Michel de Klerk and Piet Kramer, were particularly known for their designs for low-cost housing schemes which were hailed by contemporaries as 'palaces for the workers'.[29] The School's activities were geographically limited to Amsterdam, but it received much wider exposure through its monthly magazine *Wendingen* (1918-32),[30] which was devoted to all aspects of the arts, including theatre and dance. Its lavishly illustrated issues reflect the various sources that inspired the Amsterdam School designers and its striking typography was designed by its editor, H. Th. Wijdeveld.[31] Every issue had a specially designed cover by artists and architects associated with the group or by 'guest-stars' such as El Lissitsky, Jan Sluyters and Christa Ehrlich.

In the early years of the century, Dutch design debate was dominated by the utopian-socialist and rationalist ideas of the architect H. P. Berlage. The Amsterdam School architects also believed in the architect's social role, but saw themselves as artistic prophets whose expression in architecture of their own highly individual feelings would also help to achieve a better and truly modern society. For the Amsterdam School, architecture was about art rather than construction and function.

The Dutch pavilion, designed by the architect J. F. Staal, is typical of their aesthetics, with its harmonious and expressive play of forms, spaces and decoration, its integration of sculpture and its exotic inspiration (plate 15.10).[32] Its exoticism, which is most obvious in the main façade, with its curved roof-line, horizontal lacquer-red panelling, and incorporated flowerbeds and reflective ponds, owes much to the work of Frank Lloyd Wright, which was particularly popular with Dutch architects.[33] Typical also is the manner in which the design relates, in an imaginative way, to the prime function of the building.[34] The front and rear façades bear resemblance to a kiosk and a tent respectively, stressing the temporary character of the structure. The ornamental brickwork on the rear of the building includes a stylized representation of a ship at sea,

15.10 J. F. Staal, Dutch pavilion at the Paris 1925 Exhibition. *L'Art hollandais à l'Exposition internationale des arts décoratifs et industriels modernes, Paris, 1925,* Haarlem, 1925. NAL.

surmounted by an abstract rendition of the Dutch coat of arms, referring both to the Netherlands' great history as a maritime power and to the Dutch tradition of building in brick.

In the interior of the pavilion Staal achieved highly decorative effects through the interplay of rhythm, shape, pattern and colour. These bound together the design of the panelling, woodwork, polychrome upholstery, floor and wall coverings, furniture, stained glass, forged ironwork and sculpture in a true Art Deco *Gesamtkunstwerk* (plate 15.11). Hildo Krop and John Rädecker, the most prominent Amsterdam School sculptors, were responsible for the pavilion's sculptural elements.[35] Most contemporary Dutch sculptors specialized in integrated architectural sculpture, but many worked in other media as well. In Paris, A. van den Eijnde displayed a monumental silver urn and some statuettes.[36] And Krop also designed furniture, ceramics and woodcuts.[37] His fantasy heads for the pavilion are expressionist in character, but many of his designs for applied arts show a much more decorative stylization.

The selection committee sought to represent a broad range of tendencies. Work by many designers of the older generation was included, some of it dating back to Art Nouveau. Among these was the highly individual, Orient-inspired work of C. A. Lion Cachet and T. A. C. Colenbrander.[38] Cachet, who had created some of the most exclusive and ostentatious interiors around 1900, was represented by furniture recently designed for a Dutch ocean liner.[39] Typical of his work is the use of dark tropical woods inlaid with lighter wood and ivory – often combined with parchment panels decorated in the oriental batik technique – and traditional shapes combined with abundant oriental ornamentation. His cut-velvet fabric 'Mermaids', designed in 1918, received a diploma of honour.[40] Colenbrander's groundbreaking designs for ceramics and carpets in the 1880s and 1890s, which combined imaginative shapes with vibrant colours, had been influential for the Amsterdam School and other Dutch designers in the 1910s and 1920s.[41] His reputation was such that he was invited to design ceramics once again, for the Ram factory which was set up specially to produce them. The first vases were produced in 1921. A selection of decorative ceramics from the Ram factory, which drew heavily on his earlier work,

15.11 J. F. Staal, interior view of the Dutch pavilion at the Paris 1925 Exhibition. *L'Art hollandais à l'Exposition internationale des arts décoratifs et industriels modernes, Paris, 1925,* Haarlem, 1925. NAL.

was shown in Paris alongside some of his earlier designs.[42] Compared with his earlier work, the patterns on the new vases were smaller in scale and less integrated with the shapes, and the intense colours were more neatly separated by thin dark outlines. The designs achieve a greater degree of decorative abstraction; they also fit seamlessly with contemporary Amsterdam School aesthetics.

The work of other older designers, such as J. W. Eisenloeffel, had undergone a more radical change. Eisenloeffel had been a well known jeweller and designer of metalwork in the early years of the

century. His designs for metal tableware and other utensils emphasized the rationalist construction of the object in a decorative way, using only the simplest geometric ornament.[43] In the 1920s, however, he adopted a more luxurious decorative style with an oriental flavour. His monumental and profusely decorated clock shown in 1925 is one of the grandest examples of Dutch Art Deco exoticism of this period (plate 15.12). Exoticism was also represented by batiks on silk by Ragnhild d'Ailly and Agathe Wegerif-Gravestein. Produced in an Indonesian wax-resist dyeing technique, these highy

15.12 Jan Eisenloeffel, clock. Bronze, partly gilded, and enamel. Dutch, 1925. Stedelijk Museum, Amsterdam.

decorative textiles were unique pieces, intended to be hung on the wall like paintings. Other examples of an anti-rationalist approach included a tea service by Johannes Steltman; executed in hand-chased silver with a hammered finish, its striking streamlined design was based on a fish (plate 15.13).[44]

Several younger Dutch designers were inspired by the older generation's work. Jaap Gidding, who designed the upholstery of the main bench in the pavilion and some of the most striking carpets of the 1920s, employed abstract expressionist forms and strong, contrasting colours which resemble Colenbrander's carpet and ceramic designs of the 1890s (plate 15.15).

De Klerk started designing interiors in 1915 for 't Woonhuys, a company that manufactured and marketed exclusive furniture and interiors.[45] The design of a living room of 1916-17 breathes an atmosphere of ostentatious luxury with a strong oriental inspiration (plate 15.14). With its golden ceiling, the dark purple of its fabrics combined with the dark veneer of tropical woods and its Moorish-style details of furniture and fittings, the interior could have been from an illustration in *A Thousand and One Nights*.[46] A selection of furniture from this room was exhibited posthumously in Paris in 1925.[47]

The 1925 Exhibition brought international recognition to the Amsterdam School but it also marked the end of its most creative period. De Klerk had died in 1923 and while some members, such as Kramer, contributed to the spread of Art Deco in the Netherlands, others – including Staal – subsequently adopted a more rationalist approach.[48] The latter can already be observed in Wijdeveld's whitewashed interiors in the Grand Palais and on the Esplanade des Invalides, which included a gigantic streamlined showcase.[49]

Kramer's most important work is De Bijenkorf (The Beehive) department store of 1925-6 in The Hague, which is arguably the most pure Art Deco building by an Amsterdam School architect. Its main façade incorporates Kramer's typical expressionist design language, with dramatically curving walls in brick and stone and subtly integrated sculptural details; its framework, however, is almost purely rationalist. The interior of the building conveyed a similar mix of rationalist and decorative elements, with rich materials and textures and well executed details. A team of artists worked on the sculpted padouk wood panelling and the spectacular stained-glass windows of the grand staircase;[50] the dark hued wood and intense colour of the windows exuded an impression of exotic luxury particularly suited to The Hague's colonial flavour.

Although he was not a member of the Amsterdam School, Jaap Gidding had a role in spreading its decorative style to a much wider audience, especially through his designs for theatre and cinema interiors, of which the most important was the Tuschinski cinema in Amsterdam (1918-21).[51] Its intensely decorated, opulent and magical interior, including special coloured light effects, created a 'palace of dreams' that popularized the style (plate 15.16). The 'Tuschinski style' was popularly adopted for the design of wallpapers, furnishing textiles, stained glass and the decoration of glassware and pottery.

15.13 Johannes Steltman, tea service. Silver and cornelian. Dutch, 1925. Haags Gemeentemuseum, The Hague. Photo: E. Hamelink.

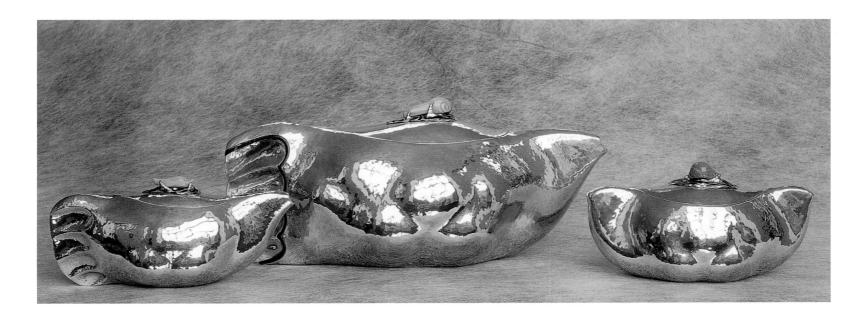

15.14 Michel De Klerk, interior
for 't Woonhuys. Dutch, 1916-17.
Wendingen, 1925. NAL.

15.15 Jaap Gidding, carpet.
Wool. Dutch, 1920. Rijksmuseum,
Amsterdam.

Alongside such tendencies, rationalism also gained ground in the Netherlands. Following the example of the Deutscher Werkbund, some architects, decorative artists and high-minded industrialists began to collaborate to create well designed mass-produced goods.[52] Jac. Jongert was the first graphic designer to collaborate intensively with industry. Initially working in a style close to the Amsterdam School, he later was to become much better known for his Modernist packaging and advertising for the Rotterdam tobacco, tea and coffee factory Van Nelle.[53] The Royal Leerdam glass factory discovered that sober, Functionalist designs of the type shown in Paris did not sell very well and soon began to produce more playfully decorative wares. Gidding designed popular products for many media, including painted glass vases for Leerdam, as well as decorative pottery, textiles and wallpapers. Other designers such as Hildo Krop and Chris van de Hoef made similarly popular decorative wares in a modernistic style, while Gidding and Jongert designed printed velvets, with striking abstract geometrical designs, for upholstery, loose covers and table cloths.[54] Large department stores, such as Vroom & Dreesman and De Bijenkorf made such articles available to a wide audience.

Under the directorship of the forward-looking Joseph de Leeuw and his son Hendrik, the department store Metz & Co. in Amsterdam and The Hague played an important role in spreading Art Deco in the Netherlands.[55] Before 1918, Metz had been the sole agent for Liberty, but after the war it sold fashionable products from France, Austria and Germany, and also imported carpets from Persia, India and Morocco. De Leeuw was always on the lookout for new developments. In 1920 he notified his customers that, besides Liberty products, the store stocked 'women's fashion and furnishings of very modern form and colour'.[56] Most of the fashion was specially ordered from the best Parisian fashion houses, while fabrics with bright and colourful abstract patterns were specially designed for Metz by Franz Cizek's pupils at the Vienna Kunstgewerbeschule. De Leeuw made many new contacts at the 1925 Exhibition. After meeting Sonia Delaunay there he began selling her fabrics, which were eventually produced by Metz itself. The store also employed its own designer, Paul Bromberg, and after 1924 Willem Penaat. Bromberg's style was close to that of the Amsterdam School, but Penaat's was more rationalist. Much of his furniture was machine produced and its design is close to that of a group of designers working in The Hague who had been influenced by the architecture of Frank Lloyd Wright and by De Stijl.

Notably absent from the 1925 Exhibition was the De Stijl group. Founded in 1917, by the painters Theo van Doesburg and Piet Mondrian, the group advocated a totally new abstract art. It opposed Amsterdam School aesthetics and sought to represent a universal truth by banning individualist and subjective influences from its art. Its strongest influence on architecture and the decorative arts was on the 'Nieuwe Zakelijkheid' (New Functionalism), the Dutch contribution to Modernism, which became an important force in the late 1920s and early 1930s. However, De Stijl's geometric compositions, which used only the primary colours red, yellow and blue, with black and white, were soon translated by others in a free, decorative way. This tendency can be seen even in some of van Doesburg's own works, such as the interior decoration of the Aubette amusement complex in Strasbourg of 1926-8 (see plate 9.10).[57] In 1925, however, De Stijl was represented only indirectly through works by two Dutch architects, Sybolt van Ravesteyn and J. J. P. Oud, and in the Belgian section, where its influence could be strongly felt in the study-interior designed by Huib Hoste and Victor Servranckx.[58] Van Ravesteyn never belonged to De Stijl, but the furniture he exhibited was strongly influenced by the work of Gerrit Rietveld and Mondrian.[59]

With the rise of Modernism, chrome-plated tubular steel and glass were deemed the only materials suitable for modern furniture, and these were combined with white walls or the bright monochrome colours of De Stijl. J. J. P. Oud's tubular steel furniture for Metz, designed in 1933-4, introduces playful, more decorative shapes. In the mid- and late 1930s, van Ravesteyn went somewhat further by introducing decoration and Baroque shapes within this otherwise Modernist idiom.[60] J. J. P. Oud's Shell building in The Hague, designed in 1938-40, illustrates the final step in this process of merging mainstream Modernism with decorative fantasy.[61]

Severe economic and political instability during the 1930s caused a return to traditional values in Germany and Austria and to a lesser extent in the Netherlands. The rise of National Socialism caused an exodus of talented – mainly Jewish – designers to the United States where, like earlier émigrés such as Josef Urban and Paul Frankl, they played a vital role in the spread of Art Deco (see Chapters 31 and 34). Meanwhile, responding to increasing financial constraints, many designers in these countries turned to mass production. They began to pay less attention to detailing and decoration and to concentrate on the use of cheaper materials. Tubular steel was abandoned in favour of wood laminate and glamour was replaced with economy, paving the way to post-war Functionalist design.

15.16 (overleaf) Jaap Gidding, foyer of the Tuschinski cinema, Amsterdam. 1918-21. © Jan Derwig.

1e BALCON — ZAAL 1 6 2
ROYAL LOGE — STALLES
FAUT DE BALC — ZU·BEN LOGE
LOGE SPECIAAL

16 Art Deco in Central Europe

David Crowley

Between the world wars, the countries of Central Europe participated in the international ebb and flow of taste, and one can find as many examples of Art Deco in popular, commercial culture in Poland, Hungary and Czechoslovakia as anywhere else in Europe. Magazine covers, advertising posters, cinema façades and consumer goods adopted the style to demonstrate their place in modern life. Glass manufacture in northern Bohemia, for instance, continued to thrive in this period, not least because its designers exploited the fashionable modern style to satisfy markets at home and abroad (see plate 18.7).

The emergence of Art Deco in post-war Central Europe was shaped by political events. Poland, Hungary and Czechoslovakia were the products of settlements made at the end of the First World War. Pre-war empires were broken up and new nations were created (or in some instances 'restored'). In the case of Poland and Czechoslovakia, independence was seen as a reward for long years of nationalist activism: in Hungary's case, a shrunken state was created by the Treaty of Trianon (June 1920) in retribution for Austria-Hungary's prosecution of the war. On the one hand, these states claimed deep historic roots and therefore legitimacy, while on the other, each was manifestly new: state agencies and institutions had to be established and an identity claimed. Involved in the 'national projection' of new states, Art Deco in Central Europe, as elsewhere, reflected tensions between past and present.

Czechoslovakia

The intellectual and stylistic origins of Czech Art Deco lie in the activities of the artistic avant-garde living in Bohemia under Habsburg rule before the First World War. One current in particular – known today as Czech Cubism – generated important ideas about the form of modern design after the First World War. This short but highly productive episode was one of the most important roots of Art Deco in the region.

The first signs of Cubist architecture and design in Bohemia emerged around 1910. It developed as both a product of Czech bourgeois affluence and as an avant-garde (and sometimes nationalist) rejection of the ideas formulated by prominent Secessionist architects in Vienna, such as Otto Wagner, who affirmed 'purpose and construction as well as poetry' in design. Josef Chochol and Pavel Janák, both architects, formulated spiritualist philosophies of design and a dynamic ideal of planar form derived, in part, from Cubist art. This 'international' current was accompanied by an interest in 'local' traditions, such as late-Gothic diamond vaulting and the Bohemian Baroque, which had a particularly dynamic form. As François Burkhardt notes, these traditions were much admired for the ways in which powerful visual and spatial effects had been achieved by the composition of massive volumes and subtle 'membranes', rather than through the application of decoration or ornament.[1]

Initially, Czech Cubism took form on the pages of art journals published in Prague. But from 1912 Cubist ideas began to be translated into actual designs by a group of architects and designers working and exhibiting with an alliance of artists, the Skupina Výtvarných Umělců (Group of Plastic Artists), which formed in that year. Early designs included Janák's reconstruction of a Baroque building (the Fára House) in Pelhřimov in 1913. Its richly plastic façade of sculpted planes, cloaking a conventional apartment house, is typical of the initial years of Cubist architecture in Bohemia (plate 16.1).

At the same time a number of architects, including Janák, Josef Gočár and Otakar Novotný, began designing furniture. Their designs reflect their fascination with oblique planes, prisms and triangular forms, which prevailed over concerns for material or technique (plate 16.2). The heavy sculptural forms of their wooden, upholstered chairs and glass and wood cabinets demanded ingenuity on the part of the cabinetmakers employed to realize the designs. The Czech Cubists abandoned the contemporary Secessionist fashion of arranging the interior as a *Gesamtkunstwerk*. Contemporary photographs of interiors arranged by Gočár, Novotný and Janák show

16.1 Pavel Janák, façade of the Fára House in Pelhřimov. 1913. Národní Technické Museum, Prague.

16.2 Josef Gočár, vitrine. Black-stained oak with mahogany veneer. Czech, 1913. UPM – Museum of Decorative Arts, Prague. Photo: Miloslav Šebek.

their striking pieces in rather conventional arrangements, accompanied by banal bourgeois furnishings. They viewed their furniture designs as expressions of their aesthetic vision – as works of art in their own right, rather than functional objects. In the early phases of Czech Cubism these angular, sculptural pieces lacked applied ornament and, consequently, had a rather monumental and even sometimes primitive appearance. Ornamental effects were replaced by the sculptural quality of the object itself. Its forms were essentially abstract, making no reference to historical ornamental languages or to nature.

Cubist designs for furniture before 1918 were largely commissioned by patrons of the artistic avant-garde in Prague – figures like Vojta Novák, a theatre director, and Václav Vilém Štech, an art critic. But Czech Cubism also found popular outlet through

Artěl, a progressive decorative arts workshop established in Prague in 1908. The ceramics, glass and metalware designed by Artěl members took a variety of forms including traditional folk art (echoing growing nationalist sentiment at the time) and the radical Modernism of Cubist designs. Vlastislav Hofman, for example, sought to realize a decorative Cubism by deforming traditional ceramic forms in a series of services and vases. The surfaces of these Artěl products were transformed with angled planes and trimmed edges (plate 16.3).

In 1914 Czech Cubism underwent what has been described as a move to 'monumentalism' and 'decorativism' which brought it into the sphere of what is now called Art Deco. The angular, planar forms of Gočár and Janák's pre-war designs evolved into circles and curves. The resulting style, known retrospectively as 'Rondo-Cubism', was adopted as a

national style in 1918, when the new Czechoslovak state emerged and its practitioners became leading figures in the architectural profession. Since its first appearance in Bohemia, Czech Cubism had been characterized as part of the national heritage – a modernization of the dynamism of the Baroque. But the new national style, which sometimes included elements of vernacular architecture and an emphatic use of colour (often the new national colours, red, white and blue), was a form of popularism, designed to meet the national mood following the formation of Czechoslovakia. The building in Prague colloquially known as the Legiobank (the Czechoslovak Legions' Bank), designed by Gočár in 1922, an example of 'official' patronage of this style, has an oppressive, classical symmetry. Massive circular decorative forms are bolted onto its façade and reappear in the overbearing decorative scheme of the interior,

16.3 Vlastislav Hofman, coffee set. Earthenware, painted in enamels. Czech, 1913-14. UPM – Museum of Decorative Arts, Prague.

16.4 František Kysela, *Pottery*. Wool tapestry. Czech, 1925. Made by Marie Teinitzerová at the Jindřichův Hradec tapestry workshops. UPM – Museum of Decorative Arts, Prague.

16.5 'Salon d'honneur' in the Czech pavilion at the Paris 1925 Exhibition, with tapestries by František Kysela and furniture by Pavel Janák. *Art et décoration*, September 1925. NAL. Photo: Marc Vaux.

16.6 Josef Gočár, north façade of the Czechoslovak Legions' Bank, Prague. 1922. Národni Technické Museum, Prague.

designed in collaboration with the painter František Kysela (plate 16.6). The emergence of Rondo-Cubism marked the final phase in the development of Czech Cubism and approximated, for a short period, to the 'official' style of the new state, as well as being an early form of Art Deco.

Many of those who had developed this self-consciously national style were commissioned to design and furnish the Czechoslovak pavilion at the Paris 1925 Exhibition. The building, designed by Gočár, took the symbolic and somewhat abstracted form of a ship, with Jan Štursa's sculpture *Victory* at its prow. The spirited exterior of the building belied the sober rooms inside. Above a conventional gallery space displaying the major exhibits, a crowded first-floor salon, designed to receive important guests, formed a striking contrast with the exterior. Modelled on a castle chamber, its ceilings were painted, its floor was carpeted with a design depicting architectural details, and its walls were hung with a series of tapestries by František Kysela on the theme of artisanal métiers. His tapestry depicting the 'plein air' workshop of the village potter evokes the planar forms of Czech Cubist furniture of the 1910s as well as vernacular tradition (plate 16.4). By contrast, most of the furnishings for this salon, designed by Janák, made no reference to this formal vocabulary.

His designs had an eclectic – even historicist – character, displaying self-consciously 'national' accents: the embroidered backs of the oak chairs and sofas in the salon suggested the pronounced parapets of Czech Renaissance buildings (plate 16.5).

If the Czechoslovak pavilion marked the triumph of a language of design that had its roots in pre-war Czech Cubism, it was also its swansong. Janák, for instance, who had once celebrated the dramatic aestheticism of his furniture designs over their capacity to function, now embraced the utilitarian qualities of Modernism. The rise of Czech Functionalism – an ideologically driven and ascetic aesthetic – did not, however, force the extinction of Art Deco, though the style ceased to have prominent advocates in the artistic and cultural elite. Czech industry in general and Czech glassmaking in particular seized upon the fashionable decorativism of Art Deco in its drive to export during the Depression years. In this period, many Bohemian glass manufacturers issued versions of a popular coloured and black opaque glassware under the brand name 'Tango'. And Art Deco aesthetics – together with new artificial materials like plastic – were also adopted by other manufacturers, including the well known Puls porcelain works.

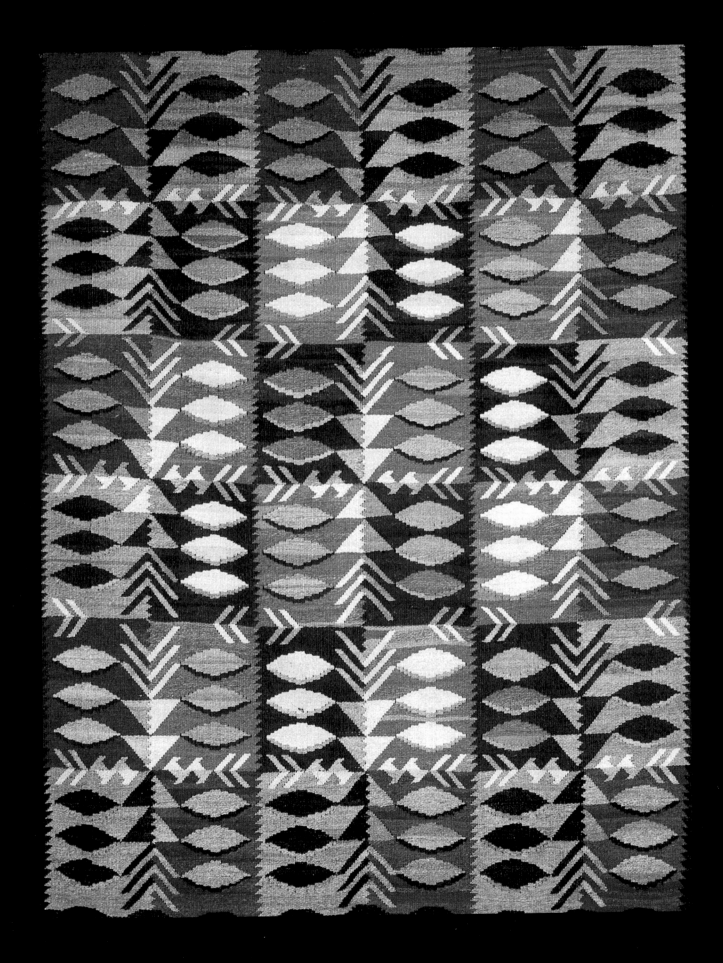

Poland

Like Art Deco in Czechoslovakia, the Polish variant had roots in the period before the First World War. Long under partition by its dominant neighbours, who had attempted to suppress the language and culture of the peoples under their rule, Polish society had a deeply established tradition of nationalism. Buildings and works of art and design had long been read in terms of their 'Polishness' – their capacity to remind the nation of its history and 'destiny'. Kraków, a southern city enjoying the relative freedom of Austrian rule, assumed the role of cultural capital. Here, at the turn of the century, artists and designers strove for the elusive and even fanciful language of a 'national style', many introducing vernacular motifs into their chic and elegant designs for furniture and interiors. For these urbane designers, the intuitive and empirical understanding of the craftsman provided a kind of inspirational model; and the art, homes and domestic utensils of the peasant a valuable repository of expressive forms and motifs. The vernacular thus offered a source for a new Polish design and thereby the pitfalls of 'international' historicism could be avoided.

When, after 1918, Polish independence was guaranteed by the Treaty of Versailles, many of these figures moved to Warsaw, the new capital, to form the new artistic bureaucracy in the Ministry of Culture or to work as teachers in the new Academy of Fine Art. Although now located in Warsaw, they continued nevertheless to be known as the 'Kraków School'. Their designs for exhibition pavilions, government ministries and even postage stamps were part of the widespread and much promoted campaign to 'rebuild the nation'. Far from ending interest in a 'national style', the achievement of Polish independence and the practical problems of rebuilding a society fractured by partition seemed to focus the energies of its most ardent enthusiasts. The new state rewarded former Kraków School activists by giving them many of the most prestigious commissions. New government buildings like the Ministry of Religion and Public Education (1928) and official institutions like the National Economic Bank (1928-35) – suitably monumental classical structures for such serious public functions – were dressed with allegorical sculptural reliefs by Kraków School artists or furnished by its designers in a modernized folk

style. In the absence of a thriving bourgeoisie (such as that which had supported the development of Czech Cubism and later Art Deco in Bohemia), the state played a key role as patron. In some instances, art and politics were combined in the work of one individual: Wojciech Jastrębowski, the leading figure in the Kraków School, designed interiors for the Ministry of Religion and Public Education as well as being director of its Department of Art and later became a prominent politician.

In the 1920s, the Kraków School developed a sophisticated design language derived from an understanding of materials and technique. The group's major theorist at this time, Karol Homolacs, published a series of articles and books about the intrinsic logic and beauty of forms that followed from the use and innate understanding of materials. His arguments were shot through with a thread of mysticism and poetry: he referred to the 'rhythmic pulse of ornament' and the 'vibration of nature'. The earlier Kraków School had been more pragmatic in its thinking.[2] Its designers had viewed certain materials as lending themselves naturally to

particular decorative forms, interpreting the chip-carved patterns traditionally used to decorate wood as 'natural' forms, and the geometric, abstract and stylized motifs along the diagonal and horizontal axes of a kilim as its 'true' vocabulary. In fact, these traditional crafts produced the essential forms that characterize Polish Art Deco, and the stepped, angular motifs that came to be known as the 'triangular style' can be found throughout Polish design of the 1920s (plate 16.7). With a footing in the practical world of craftsmanship, and having absorbed post-Cubist ideas of volume and space, a 'national style' – with the prism and crystal as its leitmotifs – was promoted by a design lobby that enjoyed a degree of state support. This was, in effect, a Polish expression of Art Deco.

The most significant expression of the Polish variant of the style was produced at the Paris 1925 Exhibition. The invitation to participate in the exhibition was viewed as a highly public demonstration of Poland's acceptance as a modern, 'western' state worthy of its independence. Kraków School designers were charged with shaping the national display. Józef Czajkowski's national pavilion was a *tour-de-force* in the new style. A long, narrow temple was capped with a glass tower constructed from hundreds of small panes, like a strange, precious gem (plate 16.8). The 'triangular style' was found throughout the pavilion: the main

16.8 Józef Czajkowski, the Polish pavilion at the Paris 1925 Exhibition, night view. Jerzy Warchałowski, *L'Art décoratif moderne en Pologne*, Warsaw and Kraków, 1928. NAL.

16.7 Karolina Mikołajczyk-Bułhakowa, *Leaves*, kilim. Wool and linen. Polish, 1926. Made by Ład Studio. Museum Narodowe, Warsaw. Photo: Jacek Gladykowski.

16.9 Józef Czajkowski, interior of the Polish pavilion at the Paris 1925 Exhibition. *Studio*, 1925. NAL.

official (another illustration of the interest of the young state in the style). From its elegant parquet floor to its diamond-patterned ceiling, this room was the ultimate expression of the carved, geometric style: the throne-like chair in which the official was to reside was upholstered with a strikingly patterned kilim and its back was capped with a deeply facetted 'crystal' arch. The Polish pavilion and other Polish exhibits elsewhere in the exhibition were warmly received, and the juries awarded 172 prizes to Polish exhibitors – the highest number given to any display. The Poles saw this triumph as a measure of the independence and vitality of their national culture. Curiously, some foreign commentators saw it as a French triumph. Gaston Varenne, in *L'Art décoratif*, detected the influence of Cubism – a Parisian invention.[3]

Ultimately, the Kraków School hopes of effecting a revolution in the tastes of Polish consumers and producers were to be disappointed. The chairman of the Polish commissioners to the 1925 Exhibition, Jerzy Warchałowski, wrote within a few months of its closing, 'This was a dream. Artists have created this Poland in Paris out of nothing, for a moment, for the honour of the name, and then, after awakening, they subsided with their efforts, back into nothingness.'[4] With a few exceptions, this national and decorative variant of Art Deco was not favoured by clients when commissioning buildings or putting new designs into production. Its decorative qualities, derived from costly handwork, were hardly suited to the impoverished conditions of the Polish economy in the 1920s. Increasingly, too, the style drew strong criticisms from the nascent but highly vocal Modernists. The leading Constructivist magazine in Poland, *Blok*, described Poland's success in Paris as a triumph of parochialism and nineteenth-century attitudes to design.[5] However, this attack did little to stem the tide of popular or commercial Art Deco in Poland, which paid no attention to the national question. In the field of poster design and production, where the Kraków School obsession with the relationship of ornament to technique was irrelevant, designers like Tadeusz Gronowski and Witold Chomicz enjoyed flourishing careers, even in the depressed 1930s, by producing witty and elegant images for commercial clients (plate 16.10).

salon, lit with flashing beams from the glass tower, was furnished with massive carved benches that suggested both Renaissance architecture and rustic construction (plate 16.9). Zofia Stryjeńska painted a calendar of frescoes on the walls, describing Slavic myths and peasant festivals (not unlike František Kysela's tapestries in the Czechoslovak pavilion, plates 16.4 and 16.5). The final, somewhat theatrical, chamber in the suite of rooms that formed the national temple was an office for a government

16.10 Tadeusz Gronowski, advertisement for
Fruzinski confectionery, poster. Colour lithograph.
Polish, c.1925. Collection of the Central Library
of the Academy of Fine Arts, Kraków.
© DACS 2002.

16.11 Sándor Bortnyik,
poster for Modiano. Colour
lithograph. Hungarian,
c.1935. V&A: E.654-1936.

Hungary

Cultural and political conditions in Hungary in the
1920s were far less auspicious than those in
Czechoslovakia and Poland. Following the collapse of
the Soviet republic, which had lasted 133 days in
1919, and the subsequent installation of a right-wing
regime under Admiral Miklos Horthy, Hungary was
isolated in Europe, cut off from exercises in
international diplomacy like the Paris Exhibition.
Moreover, many members of the artistic avant-garde
who had supported the Revolution went into exile,
including Laszlo Moholy-Nagy and Marcel Breuer.
While the regime encouraged repatriation, and some
exiles returned in the mid-1920s, culture in Hungary
laboured under the weight of conservatism – in terms
of both official tastes and the preferences of the
middle-class market. Many of the more innovative
artists and designers who stayed were unable to

secure work from the government because they had
held positions in the short-lived Soviet republic. In
Steven Mansbach's words, by the end of the 1920s
'the country's increasingly draconian social and
political climate made it almost impossible to sustain
the array of progressive art'.[6] It is perhaps not
surprising therefore that forms of historicism were
the preferred styles of the Horthy regime and
dominated into the 1930s (notably in the grandiose
interior schemes for the Hungarian parliament
building). Gyula Szekfü dubbed this taste 'neo-
Baroque', a label which, rather imprecisely, was
widely used to describe all forms of conservative
eclecticism in architecture and design.[7]

The contrast with Poland could not be more
striking. Viewed with suspicion by the state,
Hungarian Modernist designers turned to the
commercial world for their opportunities to practise.

Art Deco was to become associated with the gradual
revival of the Hungarian economy which, before the
First World War, had been one of the most dynamic
in Europe and had been critically damaged by the
post-war peace settlement. In the late 1920s, Art
Deco became the favoured style for new shop-fronts,
cafés and theatres in Budapest, as well for packaging
and other forms of commercial graphic design. Some
of the most striking works of the period were posters
advertising ordinary consumables like tea and soap.
In the late 1910s Sándor Bortnyik had promoted the
cause of social revolution in his paintings and, as a
left-wing painter, was compelled to flee the country
after the collapse of the Soviet republic. In Germany
he established close contacts with the Bauhaus.
Returning to Budapest in 1924, his opportunities to
work as an artist were limited and as a political
propagandist prohibited. Following the lead of the

16.12 Lajos Kozma, mirror. Carved and gilded wood. Hungarian, c.1920. Galerie Camoin Demachy, Paris.

Bauhaus, he turned his energies to commercial work, producing strikingly modern designs for the Italian cigarette paper producer, Modiano (plate 16.11). With their powerful use of simple, flat motifs and sans serif letterforms, Bortnyik's designs represented the commercial world through the striking images of modernity. This was a form of modern expression detached – by necessity rather than by design – from associations of activism or utopianism.

Lajos Kozma was a key figure in the development of modern design in Hungary whose career, like that of Bortnyik, reflects the ambiguous development of what is now called Art Deco in this part of Europe. His work before the First World War lay within the orbit of Art Nouveau: trained as an architect, he was associated with a group known as Fiatalok (The Young) who turned to peasant art as a source of authentic, 'national' design. Like a number of his colleagues in the 1920s, he was viewed with some suspicion by the Horthy regime – not least for having designed the Soviet republic's ill-fated bank notes – and received no major commissions from the state. In the early 1920s his designs for furniture and private interiors had a neo-Baroque character, inspired by the modest scale and character of the

buildings which typified the reconstruction of numerous small Hungarian towns in the eighteenth century, following the Ottoman occupation. This was a rather different source of Baroque inspiration from the powerfully dynamic buildings that had attracted the Czech Cubists. Kozma's attraction to this provincial aesthetic had much to do with its unpolished, vernacular character. His own designs did not directly imitate these historic models but shared some of their picturesque and unconventional qualities that Kozma took to be 'native'. Many of his furniture designs, made in the Budapesti Mühely (Budapest Workshop), were inlaid with floral swags and fantastic narrative scenes that owed much to his other career as a book illustrator. His designs for cabinets on squat cabriole legs and mirrors with expressive detailing often had an exaggerated and sometimes dramatic appearance (plate 16.12). This was not, however, a personal art: a similar combination was found in the work of others, including Gyula Kaesz's often whimsical furniture designs. Various accounts have attempted to explain the popularity – albeit short-lived – of the neo-Baroque style in the 1920s. Éva Kiss has described this Hungarian variant of Art Deco as a continuation

of Art Nouveau tastes in a society damaged by the experience and political consequences of the war. In her view, the vernacular had provided ideas about rational construction and a vocabulary for a truly popular aesthetic before the First World War; ten years later, having succumbed to 'decorativism', it offered little more than an affected and idyllic picture of national life at a time of prolonged crisis.[8]

Kozma's aesthetic took a different turn in the late 1920s, when he wholeheartedly adopted the formal hallmarks, if not the social ethos, of Modernism: tubular steel furniture designs now graced interior schemes lit by glass walls. However, as András Ferkai has noted, Kozma continued to display an Art Deco sensibility.[9] His designs in these years – perhaps best expressed in his famous Apostol Pharmacy shop-front of 1929 and Atrium cinema six years later – substituted ornament for the showy treatment of lustrous materials like glass, marble and chrome, in spaces that were lit and organized in a dramatic fashion (plate 16.13). Modern materials and design were increasingly widely used for sophisticated effects in the 1930s, to lend prestige or appeal to smart apartment buildings, luxurious shops, hotels, restaurants and nightclubs.

16.13 Lajos Kozma, remodelled shop-front of the Apostol Pharmacy, Budapest. 1929. © Hungarian Museum of Architecture. Photo: Barka Gábor.

The period that truly distinguishes Art Deco in Central Europe from the phenomenon elsewhere was a short one. The first half of the 1920s saw optimistic attempts to create national languages of design in Poland, Czechoslovakia and, to some extent, Hungary. Yet, by 1930, few traces of these aesthetic currents remained, while the more general or international forms of Art Deco thrived. Explanations for this short life are numerous, but two important ones stand out. As the Polish case shows most strongly, the origins of these national styles lay in a concern to speak for the nation through design and the applied arts at a time when its development had been restrained and culture stifled. The dialogue promoted by a chair carved with motifs drawn from history or a tapestry depicting peasant culture was, in an important sense, an 'internal' rather than an international one. When representatives of the Polish state returned to Paris in 1937 to participate in the next major international exhibition there, they chose to represent the nation in the international vocabulary of Modernism.

Reflection on Modernism also leads to the second limitation of these early 'national' versions of Art Deco. Most of those involved in their creation – unlike the Modernists – took little interest in mass production. Their designs were made largely in specialist workshops. The emphasis on handwork was given an ideological charge by some, like Jerzy Warchałowski, who saw in high craftsmanship the means to stave off the factory. In other instances this emphasis was a reflection of the economic and technical realities of Central Europe in the early 1920s: the decorativism of Kozma's early designs pandered to the parvenus, the only market left in a country broken by the war and revolution. However, as industry began to revive during the course of the 1920s, the importance of designing for mass production became obvious. Design debates were beginning to take increasing note of the possibilities of new materials and industrial processes, and Modernists were making the case for a new language of design based on the machine. In this context, the Kraków School vision of the Polish style, the Czechoslovak Rondo-Cubism and the Hungarian neo-Baroque seemed increasingly anachronistic, even to those who had once been their most ardent supporters. Kozma was not the only designer of his generation to travel from national decorativism to international Modernism: in Czechoslovakia in the late 1920s, Janák, the theorist of Czech Cubism, and Gočár, one of its leading practitioners, began to focus their energies on fully fledged Modernism and debates about industrial culture.

Art Deco was not extinguished in the region by these changing circumstances. The commercial and popular forms of the style exemplified by Gronowski's posters or Kozma's cinema interiors thrived in the 1930s, well attuned to the interests of the mass market. Such designs represented a local expression of pan-European tastes. However, for a short period in the mid-1920s, Art Deco in Central Europe was distinct from that produced elsewhere in Europe. In these years the polemical and sometimes theoretical character of design discourse, the attachment of architects and designers to the past (not least to roots in nineteenth-century nationalism), and their close relations with new official institutions (in Poland and Czechoslovakia) stimulated the design and manufacture of nationally and regionally distinctive artefacts.

17 'Lovely Neoclassical Byways': Art Deco in Scandinavia

Jennifer Hawkins Opie

Histories of early twentieth-century Scandinavian design have focused on two dominant tendencies: the survival and adaptation of neo-classical and Biedermeier traditions to contemporary needs and tastes on the one hand, and the rise of Functionalism on the other. Denmark, Finland, Norway and Sweden are not often associated with the most common perception of the Art Deco style, since its highly recognizable, jazzily geometric design rhythms and vibrant colours rarely caught Nordic imaginations. But the alternative version of Art Deco, represented elsewhere in Europe by the relaxed Mediterranean neo-classicism of René Buthaud's ceramics or Henri Matisse's paintings, has clear correspondences with its more restrained northern equivalent (plate 17.1).

Neo-classicism was the most pervasive and persistent influence on Scandinavian design. Mediated by forms established in the eighteenth century, it remained a theme in architecture and design throughout the nineteenth century, despite the overlaying of other interests. Of these interests, the most powerful arose in the years around 1900 when the four Scandinavian countries each strove to establish themselves in new political alignments independent of their neighbours. Denmark, the southernmost country, had traditionally looked towards Germany, France and beyond for its commerce and cultural interests. Norway, after four hundred years of rule by Denmark, formed a union with Sweden that was dissolved in 1905. Finland, where the population was either ethnic Finnish or Swedo-Finnish after seven hundred years of rule by Sweden, had been annexed by Russia in 1807 and was struggling for independence, which it did not fully achieve until 1917. In the cultural sphere, each of these nations sought an individual identity through the exploration and rediscovery of more ancient and local traditions. This was expressed by means of the potent and rapidly evolving forms of National Romanticism, the Scandinavian form of Art Nouveau.[1] In addition, in Sweden, where Biedermeier styles had remained popular, a revival of classicism

began in the 1880s which, interwoven with an appreciation of traditional arts, gave rise to what was known as the Late Gustavian style.[2]

In the early years of the twentieth century, these two strands slipped naturally into debates on the future course of design. Classicism, trimmed and updated, was seen to provide a secure and familiar base with which to underpin a softer and more relaxed decorative vocabulary. And while Art Nouveau was perceived as irrelevant in the rapidly changing world of multiplying technologies just before the First World War, its innate humanism, appreciation of crafts skills and celebration of local and national traditions all underpinned Scandinavian Art Deco design of the 1920s and 1930s.

Despite these countries' attempts to forge distinct national identities around the turn of the century, the First World War – so the architectural historian Eva Eriksson has argued – reintroduced closer ties within the group by isolating those Scandinavian countries that, although not engaged in the conflict, were nevertheless affected by the disruption to trade and travel.[3]

The architecture debate

These ties were reflected in architecture and in design. Here the most productive exchanges within the group were those between Denmark and Sweden. In both countries architects, designers and clients had a traditional feeling for luxury and for expensive materials, a tendency stemming perhaps from histories dominated by aristocratic and royal interests and from a more international trading history than that of their other Scandinavian neighbours. In 1731, for example, a Swedish East India Company was founded, thus establishing a trade route between Canton and Gothenburg (Göteborg), and Swedish interest in China and Chinese culture became part of the Swedish way of life. Nevertheless, it was not this empathy with exoticism that sparked the first signs of the modernization of tradition. Rather, it was a renewed interest in classicism and this new approach was first articulated in architecture.

17.1 Wilhelm Kåge, Argenta vase. Stoneware inlaid with silver. Swedish, c.1930. Made by Gustavsberg. V&A: C.129-1984.

17.2 Ragnar Östberg,
City Hall, Stockholm. 1909-23.
Photo: Max Plunger.

Eva Eriksson cites key events that contributed to the philosophical debate underpinning the formation of twentieth-century Swedish classicism. The argument around the imposition of a seventeenth-century Baroque spire on a nineteenth-century Neo-classical church sparked the debate in Denmark around 1911. This was followed by contacts between leading Danish architects Kay Fisker and Aage Rafn with the Swedes Gunnar Asplund and Sigurd Lewerentz; by the interest taken in a modest but inspirational building, the Liselund country house of 1790 on the Danish island of Mön; and, shortly after, by the design in 1914 of the museum at Faaborg by Carl Petersen, with Kaare Klint, in a fully fledged modern, yet neo-classical style.[4] Detailed drawings of the delicately classical, yet traditionally rural Liselund house were made by Fisker and Rafn and their contemporaries. These drawings, and those of Petersen's museum, with its rhythmic spaces articulated by differing heights, light and coloration, were displayed at an exhibition of Danish architecture held at the Liljevalchs Art Gallery, Stockholm, in 1918. Eriksson states that 'the importance of Petersen's work was in his belief in an interplay, at vital points, between whole uninterrupted surfaces and contrasting effects. This way of seeing things became characteristic for classicism in Sweden in the 1920s.'[5]

Probably the most celebrated building of the 1920s was Ragnar Östberg's City Hall on the Stockholm waterfront (plate 17.2). The first drawings were made during the earliest years of the debate, in 1909, though it was finally completed only in 1923, with changes made to the design almost until the last. The waterside building with its campanile was historicist in profile, but its rough construction and deep colours were a deliberately modernizing antithesis. Östberg, while articulating the vast spaces essential for civic pride and functionality, produced a building that is richly decorative, a showcase for contemporary Swedish crafts, from sculpture and weaving to mosaics. These, in turn, provided a vibrant contrast with the elegant furnishings by Asplund, Carl Malmsten and Ernst Spolén with which it was filled. This eclectic combination made the City Hall Sweden's major statement for the contemporary age.

Swedish debates were also central to design developments across Scandinavia in the 1920s and 1930s. Gregor Paulsson, director of the Svenska Slöjdföreningen (Swedish Society of Industrial Design) from 1920, was heavily influenced by the ideas of the Swedish social and educational reformer Ellen Key, who proposed a radically moral view of the relationship between design and society. Paulsson was also influenced by the Deutscher Werkbund, which promulgated closer links between art and industry. Exhibitions were held in Stockholm in 1917 and 1920 that focused on these issues. Taking an opposing view was an exhibition held in Gothenburg in 1923, to celebrate the city's tricentenary, which was unashamedly devoted to luxury goods and provoked further debate. Yet despite such social concerns, modernized traditionalism was ultimately more pervasive. With its tendency towards classical elegance, its use of the human form as a basis for proportion and ornament, and its pleasure in materials and admiration for hand skills, it entered the bloodstream of Scandinavian design. In the 1920s, it was these qualities that most closely resonated with the new style as it matured in France and elsewhere in Europe. It was this that became Scandinavian Art Deco, most characteristically in the form known as 'Swedish Grace'.

While Sweden and Denmark exchanged ideas, the debate also flourished elsewhere. In Finland, too, it was led by architects. After the 'Golden Age' of the 1890s, the country had taken some years to regain its momentum in design.[6] It had first to recover from the final separation from Russia in 1917 and the attendant economic stringencies and internal struggles that followed. With hindsight, the most interesting and unexpected of the architects testing the new style was Alvar Aalto. While it would be stretching a point seriously to claim him for Art Deco, his early work, done in collaboration with his wife Aino, nevertheless bears the lightness of touch characteristic of much early Deco. A slightly whimsical use of classical decoration and its attenuated depiction, as well as references to the Biedermeier style, were evident in Aalto's early design drawings, though they were often resolved into a more muscular style in the buildings as constructed. His Työväentalo (Workers' Club) in Jyväskylä of 1924 and Suojeluskuntatalo (House of the Civil Guard), Seinäjoki, of 1925 exemplify these tendencies. The Aaltos were deeply immersed in the design vocabularies of their time. Aino (who was older than Alvar) had been taught by the senior classical architect and designer Gustaf Nyström, while – as can be seen in his own earliest buildings – Alvar was well aware of the intelligent, considered buildings by the younger Gunnar Asplund and he remained a close friend of the Swedish architect throughout his life.[7]

The design and crafts debate

While architects were gradually feeling their way towards new forms, other areas of design were also subjected to rigorous debate, driven specially by the rivalry between design and crafts organizations. Established from the middle of the nineteenth century, by the beginning of the twentieth century there were a number of such organizations in each country: in Sweden, the Svenska Slöjdföreningen (Swedish Society of Industrial Design), the Konsthandverkarnas Gille (Artisans' Guild) and the Verkstaden (Workshop), founded in 1845, 1907 and 1918 respectively; in Finland, the Suomen Taideteollisuusyhdistys (Finnish Society of Crafts and Design) and the Suomen Käsityön Ystävät (Friends of Finnish Handicrafts) of 1875 and 1879; in Denmark, the Landsforeningen Dansk Kunst Handvaerk (Danish Society of Arts and Crafts and Industrial Design) of 1907; and in Norway, the Föreningen Brukskunst (Society of Arts, Crafts and Industrial Design) of 1918. All four countries also had schools devoted to teaching design and the crafts. These groups were active in the debates and, in many cases, were the driving forces behind them. As a result the applied and decorative arts were subjected to an intense reassessment centred on the role of design in the development of a well ordered society. This in turn focused the argument on the rival merits of hand skills and mechanization, of the unique art work and design for mass production. Here, as in other European countries at this time, some designers and makers argued that artistic individuality was endangered by the threat of anonymity that mass production posed.

Initiatives and societies, founded twenty years earlier or more to support craftsmen, adapted to represent the interests of designers, as well as to bring the two groups together. In Denmark, for example, the Københavns Snedkerlaug (Copenhagen Cabinetmakers' Guild) provided support and encouragement for the collaboration of designers with craftsmen. Initially these designers were often architects but eventually furniture design became a professional occupation in its own right. From 1927 the Guild held exhibitions and competitions on an almost annual basis. These launched the careers of several subsequently celebrated designers and makers, including Kaare Klint and later Finn Juhl, Hans J. Wegner and Børge Mogensen, who were all competition winners. However, in Denmark and Finland it was the relationship of the designer to crafts-based production, particularly in the furniture industry, that was emphasized. Neither country adopted the forms of German radicalism, which in

Sweden led to the concept of social reform via design and mass production; instead they continued to view furniture as an art. Indeed, the Copenhagen Cabinetmakers' Guild held their exhibitions at the Museum of Decorative Art for many years, thus conferring an artistic superiority by association alone.[8] Designers and makers steered a determinedly independent course with little controversy. Fashionable styles were almost universally viewed with suspicion and only an unmistakable grounding in classicism rendered them acceptable. This meant that Danish furniture took a very particular and barely admitted course around what we can now, with the benefit of hindsight, recognize as Art Deco.

Aesthetic directions were also deeply affected by commercial requirements and the degree to which manufactories were or could be mechanized. For example, in both ceramics and glass, the loyal home market absorbed sufficient production to keep the core Scandinavian factories afloat. But competition abroad was harder, and these industries were also reliant to some extent on importing materials, thus adding to the cost of production. The Swedish ceramic company Gustavsberg imported china clay from England and, uniquely outside England, made bone china as a result. Transfer prints were bought in from England and Germany, resulting in earthenware production that was no longer always regionally distinctive. New technologies from abroad also forced the pace. In ceramics, mechanized means of decorating like spray painting or aerographing altered the course of design styles. Potteries such as Porsgrund in Norway – like Susie Cooper in Britain, Sarreguemines in France and the many small potteries around the Bauhaus school at Weimar – all adopted these inexpensive techniques for their speed and commercial good sense. Of themselves, none of these technologies invited Art Deco design, but each made production faster and simpler and this put pressure on competing companies to adopt the technology where they could afford to. And design practice was changing too. Even before the end of the nineteenth century, and specially in Scandinavia, many of these industries had established the practice of inviting trained artists and architects to contribute designs in order to give their products a more individual edge. In Sweden Wilhelm Kåge at Gustavsberg, in Finland Kurt Ekholm at the Arabia pottery, in Norway Nora Gulbrandsen at Porsgrund and in Denmark Nils Thorsson at Royal Copenhagen all produced designs that subscribed to fashionable contemporary trends including Art Deco, thus improving these companies' chances of commercial success. Often, secure employment within a company, which, in Sweden specially, was combined with a commitment to the notion of social improvement through the benign influence of good design, meant that many of these professionals spent their entire careers designing for industry. In addition, the specialist design, craft and technology schools ensured a supply of designers, fully trained and familiar with a range of materials.

As elsewhere in Europe, design in the Scandinavian countries was influenced by avant-garde art. In the ceramics, glass and textile industries, for example, painters and sculptors, whose most formative experience was the training they received in Paris or Berlin, brought an educated awareness of the Ballets Russes and of Cubism and Futurism, as well as the sources behind these, to their own work.[9] Edward Hald studied in Paris with Matisse, before returning to Sweden to work at Orrefors and Rörstrand in 1917. He and the Danes, Johannes Bjerg and Kai Nielsen, all worked in bronze and adopted decorative elements culled from recent painting and sculpture from as early as 1913. Jean Gauguin and Nielsen translated these into ceramics for Bing & Grøndahl and other manufactories. As these elements entered the vocabulary of the designer regardless of international boundaries, Scandinavian decorative and applied arts were as well placed as any to express the contemporary mood. But, as in other areas, nationalistic imperatives, local preferences and temperament also dictated the degree to which this mood was adopted and the manner in which it was interpreted. And it is these local factors that give Scandinavian design of the Art Deco period its special flavour.

17.3 Aage Rafn, furniture in the Danish pavilion at the Paris 1925 Exhibition. Sycamore and mahogany. Made by Otto Meyer and Jacob Petersen. Batik wall-covering by Ebbe Sadolin. *Art et décoration*, October 1925. NAL.

17.4 Christian Joachim and Arne Malinowski, sauce tureen and dish. Porcelain painted in enamels and gilt. Danish, 1939. Made by Royal Copenhagen. V&A: Circ.274&A, 275-1939.

Scandinavia at the Paris 1925 Exhibition

As the showcase for what has become known as Art Deco, the Paris 1925 Exhibition provides a benchmark for the style. Finland, in the throes of a civil war, exhibited only one room in the Grand Palais, with Finnish furniture, decorative sculptures, textiles and ceramics. Norway did not take part. But Sweden and Denmark both invested substantially in their exhibits.

Denmark's national pavilion was built to a strikingly minimalist design by Kay Fisker, with an exterior of undecorated brickwork in a plain, horizontal bond.

17.5 Gerhard Henning, *The Chinese Bride*. Painted porcelain. Danish, 1922. Made by Royal Copenhagen. Den Kongelige Porcelainsfabrik, Royal Copenhagen Museum.
© Ole Woldbye and Pernille Klemp.

It housed a display by the touring club of Denmark. The country's main presentation was in the Grand Palais, where many of the exhibits belied this austerity with a combination of ancient and exotic influences. Neo-Greek furniture by Aage Rafn was based on the painted images preserved on Classical Greek ceramics and other artefacts, but it also had an emphatic manneristic curviness that is typical of Art Deco (plate 17.3). Ebbe Sadolin's quixotic batik, with its Indonesian-style figures and abbreviated symbols, added a curious and unexpected exoticism to an otherwise well ordered living room.

Exhibits from Royal Copenhagen and Bing & Grøndahl attracted some of the most enthusiastic critical attention. In common with most other manufacturers, Bing & Grøndahl exhibited long-admired *tours-de-force*, like the elaborately modelled porcelain of Effie Hegermann-Lindencrone and Fanny Garde, but these ornamental wares were in a style unchanged for over a decade. It was the newer generation of ceramic artists and designers that gathered the accolades. The British teacher, designer and artist Gordon Forsyth – who had done so much to encourage British designers and makers to look abroad for ideas and models – was lyrical in his admiration of the 'superlative' work in stoneware of Jais Nielsen for Royal Copenhagen and of Jean Gauguin's work for Bing & Grøndahl.[10] The elegant Chinoiserie-style design by the Swede Gerhard Henning for Royal Copenhagen was featured in *Skønvirke*, the Danish journal of decorative arts, in 1925. His model of a pagoda-like vase with two figures, 'The Chinese Bride', was illustrated as undecorated porcelain (*blanc de chine*), though it was almost certainly exhibited elaborately painted, matching Henning's own design (plate 17.5). Although Henning had been employed by the factory since 1909 and worked in much the same manner throughout, his exotic images and delicately sensual modelling exactly met the mood of 1925. Closer to the elegant neo-classicism of the interiors and furniture was the tableware by Christian Joachim, with discreet decoration by Arne Malinowski, which was awarded a Grand Prix (plate 17.4). Not all the Danish

17.6 Simon Gate, 'Parispokalen', vase with cover. Engraved glass. Swedish, 1922. Made by Orrefors. Given to the City of Paris. Musée d'Art Moderne de la Ville de Paris. Photo: Winell, Orrefors Museum.

17.7 Carl G. Bergsten, the Swedish pavilion at the Paris 1925 Exhibition. NAL.

ceramics were by the Copenhagen factories. The more experimental pottery of Herman Kahler, with its extravagantly crackled glazes and rich lustre painting by Jens Thirslund, was also exhibited. In silver, the most strikingly sensuous work was that by Christian Fjerdingstad for the Paris firm Christofle (plate 17.8).

The Swedish displays were divided between the national pavilion, which overlooked the Seine, and – within the Grand Palais – a special display devoted to Ragnar Östberg's City Hall and the general Swedish section. The national pavilion was designed by Carl Bergsten as a neo-Greek temple, fronted with attenuated Ionic columns and embellished with somewhat skittish reliefs of the Four Winds by Ivar Johnsson, in unglazed earthenware made by Höganäs. It was approached around a plain, oblong pool of water. The garden was furnished with cast iron urns in a neo-classical style designed by Eric Grate and made by the Näfveqvarns factory. The largest of these were decorated with friezes of heroic figures engaged in mining and in the production of metal objects (plate 17.7).[11] The sculptor Carl Milles provided for a fountain a naiad riding a dolphin and a lion, in bronze, partly gilded. Like many of his contemporaries, Milles worked in a variety of materials; in the Swedish display, there were also two large urns by him, manufactured by the Höganäs ceramics factory.

Within the pavilion, furniture by Carl Malmsten for the A. B. Nordiska Kompaniet of Stockholm was sparsely set around the reception hall. The large 'Parispokalen' ('Paris cup') – in fact a vase, cover and under-stand – designed by Simon Gate for the Orrefors glassworks in 1922 was the grandest work (plate 17.6). Blown by Knut and Gustaf Berqvist, engraved by Gustaf Abels and Elis Rydh, it was presented to the city of Paris and displayed in isolated splendour on a central table. The bowl was decorated with neo-classical motifs of intertwined sea creatures and classical figures, while the cover, by contrast, was embellished with a view of Östberg's City Hall. Furniture was designed by Gunnar Asplund and made by David Blomberg's workshop. Effectively

17.8 Christian Fjerdingstad (Danish), 'Gigogne', coffee pot, creamer and sugar. Silver. 1926. Made by Christofle. Musée et Archives Bouilhet-Christofle. Photo: Delage.

neo-Greek in inspiration, form and proportion, it nevertheless had the qualities of relaxed elegance so often associated with Art Deco (plate 17.9).

Manufactories of all the major materials displayed their wares in the general Swedish section. The two best known ceramics factories, Rörstrand and Gustavsberg, exhibited porcelain, earthenware and bone china designed by Edward Hald and also the progressive Wilhelm Kåge. Other factories, with a less weighty history than Rörstrand, for instance, exhibited adventurous designs that caught the style of the time. Arthur Carlsson Percy, designing for Gefle, exhibited a lively dinner service, which nodded towards neo-classicism but also fully embraced the contemporary taste for decorative sensuality (plate 17.10). Hald, and his contemporary Simon Gate,

were the designers for the Orrefors' display. Orrefors, the only Swedish glassworks represented, exhibited their exclusive Graal glass, made to a technique which, after its first successful production in 1916 under Knut Berqvist, was promoted as a factory speciality. Hald's special talent was in the design of lightly drawn scenes, often depicting contemporary city life but also using Black African motifs in a manner taken up by designers elsewhere. The company's display also included the most elaborately decorated and skilfully carved engraved glass, and it was this that caught the attention of the international press at the time. Equally, the simple, easy-to-use tableware made at the factory's other works at Sandvik, to Hald and Gate's designs of flowing shapes and subtle colours, was also well received.

17.10 Arthur Carlsson Percy, tureen. Earthenware, painted in enamels. Swedish, 1930. Similar to the one designed in 1925 and displayed at the Paris 1925 Exhibition. National Museum, Stockholm.

After 1925

In an article published in 1930, the British writer Philip Morton Shand, a Modernist critic, invented the phrase 'Swedish Grace' to identify the graceful and unmistakably Swedish design that made its first appearance at the Gothenburg Exhibition in 1923. Shand's article, a highly critical attack on British ignorance and caution, written with great relish, was primarily a defence of Modernism. In the course of it, however, he set out an appreciation of Sweden's successful adaptation of neo-classicism. In doing so, he made some telling observations about Sweden's careful orchestration of its representation at exhibitions during the 1920s. He referred to the 'perfectly edited Swedish pavilion at the Paris Exposition des Arts Décoratifs of 1925'[12] and to the national characteristics on which Swedish neo-classicism was based: 'at core the country is profoundly aristocratic – aristocratic in its instincts and its tastes, its genius for leadership'. He then went on to describe Swedish design in 1925 as a 'line characterized by its slender and almost elfin grace ... the delicate fantasy and Sleeping-Beauty charm which Swedish craftsmen had imprisoned, as with a Merlin's spell, in the exquisitely-refined glass, porcelain and textiles they so lovingly wrought'.[13]

Yet, by the end of the 1920s, design debates in Sweden had polarized. The Traditionalists found themselves increasingly challenged by the rise of the Functionalists (Tradis and Funkis, as they were nicknamed by the contemporary press). As Shand observed, 'The Swedes saw that they had wandered so far from the functional concept of the modern world along their own lovely neo-classical byways that to get back to this Weltanschauung they must forsake the fine national traditions which had inspired their most consummate achievements.'[14] Thus, 'just when the boom in "Swedish grace" is at its very zenith, Sweden calmly proceeds to jettison this halcyon godsend without so much as a "by your leave"'.[15] 'That severely functional chair ... sits oddly ... amidst furniture, hangings and crockery that perpetuate, and, indeed, over-refine, the famous Swedish grace.'[16]

17.9 Erik Gunnar Asplund, 'Senna', chair. Mahogany, leather and ivory. Swedish, 1925. Made by David Blomberg. Nordiska Museet, Stockholm. Photo: Mats Landin.

By 1930 therefore, though an interest in gentle classicism was by no means discontinued, Functionalism had emerged as the new Swedish style. The catalyst proved to be tensions between mass production for the greater social good and the exclusivity of unique works in which the skills of the maker were celebrated as well as the design. Even in factory production these tensions could arise. In 1930, Gustavsberg under Wilhelm Kåge introduced the new and expensive Argenta ceramics, characterized by classical motifs in silver inlaid into coloured stoneware – the ultimate in skilled craftsmanship and priced well beyond the average pocket (plate 17.1). Although the Föreningen Svensk Form (Swedish Society of Crafts and Design) and its directors were accused of failing to safeguard the interests of the craftsmen, in a letter signed by Simon Gate, Carl Milles, Carl Malmsten and others, change was inexorable.[17] But although the charm of 'Swedish Grace' was overtaken, the argument

never quite disappeared, as is evident from a rather sharp remark made much later by Eric de Maré: 'This has been called the New Swedish Renaissance, the period of Swedish Grace which often came to be called Pseudish Grace by the pedants of the next decade.'[18]

Sweden had signalled the break and the influence of Swedish-style Functionalism spread through design in all four countries. Faced with the rise of mechanization and growing commercial pressure, crafts co-operatives and department stores (like Copenhagen's Den Permanente and Stockholm's Nordiska Kompaniet) took an increasingly pro-active role in exhibiting and marketing design and production. In Finland the change was particularly marked in architecture. In 1926 the city buildings office in Helsinki had been responsible, under the architect Gunnar Taucher, for a vast municipal residential block on Mäkelänkatu. It had a minimally ornamented, smoothly plastered frontage which has

been described as 'a pure-bred example of 1920s classicism, and ... an important illustration of residential architecture for workers'.[19] Helsinki had as many different styles of architecture during this period as any Nordic city, but by the end of the 1930s, Modernized Classicism had been absorbed into the prevailing inter-Scandinavian philosophy of practicality as evidenced in clean, simple forms and modern materials. By 1939 the architect Aarne Ervi had designed an apartment building on Lauttasaarentie that is now described as 'one of the best examples of a humane and sensitive interpretation of 1930s functionalism'.[20]

17.11 Einar Forseth, tapestry sample. Linen, wool and gold thread. Swedish, 1924. Woven by Elsa Gullberg at the Konserthuset textile studio, Stockholm. National Museum, Stockholm. Photo: Åsa Lundén 1997. © DACS 2002.

The virtue of decoration and Art Deco transformed

Across Scandinavia, many designers and makers followed architects down the route of ornament-free practicality, but others remained firmly within traditional areas of production and committed to the use of decoration. In Finland, the *ryijy* weaving technique, so successfully re-launched as a vehicle for contemporary design around 1900, continued in the hands of weavers like Impi Sotavalta, who remained interested in maintaining and re-working traditional motifs as contemporary decoration.[21] In Sweden, the weaver Elsa Gullberg made floor coverings and wall hangings to both her own designs and those of other artists like Einar Forseth (plate 17.11). Probably the best known designer in Stockholm was the Viennese Josef Frank, who established Svenskt Tenn. This was one of the most effective and long lasting of the companies devoted to the modern concept of interior design, commissioning and selling furniture, fabrics, metalware and a variety of other household goods. Frank's trademark style was a brilliantly coloured, stylized naturalism. This almost Mediterranean flamboyance was readily adopted in his new homeland, though radically different to the far more restrained native Swedish design.

Other designers wholeheartedly embraced the very latest in fashionable decorative trends. In Norway, one of the most accomplished was Nora Gulbrandsen. Her designs in porcelain for the ceramics company Porsgrund were perhaps the most committed of any Nordic designers to the now

fashionable Moderne style. Skilfully she adopted dynamic decoration unmistakably culled from Soviet graphics and spray-shaded stripes reminiscent of the myriad mass-produced, factory-made wares of the Weimar region, home to the Bauhaus. She combined this decoration with streamlined forms, designing tablewares completely unlike any made in Norway before (plate 17.12). Sverre Petersen at the Hadelands glassworks and in the later 1930s Oskar Sørensen at the metalwork company J. Tostrup also contributed stylishly streamlined designs for glass, silver and aluminium.

Scandinavia had a justified reputation for restraint, as exemplified by its continuous preoccupation with classicism. This meant that Art Deco was met in Scandinavia by a subtle re-working of that same classicism, an inventive use of ornament and a deliberate celebration of craft skills, which made it a very particular and special contribution to this global

style. Humanism and social reform were Nordic preoccupations. The means of achieving them was the debate of the 1920s. Socially responsible design with its implications for mass production and use of the machine, perceived as liberating, formed one direction. Individuality, traditional hand skills, pleasure in materials, luxury and the familiar language of classical human proportion formed the other. Sometimes unfairly, the two words used to typify these choices were 'severity' and 'gracefulness'. In time the concept of 'social beauty', which had been promulgated as early as 1899 by Ellen Key, reconciled them; but for a few years the two directions remained clearly separate.[22] During the 1920s and for a decade or so, the most inventive and successful designers followed the path of gracefulness and luxury, celebrating the decorative, and this was Scandinavia's special contribution to the Art Deco style.

17.12 Nora Gulbrandsen, coffee set. Porcelain. Norwegian, 1929-31. Made by Porsgrund Porselaensfabrik. V&A: C.114-1987.

18 European Glass

Ghislaine Wood

The inter-war period was one of great creativity in the history of European glass. In these years glass became the most versatile and stylish of modern materials. It was blown, moulded, cast, cut, carved, sand blasted, mirrored, engraved, acid etched or enamelled, and used in an increasingly wide variety of applications. Within the interior it transformed the look of floors, walls and ceilings, and provided a stylish alternative to more traditional materials for furniture and lighting (see plate 20.9). It was used in mass-produced tableware and ornamental objects such as vases, mascots and figurines and in the craft production of expensive and unique art works. In fact, during this period, quality designed glass become affordable for all. New techniques evolved and old techniques were revived and modernized to cater for a wide range of tastes and pockets.

It was perhaps the creativity of one man that dramatically promoted the fortunes of glass. In the early years of the century René Lalique, in a search for less expensive materials, began to experiment with glass in his designs for jewellery. He quickly came to appreciate its immense adaptability. In his first vessel designs he explored the intricate process of lost-wax casting (*cire perdue*), but after 1918, when he purchased a new glassworks at Wingen-sur-Moder, he began to apply industrial techniques to glass manufacture. Adopting methods used in mass production, such as press moulding and mechanical blowing into moulds, Lalique also diversified with different object types. He developed an enormous range which included lighting, tableware, figurines and architectural glass (plates 18.1 and 18.2). Although Lalique used many techniques and colours, opalescent glass became characteristic of the company's output; it was achieved by the addition of antimony or arsenic and by controlled rates of cooling. Opalescent glass became extremely popular in the Art Deco period with many factories producing works in the technique. Lalique's highly acclaimed architectural glass displays, exhibited at the Paris 1925 Exhibition, included a monumental opalescent fountain in the Cours des Métiers (see plate 14.3). These displays, as well as prestigious commissions for ocean liners such as the *Normandie*, helped to reinforce the association between glass, spectacle and glamour (see plate 29.8). As the most successful glass company of the period, with strong markets in France and America, Lalique's influence was enormous, particularly in the area of mass production.

18.1 René Lalique, *Deux Paons*, lamp. Glass, with moulded and cut decoration, on a Bakelite base. French, c.1925. Made at the Lalique glassworks (Verreries d'Alsace). V&A: C.73-1972. © ADAGP, Paris and DACS, London 2002.

18.2 René Lalique, glasses. Pre-moulded transparent glass. French, c.1925. Made at the Lalique glassworks (Verreries d'Alsace). V&A: Circ.34-1970. ©ADAGP, Paris and DACS, London 2002.

18.3 Maurice Marinot, three bottles, flask and vase. Blown glass, decorated with internal colour, opaque enamels, acid etching and engraving. French, 1923-32. V&A: C.9&a-1964; C.2&a-1964; C.20&a-1964; C.13-1964; C.3&a-1964.

18.4 Marcel Goupy, vase. Blown glass with
opaque and translucent enamels and gilding.
French, c.1925. Made by Maison Rouard.
V&A: C.258-1987;
C.12-1979.

By contrast, the work of another great pioneer in Art Deco glass, the Fauvist painter Maurice Marinot, was mediated by a strictly artistic approach to glassmaking. Exhibited from 1911 at the *Salon des indépendants* and the *Salon d'automne*, his first works involved painting in enamel on the surface of vessels made by the Viard brothers at Bar-sur-Seine to his designs. By the early 1920s Marinot had learnt to work hot glass to create vases and bottles decorated with controlled internal bubbling and acid etching (plate 18.3). These heavy walled works explore the sculptural tension between exterior and interior profiles and the contrast between surface and internal decoration. They were extremely labour intensive but many attempted to emulate them. The Daum glassworks in Nancy also specialized in coloured and acid-etched vases but produced them on a much larger scale. The rival firm of Cristallerie de Nancy employed the jeweller and glass engraver Aristide Colotte as modeller in the mid-1920s and came closer to Marinot's artistic approach. Colotte's unusual technique combined wheel cutting, acid etching and even chiselling, and his sculptural forms are suggestive of work in other materials such as wood or stone.

Other French glass manufacturers developed distinctive approaches. Marcel Goupy at Maison Rouard in Paris experimented with enamelled glass and employed the glass worker August Heiligenstein to execute painted enamel decoration on the surface of often brightly coloured, opaque vessels. Many Goupy designs clearly reveal the attraction that the exotic and colourful imagery of the Ballets Russes exerted on Art Deco designers in 1920s (plate 18.4). Another designer to experiment with new techniques

and strong colours such as black and orange was Charles Schneider, whose glassware also sold under the name Charder and Le Verre Français.

Pâte de verre, a technique that involved melting powdered glass in a mould with metallic oxides to provide colour, was invented in the 1890s but continued to be popular until the 1930s. The principal producers of Art Deco *pâte de verre* were François-Emile Décorchemont, Joseph-Gabriel Argy-Rousseau and the Daum glassworks. Innovations in the *pâte de verre* technique by these designers enabled them to produce vessels of a substantial size. They were most often decorated with fruit, flowers or animal motifs.

In Sweden, young designers brought a new creativity to engraved glass design at the Orrefors glassworks. Simon Gate, Edward Hald and Vicke Lindstrand, employed to revitalize glass design at the factory, combined delicate wheel engraving with fresh, contemporary subjects. Hald's design for a goblet, 'Negerhyddan', reveals the contemporary fascination with exotic subjects. The shape of the vase is inspired by the form of a hut while the engraved decoration shows native figures and animals among palm trees. Another Hald design, 'Fyrverkiskålen' (Fireworks), also demonstrates the development of innovative new subjects for decoration (plate 18.5). Both works were exhibited at the Paris 1925 Exhibition and helped win Orrefors a gold medal.

18.5 Edward Hald, *Fireworks*, vase and stand. Engraved glass. Swedish, 1921-30.
Made by Orrefors. V&A: Circ.52&A-1931. © DACS 2002.

18.6 Jaroslav Horejc (Czech),
Abundance of Nature.
Cut and engraved glass.
1922-3. Made by Lobmeyr.
UPM – Museum of Decorative
Arts, Prague.

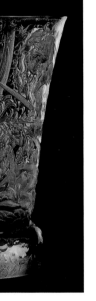

18.7 Liqueur set. Dark, smoke-coloured
glass. Czech, c.1930. Made by Moser,
Karlovy Vary-Dvory. UPM – Museum of
Decorative Arts, Prague.

Another European company that specialized in engraved glass was the Austrian firm of J. & L. Lobmeyr. In a similar attempt to modernize, Lobmeyr also turned to leading designers to revamp their output. The Czech designer Jaroslav Horejc produced a range of engraved vessels for Lobmeyr that were exhibited at the Paris 1925 Exhibition and demonstrate the restrained modernization of traditional forms typical of much Art Deco of the 1920s (plate 18.6). During the 1930s Bohemian glass manufactories were quick to respond to the rigours of the Depression years and produced cheap, stylish glass that flooded the European market (plate 18.7). Glass of the Depression years often brought a hint of the highlife, with designs for cocktail and liqueur sets, into many homes.

As a building material, glass had had a considerable history by the 1920s, especially in exhibition architecture and display. With the advent of Art Deco, the properties of glass were exploited to their full potential for illusion and spectacle and were used to dramatic effect, by day and night, in the displays of the Paris 1925 Exhibition. In an early use of glass within the domestic interior, Eileen Gray created a floor of frosted glass panels with lighting beneath which brilliantly heightened and defined the canoe-form of her famous 'Pirogue' day bed (see plate 11.11). It was not until the 1930s, however, that glass was commonly used in interior architecture, or that illumination became an integral part of building design. The foyer of the Strand Palace Hotel, designed by Oliver Bernard in 1929, is an early British example of internally lit glass architecture. Within the foyer illuminated glass columns and staircase were combined with pale marble, chrome and mirror to create a vision of sheer glamour (see plate 20.13).

19 Italian Architecture and Design

Tim Benton

It might seem that Italy would have provided the perfect seed bed for Art Deco. The *Prima esposizione internazionale d'arte decorative moderna*, held in Turin in 1902, was a model of how to create a spontaneous but unified environment full of joyful modern experimentation.[1] In many ways it was a precedent for the Paris 1925 Exhibition, with its formal insistence on modernity. The freshness and fantasy of Raimondo D'Aronco's pavilions served the needs of the industrialized world, with buildings dedicated to the Press, the Automobile and Photography. The work of the leading international Arts and Crafts and Art Nouveau architects and designers (including Josef-Maria Olbrich, Peter Behrens, Victor Horta, René Lalique, Henri Sauvage, Henry van de Velde and Louis Comfort Tiffany) could be compared with the Italian Art Nouveau designers (such as Alessandro Mazzucotelli, Carlo Bugatti and Eugenio Quarti) working in the Italian variant of the style, the Stile Liberty. Of these, Mazzucotelli's metalwork and Quarti's furniture were to develop from Art Nouveau into Art Deco. However, the path from Art Nouveau to Art Deco in Italy was disrupted by a number of factors.

The first of these was Fascism. Following the march on Rome and Mussolini's entry into government in 1922, the Fascist state slowly took over more and more control of people's lives and work. In terms of style, the consequence was not a rejection of innovation or modernity, but rather the setting of certain parameters around which all artistic debates would have to revolve. Everyone, whether Modernists or traditionalists, had to demonstrate their nationalism, which meant invoking the spirit of *italianità*, or more often a 'Latin spirit'.[2] Everyone had to pay lip service to the genius of Italian local craftsmanship and the vernacular, even though one effect of state support for the crafts was to homogenize them. The foundation of the Ente Nazionale per l'Artigianato e le Piccole Industrie (ENAPI) in 1922 had the effect of providing local craftsmen with designs and prototypes produced by artists and architects trained in the newly expanded polytechnics and art schools.[3] This was in a context where, before the First World War, many of the initiatives in design had come from master craftsmen like Alessandro Mazzucotelli and were supported by schools of arts and crafts such as the Società Umanitaria. The society had been founded in Milan in 1893 by a self-made businessman, Prospero Moisè Loria, to provide art classes and professional instruction for artists and craft workers. Its guiding principles were based on the writings of William Morris, placing emphasis on the innate creativity of the craftsman, truth to materials and a close study of nature, rather than past styles. Many of the leading craftsmen in Italy taught there at one time or another.[4] For example, the brilliant but eccentric goldsmith Alfredo Ravasco, who taught at the Società Umanitaria, was among the stars of the 1923 *Biennale* in Monza and the Paris 1925 Exhibition.

The Società Umanitaria was also behind the promotion of the *Prima esposizione internazionale d'arte decorative* in the Villa Reale, Monza, in 1923.[5] This turned into an important biennial event, until 1930 when it became the *Triennale*, held in Milan in 1933, 1936 and 1939. The first exhibitions at Monza (1923 and 1925) were organized by region, respecting the principle of the autonomy of local traditions of craftsmanship. The general opinion of the critics, however, was negative. With a few exceptions, the stimulus of the Stile Liberty in Turin, Milan or Palermo had not made its mark on the work of the master craftsmen, who preferred to produce the reproduction antiques still in demand from their patrons. But the influence of master craftsmen was giving way to that of artists and architects. By 1927, the artists and architects had taken over the *Biennale*. Displays now were more thematic and spectacular. For example, in a 'street of shops' in 1927, Felice Casorati's 'Macelleria' caused a sensation, with its radical purification of form and impact; as did the 'Sala della Grafica' by the architect Giovanni Muzio and the painter Mario Sironi in 1930, both founder members of the classicist Novecento group.[6] Casorati's 'Macelleria' was among the rooms exhibited in the *International Exhibition of Art in Industry* at R. H. Macy & Co. in 1928.

The founding of a series of schools of architecture, beginning with that in Rome (1920), along with the graduation of more and more draughtsmen from the art academies, provided industry with the design specialists they needed to meet the needs of industrial production and an expansion of their markets.[7] A sign of the times was the decision of the large ceramics firm Richard-Ginori to appoint the young architect Gio Ponti as artistic director in 1923.[8] Ponti radicalized the promotional strategy of the firm, producing a flood of fresh designs, designing advertisements, organizing the wares in 'families' strategically aimed at different markets and issuing a luxury catalogue. Similar appointments were made by the smaller ceramics firm Società Ceramica Italiana in Laveno (of Guido Andlovitz in 1923), the Venetian glassmakers SALIR (Studio Ars Labor Industrie Riunite) in Murano (of Guido Balsamo Stella) and the textile firm Carlo Piatti of Como (of Marcello Nizzoli).[9] It was the work of Ponti, Nizzoli and Balsamo Stella that caught the critics' eye in the 1923 *Biennale* in Monza and again in Paris in 1925.

Another sign of the times was the renaming of the Università delle Arti Decorative in Monza (founded in 1921 as a school for training craftsmen) as the Istituto Superiore per le Industrie Artistiche (ISIA). The ISIA soon developed a more professional approach to the education of designers, with emphasis on industrial production, promotion and packaging. Guido Balsamo Stella was a director (1929-32) and Fortunato Depero, Marcello Nizzoli, Mario Sironi, Edoardo Persico, Giuseppe Pagano and many others taught there.

The Italian pavilion at the Paris 1925 Exhibition attracted mixed reviews. Although Teofilo Rossi, who had been Vice-President of the 1902 Turin Exhibition, was in charge, the Italian contribution lacked the panache of the earlier show. The pavilion itself, designed by the Roman architect Armando Brasini in a heavy rendering of *cinquecento* architecture, was defended by the organizer of the Italian contingent, Margherita Sarfatti, as at least having the courage of its convictions (see plate 12.16). She pointed out that the materials, including the monolithic marble columns, were genuine and imposed an authentic authority, unlike the white 'staff' (reinforced plaster) used in many of the French pavilions. To most critics, however, the pavilion simply failed to meet the requirement of modernity. Sarfatti, at that time Mussolini's lover, insisted on the need to rebuild a 'stronger and more masculine style' with 'a clear logic to the forms, casting aside chaos and

responding to the native traditions in each country – which for us means classicism'.[10] Her analysis of the spirit of the age warned of the dangers inherent in abandoning tradition:

> Speedy and mechanical, modern life forces us towards a sometimes brutal simplification of language in its current usage – always peremptory, sometimes abrupt. At the same time it pushes us towards the simple and summary forms of the archaic. Primitives of a new age in which the machine will undoubtedly take an ever greater control of matter, we discover a secret but insistent longing which causes us to search out with sometimes excessive zeal the primitive exoticisms of China or Egypt or the fearful stammering of black Africa, with its embarrassed lisping full of infantile clumsiness. Everything belonging to the dawn of ancient and rudimentary civilizations seems good and new to us.[11]

This barbaric primitivism, according to Sarfatti, was not the answer for a civilized country like Italy. A purified modern style underpinned by the logic of classicism was the solution. And this was exactly what the juries in Paris appreciated in Gio Ponti's ceramics, which featured his witty 'Conversazione classica' vase, displayed in the Italian pavilion (plate 19.2). Ponti carried away the Grand Prix for porcelain. Interestingly, one of these pieces was dedicated to Fernanda and Ugo Ojetti on the occasion of Ugo's seventieth birthday. Ojetti was the foremost traditionalist critic in Italy, thundering against any implied threat to the classical style. Yet Ponti also worked in a wonderfully free and personal style. Among the pieces exhibited in Paris was one of his series 'Le mie donne'. And in the catalogue of the Italian exhibit, Gio Ponti wrote an article on the rationale of the modern style, in which he argued for the inevitability of designing for industry: 'industry is the "manner" of the twentieth century, its method of creation'.[12] Although Ponti made most of his designs, in ceramics, furniture and other media, for a discriminating Milanese bourgeoisie, he was also extremely important in educating this influential industrial class into the thinking of European Modernism.

But Sarfatti, too, went on to establish Italian avant-garde credentials, claiming that, in the exhibition, 'avant-garde art has two extreme outposts, in the Soviet Pavilion and in the Futurist stand in the Italian Section at the Grand Palais'.[13] Sarfatti, like Mussolini, had a soft spot for the Futurists and helped them secure a good place in the Grand Palais, with three large rooms near the grand staircase.[14] Giacomo Balla, Fortunato Depero

and Enrico Prampolini mixed paintings, sculptures and slogans with brightly coloured and seductive graphics, textiles and furniture. Depero's large tapestry *Serrada* (the name of an Alpine village where he liked to spend the summer) was made in 1920 and had already picked up a gold medal in Bolzano before being exhibited at the first *Biennale* in Monza (1923) and subsequently in Paris (plate 19.1). This celebration of bucolic simplicity and plenty was shown alongside the more Futurist iconography of other tapestries: *Guerra-Festa* and *Modernità* (now destroyed). Rovereto, where Depero lived and worked, was on the front line (on the Austrian side) throughout much of the war, and Depero's fierce patriotism is expressed in *Guerra-Festa*, which illustrates both the tragedy and the exhilaration of war. Like many of the Futurists, Depero sympathized with the nationalistic and militaristic yearnings of the Fascists and designed Futurist clothes and pennants for Fascist *squadri* and regiments.[15] He picked up several awards in Paris and did a brisk trade in the Parisian salons with the colourful cushions he had sent from Rovereto.[16] According to the influential critic Vittorio Pica, 'the Futurists saved Italy in Paris'. Enrico Prampolini had already moved to Paris, as had the painter Gino Severini, and it was their acceptance as a small part of the Parisian avant-garde that prepared the ground for the success of the Futurists in Paris and preserved their authority in Italy. Although the Futurists represented an isolated and increasingly marginal clique in Italy, many of the designers who made the most significant impact in Italy in the 1930s had their origins in what has been called the 'second Futurism'.

The Italian contributions to the Paris Exhibition represented two extremes of the Art Deco phenomenon. These gradually came together, with the classicists adapting new methods and introducing increasingly decorative fantasy, while the Futurists adapted to the real world of commercial design. Squeezed out were the master craftsmen. To take one influential example, Duilio Cambellotti was a Roman cabinetmaker and artist who espoused the socialist views of the Società Umanitaria and taught there in 1919.[17] He worked with disabled war veterans and insisted on celebrating the life of peasant communities in his work. Although he did a

19.2 Gio Ponti and Libero Andreotti, 'La conversazione classica'. Porcelain. Italian, 1927. Made by Manufattura di Doccia, Richard-Ginori. Museo Poldi Pezzoli, Milan.

great deal of work for the stage and as an illustrator, he tried to keep traditions of craftsmanship alive. He organized the Roman rooms in successive Biennales in Monza, designing, for example, the 'Sala degli Abitatori della Campagna Romana' at the 1925 *Biennale*. On a piece featured in this room, the 'Cofano della notte', Cambellotti carved flocks of sheep in ivory and ebony to evoke his beloved countryside. This kind of craftsmanship became less and less easy to sustain, and Cambellotti adapted to a more decorative role, serving the corporate clients of the Fascist state. His interiors for the Palazzo dell'Aquedotto Pugliese in Bari (1931-4) contain a coherent scheme of frescoes, furniture and stone carving – all bearing the iconography of flowing water – which transformed Arts and Crafts principles into Art Deco.

Eugenio Quarti and his son Mario present a typical passage through the period. Richly Art Nouveau at the turn of the century, they slowly adapted to work with interiors designed by more classical architects (Gio Ponti and Marcello Piacentini) while also evolving a decorative manner informed by Parisian Art Deco. The Banco di Mescita del Camparino, a small bar in the Galleria, Milan, 1925, is a jewel of Art Deco elegance. Its dark veneers of coloured woods with metal inlay by Eugenio Quarti match the sophisticated metalwork of Mazzucotelli and the mosaics of Angelo d'Andrea. Recently restored and expanded, it shows how the Art Deco vocabulary allowed the possibility of creating a sense of voluptuous luxury with simple means. Ten years later the Quartis would be designing within the classicizing envelope of the Novecento group.[18]

In 1925, the influential critic Roberto Papini wrote an important article in *Emporium*, in which he admitted that he had given up hope of finding genuine creativity among peasant craftsmen:

> Anyone wanting to make art today must remember that we live in an age of bold and long-awaited simplification. In other words, we are in full flood of reaction against the superfluity of useless ornaments, against complication of lines and mouldings … This explains those tendencies called neo-classical.[19]

Papini saw a clear choice for designers. Either they had to follow the road of Futurism or Cubism and strive for the utmost simplicity (following Margherita Sarfatti, he called this the 'primitive' or 'oriental' path), or they had to search for the best of the classical or neo-classical past. Art Deco in Italy was influenced by both. The latter was the chosen path of the Novecento group, based in and around Milan.[20] Organized socially in the Club degli Urbanisti, the

19.3 Giovanni Muzio, Cà Brutta, Milan. 1923-4. Photo: Tim Benton.

architects of the Novecento group would dominate commissions for office buildings and elegant condominiums in Milan for the next decade. The key figures were Giuseppe de Finetti, Tommaso Buzio, Giovanni Muzio, Piero Portaluppi and Gio Ponti, who worked in partnership with Emilio Lancia from 1927 to 1933.

Giovanni Muzio made his reputation as a fanatical advocate of a return to order in an article on architecture in Milan in the nineteenth century, in which he criticized the eclecticism and individualism which had, he maintained, spoiled the urban unity of Milan.[21] Arguing against the mere copying of old styles, however, he believed that only a full understanding of the rules of classical architecture would allow modern architects to find a new style based on the new materials and constructional methods. Paradoxically, he made his name as an architect with the purely superficial styling of a large condominium on the Via delle Moscove, dubbed immediately by the public 'Cà Brutta' (plate 19.3). The building had already been designed and approved before Muzio became involved.[22] Muzio's aim was to turn this standard Milanese block into a work of art and a rallying cry for the Novecento group. In this he was successful, attracting almost universal scorn from the Milanese press, but also the support of the young Roman architect Marcello Piacentini, who was to become the most influential

architect of the Fascist regime in the 1930s. Muzio used the colour and texture of different materials (warm travertine and white Istrian marbles, dark green and white stucco) and a collage of classical motifs to create a whole urban scenery in this one building.[23] It was Muzio who designed the building for the 1933 Milan *Triennale*, in a style that mixed ironic classicism with a thoroughly modern sense of structure and space. The work of Muzio, de Finetti, Ponti and others in the Novecento group provided Italian architects with a repertoire of forms adaptable to modern tasks. And it was the collaboration between Muzio and the painter Mario Sironi, in the 'Sala della Grafica' in the 1930 *Triennale* of Monza that showed how far he was prepared to go towards abstraction.

Meanwhile, a rival tendency to the Novecento group was developing in the form of the Rationalists. A group of young architects from Milan, Como and Turin formed the Gruppo Sette in 1926.[24] From 1930 onwards, debates raged between the classicists and the Modernists, with the Modernist critic P. M. Bardi in *Quadrante* polemicizing with Marcello Piacentini in *Architettura* (the official organ of the Sindacato Fascista degli Architetti). In fact, there is a curious convergence between the Novecento group and the Rationalists, whose hard Modernism was fuelled by a good knowledge of the European Modern Movement.[25] As architects like Muzio, Portaluppi and

Ponti simplified their classical language and adapted it to modern constructional methods, many of the Rationalists introduced elements of the 'Latin spirit' into their work, not least for political reasons. For Giuseppe Pagano, the editor of *Casabella*, the conflict was not between Novecento and Razionalismo, both of which he castigated as formalist, but between formalism and a middle way based on genuine rationalism.[26] The designs of a chair in 'buxus' (a composite material giving the impression of lacquer) by Giuseppe Pagano for the Gualino building in Turin (the headquarters of SALPA) of 1928-9 and a red lacquered chair of 1933 by Marcello Piacentini for the apartment of Fiammetta Sarfatti (daughter of Margherita) show that the gap between the defender of Modernized Classicism and the advocate of Modernism was not great (plates 19.4 and 19.5). In both cases, the values of traditional cabinetmaking were replaced by striking

forms that either exploited new materials (buxus) or imitated exotic ones (red lacquer). At the same time, however, the clear decorative effects mark these out as Art Deco rather than Modernist designs.

The strong influence of the Novecento group in the 1930s has led the leading historian of Italian decorative art, Rossana Bossaglia, to restrict her definition of Art Deco strictly to the 1920s. The historiography has let her down, however. The recent fashion for attributing the Art Deco label to an ever wider range of modernizing tendencies in inter-war architecture and design, especially in the United States, has thrown up striking similarities between Italian Fascist and American visual culture in the 1930s. The typical, stripped, Modernized Classicism with decorative trimmings of the American New Deal closely approximates to Italian Fascist examples. Italian design throughout the inter-war and Fascist period may therefore be seen to exemplify many of

19.5 Marcello Piacentini, chair. Red lacquer. Italian, 1933. Mitchell Wolfson Jr Collection-Fondazione Regionale C. Colombo, Genoa, Italy.

19.4 Giuseppe Pagano, chair. Buxus. Italian, 1928-9. Mitchell Wolfson Jr Collection-Fondazione Regionale C. Colombo, Genoa, Italy.

those features that are at the core of Art Deco: an instinct for inventive decorative expression, a rejection of 'hard' Modernism and an equal suspicion of derivative traditionalism, underpinned by a conviction that new work had to be 'modern'.

Gio Ponti, through his own designs for a wide range of clients and in different materials, and also in his editorship of the influential magazine *Domus*, retained the centre ground of Italian Art Deco throughout the 1930s. A page featuring his new black and gold design for Richard-Ginori in 1930, for example, demonstrates not only his willingness to change but also the care with which the aesthetic effect was presented on the page. His partnership with the glass and crystal manufacturer Fontana produced a number of spectacular one-off pieces of high Art Deco. But he also worked for the giant firm Montecatini, designing two office buildings for them in Milan and all the interior details, including aluminium furniture and a new range of black sanitary ware. Montecatini specialized in aluminium, a material common in Italy, which was given new importance both by its association with modernity (aeroplanes and Zeppelins) and its role in Italy's policy of economic self-sufficiency, established in response to European sanctions. Ponti also never

ceased to advocate large-scale production of
furniture at reasonable cost, working with the up-
market department store Rinascente for which he
designed the 'Domus nova' range, which became
increasingly modern in production methods and
appearance through the 1930s.

The transition of the Futurists from avant-garde
artists to Art Deco designers was not an easy one.
To survive, Antonio Bragaglia, Ernesto Prampolini
and Fortunato Depero founded craft workshops.[27]
Depero's was the most successful, despite constant
money worries, producing a wide range of products
from monumental tapestries to articles of clothing
and toys. Although the products of the Casa d'Arte
Depero were handmade, Depero was obsessed with
the potential of mass production and studied the
simple, repeatable forms and effects of colour that
might be produced in quantity with the right support.
He was also an enthusiastic student of the
techniques of promotion and advertising, composing
a 'Manifesto of Futurist Advertising' in 1932.[28] This
followed his attempt to make a career in New York
(1928-30), where he tried to move into large scale
production with a contract with the New Transit
Import and Export Company. This project, and his
Futurist House in New York, soon failed, in a culture
concerned with efficiency rather than art. He finished
up designing covers for *Vanity Fair* and *Vogue* and
trying to revive his production of tapestries, scarves
and cushions, some of these for Wanamakers
(plate 19.6). Despite the purchase of machinery to
mechanize the production of his cushions, Depero
never made the breakthrough he sought in New York
and returned to Italy in October 1930. Considering
advertisement as an extension of public art, he
never understood the promotional importance of
brand imagery and the complex factors influencing
consumption. For him, promotional art was simply a
question of producing a public art of maximum
impact:

> The art of advertising is colourful, pared down to
> essentials, fascinating, boldly proclaiming itself on
> the façades of buildings, in shop-windows, on trains,
> in the street, everywhere … Living art, not locked
> away in Museums. Art freed from academic
> restraints. Art that is playful, bold, exhilarating,
> optimistic … Advertising billboards are the symbolic
> images of a product, the ingenious plastic and
> pictorial forms to bring out its best.[29]

His work is of great interest for Art Deco, however,
because it demonstrates the application of avant-
garde ideas to the realities of commerce. There is an
astonishing transference of forms and ideas between
his commercial and artistic work. For example, the
Martellatori, exhibited as wooden sculptures in
the Paris 1925 Exhibition, originated in an advertising
campaign for the manufacturer of refractory bricks
Verzocchi in 1924 but later became part of Depero's
repertoire of humanoid-machine forms.[30] Informed
by Futurist ideas about the transforming power of
industrialization and the machine, his promotional
images depended on establishing an identity between
the product and the fantasy of the consumer.
Embedding the client's name or logo into a
decorative composition, as with his work for Daniele
Campari (plate 19.7), or creating three-dimensional
forms out of the names of the client, Depero
exemplified Marinetti's idea of 'words in freedom',
or free association poetry. The pavilion designed for
the bookshop Bestetti Treves Tuminelli and executed
for the Monza exhibition of 1927, and the pavilions
for Campari or for his own Casa d'Arte Futurista, took
these ideas to extremes (plate 19.8). These three-
dimensional celebrations of the word have strong
resonance, however, with the neon and three-
dimensional sign writing of American and European
advertising. And the one successful advertising
campaign Depero managed in New York, for the
American Lead Pencil Company, as well as the
posters for his own exhibitions, made an impact on
American graphic art, being exhibited at the
Advertising Club in Park Avenue in 1929.

Another prizewinner in Paris in 1925, who went on
to influence graphic art and textile design throughout
the 1930s, was Marcello Nizzoli. His Grand Prix in
Paris was for his silk shawls for G. Piatti, and he
went on to design for a number of textile firms.
Nizzoli's display of silk shawls in Paris employed
highly stylized mannequins, designed by himself in
the style of Archipenko. Typical of Italian Art Deco
designers, he joyously broke the barriers of the
media, fabricating full-size three-dimensional
mannequins collaged out of card, sheet metal and
whatever he could find. Similar mannequins,
constructed from cut out strips of steel, were used in
his displays for Snia-Viscosa artificial silks in 1928.
His graphic designs for Campari helped to define the
norms of the Art Deco poster, with their knowing

references to Cubism, their razor-sharp lighting and
dramatic composition.[31] By 1936, Nizzoli was
working for Olivetti as a fully fledged industrial
designer, inventing the streamlined and super-elegant
typewriters, cash machines and calculators (the key
work is the Olivetti Summa 40, 1940) which, with
very few alterations, would launch the wave of Italian
modern design in the 1950s. Nizzoli was also a
trend-setting exhibition designer, using the licence to
boast implicit in Fascist industrial exhibitions to

19.9 Luciano Baldessari, 'Luminator', standing lamp. Chrome-plated steel. Italian, 1929. MART, Trento.

manipulate light, giant photographs and projected sculptural forms in unprecedented ways.[32] All these works conform precisely to Art Deco principles by being decidedly modern but quintessentially decorative and emphatically promotional.

Typical of the best Art Deco, too, is the close proximity of abstract invention and the mechanisms of display and promotion, as seen in the work of Luciano Baldessari. Baldessari also worked for textile companies and was subject to similar influences from Paris as well as from the Bauhaus. He designed some stunning displays in the *Mostra della Seta* in Como in 1927, using semi-abstract metal mannequins designed by Archipenko and tubular steel humanoid sculptures of his own invention. One of his tubular steel display sculptures was worked up into a modernistic lighting sculpture, which he dubbed the 'Luminator' (plate 19.9).

Enrico Prampolini's work for the theatre also prepared him to become one of the foremost exhibition designers of his day. His 'Sala d'Attesa' in the *Mostra dell'Aeronautica* (Milan, 1934), for example, combines the fantasy of 'Aeropittura' with the constructional and spatial sense of the Rationalists and the decorative invention of Art Deco.[33] In some of his furniture designs, he adapted his Futurist irony to a close observation of the more outré designs shown in Paris.

Futurist ideas and fantasies illuminated much more of Italian architecture and design than might at first appear. For example, the architect who designed more railway stations and post offices than any other in the 1930s, Angiolo Mazzoni, was a close friend of Marinetti's. He wrote a 'Manifesto of Aerial Architecture' and was for a time co-editor (with Mino Somenzi) of the Futurist journal *Sant'Elia*, yet he was critical of the excesses of Futurist rhetoric and it is hard to detect Futurist elements in his public buildings.[34] However, in his adjoining technical and service buildings, and in his choice of Futurist artists to embellish the interiors with mosaics and frescoes, his Futurist associations can be detected.[35]

A text that perfectly captures the theoretical basis and aesthetic puzzle of Art Deco was the book published in 1930 by Roberto Papini, *Le arti d'oggi: Architettura e arti decorative in Europa*.[36] Papini was one of the most influential Italian critics of architecture and design and his book included a well informed and exhaustive survey of European and American architecture and decorative art, treading a fine line between Modernism and classicism. He followed a Modernist principle in focusing on icons of modernity – engineering works and bridges – before surveying modernizing decorative arts (mostly in France) and architecture (mostly in Austria and Germany). He described an entirely mythical metropolis – Universa – 'capital of the ultra-modern world spirit'. This metropolis arose, like Italian Fascism, from war and discord and was founded by 'a daring phalange of young people, conquerors and conquered'. This was the place for 'the experimentation and execution of all the most up-to-date methods discovered by modern technology for human existence . . . the home of today's men, thrusting at top speed towards the future'. Universa was organized along Fascist lines, with craft based corporations, full employment and obedience to an absolute authority.[37] It was an imaginary Fascist world where modernity and order were rigorously and positively united. But its productions were somehow international and cosmopolitan. In other words, Papini was calling for a legitimate cultural interaction with desirable foreign producers, while claiming to demonstrate Italian Fascist world leadership.

In Papini's Universa traditionalism was banned.[38] All those who copied the styles of the past were exiled. Universa's architects all understood, apparently, that architecture 'begins with the plan . . . which is developed assiduously into a harmony of aesthetics, adherence to function and obedience to the needs of this very new taste'. 'Architect and engineer are one', Papini goes on to say, in language reminiscent of Le Corbusier. But he also made clear that Le Corbusier ('this loquacious and turbulent Swiss') had been expelled from Universa. So Modernism was out, too.

The architecture of Universa was 'governed by logic but revived by fantasy' (a plausible definition of Art Deco). It was inspired by new technology, especially electric illumination. Universa was distinguished by the spectacular play of light, both by day and night,

> the city takes on fantastic characteristics; walls take on an illusory transparency; lunar gleam or dazzling glare according to the area ... direct or indirect light; spotlights or zone lighting; white or coloured light; crude or shaded light; reflected or naked neon light, fixed or flashing light, concentrated or diffused light; light, light, light.

This fascination with the glittering spectacle of the ephemeral is central to Art Deco. But the exuberance was controlled by logical use of the most modern constructional techniques, functional planning and a respect for the rules of proportion based on classical architecture. Although the women of Universa knew their place, happy to concentrate on bringing up children and making the home an ever-changing centre of delight, it was their imagination that determined the taste in Universa, while the scientists and technologists provided new colours and new materials, with new properties, for the designers to work with. Thus feminine fantasy fuelled consumption, which in turn prompted scientific and technological invention. Designers were prompted towards 'a stylization based on synthesis' and 'vigorous expression'. A vigorous expression founded on a synthesis between Nordic abstraction and oriental eroticism could serve the needs of industrialization while building consensus in the Fascist state.

Italian design between the wars well exemplifies the marriage of fantasy and technical invention that lies at the heart of Art Deco. The lead given by top designers like Ponti filtered down to everyday design at every level. Dante Baldelli's 'Vaso con arcieri' of 1933-4 is an unspectacular design, but it perfectly exemplifies the requirements of serial production and absorbs the lingua franca of Art Deco, recognizable from posters and graphic art.[39] Taste was shifted by firms like Linoleum, which employed designers like Giuseppe Pagano to radicalize their designs.[40] Advertisements like these, with their exaggerated Art Deco conventions, dramatic perspective and bright colour, lifted the appearance of architectural and design magazines such as *Domus* and *Casabella*, often in advance of the contents. Nowhere outside America were the arts of graphic design, exhibition design and advertising taken so seriously as in Italy. Serious critics like Pagano and Raffaello Giolli wrote articles about advertising and saw publicity as a medium of change.[41]

The new industries in Italy also turned to the new breed of designers to redefine their goods. Most of the early streamlining of automobiles took place in Europe, with Lancia and Alfa Romeo in Italy making important contributions. In 1935, however, the year after the ill-fated Chrysler Airflow, Fiat introduced the 1500 (see plate 34.6). This began a general process

19.10 Marcello Dudovich,
La nuova Balilla per tutti, poster.
Colour lithograph. Italian, 1934.
Courtesy of Fiat Archives.

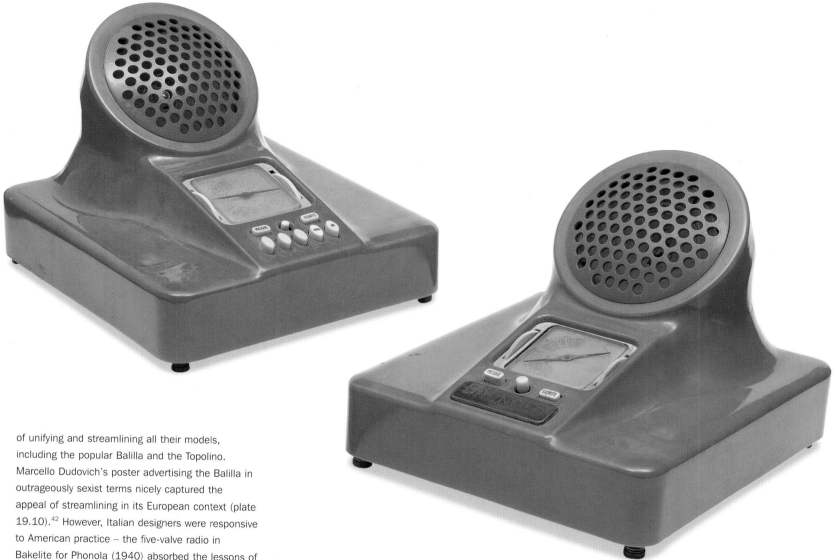

of unifying and streamlining all their models, including the popular Balilla and the Topolino. Marcello Dudovich's poster advertising the Balilla in outrageously sexist terms nicely captured the appeal of streamlining in its European context (plate 19.10).[42] However, Italian designers were responsive to American practice – the five-valve radio in Bakelite for Phonola (1940) absorbed the lessons of American streamlining and completely changed the appearance of the radio, transforming it into a piece of office equipment (plate 19.11).

The formal inventiveness of Italian industrial designers, most of them trained at the ISIA or in schools of architecture, gave Italian industrial products a more graceful, lightweight and aesthetically mature quality than their American counterparts. The high-speed train developed by the Ferrovia dello Stato and the Breda coach-building company was as sophisticated and elegant an example of streamlining as anywhere in Europe.

The low drag coefficient, studied at the new Guidonia wind tunnel and water tank, allowed the train to reach speeds of over 200 kph (125 mph) and make the Milan-Florence journey in two hours. Significantly, Breda turned to Gio Ponti and Giuseppe Pagano to work on the design, not only of the fittings but also of the overall shape of the train.[43] Characteristic of the frequent collaboration between Art Deco and Modernist designers, the result was an icon of stylish modernity, which paved the way for the dominance of Italian design in Europe after the Second World War.

19.11 Luigi Caccia Dominioni and Pier Giacomo Castiglioni, 5-valve radio. Bakelite. Italian, 1940. Made by Phonola. Collection Jeffrey S. Salmon, London.

20 Conscience and Consumption: Art Deco in Britain

Gillian Naylor

On 9 May 1925, one month after the launch of the Paris Exhibition displays, the *British Empire Exhibition* re-opened at Wembley. Addressing King George V and the 100,000 visitors at the opening ceremony, HRH The Duke of York explained the reasons for extending the celebrations:

> The Exhibition which you see set out before you has integrally the same purpose as in 1924 – to show how great are the resources within the Empire ... when we close our gates in November, it will be with the confidence that your peoples have benefited greatly, not only in regard to trade and production but also by the growth of an instructed pride in the Empire's achievements in the past, and its aims for the future.[1]

In 1925, therefore, Britain was focused on Empire trade and industry, and the exhibits demonstrated post-war hopes for an imperial future. In this context, a European exhibition of decorative arts was hardly a priority for Government support or funding, and high import duties, as well as a charge for space, discouraged many British manufacturers from participating in the Paris Exhibition displays.

Nevertheless, the organizers of the British exhibit in Paris, the Department of Overseas Trade, recognized that although the display was not necessarily representative of national achievement, it did raise several questions about the status of British design. Its *Reports*,[2] therefore, are worth some analysis, since they reflect 'establishment' assumptions about decoration and design in the 1920s and indicate design policies and achievements – such as those of Sweden and Denmark – that it was felt Britain might emulate.

Sir Hubert Llewellyn Smith, chairman of the Report Committee, was not the only critic to complain about the 'dullness and aloofness, and the absence of the spirit of adventure' in many of the British displays. British industrial art, he claimed, was impervious 'to the forces that have been sweeping over the Continent of Europe'; it was neither national nor international, and it was indifferent to foreign art movements.[3]

Neither was it an imperial display, and the reports make it clear that British designers and manufacturers were fighting, or failing to fight, on several fronts. According to Gordon Forsyth, the author of the report on pottery, British manufacturers (including Wedgwood, Adams, Copeland and Doulton) were 'staid and dull'; they needed creative designers, he insisted, if they were to lead in the various markets of the world. Sir Frank Warner and A. F. Kendrick, discussing textiles, described the contributing manufacturers as conservative, disinclined to break with the past and preoccupied with a 'world-wide market', leaving no room for experiment:

> it is obvious that the British manufacturer is coming to terms with the new order with caution and reserve ... he is searching for a middle course. It is notorious that many people, both at home and abroad, are looking for a new movement in England to take the place of that which William Morris became the typical representative ... When the change comes, it will not be the Art of Paris of 1925, but it might share some of its features.[4]

Similar problems of caution and conservatism were identified in all the categories represented (furniture, metalware, glass, bookbinding and print). The *Reports'* contributors, for the most part, recommended solutions based on the philosophies of the Design and Industries Association (DIA)[5] – an active liaison between art and industry, the integration of form and decoration, and a distrust of experiment for luxury's sake. A. Marriott Powell, who wrote about glass, maintained that Britain had lost its lead in the production of mould blown glass because its competitors 'had the sense to employ first-rate artists to design even the most simple shapes'. Sweden was his model here, while France (represented by Lalique, Daum, Baccarat and others) was experimenting with challenging new techniques, especially in pressed glass:

> The French exhibitors would seem to have devoted more time and trouble than those of any other nation to striving after new effects and even after

new methods of production, in some cases with conspicuous success, though but a few pieces shown can be described as reasonably cheap or suitable for use by any but the wealthy.[6] British design critics in the early 1920s, especially those associated with the DIA, had inherited the Arts and Crafts conscience – the moralities of practical use and fitness for purpose that had made their predecessors, in Nikolaus Pevsner's term, 'pioneers of modern design'. The extravagance of the French exhibits disturbed them – these were *objets de luxe*, 'hot-house products made under non-commercial conditions' – and examples of 'inexpensive furniture, clothing, utensils and other articles of common use were so scanty as to be practically negligible'.[7] This was certainly not decorative art for the masses; and the French had failed to acknowledge that society was changing, that there was a redistribution of wealth, a move from the rural to the urban, and a need for more and smaller houses, flats and apartments. One result, according to Llewellyn Smith, was that both the rich and the middle classes were moving from 'large and lofty to small and low ceilinged rooms'.[8]

This move from the lofty to the low had prompted the need for smaller, more flexible ranges of furniture and for built-in storage – shelf units and bookcases – as well as for coffee tables and cocktail cabinets and similar designs for a new domestic order. The British furniture on display in 1925 did not set out to meet these demands, but according to H. Shapland, the author of the furniture report, British work demonstrated truth to materials and therefore ease of production. The 'characteristic British straightness and rectangularity is the proper path of development', he wrote.[9] Sir Edward Maufe's desk (plate 20.1) for example, tasselled, gilded, gessoed and faced with white gold, was awarded a medal, and in Shapland's opinion, the design was 'essentially right'. Ruhlmann, on the other hand, 'by his very mastery and method does violence to the nature of the material in which he works'.[10]

The British lobby acknowledged that the French were aiming at the luxury market and that British industry had a wider and more eclectic remit. By the late 1920s, design reformers were mapping out several programmes for progress, as well as demonstrating differing interpretations of 'modernity'. In 1928, for example, Waring & Gillow's department store signalled its links with Paris by staging an exhibition of *Modern Art in French and English Furniture and Decoration* which gained general critical approval, including that of the Design and Industries Association. In their journal John C. Rogers

20.2 J. F. Johnson, cupboard. Macassar ebony veneer with ivory inlays. British, 1926-7. Made by Heal & Son Ltd. V&A: W.8-1975.

wrote that the exhibition was 'by far the best thing yet done in this country to re-establish the domestic crafts and to fire English designers with a new enthusiasm ... Queen Anne positively is dead, and so is Chippendale, and Sheraton.'[11]

Waring & Gillow, with their reputation for fine furniture making and interior design (for ships, hotels, clubs and embassies, as well as prestigious individual commissions) had a Paris branch at this time. It was run by the French designer Paul Follot, who was in charge of Bon Marché's Pomone pavilion at the Paris 1925 Exhibition. Waring & Gillow's 1928 exhibition marked the launch of their Department of Modern Art;[12] Serge Chermayeff was appointed head of the new department, as well as the exhibition, and Paul Follot contributed room settings to the display. According to Barbara Tilson, Follot's style 'was a mixture of the cursive and floriat Art Deco and 18th century ornamentation to produce [sic] a sumptuous effect through colour, gilding and moulding, rich

materials and strong naturalistic patterns, hardly altered by the Egypto-Cubist phase of late Deco'.[13]

While post-1960s design historians have confronted the nuances of the Art Deco style, in 1928 Waring & Gillow could confidently define the whole range of its new production as 'modern', and in the early 1920s, as the Paris 1925 Exhibition demonstrated, this modernity had many faces. Follot worked within a French tradition of modernity, while Serge Chermayeff was pioneering a more radical interpretation.

Chermayeff was born in Chechnya in 1900 and had lived in London since 1910. He was self-taught as a designer and had already travelled widely in Europe and South America when he was appointed to run the modern department. His early work for Waring & Gillow included cabinets with opulent veneers, but his room settings were more practical than those of Follot. A living room designed for Waring & Gillow around 1929 has geometric sofas and armchairs designed to maximize seating capacity and the use of space. They are fully upholstered in a Jazz Moderne fabric and are ranged around a hexagonal coffee table, which has shelving and a central cocktail cabinet; a small carpet with a geometric pattern defines the space.

If Waring & Gillow's Department of Modern Art offered its customers a cosmopolitan modernity in the 1920s, Heal & Sons was initially dedicated to the promotion of the Design and Industry Association's ideals of good design. Sir Ambrose Heal was a leading member of the DIA and in the early 1920s he sold Arts and Crafts inspired designs – in keeping with the DIA's conservative Modernism. In 1926-7, however, his designer J. F. Johnson introduced a range of bedroom furniture in macassar ebony influenced by the work of Ruhlmann, while in the 1930s Ambrose Heal designed and commissioned furniture that used new materials such as laminated wood and steel tubing (plates 20.2 and 20.3).

This eclecticism reflected wider developments in British furniture design, with an increasing number of designers working independently or in small groups. In 1927-8, for example, Syrie Maugham provided her wealthy clients with beige and white colour schemes, using screens and mirror glass (plate 20.4 and see plate 10.14). Betty Joel, who had London showrooms, was also successful with prestigious clients: her patrons included Lord Louis Mountbatten and the Queen Mother, and like the French she used eighteenth-century designs in her room settings. Other successful designers included Duncan Miller,

20.3 Leonard Thoday, dressing table. Glass and chrome-plated tubular steel. British, 1932. Made by Heal & Son Ltd. V&A: W.36-1977.

20.4 Syrie Maugham, mirrored screen. Silvered wood and mirrored glass. British, 1935. V&A: W.146-1978.

20.5 'Functionalist interior' and 'Modernistic interior'. Plates from Osbert Lancaster, *Homes Sweet Homes*, London, 1939. NAL.

Derek Patmore, Rodney Thomas, Cedric Morris and Maurice Adams. They used light woods, veneers and plywoods, and their designs for storage were innovative – built-in units, stacked units, units with curved door frames, units framing fireplaces. Maurice Adams, for example, produced an archetypal Art Deco cocktail cabinet – with rounded forms and classical references – in 1933 (see plate 2.6). In the 1920s and 1930s mass-manufactured ranges were introduced for the domestic market, including the Times Furnishing Company's 'Modern' range and P. E. Ganes's modernistic furniture, which was derived from Waring & Gillow's 'Modern Art' ranges.[14]

By the 1930s, however, designers and design reformers on the Continent as well as in Britain were assessing and evaluating the range of Twenties styles and sources of style. Serge Chermayeff, for example, had joined the Twentieth Century Group in 1930 and the MARS Group in 1933.[15] He promoted stainless steel and standardized unit furniture from Germany[16] in the Thirties and confirmed his allegiance with Modernism in 1933 when he formed a partnership with the émigré architect Erich Mendelsohn.

Modernism was widely promoted in Britain in the 1930s, when the theory and practice of contemporary Continental architects and designers was publicized, notably through the activities and writings of Nikolaus Pevsner, the German émigré art historian and critic. Pevsner was familiar with the German design reform movement and with the policies of the Deutscher Werkbund,[17] and after his arrival in Britain in 1933 the Cambridge University Press commissioned him to write a survey of design standards in British industry. He was far from complacent. 'When I say that 90 per cent of British industrial art is devoid of any aesthetic merit, I am not exaggerating', he wrote in *An Enquiry into Industrial Art in Britain*.[18] Aesthetic merit in this context related to his own aesthetic of Modernism, which, he explained, arose from 'a desire for cleanness, directness and precision': 'nothing of vital energy and beauty can be created unless it is fit for its purpose, in harmony with the materials and the process of production, clean, straightforward and simple'; 'Pursuit of these qualities is a social as well as a moral priority.'[19]

By defining Modernism, Pevsner was able to describe and condemn its alternatives, many of them, he believed, arising from that 'inexhaustible source of sham splendour' the Paris 1925 Exhibition. He deplored 'freakish angular details', 'infections of pseudo-cubism', 'atrocities of modernistic jazz patterns' and 'ceramic displays of jagged handles, square or polygonal plates, wrongly balanced pots' and 'sickening decoration'.[20]

Pevsner's *Enquiry* contributed to a crusade for good design – 'clean, straightforward' design – that was to survive into the post-war period. Its sober certainties, as well as alternative bourgeois choices, were satirized by the British elite. The illustrations to Osbert Lancaster's *Homes Sweet Homes*,[21] first published in 1939, sum up the reactions to the Pevsnerian lifestyles and their alternatives (plate 20.5). In Functionalism, the Corbusian male (identified by the spectacles and the pipe) sits on his Aalto stool, contemplating his Aalto furniture; Bauhaus designs furnish the rain-swept terrace. The electric fire is built in, the bookcases stack, the form of the radiogram blends perfectly with those of the bookcases, and there is African and abstract art. In another illustration the modernistic female, on her upholstered settee with Jazz Age cushions, confronts domestic bliss. Her coffee table to hand (with chocolates, lighter and ashtray but no books), she has a mock-Regency chair and cabinet, tasselled drapes, zigzag motifs on mirrors, lights and coving, and a mock log fire. The art, the ornaments and the pets are also Moderne.

In this context both the Moderne and the Modernist are viewed as vulgar and pretentious. The Modernist architect Leslie Martin, an editor of *Circle*,[22] was to describe the appeal of the 'modernistic' as 'the spurious appeal of surface decoration; yet another manifestation of that passion for "façade" which dragged out its life through the nineteenth century'.[23] These views prevailed among design reformers in Britain until the 1960s when Bevis Hillier published *Art Deco* (1968),[24] shocking surviving post-war pioneers and promoting a deluge of exhibitions, publications and collections. Art Deco, in Hillier's account, is associated with fun, fantasy and shopping; jazz and Cubism contributed to the style, as did the Ballets Russes, the cinema and the dance hall, as well as travel and tourism. The fall out from the Paris Exhibition, according to this interpretation, had galvanized British design in ways its guardians had never anticipated.

By the 1930s large sections of the population – including the upper and lower middle classes – had access to Art Deco. A decorative art for the select and for the masses, it had, according to Bevis Hillier, 'imposed itself universally – on hairdressers, shops, hand-bags, shoes, lamp posts and letter-boxes, as well as on hotels, cinemas and liners'.[25] There were, of course, designs that spanned the Modernist/Art Deco divide; both 'streams' on occasion promoted

craftsmen as artists, both aimed for the industrial manufacture of art for the masses, and both contributed to the transformation of the built environment. The differences relate to context and emphasis. The interior designs of Betty Joel, Syrie Maugham and the early Chermayeff, for example, might be described as Art Deco, since tradition was transformed rather than eliminated, and pattern, materials, colour and texture were used to define space (plate 20.6).

In many areas it is difficult to distinguish between Art Deco and Modernism, and for the historian the exercise can be self-defeating. Poster design and

pattern making, for example, might be interpreted as both Art Deco and Modernist, and since the designer (and client) was obviously indifferent to subsequent obsessions with classification, contemporary criticism can be helpful here. The American-born designer Edward McKnight Kauffer, for example, produced designs for carpets and posters that have been attributed to both Modernism and Art Deco (plate 20.7). His posters use Cubism, Futurism and Surrealism to convey the speed and energy of communication, and when he left the United States to come to London in 1914, he was given his first commission by Frank Pick, the design director of the

20.6 Betty Joel, carpet.
Wool. British, 1935-7.
V&A: T.296-1977.

20.7 Edward McKnight Kauffer
(American), *Soaring to Success!
The Daily Herald – The Early Bird*,
poster. Colour lithograph. 1918-19.
V&A: E.35-1973.

20.8 Gregory Brown, furnishing fabric. Roller-printed cotton. British, 1922. Made by William Foxton Ltd. V&A: T.325-1934.

London Underground. Pevsner, however, was not amused by Kauffer's work, writing 'His posters and those of a few others like Austin Cooper, looked in 1924 already exactly like the kind of thing that we are now used to calling "Paris-1925", rather wild and jazzy, but exciting and stimulating.'[26]

Pevsner associated the 'wild and the jazzy' with German Expressionism. In his opinion, Omega textiles 'were thoroughly Expressionist in pattern'[27] and Foxton Fabrics, who produced textiles for the West Indian market, also had 'a touch of the Expressionist'.[28] The DIA had included Foxton's West Indian designs on its stand in the Arts and Crafts Exhibition Society's display in the Royal Academy in 1916 and these were widely admired.[29] Their bright colours and bold patterns were totally different from those of the Arts and Crafts and Art Nouveau periods or from the contemporary English taste for neo-Georgian. Instead, their spontaneity could be related to designs for the Ballets Russes and the experiments of Paul Poiret, Raoul Dufy and the

Atelier Martine,[30] as well as to the vernacular revivals of folk art and design that had been exhibited in Paris in 1925.

British textile design in the 1920s and 1930s, therefore, had more potential than its display in the Paris 1925 Exhibition had demonstrated. The folk designs shown by several countries in the exhibition were influential for mainstream European textile design – the squares, diagonals and triangles of weaves, for example, contributing to new concepts of construction, and the block prints leading to experiments in pattern and form. Designers such as Phyllis Barron and Dorothy Larcher, Enid Marx and Marian Pepler used these methods and sold their designs through independent craft galleries. The British textile industry was also commissioning independent designers and artists to produce designs – for furnishings and fashion – that could flourish in an Art Deco context. Vibrant colours, emphatic repeats, florals and abstracts signalled the passing of William Morris's influence: this was the Jazz Age –

fabrics might be useful and beautiful, but they were also fun (plate 20.8).

Clarice Cliff of the ceramics industry, art director of A. J. Wilkinson from 1928, demonstrated a total commitment to Art Deco when she introduced her 'Bizarre' ware in 1929. Hand-painted 'Bizarre' and similar ranges that she produced in Wilkinson's Newport pottery included wall hangings, jugs and vases as well as tableware, and they celebrated the contemporary and decorative with their bold shapes and colours (particularly the Art Deco orange) (see plate 21.4). This is narrative pottery – with stories of woods and fields and flowers and castles and enchantment – and its sales, which survived the recession, were promoted in department stores as well as in specialist shops for china and glass.[31]

British ceramics, experimenting with form as well as decoration, could flout all Pevsner's conventions: Eric Slater, designing for Shelley Potteries, introduced 'Vogue' and 'Mode' in the 1930s, with polygonal plates, conical tea cups, triangular handles and

20.9 Paul Nash, Tilly Losch
bathroom, English, 1932. Mary
and Neville Ward, *Home in the
Twenties & Thirties*, 1978. NAL

sunbursts. The dressing table revealed new aids to feminine beauty – by Elizabeth Arden, for example, or Yardley – with sophisticated, tempting packaging. Mirrors were unframed and angled, usually placed over a fireplace tiled in cream or green; sometimes an electric fire (or imitation coal fire) was built in, or it perched in the hearth, also blue, cream or green, decorated with sunbursts and streamlines. The Art Deco bathroom with its stepped wall tiling, stainless steel towel rails, geometric linoleum and built-in units mimicked its aristocratic rivals in grand houses. For example, a bathroom for Tilly Losch was designed by Paul Nash in 1932 (plate 20.9).

New technologies and the electrification of the home introduced new object types, such as the radio, radiogram, telephone and vacuum cleaner. Radios and radiograms were produced with ziggurat or stepped casings. In 1931 Murphy Radios followed DIA advice by asking a designer to produce radios for them, and R. D. Russell, of Gordon Russell Ltd, introduced understated domestic designs for the middle-class home. E. K. Cole Ltd produced its alternative, the 'Consolette' (1931), designed by J. K. White in Bakelite, the winter landscape design on the tuning scale obviously relating it to Deco. Ekco's avant-garde plastic radios by Serge Chermayeff (1933) and Wells Coates (1934) were, according to Pevsner, 'the result of a careful study of function and a genuinely artistic imagination';[34] they could be considered Modernist, Moderne or Art Deco according to use and context (plate 20.10).

abstract patterns (see plate 10.8). The industry could also produce designs claimed by both Modernism and the Moderne. Keith Murray's earthenware for Wedgwood (1933-4), with its simple shapes, undecorated apart from incised circular lines, is usually associated with British Modernism, but it has also been described as being 'ornamented by the parallel horizontal bands of the streamline style'.[32] Susie Cooper, who had studied under Gordon Forsyth at the Burslem School of Art, established her own

firm in 1929 and produced designs (first patterns and then shapes) that were influenced by the theories of Continental Modernism.[33]

Designs such as these (and their imitations) became part of the middle-class domestic environment in the late 1920s and 1930s. In the Moderne house, generally in the suburbs, ceramic rabbits and Scottie dogs, glazed in emblematic green, lived on shelves and windowsills, with clocks and photographs framed in stainless steel or

20.10 Wells Coates, Ekco AD-65, radio. Bakelite. British, 1934.
Made by E. K. Cole Ltd. V&A: W.23-1981.

20.11 Edgar Brandt, 'Les cigognes d'Alsace', panel for a lift cage. Lacquer and metal on wood. French, 1928. For Selfridges, London. V&A: Circ.719-1971. © ADAGP, Paris and DACS, London 2002.

1930s. The Strand Palace, with its mirrored glass entrance and interiors, brought Hollywood to London, while the Corner Houses provided workers and shoppers with food and a contemporary setting (plate 20.13). Claridges, redesigned by Basil Ionides in 1929, demonstrated a sophisticated Deco re-interpretation of classicism for the very rich, while the Midland Hotel in Morecambe, designed by Oliver Hill in 1934, was a palace of fantasy for commoners and kings.[37] Cunard's *Queen Mary*, competing on the

transatlantic route, was also a showcase for British Deco design (see plate 29.9); the cinema brought Hollywood glamour to films and its buildings (see plates 1.12 and 3.7); the Daily Express building, designed by Owen Williams, with Ellis & Clarke, between 1929 and 1931, glamorized journalism with its cinema-set interiors (plate 20.12).

Unlike Modernism, which according to its theorists was an intellectual response to social needs as well as to the demands of materials, function and form, Art Deco in Britain was a style, in the French sense of the word, and whatever the market, it glamorized invention and creativity. The style celebrated the pleasures and possibilities of consumption – short-lived in the inter-war period, but persistent survivors in the Post-modern world.

Domestic goods could be bought in shops and department stores transformed by Art Deco. Selfridges' lifts were lined with wrought iron and bronze panels by Edgar Brandt (originally designed in 1922 and reproduced for Selfridges in 1928) (plate 20.11). Henry Wilson, reviewing the metalwork in the Paris 1925 Exhibition, recognized Brandt's adoption of innovative techniques and new approaches to form and construction. Brandt's work, he wrote, 'was no longer pure smith work, but the product of the development of autogenous soldering',[35] and his construction 'is taken up into the rhythm of design, when it comes subordinate to general form'.[36]

Art Deco in architecture is discussed elsewhere (see Chapter 22), so this summary can only give an indication of its range in Britain. New or refurbished hotels redefined luxury and pleasure for the inter-war generation. Oliver Bernard, who originally worked as a stage designer in Britain and the United States (and was technical director for the British exhibit in Paris in 1925), designed the interiors of the Strand Palace Hotel, the Cumberland Hotel, the Regent Palace Hotel and Lyons Corner Houses in the 1920s and

20.12 Sir E. Owen Williams, foyer of the Daily Express building, London. 1932. Photo: Peter Aprahamian. Courtesy Corbis.

20.13 Oliver Bernard, foyer
of the Strand Palace Hotel,
London. 1930-31.
© English Heritage, NMR.

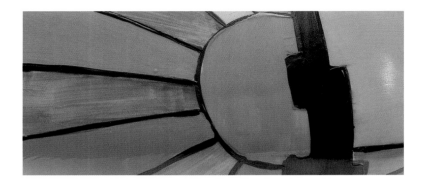

21 **British Art Deco Ceramics**

Alun Graves

In the late 1920s and the 1930s, ceramics in the Art Deco style were produced in quantity by British manufacturers. These wares were, by-and-large, made for the cheaper end of the market, where they enjoyed considerable popularity. In many ways, the acceptance of a style that was so distinctively modern, within an industry that was so notoriously conservative, was something of a breakthrough. Nevertheless, such wares have been derided for being vulgar, ugly and poorly made; for misunderstanding and debasing modern art; and for failing to adhere to the principles of good design, particularly in relation to form and function. These criticisms, still often stated, have led to the intellectual marginalization of what is in fact a rather extraordinary group of material. For rather than reaching the mass market in a watered-down form, mass-produced Art Deco ceramics represent a highly particular and often uncompromising manifestation of the style. If such wares are found lacking in sophistication or craftsmanship – and by no means all are – such defects are frequently made up for in vitality and exuberance.

For a number of reasons, there appears to have been a degree of reluctance on the part of British manufacturers to take part in the Paris 1925 Exhibition, and those displays that were mounted seem to have been regarded as somewhat dated, relying too heavily on historic styles, or characterized by the handcrafted earnestness typical of pre-war Arts and Crafts exhibitions.[1] This clearly ran counter to the exhibition's aim of promoting work of modern inspiration. The displays of certain manufacturers were, nevertheless, singled out for praise. The recently formed Carter, Stabler & Adams (CSA) of Poole, who were particularly well represented, were the recipients of a variety of awards. Sculptural works like Harold and Phoebe Stabler's 'The Bull', which was shown by CSA, represented the more robust end of the spectrum of British figurative ceramics (plate 21.1). However, it could barely be seen as reflecting the newest trends, the work having been originally modelled over a decade

21.1 Harold and Phoebe Stabler, 'The Bull'. Press-moulded stoneware. British. Designed 1914, made by Carter, Stabler & Adams, c.1921-4. V&A: C.113-1977.

previously. Also shown by CSA were vessels painted with their own particular brand of lively floral decoration. Although these exemplified the trend towards bold, hand-painted patterns, in the light of what was to follow they appear comparatively restrained. Later work by the firm, particularly that of the designer Truda Adams (later Truda Carter), was of strong Art Deco character yet it maintained a level of craftsmanship and a relatively restrained palette that kept it largely beyond reproach (see plate 7.5) – unlike some of the brasher products of Staffordshire.

It was only after 1925 that modern continental styles began to infuse the products of the ceramic industry. According to Nikolaus Pevsner, who conducted a survey of design, manufacture and marketing in the pottery industry in the mid-1930s, the influx of designs that might, broadly

21.2 Tea service. Earthenware, painted in enamels. British, c.1931-5. Made by A. E. Gray & Co. Ltd. V&A: C.295-1976.

21.3 Enoch Boulton, 'Jazz', ginger jar. Earthenware, painted in enamels and gilt. British, c.1928-30. 'Carlton Ware' made by Wiltshaw & Robinson Ltd. V&A: Circ.526-1974.

speaking, be considered as Art Deco appeared on the market around 1927-9. These he termed Modern Floral, and this itself comprised two distinct types: hand-painted designs of a rustic nature, and lithographed or hand-painted designs of a 'modern commercial character, often intermixed with some cubistic elements'.[2] The former had been introduced in order to compete with, and in imitation of, cheap imported wares from Eastern Europe. Pevsner clearly despised these various Modern Floral wares, terming them 'hideous'. Nevertheless, his report demonstrated their popularity: in one department store Modern Floral made up more than half of all sales of teaware. Pevsner noted, however, that above a certain price, sales of this type of article rapidly fell off. He also recounted with a degree of snobbishness how one supplier of picnic cases was forced to place wares with banded decoration, which were actually cheaper to produce, into his more expensive sets, while Modern Floral went into the cheapest, so as to satisfy the tastes of the various markets. Whether banded or floral, British-made earthenwares were, by the mid-1930s, almost entirely what Pevsner described as 'modern (or modernistic)' in appearance (plate 21.2). They were often marketed with evocative names such as 'Sunray' or 'Jazz' (plate 21.3). This situation contrasted markedly with that of bone china, where period designs remained dominant.

While the influence of Art Deco was eventually felt throughout a large section of the market, its introduction had been effected by a small number of progressive designers. Susie Cooper, who during the 1920s worked for the firm of A. E. Gray & Co., was among the first to promote hand-painted 'rustic' decoration. Later, around 1927-8, she introduced a range of

21.4 Clarice Cliff, 'Sunray', vase.
Earthenware, painted in enamels.
British, c.1929-30.
Made by Arthur J. Wilkinson Ltd.
V&A: C.74-1976.

21.5 Susie Cooper, ginger jar. Earthenware, painted in enamels.
British, c.1926-7. Made by Susie Cooper Pottery. V&A: C.193-1977.

geometrical patterns of a severely abstract nature, hand-painted in vibrant colours (plate 21.5). These included 'Moon and Mountains' and 'Cubist'. Cooper, however, quickly abandoned this design idiom, and it barely survived her period at Grays, which ended in 1929. The most celebrated and prolific designer associated with British Art Deco, was, however, Clarice Cliff. Born into a working-class family in Tunstall, near Stoke-on-Trent, in 1899, Cliff worked in the ceramics industry from the age of thirteen, joining the firm of A. J. Wilkinson Ltd in 1916. There, her artistic abilities were noticed, and she was placed in the design studio. A visit to Paris in 1927 was decisive, and on her return Cliff developed a range of bold, abstract, geometrical hand-painted patterns which were at first applied to a stock of otherwise unsaleable ware. The name 'Bizarre' was coined, and the initially suspicious company salesmen were persuaded to market the range from 1929, which proved an immediate success. As well as many hundreds of painted patterns, from 1929 Cliff also produced a number of geometrical pottery shapes, the first of which, 'Conical', originally incorporated the triangular fin-like cup handles that so enraged the design critics of the period. While Cliff's designs are at times somewhat crude, and she was on occasion guilty of a degree of plagiarism, her success in assembling a range of pottery that captured the mood of the period and the imagination of the public is unquestionable (plate 21.4). Though largely restricted to the production of earthenware, the stylish influence of Art Deco was also felt in the manufacture of bone china at the Shelley Potteries, thanks to the carefully considered, sophisticated and elegant pattern and shape designs of its art director, Eric Slater (see plate 10.8). The style also manifested itself in the design of mass-produced figurines, this being implemented with particular artistic success by Doulton & Co. and Wedgwood (plates 21.6 and 21.7).

21.6 Adrian Allinson, 'Diana'.
Earthenware. British, 1926.
V&A: C.538-1934. Richard Garbe,
'Spirit of the Wind'. Earthenware.
British. Designed 1932,
made by Doulton & Co., *c.*1933-9.
V&A: C.58-1988.

21.7 John Skeaping, 'A Group of Axis
Deer'. Earthenware. British, 1927.
Made by Josiah Wedgwood & Sons
Ltd. V&A: C.426-1934.

TOURISME

RENSEIGNE
MENTS DE
TOURISME·
AVIATION·
BILLETS·
DE·CH·DE
FER·NAVI
GATION·

22 Art Deco Architecture

Tim Benton

The first question to ask about Art Deco architecture is whether it is legitimate to apply to buildings a definition and concept clearly born in a different context and with a different purpose ... specifically that of the decorative arts.[1]

Is Art Deco *architecture* a useful concept, or can we only talk about buildings with Art Deco ornament?[2] This question would have been incomprehensible to most nineteenth- and early twentieth-century architects and critics, for whom architectural style was defined by its ornament. But, in the twentieth century, a split occurred between those architects for whom 'modernity' could be represented mainly in terms of architectural decoration and those for whom the 'spirit of the age' required 'architectural' solutions. This latter group included both strict Classicists and Modernists. Classicists were trained to accept rules of composition and decoration that specified the forms to be used. Modernists believed that architectural form should result from an analysis of function and an expression of new structural methods with no reference to styles of the past and preferably no ornament at all.[3] Classicists and Modernists alike sneered at the 'Moderne' or 'modernistic' application of Art Deco ornament, which they saw as 'commercial'. More recently, however, architects and critics have begun to re-evaluate the importance of the decorative in architecture, seeing it not only as a popular reflection of rapidly changing conditions but as a rich and profound expression of human feelings.

In practice, many 'Art Deco' buildings derive from Classicist, Regionalist or Modernist styles, with Art Deco sculptural or mural decorative enhancements.[4] L. H. Boileau's design for the Pomone pavilion, for example, at the Paris 1925 Exhibition, used a symmetrical, classical composition, but substituted for conventional detailing a spectacular stained-glass window with an Art Deco sunburst and an overall decorative pattern impressed into the plaster walls (see plate 14.5). Similarly, Josef Hoffmann's Austrian pavilion deployed an explicitly classical articulation, complete with pilasters and pediments but rendered decorative by the moulding of the external walls in a graceful profile (see plate 12.18). At the other end of the spectrum were 'decorative Modernist' works, based on Modernist compositional methods but rendered decorative either by applied figurative ornamentation or by a flamboyant use of colour.[5] An example of this at the 1925 Exhibition was Rob Mallet-Stevens's Pavillon du Tourisme (plate 22.1).

Most Art Deco buildings can be attributed to these two categories, 'Modernized Classicism' and 'decorative Modernism'. There are, however, some buildings in which form, structure, colour and space, as well as ornament, work together to produce modern effects without reference to past styles and these too can be called Art Deco. At the 1925 Exhibition, the Primavera pavilion by Henri Sauvage, with its concrete dome studded with glass pebbles and completely novel profile, is an example of this last – a fantastic projection into architecture of the Art Deco imagination (see plate 14.4). Similarly, the skyscrapers and the Streamline Moderne style in North America developed quite new architectural forms, with or without European Art Deco ornament. These, in turn, later had an influence in Europe, notably in the architecture of commerce and leisure. Various attempts have been made to create hard and fast distinctions between different kinds of Art Deco architecture but none has prevailed for long in the literature. I shall use the general term inclusively, but specify distinct tributaries, such as 'Modernized Classicism', 'decorative Modernism' or 'Streamline Moderne'.

Most Art Deco buildings are so named because of their ornamental decoration rather than any innate architectural quality. In Modernized Classical buildings, Art Deco detailing often derives from the exaggeration or transformation of classical ornament. The wildly decorated and illuminated Ionic capitals of the Paramount theatre, Aurora, Illinois (by C. W. Rapp and George Rapp, 1929-31), absorbed into a Chinoiserie décor, show how easily classical details could be transformed by the Art Deco imagination

22.1 Rob Mallet-Stevens, 'Pavillon du Tourisme' at the Paris 1925 Exhibition. Ink and watercolour on paper. French, 1911. Musée des Arts Décoratifs, Paris. Photo: Laurent Sully Jaulmes.

(plate 22.2). More commonly, Parisian Art Deco motifs copied from magazines were substituted for classical details. The European Art Deco style is often labelled by American writers as Jazz Moderne (or Zigzag Moderne). This adequately describes the abstract, geometric decoration characteristic of much decorative Modernism, but it underplays the floral and other organic motifs that were the staple of Art Deco ornament (see Chapter 10). Ornament of both kinds was applied in stone, concrete or terracotta relief panels and mouldings, in ironwork, and in applied surface patterns (in tile, ceramic or sgraffito) in buildings in Europe, North America and elsewhere until the Second World War (see plates 5.6, 35.4 and 38.5).

In New York, architects learned to use ornament in particular ways, according to its situation. Ely Jacques Kahn was a successful skyscraper architect who wrote extensively on form and decoration. His example can stand for countless other American architects who developed their own ornamental motifs.[6] In his otherwise rather functional 26-storey

Number Two Park Avenue building (1927) interest was achieved by applying bold and brightly coloured terracotta decoration at significant points on the otherwise bare brick walls, particularly towards the top. Kahn used the freedom of a semi-industrial building type to invent his own decorative forms. Of his first efforts to devise a new articulation he wrote, 'I was thinking of the texture of fabric.'[7] He was explicit about his methods:

> One faces the fact ... that the decoration of the tall building must produce the same agreeable effects of rhythm, symmetry, picturesqueness, sparkle ... with quite new mediums. Flat surfaces take the place of the obsolete cornices and finally color in surfaces, in proportion to the distance from the observer, mark the accents that the artist desires.[8]

The use of new materials, especially metal alloys, allowed the architect to develop a 'decorative quality' based on recognizably 'modern' means.

In the Squibb building, Kahn designed radiator covers as pure pattern. Starting from a ziggurat shape, taken from the profile of skyscrapers themselves, the

rest of the design grows logically and organically, perfectly following his theory. In a similarly functional, brick-faced building, of 13 storeys, the Film Center, Kahn reserved his most spectacular effects for the lobby. Gold painted plaster surfaces fizz with reflected light, part of the ceiling dips down in a wedge (again, to catch the light), machined stainless steel forms frame the lift doors, and red and gold mosaic and fresco focus the eye on the end wall (plate 22.3). The fluted and ribbed surfaces of the lift doors evoke not only the methods of machine production (milling, moulding and extruding) but also cans of film and stacks of coins. These milled forms are then amplified into channels, strips and flutings on the gold plaster walls and ceilings.

The forms invented by Ely Jacques Kahn and other architects derived from a wide range of sources, including French Art Deco motifs, Frank Lloyd Wright's Midway Gardens in Chicago, Moorish pattern, pre-Columbian art, German Expressionism and abstractions from classical and Gothic details. Kahn's work exemplifies the best, in its controlled

22.4 Albert Laprade, with Bazin & Ravazé, Garage Marbeuf,
Paris. 1928-9. Sepia print. *L'Architecte*, Paris, 1929.
Fonds Documentaire IFA.

use of light, its high degree of thematic development
and the precise effects that he achieved with shallow
relief on reflective surfaces.

Of the French Beaux-Arts architects who designed
Modernized Classical buildings for the 1925
Exhibition, Albert Laprade was perhaps the most
inventive. His Studium Louvre pavilion has a perfect
symmetry and classical proportion about it, with light,
airy, open pergolas on the first floor and subtle Art
Deco ornamentation of high quality (see plate 14.7).
His earlier experience (1915-20) was in North Africa,
working with Henri Prost.[9] Laprade's sympathy for
Moroccan vernacular architecture and his design of a
district for Muslim workers made him susceptible to
new ideas, and he was quick to realize the potential
of Art Deco forms in the commercial context. His
Garage Marbeuf in Paris, a showroom with five
storeys of motor cars displayed to the street via a
huge clear glass window and a zigzag array of
cantilevered balconies, picked up by a syncopated
rhythm in the flooring tiles, perfectly expresses the
essence of Art Deco showmanship (plate 22.4).
Laprade's friendship, from his Moroccan period, with
Maréchal Lyautey earned him the commission for the
Moroccan pavilion, as well as the Musée des
Colonies, at the 1931 *Exposition coloniale* in Paris
(see plate 11.2). This last, designed with Léon
Jaussely, with its stripped classical piers, and exotic
relief sculpture by Alfred Janniot, is a good example
of Modernized Classicism enlivened with Art Deco
detail. Also in 1931, Laprade designed an electricity
showroom, with Léon Bazin, for the Office Central
Electrique, on the Boulevard Haussmann in Paris
(plate 22.5). Here he abandoned classical
articulation for a sweep of light, prefiguring American
streamlining and picking up the brilliantly lit marquise
of the Galeries Lafayette department store a few
doors away. But, for all these modernistic
extravagances, Laprade remained a Classicist at
heart.[10]

Other French 'Modernizing Classicists', like Michel
Roux-Spitz, also designed commercial work of pure
Art Deco spirit.[11] These examples, which can be
matched by many others in Europe and America,
show how undogmatic and flexible Beaux-Arts trained
architects could be, capable of working in a style to
reflect the character of the commission.

22.5 Albert Laprade and
Léon Bazin, OCEL
showroom, Paris. 1931-2.
Gelatin silver print. Fonds
Documentaire IFA.

22.6 Rob Mallet-Stevens, Studio Martel, 10 Rue Mallet-Stevens, Paris. 1927. Fonds Documentaire IFA. Photo: Marc Vaux.

Rob Mallet-Stevens, by contrast, thought of himself as a Modernist, looking down on work he considered to be merely fashionable.[12] In 1911, he began publishing pochoir drawings of modern villas and other buildings in a geometric style influenced by Josef Hoffmann, Frank Lloyd Wright and Charles Rennie Mackintosh.[13] These led to an influential album, *Une Cité moderne* (1922). Unlike Le Corbusier, Mallet-Stevens had no interest in radicalizing the urban plan. He simply took each of the standard buildings of the modern town, from the fire station, via the post office and town hall to the individual house, and applied a 'modern' style to it. It is possible, however, that these illustrations proved much more influential for contemporary architects than Le Corbusier's austere urban and architectural projects. Although Mallet-Stevens thought of himself as a Modernist, his manipulation of surfaces, solids and voids, picked out with discreet ornament, for supremely decorative effect, clearly identify an Art Deco sensibility.

Mallet-Stevens's practice as an interior decorator, his articles, and the models and drawings he exhibited in the Paris Salons, drew him into a circle of influential Art Deco designers and avant-garde painters and sculptors.[14] He also cultivated friends in French avant-garde cinema, designing the sets for a number of films by Marcel L'Herbier.[15] These films contrasted an old-fashioned world of patriarchal authority, invariably set in an architectural context of pompous neo-classicism, with a youthful, dynamic and sporty world of fast cars and even faster women in Art Deco settings. Mallet-Stevens's film designs and exhibits created a fashion for 'modern' architecture in Paris. As a result, he received commissions from leading figures in the Art Deco world, including Jacques Doucet, Paul Poiret and Tamara de Lempicka; he also designed a studio for the glassmaker Louis Barillet, who decorated many of his buildings.[16] Mallet-Stevens knew how to give wealthy patrons what they wanted, a stage on which to act out their lives within a semi-bohemian

setting.[17] The street of houses he designed in Paris in 1927 was one of the most complete expressions of Jazz Moderne architecture in Europe, and Mallet-Stevens himself, as well as the Martel brothers, had their apartments and studios there (plate 22.6).[18]

Mallet-Stevens was highly influential on other architects such as G.-H. Pingusson and Charles Siclis, who designed villas, theatres and bars in a decorative modernistic style, using new materials and decorative ornament based on avant-garde art. Siclis made a name for himself with the redecoration of the Théâtre Pigalle, with its gleaming chrome tube detailing. He also designed several cafés and bars, of which the Café de la Triomphe shows his modernistic style well. It had a copper and glass staircase and a glass and stainless steel fountain designed by the metalsmith Raymond Subes, and engraved mirror-glass panels by Paule and Max Ingrand enlivening the walls and ceiling.

Cantilevered 'eyebrows' over windows and doors, banded windows, fins, ribs and moulding strips, as well as many kinds of abstract decorative ornament, came to define the decorative Modernist variant of Art Deco and were endlessly repeated all over the world in the 1930s. This repertoire of formalistic motifs was elaborated by early European Modernist architects in the years between 1912 and 1925 but progressively discarded by them after 1925.[19] By this time, avant-garde architects like Erich Mendelsohn, Walter Gropius and Bruno Taut, who had passed through an Expressionist phase before and after the First World War, had moved towards an increasingly functionalist Modernism.

The architectural historian Henry-Russell Hitchcock famously remarked in 1931 that American architects had been abandoned to 'wander for forty years in the barren wilderness of classicism and eclecticism'.[20] For John Burchard, thirty years later, Art Deco was 'somnambulant impassiveness', or even, 'a nightmare in which ornament and decoration were confused with creativity'.[21] And yet the 1920s and early 1930s saw the rise and spread of the American skyscraper, arguably the most complete expression of Art Deco architecture. The story of the skyscraper begins in Chicago in the 1880s. After the First World War, however, with the rapid development of the technologies of steel construction, high speed elevators, artificial illumination and air conditioning, New York City, and some other American cities, saw a building boom between 1925 and 1930 that led to the development of completely new forms.

By the end of the First World War, the key elements of skyscraper design were in place. The Woolworth building (by Cass Gilbert, 1913) had demonstrated how terracotta decoration could be used to clothe a very tall building (241 metres/792 feet high) to accentuate its vertical proportions, and how a sumptuously decorated entrance lobby could lend prestige and identity to the interior. In 1922, the international competition for the Chicago Tribune Tower was won by Raymond Hood and John Mead Howells with a Gothic design. Yet the competition demonstrated the limitations of both the Gothic and classical styles for the needs of this developing building type. The entry by the European architect Eliel Saarinen was widely considered the best, because it adapted Gothic articulation more freely and subtly as a means of articulating volumes. And Saarinen's example was followed when, in 1924, Raymond Hood designed the American Radiator building in New York, only 21 storeys high but pregnant with potential for future Art Deco designs (plate 22.7). Like Gilbert in the Woolworth building, Hood focused his ornament where it was needed: at the top, in bold flashes of gold detail, and on the lower storeys, where his Gothic decoration looked expensive and sophisticated. He abandoned detail in the intervening storeys, relying on the black granite surfaces and gold trim to make a spectacular impact from a distance, especially when illuminated at night. His approach to the building's night-time lighting was pure Art Deco in its stress on spectacle. He recalled trying out 'multi-colored revolving lights ... [which] produced ... the effect of the building's being on fire. We threw spots of light on jets of steam rising out of the smoke-stack. Then again, with moving lights, we had the whole of the building waving like a tree in a strong wind.'[22]

Hood's approach highlights his complete grasp of his clients' commercial needs; and yet, as the architect Harvey Wiley Corbett remarked of this building:

> If commercialism is the guiding spirit of the age, the building which advertises itself is in harmony with that spirit ... There is no reason why the term 'commercialism' would ever be considered as opposed to art. Perhaps a new kind of commercialism in its new and higher relation to human welfare.[23]

Although not Art Deco in their decorative style, the Woolworth, Chicago Tribune and American Radiator buildings set the agenda. All that was required was the development of a new style and application of ornamentation and a new approach to massing.

22.7 Raymond Hood. American Radiator building, New York. 1924. Photo: Cervin Robinson.

22.8 Hugh Ferriss, study for maximum mass permitted by the 1916 New York Zoning Law, stages 1-4. Black crayon, stumped, with brush and black ink over photocopy, varnish, on illustration board. American, 1922. Gift of Mrs Hugh Ferriss. Cooper-Hewitt, National Design Museum, Smithsonian Institution. Photo: Ken Pelka.

The New York zoning laws of 1916, which were adapted for use in over a hundred American cities by 1929, specified set-backs above a certain height (usually 38 or 46 metres/125 or 150 feet), conditioned by the width of the street, for each frontage. One quarter of the site was allowed to extend vertically without limit. Since streets and avenues framing blocks in Manhattan invariably differed in width, the zoning laws produced relatively complex forms, difficult to visualize. In 1922, Harvey Wiley Corbett asked the draughtsman Hugh Ferriss to visualize the spatial consequences of these laws and demonstrate how architects could turn these into finished designs. First published in the *New York Times* in 1922, Ferriss's drawings were repeatedly illustrated between then and the publication of his book, *The Metropolis of Tomorrow*, in 1929 (plate 22.8).[24]

Architects developed the practice of modelling these zoning envelopes in clay or Plasticine and literally cutting into the mass, first to create the vertical walls required by steel construction, then to introduce light and ventilation into the interior, and finally to rationalize the result with respect to lifts and circulation. Each slice into the clay represented a potential loss of rental revenue for the clients, though this was offset by the price that could be achieved for office space dependent on its light and view.[25] Most critics recognized that this act of modelling volumes in the air had created a new style of architecture, which they called 'modern' or 'Moderne', but which we would now call Art Deco.[26] To an extent, Ferriss became a promoter of the style he represented in his drawings. His huge charcoal renderings, with their black skies and upward-thrusting lighting, obscured all detail, focusing on the play of volumes.[27] Some architects gave Ferriss their plans to see how he would project them into the sky on the basis of the zoning laws alone.[28]

Between 1925 and 1929 a series of buildings perfected these lessons. Sloan & Robertson's 56-storey Chanin building reduced the main body of the building to sheer walls punctuated with square windows. The sculptural form of the building itself warrants the Art Deco designation, but the style is also emphatically asserted in the decoration of the lower storeys and the entrance lobbies.[29] Rene Chambellan and Jacques Delamarre worked on the copper repoussé frieze running round the bottom of the building, representing the processes of Darwinian natural selection; the lower storeys were also covered with moulded terracotta ornament (plate 22.10).

The Chanin building, strategically placed across the road from Grand Central Station, marked the beginning of a building boom in this area to rival the traditional business centre around Wall Street. William Van Alen took over the design of a skyscraper for the Chrysler Corporation in 1930, turning the 319 metre (1,048 foot) tower into the tallest building in the world and an advertising beacon for the firm (see plates 2.5 and 5.1). The white brick walls were boldly articulated with grey brick and enlivened with highly original ornamentation. The spire itself was unlike anything else in architecture, a series of sunbursts in stainless steel leading to a slender spike.[30] Bright stainless steel gargoyles in the form of eagles and a coloured frieze representing wheel hubcap motifs signalled the base of the tower 30 storeys above street level. The lobby and entrance included more stainless steel Jazz Moderne detailing and a dramatic series of frescoes illustrating modern technology and transportation.

The Empire State building (1929-30) reflects one of the most perfect solutions to the zoning formula. To maximize the amount of top rental office space, the architects – R. H. Shreve, W. H. Lamb and A. L. Harmon – handled the zoning laws by restricting the street frontage to five storeys (instead of the 10 or 16 to which they were entitled under the 1916 laws). These were followed by a deep set-back of 18 metres (60 feet) to a tall central tower 381 metres high (1,250 feet), whose offices were restricted in depth to 8.5 metres (28 feet) from external wall to internal corridor to maintain good light and air.[31] The building therefore represents the optimum economic formula for exploiting the site and has been defined by the architect Rem Koolhaas as 'automatic architecture', serving no other purpose than to concretize a financial abstraction.[32] It is small wonder, then, that the building, constructed in a record 11 months, lacks some of the formal inventiveness in profile and detail of some of its contemporaries.[33] In this and other skyscrapers, the forms of the buildings themselves became a motif in their decoration.[34] In the Empire State lobby, a marble intarsia mural shows the building radiating its influence across north-east America. Brass roundels depict the energy sources and other resources on which skyscraper design depended: concrete, steel, machinery, elevators, artists and designers (plate 22.9). Here, the dominant imagery of mechanization turned even the artist's paintbrushes into the spokes of a wheel. Geometric simplification and direct representation of the key industrial and mechanical attributes of modernization recur in much American Art Deco decoration. They allow the decorative forms to work well at an architectural scale, outside and in, and appeal to the direct and real wonder of contemporary Americans at the pace and motors of transformation. This gives Art Deco architecture a claim to realism, as well as fantasy, in its decorative attributes.

The drama of these fragile-looking towers acquired a poetic reflection of its own. The designer and aesthete Claude Bragdon described the pyramidal towers reaching up to the sky as 'frozen fountains',[35] interpreting the set-backs as rising and falling cascades, a perpetual struggle between human aspiration and the force of gravity: 'The needle-pointed *flèche* of the Chrysler Tower catches the sunlight like a fountain's highest expiring jet.'[36] Bragdon voiced a widely held view among American architects and critics that skyscraper design had evolved beyond the functional to something poetic, sublime and almost mystical: 'Economy and efficiency are not, after all, everything, so to *significant, dramatic, organic,* let us add *ecstatic,* with this for an over-word: "*Wake up and dream*" [original emphasis].'[37] The architect Frank Walker, one of the leading Art Deco skyscraper architects, stoutly defended such a 'poetic approach': 'Why should architects be ashamed of the fact that a poetic approach is necessary to appeal … to man's emotions? Why should the stress in modern thinking be continually upon the creature comforts and so little upon the mental and spiritual stimuli which we so sorely need today?'[38]

22.9 A. L. Harmon, four roundels representing the crafts of skyscraper construction, lobby in the Empire State building, New York. 1931.
Photo: Tim Benton.

Architectural Detail

22.10 Rene Chambellan and Jacques Delamarre, frieze on the Chanin building, New York. Copper repoussé. 1929.
Photo: Tim Benton.

22.11 Lee Lawrie, relief above door of the RCA building, Rockefeller Center, New York. 1931-5.
Photo: Tim Benton.

By 1930, architects and architectural critics had developed clear positions on the Art Deco (or 'modernistic') skyscraper. For traditionalists, they were showy, loud and shallow. Kenneth Franzheim labelled Van Alen 'the Ziegfeld of his profession', referring to the theatrical connotations of the Chrysler tower.[39] However, the apostles of Modernism, notably those associated with the New York Museum of Modern Art – such as Alfred Barr, Henry-Russell Hitchcock and Philip Johnson – saw them as 'illogical', 'irrational' and 'non-functional', and concluded that 'from the commercially successful modernistic architect … we may expect the strongest opposition'.[40] At issue in both these judgments was the popularity of Art Deco with the general public and the businessmen whose job it was to correctly diagnose public taste.

The apotheosis of the Art Deco skyscraper was staged at the Beaux-Arts ball in January 1931. In a spectacular festival, guests dressed in 'fire and silver' costumes were invited to 'capture the quality of rhythm and pulsation required to characterise our work and play, our shop windows and our advertisements, and all the effervescence of modern life'.[41] The high point was a ballet, *Skyline of New York*, presented by New York architects dressed to imitate their most famous buildings. Hood, Kahn, Walker and Corbett were all there, wearing identical ziggurat costumes and headgear representing their buildings. But William Van Alen stole the show with his representation of the Chrysler building, a towering model of the lantern on his head, robes made of shimmering foil and exotic woods, epaulettes representing the gargoyle eagles, and waistcoat and boots based on the interior decoration.

Nevertheless, by this time, European Modernism was finding its way into American theory and practice. Ely Jacques Kahn knew at first hand the major monuments of European Modernism,[42] and Raymond Hood eagerly read the books of Le Corbusier.[43] Both men knew and admired Frank Lloyd Wright and cultivated the friendship of European émigré architects and designers such as Joseph Urban. Hood was prepared to experiment with different styles for different jobs. For the Daily News building (1930-2), commissioned by the owners of the Chicago Tribune Company, Hood and Howells abandoned the Gothic detail of the Chicago building and went for a cool, rational form. Yet the treatment of patterned brick infill and the giant stone relief at street level substantiates a claim for the building's Art Deco status. The relief, with its Damon Runyonesque arrangement of American characters, its sunbursts and its quotation from Abraham Lincoln

('God must have loved the common man … he made so many of them'), is pure Art Deco and an excellent example of populist image making. In 1932, Hood took another step towards Modernism in the design of the McGraw-Hill building.[44] But the jazzy crowning feature of the building (with its giant lettering and heavy fins), its green ceramic tile facing and its streamlined entrance and lobby maintain this as one of the finest of the Art Deco skyscrapers (see plate 26.9).

From 1927 John D. Rockefeller had been working with the Metropolitan Opera Company to put together a very large site on which to build a new Opera House. The Depression caused the Met to drop out, leaving Rockefeller with the biggest building site in New York. Successive teams of architects worked on the project, including Raymond Hood, who is usually credited with the design of the main central slab, the RCA building (plate 22.12).[45] With his experience of sculpting elegant forms out of virtually undecorated masses, Hood subtly set back the flanks of the building, leaving a thin edge facing the central plaza. Around this 70-storey slab, lower buildings were grouped, in a symmetrical, Beaux-Arts arrangement, around internal streets and a sunken plaza. Photographs exist of a Plasticine model of what Hood would have preferred: an expressionist composition of stepped-back cubes rising from the full breadth of the site to a climax which, if completed, would have created an Art Deco 'City Crown' for Manhattan.[46] All the buildings were unified by their Indian limestone surfaces and virtually undecorated openings. A programme of art and sculpture commissions at ground level made up for this surface austerity, however, resulting in some spectacular Art Deco decorative effects (plate 22.11). The iconography for this ambitious programme, originally written by the philosopher Hartley Burr Alexander and entitled *Homo Faber*, was renamed *New Frontiers and the March of Civilisation* by the Rockefeller Center's publicity director. Lee Lawrie's relief over the central portal, based on a watercolour, *The Creator*, by William Blake, bore the pompous title: 'Genius, which interprets to the human race the laws and cycles of the cosmic forces of the Universe, making cycles of sight and sound'. Lawrie evoked these cycles in a window of cast glass panes, picked out in gold.[47]

From the late 1920s, Art Deco buildings inspired by European decorative Modernism and the example of the American skyscraper sprang up all over the world, in city centres and suburbs. In North Africa and Palestine, Australia and New Zealand, India and South Africa, European and native-born architects deployed the style to connote a sophisticated

metropolitan modernity, while adapting it to local needs and traditions (see plates 35.10 and 39.2).[48]

Many of the architects who had developed the skyscraper style found themselves involved in two national projects, the *Century of Progress* exhibition in Chicago, 1933-4, and the New York World Fair, 1939-40. The Chicago Exhibition was dedicated to the idea of progress based on scientific advance. Its promotional nature can be gauged by the chapter headings of the official picture guide: 'Forward! Ever Forward', 'Light from the Stars' (rays from the star Arcturus were meant to turn the exhibition lights on every day), 'Always Onward! Upward!', 'Even the Exhibits Move', and so on.[49] The team of architects, chaired by Harvey Wiley Corbett, included the Beaux-Arts Classicist Paul Cret, John A. Holabird from Chicago and Hood and Walker from New York. Severely constrained by the available funds, the architects first considered strictly utilitarian designs. However, as an official guidebook noted, they 'found that they were as subject to the laws of adornment as any of us, and that they were breaking their spaces with changes in form which had nothing to do with the use and could have no other value but that of adornment'.[50]

The exhibition turned into a heterogeneous display of dramatic exterior forms and controlled natural and artificial lighting.[51] A clear Art Deco decorative idiom can be detected in buildings such as the General Motors pavilion, which has a similar sunburst window to the Galeries Lafayette pavilion at the Paris 1925 Exhibition. At a late stage in the undertaking, Josef Urban was given the task of unifying the whole composition with a bright colour scheme. Admired for its vigour but generally condemned by the architectural critics as 'bitty', the exhibition succeeded in capturing the public imagination and turned in a modest profit.

The New York World Fair was a much more ambitious affair, aimed at impressing on the world the benefits of American democracy and capitalism:[52] 'It was a Fair that, from the very start viewed the people not only as observers but as potential consumers of the products it displayed. Indeed … the most popular exhibits tended to be those of producers.'[53] Most of the official buildings were designed in a Modernized Classical style, with stripped pilasters, generally symmetrical planning and

22.12 Raymond Hood & Associated Architects, RCA building, Rockefeller Center, New York, with *Prometheus* by Paul Manship. 1931-5. © Photo: Mitchell Funk. Getty Images/The Image Bank.

large, plain surfaces;[54] many of the transportation section pavilions adopted an extreme form of Streamline Moderne; but in the commercial pavilions the new breed of industrial designers had a free rein.[55] The most popular exhibits were Norman Bel Geddes's 'Futurama' exhibit (General Motors), the Theme Center exhibit of 'Democricity', designed by Henry Dreyfuss in the dramatic Perisphere, the American Telephone and Telegraph pavilion and the Ford exhibit (see plates 34.9 and 40.1).

For the European architect, the lessons of Manhattan and the American skyscraper were that anything goes in the race for public attention and profits. In England, the *Architectural Review* waged successive campaigns against commercialism in the form of advertising hoardings, Art Deco factories and cinemas and other forms of 'bad taste'. In this context, arguments in defence of both traditional and Modern architecture against 'anti-social', vulgar or commercial Art Deco were common. Establishment architects resisted Art Deco ornamentation as showy, disruptive and 'foreign'. As the President of the Royal Institute of British Architects, Hubert Worthington, put it in April 1927:

> If your so-called modernism is sensational, restless, full of aesthetic excitement and "out to tickle tired eyes"... if it is self-advertising, egotistical, non-co-operative and un-English; if it is precious, abnormal, ephemeral and inhuman, chuck it. But if it is logical, harmonious and well composed; if it is well planned and well constructed and co-operative and English; if it is sane, masculine and unaffected and human, and imbued with the quality of the eternal, let us have it.[56]

But the future lay precisely with the showy, self-advertising and ephemeral architecture offered by European and American Art Deco. In June 1928, the *Architectural Review* ran an article on the new London office block and showrooms for the American Ideal Radiator Company, designed by Raymond Hood and the British architect Gordon Jeeves. It was written by Trystram Edwards as a *comédie de mœurs*, in dialogue, between the neo-Tudor extension to Liberty's, the eclectic Dickins & Jones building and the Regency-style Palladium theatre (plate 22.13). Edwards has the Ideal Radiator building say, clearly in an American accent:

> Most of the buildings in London are just mumbling, they don't know how to shout – they haven't any advertisement value ... So many new buildings here are too dull for words. Even when they are brand new nobody looks at them, they haven't got what I call 'snap'. Now, just take a look at me – once seen never forgotten.[57]

'But don't think I pride myself upon my knowledge of architecture', the Radiator building went on, with obvious mock-modesty, 'I don't even know whether my style is good or bad. I am content not to be ignored.'[58] While Edwards mocked the brashness and naiveté of the American façade, he recognized the logic of American commercial values. If the purpose of a commercial headquarters is to advertise the brand, why not go all the way? And thoughtful architects, such as Raymond McGrath, realized that different styles suited different purposes. Reviewing the redecoration of the Savoy Theatre in 1930, McGrath wrote:

There are two kinds of architecture. Architecture which is lasting, simple and monumental in form and permanent in material, and architecture which is of-the-moment, decorated, impermanent. It is stupid to build decorated architecture to last, and it is stupid to think that decorated architecture is not just as important as that which is monumental. Without fresh, vital, contemporary decoration everywhere, the public becomes artistically anaemic and unintelligent.[59]

It is no accident that the most successful firm to design Art Deco factories in Britain, Wallis Gilbert, was a partnership formed between an American

22.13 Raymond Hood and Gordon
Jeeves, Ideal House, National Radiator
Company building, London. 1928.

22.14 Wallis, Gilbert & Partners,
Hoover factory, London. 1932-8.
© Crown Copyright. NMR.

Aumonier celebrating Beaverbrook's Empire Free Trade campaign (see plate 20.12). A few doors down, the Daily Telegraph building was a stripped classical design, similarly supplied with Art Deco detailing. In both these buildings Art Deco decoration provided mass-market appeal and a symbolism of communication.

The most effective purveyor of mass-market appeal took place in the film industry and the theatres designed to project the films. Following the early atmospheric and historicizing cinemas, American architects turned, from around 1927, to European models to develop the best internal arrangements for good visibility and sound, and to achieve dramatic night-time displays on the street. From examples such as the Tuschinski theatre in Amsterdam, by members of the Amsterdam School (see plate 15.16), they developed the richly ornamented interiors of cinemas such as the Paramount theatre, Oakland. From Hans Poelzig's Grosses Schauspielhaus (Great Playhouse) of 1919 and Capitol am Zoo Cinema (1925) and Erich Mendelsohn's Universum Cinema (1928-31) in Berlin, they – and other European architects – took lighting systems and sweeping abstract forms. Josef Urban's auditorium in the New York New School of Social Research represented these European values at their most perfectly accomplished. In Europe itself, one of the largest such Art Deco cinemas was the Gaumont-Palace in Paris, restructured by Henri Belloc in 1930-1. Its vast auditorium, measuring 34 metres in width (112 feet) and 70 metres in depth (230 feet), could seat 6,000 people in a womb-like enclosure of pink felt walls and scarlet seating. The ceiling was articulated with ripple-effect transverse fluting whose width broadened as it approached the proscenium. The sweeping curves of the balconies were picked out with hidden lighting using coloured tubes (in white, yellow or cyclamen) which could be changed to create special effects. Similar symphonies of coloured lighting could be played in the most famous theatre in Manhattan, the RCA Music Hall in the Rockefeller Center, where the whole interior arrangement, like Josef Urban's auditorium,

construction firm, Kahncrete, and a British architect, Thomas Wallis, to construct industrial buildings in reinforced concrete using the American system.[60] Most of their factories were functional demonstrations of concrete space enclosure, modelled on Albert Kahn's Ford factories in Detroit. But, around 1930, Wallis began to make a splash with a series of competitively styled showpieces on the Great West Road, London, including the Firestone (1929) and Hoover (1932 and 1938) factories, both of them symbols of the new industries that survived the Depression (plate 22.14). Such was the *Architectural Review*'s derision for this kind of

commercial Moderne that Wallis was reputed once to have visited the editor armed with a horsewhip.

Equally dramatic were the newspaper buildings on Fleet Street, competing for attention and sales. The Daily Express building, designed by the engineer Owen Williams, was a dramatic but functional concrete structure faced with black glass and aluminium strip, its stepped-back profile imitating in miniature the Manhattan Deco skyscraper. The interior design was by the classically trained Robert Atkinson, who decorated the entrance hall in a symphony of faceted stainless steel surfaces, angled to catch the light, and a glittering relief by Eric

was organized in gilded concentric curves which, with the manipulation of complex lighting effects, recreated a golden sunset before every performance (plate 22.15).[61] These 'acres of seats in gardens of dreams' brought spectacle and escapism into the heart of urban communities across the world, despite the Depression. Art Deco, with its magically illuminated surfaces supported by the latest structural sleight of hand, provided the necessary language to create this miracle, and Hollywood's use of top designers, including many European immigrants, to confect fabulous Art Deco settings for their films, completed the illusion (see Chapter 30).

The Streamline Moderne style was a variant of Art Deco particularly important in America (see Chapters 33 and 34). Innumerable small roadside structures, dependent on their dramatic external form to catch the eye, spread Art Deco imagery nationwide. Diners, high street shops and petrol stations competed for attention, often brilliantly clothed in stainless steel or rendered concrete and always dramatically picked out with neon light at night.[62]

A theme that links Modern Movement and Art Deco architecture is the dramatic use of electricity to provide a new experience, that of 'night architecture'. Where the Modernists used structural transparency to allow internal illumination to make an impact at night, Art Deco designers began to develop a new language of pure lighting. Exhibitions, cinemas and department stores gave a lead, but soon applied neon lighting and the use of lighting troughs to conceal coloured light sources began to compose the streetscape at night.

An important precedent was set by the annual *Salon de l'automobile* and *Salon de l'aéronautique* in Paris. For more than a decade, beginning in 1926, the Grand Palais was given a dramatic lighting grid by André Granet and Roger-Henri Expert. Their transformations, to celebrate the most modern forms of transportation, embraced both completely artificial decorative effects – like a coloured floral canopy – and rigidly geometrical arrangements. They were a revelation to architects (plate 22.16). To see the massive tubular steel structures required to support

these arrays of millions of light bulbs is to grasp instantly the difference between an architecture of display and one of 'rationalism'. Similarly, the lighting schemes perfected for other major national and international exhibitions after 1925 became an autonomous science of self-determining construction. Experimentally displayed in exhibition design, curving forms intended only to reflect and project light grew their own organic forms. These, and scalloped fronds, repeating step-backs in gold or silver, and syncopated contour lines in shallow relief, became the essential building blocks for the Art Deco interior.[63]

Art Deco architecture was a modern but not Modernist architecture. It developed from the application of Deco ornament to classical or Modernist buildings into a new kind of building capable of expressing the aspirations of dynamically developing consumerist societies. This was a popular style, occasionally vulgar but bursting with vitality, in striking contrast with the more austere forms of Modernism. The criticisms levelled against the latter

22.15 Donald Deskey & Associated Architects, RCA Music Hall, New York. 1933. Museum of the City of New York. Theatre Collection.

by Post-modern architects like Robert Venturi and Denise Scott Brown, from the 1960s onwards, would have been shared by Art Deco architects.[64] Venturi and Scott Brown valued the 'fun' of Art Deco architecture and played an active role in preserving it. The human values of desire, warmth, sensuality and anecdotal incident were embodied in Art Deco skyscrapers, cinemas and other commercial buildings in a way that was excluded by Modernism. The Post-modern vision of modern life as a fragmentary and illusory spectacle, as characterized by Jean Baudrillard and others, which has challenged the claimed rationalism of the Modernists, was prefigured

by Art Deco architects.[65] As one of their supporters, Edwin Avery Park, wrote in 1927: 'Life seems to have become fragmentary, a thing to be caught in passing'; and (quoting from the philosopher Will Durant), 'inductive data fall upon us from all sides like lava of Vesuvius; we suffocate with uncoordinated facts; our minds are overwhelmed with sciences breeding and multiplying into specialist chaos for want of synthetic thought and a unifying philosophy. We are all mere fragments of what man might be.'[66]

If the Modernist project was to supply the unifying philosophy, Art Deco faithfully mirrored the times and

22.16 André Granet, colour rendering of the 1928 *Exposition de locomotion aérienne* at the Grand Palais, Paris. Gouache on paper. French, *c.*1928. Fonds Granet, IFA.

gave it an imaginative spark. And, if we accept Baudelaire's definition of modernity as incorporating the ephemeral and transient alongside the universal values of art, a case can well be made for seeing the main line of modernity in the inter-war period as running from the avant-garde movements of the years around the First World War into Art Deco rather than into the ambitious orthodoxy of Modernism.

23 Art Deco Fashion

Valerie Mendes

High fashion of the 1920s became inextricably linked to an elite, international coterie of young socialites, beauties and celebrities. So powerful was the cultural impact of these slender young women, who flaunted a brittle sophistication involving cropped hairstyles, heavy make-up and short-skirted, low-waisted, tubular outfits, that they came (however misleadingly) to personify Art Deco fashion. Brimming with energy as 'flappers' or 'bright young things', they captured the attention of eminent writers who spun sometimes amusing, sometimes tragic tales about their audacious habits and touched, inevitably, on their clothes. Thus Evelyn Waugh wrote of the 'little Baroness Yoshiwara, her golden hands clasped in the lap of her golden Paquin frock'[1] and of Mrs Panrast 'who dressed with that severely masculine chic which American women know so well how to assume'.[2] F. Scott Fitzgerald depicted Daisy Fay 'drowsing asleep at dawn with the beads and chiffon of an evening dress tangled among dying orchids'.[3] The reign of these leggy, flimsily clad, straight-line heroines encompassed the Paris 1925 Exhibition but lasted no more than four years – from late 1924 to 1928. In fact, such a kaleidoscope of fashions marks the 1920s and 1930s that no one look can stand alone to signify Art Deco. The choice is legion. In addition to the stereotypical beaded and fringed 'Charleston' dress, icons of the style range from Suzanne Lenglen's Patou tennis outfits and Chanel's legendary little black dress to Vionnet's draped neo-classical *robes du soir* and Adrian's 'Hollywood Moderne' gowns for Jean Harlow. Liberated from their pre-war carapace, women now moved easily in pared-down clothes in lightweight fabrics. As fashionable *gamines* in the 1920s they frolicked in 'soft cylinder' dresses,[4] but by 1930 they had matured into svelte Art Deco *élégantes* who swept along in body-caressing gowns.

The Paris 1925 Exhibition provided the ideal opportunity for France to proclaim its continuing dominance of fashion. This was a position that it had celebrated twenty-five years earlier at the *Exposition universelle* and a reality it was to reassert at the *Exposition coloniale* in 1931 and the *Exposition*

internationale des arts et techniques dans la vie moderne in 1937. Fashion, its accessories and trimmings were allocated spacious, prime locations on the 1925 site, indicating an unswerving commitment to this enormously profitable luxury industry – at this point fashion was France's second most successful export.

The centrality of fashion was acknowledged, consciously or not, on the illustrated cover of Hachette's *Guide de l'exposition*. Dominating the composition a young woman, attired in a lavishly fur-trimmed ensemble, has the desirable 'longer-than-life',[5] androgynous physique and short hairstyle clamped by a domed, head-hugging hat (see plate 13.4). The guide asserted that fashion as a pre-eminent decorative art set the pace for other media and maintained that it was critical to 'la modernité' existing as it did on 'surprise et nouveauté'.

High-powered admission committees for fashion and its associated industries harnessed the fame and skill of top couturiers. Jeanne Paquin was vice-president of Group III, 'La Parure', and within this group Jeanne Lanvin was president of Classe XX, 'Le Vêtement', while Paul Poiret was a vice-president, and they were joined by notables from France's renowned luxury textile manufacturers including Rodier and Bianchini-Férier. Some 75 French fashion houses displayed their finest creations, eclipsing all other national attempts to show achievements in the realm of fashion and accessories. Close to the Porte d'Honneur, the Pavillon de l'Elégance highlighted the *de luxe* output of the grand couture houses, including Lanvin, Callot, Worth and Jenny. The theme of elegance was extended in a neighbouring pavilion devoted to the up-market Paris fashion magazine *Fémina*. To capture *Fémina*'s ethos, a fashion display of miniature mannequins dressed in haute couture mirrored the chic of Parisian high society in 1925. In addition to the Pavillon de l'Elégance, the main venues were the Grand Palais, *Orgues* (one of Paul Poiret's trio of barges moored in the Seine) and numerous *boutiques de vente* (notably Sonia Delaunay's Boutique Simultanée) on the Pont

23.1 Mannequin, French.
Cloche hat made by Kilpin Ltd.
Pink straw with appliqué trim.
British, c.1925.
V&A: T.3-2002; T.442-1977.

23.2 Mannequins in evening clothes by Jeanne Paquin
in the 'Pavillon de l'Elégance' at the Paris 1925 Exhibition.
Gelatin silver print. 1925. Photo courtesy of Marc Walter.

Alexandre III (see plate 13.9).

The creative ferment culminating in the Paris Exhibition inspired some notable fashion and fashion-related innovations. To considerable acclaim (even from art critics and the Surrealists, who were otherwise unenthusiastic about the exhibition) the manufacturer Siégel and its rival firm Pierre Imans produced a new generation of shop window mannequins for their respective boutiques as well as for the pavilions. Prime examples of Art Deco stylization, the mannequins ranged from semi-naturalistic figures to severe Brancusi-like abstract forms designed by the sculptor André Vigneu for Siégel. Radically new experiments led to mannequins that colour matched the dresses they wore – lamé gowns shimmered on gold and silver figures, while a glistening all-black wax mannequin was specially devised for Vionnet.

Photographic records indicate that the main fashion displays were remarkable for their languid

sophistication. Thematic tableaux in the Grand Palais celebrated the pinnacle of couture. Figures attired in magnificently embroidered and fur-trimmed gowns by Paquin prepared themselves (one ostentatiously powdering her face in a dress beaded with Chinoiserie motifs) for an evening gala (plate 23.2 and see plate 6.5). Lounging in her mirrored dressing room an 'actress' wore an expensive *déshabillé* (complete with lace boudoir cap) by Jeanne Lanvin. It was perhaps inevitable that the organizers, all long established couturiers (Lanvin, Paquin and Poiret), would promote sumptuous refinement rather than a revolutionary new look. The popular cylindrical line prevailed but the extravagant clothes descended to mid-calf or ankle length and, in essence, belonged to the early Twenties.

It was left to the Ukrainian-born Sonia Delaunay to champion youthful clothes and a vision for the future. With aplomb she continued her 'simultaneous' experiments (see Chapter 9), applying her painter's approach to fashion and textiles. Sharing a boutique with the couturier and furrier Jacques Heim, Delaunay showed a range of 'simultaneous' fabrics, clothes and accessories. In comparison with the

delicate intricacies of haute couture in the main venues her output was aggressive and forward looking. Her creations were the shortest (yet still below the knees) to be photographed at the exhibition. In acknowledgement of the advanced nature of her striking geometrically patterned outfits, on-site locations were selected to match her advanced concepts. Two Delaunay-clad models posed beneath the Martel brothers' Cubist trees (plate 23.3), while in front of Rob Mallet-Stevens's Pavillon du Tourisme an automobile painted with a 'simultaneous' check provided another suitably avant-garde location (see plate 13.8). Many Delaunay textile samples and designs have survived – mainly in French collections – but examples of her fashion and accessories are so very rare that it is tempting to speculate that potential customers found them either too extreme or overly expensive or both (see plate 13.10).

Russian émigrés made a significant impact on 1920s Paris fashion, establishing boutiques, supplying couture with elaborate embroideries and setting trends, such as the vogue for 'Russian' boots. From 1922 to about 1929 Natalia Goncharova, famed for her costumes and sets for the Ballets Russes, provided Myrbor (opened by Marie Cuttoli in 1922) with vibrant designs for highly decorative clothes (plate 23.4). Masterpieces of appliqué (embroidered in Algeria), they make ideal case studies of artistic interdependency. Described by one commentator, 'The gowns, too, are what might be called a "changing exhibit of modern art". In colour, material, line and decorative detail they are the product of dressmaking genius.'[6] Extroverts and those with bohemian tendencies were drawn to these dazzling, multicoloured creations.[7]

23.3 Models wearing ensembles by Sonia Delaunay beneath a Martel concrete tree at the Paris 1925 Exhibition. Gelatin silver print. 1925. L&M Services B. V. Amsterdam 20020402.

23.4 Natalia Goncharova (Russian), dress. Silk appliqué. French, 1924-6. Made by Myrbor. V&A: Circ.329-1968. © ADAGP, Paris and DACS, London 2002.

23.5 Paul Poiret, 'Brique', day dress.
Flecked worsted. French, 1924. V&A: T.339-1974.
© ADAGP, Paris and DACS, London 2002.

That vital precursor of Art Deco fashion Paul Poiret proved a key exhibitor in 1925. Ever an astute showman, he provided three barges, each 39 metres long (128 feet). This idea was a masterstroke and hugely popular with visitors. Poiret's post-war output has frequently been dismissed as lack-lustre and was even condemned as passé in the *Cinquantenaire de l'exposition de 1925*[8] – a criticism that can be disputed. An obvious discrepancy existed between his actual output and his professed hatred of the current look. Poiret inveighed against the 'femmes de carton' with concave silhouettes, angular shoulders and flattened breasts, maintaining that their passion for 'les allures garçonnesques' and so-called 'sportives' would kill French couture.[9] Yet archive photographs, press coverage and surviving works indicate that in spite of grave financial setbacks he kept pace with the vanguard.[10] A worsted day dress of 1924 illustrates how Poiret came to terms with the *garçonne* look (plate 23.5). Avoiding the

commonplace formula of a cylinder bisected by a conspicuous belt at hip level, he created lean but softly flared lines. Two pockets subtly delineated the dropped waist, while boldly striped braid trimming satisfied the 1920s desire for geometric decoration. His inventiveness did not desert him when – struggling with insolvency – he designed a Moderne, bias cut, ivory satin and green chartreuse velvet evening gown in 1933 that would have entranced the most seductive of Hollywood sirens. It was noted that 'M. Poiret has lost none of his striking originality and individuality.'[11]

Stars of the new generation of Paris couturiers, Gabrielle Chanel and Jean Patou, were in complete harmony with the times though not with each other. The inter-war period witnessed their rivalry and respective triumphs based upon the *garçonne* look. The term borrowed from Victor Margueritte's novel *La Garçonne* (1922) summed up the androgynous, bustless, hipless boyish shape that became the goal of so many young (and not so young) women. Chanel's idiosyncratic vision and liberated personal style informed her collections. She introduced two-piece, uncluttered costumes in easy to wear jersey in 1917 and, building on this theme throughout the 1920s and 1930s, developed daywear that combined neat, clean cut lines with comfort. Her repertoire never relied upon historical fashion but was influenced by the practicalities of occupational dress and menswear – the latter nurtured by her friendship with the Duke of Westminster and his aristocratic circle. Chanel made fashion headlines and attracted prestigious and glamorous clients such as Daisy Fellowes and Paula Gellibrand, who also found Patou's collections to their liking. In 1932 another influential customer, Loelia, Duchess of Westminster, chose Chanel's slinky blue, décolleté, sequinned evening gown decorated across the bodice with a huge *trompe-l'œil* bow[12] (plate 23.6). With the exception of some uncharacteristically elaborate evening dresses Chanel confined Art Deco pattern elements to secondary touches, particularly checked or striped linings, sweaters and banded scarves. Perhaps her most notable Art Deco coup in 1926 was to champion the little black dress[13] (plate 23.7). Fashion's predilection for black led *Vogue* to proclaim that 1926 was the year of black, and the magazine famously elevated one of Chanel's understated black dresses to 'The Chanel "Ford" – the frock that all the world will wear'.[14]

Patou returned from the First World War to resume his career in fashion having pin-pointed the fact that there was a need for clothes that retained an aura of femininity (without being fussy) yet complied with the demands of women's increasingly fast-moving lives. His approach was resolutely modern and his collections provided women (of means) who shared his outlook with impeccably constructed, streamlined clothes for all occasions. To reflect his taste he commissioned Süe et Mare to create suitably exquisite interiors for his salon and homes. One of his most famous clients, the tennis champion Suzanne Lenglen, astounded Wimbledon in 1921 in her elegant Patou attire on court. Throughout the Twenties she adhered to the Patou formula of straight-line whites with coloured cardigans and pleated skirts to just below the knee. Most distinctive was the hallmark Lenglen bandeau – a wide length of coloured chiffon wound around her head – a feature that was both decorative and functional. Patou made sportswear a speciality, providing high performance clothes for a range of sports from skiing to golfing, and like Chanel, he opened profitable boutiques in the top French resorts. For less energetic clients, chic but sporty fashions were available. Patou bathing suits and sports jumpers were prime examples of fashion meeting Cubism. Bright blocks of colour enhanced the front of V-necked jumpers, while one and two piece bathing suits enlivened beaches with their bold geometric compositions. Sonia Delaunay and newcomer Elsa Schiaparelli designed similar eye-catching and, for the time, skimpy swimwear. These daring costumes, whose Art Deco 'sleek, streamlined look'[15] was completed by rubber swimming caps, were usually photographed on fashionably tanned models posing around starkly modern swimming pools. Subtle daywear was one of Patou's major contributions to inter-war fashion. Linear aspects of Art Deco were carefully, almost imperceptibly harnessed in one-colour garments of intricate cut incorporating godets, pleats, insets and minute pin-tucking. Favoured fabrics were non-reflective, supple silks and fine wools dyed to Patou's specifications – his delicate rose-beige was all the rage in 1925. Off the body, these understated garments had little appeal but Patou (advised by the redoubtable publicist Elsa Maxwell) contracted the pretty music-hall twins, the Dolly sisters, to parade about in identical Patou ensembles and advertise the attraction of the clothes in motion.

23.7 Chanel, day ensemble.
Black wool jersey and
silk satin. French, 1926.
Gift of the New York
Historical Society.
The Metropolitan Museum
of Art, New York.

23.6 Chanel, evening dress.
Sequins on chiffon. French,
1932. V&A: T.339-1960.

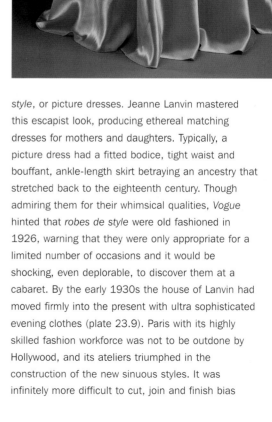

23.8 Jean Patou, evening dress. Beaded crêpe. French, 1937. V&A: T.336-1974.

23.10 Madeleine Vionnet, evening dress. Pink satin. French, 1933. V&A: T.203-1973.

Patou was credited with dispatching short skirts and 'abandoning the *garçonne*'[16] when he dramatically lowered hemlines in winter 1929. In fact, longer skirts had appeared some years earlier when designers, tired of the parallel format, changed the skirt's profile with ankle-grazing, fluttering handkerchief panels and sloping hems. By taking this trend to the extreme and by promoting slender but curvaceous lines, Patou was a forerunner of the later phase of Art Deco fashion (plate 23.8). 1929 was a turning point; the French fashion industry had to contend with financial upheavals born of the Wall Street Crash, the subsequent Depression, punitive import taxes (especially USA tariffs) and a group of talented American designers ready to break free of the hegemony of Paris.

An alternative to 'jazz style' chemise dresses with their overtones of boyishness were feminine *robes de*

23.9 Jeanne Lanvin, evening dress. Purple satin. French, winter 1935. V&A: T.340-1965.

style, or picture dresses. Jeanne Lanvin mastered this escapist look, producing ethereal matching dresses for mothers and daughters. Typically, a picture dress had a fitted bodice, tight waist and bouffant, ankle-length skirt betraying an ancestry that stretched back to the eighteenth century. Though admiring them for their whimsical qualities, *Vogue* hinted that *robes de style* were old fashioned in 1926, warning that they were only appropriate for a limited number of occasions and it would be shocking, even deplorable, to discover them at a cabaret. By the early 1930s the house of Lanvin had moved firmly into the present with ultra sophisticated evening clothes (plate 23.9). Paris with its highly skilled fashion workforce was not to be outdone by Hollywood, and its ateliers triumphed in the construction of the new sinuous styles. It was infinitely more difficult to cut, join and finish bias panels than make a dress that was little more than a straight cut tube. 1930s evening wear in monochromatic matt silk crêpe or smooth glossy satin was especially exacting to make – accuracy was crucial, as the tiniest mistakes could not be concealed. For low-key Art Deco relief, designers introduced textures, fleeting touches of embroidery or flashes of contrasting colour and perfected the all-over 'fish scale' sequinned gown (plate 23.11). Lanvin favoured techniques such as ruching and excelled in top stitching hundreds of parallel lines onto satin for collars, borders and, most difficult of all, for entire garments.

Always distinctive, Madeleine Vionnet's creations were founded on her scrupulous analysis of the structure of dress in relationship to the body. Devoted as she was to the technical aspects of couture, it is not surprising that she agreed to give educational presentations in the Salles de l'Enseignement Technique at the Paris 1925 Exhibition. Her special talents came into their own in the 1930s with the vogue for clothes of complex cut predicated on the body's contours. With mathematical precision Vionnet explored the nuances of cut (making advances that have rarely been equalled since), employing her favourite matt *crêpe Romaine*, as well as pliable, difficult to work satins and silk velvets. Hollywood films ensured that ivory satin became *the* fabric for evening. Vionnet used it for some of the most seductive cut-on-the-cross gowns, which she plunged at the front, back and sometimes at the sides to achieve a provocative, near naked look (plate 23.10). Periodicals illustrated the synergy of the new as interiors, vehicles and architecture conspired with clothes in a streamlined homogeneity. *Vogue*, *Fémina*, *L'Officiel* and *Harper's Bazaar* had Vionnet's virtuoso works photographed within environments that, like her designs, were remarkable for their honed-down purity.

Most leading Paris couturiers (Lelong, Mainbocher, Alix, Molyneux and the like) mastered the art of the bias cut in the Thirties, as did Elsa Schiaparelli. She made superb garments in a traditional vein but these were overshadowed by highly theatrical creations – the outcome of her involvement with such artists as Salvador Dali, Jean Cocteau and Christian Bérard. Thrusting her into the limelight, her surreal fantasies (from carrot shaped buttons to skeleton dresses) won press acclaim and set her apart from couture's mainstream. However, her uncontroversial classic output – tailored suits and outstanding evening wear, including a scarlet evening coat with an imposing swishing train – won her a faithful clientele (plate 23.12).

23.11 Mainbocher, evening jacket (detail). Sequinned silk. American, 1939. V&A: T.309-1974.

23.12 Elsa Schiaparelli (Italian), evening coat. Scarlet taffeta. 1939. V&A: T.52-1965.

The cinema was a potent force in both reflecting and influencing fashion. In the days of the silent movies, fans (assisted by motion picture magazines) emulated the looks and mannerisms of their favourite stars. In April 1925, for example, *Photoplay's* shopping service offered 'the wardrobes of the Stars' at reasonable prices; for those who could not afford the screen-inspired, ready-made garments, diluted versions of Hollywood styles were available as paper patterns. By the 1930s, the business of copying was widespread and encouraged by publicity-hungry studios it became a hugely profitable branch of the fashion industry. Thus Art Deco fashion (Hollywood style) was dispersed to a mass audience – Macy's claimed to have sold over half a million copies of Joan Crawford's 1932 'Letty Lynton' dress. Although direct attempts to secure the magic of Paris fashion by commissioning couturiers (most notably Chanel) to costume films were not successful, the osmotic interchange of creative ideas across the Atlantic resulted in one of fashion's 'golden' periods for both Paris couture and Californian costumiers. Hollywood's spectacular interpretations of Art Deco fashion peaked with the work of Travis Banton, Orry-Kelly and Gilbert Adrian, who designed expensive, highly sophisticated costumes for the likes of Marlene Dietrich, Carole Lombard and Joan Crawford (see plate 30.5).

Charles James never costumed a 1930s film but his dramatic, sensuous creations would have fitted the media perfectly. An itinerant Anglo-American who worked for periods in Paris, he was intrigued by the possibilities of clothing structures beyond fashion's mainstream. His work was likened to feats of engineering and architecture – 'Charlie was much more than a designer or dressmaker: he was fascinated with construction, the kind of construction that makes a bridge a thing of beauty.'[17] To achieve a bodice (with echoes of Art Deco's architectonic sunbursts) he spent months manipulating wide satin ribbon from the French silk weavers Colcombet into pleats that open around the torso like petals (plate 23.13).

Accessories, especially hats, shoes and handbags, often revealed a decorative style at its most exuberant. Their size and disposability encouraged designers to explore the far reaches of colour, pattern and form. That small but pervasive Art Deco artefact the cloche hat has come to symbolize the 1920s (plate 23.1). Decorated or plain, pulled down over the forehead, it persisted until 1930 when it grew a brim that framed the face in a becoming manner. Not everyone was a cloche devotee – 'the small crowned and close fitting hats we find so becoming nowadays press tightly against the ears and are very irksome to wear – even inflicting severe headaches on sensitive subjects'.[18] Hats were *de rigueur* throughout the period and a plethora of talented milliners in Paris, London and New York created new designs for each season.

Diminutive embroidered and beadwork bags accompanied 1920s evening outfits. Scattered with vivid stylized flowers or zigzags against black grounds, or emblazoned with golden sunbursts, they reflected successive Art Deco ornamental fads. When Howard Carter excavated Tutankhamun's tomb in November 1922, the pharaoh's 'priceless bric-a-brac of death'[19] provoked a wave of 'Egyptian' fashions (see Chapter 3). Rows of scarabs, hieroglyphs and lotus flowers – printed, woven, embroidered or embossed – broke out over handbags while fashion designers fuelled the craze with the 'Tutankhamen Over-Blouse', the 'Luxor Gown' and most eerily the 'Mummy Wrap' (plate 23.14).[20] In contrast to this decorative cornucopia, a group of 1930s exclusive clutch bags were remarkable for their refined linear decoration. Precision-made, their rectangular surfaces were pieced and hand tooled in calf leather with minimal geometric abstract designs in the manner of the finest bookbindings of the period.

23.14 Hand bag with mirror wallet. Felt, leather, satin, brass and lapis lazuli. Probably French, c.1924. V&A: T.236&A-1972.

23.13 Charles James, evening gown. Black satin. British, 1936-7. V&A: T.290-1978.

With the advent of short skirts in the mid-1920s, shoes became lively focal points and were to obtain a new artistic significance in the hands of the master craftsmen André Perugia, Salvatore Ferragamo and Roger Vivier. The most imaginative designs were saved for evening shoes. Light and made for dancing, the most coveted had the popular T-bar and Art Deco patterns in bright, eye-catching colours or gleaming silver and gold finishes (plate 23.17). As well as extraordinary shoes for 1930s cinema, Ferragamo excelled in production of innovatory footwear that epitomized the restrained streamlining that characterized the last phase of Art Deco.

Shawls were 'little less than a obsession'[21] throughout the 1920s. Hovering between fabrics and fashion, they provided warmth and another welcome accessory, but above all they were worn for their decorative appeal. Panels for shawls by the textile artists Edouard Bénédictus and Michel Dubost had huge, non-repeating Art Deco designs of semi-naturalistic flora and geometric forms, in glistening silks and metallic threads. Equally striking were appliqué shawls with vast, strongly coloured abstract compositions executed in silks, velvets and fabrics shot with silver and gold (plate 23.15). Pattern books of the 1920s and 1930s from Lyon's leading silk manufacturers illustrate thousands of superlative examples of dress fabrics and reveal the unrivalled wealth that Paris couture had at its command.[22] Fabrics of the Twenties with lavish brocaded patterns, from pseudo-eighteenth-century florals to ultra modern abstracts, equipped designers to overcome the tedium of loose, straight cut dresses. By the 1930s, ranges of plain, pliable silks in ivory, peach and duck egg blue enabled the same designers to mould gowns seductively around female contours.

Although rarefied, custom-made Paris clothes remained the province of affluent women and a fast-living international 'smart set', the rapid dissemination of ideas and a burgeoning ready-to-wear industry brought Art Deco fashion to the masses. The total Art Deco look required a svelte shape, insubstantial underwear, the latest hairstyle and the right make-up. Magazines abounded with slimming and beauty advice, and together with that powerful persuader the cinema, provided an eager audience with idols of style. Following the tenet that 'It is almost impossible for those who are too stout to wear their clothes to advantage',[23] all manner of reducing pills, potions and exercises were advertised. Nevertheless, corsets remained hidden allies – manufacturers stressed that the new, lightweight undergarments, while compressing wearers into the

23.15 Shawl. Silk, velvet and lamé. Probably French, c.1925. V&A: T.128-1980.

23.16 Cecil Beaton, *The Marquise de Casa Maury*. Cecil Beaton, *The Book of Beauty*, London, 1930. NAL.

desirable trim, sheath-like lines, did not jeopardize bodily freedom. The 1920s vogue for short hair became a burning issue. The precise geometry of a gleaming bob, or the neat cap of hair provided by a shingle or schoolboy Eton crop, was ideally suited to the rectangular dimensions of 1920s clothes. These mannish bobbed and shaved haircuts were regarded with suspicion and denounced as wicked by a vociferous and sanctimonious minority. Make-up was no longer taboo and was used in abundance by the uninhibited young, who even applied it in public. The giant cosmetic firms – Elizabeth Arden, Helena Rubenstein, joined by Max Factor (make-up artist to the stars) – vied with each other product by product. The early Art Deco face was championed by the vamps Pola Negri and Theda Bara (with her kohl-ringed eyes) and the kittenish 'It' girl Clara Bow. Louise Brooks typified the 1920s flapper with her fringed bob, big eyes and sleek appearance. Eyes were exaggerated by heavy shadow and recently introduced waterproof mascara. Skin was powdered, cheeks were rouged and dark 'kissproof' lipstick

defined hard-edged shapes – 'cupid's bow', 'bee stung' and 'V shaped' (see plate 25.8). A brash mask of make-up was affected by the most defiant, but gradually the components were toned down and the later Art Deco face with its arched eyebrows immortalized by Greta Garbo was a less abrasive composition.

The prominent society fashion photographer, diarist and dandy, Cecil Beaton chronicled the activities of the *crème de la crème*. With a penchant for exceptionally pretty or exotic women, he compiled a roll call of his sitters – beauties and leaders of fashion – many of whom were Art Deco role models. From the field of entertainment he delighted in Tallulah Bankhead, Lilian Gish, Marion Davies, Norma Shearer, Adele Astaire, Anita Loos, Irene Castle, Tilly Losch and Gertrude Lawrence; and he was in raptures over Greta Garbo, considering her to be the most glamorous figure in the whole world. Representing literature and bohemia, the aquiline features of Edith Sitwell and Virginia Woolf won his admiration. Besotted by titles, he drew enlightening

pen pictures of Lady Abdy, Lady Lavery, the Vicomtesse de Janzé and Lady Diana Cooper. However, seen through Beaton's eyes, it was the tall, svelte and immaculately groomed Marquise de Casa Maury (Paula Gellibrand) who epitomized the Art Deco look. Beaton eulogized her as follows, 'The abstract lines and contours of her face are faultless, she has the repose of Dobson's sculpture'[24] (plate 23.16). Over thirty years later he still marvelled over her as 'the first living Modigliani' he had ever seen.[25]

In the late 1930s, the bias cut, feline glamour of Art Deco fashion gave way to a panoply of historically inspired styles and, by 1938, fuller skirts, broad shoulders and drab colours were the order of the day, precursors of the sombre, inevitably utilitarian clothes of wartime.

23.17 Men's shoes. Leather inlay.
British, c.1925.
V&A: T.53, 56 and 59-1996.

24 Art Deco Jewellery

Clare Phillips

The origins of any dramatic change of style may usually, in retrospect, be glimpsed obliquely in the preceding generation. However, the jewellery produced during the 1920s and 1930s represented a very real break with the fashions of recent decades and a completely new, more austere, aesthetic. These changes were given an added edge by the transformation that women's lives had undergone since the First World War. Styles of dress had evolved to suit a freer, more active lifestyle, and lines within jewellery became streamlined and angular to complement the new, flatter silhouette. The regulations of the Paris 1925 Exhibition demanded that all exhibits should demonstrate 'a modern inspiration and a real originality'.[1] These aims were to find magnificent expression in the jewellers' art – with startling new forms, colour combinations and cuts of stones – in a distinctive style now immediately recognizable as Art Deco.

The jeweller Henry Wilson, who wrote the official British report on the jewellery and metalwork shown at the Paris 1925 Exhibition, had no doubt that the French work was by far the most interesting. He wrote,

> There was very much that was new in the French Section of Jewellery, and much that was very beautiful ... More use was made of cabochon stones than formerly; jade, black onyx and enamel were freely used to give contrast and richness. Rainbow effects of the prismatic colours natural to coloured gems were much sought after, and the combinations in most cases were rich and beautiful. In fact, colour was being sought instead of mere brilliance. In addition to this there was a tendency towards oriental effects in design, derived possibly from the use of oriental carved stones as centres of ornament.[2]

The most magnificent oriental stones shown in 1925 were three carved Mughal emeralds around which Cartier created the necklace, or shoulder ornament, with matching diadem and brooch that was the focal point of their display. A band of pearls, diamonds and black enamel linked the three emeralds that sat on the chest and on each shoulder (plate 24.2). This jewelled band was made in hinged sections, draping across the front of the mannequin with the ends hanging freely down the back, finished off with tassels of pearls, emeralds and diamonds. Although it was of incredible splendour, Wilson was not convinced of its wearability.[3] Another unusual piece created by Cartier for the exhibition was a 38 centimetre (15 inch) *broche de décolleté*, which echoed the front opening of a dress from the neckline to below the waist. Although the idea was rapidly copied in embroidery, this piece, like the emerald-set shoulder ornament, did not sell. In addition to these, and to vibrant combinations of emerald and coral, or colourful arrangements of carved gemstones, Cartier showed black and white jewellery of diamonds and black onyx. This had been

24.2 *Bérénice*, mannequin with shoulder ornament and diadem of emeralds, pearls, black enamel and diamonds by Cartier, Paris. *Gazette du bon ton*, special issue for the 'Pavilion de l'Elégance', 1925. NAL. © Cartier.

24.1 Cartier, pylon pendant. Diamonds and onyx in open-back platinum setting. French, 1913. Cartier Collection, Geneva. Photo: Nick Welsh © Cartier.

a fashionable combination for over a decade, visually striking in its own right but also appropriate for mourning wear (plates 24.1 and 24.3). The onyx, which was artificially stained black, had what *Fémina* magazine described as 'a sombre sheen [which] makes a paved diamond ground shine out more splendidly, more brightly'.[4] Cartier developed this theme into their distinctive panther skin motif, an abstract pattern that was used to great effect from 1914 onwards.

Exotic combinations of colour, doubtless inspired by the designs for the Ballets Russes, were explored in coral and hardstones by various jewellers. Among the most vibrant pieces were two substantial corsage ornaments by Boucheron in which ribbed panels of

contrasting lapis lazuli, coral, jade and onyx were set as swirling abstract mosaics, the lines picked out in brilliant-cut diamonds (plate 24.5). The exotic was even more tangible in Georges Fouquet's dramatic mask jewels (plate 24.4). Two Chinese masks were exhibited in 1925: one of blue-green jade, matching enamel, black onyx and diamonds, the other of carved, frosted rock crystal, diamonds and large pendent emeralds.

While such exhibition pieces were often innovative and calculated for maximum impact, they were not especially typical of the jewellery being made and worn on a more regular basis. Jewellery designed for stock took much more account of the wearer and was in tune with the wider fashions of the day. This

close relationship can be seen in the immediate impact that the new short hairstyles had on jewellery design. In 1925 *Queen* magazine reported, 'Hair is dressed very close to the head and the newest shingle is cut in a point at the nape. No ornament is worn in the hair for dances.'[5] The following year the *Goldsmiths' Journal* was to complain, 'Short hair is not helping the jeweller. It has lessened the demand for the tiara, the bandeau, the jewelled comb, hair ornaments, hair slides and hat pins.'[6] It was no doubt in an attempt to overcome this problem that Cartier designed a comb bandeau designed specifically for short hair. Other jewellers, too, rose magnificently to the challenge, and the tiara created by Lacloche a few years later for Loelia, Duchess of

24.3 Cartier, brooch. Carved ruby and onyx, drop-shaped pearl, briolette-cut pink tourmaline, diamonds and onyx. French, 1914. Private collection.
© Christie's Images Ltd 1981.
© Cartier.

24.4 Georges Fouquet, brooch. White gold, blue enamel and diamonds. French, c.1931. Private collection.
© ADAGP, Paris and DACS, London 2002.

Westminster's presentation at court (where tiaras were still obligatory) sat exquisitely on her stylishly short hair (plate 24.8). Alternatively, as the *Illustrated London News* pointed out, 'As the fashion for "Eton" cropped heads grows daily, long, decorative ear-rings are becoming increasingly fashionable.'[7] The other indirect advantage for the jewellers of short hair was the preponderance of hats. Hat brooches were being promoted in *Queen* by 1919: 'If one has the least pretence to smartness one cannot do without one of these hatpins. They are placed right in front of the hat and are called "*flechettes*" – because the first of the kind looked like an arrow.'[8] Hat jewels remained popular well into the Twenties. The Duchess of Westminster recalled, 'In the autumn of 1925 we wore pairs of little diamanté animals in our felt hats. Otherwise we pinned real brooches in them, which was asking for trouble as they were always falling off or getting stolen in cloakrooms.'[9] At times, particularly with evening dress, jewellery had to compete hard to be noticed on the glittering fabrics being worn. In 1925, a fashion writer described how 'Evening gowns of silver tissue have their brilliance increased by embroideries of silvered crystal beads and small discs of mirror which reflect the light', and how 'metal lace is jewelled, embroidered, and encrusted on tissue gowns so that it becomes part of the

fabric'[10] (see plate 23.16). But fabric and jewels could combine effectively, as one of the British trade journals indicated: 'Silver lamé ... the popular basis for many of the gowns, formed an ideal background for the platinum in which the jewels were set.'[11]

The abandonment of long evening gloves encouraged the wearing of richly jewelled bracelets, often several on one wrist, while the new acceptability of make-up and smoking led to the development of luxurious cosmetics cases and cigarette holders. Made of carved hardstones or enamelled and gem-set gold, these accessories became an important aspect of Art Deco fashion (plates 24.6 and 24.7). While early cosmetic cases often had a matching lipstick case and powder compact linked by chains, in the early 1930s Van Cleef & Arpels developed the *minaudière*, a compact box of several compartments which could hold cigarettes, a lighter and essential cosmetics. In contrast, many new ideas failed to catch on. In America in 1928 there were high hopes of 'the jewelled anklet, guaranteed to make walking a more interesting occupation',[12] and from Germany it was reported that 'Kneelaces are exciting considerable comment in Berlin, but with the rapidly increasing length of the frock in this country, there seems little probability of their becoming popular here.'[13] Even Cartier was to produce some curious and surprising

24.6 Cartier, vanity case. Gold, rubies, emerald, sapphire, diamonds, turquoise, mother-of-pearl and enamel. French, 1925. Private collection, Switzerland. © Christie's Images Ltd 2003. © Cartier.

24.7 Lacloche Frères, vanity case. Jade, diamonds and onyx. French, *c*.1925. V&A: M.24-1976.

24.8 Cecil Beaton, *Loelia, Duchess of Westminster*. She is wearing a diamond tiara by Lacloche. Around 1930. Courtesy of Sotheby's London.

novelties among which the 'diamants mystérieux' of 1934 stand out. These were individually mounted diamonds with clips so discreet and strong that they could be fixed securely to the thinnest wisp of hair or even to the eyebrows. Cartier recommended that ten or twelve be worn together arranged at will, pointing out that they had the potential to 'completely turn upside down our idea of ornament'[14] (plate 24.9).

One of the most distinctive and popular types of jewel at this date was the double clip, a pair of symmetrical brooches that could be worn as one or separately. Their ubiquity can be sensed in the contemporary comment that 'By the end of the twenties it had become essential to possess a pair of diamond, or pseudo-diamond, clips. They were clipped not only on to hats but on to everything else, even the small of the back, where they served to keep underclothes out of sight.'[15]

Pearls remained one of the most desirable of jewels and well matched strings were of immense value. In 1917 Cartier New York had acquired its new premises, a large Renaissance-style town house on Fifth Avenue, in exchange for a two-row oriental pearl necklace. Two years later fashion commentators noted, 'There have never been seen so many pearl necklaces, short and long' and 'Pearl necklaces no longer go round the neck. The fashion is to let them fall down to the waist, or lower still, and to twist them up in any original way.'[16] Imitation pearls, which had always been available, became extremely fashionable in the mid-Twenties. One debutante recalled,

> Then came choker pearls, the size of gooseberries.
> Up till then it had been thought good taste to wear
> small Técla pearls of a size in proportion to one's
> income, so that they might be mistaken for real.
> I was afraid that my mother would think large
> chokers vulgar so I only wore mine when I was sure
> that she wasn't about.[17]

The following year Alphonse, the Paris correspondent for *Queen* magazine, commented on the vogue for unashamedly fake pearls, larger than walnuts and stained in different shades to match one's dress.[18] Imitation or costume jewellery was being worn in society quite deliberately at this time, as is clearly shown by Chanel's provocative statement, 'It does not matter if they are real as long as they look like junk.'[19] The greatest challenge to the prestige of pearls, however, came with the arrival on the international market of the cultured pearl, developed commercially by Mikimoto Kōkichi of Japan (see plate 35.9). It delighted consumers but sent waves of alarm through the trade and prompted much debate in the 1920s over the necessity of accurate trade descriptions and protection for retailer and consumer

alike when faced with virtually indistinguishable pieces of such vastly different values.

It was during the 1920s that the rectangular baguette-cut for diamonds came to prominence. Henry Wilson had noted in 1925 that 'Much is being made to-day in Paris of diamonds cut in rod form "*taille en bâton ou en allumette*." This has only been general for the last two years, I am told.'[20] However, it is clear from photographs of work exhibited by the major jewellers such as Cartier, Fouquet and Boucheron that baguette stones were not in widespread use in 1925 and that their design potential had not yet been fully grasped. Around 1924 Boucheron had made a watch brooch in which the watch hangs on a chain of baguette diamonds individually set and arranged like rungs of a ladder,

but there are few firmly dated examples of their use at this time. As the writer and curator Henri Clouzot wrote in 1929, 'Diamonds could be baguette-cut in 1925, but we were far from suspecting that cut's implications.'[21] By 1929 the baguette had come into its own and, together with discreet platinum mounts, was at the centre of the 'completely white note' that Georges Fouquet identified as the innovation for that year.[22] The style was featured in Paris at a sumptuous exhibition of contemporary jewellery held at the Palais Galliéra the same year. It was, by all accounts, a magnificent spectacle and was written up by Fouquet for *Studio* magazine with photographs of work by Mauboussin, Chaumet and Boucheron. Conscious of the long legacy of jewels set purely with diamonds, Fouquet wrote,

A writer in the *Goldsmiths' Journal* bemoaned that 'mechanical finish has eliminated the virtuosity of technique; and, worse than that, the public have been taught to value invisible setting above visible craftsmanship ... they prefer mechanical perfection, *viz.*, sharpness, smoothness etc., before subtlety, poetry, and invention.'[24] It could be argued that these critics were simply attuned to the fundamentally conservative nature of their mainstream customers. When the Prince of Wales visited Birmingham's jewellery quarter in May 1931 he was surprised that half-hoop and cluster rings were still top sellers. He himself was reported as preferring pieces in 'the modernistic theme, where the contour is somewhat bold, geometric in style and set with square cut and baguette diamonds, together with brilliants'.[25] In the years that followed he was to indulge this taste magnificently in the jewellery by Cartier, Van Cleef & Arpels and others that he lavished on Wallis Simpson.

The 'modernistic' theme was developed to its most extreme by a small number of innovative Parisian designers whose work was distinguished by an uncompromising geometry that could, on occasions, appear almost brutally stark. At the forefront of this style were Jean Fouquet, Raymond Templier and Gérard Sandoz, all from families long established in the jewellery world (plates 24.10 to 24.19). Aiming to create a new style that was sensationally modern and rational, they broke away from the jewellery establishment and in 1930, together with other designers and avant-garde architects, founded the Union des Artistes Modernes. Drawing much of its inspiration from the strong and simple forms associated with machine production, theirs was a powerful and influential aesthetic. In 1930 Templier stated, 'As I walk in the streets I see ideas for jewellery *everywhere*, the wheels, the cars, the machinery of today. I hold myself *permeable* to everything.'[26] They argued too for the use of less traditional materials in jewellery, stating in their manifesto that 'a beautiful material is not necessarily rare or precious. It is above all a material whose natural qualities or whose adaptability to industrial processes are pleasing to the eye and to the touch, and whose value derives from judicious use.'[27]

But how new is this white stone jewellery, and how much it differs from the old! Progress has been made in working on the diamond, and this stone may now be treated like the coloured stones ... Pieces are composed and carried out which consist of a mixture of brilliants and brilliants cut in the forms of wands, triangles, or any other form, allowing the artist to obtain from diamonds whatever effect he chooses. The wand-shaped brilliants give different reflections from the round ones, and the most varied play of light may be obtained by arranging them side by side.[23]

Further contrasts of texture and lustre were achieved in the early 1930s with the addition of polished rock crystal.

In the first three months of 1929 the *Goldsmiths' Journal* published a series of articles illustrating contemporary 'modernist' jewellery. Seventy-five pieces were featured by designers designated 'progressive', including Cartier, Van Cleef & Arpels, Boucheron, Mauboussin, Vever, Sandoz, Brandt and Templier. Most were French, but Belgian, Swiss, Italian and Spanish pieces were also shown. Its tone was markedly cautious, noting that this was a more dramatic change of fashion than usually occurred and remaining non-committal as to whether it would stand the test of time. In Britain there was a degree of resistance to this new, severe style of work within the trade, particularly among those whose training had encouraged a more florid style and who now failed to recognize the very real craftsmanship required to produce such stark and minimal effects.

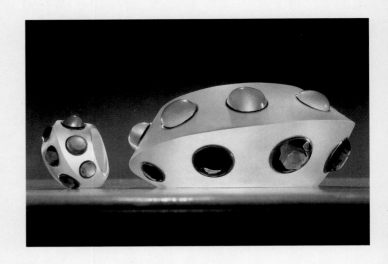

24.10 Jean Fouquet, bracelet. White gold with diamonds and aquamarines. French, c.1930. Private collection. © ADAGP, Paris and DACS, London 2002.

24.11 Jean Fouquet, bracelet and ring. Crystal, amethysts, moonstone and platinum. French, c.1930. Primavera Gallery, New York. © ADAGP, Paris and DACS, London 2002.

Modern Jewellery

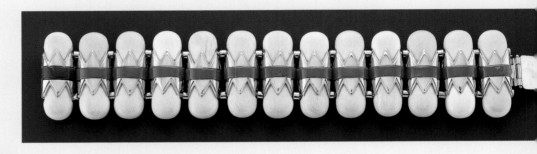

24.12 Van Cleef & Arpels, bracelet. Ivory, coral and gold. American, 1931. Esmerian Collection, New York.

24.14 Jean Fouquet, bracelet. White and yellow gold with onyx. French, c.1930. Primavera Gallery, New York. © ADAGP, Paris and DACS, London 2002.

24.15 Raymond Templier, brooch. Diamonds set in platinum. French, 1928. Collection Victor and Gretha Arwas, London.

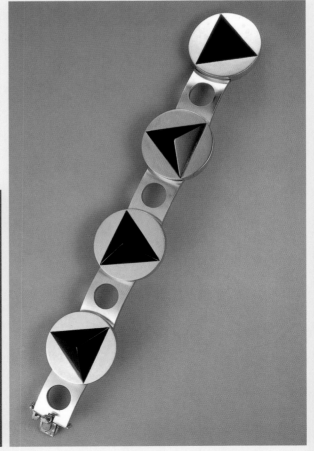

24.13 Raymond Templier, bracelet with brooch. Silver, platinum, gold, onyx and diamonds. French, c.1925-30. Gift of the Sydney and Frances Lewis Foundation. Virginia Museum of Fine Arts, Richmond. Photo: Katherine Wetzel.

24.16 Georges Fouquet, tassel necklace. Frosted rock crystal, nylon, onyx and enamel. French, 1925. Esmerian Collection, New York. Photo: © David Behl. © ADAGP, Paris and DACS, London 2002.

24.17 Gérard Sandoz, 'Guitar', pendant. Frosted crystal, labradorite, lacquer, pink and white gold and black silk. French, c. 1928. Esmerian Collection, New York. Photo: © David Behl. © ADAGP, Paris and DACS, London 2002.

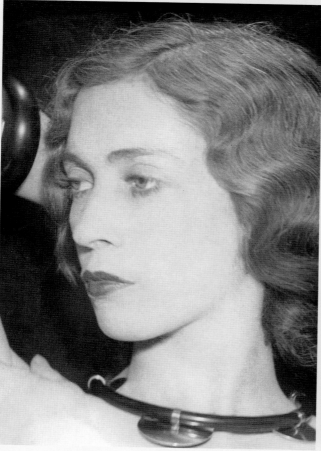

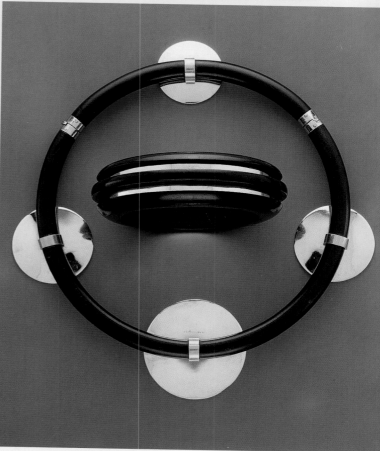

24.18 Man Ray (American), model wearing a necklace by Jean Fouquet. Gelatin silver print. Around 1931. Esmerian Collection, New York. © Man Ray Trust/ADAGP, Paris and DACS, London 2002.

24.19 Jean Fouquet, necklace and bracelet. Ebony, chrome-plated metal and gold. French, 1931. Esmerian Collection, New York. © ADAGP, Paris and DACS, London 2002.

At the more popular end of the market, adaptability to industrial processes underlay the successful production of costume jewellery in synthetic resins such as Bakelite and Galalith (plate 24.20). Their ability to imitate more precious materials and to be moulded to any form was exploited by the designers of costume jewellery with great enthusiasm and imagination.

The demand for pieces of incredible opulence continued during these decades, but the inter-war period was not an easy one for the jewellery industry as a whole. After the brief upturn following the end of the First World War, many British jewellers struggled and the trade journals indicate a mood of general gloom. A contemporary editorial reflected a widespread view:

> The motor car is, without doubt, in a great measure responsible for the lack of jewellery worn, for even were he so inclined, the possessor of a car has added to his daily expenditure that which might otherwise find its way into the hands of the jewellers, but My Lady will overcome her longing for a diamond pendant when a Rolls-Royce is at her command.[28]

The effects of the Depression, which continued until the mid-1930s, are indicated graphically in assay office figures. In Birmingham, for example, there was a 40% drop in the amount of gold and silver being hallmarked in 1920-21, with a generally downward trend until 1934.[29]

Attempts to stimulate trade in Britain included glamorous fashion parades with models wearing magnificent jewellery. In 1928 the National Jewellers' Association took part in 'a fascinating show of wonderful jewels, ravishing dresses and beautiful women' in what was termed the 'million pound jewel and dress parade' held at the Mayfair Hotel on Berkeley Street, London. Jewellers included Cartier, Garrard & Co., the Goldsmiths' & Silversmiths' Co. and Lacloche Frères, while the dresses, 'a complete forecast of the modes to be worn during the coming Riviera season', were by Paul Caret. Invitations were exclusive and strictly limited, guaranteeing great press interest.[30] A similar event followed in the following year at which 'To the music of the orchestra mannequins in beautiful frocks displayed ... gorgeous jewellery under a play of constantly moving limelights glistening on tiaras, necklaces, sautoirs, brooches, pendants, rings and earrings.'[31]

The American market appears to have been considerably more buoyant. The wealth of its high society was reflected in a comment in the London fashion press that 'The July steamers begin to leave New York with more tonnage in jewels than anybody but Aladdin could believe in.'[32] Many of the wealthiest Americans chose to buy their jewellery in Europe, particularly in Paris, but the trade at home was evidently flourishing. Even allowing for a deliberately optimistic marketing tone, trade reports originating in the Newark jewellery press had a much more positive note than their British counterparts. In 1928 it was noted that

> The most striking feature of the new jewellery is the large size of the stones, particularly in bracelets and rings ... In rings large square-cut stones are the favourites, in most cases reaching all the way to the knuckle. While obviously only one or two of these huge rings can be worn at a time, there is practically no limit to the number of bracelets that now lend distinction to the fashionable forearm. A quarter of a yard of them has been given as the proper measure.[33]

At the same time, 'There are so many new uses for brooches this year, that the feminine jewel box can scarcely be too well supplied with them.' With what seems extraordinary profligacy, it was suggested that even relatively new pieces of jewellery should 'be constantly reset or discarded for others in order to keep up with the changing mode ... The necklace that was so very smart last autumn will be unsuitable to wear with this summer's costume, and the ornament that was the making of last winter's satin or felt toque will be nothing but a menace to this season's flowered or beribboned straw.'[34] The co-ordination of fashion trends with jewellery design was something at which the French excelled:

> So determined were [the couturiers] ... about this that they brought into their establishments some of the best jewellery designers in Paris, in order that precisely the right ornaments could be created for each individual model. Patou is said to be using topaz and aquamarines on a lavish scale. Lelong's speciality ... is aquamarine and diamond buckles. And Chanel does not stop at mere ornaments – her gowns are heavily beaded with brilliants, or pearls, or coloured stones.[35]

Lady Mount Temple made a similar point when she recorded that 'Quite a number of the best French jewellers are allied in some way with one of the big dress designers, so that they have the advantage of knowing beforehand what the coming fashions are to be, and therefore what type of jewellery should be worn with them.'[36]

As these accounts make clear, the emphasis within jewellery during the Art Deco period – whether from the viewpoint of the designer or the wearer – was determinedly on the new, in the belief that modern clothes required modern jewels. This confidence in the contemporary, although it no doubt resulted in the re-setting and consequent loss of some fine historic jewellery, gave a unity to fashionable dress which has seldom been achieved since. The jeweller Henry Wilson had noted at the 1925 Exhibition that, in all spheres, historicism had been replaced by 'massiveness, severity of outline, simplicity and a certain monumental quality as impressive as it is beautiful. Everywhere one hears the cry for construction! construction!'[37] These large, austere forms may not have seemed compatible with the traditionally miniature and intimate practice of jewellery design, but they were explored to glorious effect by the finest designers of the period and they transformed ideas of fashion across the globe.

25 Photography and the New Vision

Mark Haworth-Booth

Art Deco photography is angular, commercial, decorative, innovative and in love with the same shining materials of modernity – chrome and silver, for example – used by the movement's architects and designers. The preoccupations summed up by the Paris 1925 Exhibition touched photography briefly but vividly. The first signs of the tendency were seen in a set of photographs made in Paris in 1911, when the couturier Paul Poiret designed a range of dresses in a new style – and then did something else that was new. He collaborated with Lucien Vogel, director of the journal *Art et décoration*, who hired a leading creative photographer of the day to photograph them. Thirteen photographs, by the Paris-based American Edward Steichen, were published in April 1911 and the art of fashion photography was born. Before then the photography of costume had not conceived ambitions beyond, say, standing two models side by side and having one of them hold the programme of *Schéhérazade*.[1] Steichen created soft-focus tableaux involving graceful gestures, the choreographic interplay of figures, an understanding of the clothes and an intriguingly angular presentation of space which translated readily into an orderly geometry on the printed page (plate 25.1).

Another early instance of Art Deco photography occurred the following year, when the cosmopolitan, then London-based, Baron Adolf de Meyer travelled to Paris to photograph Vaslav Nijinsky in the Ballets Russes production of *Prélude à l'aprés-midi d'un faune* (plate 25.2). As has often been remarked, if the dancer of Art Nouveau was Loïe Fuller, the dancers of Art Deco were Nijinsky and Josephine Baker. Baron de Meyer photographed them both. His Nijinsky series was published as a supplement to a London newspaper, the *Sketch*, and brought the dancing sensation to a mass audience. The sensation included de Meyer's expert representation of the final movement of Nijinsky's Faun – 'the dancer's orgasmic climax as he lay on the Nymph's scarf'.[2]

25.2 Baron Adolf de Meyer, photograph of Nijinsky as the faun. *The Sketch Supplement*, 26 February 1913. Theatre Museum, London.

25.1 Edward Steichen, *Bakou et Pâtre*. American, c.1911. *Art et décoration*, April 1911. NAL.

25.3 Alvin Langdon Coburn, *Vortograph*. Gelatin silver print. American, 1917. Royal Photographic Society Picture Library.

An impressive Art Deco experiment in photography took place in London in 1917 when the Anglo-American photographer Alvin Langdon Coburn fractured the misty mirror of Symbolism (still clouding the works of Steichen and de Meyer at this date) with his idea of a Cubist photography (plate 25.3). Another key event in 1917 took place in New York when Alfred Stieglitz, guardian of America's creative flame, published the revolutionary new work of Paul Strand in a double issue of *Camera Work*. Here was a body of photography flooded with the cold light of the new century and composed with a brusque geometry. Surely that changed everything? Certainly. However, in the context of Art Deco, the key episodes were those of 1911 and 1912. Steichen and de Meyer interpreted the works of Poiret and Diaghilev, two of the essential impresarios and creators of Art Deco, and – unlike Coburn and Strand – published their photographs in commercial magazines. The development of half-tone plates, which allowed photographs to be convincingly printed in ink, together with text, transformed photography into the dominant illustrative system of the twentieth century. 'The triumph of cheap photomechanical reproduction', as John Szarkowski has written, 'made room for a new kind of professional, who could serve radically revised potentials.'[3] These potentials included – for the leading new professionals who will be discussed here – the interpretation and diffusion of the Art Deco style.

Like all the great international exhibitions, the Paris 1925 Exhibition was extensively photographed. A 12-volume *Rapport général*, profusely illustrated with half-tone reproductions of photographs, was published in 1929.[4] The photographs illustrate the exhibits, the pavilions, the gardens and the various sites around Paris that were illuminated at night as part of the Exhibition. These photographs derive from many sources, such as publishers, magazines and freelance photographers, rather than being part of a centrally directed campaign. The only colour photographs of the event appear to be the autochromes privately commissioned by Albert Kahn as part of 'Les Archives de la Planète', his project to document the world in photographs.[5]

It seems that the organizers of the Exhibition were not sure what part photography would play in the event, but were convinced, nonetheless, that the medium had a role – or roles – to play. Thus, volume X of the *Rapport général* presents Stage Design, Photography and Film. There is an instructive text on photography. It begins with a Gallic flourish, reminding us of the Exhibition's aim to reassert French cultural supremacy after wartime invasion and occupation. Photography is 'the most striking triumph of the human spirit since the invention of writing and printing. This triumph is completely French.'[6] By 1925 photography had become, the text continues, an extension of the human eye, like a microscope applied to a vast variety of phenomena – scientific, medical, topographical, aeronautical (as begun in the war), astronomical. The high-speed chronophotography of Etienne Marey had made nonsense of the photographer's traditional plea – 'Don't move!' The *instantané* or snapshot ruled. Today, we were told, the photographer takes unprecedented risks: he photographs *contre-jour*, uses blur and double-exposures – and cinema is even more bold.

Although photography was included in a division titled 'Enseignement', the organizers embraced it as an art. A salon was designed for the photography and cinema section by the architect-designer Francis Jourdain on the first floor of the Grand Palais. Apparently designed in a neat contemporary style, it was lit by mercury vapour lamps. The generality of photographs on show were not touched by the Art Deco style. Although amateurs had been encouraged to exhibit alongside the professional studios, the representation proved meagre. Apart from France, only Spain, Monaco, Czechoslovakia and the USSR sent photographs. The French contributors did not include two of the greatest French talents of the time, who were then still virtually unknown to aficionados of photography: Eugène Atget, who was at that very moment photographing the dazzling displays of Art Deco fashions in Paris shop-windows, and Jacques-Henri Lartigue, who was – as a child in *la belle époque* – both the youngest and the greatest master of the snapshot. Instead, the contributors were Pierre Petit and Adolphe Braun, studios founded in the 1850s and specializing in – respectively – architectural views and art reproduction, and the Parisian professionals Laure Albin-Guillot, G.L. Manuel *frères* and Henri Manuel. The USSR sent works by more than a dozen professionals, of whom the best known was the inventive portraitist Moisei Nappelbaum. The most dynamic and Modernist work, Alexander Rodchenko's photomontages for books by Vladimir Mayakovsky (*Pro Eto*) and Dziga Vertov (*Kino-Eye*), appeared elsewhere, in a section on 'Graphic Arts and the Art of the Book'. Also exhibited elsewhere were portraits by Franz Löwy, elegantly displayed with other reproductive techniques from the Vienna Art School in an installation designed by Josef Hoffmann. Of all the exhibits in the photographic section, the most truly Art Deco in inspiration were by a Czech, František Drtikol.

Some of the most successful photographers associated with Art Deco had already been fluent exponents of an earlier decorative style. František Drtikol trained as a photographer in Munich in 1901-3, when it was still a major centre for Art Nouveau. He established a portrait studio in Prague in 1910. A somewhat belated practitioner of Art Nouveau, Drtikol timed his Art Deco experiments perfectly for display at the 1925 Exhibition. After the First World War, Paris exercised a great influence on Prague's artists and photographers, though they also paid close attention to Berlin, Moscow and New York.[7] A new breeze was blowing through photography. It was manifested in Prague in the excited words of the Modernist Karel Teige in an article titled 'Foto – kino – film' published in 1922: 'The beauty of photography, as well as the beauty of modern technology, is determined by simple and absolute perfection, and conditioned by purposefulness: The beauty of photography is of the same breed as the beauty of an aeroplane or a transatlantic ship or electric bulb.'[8]

The organic curves of Art Nouveau simplified, in Drtikol's studio in the mid-1920s, into the geometrical undulations of painted backdrops which play off female nudes (plate 25.4). These studio props were made in the workshops of the Národni Divadlo (National Theatre) in Prague. Vladimir Birgus has pointed to parallels for the theatrical postures of Drtikol's models in Prague's avant-garde theatre, as well as in 'the expressive dancing of Isadora Duncan and Dalcroze's eurythmics'.[9] Drtikol's contributions to the 1925 Exhibition used a new style, and his models wore the latest hats, but they were printed in a soon-to-be *passé* technique, in the form of pigment prints, which characteristically show limited resolution and broad tonal effects.[10] This printing

25.4 František Drtikol, *Composition 1925*. Bromoil print. Czech, 1925. UPM – Museum of Decorative Arts, Prague. Photo: Miloslav Šebek.

25.5 Edward Steichen,
Art Deco clothing design,
photographed in the apartment
of Nina Price. Gelatin silver
print. American, 1925.
© Vogue, Condé Nast
Publications Inc.

25.6 Edward Steichen, *Spectacles*. Gelatin silver print. American, 1927. Fabric design for Stehli Silks Corporation. V&A: Circ.970-1967.

process enhanced flat decorative patterning. His studies were rewarded with a Grand Prix. By the late 1920s Drtikol had, like most other serious photographers, abandoned pigment prints: 'A simple, ordinary glossy photograph is the best work.'[11] Like other photographers imbued with the Art Deco spirit, Drtikol designed domestic objects too – notably severely geometrical light fittings.[12]

Edward Steichen had been the star of American Pictorialist photography in his youth. After wartime service, making aerial reconnaissance photographs over the battlefields of northern France, Steichen returned to his studio in Voulangis, outside Paris, to make experimental photographs and establish himself as a painter. In 1923 he destroyed his canvases and returned to New York. During an interview by Condé Nast about taking a position as chief photographer at *Vogue* and *Vanity Fair*, the question of fashion came up. How did Steichen feel about taking fashion photographs? 'My response was that I had already made fashion photographs in 1911, for the magazine *Art et décoration*. These were probably the first serious fashion photographs ever made.'[13] Steichen created the photographic epitome of Art Deco style for publication in American *Vogue* in June 1925, using strong artificial light to illuminate the sensational Deco dress, to highlight the model's flawless skin at neck and face, her profile and slender pointing finger, and – above all – to make the whole ensemble sparkle on the printed page (plate 25.5).

Steichen combined his work for the Condé Nast publications with a contract from 1923 to 1942 with the J. Walter Thompson advertising agency. He spoke of the 'meticulous detail and biting precision' of straight photography.[14] As an art photographer, Steichen had used only natural light. Now, as a commercial photographer in his middle age, Steichen became a virtuoso of artificial lighting – as his favoured self portrait of the period shows.[15] He used his new expertise to dazzling effect in such Deco classics as his Douglass Lighter advertisement of 1928. The 30 different lighting appliances in his studio were described by a visitor. The lights were 'affixed to derricks and flash down from aloft, they peek out from every corner, they can be arranged so that they actually paint the subject of the photograph'.[16] Steichen himself spoke expansively: 'We use light to dramatise, to build up. We use it to transform. We use it to express an idea.'[17]

The 1925 Exhibition sent a strong impulse across the Atlantic, encouraging a wave of experimentation. Patricia Johnston, the historian of Steichen's work in advertising, remarks that 'Magazines covered the new "modernism" in European consumer goods and furniture design. The 1927 Machine Age Exposition in Steinway Hall [in New York] drew large crowds to view photographs, drawings, architectural models, and industrial designs created in the new style.'[18] Although this was a Modernist rather than a Deco manifestation, it helped foster a favourable climate for Steichen's entry into design. His major contribution was for a Swiss company, the Stehli Silk Corporation. Stehli invited almost a hundred artists to create designs for a new range – titled the 'Americana' print series – to be printed on fabric for women's dresses for sale in the US market. Steichen, the only photographer involved in the project, prepared at least ten designs in 1926-7 and rose splendidly to the occasion. He used raking light to create unlikely angular patterns from household objects – bottles, beans, cans, cube sugar, moth balls, poker chips, safety matches, wire-frame spectacles, cotton thread and carpet tacks (plate 25.6 and see plate 34.3). He recalled that the tacks silk 'was a very popular design and was one of the first sellouts of the Stehli designs for that year'.[19] Patricia Johnston points out that although Steichen talked up the project as a 'democratic' reaching out – like advertising – to a large audience, the fabric was obviously expensive and 'it is doubtful the material reached the wider public Steichen claimed he designed it for'.[20] On the other hand, Steichen's designs – handsomely featured in *Vogue* on 1 February 1927 – no doubt broadened the general awareness, appeal and prestige of the Art Deco style in America. The period of dramatic lighting, startling angles and fantastically glamorized products in Steichen's work was short-lived. The style suited certain products, like cigarette lighters, but did not offer much scope for the advertising of staples like Ivory Soap. Much of Steichen's advertising photography after 1930 obediently fulfilled the run-of-the-mill briefs offered by J. Walter Thompson's art directors. However, the Art Deco motifs of glamour and bright new materials continued in his work of the 1930s in another genre: his glamour portraiture. We find echoes of Art Deco in Steichen's image of Joan Crawford reclining in a *faux* fur and plexiglass chair in 1932.[21] In the same year he extended photography into large-scale public design in the form of a photomural on the theme of aviation at the RKO Roxy in New York's Rockefeller Center.

Steichen's career at *Vogue* and *Vanity Fair* is paralleled by that of Baron de Meyer, who preceded him as Condé Nast's chief photographer from 1913 until 1921, when he moved to William Randolph Hearst's magazine *Harper's Bazar* (retitled *Harper's Bazaar* in 1929). De Meyer, who also worked as a fashion designer, adopted jazzy formats for his photographs of fashion and beauty products in the mid-1920s – though he retained an increasingly anachronistic soft-focus style.[22] He was at his most inventively Art Deco in his advertising photographs for Elizabeth Arden cosmetics in a series that ran throughout the 1920s and into the 1930s. During the series, the head of a human model was, as Anne Ehrenkranz has pointed out, 'altered and manipulated almost imperceptibly in sequential photographs, and was transformed finally into a wax mannequin. Surrounded by perfume bottles or human hands, de Meyer's wax heads have a disturbing quality of constructed femininity.'[23] This idea of the model as exquisite construction goes to the heart of Art Deco (plate 25.8).

A contrasting figure, Margaret Bourke-White, operated at *Fortune* (from 1929) and *Life* (from 1936). She showed how the language of Art Deco could be used to make dramatic visual patterns on the printed page. She used this talent to display the structures that began soaring above Manhattan at exactly the moment her career took off – the George

25.7 Man Ray (American), *Lee Miller*, solarization. Gelatin silver print. 1929. Lee Miller Archives. © Man Ray Trust/ADAGP, Paris and DACS, London 2002.

25.8 Baron Adolf de Meyer, advertisement for Elizabeth Arden cosmetics. Gelatin silver print. British, *c*.1927. National Gallery of Australia, Canberra.

Washington bridge, the Empire State building and, most of all, the Chrysler building (see plate 5.1). She photographed the famous Chrysler eagle gargoyle from her studio on the 61st floor. The studio, with custom-built furniture designed by John Vassos, was as full-bloodedly Deco as the building and was featured in *Architectural Forum* in January 1932. Bourke-White also posed with her camera on the gargoyle in much-reproduced photographs by Oscar Graubner.[24] The patterns she recognized in industrial buildings and mechanized production became symbols, in her photographs, of epic changes in industry and society between the wars. She playfully acknowledged the role of such patterns in her career in a photographic dress in an 'Industrial-Deco' style which she wore to an artists' ball in Greenwich Village in 1934.[25] She used these forms to grander effect in the photomurals she composed on the theme of 'Radio' for NBC at the Rockefeller Center.[26]

Enterprising American photographers were active in Paris during the period. Man Ray is the central figure. He had one foot in the art world, the other in magazines and publicity – and a finger, at least, in pornography. He was able to apply his inventive techniques, such as the 'Rayograph' (or photogram)

and solarization, to portraiture and publicity. Rayographs showed objects, laid on photographic paper and briefly exposed to light, magically transformed into black and white pattern. Solarization reversed tones, so that a strong highlight printed as black. A photograph could appear to be simultaneously positive and negative. With this technique Man Ray, and his many associates and followers, presented beautiful women – such as Lee Miller and Meret Oppenheim – as if cast in chrome (plate 25.7). His photograph of arum lilies suggests polished aluminium. Man Ray's radical cropping of his images demonstrates his ability to create pattern under the enlarger and later on the printed page.[27] His sense of fashionable life, the role of negrophilia – Kiki with an African mask, Nancy Cunard with bangles – and the ease with which he imagined reversing positives to negatives and back, all place him at the centre of Deco, as well as Surrealist, Paris (plates 25.9, 25.10 and see plate 24.18). He photographed models and Siégel mannequins, clad in fashions by Poiret, Lelong and Boulanger, in the Pavillon de l'Elégance in the Grand Palais that were published in Condé Nast's newly inaugurated French *Vogue* (21 August 1925). In 1931 he was

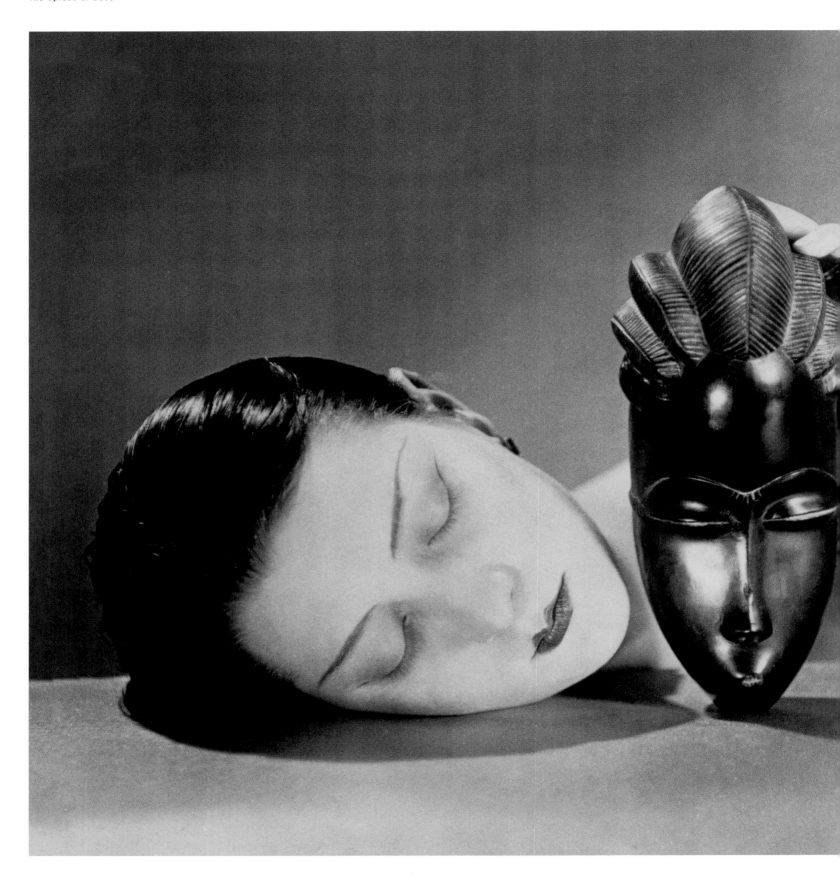

25.9 Man Ray (American), *Noire et blanche*. Gelatin silver print. 1926. Zabriskie Gallery, New York. © Man Ray Trust/ADAGP, Paris and DACS, London 2002.

25.10 Man Ray (American). *Noire et blanche*. Gelatin silver print, negative. 17.7 x 23.6 cm. 1926. Centre Georges Pompidou, Paris. MNAM. Photo: CNAC/MNAM dist. RMN. © Man Ray Trust/ADAGP, Paris and DACS, London 2002.

commissioned by the Paris Electricity Board to make a portfolio of ten images titled *Electricité*. The images ranged from domestic appliances through electric currents leaping across a nude female torso to superimposed images of neon-lit Paris (plate 25.11). Man Ray developed a taste for artificial lighting to rival Steichen's, relishing the lavish technical support provided for his fashion shoots by *Harper's Bazaar*. In later years he recalled that having a lighting crew and models at his disposal made him feel like a movie director.[28] Merry Foresta and Willis Hartshorn have written: 'Man Ray's methods were extreme. Models were decapitated; hands were separated from bodies; camera distortions made arms look long, and angular gestures seem more like contortions than sophisticated poses. The clothes were never as interesting as the pose to Man Ray.'[29] They also note that, despite its apparent freedom, fashion maintained its own iron codes. Man Ray's Haitian lover, the beautiful Adrienne Fidelin, appeared in only one magazine article: 'her mulatto colouring

prevented her from receiving most couture assignments'.[30]

Laure Albin-Guillot did not invent any of the new styles in photography, but she served the moment of Art Deco in important ways. At the 1925 Exhibition she showed (in addition to some feeble artistic photographs) her more than capable portraits of the Exhibition's leading figures: the Director General of Fine Arts, Paul Léon; the architect and designer Pierre Chareau; the architect Pierre Patout; the *dinandier* (coppersmith) Jean Dunand; the *orfèvre* (gold- and silversmith) Jean Puiforcat; the architect and designer Francis Jourdain; the ceramicist Emile Decœur and the quintessential designer Jacques-Emile Ruhlmann. A portfolio of these portraits appeared in *Art et décoration* in 1926.[31] Albin-Guillot represents Parisian professional photography, and its rapidly expanding infrastructure in France after 1925, in a number of ways. She contributed to the first *Salon indépendant de la photographie* (also known as the '*Salon de l'escalier*') in 1928, alongside a galaxy of *immigré* photographers, such as the

25.12 Florence Henri, advertisement for Lanvin perfume. Gelatin silver print. French, 1929. V&A: PH.272-1982.

Hungarian André Kertész, the White Russian George Hoyningen-Huene, the German Germaine Krull, the Americans Berenice Abbott, Paul Outerbridge and Man Ray, and the Viennese Mme d'Ora. Her work was published in the new magazines – *Arts et métiers graphiques* (founded 1928), *Vu* (founded 1928), *L'Art vivant* (founded 1925), *Photographie* (founded 1930) and *La Revue du médecin* (founded 1929). Rob Mallet-Stevens designed a house for her in 1930 in Boulevard Beauséjour, decorated – in wood and chrome – by Jules Leleu. In 1932 she mounted an exhibition entitled *Pour la constitution des artistes photographes*, featuring major *auteur photographes* (creative photographers) working in Paris. The exhibition led to the formation of the Société des Artistes Photographes, which included many of the liveliest talents of the day: Nora Dumas, Germaine Krull, Ergy Landau, Ylla, François Kollar, Man Ray, Kertész, Maurice Tabard, Roger Schall, René Zuber, André Vigneau, Dora Maar (Kéfer), Georges Saad, Jean Moral and Harry Meerson. She published the first book in French on photography and advertising in 1933, exhibited in *La publicité par la photographie* at the Galerie de la Pléiade in 1935 and in the large section on 'Publicité' at the 1937 *Exposition internationale des arts et techniques dans la vie moderne* in Paris.

Albin-Guillot's most compelling work is an album of photographs published in 1931 as *Micrographie décorative*. According to her biographer Christian Bouqueret, Albin-Guillot intended to call the volume simply *Micrographie*. Her publisher and printer,

25.11 Man Ray (American), *Electricité*. Photogravure. 1931. From the *Electricité* portfolio published by the Compagnie Parisienne de Distribution de l'Electricité. V&A: E.1653-2001. © Man Ray Trust/ ADAGP, Paris and DACS, London 2002.

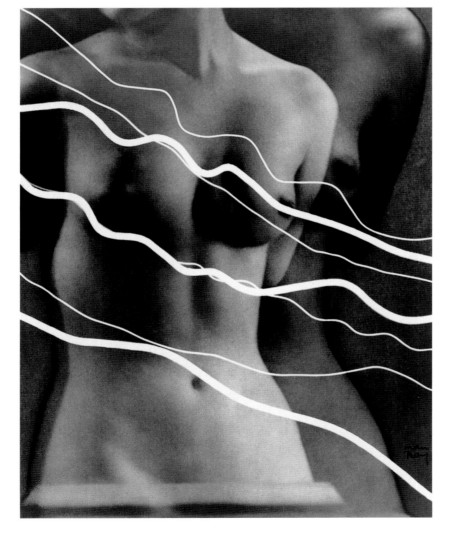

Draeger, with an understandable desire to market the lavish volume, added the adjective. The word 'decorative' was fully justified, however, because Albin-Guillot's microphotographs were printed on a range of coated papers, some in silver and gold. Albin-Guillot literally fulfilled the vision of the writer – quoted earlier – who spoke of photography applying a microscope to reality. The plates in her own copy, (V&A Collection) are printed with extraordinary richness in the permanent Fresson process (unlike the coloured photogravure used for the rest of the limited edition). The volume's considerable success led to a commission to Albin-Guillot to supply decorative screens – using the same technique – for the interior of the ocean liner *Normandie*.[32] Albin-Guillot is representative of a photographic 'Ecole de Paris' which comprised not only those already mentioned but also Pierre Dubreuil, Roger Parry, Emmanuel Sougez, Maurice Tabard[33] and other outstanding women photographers such as Ilse Bing and Florence Henri (plate 25.12).[34]

A photographer who made no artistic claims but whose contribution became an essential part of the infrastructure of photography in the newly developing heyday of the picture press was another American, Therese Bonney. She photographed prolifically in Paris between the wars and set up a press service, with its own staff photographers, to supply newspapers and magazines. Bonney's coverage included portraiture, couturiers' salons, the Paris 1925 Exhibition, the 1931 *Exposition coloniale*, interiors, decorative arts (including, for example, the Stehli Silks series to which Steichen contributed), architecture and store fronts.[35]

Publications were vital international conduits of Art Deco imagery. The most important of the new French magazines was *Vu*. Founded and edited by Lucien Vogel, *Vu* adapted and improved German innovations in magazine design – especially in the layout of photos and text. Stylish, large-format and ambitiously edited, *Vu* furthered in its typographic style, its favoured subjects and its photographs the international diffusion of Parisian design innovation.[36]

London, like Paris, was enlivened by talented photographers from elsewhere who welcomed the new possibilities offered by commercial outlets and the printed page. The most notable was the Munich-born E. O. Hoppé, who evolved from salon and society photographer to advertising and editorial photographer and then transformed himself into an archive and agency.[37] Two innovative Americans, Francis Bruguière and Curtis Moffatt, came to London in the 1920s and became leaders in experimental and advertising photography. Moffatt

was a specialist in tri-carbro colour photography, which he used for advertising and personal work, but he also promoted modern design and sold African sculptures at his gallery at 4 Fitzroy Square, London W1 from 1929 to 1933.[38] Bruguière produced cut-paper abstractions and experimental books and films in addition to commercial photography.[39] Home-grown British photographers in the orbit of Art Deco included John Havinden in advertising, Paul Tanqueray and Dorothy Wilding in portraiture and fashion, and – above all – Cecil Beaton.

Beaton discovered de Meyer's photographs in American *Vogue* around 1920: 'A new silvery world was opened to me.'[40] Beaton recalled 'running amok among the theatrical fabrics at Burnet's store' in Covent Garden, discovering materials for photographic backgrounds which 'created an extraordinary atmospheric effect of shimmer, like sunlight on water'.[41] He also found shimmer in props like the white balloons and sheets of cellophane in which he draped the 'bright young things' – including his sisters – during many photographic sessions in the 1920s. His photograph of 'Nancy Beaton as a

Shooting Star', dressed for a 'Galaxy Ball' in 1929, is characteristic of Beaton (plate 25.13). It reminds us of the considerable invention – and stupendous expense – often lavished on such ephemeral occasions in the heyday of exotic creatures of the period like the Marchesa Casati and Beaton himself. With such photographs, Beaton – along with other new professional photographers – created his own silver world (plate 25.13 and see plate 24.8).[42]

Art Deco touched photography over some twenty years, leaving its vivid signature on innovative photographers in cities as far apart as Prague and New York, as well as on the new breed of pioneering commercial photographers who picked up the style and filled it with energy and ideas, before casting it aside and moving on. At the height of Art Deco photographers contributed to its prestige and international diffusion – and made some of its masterpieces.

25.13 Cecil Beaton, *Nancy Beaton as a Shooting Star*. Gelatin silver print. British, 1929. V&A: PH.965-1978.

26 Art Deco Graphic Design and Typography

Jeremy Aynsley

Commerce is the god of the modern world and publicity, though a woman, is its prophet. Today there is no road nor square, there is not a crossroads, boulevard or an arcade, there is not a bare piece of wall where the curiosity of the passer-by is not arrested by the particulars of some new invention adding to the great works of nature or the accumulated treasures of human labour. There is not a station hall, a hotel entrance lobby, a metro station, there is not a shed where some image, or calligraphy, or typography does not offer us exactly that which is missing for our good fortune.[1]

When Charles Imbert made these comments in the official commentary to the French contribution to the Paris 1925 Exhibition, his observations were not unusual. Indeed, they conformed to an international perception of the imperatives of commerce and the growing significance of graphic design to this field, as well as to the idea, often expressed in contemporary texts, that the street was the 'art gallery for the public'. Furthermore, the gendered characterization of publicity was not unusual – in the early years of the century similar parallels had been drawn between women, fashion and style by the economist and social critic Thorstein Veblen and the architect Adolf Loos, often disparagingly.[2] Yet, in the years immediately before 1925, the rapid proliferation of advertising in everyday life had been greeted with enthusiasm in many quarters as a sign of modernity. So it was not surprising that an international exhibition dedicated to modern decorative and industrial arts should devote attention to an area of design increasingly receiving recognition and professional attention.

The section of the exhibition devoted to graphics was divided into familiar categories: 'Les Arts du Livre' and 'L'Art de la Publicité'. According to one British reviewer,

In the *Grand Palais*, France made a feature of her posters. The walls of the large *Salle des Congrès* were hung with posters to a height of about forty feet above from the gallery, by the Union de l'Affiche Française, a national group of artists, publishers, printers, and posting agencies concerned with the development and protection of the art and industry of the posters.[3]

In addition to posters – clearly the most visible form of graphic design on display – attention was given to the relatively esoteric field of fine book arts, a genre in which France had traditionally excelled and had recently revived. In the Pavillon du Livre, besides examples of typography and illustration, a substantial number of bookbindings was exhibited by designers including Rose Adler, Pierre Legrain, Gérard Sandoz and Jacques Nathan-Garamond[4] (see plates 27.5 and 27.6). These included distinctive abstract designs exquisitely executed in luxury materials. Such ornamental schemes linked the luxury book with decorative designs in other media, such as metalwork and textiles.

Elsewhere in the exhibition, graphic designers' work could be seen in the national and commercial pavilions. The magazines *Le Monde illustré, Fémina, L'Illustration* and *Art et décoration* marked an important presence with their pavilions, as did the leading department stores, whose model of marketing – which incorporated purpose-designed packaging and publicity, window display and shop interiors – offered a commercial message that would be taken from the exhibition, especially to New York.[5]

To design the official exhibition posters, the jury chose the young poster artist Charles Loupot and the fashion illustrator Robert Bonfils. Their contrasting solutions can be taken as representing the variants of the Art Deco graphic style as it had emerged by 1925 (plate 26.1 and see plate 10.1). Bonfils was an established fashion illustrator, having worked for the *Gazette du bon ton, Journal des dames et des modes* and other fashion magazines. His poster's iconography of a dancing figure and faun depicted in a graceful manner conformed to the modernized classicism seen in other objects on display. Bonfils gave his design a modern inflection through a geometrical emphasis in the stylized lettering.

26.1 Charles Loupot, poster for the Paris 1925 Exhibition. Colour lithograph, French, 1925. V&A: E.1201-1925.

26.2 Cortý, *Assuh Zigarette*, poster.
Colour lithograph. German, 1920-5.
V&A: E.1502-1926.

By contrast, Loupot's design predicted a second, Moderne Art Deco graphic style, which in 1925 was less resolved. His image of a factory with a rose emerging from the smoke was intended to symbolize co-operation between the decorative arts and industry – the underlying intention of the exhibition, which was belied by the luxury character of many of the displays.

In 1997 the graphic design historian Steven Heller wrote that 'the confluence of a high Deco elegance and a mass-market wit made French fashion graphics the most enticing in the world'.[6] This association with fashion and France was clearly established from the outset. In formal terms, one commentator has summarized the characteristics of Art Deco graphics as including geometric and linear formality, optical simplicity, distortion or transformation of reality and a concern for contemporaneity.[7] This adequately covers the Moderne wing of Art Deco but needs to be broadened if it is to encompass work of a historicist or eclectic tendency – like that of Bonfils – which was initially as important for the new style as the search for the straightforwardly modern.

Art Deco's eclecticism in other areas of design is well recognized, and graphic design was no different in this respect. References for ornament were drawn from a wide range of sources that together constituted a curious blend of the modern and ancient, the geometric and the exotic, and included Art Nouveau, European folk sources and avant-garde art. Similarly, contemporary events and fashions, among them modern dance and theatre – especially Diaghilev's Ballets Russes – and the Egyptomania of the early 1920s made an impact on the graphic version of the style (plate 26.2).

Paris was a significant *locus* for the style, but could not lay exclusive claim to its origins. References to folk art, for instance, had been common in Russian Futurism and early Expressionism, where stylized figure drawing was combined with highly coloured decorative designs. And many parallels can be drawn between French decorative illustrations and those by Polish, Hungarian and Czech designers (see Chapters 9 and 16).[8]

Finally, commentators often distinguish two stages in the history of Art Deco graphics: the years before 1925, when the style was being defined almost exclusively in France, and the years following the exhibition, when the style exploded internationally as it moved from a context exclusively defined by art and design to a wider commercial and industrial application. An early form of Art Deco in graphic design was closely associated with France and the traditional artisanal skills, such as those involved in lithography. After 1902, the annual exhibitions organized by the Société des Artistes Décorateurs (SAD) provided an opportunity to show the products of the various *métiers* – artists' books, bookbindings and print portfolios – in displays that removed them from their immediate social and commercial setting. This emphasis on skilled handcrafts and an art for art's sake approach contrasts with the situation in Germany, where the activities of an equivalent body, the Deutscher Werkbund, stressed design's application to industry in the interests of the national economy.[9]

Among graphic items selected for exhibition by the Société des Artistes Décorateurs, pochoir prints became a distinctive feature. Pochoir, a stencilling process, was an ancient technique, older than type itself, and it had been employed by the early *cartiers* for colouring playing cards. The technique enabled the freshness of any original colours used by an artist to be preserved in reproduction. The colours, matching those in the original, were applied by hand in various techniques such as stippling, sponging and so on. This was done either by the artists and illustrators themselves, or by master printers. Whether in watercolour or gouache, a quality and consistency could be achieved by hand that was hard to imitate in mechanized printing.[10]

An important French agent for the popularization of the pochoir print in the world of design was the fashion designer Paul Poiret. Among his circle were several prominent fashion illustrators. From two of these he commissioned the important luxury brochures, *Les Robes de Paul Poiret* by Paul Iribe in 1908 and *Les Choses de Paul Poiret vues par Georges Lepape* in 1911 (plate 26.3 and see plate 8.8). Both were to act as influential models for the promotion of fashion and design in subsequent years, when mainstream French fashion magazines such as the *Gazette du bon ton* (1912-25) and *Fémina* (1901-38) published illustrations in the style of these elite editions. Characteristically, fine typography accompanied the illustrations but was reduced to a minimum to express a sensibility of refined elegance. In Art Deco fashion illustration of this period, too, the depiction of mannequins with closely shaped heads above a loosely styled body (derived from Poiret's designs and giving freeform to the figure) became a central trope. Inspired by these fashion illustrations, photographers such as Man Ray, Horst and Hoyningen-Huene interpreted the subject of mannequins. By the 1920s, several articles on mannequins had appeared in the press and many artists in the Pittura Metafisica and Surrealist groups incorporated references to them.[11]

How quickly this Deco style of fashion illustration spread internationally is shown in the case of the Russian-born Erté (Romain de Tirtoff). Erté began his professional life as an illustrator for the *Gazette du bon ton* in 1913 (plate 26.4). Then, in 1916, still in Paris, he sold illustrations to New York and was published in Condé Nast's *Vogue* for six months before establishing a substantial contract with William Randolph Hearst to provide cover designs for the competing magazine *Harper's Bazaar*.[12] Through fashion journalism the worlds of Parisian haute couture, New York business and the burgeoning Hollywood film industry were connected, reinforcing Paris as fashion capital and, in turn, centre of this particular graphic style (see Chapter 30).

The later development of Art Deco graphics was particularly associated with poster designers. In the 1920s France was home to a dynamic group of poster designers, including Jean Carlu,

A. M. Cassandre, Paul Colin, Charles Loupot and Maurice Moyrand, who were members of the Union des Artistes Modernes (UAM) and were attempting to promote a new spirit in the graphic arts. They distinguished themselves from the more traditional French Deco graphic artists like Bonfils by self-consciously borrowing ideas and forms – such as 'contrasts of forms', 'simultaneity' and geometry – from recent and contemporary avant-garde fine art movements, including Cubism, Futurism and Purism.

The UAM represented a reaction against the more established SAD,[13] and its members included notable French Modernists. They advocated a new machine art, but in practice much of their output was handmade or concerned with archetypal Art Deco lifestyle themes. The latter was particularly true of the designers associated with the UAM who devised large-scale, prestigious posters for department stores; drinks companies (in particular to promote the new

aperitifs of the 'cocktail age'); other foodstuffs; cosmetics and perfumes; travel (especially by train and ocean liner) (see plate 29.1); and the theatre and other performing arts.

Cassandre (Adolphe Jean-Marie Mouron) was awarded the first prize at the 1925 Exhibition for his poster *Au Bûcheron*, made in 1923.[14] This has been celebrated as the first modern poster to be seen on the streets of Paris that incorporated words and images in a post-Cubist way. Cassandre's designs often appeared deceptively simple but were the result of meticulous composition; he applied the principles of the Golden Section, inspired by the mathematician Matila Ghyka. He was also influential

26.3 Georges Lepape, plate from *Les Choses de Paul Poiret*, Paris, 1911. Calotype with letterpress, line block and stencil. V&A: Circ.267-1976. © ADAGP, Paris and DACS, London 2002.

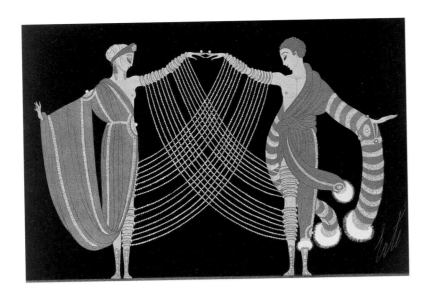

26.4 Erté (Romain de Tirtoff), plate from *L'Illustration*. Paris, Christmas 1926. NAL.

26.5 Cassandre (Adolphe Mouron), *L'oiseau bleu, Train Pullman*, poster. Colour lithograph. French, 1929. V&A: E.225-1935.

in the spread of Moderne graphics (plate 26.5). In 1936, at the time of a retrospective of his work at the Museum of Modern Art in New York, Cassandre settled in the city. There he designed covers for *Harper's Bazaar* (following Erté) and also took on work for the Container Corporation of America, two of the most established routes by which contemporary European graphic design ideas were transmitted to the United States.[15]

By contrast, Paul Colin specialized in figure drawings that he adapted to theatre and entertainment posters, particularly in his work for the Théâtre des Champs-Elysées. In 1925, he collaborated with the black American dancer Josephine Baker, whose premiere of *La Revue nègre* opened in Paris to tumultuous success in 1925 and who became the epitome of the Jazz Age. He also produced *Le Tumulte noir* in 1927, a portfolio of 45 hand-coloured lithographs for Josephine Baker (see plate 11.14).[16]

The UAM poster designers found a particular inspiration in the work and ideas of the French Purist painter Fernand Léger (see plate 9.3). In the 1920s Léger led the Atelier Moderne, where a generation of artists and designers trained, many to become contributors to the spread of the Art Deco style. In 1923 he wrote: 'We live in a geometric world, it is undeniable, and also in a state of frequent contrasts. The most striking example is the advertising billboard – sharp, permanent, immediate, violent – that cuts across the tender and harmonious landscape.'[17]

Léger was especially intrigued by the way advertisements intruded on conventional space, distracting the viewer by introducing new reflexes and thoughts. He was distinctive among the many artists investigating the implications of Cubism and Futurism and became important for graphic and poster artists

because he combined objects and typographic elements – often stencilled letters – in his paintings and graphic work.[18] His 1919 version of Blaise Cendrars' poem *La Fin du monde (filmée par l'ange)*, for Jean Cocteau's Editions de la Sirène, was a dramatic demonstration of the power of figurative and abstract components combined to convey a visual narrative in book form (plate 26.6).[19]

By the mid-1920s, through the borrowing of such ideas as the post-Cubist integration of word and image in visual compositions, a Moderne poster style had emerged in several European countries – among them Belgium, the Netherlands, Spain and

Switzerland – frequently through direct contact with Paris. The American designer Edward McKnight Kauffer, who had trained in Paris and worked for much of his professional life in London, applied these principles of composition to many remarkable posters, often for transport services (see plate 20.7).[20] A different set of circumstances informed Moderne poster designers in Italy. For them, the Vienna Secession – rather than Paris – and Italy's own national design movements, Stile Liberty, Futurism and Rationalism, were major sources of inspiration. Italian Art Deco posters were distinguished by their tendency towards smooth surfaces, monumentalist compositions and an architectural approach to lettering. Designers such as Marcello Nizzoli, Fortunato Depero and Sepo (Severo Pozzati) were equally at home making designs for exhibitions and the stage, for the applied arts, and for posters for major commercial companies and cultural or political events (see plate 19.6).[21] In the years of Mussolini's Fascism, the result was a style that blended the modern with the archaic.

The new print culture of the 1920s was to some extent determined by the type-foundries, who provide the basic ingredients of printing – the typefaces – and thereby can determine the foundations of a style or its infrastructure. Art Deco coincided with a period of increasing internationalization in type design. Another contemporary development was the speeding up of type composition and distribution through the introduction of Monotype and Linotype, the mechanical composition systems that had become widespread in Europe by the 1920s. Thus, increasingly, styles of typography could be quickly exchanged between countries.

By 1928 French type-foundries had established a range of Art Deco typefaces. However, the favourite typefaces were by no means all French. In America, the American Type Founders Company (ATF) produced M. F. Benton's *Broadway* (1929), a high contrast, modified sanserif letterform with a distinctive thick body, which has been considered the archetypal Art Deco typeface.[22] Other widely used designs included Rudolf Koch's *Kabel* (1927), William A. Dwiggins's *Metro* (1929) and Lucian Bernhard's *Fashion* (1930). Interestingly, Bernhard, a German graphic designer working in New York, was able to bridge European and American tastes in printing through his understanding of the two continents' traditions.[23]

Nevertheless the French played a significant part in defining a distinctive Art Deco print culture. The lead came from two members of UAM, Maximilien Vox and Charles Peignot, who represented the interests of modern typography. Peignot was a director of the

26.6 Fernand Léger, 'C'est le 31 Décembre'.
Illustration for Blaise Cendrars, *La Fin du monde (filmée par l'ange)*, Paris, 1919. NAL.
© ADAGP, Paris and DACS, London 2002.

commissioned Cassandre, who devised three typefaces, *Bifur* (1928), *Acier* (1930) and *Peignot* (1937). The most distinctive, if not the most financially successful, was *Bifur*, which was much admired and incorporated in many designs of a Moderne flavour, especially press advertisements in black and white.

The letters of *Bifur* were reduced to geometrical forms with about half of each letter omitted and replaced by striking parallel lines (plate 26.7). These gave the illusion of light and faceting, creating the jewelled effect of decorated metalwork. But despite its distinctive Art Deco qualities, Cassandre himself attributed startlingly Modernist credentials to this typeface, writing that: 'Bifur was conceived in the same spirit as a vacuum cleaner or an internal combustion engine'; that 'It is meant to answer a specific need, not to be decorative. It is this functional character that makes it suitable for use in the contemporary world'; and also that, 'Bifur was designed for advertising. It was designed for a word, a single word, a poster word.'[25] In contemporary print design circles, such an interpretation was not uncontroversial, as Cassandre's defensiveness about the possibility that the typeface could be interpreted as decorative betrays.

In the years following *Bifur*, similar decorative motifs recurred in the design of architectural lettering. Among the best known examples are those on New York skyscrapers, such as the McGraw Hill building (1930-31), the Rockefeller Center (1931-40) – where the letterforms were realized in aluminium – and the RCA Music Hall (1932), where the accentuated lines in the letterforms held strips of neon for night-time illumination (plate 26.9). More generally, three-dimensional lettering, either for discreet labelling or overt advertising, was incorporated in many Art Deco buildings in the late 1920s and 1930s (see plate 19.8). As the American architect Raymond Hood wrote in 1931, 'The incorporation of publicity or advertising features in a building is frequently an item for consideration. This feature as an element of modern architecture was first notably incorporated in the Woolworth building.'[26] While contemporary observers such as Siegfried Kracauer and Walter Benjamin commented on this attention to surface in modern urban life, simultaneously repelled by and attracted to its ephemeral character of allure and distraction,

distinguished Paris type-foundry Deberny et Peignot. In the 1920s, the foundry began commissioning modern typefaces that could be employed in contemporary advertising and publicity – as well as providing for the more established demands of book typography – thereby giving a more public profile to typographic diversity and also increasing sales. Their typographic experiment was promoted through two periodicals. *Les Divertissements typographiques* (1928-33), edited by Maximilien Vox, acted largely as a showpiece for new typefaces by Deberny et Peignot. The more substantial publication was *Arts et métiers graphiques* (1927-39). Issued six times a year, this periodical established itself as France's major typographic magazine, covering a range of international and historical issues on the book arts,

printing, publicity and typography. Peignot's role in defining, interpreting and promoting French Modernist – as well as Art Deco – graphic design should not be underestimated. Although he introduced *Sphinx* (1925), an Egyptian typeface with heavy proportions that was used in much publicity associated with Art Deco in its early days, he was aware of the need to compete with the artistic movement of the Bauhaus and 'the new typography' in Germany and other European countries. He thus bought the rights for Paul Renner's famous sanserif typeface *Futura* (1926), which he re-named *Europe* for distribution to the French market.[24] On the basis of revenue from this and other staple typefaces, Peignot could embark on greater artistic experiment in the design of Art Deco typefaces. He

many designers also became increasingly aware of it as a growing field of specialization.[27]

The concern for luxury that was so often a feature of Art Deco ran counter to print culture as it was developing internationally in the mid-1920s. At this time, printing and commerce had a complex and, at times, uneasy relationship. In some parts of Europe, the rise of Modernism had prompted debates about the social responsibilities of design. At the Bauhaus and elsewhere, graphic design and typography were used in the service of a more committed and ideological cause, though there were exceptions too. The Modernist Herbert Bayer understood and used Art Deco strategies, where appropriate – including stylized lettering and exotic decoration – in his designs for magazines, packaging and advertising.[28]

In contemporary reviews of its development, Moderne typography, associated with Art Deco, was cast as an illicit intruder on Modernism. It did not fit well within the schema defined either by the deeply rooted Arts and Crafts principles of printing in Britain and the United States – where truth to materials and a respect for neo-classical typefaces informed book design – or the Constructivist principles adopted by avant-garde typographers in the USSR, Germany and the Netherlands. In the latter, graphic design was considered as a form of industrial design and its commercial application was sometimes perceived to be a distraction from committed designers' more serious intentions.[29] In Germany especially, following a movement to promote 'form without ornament' in

26.7 Cassandre (Adolphe Mouron), *Bifur* typeface. French, 1929. Made by Deberny et Peignot. *Arts et métiers graphiques*, Paris, 1929. NAL.

the early 1920s, the stylistic inflections of Art Deco and its use of typographical elements as pure style – as well as its allegiance to advertising, promotion, marketing and cycles of fashion – were considered decadent by some critics and designers.[30] Yet, paradoxically, Art Deco posters conformed to recommendations made by contemporary marketing

and advertising specialists and, in this respect, could be seen as more 'functional' than many Modernist examples. Studies of retail psychology stressed the significance of visual exactitude, the reduction of imagery to essentials and the need for striking imagery to attract the eye of the consumer, all of which Art Deco fulfilled.[31]

Two key contemporary texts, Douglas McMurtrie's *Modern Typography and Layout* (1929) and Alfred Tolmer's *Mise en Page* (1931), promoted an approach to graphic layout that was in tune with Art Deco practice, turning many of the attributes of Modernist typography into pure style (plate 26.8).[32] For these authors, asymmetry, geometric devices, associative decoration and sanserif letters were used for their modishness, rather than as principles. And their recommendations were often considered less constraining by printers worldwide than those of the Modernists because they were free of dogma and ideology.

Tolmer's *Mise en Page* – frequently spurned by Modernists – was a 'how to do it' book. Written by a French printer familiar with developments in modern painting, especially Cubism and Futurism, it offered a new approach to the theory and practice of layout in book design, publicity and advertising. It was published in England, with a supplement of the text in French, and was also distributed in the United States. The book was arranged as a series of visually driven chapters, with each layout epitomizing the preferred approach, and it was influential for designers and draughtsmen in many parts of the world. It is especially interesting for its comparisons between contemporary design and the art of the past and non-western art.

Until the early 1930s American domestic graphic design was driven more by business sense and the need to satisfy successful marketing strategies than by avant-garde artistic styles. Art Deco offered a way to reconcile these previously conflicting approaches. By this time, with the rise of the art director in the design of fashion magazines, and the designers' ready acceptance of the new, Art Deco graphics had travelled from Paris to New York. Well recognized routes into the USA included working for the art directors Alexei Brodovitch at *Harper's Bazaar* and Mehemed Fehmy Agha at *Vogue*.[33] And, no doubt inspired in part by the visual novelties of full-colour

26.8 Alfred Tolmer, plate from *Mise en Page: The Theory and Practice of Layout*, London, 1931. NAL.

magazine covers, American advertisers adopted Art Deco as a visible marketing tool, most obviously for goods aimed towards the female consumer.

The Art Deco graphic style was also transmitted by the movement of European designers, whether in response to professional career opportunities or to political difficulties. In the United States some of these individuals took up key positions in the design departments of commercial concerns, while others established themselves in their own design studios. In the early 1930s, too, the emergence of professional industrial design offered new opportunities for graphic designers. Thus the French-born designer Raymond Loewy was able to extend his skills as an illustrator on arriving in New York. Realizing that it was a short step from drawing a product for advertising purposes to re-styling it for production, Loewy was among the first graphic designers to make this transition.[34] Thus, during the 1930s, his design office moved from advertising and

window display for Macy's and Saks of Fifth Avenue to applying the aesthetic of streamlining to the design of products (see Chapter 34).[35]

Undoubtedly packaging was the most ubiquitous form of Art Deco graphic design. In early Depression America, manufacturers quickly learned that significant alterations could be made to a product's identity through the design of packaging. This could make the product appear fresh to the consumer and so enhance sales without the costs of re-tooling. This perpetuated the association between Art Deco and the commercial, the superficial and the ephemeral, an ambiguous identity that makes it all the more fascinating to investigate and evaluate today.

As Charles Imbert predicted, the graphic arts infiltrated all walks of life in the inter-war years – not only in the form of posters, press advertisements and packaging, but also as permanent aspects of a built environment in which the distinction between graphic and structural form was becoming increasingly

blurred. Advertisements in mirrored glass and enamel, illuminated signage and tiled lettering all meant that Art Deco graphic and typographic imagery could be encountered in a wide range of everyday circumstances – at the garage, the fishmonger or the post office, in banks, cinemas or railway stations – just as much as in posters or on the printed page. Through commercial architecture's preoccupation with the graphic sign, trademark or lighting, Art Deco lettering became an integral feature of major cities worldwide. In these contexts, the style escaped the particularity of feminized associations with fashion and became part of an Americanized business culture, which in many ways was its true home.

26.9 Raymond Hood, entrance of the McGraw-Hill building, New York. 1930. Photo: Cervin Robinson.

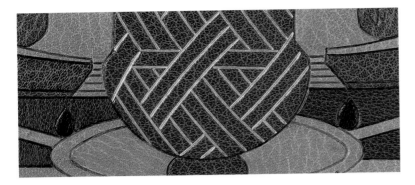

27 Art Deco Bindings

Rowan Watson and Annemarie Riding

The World Fairs of the nineteenth century had always included bindings as well as books – and the machines that made them – among the artefacts that signalled modern advances in art and industry. From the 1880s, collectors, led by the binder Henri Marius-Michel, promoted the notion of 'art binding', *reliure d'art*, to combat the perceived vulgarity of industrially produced books. Binding was taught as an expressive art in design schools; prizes were awarded at exhibitions that were reviewed in the art press.

A prominent category in the Paris 1925 Exhibition was that of 'Art et Industrie du Livre', and French bindings in particular were presented in terms of a 'new renaissance'.[1] The most noteworthy practitioners were artists and decorators, used to working in a variety of media and keen to provide designs for bindings that were then made by bookbinders. The designers tended to use the same motifs on bindings as on other artefacts: thus Pierre Legrain used a circle motif on both an armchair of 1912 and on his binding for *L'Annonce faite à Marie* (1917-19).[2] Robert Bonfils worked as a painter, costume designer and illustrator, while also providing designs for Sèvres porcelain and bindings. Paul Bonet had been a modeller of fashion mannequins before designing bindings. This variety of backgrounds doubtless lay behind these designers' use of exotic materials: not only unusual leathers (crocodile, sharkskin, snakeskin) but metals, from nickel and platinum to aluminium and steel, rare woods and inlay of mother-of-pearl and lacquer (the latter favoured especially by François-Louis Schmied). Styles were eclectic, though the use of abstract and geometric decoration and lush colours gave coherence to the work. Bonfils produced geometric, stylized versions of traditional floral motifs and even a modernized representation of an eighteenth-century Rococo silhouette that imitates an African sculpture (plates 27.1 and 27.8). Bonet's work by 1932 could use commercial Modernist lettering in metal, set against strips of coloured leather like neon signs, in a binding with double, independently opening boards for each cover (plate 27.2). When handled the book felt like a small sculpture. Legrain, by 1925 hailed as the leader of a 'new movement' in bookbinding,[3] had exhibited bindings at the 1919 exhibition of the Société des Artistes Décorateurs, his work showing affinities with the forms and motifs that preoccupied avant-garde painters (see Chapters 7 and 9). It included, too, reference to the exotic locations that air travel had made easily accessible to the wealthy: a Mayan monument was the source

27.1 Robert Bonfils, binding for Abbé A. F. Prévost, *Manon Lescaut*, Paris, 1931. Red morocco with gilt tooling, black onlays and watered silk doublures. French, 1931. Collection Victor and Gretha Arwas, London.

27.2 Paul Bonet, binding for Guillaume Apollinaire, *Calligrammes: Poèmes de la paix et de la guerre (1913-1916)*, Paris, Gallimard, 1930. Green morocco, lacquer and aluminium. French, 1932. Private collection. Photo: David Heald. © ADAGP, Paris and DACS, London 2002.

for the temple on the binding of *Le Jardin des caresses* (plate 27.6). Rose Adler worked in a similar vein in the 1920s, matching geometric forms with lettering in a playful Modernist idiom (plate 27.5). The English binder Sybil Pye, called a 'Constructivist' by Apollo magazine, was described at the 1925 Exhibition as 'working before the altar of Cubism'. Unlike other exhibitors, she made her own bindings and her own set of tools gave her output a stylistic unity (plate 27.4). Like painters, these binders articulated their aims. Bonet spoke for all in defining his goals as 'to serve all forms, to employ all materials, not to restrict oneself to precedence and to innovate continuously', provided the laws of 'balance and proportion' were respected (plate 27.3).[4]

These bindings were commissioned and bought by art collectors. The most celebrated was Jacques Doucet, the leading fashion designer of the day, who donated his eighteenth-century library to Paris University in 1918 in order to collect contemporary writing.[5] For these new books, he commissioned bindings to complement both their texts and the modern furnishings of his flat. Pierre Legrain designed some 370 bindings for

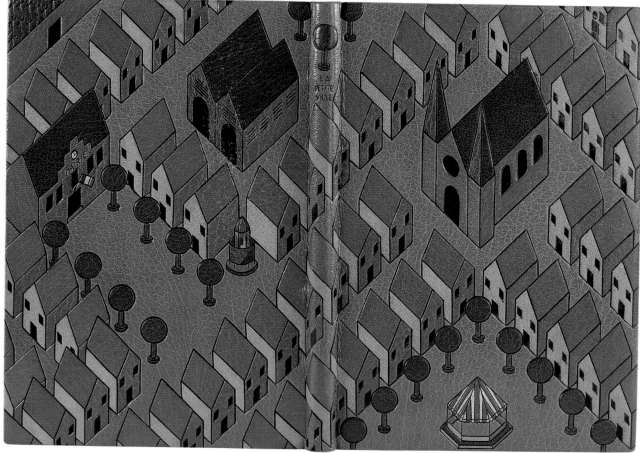

27.3 Paul Bonet, binding for André Marty, *La Petite Ville*, Paris, 1927. French, 1927. Esmerian Collection, New York. © ADAGP, Paris and DACS, London 2002.

Doucet's library between 1917 and 1919, all subsequently executed by high-class commercial binders using traditional methods of handcraft production. Doucet's bindings were for display: they were featured in Ruhlmann's 'Hôtel d'un Collectionneur' in the 1925 Exhibition and were sent to the gallery of Jacques Seligmann in New York in the same year. Paul Bonet and his patrons took a similar approach. Having exhibited in the Paris Salons, Bonet was approached by R. Marty, a rich collector, to provide bindings for his library. It was perhaps Marty's sale of over 50 bindings in 1930 that brought Bonet to general notice. Bonet similarly worked for the Argentinian businessman Carlos Scherrer, whose interest was in bindings rather than in texts. Later, Bonet designed bindings for the Surrealist works owned by the Belgian collector René Gaffe.

The limited, numbered, *de luxe* edition was an established feature of French publishing by the 1920s. Schmied trained as a wood engraver and set up his own press to produce limited editions. Rich colours and monumental page layout distinguish his works, where each page spread is treated as a coherent whole. Some copies of these books were also lavishly bound to his designs (plate 27.7).

As personal commissions, the bindings reveal the horizons of their owners: they were intimate, private objects yet designed for public exposure. The works they cover range from light literature to the most avant-garde writing of the day. The bindings often play with allusions that show engagement with the texts before the volume is even opened.

The Depression seriously undermined all luxury crafts, including binding. Prices in the salerooms fell. Schmied tried to buy back many of his works to maintain their value, but without success. Bonet returned to his former activity as a mannequin designer.

27.4 Sybil Pye, binding for *The Apocrypha*, London, New York, Nonesuch Press, Dial Press, 1924. Black morocco with orange onlays and gold tooling. British, 1924. NAL: L.494-1938.

27.5 Rose Adler, binding for Sidonie-Gabrielle Colette, *Chéri*, Paris, Editions de la Roseraie, 1925. Morocco, stamped and foiled. French, 1925. Gift of Sydney and Francis Lewis. Virginia Museum of Fine Arts, Richmond. Photo: Katherine Wetzel. © ADAGP, Paris and DACS, London 2002.

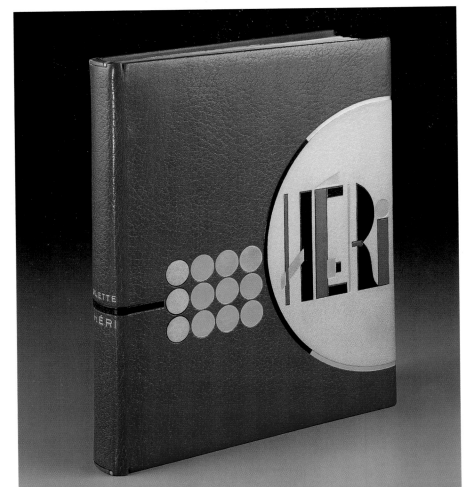

27.6 Pierre Legrain, binding for Franz Toussaint, *Le Jardin des caresses*, Paris, H. Piazza, 1914. Calf inlaid with morocco, gilt tooling. French, c.1914. NAL: Circ.663-1972.

27.7 Louis Creuzevault, inside cover for a *de luxe* edition of *Le Cantique des cantiques*, translated by Ernest Renan, Paris, François-Louis Schmied, 1925. Black calf with gold-tooled lettering, inlaid leather inside. French, 1925. NAL: L.2564-1983.

27.8 Robert Bonfils, inside cover for Henri de Régnier, *Les Rencontres de M. Bréot*, Paris, Kieffer, 1919. Morocco with inlays and onlays, gilt and blind tooling. French, c.1919. NAL: 902-1984.

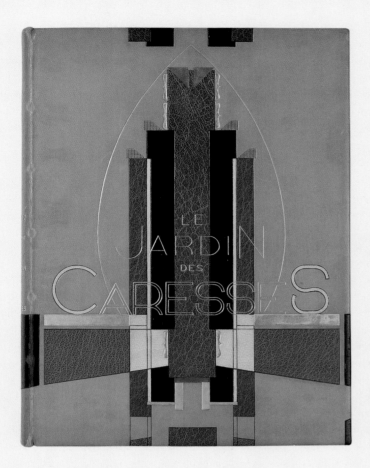

28.1 Designer unknown, book jacket for Harvey Fergusson, *Hot Saturday*, London, printed in New York, Alfred A. Knopf, 1926. Halftone letterpress. V&A: AAD 1995/8/4.

28 Art Deco and the Book Jacket

Rowan Watson and Annemarie Riding

28.2 Edward McKnight Kauffer, book jacket for Walter S. Masterman, *Green Toad*, London, Victor Gollancz, 1928. Colour lineblock. V&A: AAD 1995/8/5.

Printed jackets first appeared in the book trade from the 1890s. They were especially favoured for series, such as Dent's hugely successful Everyman's Library, first published in 1904. In the early years jackets carried promotional texts, a 'blurb' (a word coined in the United States in 1907) and even graphic images to suggest the character of the text. This sobriety was replaced in the 1920s with bright, colourful designs that would persuade bookshop managers to give prominence to certain titles and so attract the attention of a browsing public (plate 28.1). This development was part of a wider transformation of marketing methods in modern urban life and represents the transfer of graphics from the rapidly expanding advertising industry to the matter of selling books.

By the 1920s, the practice of supplying the advertising industry with images and designs was becoming recognized as a profession (see Chapter 26). It had its own journals. *Commercial Art*, for instance, first appeared in 1922 and proclaimed its mission to enliven business by 'the great revivifying force of art'. The work of commercial artists was shown in exhibitions and, especially in America, art school courses were devised to supply the industry.

Increasingly, publishers recognized the value of adopting a coherent style for the design of book jackets and they began to recruit commercial artists. Edward McKnight Kauffer had arrived in Britain from the United States in 1914. His abstract, geometric patterns, lettering and bright colours could be seen on the advertising hoardings of Messrs Eastman & Co. and on the platforms of the new London Underground; Shell and British Petroleum were among his clients, as were American Airlines in the USA (see plate 20.7). In the 1920s and 1930s, he produced designs for the contemporary writing and current affairs books of publishers like Victor Gollancz and Faber & Faber. Both were alive to the importance of graphics in making their wares distinct in the marketplace, and McKnight Kauffer had a special knack for translating the languages of avant-garde fine art movements, from Cubism to Surrealism, into compelling graphic images for the High Street (plates 28.2 and 28.3). His career was paralleled by that of his disciple Theyre Lee-Elliott, who gained immortality by the Speedbird device he produced for

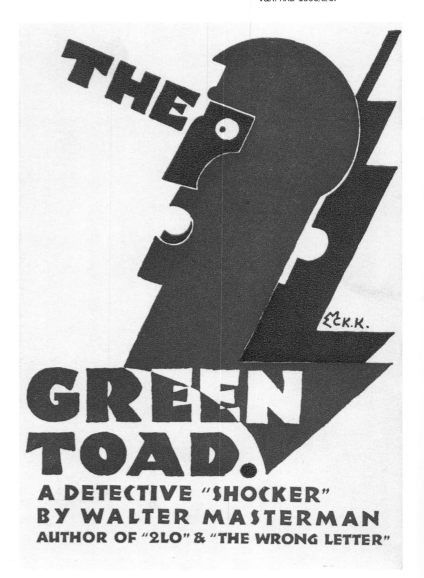

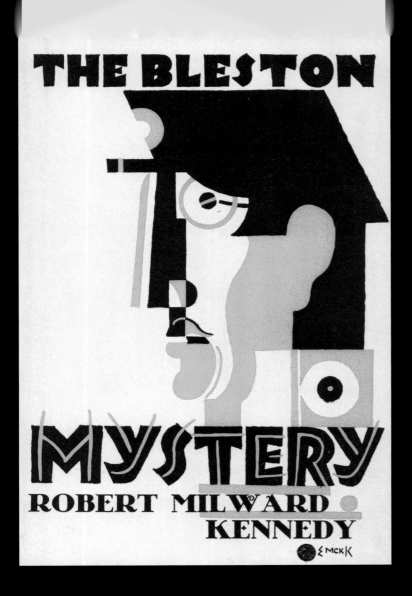

28.3 Edward McKnight Kauffer, book jacket for Robert Milward Kennedy, *The Bleston Mystery*, London, Victor Gollancz, 1928. Colour lineblock. V&A: AAD 1995/8/5.

28.4 Theyre Lee-Elliott, book jacket for Georgette Heyer, *Pastel*, London, printed in USA, Longman, 1929. Colour lineblock. V&A: AAD 1995/8/6.

Imperial Airways in 1935 and also designed book jackets for Longman and Lovat Dickson (plates 28.4 and 28.5). Another poster artist who designed book jackets was Irene Fawkes, who worked for London Underground in the 1920s (see plate 2.2).

Within a publishing house those responsible for design grew in importance. It was recognized that book jackets not only sold the product but also identified the publisher. Alfred A. Knopf, a rapidly expanding American publisher in the 1920s, attributed his success to his view of the book as the product of a complete design process, the book jacket being most important of all. W. A. Dwiggins, the Boston typographer and illustrator whose *Layout in Advertising* (1928 and later editions) was the bible of graphic designers, designed over 400 books for Knopf and a large number of jackets. The same endeavour to identify a company through modern design can be seen in the Mystery League series published in the early 1930s and distributed only through the United Cigar Stores Company.

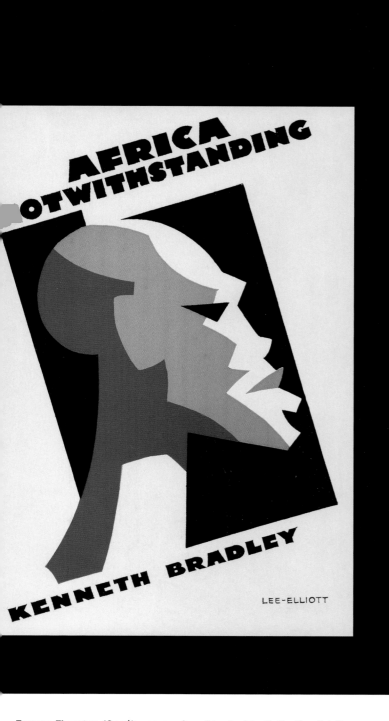

Eugene Thurston (Gené) was employed to design distinctive Art Deco
jackets for the series. Thurston, who taught commercial art at the El Paso
Technical Institute, also worked for publishers such as Payson & Clarke
(plate 28.6).

Designers of book jackets, and indeed packaging in general, capitalized
on the ease with which characteristic elements of the luxurious 1925 Art
Deco style could be abstracted and streamlined into simple motifs suitable
for mass production. Books thus joined the world of consumer goods whose
commercial success depended on eye-catching design. Colourful jackets
were used above all for modern fiction and detective stories, in particular
for works of little known writers where more than the author's name was
needed to attract attention. Through lettering, image and pattern, books
came to be associated with the new age of motor transport, flight, the
wireless and film, and with the glamorous lifestyle that was being proposed
visually by the marketing campaigns of the day.

28.6 Eugene Thurston (Gené),
book jacket for Nard Jones,
Oregon Detour, New York, Payson
& Clarke, 1930. Colour lineblock.
V&A: AAD 1995/8/5.

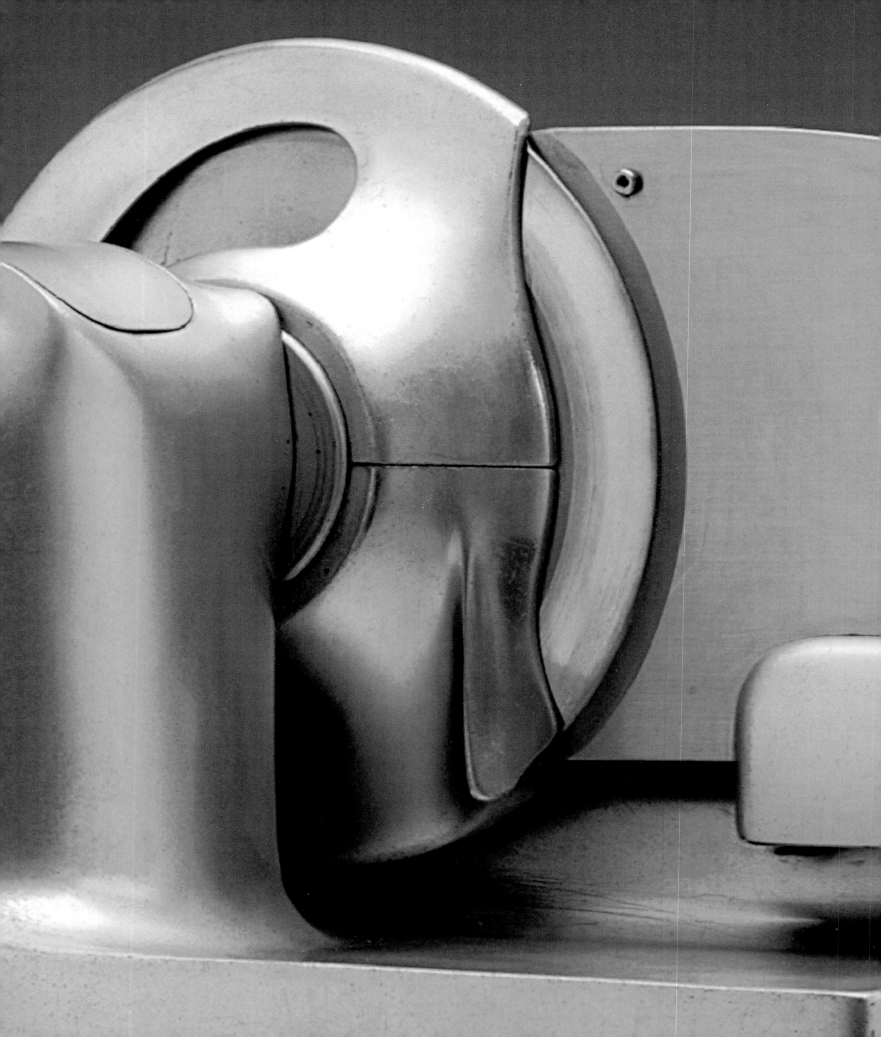

The Deco World

CHEMIN DE FER DU NORD
A.M.CASSANDRE 27
NORD
EXPRESS
HACHARD & Cie PARIS
SOUTHERN RAILWAY = CHEMINS DE FER BELGES
DEUTSCHE REICHSBAHN GES. = POLSKIE KOLEJE PAŃSTWOWE
LONDRES BRUXELLES
RIGA
PARIS LIEGE BERLIN VARSOVIE
COMPAGNIE DES WAGONS-LITS

29 Travel, Transport and Art Deco

Paul Atterbury

A defining characteristic of Art Deco is the application of streamlining, as an evocation of speed, to domestic and commercial objects whose functions rarely included the need for significant movement. Streamlining reflected contemporary enthusiasms for science, technology, engineering and, above all, travel and transportation. The rapid expansion of mass travel by train, ship, bus, car and aircraft was a phenomenon of the Art Deco period.

However, the real revolution in the field of public transportation had occurred in the nineteenth century, with the creation of the major international shipping routes and railway networks, along with the principle of genuine public transport that was accessible to all levels of society. In the Victorian period mass travel on a global scale had become a reality, but much of that travel, for example migration from Europe to the New World, had been driven by social or economic necessity. The twentieth century added flexibility, diversity, increased leisure opportunities and, in the motor car, a greater degree of personal freedom. It also brought to the process of travel a new sense of elegance, luxury and exclusiveness, in which the concept of modernity was expressed by the visible symbols of speed. In fact, trains and ships did not travel significantly faster during the 1920s and 1930s. Before the First World War trains could travel at over 100 miles per hour and ships could cross the Atlantic in five days. Twenty years later these speeds had not altered materially.

Naturally, cars and aircraft had added a new dimension but far more important was the sense of speed created by the pace of social, cultural and technological change and the image of travel as a symbol of modernity and internationalism. This image was itself the product of the new and infinitely more sophisticated marketing techniques that became commonplace during this period. In many ways, the posters and publicity material generated by travel companies and vehicle manufacturers at this time are far more significant and memorable than the actual locations, routes and means of travel that they

promoted. For example, the famous images created by poster artists such as Cassandre, McKnight Kauffer, Roger Broders and Claude Flight are far better known today than the services they were designed to advertise, standing as they do as enduring symbols of modernity (plates 29.1 and 29.2). It is an irony that these essentially ephemeral objects are often the only tangible record of methods of travel that vanished almost without trace many decades ago. The posters, and the image they created, played a major role in underlining the perceived links between travel, speed, luxury and modernity. They also expressed in a direct way the

29.2 Roger Broders, *Le tour du Mont Blanc*, poster for a bus tour run by the Paris–Lyon–Méditerranée. Colour lithograph. French, 1927. V&A: E.519-1929.

29.1 Cassandre (Adolphe Mouron),
Nord Express, poster.
Colour lithograph. French, 1927.
V&A: E.223-1935.

29.3 Gordon Miller Buehrig, Auburn 851 'Boat Tail' Speedster. American, 1935. National Motor Museum, Beaulieu.

almost universal understanding of a design language based on abstract, stylized and symbolic imagery. In the process, they did much to establish the idea of streamlining as the expression of modernity.

The principles of streamlining were appreciated in a rudimentary way before the First World War and rather basic rounded or contoured bodywork was sometimes applied to racing motor cars and other vehicles designed for speed. During the First World War streamlining had an impact on aircraft design, but even then the principles of aerodynamics were inadequately applied to machines whose design

criteria were not determined by speed alone. In the 1920s the achievement of land, air and sea speed records became increasingly important, underlining both a new enthusiasm for national and international competition in the sporting arena and the rapid improvements in technology. This brought a more thorough application of streamlining in engineering terms and a wider appreciation of the apparent modernity of rounded forms. For example, Britain's achievement in winning outright in 1931 the international Schneider Trophy seaplane race aroused enormous popular interest. The streamlined shape of Reginald Mitchell's design for the winning Supermarine S6B, the first aircraft in the world to fly at more than 400 miles per hour and the forerunner

of the famous Spitfire fighter, not only reflected this popular wish for modernity, but actually made the aircraft much more efficient and faster than its rivals. Through this period, streamlining was applied increasingly to all high-speed vehicles, boats and aircraft, resulting in the achievement of ever-greater speeds in both domestic and international competitions. As a result, streamlining and speed became synonymous in the public mind, and so streamlined forms were widely applied to domestic motor vehicles despite having little or no impact on their actual performance. Typical examples are the Chrysler Airflow, the Hudson Terraplane, the Cord car series, the Auburn Speedster and the Indian motorcycle (plate 29.3 and see plate 34.6). At the

top end of the market individual coachbuilders vied with each other in the production of distinct and modern-looking body shapes for expensive motor cars, while in the mass market even ordinary cars such as the Austin Seven and the Morris Minor featured rounded forms, as did a wide range of commercial vehicles and buses. In effect, as in many areas of product design, the streamlining of vehicles became merely a fashion statement.

The streamlined train was also a phenomenon of the Art Deco period. Here, speed was clearly an issue, but far more important was the image that streamlining represented. During the 1930s and 1940s streamlined trains went into service in practically every country of the world, with notable examples in Britain, France, Germany, the United States, Canada and Japan. However, the speeds achieved by these trains were, in general, not significantly increased, and it was quickly appreciated by engineers that it was good track-work rather than streamlining that enabled trains to travel faster. The streamlined trains of the United States, for example the Twentieth Century Limited, were famous throughout the world as symbols of modernity but they did not, in reality, go very fast (plate 29.4). Faster timings were regularly achieved by unstreamlined trains in European countries. That the image of speed was more important than the reality was underlined by the application of stream-lining to the interiors of railway passenger vehicles,

29.4 Henry Dreyfuss, *Twentieth Century Limited*, locomotive. American, 1938. Hulton Archive/Getty Images.

where contoured forms, smooth surfaces and modern materials became synonymous with luxury and comfort.

In Britain in the late 1930s, there were two classic streamlined trains, operating on competing routes between London and Scotland. The London, Midland and Scottish Railway ran its *Coronation Scot* along the west coast route from Euston, while the London and North Eastern Railway's east coast services from King's Cross featured Sir Nigel Gresley's even more famous A4 Pacific locomotives. In 1938, one of these blue-painted locomotives, the *Mallard*,

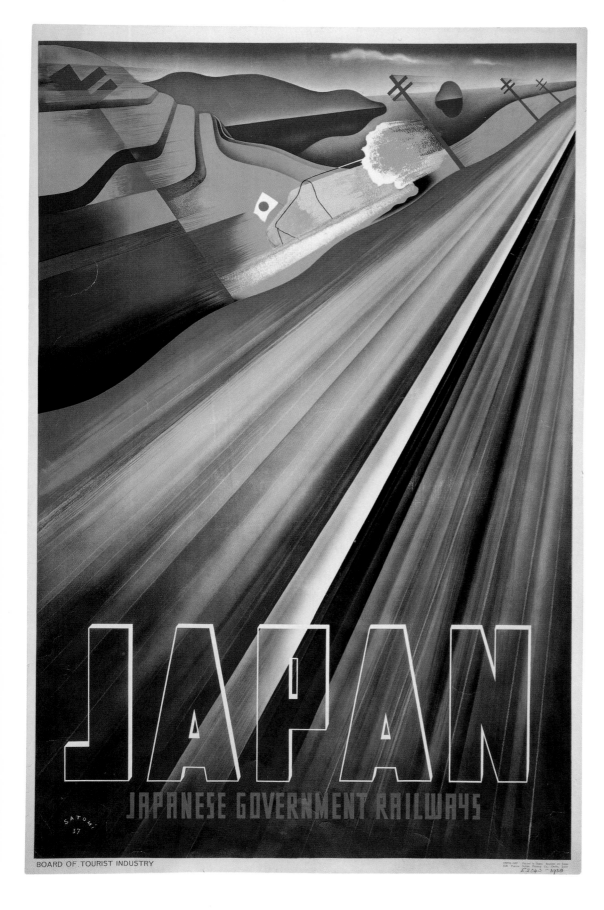

JAPAN
JAPANESE GOVERNMENT RAILWAYS
SATOMI 37
BOARD OF TOURIST INDUSTRY

29.5 Satomi, poster for Japanese
Government Railways. Colour
lithograph. Japanese, 1937.
V&A: E.2043-1938.

established the world-record speed for a steam train, 126 mph, a record that has never been challenged. Yet, it was known at the time that the streamlining that made these locomotives so distinctive had only a limited effect upon the speed achieved. The air-smoothed casing also hindered routine maintenance. Subsequently, the rival LMS Coronation Scots were all rebuilt in an unstreamlined form without any impact upon running speeds.

In 1937 the American industrial designer Raymond Loewy wrote a book entitled *The Locomotive*. It was published in Britain by The Studio in its New Vision Series, which also included a title on aircraft by Le Corbusier. In this study of the world's streamlined trains, Loewy based his judgments on appearance as much as operating efficiency. He was critical, largely on aesthetic grounds, of the design of many of the great trains of the world: Gresley's record-breaking A4 Pacifics, the French Paris-Lyon-Mediterrannée locomotives, the streamlining efforts of German State Railways and Japanese Railways, and some of the most avant-garde of the named trains of the United States, including the Milwaukee Road *Hiawatha*, the New York Central *Commodore Vanderbilt* and the Burlington *Zephyr* (plate 29.5 and see plate 34.5). Most favoured were his own designs for steam and electric locomotives for the Pennsylvania Railroad, an effective blend of aesthetics and mechanical efficiency, achieved through an extensive programme of wind tunnel testing that underlined his belief that design is more than packaging.

The foundations for the use of streamlining as a matter of style rather than efficiency had been laid at the end of the nineteenth century, with the development of a new kind of luxury train that offered passengers more than just a journey. The pioneer was the American George Mortimer Pullman, the creator of the first sleeping cars. During the 1870s and 1880s the first Pullman cars went into service in Europe, and soon dedicated Pullman services of sleeping cars and dining cars were operating in Britain, France and other parts of Europe, in many cases run by the recently formed Compagnie Internationale des Wagons-Lits. One of the first international routes, started in 1882, was between Paris and Vienna. From this developed the famous

Orient Express, running regularly between Paris and Constantinople and Athens from 1889. The network of routes rapidly expanded before the First World War, following the opening of the Simplon tunnel in 1906, and by 1908 wagons-lits were operating regularly on the Trans-Siberian railway.

During the 1920s many new luxury routes came into operation, mostly centred on Paris and serving all parts of Europe and the Middle East (plate 29.1). Notable were the Simplon Orient Express and the Arlberg Orient Express (rivals to the original Orient Express), the Carpathian Express, the Etoile du Nord, the Mozart Express, the Rome Express, the Taurus Express and the Train Bleu. The network also had connections with Russia and China, and through the eastern Mediterranean to Cairo. During the same period an extensive Pullman network was established in Britain, including the famous Brighton Belle. However, best known was the Golden Arrow from London to Dover, connecting from 1929 with the Flèche d'Or from Calais to Paris via a dedicated steamer service. Even more direct was the famous Night Ferry introduced in 1936 to link Paris and London, whose wagons-lits crossed the Channel on a train ferry while their passengers were asleep.

The British Pullman trains and the great international routes served by the wagon-lit carriages established new standards for elegance and comfort, standards that were echoed by railway companies all over the world. In these trains the definition of modernity was no longer speed but style. The carriages built during the 1920s were notable for their stylish design and fittings (plate 29.6). A number of designers and manufacturers were involved, but all reflected the contemporary enthusiasm for decorative Modernism. Particularly memorable was a series of wagons-lits with interiors designed by René Prou, featuring lavish panelling in exotic woods inlaid with ivory-coloured Art Deco designs of stylized fruit and flowers, matched with metalwork with similar motifs. Made at the same time, the late 1920s, were dining cars with glass panels by René Lalique. These fashionable carriages initially went into service on the most prestigious routes, the Train Bleu and the Côte d'Azur Pullman to the French Riviera, the Sud Express to Spain, the Etoile du Nord to Amsterdam, the Flèche d'Or to Calais (for London) and the infamous Deauville Express (a sleeping car train that left Paris in the mid afternoon!). Some wagon-lit carriages were built in Britain. These featured a more conventional, and less exotic, approach to Art Deco, along with some dramatic Chinoiserie effects in the style then fashionable in 1920s Britain.

29.6 Marquetry panels in the Orient Express (modern restoration). French, c.1925. © VSOE Ltd.

More diverse were the Pullmans built to operate on British routes, with their marquetry panels of landscapes, flower sprays, classical cameos and French-inspired patterns in a mixture of revived eighteenth-century and modern styles. The most elegant were used for services such as the Golden Arrow, the Brighton Belle and the Queen of Scots Pullman, for ocean liner trains and for transporting members of the Royal Family and visiting Heads of State. Outside Europe, long distance and luxury trains tended to be more functional in their décor, reflecting a more mechanistic approach to interior design. Steel, chromium, aluminium and other factory materials were used to underline the industrial ethic inherent in aspects of Art Deco design. At the same time, luxury trains operating on both national and international routes were frequently seen as symbols of value and prestige by national governments. In effect, the modern train represented a modern state. Particularly expressive of this political interpretation of modernity were the railway networks of Italy and Germany, along with individual trains such as Japan's *Asia*.

The impact of these trains as the symbol of modernity was considerable and it gave them a distinct cultural identity. Throughout the period trains appear as the title, or the setting, for novels, poems, theatre and ballet, films and pieces of music, particularly jazz (*Murder on the Orient Express*, *Night Mail*, *Le Train Bleu*, *Shanghai Express*, *Coronation Scot*, *Superchief*). However, even more definable in

this context was the ocean liner, a setting much favoured by Hollywood, especially for musicals. For this, and many other reasons, the great ships of the 1920s and 1930s, sailing to and fro across the North Atlantic, are remembered today as the perfect blend of Art Deco style with speed and engineering excellence. Yet, these ships were, in effect, dinosaurs, representatives of a mode of travel already in decline. The most successful period in the history of the ocean liner on the North Atlantic was the Edwardian era. There were more ships in service than hitherto, and standards of speed and comfort were improved by a new generation of four-funnel liners bigger than anything the world had ever seen before. These great ships, operated by British, German and French owners, included the *Olympic*, the *Mauretania*, the *Aquitania*, the *Imperator*, the *France*. It was this generation of ships that established the concept of the liner as a floating luxury hotel.

Many of the best ships on the North Atlantic route in the 1920s had been built or planned before the First World War and were, as a result, often seen as old fashioned in terms of style and interior decoration. The designers of that generation of liners copied or adapted shore-based styles, drawing inspiration from sources both predictable and surprising: Tudor, eighteenth-century French, classical, Renaissance, oriental, Moorish, Egyptian, Spanish-American and many more were all to be found, often freely mixed together. The mixture of

29.7 J. R. Tooby, *Empress of Britain, Canadian Pacific Railway*, poster. Colour lithograph. British, c.1931-40. V&A: E.2215-1931.

styles was also a result of the constant refitting that has always been a part of any liner's active life. This meant that there was no definable liner style until the latter part of the 1920s.

The point of change was 1927, with the arrival in service of the Compagnie Générale Transatlantique's *Ile de France*, a ship that defined, for the first time, a new and distinct kind of Modernism in maritime interior design. Outwardly conventional, the *Ile de France* was internally the living embodiment of contemporary French Art Deco, expressing in its style and its use of exotic materials the spirit of the Paris 1925 Exhibition. Immensely popular and highly acclaimed by press and public, she also set new standards in luxury and comfort. When Cole Porter wrote the line 'You're as hard to land as the *Ile de France*' he knew he was using a popular and familiar image. The 'ocean liner style', created by the *Ile de France* on the North Atlantic, was quickly copied by interior designers ashore, reversing the usual process. From this point, architecture and the interior became for a time distinctly maritime. The image of the ocean liner was to be seen in buildings with exteriors designed like the superstructures of liners and with details such as porthole windows and balconies like ships' bridges; and the visual metaphor was carried through in the design of interior fittings.

On other routes, particularly east of Suez, more traditional attitudes still prevailed. The *Viceroy of India*, completed for P&O in 1929, was widely regarded by both passengers and crew as one of the most comfortable and elegant ships ever built. Among her many features was the first indoor swimming pool. Yet, in design terms her interiors were almost deliberately old fashioned, to emphasize the importance of traditional concepts of comfort on long sea voyages.

On the North Atlantic, the *Ile de France* was not alone for long. Government backing for the route was now a fact of life and it was a matter of national prestige to have the fastest and most stylish ships. A number of countries decided to have new ships to fly the national flag. First came North German Lloyd's twin ships, the *Bremen* and the *Europa*, which entered service in 1929 and 1930, having been paid for by German and American government money. These two large liners (each over 50,000 tons) were designed for speed and for an international clientele increasingly attuned to the modern style. On her maiden voyage to New York in July 1929 the *Bremen* captured the coveted Blue Riband for the fastest crossing by a passenger ship, long held by Cunard's elderly *Aquitania*. She held on to it until 1933, much to Hitler's delight. The next great ship to enter the Atlantic arena, in 1931, was the *Empress of Britain*, the new flagship of the Canadian Pacific Line (plate 29.7 and see plate 6.8). Famed for her lavish and spacious interiors, this ship helped to encourage a wider enthusiasm for the modern style, particularly as she also had a pioneering role as a cruise ship during the winter season. The success of the

29.9 A bar on the *Queen Mary*. The bar is made of macassar ebony with a mural by Alfred R. Thomson behind. 1936. Hulton Archive/Getty Images.

29.8 J. Simont, Grand Salon of the *Normandie*. Plate from *L'Illustration*, special issue on the *Normandie*, 1935. Colour print. NAL.

Probably the ultimate ocean liner, the *Normandie* remained the most famous ship in the world and a potent symbol for modern France. However, in commercial terms she was not a success. She often sailed half empty and was unprofitable throughout her four years on the North Atlantic. For many she was too grand, too luxurious, too modern, too extreme, too demanding. Her rivals also suffered on this highly competitive route, but national prestige was often more important than realistic cost control. Partly because of her short life (she was destroyed by fire and flooding in New York harbour in 1941), the *Normandie* has become the subject of myth and legend. Widely seen as the greatest creation of the Art Deco style, the ship was, in reality, a glorious folly and a great white elephant.

In Britain the fortunes of Cunard's North Atlantic business in the 1920s were still based on their increasingly costly and outmoded fleet of pre-First World War veterans, the *Aquitania*, the *Mauretania* and the *Berengaria*. Responding to the threat posed by modern German and Italian ships, and encouraged by government support in return for the takeover of the once great White Star Line, Cunard commissioned the first of two new super-liners from John Brown's Clydebank shipyard in December 1930. After years of delay and uncertainty, and the input of huge sums of government money, the first ship was finally launched in September 1934 as the *Queen Mary*. In May 1936 she sailed on her maiden voyage to New York.

Always popular, this massive 80,000-ton vessel was, externally, quite old fashioned. Her upright looks echoed the Cunard style of a previous generation, and her decks and superstructure were conventional. The three tall funnels had none of the refinement of those on the *Normandie*. However, despite her looks, the *Queen Mary* was a fast ship and she was soon to capture the Blue Riband from the *Normandie*. Her fastest Atlantic crossing was 3 days, 20 hours and 40 minutes. Internally the *Queen Mary* was a modern ship, but her Art Deco styling was less extreme and more restrained, representing in many ways the popular face of Modernism. Her interiors, elegant and well mannered, expressed the by then well established taste for the contemporary look made familiar in Britain by modern houses, plywood furniture, cinemas, hotels, department stores, offices, abstract-patterned textiles and tablewares, radios and popular motor cars (plate 29.9). In her own way the *Queen Mary* was distinctly stylish, even if she lacked the lavish opulence of the *Normandie*, and she was clearly a more popular and successful ship, destined for a far longer and more adventurous life.

Empress was limited by the fact that, as a Canadian ship, she sailed from Canadian ports. Most transatlantic travellers still wanted to sail to or from New York.

Italy, driven by the global ambitions of Mussolini, now entered the fray. Built almost regardless of expense, the 51,000-ton *Rex* and her slightly smaller sister, the *Conte di Savoia*, joined the North Atlantic route in 1932. These ships were designed virtually as floating resorts and so brought new standards of comfort and service into what was already a highly competitive market. Their modernistic interiors had, inevitably, echoes of the stylized Roman classicism favoured by Mussolini but they were combined with fashionable streamlining and contouring. Between 1933 and 1935 the *Rex* held the Blue Riband, the only Italian ship ever to capture this prize upon which so much national pride depended.

Meanwhile, the focus of attention had switched to France with the launch in October 1932 of the *Normandie*. A sensation throughout her short life,

this ship was always in the headlines. The largest ship afloat, fast, elegant and the ultimate statement in luxury, the *Normandie* was the epitome of the kind of Art Deco that the French had made distinctly their own in Paris in 1925. Her interiors, beautifully made in lavish and exotic materials, were the best that leading French artists and designers such as Lalique, Jean Dupas and Jean Dunand could produce (plate 29.8 and see plate 3.6). The ship cost over $60 million, and critics referred to her as France's floating national debt. Even the exterior was revolutionary in its clean-cut and almost streamlined simplicity. The decks were free of the conventional clutter of masts, ventilators and winches, and even more radical were the funnels that graduated in size towards the stern to emphasize the sense of movement, and the sharply raked bow that improved both speed and style. The fastest liner in the world, she easily captured the Blue Riband from the *Rex* in the spring of 1935, with an average speed to New York of 28.92 knots (33 mph).

29.10 Douglas DC3 airliner,
American. First produced 1935.
Photograph 1945.
Hulton Archive/Getty Images.

During the 1930s the spread of airlines began to make inroads into areas of transport previously dominated by rail. This was particularly notable in North America, and on shorter routes in Europe, as aircraft became faster, more reliable and larger. In the early 1920s most airliners were still derived from military types but by the end of the decade a new generation of large multi-engined biplanes were in service around the world. A notable example was the British Handley-Page 42, the mainstay over many years of Imperial Airways' European and Empire routes. Such aircraft were comfortable and well fitted, but rather slow. The HP 42 could carry up to 38 passengers at just over 100 miles per hour. In the 1930s a new series of sleeker, faster monoplane airliners appeared, offering infinitely improved services. However, their capacity was still limited,

usually to under 30 passengers. Typical were the American Douglas series, the DC1, DC2 and the ubiquitous DC3, used by airlines all over the world in the late 1930s (plate 29.10). In Britain, the Armstrong Whitworth Atalanta, a high-winged, four-engined monoplane, gave a new look to the Imperial Airways fleet from 1933. This was followed in 1939 by the even more elegant and modern looking Ensign, an aircraft that would not have looked out of place in the 1950s. Of similar date and appearance was the De Havilland Albatross. German, Italian and French manufacturers all made modern looking airliners at this time. Externally streamlined for practical reasons, these aircraft also brought a Modernist look to their interior fittings as wicker chairs gave way to aluminium. Air travel was perceived to be modern, so travellers expected a contemporary look. Even the great flying boats of the late 1930s that flew the Imperial Airways Empire Mail routes to Africa and elsewhere featured in their interiors a blend of contoured Modernism and the fashionable industrial look with traditional comfort. Tubular steel, aluminium and other materials reflecting modernity were also very evident in the interior design of the *Hindenburg*, the great German airship briefly in transatlantic service until the disaster at Lakehurst, New Jersey, on 6 May 1937 which brought commercial passenger airship travel to an end (plate 29.11).

It is difficult today to measure the true impact of Art Deco on travel and transport during the inter-war period. Of the great liners, only the *Queen Mary* survives, converted into a hotel in Long Beach, California. Some of her interiors are complete, but

they inevitably reflect post-war refittings. Lacquer panels and other decorative elements saved from the *Normandie* give a hint of what that ship may have looked like. A few preserved 1930s airliners suggest the excitement and the sense of modernity associated with that means of transport. There are, luckily, plenty of preserved 1920s and 1930s railway vehicles, reflecting the universality of Art Deco at the time. Motor vehicles also survive in large numbers, allowing a more accurate measure of the impact of Modernism and streamlining upon both cars and public service vehicles such as buses and coaches. It is apparent from these that streamlining and Modernist styling did not become commonplace until the latter part of the 1930s. The great Bentleys that won the Le Mans race so conclusively between 1927 and 1930 are remarkable for their complete lack of

streamlining, and even famous record breakers like Sir Malcolm Campbell's *Bluebird* were streamlined in a rather angular manner that was notably lacking in rounded contours. The use of streamlining based on sound aerodynamic principles appears in the late 1930s, for example with John Cobb's Napier-Railton car, which raised the world's land speed record to 369 miles per hour at Utah in 1939. In the field of popular motoring, streamlining and a modern look were always more about style than performance, a principle that can perhaps be applied to the Art Deco period as a whole.

29.11 *Hindenburg* airship (LZ-129) flying over the Hudson river and Downtown Manhattan. 1936. Hulton Archive/Getty Images.

30 Art Deco and Hollywood Film

Ghislaine Wood

'Long life to the cinema – where else will we find our illusions?'[1]
Ruth Vassos, *Contempo*, 1929

Film, the most powerful medium of the modern age, established Art Deco as a mass style. Many European and American films of the 1920s and 1930s explored Art Deco as the main visual idiom to convey modernity, but it was in Hollywood films that the style reached its full potential for fantasy, glamour and mass popularity. In films such as *Our Dancing Daughters* (1928), *A Woman of Affairs* (1928), *Grand Hotel* (1932), *42nd Street* (1933), *Gold Diggers of Broadway of 1933* and the musicals of Fred Astaire and Ginger Rogers, Hollywood wove a magical web with tales of luxury, youth and beauty, upward mobility, individualism, sexual liberation and rampant consumerism. The backdrops for this exploration of contemporary dreams and aspirations were fantastic Deco-styled hotels, night-clubs, ocean liners, offices, apartments and skyscrapers. Offering a heady cocktail of modern themes and chic style, these films proved irresistible to millions worldwide. In fact, Hollywood's success was so rapid and far-reaching that by 1932 the League of Nations could report that 'only the Bible and the Koran have an indisputably larger circulation than that of the latest film from Los Angeles'.[2] But while the 'illusions' these films conveyed were thoroughly grounded in American values and transmitted American culture worldwide, their design was dominated by Europeans. Promulgated by successive waves of émigré designers, directors and producers, a European aesthetic governed the design of Hollywood films in the 1920s before being gradually superseded by a more distinctively 'home-grown' idiom in the 1930s.

In the early years of the century many European countries developed film industries. The two most powerful before the war were those of Italy and France but by the early 1920s there were thriving studios in Russia, Czechoslovakia, Germany, Austria and Britain. As distinct national schools and styles evolved, many directors and designers explored the use of contemporary art and design to denote modern themes. In Berlin the UFA studios established a unique movement with German Expressionist films. Neo-romantic or mythical plots were filmed in artificial and highly stylized sets defined by heightened contrasts of light and shadow. The supernatural, mysterious or psychologically disturbing – other common strands in Expressionist film – were explored in the most famous example of the style *The Cabinet of Dr Caligari* (1919), directed by Robert Wiene. In Russia films such as the science-fiction adventure *Aelita Queen of Mars* (1924), directed by Jakov Protazanov with kinetic costumes designed by Alexandra Exter, brought Constructivist design to a wider audience. But it was in France that one of the earliest coherent uses of Art Deco on screen appeared in the work of the avant-garde director Marcel L'Herbier. In films such as *L'Inhumaine* (1923) and *Le Vertige* (1926), L'Herbier used Art Deco sets and costumes to symbolize modern themes and modern lifestyles. The femme fatale of *L'Inhumaine*, for instance, inhabits an ultra-modern house designed by Rob Mallet-Stevens symbolic of her liberated lifestyle. L'Herbier later declared of *L'Inhumaine* that 'we wanted [it] to be a sort of résumé ... of all that was happening in the visual arts in France'.[3] Many leading artists were involved in the design of his films including Rob Mallet-Stevens, Fernand Léger, Claude Autant-Lara, Alberto Cavalcanti, Sonia and Robert Delaunay, Pierre Chareau, Michel Dufet, Paul Poiret, René Lalique, Jean Puiforcat and Raymond Templier (plate 30.2). Despite L'Herbier's early identification of the essential ingredients for the successful film – racy subject matter, high Deco style and plenty of melodrama – by the mid-1920s Hollywood led the way in the fusion of modern themes and glamorous settings and, as a result, dominated world markets.

The reasons for Hollywood's rapid and phenomenal success were many. As Europe slowly recovered from the effects of the First World War, the American economy boomed; and while European critics and artists debated the nature of film and hoped to

30.2 *L'Inhumaine*, directed by Marcel L'Herbier,
set design by Fernand Léger. 1923.
Art et décoration, October 1926. NAL.

experience for ever larger audiences. And it was with this shift of emphasis from art to commerce and industry, that film became one of the most powerful signifiers of modernity.

The film industry in America was largely the creation of pioneering Jewish immigrants, many with a background in the New York textile or clothing industry, whose status on the peripheries of American business gave them an entrepreneurial advantage in a fledgling industry as yet unclaimed by class or ethnic group.[6] As heads of independent film companies, Adolph Zukor, William Fox, Carl Laemmle, Samuel Goldwyn and Louis B. Mayer oversaw a series of business mergers that ushered in the Golden Age of the great Hollywood studio.[7] Hollywood had existed as a centre of production before the First World War, but it was not until the creation of these larger companies that the industry could expand to supply the world market. Under these 'movie moguls' Hollywood flourished. They industrialized the system of production, established control over distribution and exhibition networks and created a vertically integrated structure, the commercial nature of which was well understood by all those involved. The director of the Roxy theatre, lecturing at New York University in the mid-1930s, entitled his talk 'Why the motion pictures are not an art'. He emphasized that the films he chose were selected not on aesthetic grounds but solely on account of their box office value: 'as we sit in our projection room, we are more like shoe buyers looking over the fall line than connoisseurs inspecting works of art. For the fact is that we, along with the shoe buyers, have only one thought uppermost – will the public pay its money for this article?'[8]

The Hollywood 'dream factory' was built on ruthless business techniques instituted to ensure that the American product dominated markets.[9] It was through practices such as block booking and blind booking[10] that Hollywood films saturated world markets and created a global taste for modern American culture and with it Art Deco as the style that represented that culture. Many countries responded to the erosion of their native film industries by introducing legislative controls.[11] Germany, with the largest film industry outside America, was the first to respond, quickly followed by Britain where the Cinematograph Films Bill, debated in the House of Commons in 1927, revealed the

preserve it as a form of high art, or – as we have seen with L'Herbier – adopted it to promote high art, dynamic American businessmen realized the potential of the medium for making money.[4] Their identification of film as a manufactured 'product' like any other, to which the rules of business could be applied, led to the rapid development of the industry in America. Harnessing an increasing understanding of consumer psychology to commercial imperatives, they also exploited the power of film for propaganda and persuasion. As the early film historian Paul Rotha

opined, 'under the thin veil of entertainment, the hard fact is apparent that the film is the most influential medium yet discovered for persuading an audience to believe this or to do that'.[5] Hollywood rapidly recognized that the voracious appetite of contemporary consumers for the 'new' could be stimulated through a constant stream of new stars, new fashions, new themes and new experiences. The inexorable progression of film technology, and the dramatic leap forward with the introduction of the 'talkies' in 1928, created an ever more sophisticated

anxiety many countries faced as audiences for home-grown films dwindled. As one speaker put it,

> From the trade point of view, the influence of cinema is not less important. It is the greatest advertising power in the world. Just let the House imagine the effect upon trade of millions of people in every country, day after day, seeing the fashions, the styles and the products of a particular country.[12]

Another speaker commented that the British public 'talk American, think American, and dream American. We have several million people, mostly women who, to all intent and purpose, are temporary American citizens.'[13] Yet such was the draw of the Hollywood product, over that of films from elsewhere, that desperate exhibitors all over the world committed to blind booking. One British critic bitterly commented,

> The film industry in America grew with the rapidity of her Californian asparagus. Whether for good or ill, therefore, it became the province of American films to influence fashions, habits, manners, and outlook in the four corners of the earth. And it should be borne in mind that countries such as China and Russia, too quickly acquired a taste for the photoplay. America, building without rivalry, on the solid foundation of producing, distributing, renting and exhibiting organisations, made cinema a great industrial success.[14]

It was not simply a matter of sharp business practice that ensured the success of the major Hollywood studios. Equally important was the creation of narratives and a style with an international and mass appeal. In the late 1920s the director King Vidor identified the task: 'we must seek a great common denominator, a means of telling a story that is understandable to all classes of audience – the poor, rich, old, young, European and American'.[15] The need to appeal to a heterogeneous and multi-ethnic domestic market in America undoubtedly helped in the creation of a style that could be readily consumed across the world. This was achieved through the development of formulaic genres and clear narratives, based on modern themes set within the simulacrum of real time and space, and Art Deco designs played a vital part in its creation. These components were established by 1928 but were given a tremendous boost with the introduction of the 'talkies', when movie narratives shifted from simple story lines to the complex and sophisticated dramas made possible through dialogue.

An important factor in this development of an internationally accessible style was the role played by recent European émigrés. In their positions as studio producers, writers, artists, directors, designers and composers, they were able successfully to adapt their knowledge of European tastes and film styles to the demands of commerce. Placing a clear emphasis on realism and modernity, they created a successful formula for the development of film as a mass cultural form.

The culture these films explored and transmitted – upward mobility, sexual liberation and conspicuous consumption – fuelled the desires of audiences and became inextricably linked with Art Deco. The Depression fantasy of escaping poverty was often played out in the modern penthouse apartment, night-club, luxury hotel, ocean liner or resort, with Art Deco styling providing the mise-en-scène for escape from a restricting morality to a fast, new, glamorous and sexually liberated modern age. Luxurious Art Deco sets for films such as *Our Dancing Daughters*, *Swing Time* (1935) and *Dodsworth* (1936) did not attempt to create a real or viable vision of the style as it existed on the street, but instead gave a sense of heightened reality to the dreams the films conveyed. As one contemporary historian observed, 'Hollywood is in the business of building illusion ... Hotels more sumptuous than the Waldorf-Astoria or the Ritz, liners outvying the pretentions [sic] of the Normandie; speed that sets Malcolm Campbell to shame.'[16] In this world enormous night-clubs stretched away into the distance, vast metropolitan offices and apartments sprawled across the screen, and stage sets expanded beyond the realms of possibility. The living room from *Our Modern Maidens*

30.3 *Grand Hotel*, directed by Edmund Goulding.

BFI Stills, Posters and Designs.

© (1932) Turner Entertainment Co.

An AOL Time Warner Co.

All Rights Reserved.

(1929), more reminiscent of a theatre than a living room, brilliantly demonstrates the use of Deco architecture to create a fantasy of modern life (plate 30.1). Designed under the auspices of Cedric Gibbons, the supervisory art director at MGM, the film's décor was given glowing reviews,

> The setting is ultra and neo. If the players depict the development of flapperism, their environment is not lagging. We believe it is the first time that the screen has shown such a faithful picture of the great revolution the French mode in home furnishings is about to effect. The moderniste motif is carried out even to architectural details, and it will afford no end of keen amusement to see square, solid, severe lines and the quixotism of strange lighting arrangements.[17]

Gibbons, an American, and one of the first of the new breed of specialist art directors, was widely credited with introducing the new style in film. He developed a unified conception of the Art Deco interior that included real furnishings and furniture and gave meticulous attention to the detailing of sets right down to the selection of European Art Deco paintings, sculpture and design. Many of his films carefully incorporated typical Deco iconography and helped to spread the repertoire of motifs worldwide (see plate 10.6). He was not, though, the first to adopt the style in Hollywood. Earlier films such as Cecil B. De Mille's *Male and Female* (1919), designed by Wilfred Buckland, had contained Art Deco elements and, with his keen sense of popular tastes, De Mille was the first director consciously to use Art Deco to signify shifting morality. While his sets represented the height of classic French Art Deco and often included works by leading designers, the plots set the standard for films of the next decade as he 'visualised more sex and displayed more consumption than any previous photoplays'.[18] The famous bathroom scenes created for *Male and Female* and *Dynamite* (1929) both presented the femme fatale in luxurious marble-clad Art Deco surroundings. The bathroom in *Dynamite* was thought particularly risqué in its combination of black marble, gilt swag decorations and a transparent glass bath.

De Mille was also one of the first to import leading Art Deco designers from Europe. In 1921 he commissioned Paul Iribe, a pioneer of the style in France, to design the sets and costumes for the historical drama *The Affairs of Anatol*. Iribe's designs owed much to the Ballets Russes and to Art Nouveau, though he incorporated Art Deco forms in some of his designs for furniture. The same year saw Joseph Urban, an Austrian émigré, create sets for *Enchantment* (made by the East Coast company

30.4 *Grand Hotel*, directed by Edmund Goulding. BFI Stills, Posters and Designs. © (1932) Turner Entertainment Co. An AOL Time Warner Co. All Rights Reserved.

Cosmopolitan Pictures) that were described at the time as 'ultramodern in every sense of the word'.[19] His designs adhered to the style of the Wiener Werkstätte, with the set for the tea-room adopting the floral patterns and linear geometry of the Austrian model. The central motif of the scheme, the grid, gave the room a restrained but sophisticated symmetry. Urban, one of the most influential of all the émigré designers, had been retained as the house designer for the Broadway producer and showman Florenz Ziegfeld. His designs for Art Deco sets that combined bold colour with outrageous fantasy provided a look for the hugely successful female revue, the Ziegfeld Follies. It was a look that was emulated in theatres everywhere. His side step into film came at the invitation of the newspaper tycoon and owner of Cosmopolitan Pictures, William Randolph Hearst, who employed Urban to design sets and costumes. Although few

of Urban's set designs were in the Deco style, as most were for historical dramas, he was well aware of the potential of film for embracing modern design, 'The motion picture offers incomparably the greatest field to any creative artist in brush or blueprint today. It is the art of the twentieth century and perhaps the greatest art of modern times. It is all so young, so fresh, so untried.'[20]

Metro Goldwyn Mayer (MGM), the richest of the Hollywood studios, with the greatest roster of stars, keenly promoted the new style from the early 1920s. In 1924 Louis Mayer imported Erté, at great expense, to become head of the MGM art department. Famous for his fashion illustrations for *Harper's Bazar* and *Vogue*, and like Urban hot from recent successes designing Broadway shows, Erté found it difficult to work with precocious stars who refused to wear his costumes and conservative studio directors who wanted to temper his designs. He left

MGM within a year and was replaced by Gibbons who, through a strict division of labour, turned the MGM studio into the most productive in the business. Employing many talented designers, including Merrill Pye and Richard Day, the studio created luxurious Art Deco designs for films such as *Our Dancing Daughters*, *Our Blushing Brides* (1929), *Susan Lenox: Her Fall and Rise* (1931), *Men Must Fight* (1933), *The Easiest Way* (1931), *The Thin Man* (1936), *Dodsworth* and most famously *Grand Hotel*. These clearly reveal the evolution of the style in film, from its use as a signifier of the fashionable, modern interior – created through set detailing and Deco furnishings and brilliantly exemplified in *Our Dancing Daughters* – to its streamlined incarnation in the early 1930s, where decorative detail has been subsumed by a preoccupation with materials, surface and overall architectural form. The advent of streamlining in America profoundly affected the design of Hollywood films, providing them with a native design idiom.

Other studios also developed a considered use of Deco sets and costumes to signify a racy modern world. Paramount, a studio renowned for its high proportion of émigré artists, set its witty comedies in Art Deco surroundings. The German designers Jock Peters and Kem Weber were both employed by Paramount during the Depression. Contemporary critics associated some of the most progressive designs with the Paramount art department,

> the majority of the interior sets of American pictures are the essence of spaciousness and modernism. Their appearance is always polished and slick, appealing to the audience to achieve a similar standard of living. The sets in all Paramount's sophisticated comedies are noteworthy for their brilliance of design and surety of decoration.[21]

Hans Dreier, head of the art department from 1932, had been a designer at the UFA studios from 1919 to 1923. Schooled in German Expressionism, he used lighting to its full dramatic potential in the creation of a spare, brilliant style. In the early 1930s the studio developed the predominantly white set, reflecting the taste for all-white Deco interiors (see plate 10.14). This became technically feasible with the development of incandescent lighting and improvements in film stock, which enabled designers for the first time to use pure white as the defining feature of a set. Panchromatic film also offered greater image definition and produced the glossy, lustrous quality that became so central to the Hollywood style. It led to a rash of films in which every aspect of the styling from the platinum blonde, white-skinned actress, to clothing, backgrounds and

furniture, was a sophisticated orchestration of shades of white.

A film that used panchromatic film to full effect was the hugely successful *Grand Hotel*. Winning two Academy Awards and grossing $1,650,000, it was the quintessential streamlined Art Deco movie of the early Depression years. Like many films of this period it attempted to attract audiences back in to the theatres after the post-Crash slump with sheer glamour and more sex. Every aspect of the design was conceived in the Deco style, from the chic costumes created by MGM's in-house fashion designer, Adrian, to elegant suites furnished with French furniture.[22] The lobby, with its streamlined forms, circular reception desk and intricate chrome-strip and glass-panel detailing, was styled to represent a hotel in any modern city (plate 30.3).

As one character declares, 'There's a Grand Hotel in every town'. The film explored a modern world of sexual frankness and availability, avaricious consumerism and the instability of wealth – in which morality was mediated by pragmatism. The luxury hotel, one of the most potent symbols of the Deco age, eroded the boundaries, both physical and psychological, between class and sex. The plot intertwined the lives of five very different characters, for all of whom luxury and glamour were attained at a certain cost, and the design of costumes and interiors was subtly used to differentiate story lines and characters. For Joan Crawford's worldly-wise stenographer, propositioned in *the* contemporary site of decadence and frivolity – the cocktail bar – the reality of sex as business is clear. In a later scene, her dimly lit, en-suite bedroom and dark negligee

30.5 Adrian, dress for Joan Crawford in *Letty Lynton*. White silk crêpe and black bugle beads. American, 1932. Museum Collection, Fashion Institute of Design and Merchandising, from the Department of Recreation and Parks, City of Los Angeles.

present a tough image of the purely sexual nature of her transaction. By contrast, Greta Garbo's forlorn ballerina is sexually liberated but desperate for love. Her luxurious Art Deco suite, shot in a filtered white light, is the site for a one-night affair, its satin surfaces and rich furnishings reinforcing the association of glamour, sensuality and romance, as does her pale and diaphanous clothing (plate 30.4).

The practice of using Art Deco settings for modern themes was reiterated in a vast number of Hollywood films in the late 1920s and early 1930s. Another Garbo vehicle, *Susan Lenox: Her Fall and Rise*, explored a favourite Art Deco playground of ill gotten gains – the luxury penthouse. Designed by Gibbons, the film developed a more coherent approach to the design of interior spaces. An elegant, streamlined style was carried throughout the apartment, from the steel and glass walls of the living room to the lustrous lacquered bedroom. Brilliant metallic surfaces combined with the reflective sheen of Garbo's costumes to create an irresistibly stylish and quintessentially Deco image that firmly positioned this immoral character within her luxury surroundings. Like the objects in her apartment, she is an expensive decorative fixture. Films such as these promoted new lifestyles that explicitly linked sex and money. In challenging traditional values they did not go uncriticized. With the introduction of the censorship code, and the

establishment of the Breen office in 1934 to enforce the code, the narratives of films shifted to more conservative territory – the comedy and the Western – but in so doing sacrificed the more complex and sexually empowered female so brilliantly embodied in Greta Garbo's characters.

For many it was not the morality of the movies that offended but the sheer commercialism. F. Scott Fitzgerald scoffed, 'Throughout the Jazz Age the movies got no further than Mrs Jiggs, keeping up with its most blatant superficialities'.[23] This 'superficiality', the constant changes in fashion and the endless stream of 'looks' powerfully affected consumption. Hollywood both initiated new fashion trends and popularized existing ones, with the star system adding to their glamour and desirability. Fan magazines presented fashion features, often with stars shot in Art Deco settings, while promotional material such as press books featured film styling and costume as prominently as the stars and story line. The *New Survey of London Life and Labour* noted in 1935,

> The influence of films can be traced in the clothes and appearance of the women and in the furnishing of their houses. Girls copy the fashions of their favourite film star. At the time of writing, girls in all classes of society wear 'Garbo' hats and wave their hair *à la* Norma Shearer or Lilian Harvey.[24]

A young shorthand typist when interviewed reported:

'regarding fashion, I myself have taken dozens of clothes and hairstyles from films, and will continue to do so, as I believe that this is a sure way of keeping in step with fashions'.[25] The effects of films such as MGM's *Letty Lynton* (1932), one of the most beautifully styled for Art Deco clothes and accessories, were hard to resist (plate 30.5). Joan Crawford started a nationwide fad for frilly-sleeved white dresses after she appeared wearing an elaborate creation by Adrian in the film. Cheap versions appeared on every high street. The impact on popular fashion of film was further promoted by merchandizing. Companies such as Modern Merchandising, founded in 1930, created new lines, 'Cinema Fashions', which were sold in cities all over America. Margaret Farrand Thorp, analyzing the effect of merchandizing in *America at the Movies*, reported that 'Cinema Fashions appear in the big cities but their strongest influence is in the small towns. There the movies have little else to compete with as the dictators of fashion'. And it was not just specialist merchandizing companies that responded to the dictates of cinema: 'individual manufacturers of every sort of apparel and accessory are constantly attending previews of important pictures and obtaining permission to reproduce this or that article of dress. Even Fifth Avenue shops find a motion picture name now and then to their advantage.'[26]

The film genre that lent itself most easily to fantasy was the musical and it was in this sphere that some of the most elaborate Art Deco film sets were conceived. A distinctly American creation, the musical had an enormous resurgence of popularity in the early 1930s, largely as a result of a gritty, post-Crash revision of story lines and characters. The move towards narrative realism demanded by the Wall Street Crash resulted in films whose subject matter was most often the on- and off-stage action of Broadway musical companies. *42nd Street* (1933), *Footlight Parade* (1933), *Gold Diggers of Broadway of 1933* and *1935*, *Broadway* (1929), *Broadway Melody of 1936* (1935) and *Broadway Melody of 1938* (1937) all explored the trials and

tribulations of the 'Great White Way' and provided a believable framework for spontaneous song and dance. The head of production at Warner Brothers, Darryl F. Zanuck, was quick to realize that the musical combined extremely popular elements – semi-clad chorus girls, illicit sex, glamour, music, dance and escapist narratives – that provided audiences with a dream of upward mobility. The formula was hugely successful for Warner Brothers with *42nd Street* becoming the top grossing film of 1933.

A distinct development in the film musical was the use of mechanical sets. The scale and complexity of sets needed to stage musical action produced novel

solutions not only in design but also in filming and editing. The great staged dance pieces, most famously conceived and choreographed by Busby Berkeley and shot from an aerial viewpoint, often depended upon mechanical sets to create the geometrical forms that represent Art Deco film design at its most abstract. Berkeley elided figures and sets in editing to create formal patterns that clearly explore the imagery of the modern world. Industrial technology preoccupied many artists and fed the search for a new repertory of symbols. The factory assembly line, brilliantly satirized by Charlie Chaplin in *Modern Times* (1936) (plate 30.7), was given an altogether different interpretation by

30.7 *Modern Times*, directed by Charlie Chaplin. 1936. BFI Stills, Posters and Designs. © Roy Export Company Establishment.

Berkeley, whose complex, erotically charged, synchronized dance routines were executed and shot with machine-like precision in films like the *Gold Diggers of Broadway of 1933* and *Footlight Parade* (see plate 2.7). Siegfried Kracauer's study of film, *The Mass Ornament* (1963), made the analogy between the mechanics of industry and the dance of the Tiller Girls:

Not only were they American products; at the same time they demonstrated the greatness of American production ... When they formed an undulating snake, they radiantly illustrated the virtues of the conveyor belt: when they tapped their feet in fast tempo, it sounded like *business, business*: when they kicked their legs high with mathematical precision, they joyously affirmed the progress of rationalization; and when they kept repeating the same movements without ever interrupting their routine, one envisioned an uninterrupted chain of autos gliding from the factories of the world, and believed that the blessings of prosperity had no end.[27]

While designers such as Jack Okey and the Polish-born Anton Grot explored an abstract and often surreal Deco style at Warner Brothers with the musicals of Busby Berkeley, RKO was establishing an equally fantastical approach. The immensely popular musicals of Fred Astaire and Ginger Rogers – *Flying down to Rio* (1933), *The Gay Divorcee* (1934), *Top Hat* (1935), *Swing Time* (1935), *Follow the Fleet* (1936) and *Shall We Dance* (1936) – relied on highly stylized Art Deco sets that revealed the increasingly widespread acceptance of streamlining as a contemporary design idiom and metaphor of modernity. The Hotel Bella Vista in the *Gay Divorcee*, with its long, low, curving wings accentuated by flowing balconies, was composed of a sophisticated play of light and shadow (plate 30.8). The contrast of black and white represented so boldly in the architecture was carried through the entire set, including the stunning costumes designed by Walter Plunkett. Van Nest Polglase, the art director at RKO, assisted by Carroll Clark, created a style for the Astaire/Rogers films that played on contrast and surface sheen. It was perhaps most brilliantly explored in the sets for the Depression romance *Swing Time*. The action for this film takes place in a series of fabulous night-clubs set in skyscrapers high above Manhattan where every surface from the cellophane-wrapped tables to the Bakelite dance floors radiate the glossy, lustrous quality so characteristic of much Deco. It is in one of these nightspots, the Silver Sandal, that Astaire performed 'Bojangles of Harlem', one of his most memorable solo dance sequences. 'Bojangles' is emblematic of the sculptural use of light and shadow that epitomized the design style of the Astaire/Rogers films. Astaire plays the black Harlem hoofer Bill 'Bojangles' Robinson on a Cubist-inspired set composed of black and white planes. The set opens to reveal an enormous backdrop onto which Bojangles' giant silhouette is multiply projected. As these silhouettes break away and dance independently, shadow as the dominant design device is made autonomous. *Swing Time* encapsulated many of the themes that made the Astaire/Rogers films so successful. It represented the aspirations of the Depression era by portraying an out-of-work man, Astaire, and an independent working girl, Rogers, conquering Manhattan, yet the action takes place in an ultra-sophisticated world, metaphorically and physically high above that of ordinary people. *Swing Time* ends with the couple looking out over the Manhattan skyline, indelibly fusing glamour and romance with that icon of modernity, the skyscraper metropolis.

Nothing was more frequently depicted than New York in the search for a resonant modern imagery in film. Fritz Lang described his first impressions of the metropolis:

> The view of New York by night is a beacon of beauty strong enough to be the centerpiece of a film ... There are flashes of red and blue and gleaming white, screaming green ... streets full of moving, turning, spiraling lights, and high above the cars and elevated trains, skyscrapers appear in blue and gold, white and purple, and still higher above there are advertisements surpassing the stars with their light.[28]

From the impassioned visions of a technologically driven future in Lang's *Metropolis* (1926) to the light-hearted and frivolous skyscraper costumes and sets in *42nd Street*, *Broadway* and *Broadway Melody of 1938*, the city became a leitmotif in film of the 1920s and 1930s (plate 30.6). Its new skyscrapers fulfilled the desire for a native and modern iconography in the world of film, while film played a vital role in transmitting and naturalizing this imagery (see Chapter 31).

One of the most interesting representations of New York in any Hollywood film was to be found in the final scenes of the RKO hit of 1933, *King Kong* (plate 30.9). Using all the latest technical developments, including miniature projection, stop-motion photography and split screen photography, *King Kong* was the most technically advanced film of its time. But its underlying theme, the conflict between primitivism and modernity – a theme explored in extremely diverse contexts in this period (see Chapter 11) – struck a popular chord. In *King Kong* it reached truly epic proportions. The conflict was symbolically played out when Kong, at large in the heart of the modern world, wreaked havoc in Manhattan, destroying symbol after symbol of progress from trains and cars to electricity pylons and buildings. The final scene has Kong scaling the most modern of skyscrapers, the Empire State building. His destruction, shot down by planes against the backdrop of Manhattan, is less a victory for the modern world than the loss of an irreplaceable primal force. *King Kong* was as powerful a warning of the destructive force of technological progress as *Metropolis*.

Hollywood movies were created for a mass market and, at their peak in the mid-1930s, were seen by over 80 million people per week. Through them, Art Deco reached an enormous and receptive audience. Ironically, it was Art Deco and not Modernism that was assimilated into popular culture and achieved the mass appeal that its more radical and utopian sibling so desired. But the story of Art Deco in Hollywood is the story of the birth of the most important mass culture of the twentieth century. Hollywood transmitted American values and American ideals and eventually American style, in the form of streamlining, worldwide. As F. Scott Fitzgerald stated in *The Jazz Age*, 'We were the most powerful nation. Who could tell us any longer what was fashionable and what was fun?'[29]

30.8 *The Gay Divorcee*, directed by Mark Sandrich. BFI Stills, Posters and Designs.
© (1934) RKO Pictures, Inc. The appearance of Mr Fred Astaire has been arranged through a special license with Mrs Fred Astaire, Beverly Hills, California. All Rights Reserved.

30.9 *King Kong*, directed by Merian C. Cooper and Ernest B. Schoedsack. BFI Stills, Posters and Designs.
© (1933) RKO Pictures Inc. All Rights Reserved.

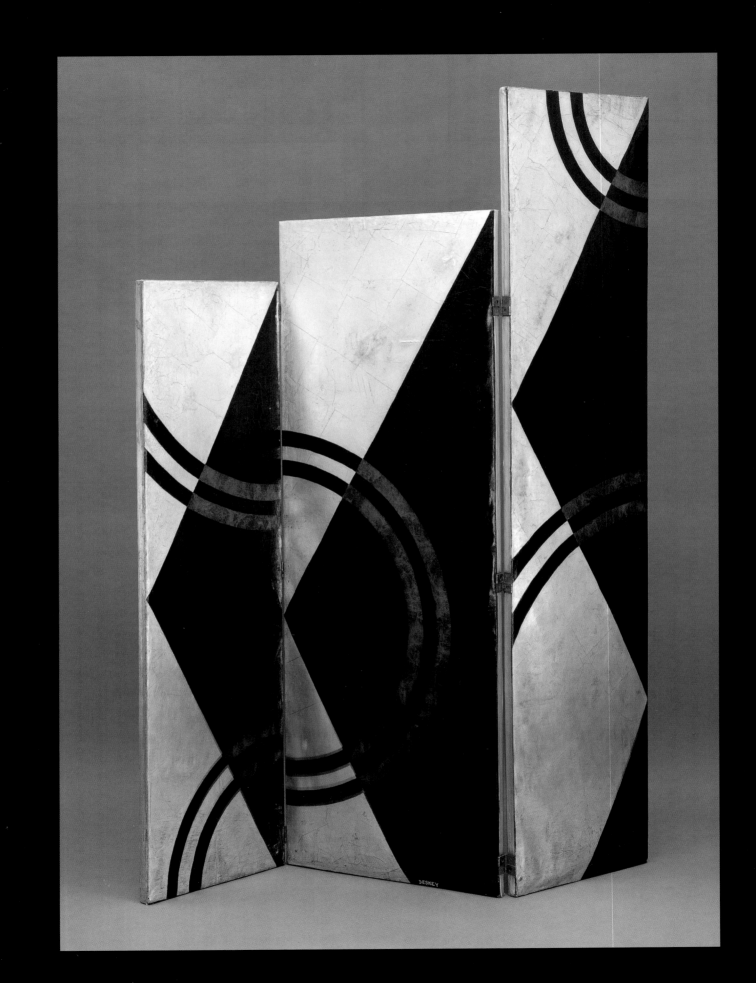

31 'The Filter of American Taste': Design in the USA in the 1920s

Wendy Kaplan

As an article in the *New Yorker* – that arbiter of culture and taste – declared: 'Nineteen-twenty-six was a propitious year for a decorative artist and industrial designer aware of ideas current in Europe and full of enthusiasm to return to America ... Commerce was going in for art; and a boom time was coming.'[1] The most direct inspiration for what was called 'modern', 'modernistic' or, in acknowledgement of the debt to France, 'Moderne' was uncontested in the interior decoration and fashion magazines of the time. As *House Beautiful* pointed out, 'little attention was given the modern style until the Paris show of 1925 brought it so vividly to our knowledge'.[2] The United States famously had not participated in this hugely influential exhibition because its government had declared that 'American manufacturers and craftsmen had almost nothing to exhibit in the modern spirit'.[3] This essay will examine how, why and in what ways this stagnant situation was rapidly transformed in the latter half of the 1920s.

Sources for transmission were many. A great number of American designers visited the 1925 Exhibition, the show was exhaustively reported in newspapers and magazines, and the very next year Charles Richards, director of the American Association of Museums (AAM), organized a tour of over 400 objects that had been displayed at the exhibition. Richards had also been the leader of the commission President Hoover sent to Paris to report on the show and had come away sufficiently impressed to 'hope that a parallel movement may be initiated in our own country'.[4] The AAM exhibition travelled to nine major art museums, including those in Philadelphia, Boston, Chicago, Cleveland and Minneapolis, as well as to New York's Metropolitan Museum of Art.

In order for the new modern style to flourish, a market for its products would have to be created. Museum shows were instrumental in these efforts, especially those in the New York area at the Metropolitan, Brooklyn and Newark art museums. The AAM tour was only the first of many after 1925

that promoted new developments in design. An important legacy of nineteenth-century design reform movements had been the mandate that museums play an active role in stimulating new design and forging new ties between art and industry. In 1918 the Metropolitan Museum of Art hired Richard Bach to serve as a liaison with manufacturers, retailers and designers and to organize annual exhibitions with the goal of improving American standards in design. Although at first the products in these exhibitions were supposed to be inspired from the Metropolitan's own collections, by 1926 the focus had so much shifted that no copies of objects were even allowed. The titles of the exhibitions reflected this change, having been called before 1924, *Exhibition of Work by Manufacturers and Designers Based upon Study in the Museum* and then until 1929, *American Industrial Art: An Exhibition of Current Manufactures Designed and Made in the United States*.[5]

The most critically important role, however, was played by department stores. According to an article in the trade magazine *Good Furniture* in 1928: 'Lord & Taylor of New York reported their Exposition of Modern French Decorative Art was attended by more than 200,000 people. In one week R. H. Macy Company counted 100,000 visitors to their International Exposition of Art-in-Industry.' (Macy's exhibition the previous year, *Art-in-Trade*, was organized in collaboration with the Metropolitan, further attesting to the close ties between museums and retailers in promoting new design.) The article went on to list department stores throughout the country – in Los Angeles, Atlanta, Seattle, St Louis – that 'have featured modern exhibits within the last year'.[6] The introduction to the catalogue of Lord & Taylor's exhibition was forthright about its goals. The store wanted to 'appraise the attitude of the American public toward Modern Art. Specifically, the aim is to ascertain whether or not there is ... sufficient interest to justify activity on the part of American artists, manufacturers and merchants in the production and presentation of such merchandise as a business venture.'[7] In other words: if we make

31.1 Donald Deskey, screen. Wood, canvas, paint and metal fittings. American, *c.*1930. Collection John P. Axelrod, Boston, MA. Courtesy Museum of Fine Arts, Boston.

it, will they buy? The success of Lord & Taylor's new products answers this question. While the exhibition provided a paradigm for the transmission of the new French style, Lord & Taylor's retail floors provided one for its dissemination.

Lord & Taylor had rounded up examples from most of the leading French practitioners of the high luxury style – including Ruhlmann, Dunand, Süe et Mare and Chareau – but what the store actually manufactured was quite different. Its market was more middle class. Although upwardly mobile clients might long for the sharkskin, macassar ebony and gilded surfaces of French imports, they could not afford them. They could *approximate* it, however, as demonstrated by the dressing table purchased by the newly engaged Marie-Louise Montgomery (later, Osborn) for her marital home (plate 31.2). The dressing table she ordered, probably from Lord & Taylor, was an adaptation of a design by Léon Jallot, one easily accessible since it had been published in *Good Furniture* in December 1928. As Louise had noted in a letter, department stores and other retailers were only too happy to 'make up any sort of modernistic furniture you desire from sketches'.[8] A photograph would serve as well, and the result was furniture in the modern taste, without the expensive materials or custom design costs. For the dressing table, imitation Chinese red lacquer had to stand in for sharkskin, but the Osborns would still be the proud possessors of a 'Cubist', sleekly geometric look.

Of course, wealthier Americans could buy luxury French goods at department stores such as Lord & Taylor and Macy's in New York, Marshall Field in Chicago and Barker Brothers in Los Angeles; all had increasingly successful departments of modern interior decoration. Alternatively, they could turn to local makers of similar wares such as Eugene Schoen (see plate 33.2). Trained as an architect in his native New York, Schoen received a scholarship for European travel after graduation. He returned later to visit the Paris 1925 Exhibition and then established an interior decoration practice in New York. The influential critic Nellie Sanford summarized Schoen's role as a pioneer in bringing *art moderne* to the United States, saying that he had 'adapted to American tastes the best features of the French mode – the use of fine woods, beautiful inlays, sweeping, highly polished surfaces, and a practical utilization of each piece as a space saver in the modern *ménage*'.[9]

Schoen was both commercially successful and critically acclaimed, but many articles about his work have reservations about its elitist nature. Sanford observed, 'He steadfastly clings [to] the slogan of "no duplication" ... Restricting his work to the demands of those who must have unique pieces necessarily eliminates him as a commercial factor.' While most museums, retailers, critics and designers were committed to a broader distribution of modern design, in the 1920s this goal was premature. Although Sanford optimistically declared, 'It really costs no more to be modern', she had to concede, 'of course, it will cost a whole lot less when the quantity producers take up the fashion in earnest.'[10] This, however, would be a story of the 1930s – during the previous decade, most modern design (even if it looked 'machined') was custom made. During the Great Depression, the taste for and ability to buy luxury goods precipitously declined, and mass production of a machine aesthetic using new industrial materials became an important tool of economic recovery.

Despite America's modest disclaimer that it did not have modern art to display in 1925, this was not entirely true. An essential and early source for the transmission of Art Deco, and for the goal of combining technology with an improved way of life, were the émigré designers. Joseph Urban and Paul Frankl had come from Vienna; Kem Weber, Winold Reiss and Oscar Bach from Germany; and Ilonka and Mariska Karasz and Hunt Diederich from Hungary. Rena Rosenthal, though American-born, had lived in Austria for ten years and married there before returning to New York in 1914. (Several years later she opened the Austrian Workshop, which was followed in the early 1920s by the very influential Rena Rosenthal Studio that specialized in selling the latest European designs.) All these designers were working in the United States by the end of the First World War and were considered harbingers of the new style. (Many more émigré designers and craftspeople would come over during the 1920s.) Furthermore, all were recognized at the time for bringing their German or Austro-Hungarian sensibility to the establishment of American modern design.[11]

The importance of these designers cannot be overstated. Far more than the French, with their country's grand tradition of luxury goods and specialized craftsmanship, the German and Austrian designers contributed to the establishment of what became a characteristically American machine aesthetic. The ideals of an alliance between art and industry and the production of quality objects for everyday use were not new – they had been central to the ideology of the nineteenth-century Arts and Crafts Movement. However, a working programme for their realization was only introduced by organizations such as the Deutscher Werkbund, which had been founded in 1907 to bring together the diverse interests of art, craft, industry and commerce. As early as 1912 the Newark Museum displayed over 1,300 German and Austrian objects by Werkbund members, and this influential exhibition toured many other museums throughout the United States.

German and Austrian émigrés, many of whom had actively participated in the Werkbund, played a central role in the establishment of the most progressive new organizations. In 1927 the American Designers' Gallery was established 'as a connecting link between the artist and the manufacturer' and to display modern products only.[12] The list of the participants in the Gallery's first exhibition, held the following year, reads like a 'who's who' of progressive American design, with Donald Deskey, Hunt Diederich, Paul Frankl, Ilonka Karasz, Ruth Reeves and Joseph Urban. (If these designers were not émigrés themselves, they had all spent considerable time abroad; for example, Ruth Reeves was in Europe for most of the 1920s and studied with Fernand Léger in Paris.) In 1928, the American Union of Decorative Artists and Craftsmen (AUDAC) was formed, a larger organization with a broader member base (for example, it included photographers), but also run by designers and artists. In addition to mounting two exhibitions, the latter at the Brooklyn Museum in 1931, AUDAC published a book of its members' work, *Modern American Design*.

Some of the founding members of both organizations, such as decorator and graphic designer Lucian Bernhard, had had leading positions in the Werkbund before moving to the United States. Bernhard, together with the German designer Bruno Paul (who did not emigrate, but was a hugely influential figure internationally (see plate 15.2)) and others, was also a founder of Contempora, Inc., which mounted an exhibition of 'Harmonized Rooms' in 1929. Each of the eight rooms displayed was available for mass production: the client could order its complete contents in any of the six available colours at a very reasonable price.[13] All three

31.2 Dressing table and bench. Red 'lacquered' wood, glass and chromium-plated metal. American, c.1929. Adapted from a design by Léon Jallot and distributed by Lord & Taylor. Gift of Mr James M. Osborn. Cooper-Hewitt, National Design Museum, Smithsonian Institution.

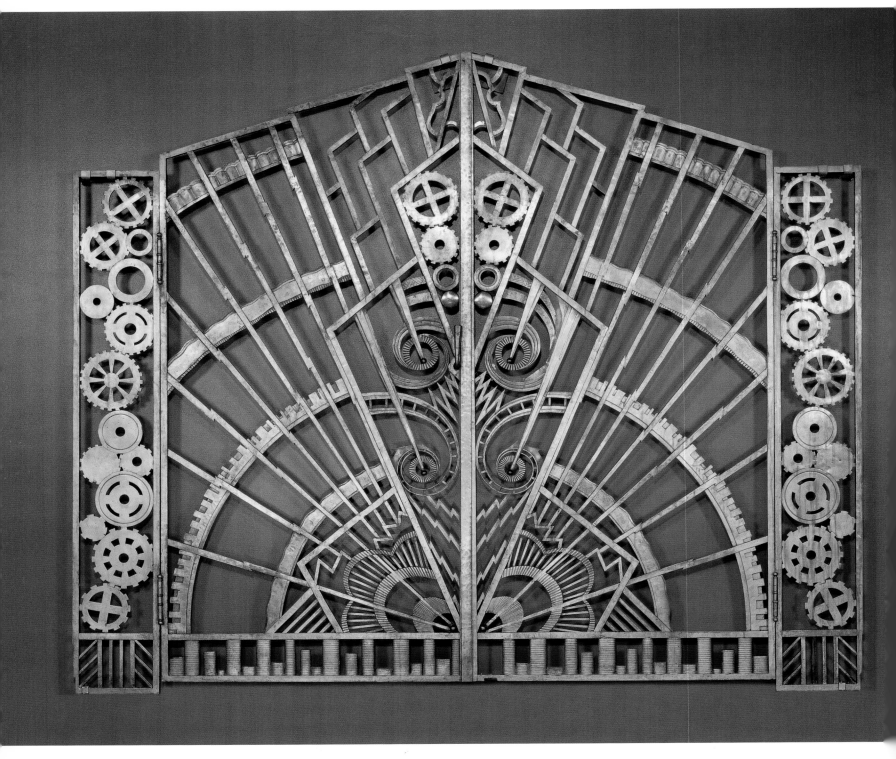

31.3 Rene Paul Chambellan, entrance gates to the executive suite of the Chanin building, New York. Wrought iron and bronze. American, 1928. Gift of Mr Marcy Chanin. Cooper-Hewitt, National Design Museum, Smithsonian Institution. Photo: Dennis Cowley.

organizations were short-lived, but they were critically important not only in the articulation of a self-consciously American interpretation of modern design, but also in promoting a broad definition of what constitutes industrial production. A description of Donald Deskey, a founder of both the American Designers' Gallery as well as AUDAC, sums up the approach that would pave the way for mass production of the new style in the 1930s: 'He has designed beautiful single pieces, but fundamentally he believes in the union of the craftsman and the manufacturer and sees no reason for hostility between them ... He himself has worked on textiles, lighting fixtures, slot machines, wallpaper, and combs, brushes, and mirrors.'[14]

What kinds of objects expressed this emerging American modern sensibility? In Europe, avant-garde artists, architects and designers believed the future must be a machine age. Working from the shared belief that the machine would establish a new structure for society, American designers chose different directions. While some rejected the past

absolutely and abhorred all decoration, such a purely Functionalist aesthetic was seldom acceptable in America in the 1920s. During that decade, no significant distinctions were made between 'modern', 'Modernist', 'modernistic' and 'Moderne' – terms that would soon become fighting words as designers associated with the International Style relegated any use of decoration to the historical scrap heap. Led by the curators at the Museum of Modern Art in New York, the passionate advocates of pure Functionalism denigrated the kinds of objects discussed in this essay as 'modernistic', a term that became one of disparagement in the 1930s.

But in the America of the 1920s, the church of modern design was catholic. Furnishings could range from the most conservative evocations of the French eighteenth-century past (if updated by a simplified geometry and smooth surfaces) to translations of avant-garde fine arts styles such as Cubism, Suprematism and De Stijl (plate 31.1). Yet, they would all come under the rubric of the modern. All were considered celebrations of contemporary life –

its speed, dynamism and technology – and when they contained references to the machine, they were characterized by decorative imagery rather than the abstract machine forms embraced by the purists. The gates that guarded the entrance to the executive suite of the Chanin building, a New York skyscraper, provide a good example (plate 31.3). The zigzag lines and lightning bolts suggest the energy of the modern world, the cogs and wheels represent the machinery that actually powers it, and the stacks of coins on which they all rest attest to the healthy economy that metaphorically fuels the entire operation.

The exhibitions discussed earlier demonstrate the ways that designers celebrated the modern world. At the American Designers' Gallery in 1928, ten designers installed complete room settings and many others displayed groups of objects. Donald Deskey's 'Man's Smoking Room' received enormous acclaim (plate 31.4). His furnishings seemed the embodiment of the modern: the lines were horizontal (which was deemed 'expressive of the style of today'), the forms geometric and rhythmic – the

31.4 Donald Deskey, 'Man's Smoking Room' for the RCA Music Hall. Exhibited at the 1928 American Designers' Gallery exhibition, New York. Donald Deskey Collection, Cooper-Hewitt, National Design Museum, Smithsonian Institution.

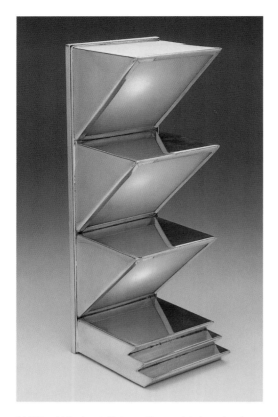

31.5 Donald Deskey, table lamp. Chrome-plated metal and glass. American, c.1927. Made by Deskey-Vollmer. Collection John P. Axelrod, Boston, MA. Courtesy Museum of Fine Arts, Boston.

lamp, in particular, a jazzy saw-tooth machine of chrome-plated steel and glass (plate 31.5).[15] While all the furnishings were produced to order, they were largely made of new or newly inexpensive materials that would soon enable modern design to be more accessible. When Deskey began collaborating with large manufacturers in the early 1930s, the materials used in the 'Man's Smoking Room' – aluminium for the ceiling, cork for the walls, chrome-plated metal for furniture, Vitrolite and Bakelite for the table tops, linoleum for the floor – would truly become indicators of modernity for the middle classes.

This vocabulary of angularity, of abstracted geometric forms, was recognized at the time as a commercial dissemination of the principles of Cubism. Assessing what he considered the dominant style of the Paris 1925 Exhibition, one reviewer declared, 'architects, furniture makers, and decorative designers uniformly apply the principles of composition introduced by Pablo Picasso, Georges Braque, and Juan Gris'.[16] In addition to Deskey, other American designers mastered these principles as well. At the American Designers' Gallery exhibition, Ilonka Karasz provided the cover of the catalogue and showed work in a wide range of media, among them Cubist-inspired silver plated vases, bowls and candlesticks (plate 31.6). Born and trained in Budapest, Karasz was well steeped in other currents of the avant-garde and manipulated them to form her own distinct style. A bold, sanserif Bauhaus typography distinguishes her catalogue cover; textile designs reveal the influence of German Expressionist painting as well as traditional folk art. Karasz was the only woman designer commissioned to supply complete rooms at the exhibition. Her geometric, brightly coloured children's nursery was considered 'one of the gayest, jolliest and most practical rooms ever designed for a child';[17] Arts and Decoration declared it the first nursery 'ever designed for the very modern American child'.[18]

Many critics, designers and style-conscious consumers welcomed the adaptation of the latest European fashions, and they were convinced that these permutations could be developed 'into a distinctive and distinguished style as subtly different from its European inspiration as Early American furniture and interiors are different from their English and French ancestry'.[19] Even more desirable, however, would be a style that came more directly from the country's own experiences and achievements. By 1930, many articles and books addressed the issue of a distinctly American expression of modernity – what designer Paul Frankl called the 'new spirit manifest in every phase of American life'. As he elaborated in his influential book Form and Reform: A Practical Handbook of Modern Interiors: 'This spirit finds expression in skyscrapers, motor-cars, aeroplanes, in new ocean liners, in department stores and great industrial plants. Speed, compression, directness – these are its attributes.'[20]

Frankl was one of the designers who embraced the Manhattan set-back skyscraper as the building type that most captured the spirit of American innovation – and then adapted it to furnishings. With its characteristic form a response to a city ordinance requiring all buildings over a certain height to be set back so that light could reach the street, the skyscraper embodied civic pride, industrial prowess and a complete break with the past. Although Frankl's line of 'skyscraper' furniture was all custom made and, therefore, too expensive for wide distribution, it still reached a large audience through exhibitions and publications (plate 31.7). He displayed a whole room of skyscraper furniture at Macy's 1927 Art-in-Trade exhibition as well as at the American Designers' Gallery exhibition in 1928. Good Furniture was only one of many journals that wrote admiringly of the skyscraper line, declaring it was 'as American and as New Yorkish as Fifth Avenue itself'.[21] The skyscraper was depicted in every possible medium – ceramics, metalwork, textiles, paintings, photographs and prints as well as furniture.

31.6 Ilonka Karasz (born in Hungary), vase, bowl and candlestick. Silver-plated metal. American, c.1928. Cooper-Hewitt, National Design Museum, Smithsonian Institution.

31.7 Paul T. Frankl (born in Austria), desk and bookcase. Walnut, paint and brass handles. American, c.1928. For Frankl Galleries, New York City. Collection John P. Axelrod, Boston, MA. Courtesy Museum of Fine Arts, Boston.

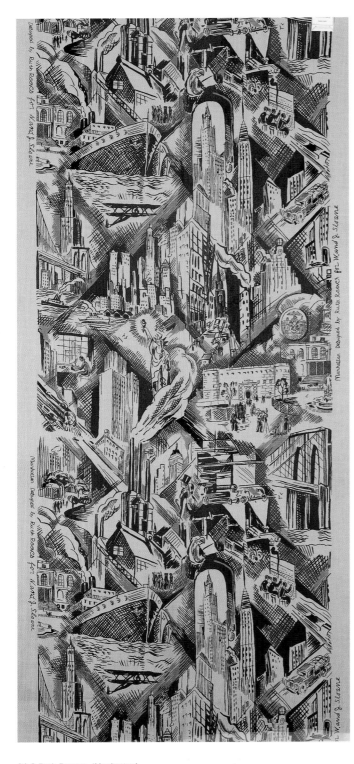

31.8 Ruth Reeves, 'Manhattan',
furnishing fabric. Block-printed
cotton. American, 1930. Made by
W. & J. Sloane. V&A: T.57-1932.

The 1920s were characterized not only by a
preoccupation with the skyscraper but also by a
giddy intoxication with the entire experience of city
life. Hugh Ferriss produced an ode to urban living
in his 1929 book *The Metropolis of Tomorrow*,
with its seductive drawings of skyscrapers and a
rhapsodic text. The German architect Erich
Mendelsohn celebrated the urban landscape (and
marvelled at grain elevators) in his book of
photographs, *Amerika*. But it was New York City that
epitomized the ultimate American urban experience.
In her textile 'Manhattan', Ruth Reeves used the
interpenetrating planes of Cubist design to create a
dynamic depiction of skyscrapers, the Statue of
Liberty, bridges, high-speed trains and aeroplanes
(plate 31.8).

Viktor Schreckengost's 'Jazz Bowl', with its
allusions to speakeasies, African-American music and
cocktail glasses, embodies the nervous energy – and
sometimes illicit pleasures – of the city (plate 31.9).
As the *New York Times* observed, 'Today is not
only an age of tall buildings, plain surfaces and
geometrical forms, but also of artificial lighting.'[22]
Without this technological marvel, the glamorous
nightlight depicted on the bowl, where radiant street
lamps loom over a clock recording 3:30 (presumably
3:30 in the morning), would not have been possible.
Schreckengost designed this bowl in 1931 while
working for the Cowan Pottery in Rocky River, Ohio,
which had received a commission from a woman who
wanted something 'New Yorkish'. After executing the
design, and receiving a request for two more like it,
Schreckengost learned both orders had come from

31.9 Viktor Schreckengost, punch
bowl from the 'Jazz Bowl' series.
Glazed porcelain with sgraffito
decoration. American, 1931.
Made by Cowan Pottery.
Gift of Susan Morse Hilles in
memory of Paul Hellmuth.
Museum of Fine Arts, Boston.
© Viktor Schreckengost.

Eleanor Roosevelt. Art historian Henry Adams recounts that, 'Franklin was making plans to run for president and she wanted a present to celebrate his victory, since she was sure he was going to win.'[23] The bowl received so much attention that Cowan Pottery put it into limited production. At least fifty were made, though all required laborious hand carving.

A dazzling combination of Cubist motifs and skyscraper imagery, the coffee service designed by Danish émigré silversmith Erik Magnussen for the silver company Gorham was considered a quintessential example of American Modernism (see plate 32.2). It was known as the 'Cubic' service and first displayed in November 1927 in Gorham's shop window on Fifth Avenue in New York. The following month, a New York Times article stated that the service had 'been poetically named "The Lights and Shadows of Manhattan" because of its suggestion of metropolitan architecture and the play of light over its variegated surfaces'.[24] The effect was spectacular: to enhance the faceted composition, Magnussen had gilded some of the silver panels to create highlights and oxidized others for dramatic contrast. He explained that his inspiration came from taking a plane ride over New York and finding that 'the entire city made a picture of triangular patches of sun and shadow'.[25] What could more eloquently express the modern – a form inspired by American building innovation, with specific imagery made possible by the new technology of air transportation, in a style called 'Cubic'. Although only one was ever made, the Gorham set became a Modernist icon. It was a prototype: the company had planned 'Cubic' as a line, and had also produced a salad set, spoon and fork, but it was much too expensive and perhaps too radical to generate other orders.

Not everyone loved the 'Cubic' service or the skyscraper style. Describing Magnussen's service, an editorial writer in the New Republic declared: 'Our skyscraper worship has produced some pretty sad results; but I think this cubistic claptrap in silver is about the worst I have seen.'[26] Even the almost worshipful interior decoration magazines, which had much to gain from an American conversion to the new style, had some reservations. In House Beautiful, critic Adolph Glassgold was relieved that Frankl had expanded his designs beyond skyscraper furniture 'which threatened for a time to become his symbol'. Glassgold did not consider the skyscraper line particularly appropriate for 'the development of the contemporary style in America, where simplicity and not dramatics is the great requisite'.[27]

However, imitations of the skyscraper style followed almost immediately after its introduction, and companies such as Bernard Rice's Sons made the style accessible by using less expensive materials like silver plate in their 'Apollo Sky-Scraper' line (see plate 32.3). The advertisement for the line epitomizes the marketing of the modern in America (plate 31.10). Within the bold outline of a set-back building, the text proclaims 'the Modernistic Movement is the expression of our modern scheme of life/ The sky-scraper is the inspiration of modernism/ Hence, the Apollo Sky-Scraper line'. Lest the reader not quite get the visual connection, the advertisement points out that the bodies of the silver-plated wares look like skyscrapers, 'with black smoke-stacks as handles'.

Since the eighteenth century, American life had been characterized by the belief that change was good and would lead to a better future, that one's destiny could be controlled by personal effort. Because of the nation's economic prosperity and ever-growing confidence in its role as a world leader, the belief in progress was particularly strong in the 1920s. It created an environment conducive to embracing the new, and the new was ubiquitous. The automobile, aeroplane, high-speed train and ocean liner had dramatically altered people's conception of distance. Instantaneous forms of communication – telephone, radio, film – were radically changing their experience of time and proximity to world events. In this respect, America was poised for the introduction of modern design.

Yet, along with the exhilaration of modernity, and despite Americans' long love affair with the new, came the natural fear about the rapidity and consequences of unprecedented technological innovation. As the historian Jeffrey Meikle has pointed out, one way to 'domesticate' modernity and make it more familiar was to miniaturize it; for example, to shrink the skyscraper and put it into the home as furniture or tableware.[28] Another way was to take the qualities that people associated with being American and apply them to the new modern style. During the 1920s, the periodicals, exhibition catalogues and books proselytizing for the adoption of modern design claimed that it was simple, useful and, above all, practical to be modern – these were all adjectives associated with the American spirit. It was not only a fashion statement, but also provided a way of being comfortable in the modern world. In a 1928 article for Vogue, the critic Helen Appleton Read maintained that twentieth-century design would need to pass through 'the filter of American taste' to develop into a distinctive form in the United States. Read's statement aptly summarizes America's role in refining European-originated modern design into a bold new expression of national identity.

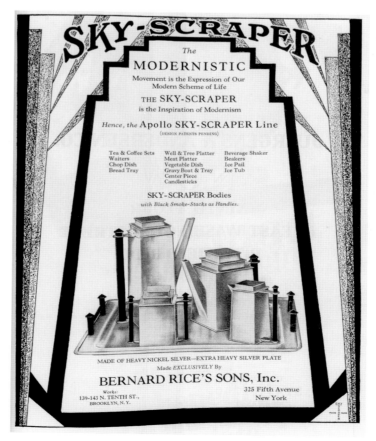

31.10 Advertisement for the 'Apollo Sky-Scraper' line made by Bernard Rice's Sons, Inc. The Keystone, May 1928. General Research Division, The New York Public Library. Astor, Lenox and Tilden Foundation.

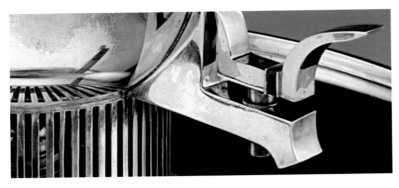

32 American Metalwork between the Wars

Jeannine Falino

Silversmithing and silver-plating firms in the north-eastern United States flourished during the 1920s, as disposable incomes rose and manufacturing costs remained constant or decreased. However, the Great Depression and the availability of inexpensive metal goods cut into the luxury market for silver.[1] Aluminium, pewter and chromium-plate manufacturers, such as Kensington Ware (founded 1934), Russel Wright, Inc. (founded 1935) and the Chase Brass & Copper Company (founded 1936), took advantage of this shift by selling attractively priced goods styled by leading designers. Chromium, known generally as chrome, was well suited to the machine age aesthetic, for it was characterized by a hard, reflective surface that needed no polishing, ideal for modern, servantless households.[2]

The field of domestic silver had changed considerably from previous decades, when an emphasis on hand craftsmanship during the Arts and Crafts era had briefly enabled studio artists to achieve some renown even as the larger manufacturing concerns such as Gorham and Tiffany continued to grow. By the 1930s, the few arts and crafts studios that continued in existence included the workshops of Arthur Stone in Gardner, Massachusetts, George Gebelein in Boston and the Danish émigré Peer Smed in New York, as well as the Kalo Shop of Chicago (founded 1900). Their designs were inspired by colonial forms, the Danish silver of Georg Jensen, or by an Arts and Crafts formula that continued to find a market among those who preferred the old fashioned comfort offered by pre-industrial styles.[3]

Progressive design ideas from France, Scandinavia and Central and Eastern Europe took root in America from the mid-1920s, as recent émigrés from these countries and regions began to participate in exhibitions and created stage sets, buildings and furnishings. The new waves of design that they introduced to the public were both exciting and strange to their American audience. It was not long, however, before these strains of influence developed into an American idiom that owed a debt to Scandinavian, Wiener Werkstätte and Bauhaus sources.

As in the Arts and Crafts period, small workshops of independent metalsmiths and teachers continued to thrive. Each of these artists developed their own personal interpretation of the evolving modern styles while remaining essentially true to traditional handcraft methods. For

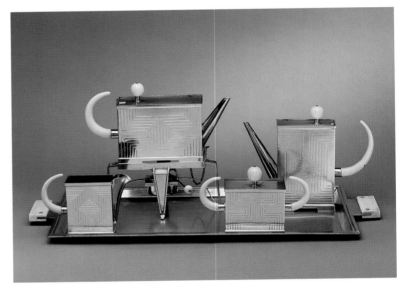

32.1 Peter Müller-Munk (born in Germany), tea service. Silver and ivory. American, 1931. Gift of Mr and Mrs Herbert R. Isenburger, 1978. The Metropolitan Museum of Art, New York.

example, American-born Janet Payne Bowles of Indianapolis, Indiana, produced an idiosyncratic body of work that was, in turn, organic and geometric in form. Marie Zimmermann of New York and William Brigham of Providence, Rhode Island, created vessels and jewellery that often incorporated jade or other exotic elements.[4] Arthur Neville Kirk, a professor of the London Central School of Arts and Crafts, taught at the Cranbrook Academy of Art in Michigan, but his Arts and Crafts aesthetic conflicted with the goals of the Modernist architect and designer Eliel Saarinen, who had been appointed President of the Academy in 1932, and he departed in 1936. Kirk was succeeded by Italian-born Harry Bertoia, who produced a distinctive body of volumetric forms.[5] Kansas-born Margaret Craver followed her education with specialized study at the workshops of several silversmiths and jewellers, including that of Arthur Stone. She went on to a long and fruitful career in her field as a teacher, silversmith and jeweller.[6]

32.2 Erik Magnussen (born in Denmark), 'Cubic', coffee service, or 'The Lights and Shadows of Manhattan'. Silver, silver gilt and oxidized silver. American, 1927. Made by Gorham Manufacturing Co. Museum of Art, Rhode Island School of Design, Providence. Gift of Textron Inc.

32.3 Louis W. Rice, 'Skyscraper', cocktail shaker. Electroplated nickel silver. American, 1928. Made by Bernard Rice's Sons, Inc. John C. Waddell Collection. Promised gift of John C. Waddell. The Metropolitan Museum of Art, New York.

Among Central and Northern European émigrés, Peter Müller-Munk of Germany was especially influential. He arrived in New York about 1926 and created a small body of custom silverware until economic conditions forced him into the field of industrial design. His early hollowware revealed an interest in strong rectilinear shapes with unexpected curvilinear contrasts (plate 32.1). Müller-Munk's chrome-plated 'Normandie' water pitcher of 1935 (see plate 34.7), fashioned after the ocean liner's teardrop-shaped smokestack and manufactured by the Revere Copper and Brass Company (founded 1929), was his most celebrated design.[7]

A modern neo-classical style was advanced by another émigré, the Dane Erik Magnussen, who worked briefly for Georg Jensen before moving to Gorham in 1925. Magnussen created 'The Modern American' service for Gorham, which was simply ornamented with a triglyph-style border on smooth cylindrical and conical forms.[8] The line was intended for conservative consumers who were seeking modestly updated styles. Modernized neo-classical forms based upon the Grecian column were developed by a range of designers, including Ilonka Karasz for Paye & Baker (founded 1901) and Walter von Nessen, whose 'Diplomat' service was produced by Chase Brass & Copper Company. A hand-wrought silver service in a faceted columnar design may have been one of the few uncharacteristically Art Deco designs ever fashioned by Arthur Neville Kirk.[9]

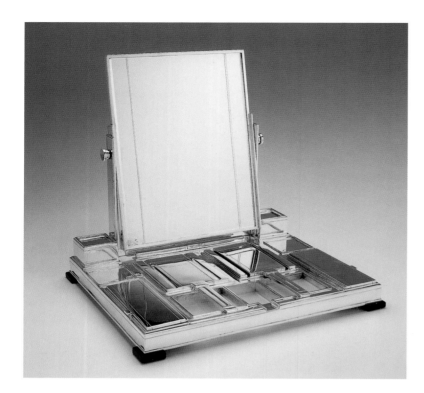

32.4 Tiffany & Co., vanity set. Silver, mahogany and velvet. American, 1935. Collection John P. Axelrod, Boston, MA. Courtesy Museum of Fine Arts, Boston.

32.5 Norman Bel Geddes, 'Manhattan', cocktail set. Chrome-plated brass. American, 1937. Made by Revere Copper & Brass Company. Gift of John C. Waddell, 1998. The Metropolitan Museum of Art, New York.

Far more radical than the soothing lines of 'The Modern American' was Magnussen's 'Cubic' coffee service of 1927, a sharply angled and richly gilt extravaganza that looked to Cubist paintings for its inspiration (plate 32.2). Dubbed 'The Lights and Shadows of Manhattan' by the New York Times, 'Cubic' garnered favourable media attention for Gorham, but proved too avant-garde for public consumption.[10] At least one variation on 'Cubic' was attempted on a simpler scale. Designer Elsa Tennhardt patented a bold triangular template in 1928 that could be employed in the fabrication of vessels. She then created a series of shapes based around the triangle and used them in a silver-plated brass cocktail set, salts, a centrepiece and matching candlesticks. These pieces were manufactured by the E. and J. Bass Company of New York.[11]

The growth of skyscrapers in New York prompted a parallel development of similar vertical forms in domestic goods, most notably in the furniture of Paul Frankl (see plate 31.7). Among American silver manufacturers, the skyscraper form served several functions. Louis Rice, president of Bernard Rice's Sons (founded about 1899), developed a line of silver-plated 'Skyscraper' tableware (plate 32.3), whose vessels were unadorned rectangles capped with set-back forms that echoed New York architecture. In contrast, Tiffany & Co. produced a smooth façade for their silver vanity set (plate 32.4). Like so many small buildings, the base of the vanity is composed of squares that mark the places of brush, hand mirror, containers and ashtray that lie below a monolithic, tilting mirror.

Other designers chose to mass their vessels in order to emulate clusters of skyscrapers, as in the 'Diament' coffee service created in the late 1920s by Gene Theobald for the Wilcox Silver Plate Company (founded 1865).[12] In such cases, a coffee pot forms the central focus, flanked by supporting forms such as sugar bowls and creamers. A shaped serving tray held the group in a fixed arrangement. A more flexible design was offered by Norman Bel Geddes in his chrome 'Manhattan' service (plate 32.5), manufactured by Revere Copper & Brass Company, which made use of a tall, cylindrical

cocktail shaker and simple cylindrical stemmed cups.[13] Bel Geddes's stepped serving tray, 'Manhattan', was sold with the service to create a plaza-like set design on which the cocktail service could be arranged like so many architectural elements.[14]

Streamlined forms, with soft curves and an emphasis on horizontal banding and spheres, found favour with numerous designers, among them Russel Wright, Paul Lobel and Eliel Saarinen (plate 32.6). Wright was among the first to experiment with a sphere and cylinder design in 1931 when he designed a cocktail shaker and cups made of spun, chrome-plated pewter. The Metropolitan Museum of Art's 1934 exhibition on industrial design featured a spherical beverage service designed and made by Lobel. Also seen in the same exhibition was a futuristic orb-like coffee urn and tray in silver designed by Eliel Saarinen. A variant of the urn was designed several years later by Walter Von Nessen in chrome and manufactured in 1938 by the Chase Brass & Copper Company.[15] The sphere embodied contradictory ideas and emotional responses, signifying the comfort of the womb and at the same time a desire for planetary exploration. These globular and angular vessels of the 1920s and 1930s may have anticipated the celebrated Perisphere of the 1939 New York World Fair which stood beside the rocket-shaped Trylon, whose piercing form was emblematic of an adventurous modern age (see plate 40.1).

32.6 Eliel Saarinen (born in Finland), tea and coffee urn and tray. Electroplated nickel silver, brass and Bakelite. American, c.1934. Made by International Silver Company, Wilcox Silver Plate Company Division. Purchase, Mr & Mrs Ronald Saarinen Swanson and John C. Waddell Gifts, and Gift of Susan Dwight Bliss, by exchange, 1999. The Metropolitan Museum of Art, New York.

The aerodynamic aspect of the streamline style was pursued by Bel Geddes in his 'Soda King' siphon bottle. The vessel's missile shape is similar to the pencil sharpener designed by Raymond Loewy, yet the airflow design was an illogical choice for these stationary objects (plate 32.7). For these designers, and the others who worked for Reed & Barton (founded 1840), International Silver (founded 1898) and Towle Silversmiths (founded 1882) – to name but a few of the most prominent manufacturers – the irrelevance of the design to the function of these objects was of little consequence. Their role was to create demand for merchandise by dressing traditional objects in new, exciting and affordable garb.

The variety of Art Deco design in metalwork offered consumers the opportunity to select a form of their choosing for use in the home or office. Produced in silver, pewter, aluminium or chrome plate, and priced accordingly, these objects brought modern designs to a wide audience.

32.7 Raymond Loewy (born in France), prototype pencil sharpener. Metal. American, 1933. © Christie's Images Ltd 2000.

33.1 Edgar Brandt, *Oasis*, screen.
Iron and brass. French, *c.*1924.
Private collection, Paris.
© Christie's Images Ltd 2000.
© ADAGP, Paris and DACS,
London 2002.

33 New Materials and Technologies

Jeffrey L. Meikle

Some historians emphasize Art Deco as an exotic flowering of intricate veneers and Fauve-inspired patterns. Others, pointing out the stylized precision of much Art Deco, regard it as a stimulus to frankly decorative, machine-oriented design vocabularies. Although many classic examples, ranging from cigarette cases to skyscrapers, display figurative or representational motifs, they often intentionally exploit inherent aesthetic qualities of particular materials. While French Art Deco favoured rare traditional materials worked by skilled craft methods (see plate 1.4), American designers tended to rely on new materials and technologies. Even so, European and American variants were closely linked. Although the decorative motifs of French Art Deco inspired American designers, specifically American references soon emerged. As the style was democratized, designs for batch or mass production echoed surface effects that were typical of expensive French Art Deco designs (see Chapter 31).

The metalworker Edgar Brandt afforded a link between the Paris 1925 Exhibition and the machine-age future envisioned by New York designers. His exquisite wrought iron screens revealed an assembly-line repetition of forms derived partly from mechanical stamping processes. Employing a hundred designers, drafters and artisans, Brandt relied on oxyacetylene-torch welding and on the newer electric-shot welding process to join the complex pieces of assemblages without heating them at the forge. He obtained varied effects of colour and hue by electroplating with brass, silver, zinc and nickel. Brandt's most impressive exhibit at Paris was *Oasis*, an exotic five-panel screen fabricated from iron and bronze. Its flat, stylized shapes represented water jets cascading from a high central fountain against a backdrop of palm leaves, with low floral bushes spreading to either side (plate 33.1). Brandt's decorative use of metallic surfaces and textures was compelling. The intricacy of fountain and flowers contrasted with the bronze smoothness of palm leaves. Their precision invited viewers to think beyond organic references towards an inorganic realm of radiating force lines, gears and rotating propellers – suggested as much by the decorative effects of refined surfaces, incised lines and repeating metal patterns as by formal analogies to modern technology.

The very materials of Brandt's work appealed to Americans seeking to express decoratively the spirit of the machine age. Brandt capitalized on this interest by opening Ferrobrandt, a New York studio that created interior grilles, lighting fixtures and hardware for Manhattan's new skyscrapers. Even more resonant with modern times was the work of Rene Chambellan, a sculptor from New Jersey who fabricated heating grilles, figurative bas-reliefs and other interior accents for the lobby of the Chanin building. His wrought iron and bronze gates at the entrance to the executive suite on the 52nd floor effectively reinterpreted Brandt's *Oasis* screen for an American context (see plate 31.3). Zigzag lines radiate in a burst of energy waves from a central point at the bottom of the gates. Concentric arcs suggest giant flywheels. Framing the gates are narrow panels portraying intermeshed cogwheels. Despite the bold symbolism, the gleaming material also spoke for itself, as it did in other American wonders of the age, like the Chrysler building with its soaring science-fiction spire of stainless steel, as much an icon of modernity as the Bauhaus (see plate 5.1).

An Austrian émigré designer, Paul Frankl, claimed that had the United States exhibited a full-sized skyscraper at the Paris Exhibition, 'it would have been a more vital contribution in the field of modern art than all the things done in Europe added together'.[1] Quick to adapt the French style to the 'new American tempo',[2] he provoked controversy in the late 1920s with his so-called 'skyscraper' furniture (see plate 31.7). Although Frankl applied traditional veneers and lacquers to his custom furniture's symbolic forms, he also portentously referred to 'materia nova', maintaining that Bakelite, aluminium, Monel metal alloy and Vitrolite glass comprised 'the vernacular of the twentieth century'. With 'base materials ... transmuted into marvels of new beauty' through science and engineering, designers now had 'to create the grammar of these new materials'. Above all, he insisted, 'new materials demand new forms' because 'a new technique of living requires a dress consistent with itself'.[3] In these last two clauses, Frankl seemed to confuse substance with surface. Would designers indeed use innovative technologies to create unprecedented forms, or would they merely use new materials in old ways for decorative effect?

33.2 Eugene Schoen, étagère. Bakelite, bronze and chestnut wood. American, 1929. Gift of Robert and Meryl Feltzer Fund. The Metropolitan Museum of Art, New York.

Critics often attacked new materials, especially plastics, as imitative substitutes for natural substances. Celluloid had long served as a substitute for ivory and tortoiseshell, with manufacturers devising ingenious visual simulations. Even Bakelite, a hard, durable, synthetic plastic marketed as the 'material of a thousand uses', initially substituted for hard rubber and shellac. Many early Art Deco applications of new materials simply replaced the old with the new for purely decorative purposes, as when Bakelite replaced ebony for drawer pulls or the handles of tea and coffee urns. Even a piece of furniture like Eugene Schoen's étagère of 1929, a dynamic, asymmetrical, semi-Constructivist assemblage of horizontals and verticals arranged in apparent defiance of gravity, displayed a use of plastic that might be considered imitative (plate 33.2). More radical in form than Frankl's skyscraper bookcases, it had smooth reflective surfaces of thin black Bakelite laminate visually indistinguishable

from the lacquer Frankl had used on his own furniture. However, the front edges of shelves and partitions were trimmed with chrome-plated strips whose industrial sheen accented the artificiality of Bakelite. Schoen was striving to devise a vocabulary balanced between the decorative and functional uses of new materials.

Other American designers with similar goals included Gilbert Rohde and Donald Deskey. Each was inspired by French Art Deco, with Deskey attending the 1925 Exhibition and Rohde visiting Paris afterwards. Each was also attracted by contemporary German Modernism and became involved in adapting the purist aesthetic of Marcel Breuer's and Mies van der Rohe's chromed-steel tubular chairs to a visually and physically more comfortable standard. They were not alone, as numerous American and European designers sought to moderate the Bauhaus model. The German Hans Luckhardt, for example, designed a sweeping cantilevered adjustable tubular armchair

33.3 Hans and Wassili Luckhardt, tubular chair. Chromed steel and painted wood. German, 1931. For DESTA, from the music room of the Maharaja of Indore's palace. V&A: W.49-1984.

as part of an ensemble for the Maharaja of Indore (plate 33.3). And Kem Weber, a German émigré in Los Angeles, designed a leather-upholstered armchair in 1934 with seat and slanted back suspended left and right between extravagantly teardrop-shaped open loops of chromed-steel (with each loop composed of three tubes running side by side). Rohde and Deskey were usually not so extravagant. Neither wandered far from the Bauhaus model while also insisting on comfort. Both employed various materials, including standard chromed 'bicycle' tubing and flat steel bands curved in tension. Both also experimented with cast frames and legs of lightweight, durable aluminium – a metal only recently inexpensive enough for everyday use. As a trade journal observed, aluminium enjoyed the status of its use in 'airplanes, dirigibles, motor cars, [and] truck bodies' even though it was also, to be sure, 'a decorative metal'.[4] Surfaces were chromed, bronzed, brushed, polished or otherwise invested with what seemed a perfect industrial finish. Both Rohde and Deskey employed moulded armrests of Bakelite, whose warm touch alleviated the discomfort of cold, narrow metal arms. In custom work and in batch-

33.4 Donald Deskey, model dining room for the 1934 exhibition *Contemporary American Industrial Art*, New York. The Metropolitan Museum of Art, New York.

produced furniture, both designers highlighted the contrast of gleaming metal and black Bakelite, which was used to best effect, often under the Formica trade name, as a laminated surface for cabinetry and table tops.

This relatively sober American approach to Art Deco was epitomized in Deskey's model dining room for an exhibition entitled *Contemporary American Industrial Art* at the Metropolitan Museum of Art in 1934 (plate 33.4). Along one side, however, ran a wall of translucent glass brick lit from behind. As another designer observed, such a wall 'sparkles and shimmers softly with an ever-changing radiance'.[5] But this was no gossamer substance. Glass, one of

humanity's oldest materials, assumed a new guise as a product of modern engineering, with the 'structural stability of masonry' and a capacity for encapsulating the pristine artificiality of modern interiors.[6] Used mostly in public or industrial buildings, where it blocked workers from distracting views or prevented outsiders from looking past a gleaming facade into a cluttered factory or warehouse, glass brick also lent itself to decorative accents around entrances of retail establishments.

As retailers across the United States and elsewhere sought to improve appearances, both to keep up with cosmopolitan trends and to stimulate business after the stock market crash of 1929, they turned to coloured glass exterior wall panels with stainless steel fittings as a way 'to modernize main street'.[7] Among the American contenders in the glass industry was Libby-Owens-Ford, who offered Vitrolite glass, one of Frankl's key 'materia nova', in a range of colours from light pastels to deep purple and black. In 1935 the company sponsored an architectural competition for the use of Vitrolite in storefront design. Winning entries employed contrasting colour fields, horizontal display windows ending in semicircles, inward-curving entrances, horizontal metal accent lines and Moderne lettering in gleaming or brushed metal projecting from reflective glass surfaces – all arranged in two-dimensional compositions suggesting stylized variants of French Art Deco exteriors from 1925. The designer Walter Dorwin Teague, whose office prepared storefront prototypes for the Pittsburgh Plate Glass Company, predicted an 'all-glass house ... inside and out, glass furniture and equipment, colorful, translucent, hygienic', with 'glass pipes' to 'eliminate the hidden horrors that lurk in our so-called "sanitary" plumbing'.[8] Such wonders never materialized; nor did American designers ever use glass in furniture so dramatically as the British designer Denham Maclaren, whose gravity-defying armchair suspended a heavy-looking zebra skin seat and back cushion between two sharply angled slabs of transparent glass (plate 33.5). The most impressive American use of glass was the architect George Fred Keck's three-storey Crystal House for Chicago's *Century of Progress Exposition* in 1934. Framed in steel with

33.5 Denham Maclaren, chair. Glass and zebra skin. British, 1931. V&A: W.26-1979.

reinforced concrete floors and roof, it had walls – inside and out – of transparent or translucent plate glass. Although Keck attracted considerable publicity, his engineering approach remained a minority position in a culture that preferred to see technological progress signified by the familiar surface treatments of machine-age Art Deco.

The allure of new materials was also represented at the *Century of Progress*, in mosaics celebrating the Westinghouse Electric Company (plate 33.6). The background material in each panel was black Micarta laminate manufactured by Westinghouse. Images were composed of pieces of aluminium in several shades of silver and bronze. Although the bright lines and forms seemed to project from the dark background, aluminium and Micarta were seamlessly fitted to present a smooth surface. If the fabrication suggested the artificial perfection of the machine, so too did the mosaic's themes and forms. For example, a classically stylized male figure dominates the centre of a triptych devoted to railway electrification. At his feet, thick lightning bolts rise diagonally from a circular device signifying a turbine. The energy of the turbine is transmitted to driving wheels represented symmetrically in the mosaic's side panels by three concentric circles, each associated with a tiny electric locomotive moving outwards from the centre. As a composition, this mosaic, with its stylized

abstractions of mechanized power and its central source from which all benefit flows, recalls both Chambellan's gates for the Chanin building and Brandt's *Oasis* screen. Unlike those earlier celebrations, however, this was intended for an audience of ordinary citizens. As Art Deco became a democratic style, moving from custom furniture and architectural decoration to the stuff of everyday life, its development passed to a different sort of designer oriented economically as well as aesthetically, with different ideas about how to exploit new materials.

The commercial design profession of the 1930s relied on Bakelite and other plastics as durable materials cheaper to process and assemble than wood, brass, iron or steel. An American industrial designer described his profession as a 'depression baby', meaning that it answered manufacturers' pleas for new product designs to stimulate consumption during hard times.[9] The business magazine *Fortune* likewise referred to the plastics industry as a 'child of the depression'.[10] Designers' comments about plastics reflected their own attitudes about the shaping of consumer products. While Lurelle Guild recommended plastics as ideal for 'tricking up design',[11] Teague insisted there was 'no need to apologize for a material that can be moulded in many different forms, that is hard, durable, colorful, light, pleasant to the touch and relatively

inexpensive'.[12] Whatever the case, it was true, as the German émigré designer Peter Müller-Munk recalled, that plastics became 'the hallmark of "modern design" ... the mysterious and attractive solution for almost any application requiring "eye appeal"'.[13]

Bakelite itself was a trade name for a phenol formaldehyde resin for which Leo Baekeland, a Belgian émigré chemist, had received a patent in 1909. He had already licensed its production in Germany, with Great Britain and other European countries soon to follow. As a thermosetting resin, Bakelite became hard, durable and chemically inert under intense heat and pressure. Used as a liquid to saturate stacked sheets of paper, it yielded a thin, hard, laminated surfacing material. Reinforced with wood flour, asbestos or powdered slate, it could be moulded under pressure into complex shapes (limited to dark hues that concealed the fillers). When cast as a liquid and cured under pressure, phenol formaldehyde could assume a complete range of rich colours. The Catalin brand of cast phenolic yielded long rods, variously shaped in section, from which colourful buckles, napkin rings and bracelets could be 'sliced' and then cut, incised or polished using small power tools. After Baekeland's patents expired in 1927, several suppliers produced the resins used by small moulding and fabricating companies to make plastic parts for consumer goods. Other new

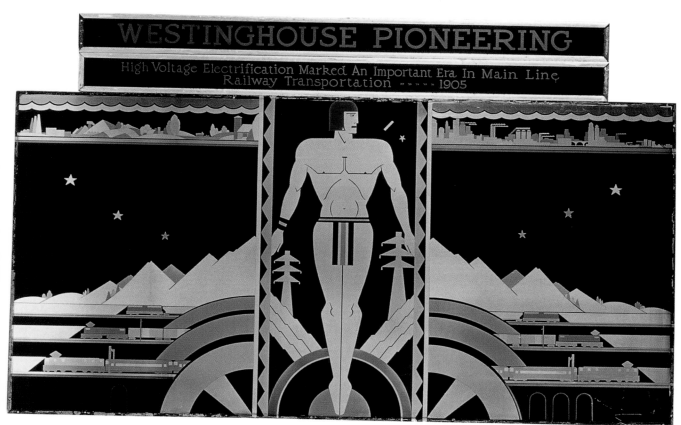

33.6 *High-Voltage Railway Electrification*, mosaic panel. Aluminium and Micarta laminate. American, 1933. From the Westinghouse pavilion at the 1933 *Century of Progress Exposition*, Chicago. The Mitchell Wolfson Jr Collection, The Wolfsonian-Florida International University, Miami Beach, Florida.

33.7 Fisk Radiolette, model 33.
Black and green phenolic. Australian,
c.1936. Harold Van Doren and John
Gordon Rideout, Air-King radio.
Plaskon urea formaldehyde.
American, c.1934.
Made by Air-King Products Company.
Collection Jeffrey S. Salmon, London.

33.8 Fada Bullet or Streamliner,
model 115. Catalin. American, 1940s.
Made by Fada Radio & Electric Co.
Inc. V&A: W.26-1992.

synthetics, thermoplastic materials such as cellulose acetate, polyvinyl chloride and polystyrene, were nearing commercialization by 1939. Although their cheapness and lack of durability gave plastics a dubious reputation after the Second World War, Bakelite was marketed and widely accepted as a machine-age miracle material during the 1930s.

Manufacturers adopted plastic to enclose consumer products like small table radios. The use of a one-piece moulded cabinet eliminated expensive hand assembly. Moulds were machined from solid blocks of case-hardened steel and designers quickly learned that geometric shapes entailed less work and expense than intricate shapes. The moulding process thus encouraged designers to select simplified Art Deco forms and motifs. One of the earliest table radios was the Air-King, designed by Harold Van Doren and John Gordon Rideout and moulded from Plaskon urea formaldehyde, a synthetic resin chemically similar to Bakelite that was developed to enable the moulding of colour-fast pastels, ivory and other light hues (plate 33.7, right). The cabinet of the Air-King radio, introduced in 1933, was the largest single-piece compression moulding yet produced in the United States. Its dramatic vertical form consisted of a central pylon flanked by two receding set-backs on each side. A band of seven sharply incised parallel ribs extended up the front, creating a crenellated effect inspired by the only Art Deco skyscraper in Toledo, Ohio, which the designers viewed daily from their office windows. A similar set-back skyscraper motif marked the boxy Fisk Radiolette, an Australian model with a cabinet of black phenolic plastic (plate 33.7, left). Its accents in luminescent green were probably machined from cast phenolic. Ironically imitating jade, these accents included stubby feet and a fretwork speaker grille featuring stylized French Deco motifs.

As the 1930s progressed, moulded plastic housings shifted from vertically oriented, geometric skyscraper forms to horizontal forms with rounded corners and edges. While the curvilinear forms of some radios directly echoed those of streamlined trains and aeroplanes, one of the most directly representational radios was the Silvertone Turbine model of 1938. It was designed by Clarence Karstadt for Sears, Roebuck, with an industrially smooth, black cabinet evoking the form of an electrical turbine with cooling fins and spinning rotor. For the most part, however, the trend in plastic cabinet design during the 1930s was towards more abstracted, streamlined shapes. The Ekco model AD65 radio designed by Wells Coates in 1934 and the Radio Nurse intercom designed by Isamu Noguchi in 1937 seemed quite distinct in this

regard – the former revealing an essentially flat, circular composition, the latter a fully-rendered sculptural whole. Such curvilinear plastic radios perfectly expressed a relatively new technology and communications medium. Perhaps best known is the Fada Bullet or Streamliner, introduced briefly in 1941 but not widely sold until 1946 (plate 33.8). Viewed from the front, its semicircular right side frames a round tuning dial, with moulded-in speed lines flowing horizontally to the left through the speaker openings and then wrapping around the left side. Although the Bullet evokes the speed of communication conflated with that of transportation, its form is abstract rather than representational. Despite its fame, the Bullet is not typical of most plastic radios. Its cabinet, available in dramatically contrasting colours, was assembled from several pieces of cast phenolic instead of being moulded in one single piece.

The forms of most curvilinear radios were functional as well as expressive. Plastic moulders preferred to work with generously curved shapes. A rounded mould for a one-piece cabinet was easier to machine than one displaying the geometric ribs and set-backs of the early 1930s. It facilitated the even flow of molten resin during the moulding process. A curved plastic piece could be removed more easily from the mould and was more easily polished. Its rounded form, devoid of corners or points, was durable under conditions of use. Technically, as a plastics executive noted in 1935, streamlining approached 'the ideal contour which designers have always claimed that plastics should take'.[14] The use of plastics also transformed designers' aesthetic conceptions of their work. Müller-Munk observed that the 'large flowing curves' of plastic were leading designers to abandon a 'purely façade type of design' in favour of 'a really

plastic conception of the machine as an object to be seen from all angles'.[15] It is remarkable how much the impact of popular design revolved around the modern materials employed. As economic and technical factors dictated ever more limited, stylized and abstracted decorative motifs for consumer goods, attention remained focused, as before, on surface rather than substance, on the rich depth of Bakelite's integral colours or on the highlights reflected from its wide-radius curves. The machine-age world was one of evocative surfaces and textures that afforded their own ornament.

A similar shift in decoration and ornament from figurative or iconic reference to an emphasis on surface qualities of new materials occurred in objects made primarily of metal. A classic example of the earlier approach in a traditional metal is the Zephyr clock attributed to Kem Weber (see plate 10.13). Its low, sleek brass case, with a 'ribbon window' displaying the time digitally on revolving plastic tumblers, was little more than a rectangular box. However, the designer provided the case with two interlocking curves, accented with indented speed lines across the front. While not literally representing anything, these devices drew attention to a common perception of time accelerating. Other examples of durable consumer goods – manufactured from aluminium for its ease of casting and extreme lightness compared with brass or steel – revealed industrial designers endowing even the most functional objects with symbolic import. Lurelle Guild designed an Electrolux vacuum cleaner, model 30, whose horizontal aluminium tube, accented with cast-in speed lines and slanted at the front, recalled a streamlined passenger train (plate 33.9). More iconic than representational was the Waterwitch, an

33.9 Lurelle Guild, vacuum cleaner, model 30. Chrome-plated steel, aluminium, vinyl and rubber. American, 1937. Made by Electrolux. Collection of John C. Waddell. Photo courtesy of the Metropolitan Museum of Art, New York.

33.10 John R. Morgan, Waterwitch outboard motor. Steel, aluminium and rubber. American, 1936. Made by Sears, Roebuck & Co. Gift of John C. Waddell, 1998. The Metropolitan Museum of Art, New York.

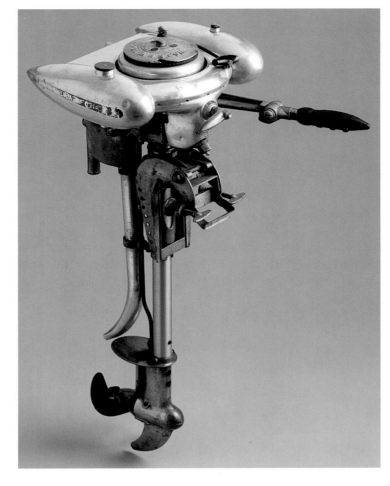

33.11 Russel Wright, spherical vase, planter and cocktail shaker. Spun aluminium and cork. American, c.1932. John C. Waddell private collection. Promised gift to the Metropolitan Museum of Art, New York. The Metropolitan Museum of Art, New York.

outboard motor designed by John R. Morgan, an in-house designer at Sears, Roebuck (plate 33.10). Although the typical weekend fisherman probably did not consult style trends when purchasing a motor for his boat, Morgan created an object later praised by the art historian Richard Guy Wilson as a piece of 'machine age sculpture'.[16] With a semi-circular engine housing flanked by two teardrop fuel tanks, it reminded later generations of the starship *Enterprise* in *Star Trek*. In 1936, however, it brought boating some of the glamour of modern transportation.

Although many American Art Deco products of the 1930s, from irons to refrigerators, made reference to recognizable formal analogues, other objects fabricated from aluminium relied for their attractive-ness almost entirely on the surface qualities of their material. Noteworthy in this regard was the RCA Victor Special, a portable phonograph designed by John Vassos (plate 33.12). This high-style variation on the old fashioned hand-wound record player came mounted for high-impact resistance in a rectangular, round-edged aluminium case. Devoid of direct visual references to streamlined vehicles or other machine-age icons, the Special's every detail evoked modernity, especially the mirror inside the lid that, when open, enabled an operator to gauge visually how much playing time remained on a record. An owner of a Special could take pride in possessing a piece of equipment that looked as if it belonged on the *Graf Zeppelin* airship (see plate 29.11).

Even more dependent on the material itself for aesthetic effect were the pitchers, urns, cocktail shakers and other aluminium serving pieces spun by Russel Wright on his own lathe in the late 1920s and early 1930s (plate 33.11). Starting from thin, lightweight tubes of metal, the young artisan transformed the era's most high-tech material into objects whose delicacy belied the aura of the machine shop they retained. Although Wright rendered these pieces vaguely organic by stretching their forms and supplying them with wooden handles, such effects drew attention by contrast to the surface of the material itself, a muted silver-grey but enriched by finely brushed horizontal lines. As American designers adapted the luxurious motifs of Paris 1925 for a middle-class market, they retained Art Deco's central emphasis on decorative effects. However, economic constraints forced them to do more with less, to stylize mercilessly, to suggest rather than to execute, and finally to rely on innovative surface effects achieved with such new materials as aluminium, stainless steel, chrome plating and synthetic plastics, all of which depended on new technologies. The inherent tension between

33.12 John Vassos (born in Romania),
portable phonograph, model RCA Victor
Special. Aluminium, chrome plated steel,
plastic and velvet. American, c.1937.
Made by RCA. V&A: W.1-1997.

33.13 Walter Dorwin Teague, desk lamp. Bakelite and aluminium. American, 1939. Made by Polaroid Corporation. Gift of John C. Waddell, 2001. The Metropolitan Museum of Art, New York.

33.14 American diner, Massachusetts. Photo: Elliott Kaufman.

material and form is illustrated by a desk lamp designed by Teague in 1939 for the Polaroid Corporation (plate 33.13). Composed of three simple parts, the lamp possesses a small rounded base of matte black Bakelite, out of which rises a widening conical pillar of brushed aluminium supporting a flared Bakelite hood. If it were not for the hood's attenuated reference to the teardrop motif and the aluminium cone's dramatic angle, the lamp's simple forms would evoke the timeless purity that Le Corbusier sought in modern engineering. As it was, Teague, who greatly admired Le Corbusier, succeeded in so reducing the formal references of his design that anyone who seeks to explain the lamp's considerable aesthetic presence must recognize the decorative impact of contrasting silver and black materials in a composition that ultimately refers back not to Le Corbusier but to the 1925 Exhibition.

This attenuation of Art Deco under the influence of new materials and democratization attained full expression in the roadside diner, the most typical of American machine-age sites. Scores of such diners, loosely based on the railway dining car, were factory-built during the 1930s and trucked to cities and towns across the United States for final assembly. Anonymous designers outfitted them throughout with

modern materials. Diners often had stainless steel exteriors with glass brick curving around the ends or accenting entranceways; counter and table tops of easily maintained Formica laminate; linoleum floor tiles in geometric patterns; and squat round stools mounted on tubular steel shafts, their seats covered with Fabrikoid artificial leather and rimmed with chromed steel. Most obvious, surfacing all the interior walls and display cases, was the panelling of gleaming stainless steel (plate 33.14). Unable to afford any ornament beyond effects attainable through the inherent qualities of materials, designers of roadside diners often embossed this panelling with wavy patterns whose reflections vaguely suggested sunbursts, fantails and diagonal strafing lines. The designers most likely did not know they were echoing, in the most attenuated stylization possible, the forms of Chambellan's Chanin gates and even Brandt's *Oasis* screen. A weary traveller might allow drifting eye and reverie to follow these flowing patterns in stainless steel without ever actually discerning a representational form. In American Art Deco's most vernacular or populist site, the new materials of machine-age technology attained a state of decorative expression that approached the Modernist ideal of truth to materials.

34 The Search for an American Design Aesthetic: From Art Deco to Streamlining

Nicolas P. Maffei

Streamlining was not an American invention, but its widespread application in the 1930s to the design of vehicles and stationary consumer goods was America's distinctive contribution to the development of Art Deco. It emerged in the context of serious and often contentious discussions – which raged among American cultural commentators, museum curators, designers and others – concerning the need for an authentic national aesthetic to replace the United States' artistic dependence upon Europe. These debates were not new. Writing in 1935, the cultural historian Constance Rourke noted that America's 'obsession' with 'aesthetic fulfilment' originated 'almost from the close of the Revolution', and that the country's 'mixed attitudes' towards European culture expressed both 'our languishing wish to conform to European standards and our sensitive belligerence'.[1] However, they were given a new impetus in the inter-war years by the impact of the Paris 1925 Exhibition (see Chapter 31) and by the presence of a number of influential European-born designers. In 1924 the Austrian-born Paul Frankl, one of the key figures in the story of American inter-war design, opened a New York gallery where he showed the work of American and European designers. His own designs reflected and responded to modernity, which he viewed as a characteristically American phenomenon, writing that 'modernity and America have in fact come to mean, in the mind of the world, one and the same thing' (plate 34.2).[2] Frankl's best known designs are those for skyscraper bookshelves and desks, made in the late 1920s, which evoke the dynamism of the contemporary American city (see plate 31.7). After thirteen years in the United States, Frankl viewed himself as an American, writing 'we [the American people] ... have been rather reluctant in our welcome to the modern movement in the field of decorative arts'.[3]

Frankl's stress on his American pedigree was perhaps not surprising at this date. By 1929, the exhibitions of European applied art in American department stores and museums had prompted the question 'who are our designers?' This became the central concern of an editorial in *Good Furniture Magazine* that year.[4] Its author wrote that the great department store exhibits had 'ruffle[d] the placid surface of our industrial art'; it was only then that we 'started the search for talent in our own country to compete with the very evident European talent seen in the exhibits'. This particular author believed that 'an answer appeared in the textile field' in the form of the 'Americana' print series made by Stehli Silks (plate 34.3).[5] He did not, however, view designers like Frankl as American. Referring to the exhibits of modern decorative arts recently shown at department stores and elsewhere, he noted that there:

> we have the chance not only to see what American designers have done, but to compare with similar work by European designers. When Eugene Schoen, Joseph Urban, Paul Frankl, Lucian Bernhard, Winold Reiss and Pola Hoffmann appear in these showings of American designers, it should be remembered that, by years of training, practice and experience, this group is 'American' only in the matter of citizenship.[6]

This view was not unusual in the climate of nativism that existed in America in the 1920s and favoured the interests of the established inhabitants over those of immigrants. Created by a mixture of First World War propaganda, post-war immigration, labour unrest, political radicalism and the growth of the Ku Klux Klan, this climate resulted in immigration restrictions, 'Americanization' initiatives and deportation drives.

Proponents of a specifically American design presented their country in the late 1920s as underdeveloped but full of promise. In the same 1929 issue of *Good Furniture Magazine* N. C. Sanford reminded readers that modern European design was not adaptable to American conditions, writing that the public was 'baffled' by the 'constant series' of modern applied arts exhibits touring America from 'France, Germany, Austria, Italy and England'. 'In them', she wrote, people 'have found ... little of practical value for the American home.'[7] Sanford's conservatism was economically motivated; she

34.1 Kem Weber (born in Germany), airline chair. Wood and Naugahyde. American, 1934. Made by Airline Chair Company. Collection John P. Axelrod, Boston, MA.

34.2 Paul T. Frankl (born in Austria), dressing table. Lacquer, brass and mirrored glass. American, c.1930. Collection John P. Axelrod, Boston MA.

believed that the 'startling and bizarre' modern design of recent years had frightened the 'general public [which] was a bit shy'. Now, however, she felt that 'customer demand' was in the 'first formative stage' and that good American design struck a 'graceful compromise between tradition and modernism' which could appeal to this demand.[8] Her stance was in harmony with America's protectionist trade practices that would intensify during the Depression.

The critique of the new European design continued in the pages of *Good Furniture Magazine*. In May 1929 the design journalist Matlack Price penned a harsh attack against the German architect Bruno Paul and the German-American graphic artist Lucian Bernhard (see plate 15.2). Responding to the designers' statement that 'the whole interior is more important than any of its parts' and their 'announcement' that the designs were 'appropriate for the modern American interior', the author accused the European-born designers of 'standardization or regimentation'. Price promoted a more moderate approach, showing a marked preference for American goods with 'individuality' that were 'neither imported nor copied'.[9] However, at least in the pages of decorative arts magazines, such explicit nativist sentiment was quelled as the following decade witnessed increased naturalization and decreased immigration.[10]

Whereas writers in *Good Furniture Magazine* in the late 1920s had cautioned their readers against the work of Europeans and European émigrés, Paul Frankl proclaimed, in his book *Form and Re-Form* (1930), that both European émigré and native-born American designers had contributed to a vigorous modern American design movement. He wrote that 'our country assimilates artists of many countries – Hungarians, Russians, Germans, Viennese, Frenchmen, Japanese. *Je prends mon bien où je le trouve.*'[11] And he presented the work of a number of émigrés alongside that of native-born American designers.[12] By 1931 Adolph C. Glassgold could write that the exhibit by the American Union of Decorative Artists and Craftsmen (AUDAC) at the Brooklyn Museum proved that American design had coalesced into a 'powerful and conscious movement' which was no longer 'a series of sporadic explosions of individual whimsy'. AUDAC, which was formed in 1928 in Frankl's gallery in New York City, has been viewed as crucial to the development of a unified American design movement, despite the fact that many of its members were émigrés and its meetings were often held in German.[13] And, in contrast to conservative critics, Frankl claimed that 'extreme ideas in modernism are not all imported from Europe; artists of American stock are often the most daring radicals of the "left wing"'. He offered a list of

American extremists, including the ceramicist Henry Varnum Poor and the textile designer Ruth Reeves – 'who dares to be "profoundly passionately" herself'.[14] In an attempt to find a balance between extremism and human warmth, Frankl defined American radical design as courageous, passionate and uniquely personal.

While the idea that a unique quality of American design was 'strong personality' gained currency for a time, the 'harshness' and 'angularity' of many American Deco designs of the late 1920s were strongly criticized by Charles R. Richards, a tireless educator and leading promoter of design. Referring to a display of American 'rooms' in a recent New York department store exhibition, Richards wrote that most products of the 'new movement' in American design 'indicate either the effusions of insanity or the exuberance of adolescence'. He added that 'the highest expression of modernism is the highest expression of eccentricity' and that 'various European examples' of applied art shown 'at our great department stores in New York and elsewhere have left a very confusing impression on the public mind'. The result, he claimed, did not 'appeal to our American needs and tastes'.[15] Adopting a cyclical view of history, he saw this as a 'transition stage' that would be followed by a period of 'maturity and sanity', when design would become rational

34.3 Edward Steichen, 'Americana' print, 'Moth Balls and Sugar', dress fabric. Crêpe de Chine. American, 1927. For Stehli Silks Corporation. V&A: T.87P-1930.

and restful rather than insane and confused.

Ruth Reeves – singled out by Frankl for her individuality – is best known today for 'Manhattan', her cubistic textile design depicting an American cityscape (see plates 9.11 and 31.8). By the early Thirties, however, Reeves's work was increasingly presented as an example of the more moderate approach and referred to as 'agreeable', 'elegant' and 'individual'. Frankl, too, came to recognize the need for a more restful attitude, writing that 'Simple lines are modern. They are restful to the eye and dignified and tend to cover up the complexity of the machine age.'[16] His designs and those of Kem Weber of the early 1930s for simple, horizontal furniture reflected this belief (plate 34.1). A stress on 'charm' became a means of claiming equal status for

American design with that of Europe and of countering notions that the former was naturally brash. Thus, in 1932 Walter Dorwin Teague's designs for glass for Steuben were presented as 'casual', 'charming', 'subtle', 'poised and graceful', and of 'equal distinction' to those of Europe. They were described as 'modern' but 'not bizarre', as 'decidedly American as Orrefors is Swedish'.[17] Increasingly, American decorative arts journals showcased the work of American designers, presenting their work as equal in quality to that of European designers, as well as more appropriate to American tastes.

Not everyone accepted 'charm' as an essential element in modern American design, however. In an effort to put an end to being 'deceived by the external charms of decoration', an article in

the American Magazine of Art recommended the elimination of ornament and the reduction of an object to its 'primary form'.[18] In the following years the promoters of Modernist design would become even more vocal. Yet the notion of charm was not altogether lost; instead, it was transformed, with the rise of notions of styling. As Norman Bel Geddes, one of the leading stylists, observed, styling addressed the 'psychological' dimension of design to 'appeal to the consumer's vanity and play upon his

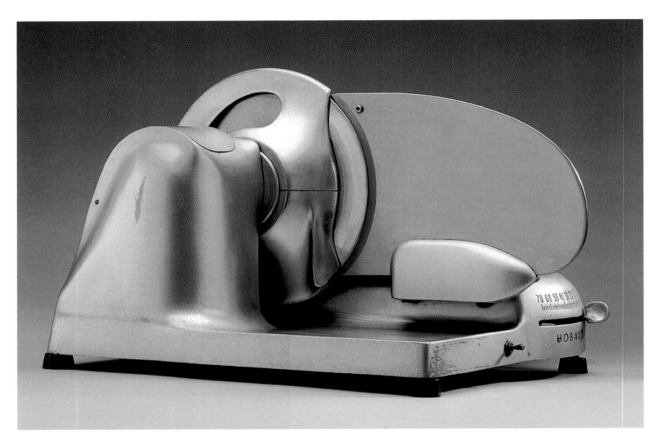

34.4 Egmont Arens and Theodore C. Brookhart, 'Streamliner', meat slicer. Aluminium, steel and rubber. American, designed in 1940. Made from 1944 by Hobart Manufacturing Company. Gift of John C. Waddell, 2002. The Metropolitan Museum of Art, New York.

imagination'.[19] One of the devices frequently deployed by stylists was streamlining; while offering a symbol of science and rationality, it was also used to appeal to irrational desires and thereby seduce potential customers.

After the 1929 stock market crash the need for mass production and for ways to appeal to the consumer by active salesmanship meant that new approaches to design were vigorously promoted. The example of annual fashion changes in Parisian couture intensified American manufacturers' and retailers' interest in the economic value of stylistic obsolescence. Towards the end of 1930 the *American Magazine of Art* published Earnest Elmo Calkins' plan for jumpstarting the economy. Calkins had founded the Calkins & Holden advertising agency in 1901 with Ralph Holden and had long been an ardent promoter of the cash value of art in industry. His article explained how consumer dissatisfaction could be generated through the styling of products – the 'new merchandising device' known as 'styling the goods'. Goods were to be 'redesigned in the modern spirit ... to make them markedly new, and encourage new buying'. This would result in the displacement of 'still useful' things which are now 'outdated, old-fashioned, obsolete'. The application of 'modern' design allowed products to express abstract qualities that consumers found irresistible and a 'new field',

that of the industrial designer, was emerging to facilitate this method of stylistic obsolescence.[20] In 1932 Calkins reiterated his views in Roy Sheldon and Egmont Arens' book, *Consumer Engineering*, stressing the need to manipulate psychologically consumers' 'latent and unsuspected demands and desires' by using styling to raise goods 'from the commonplace to the distinctive'. The book also recommended the use of psychology to reduce friction at the point of sale and thus 'streamline' consumption (plate 34.4).[21]

The adoption of such views by American manufacturers in the early 1930s aided the success of the emergent genre of the 'industrial designer' or 'stylist'. Often decorative, theatrical and advertising artists by background, they included Walter Dorwin Teague, Norman Bel Geddes, Henry Dreyfuss, Harold Van Doren and the French-born Raymond Loewy. This first generation of American industrial designers opened their offices in the late 1920s, often finding clients through advertising agencies and self-promotion. They came to be seen as the logical and mature leaders of the country's indigenous design movement, who had 'grown up' past the need for 'childish effort' in decoration.[22] It was with the promotion and development of their work, spurred on by the increased commercial competition during the Depression, that the self-conscious comparisons

of American and European design began to wane. An emphasis on styling to promote mass consumption and mass production came to be seen as the hallmark of American design.

Harold Van Doren, a leading first generation industrial designer, wrote that the term 'streamline' first appeared in print in 1873 in reference to hydrodynamics, and that by 1909 automobile manufacturers were using the term to refer to the 'sweeping lines' of their products.[23] Although streamlining was eventually widely adopted for the design of consumer goods and services, it made its greatest impact on the public imagination in the area of transportation (see Chapter 29). By the early 1930s American railroad companies had lost many of their passengers as a result of the Depression and increased competition from automobiles, buses and aeroplanes. Several companies introduced streamlined locomotives and rolling stock to modernize and make more glamorous the image of their services. Streamlined trains, such as the Union Pacific's M-10,000 and the Burlington *Zephyr*, were exhibited at the Chicago World Fair of 1933-4 and helped to popularize both rail travel and the new style (plates 34.5 and 34.6). During the second year of the fair these streamliners made extensive tours of American cities where millions clamoured to see them, further popularizing the style across the

34.5 Burlington *Zephyr* locomotives of the Baltimore and Ohio railroad (renamed *Pioneer Zephyr* in 1936). American, 1934. Hulton Archive/Getty Images.

34.6 The Chrysler Airflow next to a Union Pacific 'Streamline Express' train. American, 1934. Photo courtesy of DaimlerChrysler Corporation.

nation. The application of contoured lines, smooth surfaces and horizontality was intended not only to decrease the vehicles' air resistance but also to provide a style expressive of modernity, while at the same time suggesting comfort and restfulness. Streamliners proved highly successful during the Depression, sometimes having to turn passengers away – though railroads as a whole were then underused.[24] Streamlining was often applied to the total 'package': exteriors, interiors and accessories. Among product engineers the term 'package' engineering was synonymous with industrial design as early as 1931.[25] Significantly many American industrial designers, including Teague, Van Doren and Dreyfuss, had backgrounds in packaging design, a practice that was particularly applicable to the styling of vehicles.

Although streamlining had been actively explored by product and vehicle designers for some years, Norman Bel Geddes's book *Horizons* (1932), with its spectacular visionary designs of streamlined trains, planes and cars, did much to popularize the style.

Horizons was widely reviewed, and its striking images of streamlined vehicles were reprinted in the Sunday supplements. Like many other first generation American industrial designers, Bel Geddes had been to Europe in the 1920s; the horizontal lines and rounded corners in his designs for streamlined vehicles have precedents in the expressive architectural sketches made during the First World War by the German architect Erich Mendelsohn.[26] But Bel Geddes's visionary book strikingly encapsulated contemporary American aspirations. Significantly, *Horizons* found its way onto the desks of automotive engineers at Chrysler and General Motors. In 1933 Chrysler's head of engineering, Fred M. Zeder, claimed the book was an inspiration to him and his associates. He made his senior engineers read it and said that *Horizons* gave him the courage to go forward with the first streamlined production car, the Airflow.[27]

1934 was a watershed year for streamlining. In addition to the excitement surrounding the streamliners, the 1934 annual meeting of the Society of Automotive Engineers adopted streamlining as a major conference theme. The same year saw the production of the Chrysler Airflow, which was visually, aerodynamically and structurally streamlined (plate 34.6). Its exterior was integrated into a visible whole in order to direct air currents and reduce turbulence, and its chassis and framework were fused to add body strength. In an advertisement for the car Bel Geddes was shown sitting in it, holding an open copy of *Horizons*. The text read: 'Norman Bel Geddes [sic] famous book "Horizons", in which he forecast the Airflow motor cars'.[28] Bel Geddes emphasized the application of honesty, utility, simplicity and the rejection of ornament, calling the Airflow the 'first sincere and authentic streamlined car', its 'new style ... bound up with usefulness'. He concluded that 'gingerbread carving stuck on a building is not great architecture. Meaningless surface design on a motor car is not great style.' Airflow promotional material included an excerpt from *Horizons*, proclaiming that whoever manufactured the first streamlined car would dominate the automotive field, but despite its stylistic and technical innovations, the Airflow was not commercially successful. Although it was recognized as an important step in 'educating' the public to streamlining, it was considered too radical visually to appeal to the average consumer. Poor sales forced it to be withdrawn from production in 1937. Ironically, the failure of the Airflow led to Chrysler's withdrawal from radical styling. Far from leading the field, it would become the most conservative of the big three

automotive manufacturers in the following decades. Despite the failure of the Airflow, however, streamlined automobiles such as the 1938 Cadillac 60 Special found wide consumer appeal. And in the following decade the essential elements of the Airflow would become standard features of most production automobiles, including the lower silhouette, the all-steel frame and body, and the unified exterior shell.

On the one hand streamlining expressed the dynamic qualities of modernity, such as speed and technological progress. On the other, it domesticated the machine, concealing its operating parts, providing 'restful' horizontal lines and removing sharp projections.[29] In *Product Engineering* in 1933 Franklin E. Brill, a publicist for General Plastics Inc., suggested that industrial designers were 'so successful' because 'their designs are extremely simple, and are restful to the eye', and that designers should end the 'assault [on] the consumer's eye ... [with] zigzags, bumps and notches'.[30] Bel Geddes's 1933 stove design for the Standard Gas Equipment Corporation exemplified this emphasis on visual harmony, or 'cleanlining', through the removal of protrusions in order to create continuous surfaces. The design employed sheet metal clipped onto a tubular frame to achieve clean lines and level surfaces. The corners were rounded and the skirt was extended to the floor. Even the

protrusions of the gas hobs were covered with a flush, removable metal top. Raymond Loewy's design of the 1934 Sears Coldspot refrigerator showed how horizontal lines could be used to restyle a vertical appliance. The model was shaped using Plasticine upon a wooden block. This use of a pliable material allowed for the development of gently rounded corners, the horizontal lines of the doors and the tapered handle. The restyled refrigerator was a huge success, doubling sales in the first year of its production (see plate 10.4).[31]

By the mid- to late 1930s the projectile imagery of streamlined vehicles was evident in designs for stationary objects. Henry Dreyfuss's Hoover 150 vacuum cleaner (1936) displayed the rounded and horizontal forms of streamlined trains, as did Lurelle Guild's Electrolux Model 30 (1937) (see plate 33.9). Dreyfuss's design for Hoover incorporated an operable headlight, while Guild's design boasted its own rails in the form of metal glides attached to the base. Such references to modern transportation may have brought some glamour to often mundane housework. The symbols of modernity were also evocatively applied to the American domestic landscape by some émigré designers. The 'Normandie' water pitcher (1935), by the German-born designer Peter Müller-Munk, miniaturized the allure of one of the century's great ocean liners (plate 34.7).[32]

34.7 Peter Müller-Munk (born in Germany), 'Normandie', water pitcher. Chrome-plated brass. American, 1935. Anonymous gift, 1989. The Metropolitan Museum of Art, New York.

While Calkins had promoted the commercial potential of novel design and many saw the adoption of styling and streamlining as America's distinctive contribution to contemporary design, others criticized the industrial designer for overvaluing salesmanship above more elevated and lasting factors, as well as for misapplying streamlining. In 1931 Richard Bach, an active promoter of industrial arts and curator at the Metropolitan Museum of Art, censored consumers for being seduced by those who sold goods with 'eye value' rather than for the 'continuing satisfaction of ownership' or 'cultural potentiality'. And design purists at the New York Museum of Modern Art (MOMA) rejected streamlining as excessively commercial and 'misapplied to a fantastic variety of objects ... such as cocktail shakers and fountain pens where its use is nonsense'.[33] In 1934, as streamlining developed into a full-blown craze, MOMA's *Machine Art* exhibition presented a display of American machine parts and industrial design whose elementary geometric forms resembled those of Bauhaus Modernism. This attempt to identify an American machine vernacular as a source for modern design paralleled the work by Rourke and others to develop an American design movement with roots in the country's folk and industrial cultures. In his catalogue essay Philip Johnson, one of the exhibition's organizers, rejected both the '"modernistic" French machine-age aesthetic' and American 'principles such as "streamlining"'.[34] And Alfred H. Barr Jr quoted Plato to suggest that the exhibits, derived from elementary geometric forms, could be characterized as 'classical', implying, at a time when American intellectuals worried that they lagged behind Europe culturally, that America's machine-age civilization was comparable to that of Classical Greece.[35]

In the wake of MOMA's critique of streamlining, proponents of the style more vigorously defended it, both as *the* expression of the age – representing speed, efficiency and science – and on aesthetic grounds. In their overview of American industrial design, *Art and the Machine* (1936), the historians Sheldon and Martha Cheney defended streamlining in the design of vehicles and stationary products. They wrote, 'we subjectively accept the streamline as valid symbol for the contemporary life flow, and as a badge of design integrity in even smaller mechanisms, when it emerges as form expressiveness'. For them, the essential task of the industrial designer was to express in everyday objects the most vital of contemporary values: 'In its own smaller and often more menial form' an ordinary streamlined product was as 'conspicuous a symbol

... of the age' as the 'symbol of the cross' was to the 'medieval mind'.[36] They suggested that if religion were the essence of the medieval age, then movement, change and progress were the essence of theirs. They also recognized the aesthetic influence of Europe, writing that 'common principles' of form and expression could be found whether comparing Norman Bel Geddes's stove for Standard Gas with Piet Mondrian's paintings, or the American-born, Paris-trained, George Sakier's 'plumbing fixtures' with Constantin Brancusi's sculpture (plate 34.8).

Harold Van Doren also defended streamlining, claiming that what many attacked as a 'faddish style' was actually the 'technological result of high-speed mass production'. He explained that in plastic-moulded and pressed sheet-steel products it was more efficient to employ designs with gentle curves and rounded corners, writing that 'what may thus appear to be a captious preference for voluptuous curves and bulging forms in place of a more athletic spareness proves to be one result of the evolution of fabricating methods and assembly-line techniques'. Additionally, Van Doren defended the style on aesthetic grounds, seeing streamlined form as a visual metaphor for progress, and the egg-shape it often depended on as a more 'dynamic' shape than the 'static' circle and sphere found in classical design.[37]

In practice, a range of styles suggesting modernity competed in the 1930s. In 1933 the industrial designer Russel Wright differentiated between 'modernistic', 'modern' and 'classic modern' design.[38] In 1934 'classic modern' was defined as the 'tendency to simplify the classic styles' and 'decadent fashions of yesterday', making it a 'halfway house' between Modernist and period styles (see plate 33.11).[39] An *Arts & Decoration* article of the same year offered a compromise between 'machine art' and styling, expressing a strong reaction against 'the too rigid pattern' of geometric design. This was one of the first articles in the magazine to profile a leading stylist, Walter Dorwin Teague, who was also a promoter of 'classical' geometric forms. In it Teague outlined his efforts to find a compromise between 'geometric perfection,' 'charm' – described as the 'human element' – and an 'attention to detail'.

34.8 Constantin Brancusi (born in Romania), *Le Coq*. Bronze, wood and stone. French, 1935. Centre Georges Pompidou, Paris. MNAM. Photo: CNAC/MNAM. Dist. RMN.
© ADAGP, Paris and DACS, London 2002.

34.9 The General Motors building and the ramp to the Ford building at the New York World Fair, 1939. *L'Illustration*, 10 June 1939. NAL

By the end of the decade streamlining and geometry shared the same stage at the New York World Fair of 1939. The show significantly increased the profile of industrial design by associating the new profession with the vision of the future. This was the theme of the fair, developed by Teague, who served on the Board of Design alongside six architects. 'Focal exhibits' within the major buildings were provided by Teague and other leading industrial designers, including Dreyfuss, Rohde, Russel Wright, Egmont Arens, Donald Deskey, George Sakier and Raymond Loewy. The fair's architecture reflected the popularity of streamlining as well as Teague's own preference for geometric forms. Exemplifying the streamlined style was the hook-shaped General Motors building, designed in association with Norman Bel Geddes and containing his 'Futurama' exhibit, a vast diorama of the world of tomorrow dominated by superhighways, teardrop-shaped automobiles and tower cities (plate 34.9).[40] In contrast were the Perisphere, a sphere 55 metres in diameter (180 feet), and Trylon, a triangular tower of 186 metres (610 feet), designed by the architects Wallace K. Harrison and J. André Fouilhoux, representing the 'classical' geometric aesthetic (see plate 40.1).

The New York World Fair is usually seen to mark the end of streamlining. In the years after the Second World War, however, aerodynamic automotive design continued to develop, eventually leading to an orgy of non-functional styling. The 1948 Cadillac Coupé was the first post-war car to show tailfins. Designed under Harley Earl's team at General Motors, it initiated a mad rush among Detroit manufacturers exuberantly to express speed and flight in automobiles. Such design was often derided by critics and designers. Already in 1948 the historian Sigfried Giedion considered streamlining and the Detroit look retrogressive. Since its inception the streamlined style had been presented as alternately restful and an expression of speed, as well as the natural outcome of science. But Giedion noted that all styles, even streamlining, had a history. Rejecting the popular assumption that streamlining was based solely on the image of speed, he suggested instead that it derived from Art Deco products shown at the Paris 1925 Exhibition. The streamlining in American automobiles, refrigerators and even furniture from about 1935 was a direct outcome of the 'declining art décoratif approach'.[41]

He found formal resemblances between the bulbous design of an American vacuum cleaner of 1943 and a curved French Art Deco lighting fixture 'with its swollen profile thrice repeated'. The irony of the streamlined form, Giedion pointed out, was that while in its scientific sense it aimed at the 'utmost economy of form, at a minimum of volume', when applied as a style it produced an 'artificial swelling of volumes'.[42] This tension, Giedion believed, could not be sustained within product design.

In 1959 Henry Dreyfuss, an innovator of streamlining in the 1930s, was asked if America had a 'heritage of good design'. He answered in the affirmative, claiming that it was rooted in the 'pioneer tradition' of America's European settlers which resulted in designs of great 'simplicity, toughness, efficiency and good workmanship'. Ignoring his previous forays into streamlined design, he added that American design had devolved into the 'Detroit' look of 'motorized jewellery', which had begun to 'infect other types of products ... [including] refrigerators and washing machines'. Other 'deviations' included 'the many attempts to introduce European styles of lush decoration'.[43] Streamlining was now effectively defined in opposition to 'good design'. But Dreyfuss also emphasized the importance of drama and power, adding that American design expressed 'cleanlines, dramatic shapes, and powerful forms', echoing the expressive values of American design which the Cheneys had appreciated in the streamlined style.

As early as 1935 Constance Rourke had argued that early Americans, though restricted by the need for economy, had practised a 'free sense of personal decoration' and valued material goods, such as 'portraits or clocks with glass paintings or delicate china', for the emotional and symbolic meanings they evoked and the 'pleasure' they provided.[44] In other words, they enjoyed goods with charm and personality. Rourke's perspective helped to define an American art that was diverse and expressive without denying non-native influences. In this expansive view we can recognize American streamlining, not as a purely American style without a history, but as a complex product of twentieth-century modernity – a product of a transatlantic collaboration that embodied the contradictions of modernity. Both restful and dynamic, streamlining reflected and responded to the fluid changes of a modern world.

35 Art Deco in East Asia

Anna Jackson

Shanghai, city of amazing paradoxes and fantastic contrasts; contradiction of manners and morals; a vast brilliantly-hued ... panoramic mural of the best and the worst of Orient and Occident. Shanghai, with its modern skyscrapers ... modern department stores ... modern motors ... is the Big Parade of Life.[1]

Tokyo has none of the characteristic, often sordid, aspects of a so-called Eastern city ... To the newcomer the city may seem a heterogeneous medley, at once ultra-modern, quaint, colourful, even bizarre – a 'cocktail' sort of city ... The true explanation is that Tokyo is unique.[2]

Japan and China were both represented at the Paris 1925 Exhibition, but their displays were something of a failure and attracted little attention. In the eyes of a western audience the 'modern Japanese house'[3] seemed very traditional and the overall 'lack of new endeavour was a source of great disappointment to those who expected Japan to take her accustomed place as a leader in the applied arts'.[4] The Chinese display was organized by two artists' groups, the Association des Artistes Chinois en France and the Société Chinoise des Arts Décoratifs à Paris.[5] Their catalogue expressed the hope that visitors would have 'a nice surprise when they see the rapid and unexpected evolution of our arts towards modernization. Our vast country is transforming itself towards modern progress: to new times and new conceptions.'[6] This vision of the future was not fully realized by the exhibit, however, nor comprehended by those who saw it. The striking settings created by the young Chinese artists were lost among the displays of 'familiar styles of craftsmanship'[7] supplied by a number of Chinese import-export houses based in Paris, London and Shanghai (plate 35.2).[8] The virtual absence of Art Deco in the Japanese and Chinese displays of 1925 does not mean, however, that the style had no impact in the East. In fact, the opposite is true. Art Deco designers in Europe and America had found an important source of inspiration in the arts of East Asia (see Chapter 6). This stylistic affinity meant that Art Deco had a special resonance in Japan and China. The style appeared on the cultural landscape at a crucial point in the history of the two countries, when lifestyles were changing and concepts of modernity were being defined. In major cities such as Tokyo and Shanghai, Art Deco had a particular relevance and developed in a distinctive way.

The Taishō period (1912-26) was one of confidence and optimism in Japan.[9] Industrial development was stimulated by the First World War, in which Japan participated as one of the victorious allies. Economic prosperity was matched by political democratization and the broadening of suffrage. It was a period of great urban growth, particularly in the capital, Tokyo. People moved to the suburbs, commuting on expanding railway networks to new types of office and factory jobs. Women entered the work force in large numbers, employed as typists, bank clerks, bus conductors and shop assistants. These workers were the consumers of a new mass urban culture centred on the café, the cinema and the department store. Culture itself became a commodity, seen in the use of the adjective *bunkateki*, 'cultural', for many accoutrements of everyday life.[10]

The main 'cultural space' was the Ginza, the most fashionable district of Tokyo. The home of the biggest department stores and the smartest cafés, it was a site of consumption and spectacle encapsulated in the word *gimbura* or 'wandering the Ginza'.[11] This was the world of the 'modern boy' and the 'modern girl', popularly abbreviated to *mobo* and *moga*, who wore western clothes and read western novels. The boys wore their hair long and the girls, more shockingly, cut their hair short.[12] The *mobo* and *moga* enthusiastically participated in all aspects of contemporary Taishō culture. *Modanizumu*, 'modernism', became the catchword of the period and the latest trends in western art and literature were eagerly followed. Attraction to the West was not based on the fact that *it* symbolized the modern, however. The *modan* was something being

35.1 Ban'ura Shōgo, partition screen. Lacquer on wood. Japanese, 1930. Private collection.

35.2 Room from the Chinese display at the Paris 1925 Exhibition. *La Chine à l'Exposition internationale des arts décoratifs et industriels modernes à Paris 1925*, Paris, 1925. NAL.

shattered just before midday on 1 September 1923. A major earthquake struck the Tokyo and Yokohama area, killing 60,000 people in the capital alone. Much of the city was destroyed, though the Imperial Hotel survived.[16] The reconstruction of Tokyo not only physically altered the streets of the city, but also created an even greater awareness of notions of *modanizumu*. Many Art Deco buildings, including Satō Kōichi's Hibiya Hall and Matsui Kitarō's Sanshin building, both of 1929, were erected in the years following the earthquake, the style seeming a fitting choice for the construction of a sophisticated, fashionable, modern city that aimed to rival Paris, London and New York.[17] Architects, inspired by the example of the Imperial Hotel, used terracotta to create Art Deco ornament on buildings such as the Ministry of Home Affairs (plate 35.4).

The 1920s saw the development of two architectural camps in Japan. The Bunriha Kenchikukai (Secessionist Architectural Group) was formed in 1920 by a group of young practitioners. It took its initial inspiration from the style and spirit of the Vienna Secession, but gradually came under the influence of emerging European Modernism. Some Bunriha buildings, such as Ishimoto Kikuji's Shirokiya department store of 1931,[18] echoed the geometric patterning of the Deco style. However, it was other, more conservative architects seeking to apply western stylistic elements in a way that expressed an underlying Japanese spirit of design who found in Art Deco, a modern style partly inspired by the East, an appropriate source of inspiration. The influence of Art Deco was apparent in the National Diet, the most important public building of the period, which had a stepped pyramid roof and stylized terracotta ornament. In the 1930s this search for indigenous interpretation and identity was harnessed to the growing nationalism of the Shōwa period (1926-89).[19] The government demanded that new buildings be conceived in what became known as *teikan yōshiki* (Imperial Crown Style), a rather eclectic mix of Japanese and western classical and Deco elements which was employed most famously by Watanabe Jin in his Imperial Museum of 1937.[20]

Art Deco was seen most commonly on the streets of Tokyo, and other Japanese cities, in places of leisure such as the cinema, dance hall and café. The café was viewed as *the* quintessential space of modernity, a site that symbolized freedom, youth and

experienced in Japan, not something copied from abroad, and the interest in western ideas resulted from indigenous developments and experiences.

Art Deco and other new European art movements were disseminated in Japan through exhibitions and publications such as *Bijutsu Shinpō* (Art News). Japanese artists worked in the West and western artists came to Japan. In 1917 Frank Lloyd Wright, a great admirer of Japanese art and architecture, arrived in Tokyo to begin work on the new Imperial Hotel.[13] Wright intended his design to be a bridge between East and West, later stating that 'no single

form was really Japanese but the whole was informed by unity. The growing proportions were suitable to the best Japanese tradition.'[14] In its symmetrical plan, articulation of space and integration of buildings and gardens the hotel did echo some elements of traditional Japanese architecture.[15] However, Wright's rich 'organic' ornamentation had no such precedent. The hotel, completed in 1923, became a major social centre of the capital, popular with both locals and foreigners, and an important symbol of the modernization of the nation (plate 35.3).

The confident spirit of the Taishō period was

the future.[21] The number of cafés in Tokyo rose dramatically after the 1923 earthquake. Famous places such as the Café Maru and the Ginza Palace proclaimed their glamorous modernity through the use of bright neon lights and surfaces of stainless steel, aluminium and glass. What distinguished such establishments from their European counterparts was the role of the waitresses, for the Japanese café was a sexualized space. In some respects, work as a café waitress liberated women from traditional social and economic restraints, but circumstances often pushed them into prostitution. It was certainly the lure of the erotic that drew male customers to the cafés. They were a major site of *eroguro nansensu*, 'erotic-grotesque-nonsense', the term used to describe the Japanese equivalent of the 'flapper' age. The waitress, and her sisters in bars and dance halls, embodied the image of the *moga*, a focus not only of fascination, but also of anxiety about the modern. Reactionaries called for a return to past values, while the experiences of the eroticized and victimized 'modern girl' were the subject of social critique, fiction and films. Mizoguchi Kenji's *Naniwa Hika* (Osaka Elegy) of 1936, for example, tells the story of a girl who sells herself to support an ungrateful family.

In Japan in the 1920s and 1930s concepts of tradition and modernity, East and West, worked together, rather than in opposition, in complex ways.

In *Hama Kōen* (Hama Park), the novelist Kawabata Yasunari asked a companion whether it was no longer possible to erect a building in a purely Japanese style in the capital, the reply being 'but all these American things are Tokyo itself'.[22] The influence of America, particularly of Frank Lloyd Wright, is seen in many of the buildings of early Shōwa Japan. It was French Art Deco, however, that inspired the residence of Prince Asaka, who studied in Europe in the 1920s and visited the Paris 1925 Exhibition. On his return to Japan in 1931 he set about building his own house in the Art Deco style.[23] Most of the interiors were designed by Henri Rapin, a leading French architect and artist-decorator, and many of the glass doors and light fittings (including some by Lalique), wallpaper, paintings, mirrors and heating devices were imported directly from Europe (plate 35.5). Rapin never visited Japan, however, and the realization of his designs was entrusted to craftsmen of the Imperial Household Department.[24] The overall design for the residence, including the plan and elevation, was the work of Gōndo Yōkichi, an engineer in the Department who, like the Prince, had visited the 1925 Exhibition.

Concepts of art and design changed dramatically in Japan in the first decades of the twentieth century as Confucian ethics, which placed the interests of the state above personal welfare, were challenged by new ideologies of individualism. Freedom of artistic

35.3 Frank Lloyd Wright, main façade of the Imperial Hotel, Tokyo. 1913-23. Photo courtesy of the Imperial Hotel, Tokyo.

35.4 Terracotta ornament on the Ministry of Home Affairs, Tokyo. 1933. Made by INA Ceramics Manufacturing. Courtesy of the INAX Corporation. Photo: Yukinobu Takada.

expression was espoused most famously by the poet and sculptor Takamura Kōtarō in his groundbreaking essay *Midori-iro no Taiyō* (Green Sun) published in 1910. Takamura had a strong influence on his younger brother Toyochika, who studied metalwork under Tsuda Shinobu, a professor at Tokyo School of Fine Arts. Tsuda was in Paris at the time of the 1925 Exhibition and was asked to serve on the international jury. He wrote enthusiastically about what he saw in the official report[25] and on his return to Japan played a crucial role in introducing the Art Deco style to the next generation. In 1926 Takamura Toyochika and other of Tsuda's students formed Mukei, one of the groups involved in what is known as the Shinkō Kōgei Undō (New Craft Movement).[26] Members of Mukei, which means 'formless', aimed to destroy convention and embrace the new, declaring: 'Now is now, the moment that we fly away. Love this moment. Create the craft art that breathes in this moment, and defend it.'[27] The influence of Art Deco is evident in the work of Mukei members such

35.5 The grand guestroom
of the Asaka residence,
Tokyo. 1931-3.
© MASUDA Akihisa.

as Naitō Haruji, Toyoda Katsuaki and Yamazaki Kakutarō (plate 35.6 and see plate 6.16).[28] The style was only one of those being absorbed in Japan at the time, however; Russian Constructivism, Cubist sculpture and Bauhaus design were all influential. These styles were collectively termed Kōsei-ha (Constructivism) in Japan. For Mukei practitioners such as Yamazaki it was crucial that such influences were employed within a theoretical framework. In his 1929 essay *Mujun o Kataru* (About Contradiction) Yamazaki criticized those Kōsei-ha artists whose use of new styles had become nothing more than the incorporation of superficial details.

Although Art Deco in Japan is most readily associated with the new Tokyo that arose from the ashes of the 1923 earthquake, it was in Kyoto that some of the most striking Art Deco objects were produced. The old capital, for centuries the centre of luxury craft production, was often seen as the bastion of Japanese decorative traditions. Here too, however, the crafts were transformed during the inter-war period.[29] Art Deco, a style largely based on decoration, found particular resonance in Kyoto, as can be seen in the stylized floral designs of the potter Kiyomizu Rokubei VI (plate 35.7). Japanese lacquerwork had been a great inspiration to Art Deco artists in the West (see Chapter 6), so it is not surprising, therefore, that in Japan some of the most remarkable Deco pieces were made in that medium. Kyoto lacquer artist Ban'ura Shōgo developed a particularly dynamic personal style that featured powerful stylized forms and bright, bold colours (plate 35.1). In 1935 Ban'ura, Kiyomizu VI and others formed Sōjun-sha which, like its Tokyo counterparts, aimed to break down the boundaries of craft production.[30] Another leading Kyoto lacquer artist, Suzuki Hyōsaku II, was a member of Ryūkeiha Kōgeikai (Streamline School Craft Association), which aimed to produce objects in keeping with modern life (see plate 1.15).

35.6 Naitō Haruji, wall clock.
Cast bronze. Japanese, 1927.
National Museum of Modern Art, Tokyo.

35.7 Kiyomizu Rokubei VI, vase.
Earthenware, painted in enamels.
Japanese, 1933. Kyoto Municipal Museum.

35.8 Sugiura Hisui, *The Only Subway in the East*, poster. Colour lithograph. Japanese, 1927. National Museum of Modern Art, Tokyo.

The Art Deco style is also apparent in Japanese graphic design, which developed rapidly in the first decades of the twentieth century. One of the pioneers of the new art form was Sugiura Hisui, who produced numerous posters and book and magazine covers. Sugiura founded *Affiches*, a journal that introduced European and American poster design to Japan, and was a member of the editorial committee of the most influential design compendium of the period, *Gendai Shōgyō Bijtsu Zenshū* (The Complete Commercial Artist). His 1927 poster advertising the first subway in Asia depicts, in striking perspective, a line of waiting passengers that includes women in both kimono and western dress in a telling reflection of the fashions that jostled on the streets of Tokyo at the time (plate 35.8).[31] Much of Sugiura's work was for Mitsukoshi, Japan's leading department store. Mitsukoshi established its own design department, with Sugiura as chief designer, in 1909 and also played an important role in familiarizing Japanese audiences with modern art and design through its regular art exhibitions. In 1928 it staged the *Furansu Bijitsu Tenrankai* (French Art Exhibition) which included works by leading Art Deco designers such as Dunand and Ruhlmann. The new Japanese lifestyle required new furniture and to aid customers Mitsukoshi produced a range of relatively inexpensive furniture 'sets'. After the 1928 Exhibition, the Art Deco 'set' became a bestseller.

The cosmetics company Shiseido was at the forefront of Japanese design trends and through its products, magazines and parlours it promoted a modern, sophisticated lifestyle that appealed directly to the *moga*. Fukuhara Shinzō took over as head of the company from his father in 1915 and the following year established the Shiseido design department to create a coherent approach to advertising and packaging. In the late 1920s and 1930s company designers such as Maeda Mitsugu and Yamana Ayao made a lyrical Deco style the core of Shiseido's corporate image. Art Deco graphics also featured on the covers of *Pearl*, the catalogue of the Japanese jeweller Mikimoto Kōkichi. Mikimoto displayed his cultured pearls at the Paris 1925 Exhibition and they rapidly came to dominate the western market, a long necklace of such pearls being a major accessory of the 1920s woman (see Chapter 24).[32] Designs for Mikimoto's Art Deco jewellery were illustrated in *Pearl* and then ordered by clients through shops in London, New York and Paris as well as on the fashionable Ginza (plate 35.9).

In the inter-war years Europe, America and Asia were linked by sea routes plied by the great ocean liners of the day (see Chapter 29). The interiors of

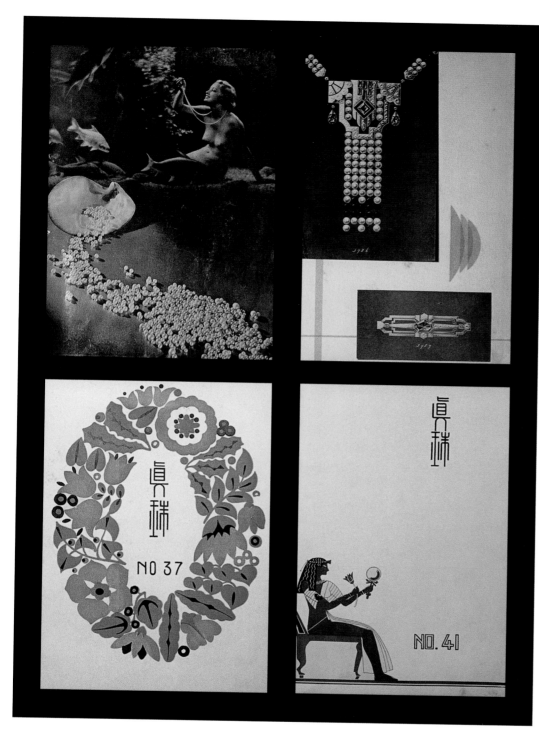

35.9 Four covers and pages
from copies of *Pearl*.
Photo courtesy of Mikimoto
Pearl Island Co. Ltd.

Japanese ships such as the *Nishiki-maru* were designed by Nakamura Junpei, who created Art Deco salons in which Japanese lacquer and inlaid mother-of-pearl were combined with metal, glass and resin. East and West were also linked by rail and it became possible to travel from Tokyo to Paris, via the Siberian railway, in about twenty days. Part of this route was operated by the South Manchurian Railway Company Ltd, or Mantetsu as it was known. Along these tracks ran 'the ultra-modern, streamlined super express *Asia*'.[33] The train, with its sleek exterior shape and luxury Art Deco interiors, was the fastest on the continent (see plate 29.5).

This railway construction was part of Japan's development of Manchuria, the region in northern China it seized in 1931. In Manchuria Japan set about creating a politically, economically and culturally advanced state.[34] The *Asia* was one of the two great symbols of this modernity, the other being the development of cities such as Xinjing, the new capital, where the State Council building was constructed in the grandiose Imperial Crown style.[35] The new state became a popular tourist destination for many Japanese, while those at home could experience it vicariously at the 'Salon Manchuria' on the second floor of the Ginza Palace café.

Manchuria, and the rest of China as Japan increasingly encroached upon it, became an exoticized, and often eroticized, 'other' for Japan. Certain cafés in Tokyo featured Chinese style decoration and waitresses dressed in Chinese costume, while Yamaguchi Yoshiko, a Japanese woman born in Manchuria, became the exotic and sexy 'Chinese' movie star Ri Ko-ran.[36]

At the same time, in one of the great cities of China, other myths were being forged. The first decades of the twentieth century were a period of great instability in China. The last imperial dynasty fell and a republic was declared, but the nationalist Guomintang, lead first by Sun Yat-sen and then by Chiang Kai-shek, found itself battling northern warlords, the growing Communist party and Japanese expansionist policies.[37] As the rest of China collapsed into chaos, however, Shanghai thrived.

Shanghai was a treaty port, controlled by foreign traders since China's defeat in the Opium War of 1839-42. The British, French and Americans had originally ruled separate areas of the city, but in 1863 the British and American concessions merged to become the International Settlement. The city became one of the most prosperous and cosmopolitan in East Asia, a centre not only of business but also of pleasure. By the 1920s Shanghai's free-for-all capitalism and reckless hedonism had become legendary. The city boasted the longest bar in the world, the shortest street, the best restaurants, cafés and cabarets, metered 'taxi dancers', 'sing song' hostesses and 'a blatant cacophony of carnality from a score of dance-halls'.[38] Such potent images of the exotic and erotic made Shanghai a major tourist destination. Here, as Christopher Isherwood recounted, the

> tired or lustful ... will find everything to gratify his desires. You can buy an electric razor, a French dinner or a well-cut suit. You can dance at the Tower Restaurant of the Cathay Hotel ... you can attend race meetings ... see the latest American films. If you want girls, or boys, you can have them, at all prices, from the bath-houses and the brothels. If you want opium you can smoke it in the best company, served on a tray like afternoon tea ... there is enough whisky and gin to float a fleet of battleships. The jeweller and the antique dealer await your orders.[39]

35.10 Palmer & Turner, Peace Hotel, former Cathay Hotel, Shanghai. 1932. Private collection.

In the inter-war years Shanghai was known as the 'Paris of the East'. Even more than in Tokyo, however, the dominant influence imprinted on the architecture of the period was America. The exuberant, decorative spirit of Art Deco was perfectly at home in the Shanghai of the 1930s, but the specific characteristics the style bore in the city reflected a fundamental shift of power as British imperialism was challenged by American capitalism. The Art Deco buildings of Shanghai were a symbol not so much of colonial authority as of the new doctrine of wealth.[40] The Cathay Hotel mentioned by Isherwood was the most fashionable place to stay.[41] It was the showpiece of Victor Sassoon, the richest and most prominent businessman in Shanghai. He bought vast amounts of land, pulling down nineteenth-century buildings to put up new hotels, apartment blocks, offices and department stores, which were built in the Art Deco style that dominated the city in the 1930s. The Cathay Hotel set the standard for the luxury and glamour that, along with the skylines Sassoon helped create, became the chief characteristic of Shanghai (plate 35.10). Standing on the Bund, the thoroughfare alongside the Huangpu River that marked the seat of foreign power, the hotel was built in 1932 by the architectural firm of Palmer & Turner, pioneers of new techniques that allowed the construction of high-rise buildings in the city.[42] The Cathay rose 12 storeys, its square tower surmounted by a sharply pitched, green, pyramidal roof. The Art Deco ornament on the exterior was matched by an interior that featured light fixtures by Lalique. Palmer & Turner were also responsible for many other Art Deco buildings in the International Settlement including the Metropole Hotel, Hamilton House, Embankment House and Broadway Mansions, a massive 22-storey, ziggurat-shaped apartment hotel completed in 1934.[43] These new skyscrapers gave the waterfront city a resemblance to New York, but it was the Chicago style that particularly influenced another leading Shanghai architect, the Czech-Hungarian émigré Laszlo Hudec.[44] Hudec was responsible for the Park Hotel, completed in 1934. The tallest building in Asia, it was equipped with the latest modern amenities and stylish Art Deco interiors.

While the International Settlement represented the commercial side of Shanghai, the French Concession, with its leafy avenues and café society, was the most popular place to live. Many Art Deco apartment blocks were built in the area including Grosvenor House,[45] also by Palmer & Turner, Empire Mansions, the Savoy, the Gascogne and the Astrid (plate 35.11). The Cercle Sportif Français was *the* club to belong to in Shanghai and, although the exterior was designed in the Beaux-Arts style, the interiors boasted various Art Deco features.[46] Furniture and fittings for these buildings were often

35.11 Levin, Astrid apartment block, Shanghai. 1933. Photo courtesy of Deke Erh, Old China Hand Resources, Shanghai.

imported from Europe and America, but such foreign examples provided a blueprint for local craftsmen who were able to create native designs to suit the fashionable Art Deco interiors. The Soy Chong company, for example, provided stainless steel doors, light canopies and ornamental wrought ironwork for the Park Hotel. These apartments were built predominantly for the foreign community, however. A 1939 list of the tenants of the Astrid apartments, for example, reveals only one Chinese name.[47]

The elite members of Chinese society were able to share the high life of the foreigners. The godfather of the underworld, Du Yuesheng, exemplified the political and social ambiguities of Shanghai. Du controlled the city's prostitution, drug and protection rackets, but was also a member of the Municipal Council of the French Concession and a prominent figure on the business and social circuit. One of his luxury residences bore a number of Art Deco features.[48] In December 1927 Du, along with the rest of Shanghai society, attended the wedding banquet of Chiang Kai-shek and Soong May-ling, which took place in the ballroom of the fashionable Majestic Hotel. The new Mme Chiang vied for the position of the most fashionable woman in China with Koo Huilan, the wife of China's Foreign Minister.[49] Both women were great collectors of jade, but Huilan was also very fond of wearing her 'sapphire and diamond necklace from Boucheron, and ... huge earrings to match'.[50]

In the late 1920s western businessmen in the city started to invite young Chinese men and women to social gatherings. 'The Chinese girls ... came shyly at first ... carrying gold and enamel French compacts in their hands, symbols of a new day. Now they circulate around the town quite freely, smoke, drink, drive their own automobiles.'[51] For many of the emerging Chinese bourgeoisie, however, the glittering lifestyle embodied in Art Deco remained something of a fantasy. American magazines and Hollywood movies provided a source of such dreamscapes, but they were also transformed into indigenous cultural mediums. A Chinese taste for the modern, or *modeng*, was conveyed through magazines such as *Shanghai Huabao* (Shanghai Sketch) (plate 35.12) and *Liangyou* (The Young Companion), which featured photographs of the latest fashions and the Art Deco interiors of the 'typical modern home'.[52] The Chinese inhabitants of Shanghai were also able to enjoy many of the pleasures that the modern city had to offer. The big department stores on the Nanjing Road, some built in Deco style, were a major attraction where one could buy, or at least look at, the latest clothes, shoes and cosmetics by

35.12 Zhang Zhengyu,
Kuangwu (Crazy wild dancing).
From *Shanghai Huabao*
Fascimile copy. May 1929.
British Library.

35.13 Portrait of the Chinese actress Ruan Lingyu. *Dian Ying Nu Ming Xing Zhao Xiang Ji, Ruan Ling-yu*, Shanghai, 1934. Private collection.

companies such as Shiseido, which produced their 'Rose' and 'Bluebird' ranges for the Shanghai market. Social dancing also took the Chinese community by storm.

The most important place of entertainment, and another site where the native Chinese were increasingly able to cross the colonial boundaries, was the cinema. By the 1930s the film theatre had become an important addition to the architectural landscape of Shanghai. Many were built in the Art Deco style, the most famous being the Grand Theatre designed by Hudec. With its spacious marble lobby, neon-lit marquee and comfortable sofa-seats, it created a dazzling spectacle in itself. Hollywood films were very popular among Chinese audiences, though the stereotyped portrayal of China in *Shanghai Express* caused a furore when it was screened in the city. Native cinema also thrived, creating stars out of movie actresses such as Ruan Lingyu, whose appeared in films such as *Xin Nuxing* (New Woman, 1935) (plate 35.13). Her suicide in 1935 stunned the whole of China and left an indelible mark on public consciousness.

Photographs of Ruan Lingyu show her as the epitome of the modern, urban woman, wearing Art

Deco earrings and the quintessential Chinese garment of 1930s Shanghai, the *qipao*, or *cheongsam* as it is more commonly known in the West.[53] The design of the *qipao* evolved over the first decades of the twentieth century, becoming more form fitting by the 1930s. Fabrics and patterns also varied, ranging from traditional flower motifs to fashionable Art Deco designs. The advent of the *qipao* coincided with women's emergence into the public sphere. The garment became the focus of debates about what women should wear, in which questions of morality, national identity and Chinese modernity were articulated through dress, shoes and hairstyles.

The image of glamorous, sophisticated Chinese women was used on calendar posters to advertise products such as cigarettes, alcohol and medicine (plate 35.14).[54] Often placed within Art Deco settings and sporting a *qipao*, high heels and a permanent wave, the women signified the modern world to which the new bourgeoisie aspired. Such depictions of women as the vanguard of modernity, produced in a city that was the centre of the campaign for sexual emancipation, could be seen to reflect a newly liberated position. However, they can also be viewed as an attempt to regulate the impact of the 'new

woman' and to signify her sexual availability. The woman is a commodity, something that can be acquired along with the product.[55]

These posters are only one example of the graphic arts that flourished in Shanghai in the 1920s and 1930s, appearing on billboards, matchboxes, and magazine and book covers. Artistic links with Japan played a part in introducing new graphic styles, including those influenced by Art Deco. Many Chinese art students studied in Japan, while numerous Japanese artists, along with writers and intellectuals, visited Shanghai.[56] The stylistic roots of Art Deco lay, in part, in traditional Chinese art, and its absorption into contemporary practices in China was quite a natural evolution. Patterns and motifs from Chinese art were combined with Deco-inspired imagery to create a new, dynamic visual vocabulary. Typography was also influenced by Art Deco. Chinese characters had always lent themselves to expressive manipulation, but in the 1920s and 1930s creative distortion produced extremely stylized characters (plate 35.12). The Shanghai graphic style accompanied the development of the New Literature and Design Movement, led by the writer and scholar Lu Xun, which sought to create new styles for a new, modern nation.[57] In China, as in Japan, Art Deco acted as a signifier of modernity, and its use did not simply connote 'the West'. The incorporation of the style into modern Chinese design led to the creation of something native rather than foreign. In both East Asian countries Art Deco acted as a stylistic mediator of concepts of traditional and modern, of East and West. While western Art Deco artists had absorbed and appropriated East Asian art in the evolution of the style, artists in China and Japan then reabsorbed and re-appropriated it as an exotic 'other' in the construction of an indigenous 'modern'.

By 1937 fighting between China and expansionist Japan had escalated into full-scale war. Until then the foreign settlements of Shanghai had remained fairly untouched, but on 14 August 1937 bombs fell on the concessions for the first time, one even hitting the Cathay Hotel. In 1941 the Japanese took over the city and two years later interned any Allied nationals who remained. The exciting worlds, both real and imaginary, in which Art Deco blossomed in East Asia, were irrevocably lost. Tokyo was virtually destroyed in the Allied air raids of the Second World War, though some traces of the style remain. In Shanghai, despite the Japanese occupation and the troubled years of the Cultural Revolution, the architecture of the 1920s and 1930s has survived, making the old treaty port now, as before, one of the great Art Deco cities of the world.

35.14 Hang Zhi-ying, poster
for the Qicong Tobacco
Company. Colour lithograph.
Chinese, late 1930s.
Powerhouse Museum, Sydney.
Photo: Penelope Clay.

36 Indo-Deco

Amin Jaffer

India in the 1920s and 1930s was socially deeply conservative, economically largely unmodernized, and impervious to western secularism. Nevertheless she embraced modern design tendencies with tremendous zeal. Although the social and cultural conditions that inspired the development of Art Deco in the West were largely absent in the Indian social and cultural environment, the novelty and allure of the style was still appreciated by a people who, albeit traditional in many respects, were also highly receptive to foreign visual and artistic influences. Since India was a colony, the influence of western design was articulated principally through Britain, which was appreciably slower than her continental neighbours in subscribing to the new design strategies of the early twentieth century. But Art Deco was also promoted in India by émigré designers from Central and Eastern Europe, who sought patronage in India and brought with them knowledge of the style and its manifestations in Europe and America.

If in the West Art Deco was originally perceived as an elite style, then this was doubly true in India, where early support for the style was confined to the westernized ruling classes and mercantile communities. The epicentre of Art Deco was Bombay, which after the opening of the Suez Canal in 1869 became India's principal port and centre of international communication. The walls of its eighteenth-century fort had been knocked down in 1862 and the city had subsequently developed on a grand scale, with spectacularly ornamented civic and commercial buildings in neo-historic styles. By the second decade of the twentieth century, however, Bombay was experiencing serious congestion. This was partly remedied when, after much controversy and prolonged delays, the Development Trust

reclaimed 439 acres along Back Bay, on the island's western side, marked with a corniche appropriately named Marine Drive.[1] The Back Bay reclamation area was developed, piecemeal, from 1929, reaching a peak between 1935 and 1940. Although it was built by several different speculators, strict regulations were laid down concerning the materials, style and appearance of buildings, to ensure 'uniformity and harmony of design'.[2]

The development of Back Bay in a consistent architectural style resulted in a coherent Art Deco cityscape second in size only to Miami's South Beach (plate 36.2). Its buildings are all characterized by concrete construction, flat roofs and curved fenestration. That Art Deco was so firmly adopted in Bombay was the result of several factors, including the establishment of the city as the centre of the architectural profession in India. This was led by the Indian Institute of Architects, founded in 1929, whose membership included both Indian and British

36.2 Marine Drive, Bombay. Photo: A. L. Syed. From Sharada Dwivedi and Rahul Mehrotra, *Bombay: The Cities Within*, Mumbai, 2001.

36.1 Canopy bed. Silver-covered wood. Indian (attributed to craftsmen from Udaipur, Orissa), 1922. Talisman Antiques.

architects familiar with the new idiom.[3] As the country's centre of communication, Bombay was exposed to European currents in fashion transmitted by the regular waves of people who arrived there, including architects and designers in search of work. Prosperous business people, whose success under British rule had given them a high regard for western thinking, were particularly receptive to European tastes and it was precisely this group that financed the development of the city. Within India, Bombay epitomized modernity, reflecting it visually in its new architecture, whose elegant streamlined forms, sparse but potent ornament and machine aesthetic glamorized the new age and its technologies. The drive for a new aesthetic in the city may also be seen as a reaction against the dominating Victorian cityscape, with its richly ornamented façades.[4]

The boom in Bombay and the consequent shortage of land meant that, more than anywhere else in India, its residents experienced the spatial constraints felt in many western cities. This resulted in the development of Back Bay into rows of high-rise apartment buildings, a radical departure from the convention of living in bungalows with verandas positioned in substantial compounds. The electric fan meant that rooms no longer needed to be as lofty as in former times, when ceilings were hung with a *punkah*, a suspended rectangular fan rocked with a pulley. Air conditioning likewise made it possible to live comfortably in rooms that were neither large enough for air to circulate nor had access to fresh air. The flats themselves were often designed in set European or Hindu styles; the former with a joint living and dining room and small servants' quarters, the latter with a large, long central hall and small bedrooms.[5]

As important as the technological advances that made apartment living possible were the changes in outlook that permitted Indian families to live as single units rather than forming part of a larger joint family. An editorial in the *Journal of the Institute of Indian Architects* of 1938 explained that:

> Young people, fed on the international outlook day by day, by the newspaper, the cinemas and the radio, with the speed lines of the motor car and the aeroplane as familiar as were once the family bullock cart and the richly caparisoned elephant, bearing aloft its purdahed howdah, are not satisfied with the old traditional family home that took generations to come to its fruition. They require a little home of their own and one that does not require a great deal of time and an army of servants to keep tidy.[6]

Newspaper advertisements and surviving Bombay interiors of the period suggest that by the early

36.3 Advertisement for the *Army and Navy Co-operative. Journal of the Indian Institute of Architects*, April 1934. RIBA.

1930s the public was well served for Art Deco furnishings and accessories. Leading cabinetmakers such as John Roberts & Co., McKenzie's and William Jacks & Co. advertised their ability to work in contemporary styles. The latter stated expressly that the firm was staffed by 'expert trained European decorators who will be happy to help you choose the trend of the day'.[7] The Army and Navy Co-operative was likewise prepared to provide customers with estimate 'sketches, patterns and specimens if desired' (plate 36.3).[8] Modern furnishings were the object of intense interest at Bombay's *Ideal Home Exhibition* organized by the Indian Institute of Architects in 1937 with the purpose of providing the public with clear ideas about contemporary living. In spite of its success, the exhibition cannot have had much meaning except for the moneyed westernized minority who were able to devote means and time to matters of style; a census of 1931 showed that in

that year 80 per cent of the city's inhabitants lived in single-room tenements.[9]

The 'trailblazers' of Art Deco in Bombay were the cinemas, of which nearly 300 existed by 1939.[10] More than ordinary commercial and domestic buildings, cinemas – temples to the new art of the talking picture – became beacons of modernity, fantasy and glamour. Nowhere in Bombay was modern technology treated more stylishly than in these buildings which welcomed viewers into an atmosphere of Hollywood chic that paralleled the escape from reality offered by the films themselves. The Parsee-backed Regal cinema (1933) designed by Charles Stevens Jr, for example, offered patrons underground parking with a lift and air-conditioning throughout.[11] The interiors, designed by the Czech émigré artist Karl Schara, who decorated the auditorium in jade green and orange artfully worked with solar rays and waves, all bathed in orange light,

36.4 Bhedwar & Sorabji, Eros cinema, Bombay. 1938. Photo: Jon Alff. Reproduced from *Bombay to Mumbai: Changing Perspectives*, Mumbai, 1997.

bore the stamp of international Art Deco. The Eros cinema (1938), designed by the Indian firm of Bhedwar & Sorabji, went one step further with its inclusion of a ballroom, ice-skating rink, restaurants and luxury shops (plate 36.4).[12] The building was positioned on a corner site, a graduating tower marking the entrance, which was of white and black marble with bands of gold. India was integrated into the cinema's decorative scheme through murals depicting lush vegetation, the Taj Mahal and South Indian temples.[13] Once again, control over the interiors was given over to a European designer, Fritz von Drieberg, who had started his career in Bombay working under local cabinetmakers John Roberts & Co.[14] Bombay was not the only city to enjoy modern cinema houses. The Roxy and Metro in Calcutta, the Relief in Ahmedabad, the Mayfair in Lucknow and the

Hind in Patna were all configured in a streamlined, modern style emblematic of the new age.

It was not only new buildings that carried the stamp of Art Deco. Stylistically outdated structures were also modernized at the hands of designers, both European and Indian. The German engineer E. F. Messerschmidt, who advertised himself in 1934 as a 'modern interior decorator', enjoyed a successful career in Bombay re-styling the city's leading restaurants, offices and residences including the interiors of the Taj Mahal Hotel, while Karl Schara, of Regal cinema fame, modernized the tea- and ballrooms of the Cornaglia restaurant.[15] The work of the prolific architect G. B. Mhatre shows that Deco re-styling was not confined to western-style buildings intended for elite or commercial use. His projects for 1935, for example, included updating a monastery at Banganaga, Walkeshwar, which he endowed with a streamlined fountain worthy of any Hollywood film set and a minimal concrete gateway modelled after the gate at the renowned Buddhist stupa at Sanchi.[16]

The highlight of this project was the bedroom designed for Swamiji, the head of the monastery, which was 'finished internally in wood panelling with chromium strips running horizontally'. Mhatre's other projects included re-styling temples in Bombay such as Gamdevi Devalaya and Worli Gopchar Bhoye Sansthan at Prabhadevi.[17]

As might be expected, the most significant patrons of Art Deco architecture in India were its princes. From the earliest days of direct interaction between European and Indian rulers, the latter showed themselves to be appreciative of western articles such as oil paintings, mirrors, clocks and scientific instruments.[18] However, with the gradual subjugation of the subcontinent by British forces, Indian princes increasingly came to adopt aspects of western lifestyle, including building in western architectural styles.[19] By the time the British Government came to rule India directly, following the uprisings of 1857, Indian princes were, as a matter of course, abandoning their former residences for new palaces. Typically, these were designed for them by British engineers and configured partly in a western style, with function-specific rooms for durbar, dining, entertaining and sleeping. The appearance of such buildings varied depending on the taste of the individual ruler, the choices available to him and the fashions of the day, but included revivals of Louis XIII, Palladian, Gothic, Baroque and Baronial styles.[20] 'Indo-Saracenic', a style that used indigenous architectural forms such as domes, *chhatris* (domed pavilions), *chhajas* (overhanging eaves), *jalis* (pierced lattice screens) and *bangaldar* (bowed Bengali-style) roofs was particularly popular as it seemed at once to preserve an element of indigenous architectural traditions while allowing innovations in the use of space.[21]

The adoption of a western lifestyle among Indian princes was partly motivated by an attempt to swim with the political tide, but also the result of the Government's official programme of instilling rulers with western values. This was achieved above all by establishing institutions for the education of princes, such as Rajkumar College, Rajkot (1870) and Mayo College, Ajmer (1872), which were based on English public schools and taught a western curriculum. Direct links with the West were struck increasingly from the closing years of the nineteenth century, when it became common for the Indian elite to travel to Europe to enjoy the Season, sightsee and pay homage to their Sovereign. An integral part of such trips was the acquisition of western luxury goods. Under British rule, India's princes were relieved of any need to wage war against each other,

36.6 Bernard Boutet de Monvel, *The Maharaja of Indore in Maratha Dress*. Oil on canvas. French, 1934. Private collection. Courtesy of the Musée des Années 30.

36.5 Bernard Boutet de Monvel, *The Maharaja of Indore in Occidental Dress*. Oil on canvas. French, 1929. Private collection. Courtesy of the Musée des Années 30.

and were thus able to divert their substantial incomes to building projects and stylish objects. The great luxury shops of London and Paris were natural targets for their attention. A handful of princes including the maharajas of Baroda, Cooch Behar, Indore, Kapurthala, Nawangar and Patiala epitomized this taste for lavish spending. Their acquisition of jewels, pictures, motor cars and aeroplanes provides a good idea of the zeal with which they adopted western manners and aesthetic priorities. The House of Cartier's observations about how ready they were to drop their own decorative traditions applies to jewellery as well as other luxury goods: 'Indian rulers were exclusively interested in Parisian jewelry and had no hesitation in handing over their family treasures for reworking in fashionable European styles.'[22]

The yen for the fashionable extended, of course, to architecture and interior decoration. As with Bombay cinema interiors, the successful handling of such stylistically ambitious projects invariably depended on western or western-trained designers. The quest for novelty and modernity is perhaps best seen in the commissioning of a new palace, Manik Bagh, by Yeshwant Rao Holkar, Maharaja of Indore in 1930, the year he reached his majority.[23] Society painter Bernard Boutet de Monvel's portraits of the prince in traditional Maratha and western evening dress captures his elegant and self-assured style in both worlds (plates 36.5 and 36.6). Holkar, who was educated at Charterhouse and Christchurch, Oxford, developed a passion for the avant-garde, befriending Brancusi and commissioning portraits from Man Ray.[24] Manik Bagh proved to be an expression of his

artistic interests. The German-born architect Eckart Muthesius, son of Hermann Muthesius, designed a fully air-conditioned, U-shaped structure with steel frame and steel-framed windows, concrete walls and wooden roof. The interior was stylistically integrated, much of the furniture and accessories such as light fittings, switches and door handles designed by the architect and made at factories in Germany. Furnishings chosen by Muthesius for the palace included carpets by Ivan da Silva Bruhns and silver by Jean Puiforcat, while Holkar himself chose works of art including Gustave Miklós's *Tête de reine* and Brancusi's *Bird in Space*.[25] The furniture for the Maharaja's study was of macassar ebony designed by Ruhlmann; chairs for the ballroom were by Wassili Luckhardt and chairs for the billiard room were by Michel Dufet, while the Maharaja's bedroom was equipped with Eileen Gray's 'Transat' armchair and Le Corbusier and Charlotte Perriand's chaise longue (see plates 1.9 and 33.3).[26] The interiors of Manik Bagh featured both highly simplified, functional, serially produced furniture and more decorative, individual pieces in exotic materials in the high French style. The latter included metal, glass and lacquered screens and reflective metallic canopied beds designed by Louis Sognot and Charlotte Alix for the Maharaja and Maharani's bedrooms (plate 36.7).[27] Manik Bagh was only part of Holkar's equipage for modern living, which included two aeroplanes, a hunting caravan and a railway car (built by the Gloucester Railway and Carriage Company), all designed by Muthesius in a similar style.[28]

Manik Bagh contrasts strongly with the exuberant New Palace in Morvi, a carnival of de luxe Art Deco commissioned by Maharaja Mahendrasinhji Lakhdiraj and built between 1931 and 1944.[29] The building lies long and low, the exterior of pink plaster defined by strong horizontal lines and curved corners (plate 36.8). The interior epitomizes charmed living in the cocktail age. The atmosphere belongs more to a Deco pleasure dome than to a private palace and

36.7 Louis Sognot and Charlotte Alix, the Maharani of Indore's bedroom at Manik Bagh, with psyche and swivel chair. Around 1933. Photo: Descharnes & Descharnes.

36.8 New Palace, Morvi. 1931-40.
© Photo: Antonio Martinelli.

reflects the styling of ocean liners, luxury hotels and cinema interiors of the period. The interiors include, in addition to the suites of rooms expected in any palace, a lounge with dining booths for more relaxed meals, two bars, both with triple-decker cushioned barstools, a gym and a swimming pool (plates 36.9, 36.10 and 36.11). In accordance with the Deco tradition of incorporating flat art into interior schemes, the furnishings are set off by sensual murals and oil canvases by Polish poster artist Stefan Norblin. They vary in theme, but the painting on the cupola above the entrance transposes Krishna for Apollo riding his chariot across the sky, a clever manipulation of western and Hindu imagery. The bars and swimming pool are enlivened with murals of writhing and dancing bare-breasted women, their lower bodies wrapped in luxuriant diaphanous textiles; and the gaming and billiard rooms include canvases with Indian themes featuring tiger hunts and caparisoned elephants.

36.9 The Maharaja's bedroom,
New Palace, Morvi. 1931-40.
© Photo: Antonio Martinelli.

36.10 Upper bar, New Palace,
Morvi. 1931-40.
© Photo: Antonio Martinelli.

36.12 Umaid Bhawan, Jodhpur.
1929-44. © Photo: Antonio Martinelli.

36.11 Blue and silver mirrored
furniture, New Palace, Morvi. Indian,
1931-40. © Photo: Antonio Martinelli.

Umaid Bhawan, built by Maharaja Umaid Singh of Jodhpur between 1929 and 1944 as an employment project during a period of prolonged drought, offers a curious synthesis of Art Deco and indigenous architectural and decorative traditions.[30] The 347-room palace was built of local red sandstone and configured with a central soaring dome flanked by two vast wings (plate 36.12). Its architect, Henry Vaughan Lanchester, was an experienced designer of grandiose civic buildings and had been a contender for the job of building New Delhi.[31] Lanchester expressed a marked appreciation for India's architectural heritage and a disdain for the manner in which the country had become overrun with buildings in unsuitable western styles.[32] For Umaid Bhawan, he rejected Indo-Saracenic architecture 'in view of the fact that the States of Rajasthan only came to a very limited extent under Muslim domination'.[33] Instead he drew inspiration from the Hindu tradition of the temple-mountain palace, a structure typically raised high on a hill and representative of both purity and proximity to the cosmic forces.[34] The layout

conformed with the *vastu sastras*, medieval Hindu architectural treatises derived from the *Puranas*, a collection of ancient texts expounding on aspects of Hinduism.[35] In accordance with precedent, the palace's principal entrance is from the east, while the zenana (where ladies of the Maharaja's family lived in seclusion) and quarters for the staff are disposed in the south and north respectively. The subterranean swimming pool with mosaics of figures from the zodiac, meanwhile, was built directly beneath the palace's central rotunda (plate 36.13).

The architectural detailing of Umaid Bhawan is principally Indian, but the clean lines and streamlined, cool treatment of sculptural elements are entirely Deco in style. Chains of lotus flowers, lions, elephants, boars, horses, peacocks and interlacing patterns were all defined in minimal modern lines.[36] Carved motifs were chosen from local temples by G. A. Goldstraw, whom Lanchester had brought to Jodhpur as resident architect to ensure the stylistic consistency and integrity of the design.[37] The styling of motifs was handled by the sculptor

36.13 Swimming pool, Umaid
Bhawan, Jodhpur. 1929-44.
© Photo: Antonio Martinelli.

Norblin was not the only European artist in India
who was asked to design Deco interiors. Verandah
furnishings for Indira, Maharani of Cooch Behar were
made for her by a friend, Alister Maynard, then ADC
to the Governor of the Punjab. He objected to her
rooms 'absolutely crammed full of Victoriana' and
persuaded her to employ him to design furniture 'in
a more reasonable up-to-date style'.[41] The success
of this commission was followed by more work for
Maynard from the Maharani and other Indian princes
and led to the beginning of Maynard's career as a
professional designer. The influence of a European
designer is certainly felt in one of the most elaborate
and spectacular pieces of Indian Art Deco furniture,
a silver-covered canopy bed attributed to craftsmen
from the princely state of Udaipur in central India
(not to be confused with the better known state of
Udaipur in Rajasthan) (plate 36.1). The bed
continues the Indian royal tradition of covering
furniture with precious metals. However, its shape,
defined by a succession of rectangular planes, and
its ornament, of intersecting circles, fans, vertical
and horizontal lines, epitomize the Deco aesthetic.
According to tradition it was made in Udaipur to a
French design as a present for the Maharaja of
Surguja on his marriage in 1922.

Although the most significant and best known of
India's Art Deco palaces, Manik Bagh, New Palace
and Umaid Bhawan are by no means the only
residences erected in this style. On a smaller scale,
Karni Bhawan in Bikanir, Anant Niwas in Poorbander,
Sardar Samand in Jodhpur and Oasis House in
Wankaner all reflect the contemporary princely
penchant for Deco and its effects. However, equally
popular among India's rulers was to build in a
traditional Indo-Saracenic style, but pared down and
streamlined. Shiv Mahal in Baroda and Kusum Vilas
in Chotta Udaipur are typical of this trend. The
interiors of the lesser Deco and simplified Indo-
Saracenic palaces reflected the architecture. An
indication of exactly how these were furnished is
evident from a set of estimates provided in 1932 by
Waring & Gillow for Hyderabad House, built by Lutyens
for Mir Osman Ali Khan, Nizam of Hyderabad.[42] The
estimates reveal how Art Deco was perceived by
Indian princes as a style suitable for personal spaces
– bedrooms, dressing rooms and smoking rooms –
but inappropriate for formal ones such as reception
rooms, drawing rooms and waiting rooms, which
were furnished in eighteenth-century French and

L. F. Roslyn, who was brought to Jodhpur and asked
to train local sculptors to work in a Deco idiom. Not
all of the motifs were indigenous. To celebrate the
Maharaja's passion for flying, Lanchester cleverly
worked aeroplanes and propellers into aspects of the
scheme.[38] As at Morvi, the principal rooms at Umaid
Bhawan were enlivened with murals and canvases
by Norblin, who turned his hand to episodes from the
traditional Hindu epics and the history of Jodhpur
(plate 36.14).

Umaid Singh appointed Roslyn to devise an
appropriate scheme for the interior.[39] The sculptor
chose Maples – conveniently located within walking

distance of Lanchester's London office – which
provided estimate sketches for the various rooms in
Art Deco and simplified classical revival styles.
Although commissioned and made, the furniture,
carpeting, fixtures, lighting, linen and porcelain were
never to arrive; the vessel on which they were
dispatched left England in August 1942 and was
sunk by a German torpedo off the coast of Africa.[40]
Without any prospect of importing more furniture due
to the war, the Maharaja turned to Norblin who,
working from Maples's original sketches, prepared
a set of perspective schemes which were realized by
local carpenters.

English revival styles. The billiard room, by contrast, was conceived in a mock-Tudor style. According to the estimate, fibrous plaster detailing, curtains, metalwork, parquetry floors, electrical goods (including an HMV gramophone and a 'Magicoal' electric log fire) and revival furniture were to come from England; while the Deco furniture was to be made in India 'of selected teak celluloid to an approved colour to designs as illustrated on drawings'.[43] The Nizam objected to the high cost of the project, whereupon a more modest scheme was devised:

> The furniture (with the exception of a few selected period pieces which we are at present unable to make in India) will be manufactured in our Delhi workshops from the finest selected timbers, under the direct supervision of our representative who has now had 24 years experience manufacturing furniture in India … [These pieces will be] copied from actual selected models taken from our famous *Gillow Galleries* for this purpose.[44]

With the drive towards self-rule in the 1930s and 1940s and the consequent rebellion against British cultural hegemony, the question arose of the appropriateness of western-style architecture in India. The Poona engineer R. S. Despande, who published a series of modern house designs in 1931, championed the International Style, having seen fine examples while travelling around the world in 1936-7. According to him, it was a 'natural and inevitable evolution' in architecture, as valid in India as anywhere else in the world.[45] But Arthur Shoosmith, a follower of Lutyens and architect of the monolithic and towering St Martin's Garrison Church, New Delhi, argued that western modern architecture was not universal, but the product of circumstances in Europe which had no bearing on India. He questioned, too, whether it could ever be properly adopted since 'rigorous geometry' and sparse ornament are antithetical to India's own architectural and decorative traditions.[46] Feelings about the inappropriateness of western architecture were expressed in the *Journal of the Institute of Indian Architects* in 1939, partly as a response to the appointment of a German architect in Mysore to a post that many felt might have been easily filled by an Indian:

> the West is not the East, and the spirit that is India is not of the spirit of a Le Corbusier or a Gropius, or of a Frank Lloyd Wright or a Dudok … In India, cultural and material influences are different, and while we have a great deal to learn from men such as these, a philosophy of Architecture that would admirably serve the west would more likely be not in harmony with our needs here.[47]

36.15 Narotamdas Bhau, tea service. Silver and celluloid. Indian, c.1920-29. The Mitchell Wolfson Jr Collection. The Wolfsonian-Florida International University, Miami Beach, Florida.

An attempt to bridge Indian traditions and contemporary western architecture is found in the work of Walter Burley Griffin, protégé of Frank Lloyd Wright and architect of Canberra, who arrived in Lucknow in 1935 to build a new university library there. Griffin, too, railed against the movement of Indian architecture towards 'stark, logical, modernism' and sought to incorporate local decorative and structural elements into buildings that reflected local traditions but were also suitable for modern use.[48] His Indian designs (few of which were realized due to his untimely death in 1937) included the proposed library; additions to the palace of the Raja of Jahangirabad; a manuscript library and museum for the Raja of Mahmudabad; offices for the *Pioneer* newspaper; pavilions for the *United Provinces Industrial and Agricultural Exhibition* of 1936; and houses for faculty members of Lucknow University. Some of these are characterized by cubic forms married with local elements, such as pointed arches in the early Mughal style and domes inspired by mosque and stupa architecture. For surface decoration Griffin relied on repeating geometric patterns – some locally inspired and others international in flavour.

The nervous attitude to western design in the late 1930s and 1940s is symptomatic of India's ambitions to forge a new future and a new political, cultural and visual identity. In spite of this, however, western design infiltrated many aspects of Indian material culture, from film posters and window grates to sari fabrics and tea services (plate 36.15). Art Deco appealed to the elite for its cosmopolitanism, sophisticated styling, associations of luxury and glamour and conscious machine-age aesthetic, as well as its ability to assimilate and modernize local decorative traditions. It could be easily copied and worked in various media and in less expensive ways for wider consumption; as a result, the style was influential throughout India, if sometimes in a watered-down manner, and well after it ceased to be fashionable in the West. Thus traces of Deco may be seen from remote Indian villages in Gujarat to merchants' houses in Chettinad, where intersecting circles, sunrays, fans and curved lines demonstrate its popular appeal.

37 Ambiguously Modern: Art Deco in Latin America

Rafael Cardoso

Anyone doubting the powerful influence of Art Deco in Latin America has only to call to mind what is perhaps the most ubiquitous man-made symbol of the region – the monument to Christ the Redeemer atop Corcovado peak in Rio de Janeiro (plate 37.1). With a height of 38 metres (125 feet) and its famous outstretched arms, the statue has become so immediately recognizable as a signifier of place that few bother to look at it as anything other than that. Yet, like any monument, it too has a history and, like any work of art, a formal and stylistic affiliation. Designed around 1924 by the French sculptor Paul Landowski, the monument took over five years to build and was only inaugurated in 1931.[1] Both in period and in style – with its bold, flowing lines, smooth surface and stylized treatment of features – the Christ statue is a rare example of Art Deco sculpture on a monumental scale.

The reasons behind its undisputed resonance as a symbol are, however, far from clear or straightforward. Just what does it symbolize? The statue is most certainly an affirmation of the power of the church in a country often referred to, at least in the twentieth century, as the 'largest Catholic nation in the world'. Curiously enough, though, it was conceived at a time when the political sway of the Roman Catholic church was at a low ebb in Brazilian history. The Positivist-inspired Republic of 1889 had instituted the separation of church and state, paving the way for a distinct erosion of the church's temporal power over the following decades. Throughout the beginning of the new century, Catholic intellectuals struggled against what they considered the godless republicanism of the state. The tide began to turn in their favour precisely at the time when the statue was commissioned, ultimately culminating in a major rehabilitation of state-supported Catholicism after the rise to power of the authoritarian populist leader Getúlio Vargas.

The building of the Christ statue was conceived in conservative intellectual circles as an affirmation of Brazil's Catholic heritage. It was financed by the contributions of the faithful, who also contributed

their labour – with leagues of Catholic ladies patiently cementing the thousands of pieces of soapstone to panels that make up the statue's surface. It is therefore perhaps surprising that the style chosen for its execution was so manifestly modern for its time. Modern, yes, because there can be little doubt that Landowski's design conveys an image attuned to both the unsentimental vision of Christ then favoured by the Vatican and the aspirations towards artistic modernity so strongly felt in Latin America during the 1920s.[2] Modern, also, in building technique, as the monument's reinforced concrete structure represents an engineering triumph for its time. If, on the one hand, the statue's symbolism is 'reactionary' – to use ideological terminology – it is, on the other, also 'progressive'.

The Christ statue is no anomaly. Ambiguity is a characteristic of Art Deco in Latin America, and the myriad expressions of the style express a complex tangle of secondary meanings and contradictory connotations hidden within the umbrella-like simplicity of a concept as broad as 'modernity'. The triumph of high Modernism in the region during the 1930s and particularly after the Second World War has tended to subsume Art Deco as a mere precursor of things to come, a doomed tributary in the stream of evolution from a 'functional tradition in the nineteenth century'[3] to full-blown Functionalism. This teleological view of Art Deco as a sort of misguided early Modernism is still present in some of the terms used to discuss the architecture of the period in Latin America, such as 'pre-modern' or 'proto-modern'.[4] Obviously, nothing is ever designed, at the time of its making, to be simply a precursor of anything else; so, the first step to understanding the real significance of Art Deco is to move away from this historicist interpretation.

Rather than as a precursor of Modernism, Art Deco in Latin America is probably best understood as belonging to a complex of ideas and initiatives that Argentinian architectural historian Jorge Ramos has termed 'the other modernity'.[5] The idea of Art Deco as a phenomenon standing apart from – and, to

37.1 Paul Landowski, monument to Christ the Redeemer, Corcovado peak, Rio de Janeiro. 1924-31. © Thierry Cazabon/Getty Images/Stone. © ADAGP, Paris and DACS, London 2002.

some extent, in opposition to – the accepted paradigm of high Modernism and its genealogy is an important one, throwing into relief the increasingly evident fact that modernity was never so simple an affair as Modernist commentators would have us believe. Deep as we are into a period content to describe itself as Post-modern, we are still not completely at ease with the idea that modernity has always meant different things to different people.

Modernizing the built environment

Art Deco architecture arrived in Latin America in the mid-1920s bringing with it an incontrovertible sense of novelty and fashion. From Vicente Mendiola in Mexico City to Alejandro Virasoro in Buenos Aires, architects all over Latin America quickly incorporated the style. Some of the earliest designs were for the private houses of wealthy patrons; but by the end of the decade notable examples of banks, office buildings and residential buildings had sprung up in virtually every major city in the region (plates 37.2 and 37.3).[6] Given the enduring sway of French culture over Latin American elites at the time, the echoes of the Paris 1925 Exhibition were clearly in the air. However, the overriding influence on most of the architects who chose to conjugate the Deco idiom into local building projects appears to have been a North American one, conveyed by the medium of film. The skyscrapers soaring up in New York and Chicago exerted a powerful attraction for a generation fascinated by the possibilities of technological progress and in awe of the fact that the United States – also a former European colony – had emerged from the First World War as, arguably, the world's greatest power.

The post-1918 cultural context of Latin America was unique and, in some senses, increasingly divorced from the European experience. For most Latin American nations, the period between 1920 and 1924 marked the centennial of independence from Spain and Portugal. This sparked civic celebrations of the exploits of San Martin, Bolivar and other national heroes, as well as a good deal of soul-searching about the patent failure of the region to attain its post-independence expectations of glory and prosperity. Most Latin American countries had remained completely within the European – and particularly British – sphere of economic and political influence during the nineteenth century. The steady rise of the United States as an industrial power was widely perceived, after the 1870s, as providing an alternative to the old colonial hegemony, even in monarchical Brazil, which of all the nations in the region had maintained itself most distant from the republican values of the great neighbour to the north.[7]

Before the Great War, much of the cultural debate had been concerned with making Latin America more 'European' (i.e. French, British or German) and, therefore, more 'civilized'. The architectural practice ensuing from that vision had enshrined the ideal of copying Parisian models, even to the extent of undertaking massive urban reform and public works projects like the neo-Haussmannian transformation of central Rio de Janeiro during the first decade of the twentieth century.[8] For the post-1918 generation of artists and architects, however, the idea of Europeanizing Latin America seemed to be not only improbable but frankly undesirable. In the climate of patriotic bluster surrounding the centennials, national style came to the fore as the great concern of a large number of cultural policy makers, ranging across a broad political spectrum that included representatives of both left and right. During the 1920s, the political polarization of nationalism and internationalism was still not at all clearly defined; and many, if not most, of the younger Latin American intellectuals felt no contradiction in aligning themselves both with modernity and nationalism.[9]

The pressing issue of defining national style sparked a renewed interest in the Iberian traditions prior to independence, and even in the indigenous cultures of Latin America. So-called 'neo-colonial' architectural movements sprang up in virtually every major country in the region, sometimes applying decorative motifs of local native origin to re-workings of the forms and spaces of the colonial past.[10] The partisans of 'Neocolonialismo' or 'Criollismo' were careful, nonetheless, also to employ the latest industrialized building techniques. Although the formal tradition of the past held an ideological attraction, few advocated a return to the materials, scale or even, necessarily, the spatial distribution and floor plans of bygone days. Thus, a nationalist visual aesthetic was adapted to contemporary standards of building design.

37.2 Ricardo Wriedt, Novo Mundo building, Avenida Presidente Wilson, Rio de Janeiro. 1934. Arquivo da Cidade do Rio de Janeiro.

37.3 Arnoldo Gladosch, entrance to the Itahy building, Rio de Janeiro. 1932. © Photo: Cadu Pilotto.

Apart from national style, the other great parameter for architectural debate at the time was modernity, both in the narrow technological sense of making buildings comfortable, attractive and durable, and as a broader ideological project of asserting novelty and change. These two aspirations would eventually come into conflict, as the strident nationalism of Fascist ideology collided with the increasingly internationalist bent of Modernism. Nevertheless, partisans of national style and of modernity often managed to find common ground in Latin America during the 1920s, insofar as they were perceived as being mutually opposed to the lingering influence of Beaux-Arts eclecticism. The skyscrapers of the Jazz Age were, at once, modern and non-European; and they spoke of a time in which the Americas would come into their own as the new epicentre of world progress. The first skyscrapers to spring up in places like Rio de Janeiro (Elisário da Cunha Bahiana's Edifìcio A Noite, 1928) or Mexico City (Manuel Ortiz Monasterio's Edifìcio La Nacional, 1932) marked a bold break indeed with the timid scale of the colonial city; yet they were also powerful symbols of a distinctly American – and Pan-American – identity, liberating in its denial of traditional values.

This is the architectural stage upon which Art Deco was to make its debut in Latin America. On the one hand, Art Deco was modern: it is no coincidence that the main vehicle for its dissemination in Mexico was the journal *Cemento*, which propounded the style along with the virtues of modern materials like reinforced concrete and stainless steel.[11] On the other hand, Art Deco could be nationalized, made native, by the application of indigenous motifs, as became common practice from Havana to Rio de Janeiro, from Santiago to Mexico City, particularly since much of the traditional ornament of Native Americans – Aztec, Inca, Marajoara, Mapuche and others – was broadly geometrical and abstract, well suited to the conventionalized treatment already in vogue in Europe and North America. In some places, like Mexico, this 'nativized' Art Deco appears to have functioned as an alternative to neo-colonialist nationalism. In others, like Chile and Argentina, a curious coalition appears to have taken shape between neo-colonialism and Art Deco against what was perceived to be the staid academic establishment of architecture.[12]

37.4 Lobby of the Palacio de Bellas Artes, Mexico City. Around 1928. Courtesy of the Museo del Palacio de Bellas Artes, INBA. © Photo: Javier Hinojosa.

37.5 Aerial view of site demolished for construction of the Avenida Presidente Vargas, Rio de Janeiro, 1944. Arquivo da Cidade do Rio de Janeiro.

In any event, Art Deco was able to encompass these competing aspirations and fuse them into a package that was novel and exciting, yet unlikely to provoke the wrath of those segments of society so often suspicious of innovation and change. Linked in the popular imagination to the great symbols of technological fantasy of the time – skyscrapers, cinema, transatlantic luxury liners, flying clippers, aeroplanes, automobiles – the style encountered little resistance in Latin America and was rapidly assimilated by both public and private sectors, rich and poor, as a building aesthetic suited to the changing times.[13] Not surprisingly, among the main expressions of the Art Deco style are new building types such as cinemas and garages, as well as those linked to leisure and pleasure such as hotels, museums, casinos and resorts (plate 37.4). By the 1920s, Hollywood-inspired styles and fashions had made notable inroads in the Latin American imagination, creating a curious cocktail of frivolity, luxury and modernity that found its visual translation in the Deco idiom of cinema foyers and stage-set interiors.[14] As elsewhere in the world, movies and motor cars were instrumental in ushering in a new culture of fun and fashionable cosmopolitanism, largely based on superficial appearances and therefore readily accessible to a growing mass public.

The impact that style rather than substance could have on the masses was central to the subsequent development of Art Deco architecture, as is made evident in the context of 1930s Brazil.[15] Getúlio Vargas rose to power with the so-called Revolution of 1930 and finally consolidated that power into a full-blown dictatorship after 1937 with the advent of the self-styled 'Estado Novo' (New State). The story of Vargas is distinctly Brazilian in its flavour and detail; yet it ties into a broader international zeitgeist of political populism and the cult of personality. There are obvious parallels with Perón in Argentina and Roosevelt in the United States, as well as less flattering ones with dictators such as Franco, Mussolini, Hitler and Stalin. Architectural historians have long pointed out the consistent partnership between political authoritarianism and building on a monumental scale, a relationship borne out in the Latin American experience just as much as in Europe and North America in the 1930s. What is perhaps less evident elsewhere, but disturbingly clear in Brazil, is the way in which the Art Deco style was applied to the architecture of monumentalism as a means of masking the politics of reaction with a veneer of progressive modernity.

The great urban reform project under Vargas was the opening up of an avenue bearing his own name in the centre of Rio de Janeiro, then the national capital (plate 37.5). It is 16 lanes wide and several kilometres long. The building spanned four years[16] and entailed the destruction of whole streets and dozens of city blocks, including hundreds of buildings, old and new, as well as historic churches,

Modernity before the dictates of Modernism

Given their eventual parting of ways, the relationship between Art Deco and Modernism is a point particularly worthy of investigation. Brazilian Modernism in the visual arts officially traces back its genealogy to 1922, when the Semana de Arte Moderna (Modern Art Week) was held in São Paulo, bringing together the first generation of self-declared modern artists in the European avant-garde vein. These artists positioned themselves as establishing a rupture with Brazilian art of the preceding century and, particularly, its purported habit of slavishly copying outdated European models. (That they themselves were copying Cubist, Expressionist and Constructivist models, often with a lag of a decade and more, seems not to have made a dent in their earnest rhetoric.) Despite the hallowed place of 1922 in the annals of Brazilian Modernism, the contemporary importance of the Modern Art Week has been largely overestimated by the Modernist commentators who subsequently wrote it into history.[19] Nonetheless, the movement's capacity to embrace Art Deco reveals something about the slippages between differing visions of modernity.

Decorative art and interior design provided intimate arenas for the mingling of Art Deco style and Modernist ideals; and the work of the artist couple John Graz and Regina Gomide has been rightly singled out as a prime example of this interplay. Swiss-born Graz distinguished himself in the 1920s and 1930s as a designer of furniture and interiors, mostly executed for wealthy São Paulo patrons and often embellished with textiles designed by his wife.[20] His work occasionally combines angular geometric ornament with figurative motifs representing stylized indigenous characters, reflecting a curious amalgam of Modernist formal conventions and nativist rhetoric of a Romantic vein. This revealing juxtaposition of past and present is not limited to the work of Graz and Gomide, but also crops up in the decorative work of other contemporary artists like painter Vicente do Rego Monteiro or sculptor Hugo Bertazzon. Like their architectural counterparts, many fine and decorative artists appear to have perceived Art Deco as a particularly suitable idiom for reconciling the traditional opposition between modernity and national identity, however uneasy that co-existence may eventually have proved.

If Modernism had an impact on the decorative arts, it did not entirely set the tone of cultural production in Brazil during the 1920s and 1930s. A significant upsurge of industrialization during these decades ushered in new products and created new

37.6 Roberto Magno de Carvalho, Gare D. Pedro II, 'Central do Brasil', Rio de Janeiro. 1937. © Photo: Cadu Pilotto.

a large section of park and the mythical location of Praça Onze, epicentre of popular entertainment, music and nightlife at the time.[17] To line this great axis, the government commissioned a number of monumental buildings, including the railway station popularly known as 'Central do Brasil' (1937), which clearly partakes of the Deco idiom (plate 37.6) and is perhaps the best-loved architectural product of the Vargas years. Though monumental in scale, it possesses a lightness and grace that stand in stark contrast to the heavy-set boxiness of the neighbouring Ministry of War building (1937), a less successful attempt to blend Deco effects with monumentalism.

Like its more famous contemporary, the Corbusier-derived Ministry of Education (1937), the Central Station building is a part of the broader attempt by Vargas to refashion capital and nation in the image of his 'New State'.[18] That the architectural portion of

this programme to meld dictatorship and populism could include, at one and the same time, quasi-Fascist buildings like the Ministry of Finance – monumental and vaguely neo-classical – and the putative Functionalism of Le Corbusier attests to the profoundly contradictory nature of the idea of an authoritarian state as protector of the people and their culture. That the Art Deco style, for all its appeal as a symbol of progress and modernity, could lend itself successfully to the very same building programme attests to the ambiguity of its legacy in Latin America. Like the monument to Christ the Redeemer, Central Station stands out as a weird symbolic amalgam of brute institutional power and genuine popular enthusiasm. Both are material vestiges of a time when industrial civilization was undaunted by the prospect of translating the pipe-dreams of the few into public policies sealing the fate of millions.

consumer expectations and habits. These products were culturally modern – that is, formally and conceptually distinct from earlier products and often relying on new methods of production – and they reached constituencies much wider and more heterogeneous than the traditional elites. They included not only new types of domestic goods, such as phonographs and radios, but new – or modernized – visual media such as photography, film and graphic design. Illustrated magazines stand out as a particularly rich, yet little studied, example of the proliferation of a visual culture that was not affiliated with international avant-garde circles yet was both modern and accessible to a popular audience.

The noted book collector and author José E. Mindlin has remarked upon the importance of illustrated periodicals in disseminating political and cultural change in Brazil from the late nineteenth century onwards.[21] This observation is not only apposite in general but, to my mind, particularly revealing of the paths by which the Art Deco style came to be construed as a signifier of modernity in the Latin American context. From the early years of the twentieth century, Brazil experienced an undeniable boom in the production and consumption of illustrated magazines, which can be broadly attributed to both technological factors such as new methods for the printed reproduction of photographs and demographic factors such as urban growth. Arguably, by the 1920s, something approaching a modern publishing market was in place. Besides a generalized increase in the numbers of titles and readers, illustrated magazines began to move away from the previous emphasis on political satire and social or literary commentary. Instead they targeted specific segments of the public, such as women or children, and special interests, such as industrial technology or modern art.[22] By the end of the decade, a new culture of illustrated magazines was clearly consolidated, providing a vehicle for the work of an entire generation of talented illustrators and graphic artists. It included names like di Cavalcanti, Paim, Belmonte and, above all, J. Carlos (José Carlos de Brito e Cunha), perhaps the leading Brazilian caricaturist of the period (plate 37.7).

Not coincidentally, many (if not most) of the great graphic artists of the period were influenced to some extent by the evolving Art Deco style, disseminated worldwide in record time by the rapidly changing technologies of visual communication. Most popular magazines of the 1920s are filled with illustrations that bespeak a curious slippage between the visual idioms characteristic of Art Nouveau and those of Art Deco. The opposition between these styles was never

37.7 J. Carlos, cover of *Para Todos*, 28 May 1927. Fundação Casa de Rui Barbosa. © Photo: Cadu Pilotto.

PARA TODOS...

NA TERRA DO MAXIXE   Dese
I—Sururú no botequim   Roberto Rodrig

37.8 Roberto Rodrigues, 'Na Terra do maxixe. I. Sururu no Botequim', *Para Todos*, 31 March 1928. Fundação Casa de Rui Barbosa. © Photo: Cadu Pilotto.

37.9 Emiliano di Cavalcanti, cover of *O Malho*, 9 August 1919. Fundação Casa de Rui Barbosa. © Photo: Cadu Pilotto.

garçonne is revealing of how Art Deco imagery was linked in the popular imagination to a very specific brand of modernity. This was a modernity that was cosmopolitan and unashamedly frivolous, a fun-loving vision of modern living far removed from the dour cerebralism and mystical asceticism of much avant-garde culture. The prevalence of such magazines is an unambiguous indicator of the existence of that 'other modernity' mentioned at the start of this text, a modernity un-tinged by the later sectarian politics of high Modernism.[24]

The illustrated magazines of the 1920s appear equally to be free of another type of polarization typical of Latin America. Historically dependent upon cultural models far removed from their day-to-day experience, Latin American elites have traditionally veered between a conservative position of reverentially preserving the legacy of their European heritage and a radical position of affirming supposedly native values as an antithesis to imported ideas and an antidote to their continued dominance. The opposition between these two views dates back to colonial times and has generated certain

as clear-cut in Brazil as in Europe, and a seamless continuity between them as signifiers of fashionable cosmopolitanism comes through in the pages of magazines like *O Malho*, *A Maçã* and *Para Todos*, three of the bestselling illustrated periodicals of the decade (plates 37.8 and 37.9). The case of *A Maçã* (The Apple) is particularly interesting. Edited by the popular writer Humberto de Campos, this gentleman's magazine specializing in piquant social

satire allied exquisite cover illustrations, largely in an Art Deco vein, with an extremely innovative layout. This was characterized by geometrically constructed one- and two-page spreads and by a bold interchange between typography and image as elements of visual structure (plate 37.10).[23] Delightfully naughty by the parochial standards of the time, the magazine's manipulation of the perceived erotic charge of flappers in garters and hairdos *à la*

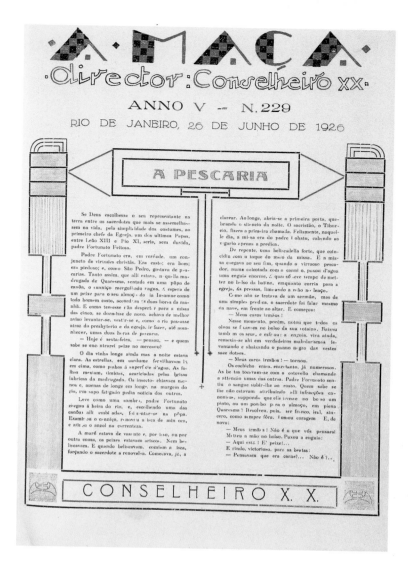

young woman stands next to an armchair in which a wealthy older man is just nodding off, his eyes closed and fingers barely grasping the edge of the newspaper as it drops to the floor. Left hand on hips, the young woman's right index finger touches the mouth of a little monkey poised on a wooden perch. The caption is a dialogue in which she comments: 'These African monkeys can't survive our climate.' 'Why?' asks the man. 'They are soon worn out here', she replies, in a clever play on words.[25] The suggestion is that both monkey and man have been worn out by her cosmopolitan femininity (and implied sexual availability), signified by the combination of high heels, stockings, garters, diminutive *robe de chambre* and short hair. Pictorially, her body is the main site that links man and beast, respectively of European and African origin. The Deco patterns of both armchair and robe play an essential part in this comic representation of the power of the other modernity to subdue the brutes of the past.

anomalies: on the one hand, the tendency to perpetuate European customs long after they have been abandoned even in Europe; on the other hand, the tendency to deny the obvious ascendancy of those same customs and affirm – often with dubious validity – a claim upon the indigenous or African origins of the non-elite segments of society. To a great extent, this conflict mirrors that between 'academic' and 'modern', upon which high Modernism long premised its legitimacy in Latin America. Art Deco has proved to be resistant to these simple dichotomies of traditional versus modern and imported versus native. More akin to the multifaceted complexity so prized in Post-modernity, it remains ambiguously modern: genuine in its enthusiasm for the present, but not entirely convinced of its power to bury the past and reshape the future.

A wonderful cover of *A Maçã* (plate 37.11) provides a fitting epilogue to the sophisticated way in which the 1920s generation made use of humour and sexual politics to resolve abiding cultural dilemmas. A scantily clad and decidedly modern

38 'A Growing Enthusiasm for Modernity': Art Deco in Australia

Christopher Menz

Australia's reaction to Art Deco was multifarious. The style had a strong and lasting impact in all areas of the visual arts, especially in architecture and architectural decoration. Its first manifestations appeared in Australia in the mid-1920s – initially in the major population centres of Sydney and Melbourne and later in cities and towns throughout the country – and continued throughout the 1930s.

The mixed response to the style may be attributed in part to the fact that Australia did not participate in the Paris 1925 Exhibition – an omission noted at the time by at least one Australian visitor[1] – with the result that artistic and design developments in Paris were not followed so strongly in Australia as they might otherwise have been. Furthermore Britain – where Art Deco was relatively slow to develop – remained a major influence on Australian culture during the first half of the twentieth century. Isolation from Europe and North America meant that first-hand exposure to novel and progressive tendencies in international design was limited to those able to travel, or to recent immigrants and visitors from Europe who had been exposed to modern art and design. However, in progressive circles in Australia, there was a great interest in the latest in overseas design. North American architecture was followed keenly, and contemporary developments found supporters and promoters among artists and designers, as well as magazine editors, importers and retailers. In parallel to this interest in modernity, however, there was a flourishing market in historical revivals and a culture embedded in many of the art and design teaching institutions that drew on the philosophy and practices of the Arts and Crafts Movement.

For most designers in Australia and New Zealand, knowledge of the latest trends in European design was derived from the study of imported objects or secondary sources such as articles and illustrations in magazines and books. A number of Australian publications kept their readers informed about new tendencies. *Art in Australia* (1916-42), for example, and the two magazines that it spawned – *The Home*

and *Architecture* – often included material on contemporary international architecture and design. *Art in Australia*, though primarily concerned with painting and sculpture, regularly carried features on architecture and interior design. *The Home*, while focusing on Australian subjects, also ran illustrated articles on the *Salon d'automne* and on modern European designers such as Paul Poiret and Jean Patou. *The Home* also featured stylish covers and advertisements for Australian concerns that promoted the new trends — notably the department store David Jones. Many of those covers in distinctly Art Deco mode were designed by Thea Proctor or Hera Roberts.

Art in Australia's coverage included articles on modern French shop-front design. But it made no distinction between what we would now call Art Deco and Modernism. In 1929, for example, a special issue contained a section entitled 'Industrial and Applied Art Section'. It illustrated a range of contemporary European and Australian objects, including ceramics, glass, textiles, metalwork and jewellery, book design, graphic design and automobiles. The selection consisted of work whose modernity was accentuated by captions such as 'Group of modern design in Lallemant Ceramics'. (The most intriguing entry was for two Ford Sports Roadsters with colour schemes designed by Australian artists.) In 1935, the magazine illustrated British design from the *British Art in Industry* exhibition at the Royal Academy[2] and the popular 'Circus' set designed by Laura Knight which was sold in Australia.[3] Other issues contained occasional illustrated articles on architecture, interiors and furniture design. In 1936, the author of an article titled 'Australian Furniture' could write that there was 'a growing enthusiasm for "modernity"'.[4]

Art Deco's reception in the region was not passive, however. Its advent coincided with a growth of regional consciousness and a wish to develop an indigenous style. Art Deco's combination of modernizing and traditional impulses offered a powerful example of other possibilities of synthesis.

38.1 Rayner Hoff, *Sacrifice*, central sculpture in the Hall of Silence, Anzac Memorial, Sydney. Bronze. Australian, 1934. Photo: Patrick Van Daele.

38.2 W. Hayward and Robert Casboulte, detail of stone goannas entwined between waratahs and ferns, forming the capitals of the columns and pilasters of the façade of the National Film and Sound Archive, Canberra. Australian, 1930. Photo: Patrick Van Daele.

The blend of internationalism and regionalism in the visual arts was championed by a major Australian artist of the day, Margaret Preston. In an article titled 'The Indigenous Art of Australia', which appeared in *Art in Australia* in 1925, Preston argued cogently, through text and images, for both the importance of Aboriginal art as a source of truly Australian art and the need for modernization. Warming to her theme, she asked:

> Would France be now at the head of all nations in art if her artists and craftsmen had not given her fresh stimulus from time to time by benefiting from the art of her native colonies, and not only her own colonies, but by borrowing freely from the colonies of other countries?[5]

In practice, just such a synthesis of internationalism and exotic regionalism as Preston proposed produced some of the more arresting and original works of the period, particularly in architecture. Thus, in some local variants in both Australia and New Zealand, an Art Deco neo-classical architectural vocabulary was combined with indigenous motifs in decorative details and modelling. In Canberra, heads of Aboriginal figures appear as details in the Australian War

Memorial (1933-6). A wealth of Australian flora and fauna – including rare images of the platypus, goanna and wombat – was used to decorate the Institute of Anatomy (1930), now the National Film and Sound Archive (the building's neo-classical façade is also decorated with geometrically patterned, Aboriginal-style glazed panels) (plate 38.2). In Macquarie Street, Sydney, Australian flora adorns the Art Deco British Medical Association House (1930); and in Napier, New Zealand, Maori motifs appear in the former Bank of New Zealand and on the Ross & Glendinning buildings (1932). This interest in the decorative possibilities of the indigenous flora and fauna, and in the culture of the native peoples of the region, was firmly rooted in the nineteenth-century tradition of applied decoration but was given a new impetus with the advent of Art Deco and its fondness for decoration.

The early inter-war period in Australasia saw a partial building boom during the 1920s, followed by renewed building activity after the Depression. Besides architecture, the major field of the visual arts to be influenced by Art Deco was sculpture, particularly in the 1930s. Around Australia,

memorials to the fallen of the First World War, many of them collaborations between architects and sculptors, represent some of the great Art Deco monuments. The most splendid examples are the Anzac Memorial in Sydney's Hyde Park (C. Bruce Dellit with Rayner Hoff, 1931-4), the Australian National War Memorial in Canberra (Emil Sodersteen, 1933-6) and the Shrine of Remembrance in Melbourne (Hudson & Wardrop, 1927-34) (plate 38.3). The National War Memorial in Wellington, New Zealand (Gummer & Ford, 1931-2) – a bell tower – also shows strong Art Deco influences.

Rayner Hoff was the most significant and successful sculptor to work in Australia during the inter-war period. Described as producing work with a 'synthesis of Classicism and Vitalism, of radical sexuality and Art Deco', he came to Australia from Britain in 1923.[6] Through his work as a sculptor and teacher, his influence on Australian sculpture was vast. His school included many sculptors with strong Art Deco elements in their work, among them Jean Broome-Norton and Barbara Tribe (plate 38.4). Hoff was involved in many major building commissions, but some of his most impressive work was to be

38.3 C. Bruce Dellit and Rayner Hoff,
Anzac Memorial, Hyde Park, Sydney.
1931-4. Photo: Patrick Van Daele.

38.4 Jean Broome-Norton, *Abundance*.
Bronze. Australian, 1934. Art Gallery of
New South Wales. © Jean Broome-Norton.
Photo: Christopher Snee for AGNSW.

found in schemes for war memorials. He worked on
Dellit's Anzac Memorial in Sydney and also designed
the sculptures for the National War Memorial,
Adelaide (1927-30).[7] The Sydney memorial,
described as a 'unique statement of architectural and
sculptural unity, a masterwork of Art Deco work in
Australia', houses Hoff's *Sacrifice*, one of Australia's
finest civic sculptures (plate 38.1). The memorial's
success lies in the synthesis of Dellit's monumental
architecture and Hoff's sculpture. Hoff used both
classical and contemporary imagery and stylized
geometrical forms. The battle scenes in low relief,
with the figures in modern dress, form a link between
an ancient mode of representation and modern life.
Similarly, Dellit's building echoes ancient military
monuments, with its steps, columns, arches and
ziggurat-like top (the latter a favoured Art Deco
form). It achieves its effect through the interplay of
these massive forms and Hoff's decorative reliefs.

38.5 L. P. Burns, terracotta decoration on Elmslea Chambers, Goulburn, New South Wales. Australian, 1933. Made by Wunderlich Ltd.
Photo: Patrick Van Daele.

chromed steel, granite and terracotta, were ones that possessed – or could be given – the surface brilliance so characteristic of Art Deco.

Architectural terracotta, introduced in Australia during the 1920s, was used extensively as a decorative material, often to cover entire façades of buildings. In Goulburn, New South Wales, famous for its fine wool, Wunderlich Ltd, tile manufacturers, in conjunction with the architect L. P. Burns, rose to Dellit's challenge and produced a rich polychrome ornamental façade for Elmslea Chambers (1933); neo-classical pilasters surround a design based on a ram's head (plate 38.5). Ernest Wunderlich had visited the Paris 1925 Exhibition and recorded:

> It is a pleasure show like all French Exhibitions ... full of novel conceits and, but for the modern sculpture, which is uniformly vile, pleasing and striking. In furniture and interior decoration, especially in lighting effects, many ideas could be picked up. Even when the designs are *outré* they are always artistic and possess a cachet of their own ... and the *palais des marbres et mosaïques* is gorgeous.[9]

The firm's subsequent work and their showroom were much influenced by what Ernest Wunderlich had seen at the exhibition. In addition to architectural terracotta, used to clad and ornament several buildings, Wunderlich promoted Art Deco designs in their decorative pressed metal ceilings.

Napier Waller and his wife, Christian, were the most important Australian artists in stained glass during the 1920s and 1930s. Both worked in other media including printmaking; Napier was also a painter. They had been exposed to contemporary ideas about stained-glass design while studying at Whall & Whall in London in 1929 and were strongly influenced by contemporary international design tendencies more generally. After their return to Australia in 1930, there was a pronounced change in Christian's style. Her graphic work – prints, illustrated books and bookplates – with its emphatic geometry and often elongated forms, was strongly influenced by Art Deco. Her remarkable group of illustrations for the book *The Great Breath* (1932) are based on theosophical thought and, like many Art Deco designs, also drew on ancient Greek and Egyptian art (plate 38.6). Similarly, the Wallers' stained glass shows the same preoccupation with geometric form, apparent in the leading as much as in the figure and decorative work. Napier Waller's most pronounced statement in the style was the Leckie window for Wilson Hall in the University of Melbourne (1935).[10] Its complex design draws on Greek mythology and biblical images to illustrate the Creation and the evolution of European culture (plate 38.7).

The Anzac Memorial appears to be made of stone but is largely of reinforced concrete. The possibilities opened up by new materials and technologies were welcomed by Dellit, who advocated that architects should exploit them: 'Modernity has produced such wonderful materials and methods ... glass, electric light, synthetic materials, highly finished materials, structural steel, reinforced concrete, terra cotta – each with possibilities unknown to the ancients – mechanical inventions and mass production.'[8] Many of the materials to which Dellit referred, such as

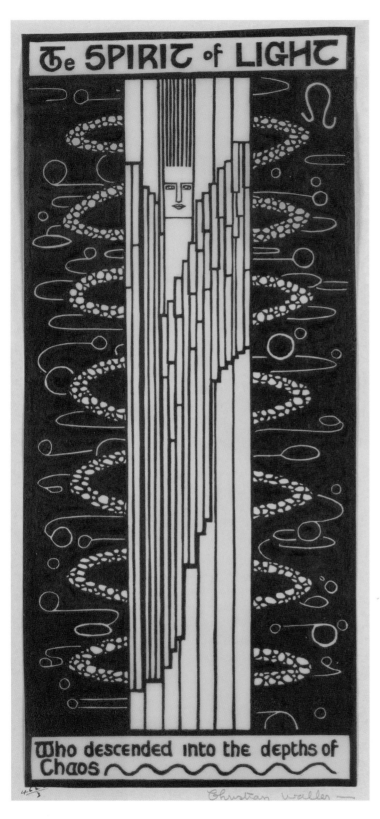

38.6 Christian Waller, *The Spirit of Light*. Linocut. Australian, 1932. Plate 1 of *The Great Breath*, Melbourne, 1932. National Gallery of Victoria, Melbourne.

38.7 Napier Waller, detail from *Ceres*, Leckie Window, University of Melbourne. Stained glass and lead. Australian, 1935. University of Melbourne Art Collection. Gift of John E. Leckie.

Large-scale building decoration in the Art Deco style was not confined to stained glass and terracotta. Napier Waller's scheme *The Pastoral Pursuits of Australia* (1927) was a vast mural decoration painted for the Menzies Hotel in Melbourne.[11] His mosaic with the text 'I'll put a girdle round about the earth' (1933), for the façade of Newspaper House, Collins Street, Melbourne, was similar in scale (plate 38.9). Both wall decorations drew on classical art for the poses of the figures (located in a classicized Australian landscape in the painting and in a Modernist urban landscape in the mural), yet both are Art Deco in their overall content and feel. Waller's interest in the cult of the body and its regenerative force – a theme common to both Art Deco and Modernist art and design – is evident in much inter-war Australian visual art.

A major attempt to promote new tendencies in design in Australia was the series of rooms created as part of the Burdekin House Exhibition in Sydney in 1929. This loan exhibition – predominantly of antiques and historic works of art, shown in an elegant Sydney colonial town house – included six contemporary rooms created by Sydney artists and designers. The artists Roy de Maistre, Thea Proctor, Hera Roberts and Adrian Feint created designs, while well known Sydney furniture makers, not otherwise

recognized for progressive design work, made the furniture (plate 38.8). As Sydney Ure Smith stated in his foreword: 'Nothing as complete as these rooms has been seen previously in Sydney and they prove conclusively that good modern furniture can be made in Sydney.'[12] The artists in the exhibition and commentators in the catalogue were clearly *au fait* with the latest in French and North American Art Deco design. To underscore this, the Australian-made furniture was supplemented by French lamps and textiles. Comments in the exhibition catalogue clarify the ideas behind the design processes. Leon Gellert, in his text 'The Modern Interior Decoration', analyzed modern design, stating that:

> Modern interior decoration ... eliminates all that is unnecessary and is in agreement with the whole world-movement towards simplification in modern dress, modern architecture, modern art ... Furthermore, it gives ample scope for the application of colour. Its furniture is based ... on the simple primary forms – the cube, the prism, the cylinder, the cone, the pyramid, the sphere – and restricted variations of these forms. An analysis of the greatest examples of architecture in the world's history discloses that they have achieved their purpose through the judicious use of these elementary shapes.[13]

38.8 Hera Roberts, interior from the 1929 Burdekin House Exhibition, Sydney. *The Home*, October 1929. By permission of the National Library of Australia.

38.9 Napier Waller, *'I'll put a girdle round about the earth'*, Newspaper House, Melbourne. Mosaic. Australian, 1933. Photo: Patrick Van Daele.

Furniture in the living room by Hera Roberts is similarly described: 'Tables – These tables are based on the simplest primary forms – cylinders, cubes, prisms and pyramids. Armchairs – represent the halves of a cylinder divided diagonally. Bookcase and Cabinet – These are modern forms which owe their origin to the set-back architecture of American skyscrapers.'[14]

The modern rooms at the Burdekin House Exhibition built on an existing relationship between artists and department stores. Grace Bros. had used Roy de Maistre and Thea Proctor to design interiors in 1927, and the success of the Burdekin House Exhibition can only have encouraged other stores to follow suit. Art Deco graphic design and advertising were used by department stores such as David Jones and Grace Bros. from the 1920s onwards.

By the mid-1930s, as an article in *Art in Australia* indicated, furniture by several Australian designers reflected 'simplicity of form, and interest obtained by the use of fine materials rather than applied pattern or ornament'.[15] Designs by Molly Grey, Hera Roberts and the H. Goldman Manufacturing Company reflected the Art Deco style in this respect. The luxury aspect of Art Deco, which was such a feature of French design and demanded a wealthy clientele, was not prevalent in Australia. Nevertheless, elements of a luxurious finish and use of materials are to be found in furniture made in sumptuous combinations of timbers (both Australian and exotic) and with veneers such as burr walnut. In 1936, *Art in Australia* illustrated a desk designed by Hera Roberts in which she augmented the impression of luxury with an inlay of synthetic ivory.[16] In Melbourne, Goldman produced furniture of high quality, frequently to architects' designs. The firm exhibited at the *British Empire Exhibition* at Wembley in 1924, winning a gold medal. Goldman probably supplied some of the finely detailed and veneered furniture to the house known as Burnham Beeches in Victoria (1930-33). The house was designed by the architect Harry Norris and, with its arresting interplay of geometric forms and refined decorative details and furnishing, was one of the most complete essays in Australian Art Deco domestic architecture. Expensive materials may not have been widely taken up in Australia, but many of the characteristic forms and decorative motifs of Art Deco – such as sunbursts and zigzags – were adopted. Yet, to some extent, Modernism, with its undecorated forms and simpler materials, was more suited to Australian tastes and conditions. This is particularly evident in progressive furniture designs such as those by Fred Ward.

Despite the lack of a highly developed industrial base, Art Deco in Australia can be found in all aspects of the decorative arts, crafts and design. Commercial ceramic factories – such as the Hoffman Brick Company in Melbourne, and Bakewell's and Mashman Bros. in Sydney – produced a range of functional domestic wares that drew on the geometric volumes and forms of international Art Deco, but were often given an Australian flavour through the incorporation of local flora and fauna in moulded relief. Both the angular and the streamlined design aspects of Art Deco also appear in many Australian handcrafted objects. The use of moulds became a feature of pottery teaching, and in studio ceramics angular forms and a concern with volume influenced the work of several potters, including Doreen Goodchild, Margaret Mahood, Allan Lowe, J. A. Barnard Knight, Klytie Pate and Loudon Sainthill, in the 1930s. Art Deco designs can also be found in ceramics decorated by Napier Waller during this period and in china painting, notably in the work of Olive Nock, who had visited the 1925 Exhibition.

The Australian glass industry between the wars was not large. Much glass was imported and production was dominated by Australian Glass Manufacturers under its subsidiary Crown Crystal Glass. Among its varied range, Crown Crystal produced some Art Deco forms, reminiscent of the popular frosted surfaces of Lalique, whose work was known in Australia through imports such as the 'Bacchantes' vase. Jewellery, like glass, was imported in quantities, but Art Deco jewellery – notably that which included Australian opals – was also made by some local firms. Much of the handcrafted Australian jewellery made during the 1920s and 1930s, however, followed the linear styles popular in the Arts and Crafts Movement.

Textiles, too, reflected the influence of Art Deco. Australian-born Kathleen O'Connor lived in Paris during the 1920s and was there at the time of the 1925 Exhibition. Although primarily a painter, in the mid-1920s she was involved in interior decoration and fabric painting, some of which she did in Sydney on a return visit in 1927. In Paris, she also produced painted fabrics for Paul Poiret. British-born Michael O'Connell worked in Australia from 1920 until 1937 and produced a large number of hand-printed fabrics. After his trip to London and New York in 1929, the printed fabrics, some using angular, frieze-like figurative compositions, began to reflect the modernistic imagery of the Jazz Age. Like many Art Deco designers, however, his sources were wide-ranging. Other designs and images derived from Australian flora and fauna and from Aboriginal figures, as well as from Anglo-Saxon and Norman coins (plate 38.10). This interest in ancient and 'primitive' cultures was noted in a contemporary review of O'Connell's work: 'there were pleasant touches of the barbaric. It was a barbarism tempered by the wit and the self-conscious aloofness of viewpoint which are characteristic of contemporary art. Little dancing figures of aborigines brought these qualities most sharply into focus.'[17]

Lingering influences of the British Arts and Crafts Movement pervaded the teaching in many of the art schools where the crafts were taught. Although the schools were often conservative in outlook and practice, some of the preoccupations of 1920s Modernist and Art Deco design – such as smooth surfaces and angular forms – began to be incorporated into the techniques and design philosophy inherited from the preceding generation. These can be seen in ceramic production, china painting and woven textiles. The need to train art students to have viable careers, and with it the commercial importance of design, was increasingly recognized. A promotional review of the Department of Art at the East Sydney Technical College stated:

> Art must go hand in hand with industry as it has always done during periods of great artistic achievement ... Many [students] have made their mark here, in Europe and America. They are decorating offices and public buildings with paintings and sculpture; illustrating books, designing fabrics, wall papers, glass, metalwork and every other material; and are working either in their own or other advertising art studios which are helping to sell goods.[18]

Numerous cinemas were either built or remodelled during the 1920s and 1930s, many in the Art Deco style. They were strongly influenced by cinema design from the United States: the Metro theatre (1939) in Adelaide, for instance, was designed in New York and built under supervision of an Adelaide architect. Major examples include the Hayden Orpheum, Sydney (1935); the Astor theatre, Melbourne (1938); and the Piccadilly, Adelaide (1940). But the cinema whose design towered above all in its complexity, originality and modernity was the Capitol, Melbourne, designed by Walter Burley Griffin and opened in 1924. Robin Boyd later described it as 'The best cinema that was ever built or is ever likely

38.10 Michael O'Connell, 'Bacchantes', furnishing fabric.
Printed cotton. British, 1937. Made by Edinburgh Weavers.
V&A: Circ.472-1939. © 2002. All rights reserved, DACS.

38.11 Walter Burley Griffin, interior of the Capitol theatre, Melbourne. 1924. Courtesy of Mrs M. Ferme and the Powerhouse Museum, Sydney.

to be built.'[19] Although much altered, the dramatic ceiling survives today. Its artfully lit, tiered recesses contain a wealth of carefully modelled prismatic crystalline forms, which are part of a magical light show (plate 38.11).

Architectural essays in Art Deco in Australia were limited to individual buildings, notably cinemas, office buildings, department stores and hotels, where it was important to project an image of modernity. But across the Tasman Sea a major natural disaster precipitated the creation of a complete urban streetscape in the Art Deco style. Napier, New Zealand, is situated on Hawkes Bay on the north island. The town developed as a seaside resort during the late nineteenth and early twentieth centuries. On 3 February 1931, however, an earthquake struck Napier, destroying most of the city and killing 258 people. The ensuing fires and devastation were dramatically reported: 'With one

gigantic sweep the earthquake has reduced the whole town to a heap of ruins, still blazing and crumbling at each shake ... Napier as a town has become wiped off the map.'[20]

The Napier Reconstruction Committee was formed in July 1931. Given the opportunity for extensive rebuilding, there was much discussion as to how the new city should appear. Handled adroitly, there was a chance to achieve stylistic homogeneity. Santa Barbara in California provided a model, as it too had been extensively rebuilt after an earthquake in 1925. As early as 16 February 1931 it was reported that:

The attractiveness of Santa Barbara ... is behind the suggestion that all permanent buildings erected in Napier of the future should conform to a uniform style of architecture. A handful of enthusiasts are working unobtrusively in the advancement of the proposal and have already succeeded in exciting and encouraging interest among architects in the city.[21]

The rebuilding of Napier involved widening several major streets, a process that had begun before the earthquake. The central business district was almost entirely rebuilt. Not surprisingly, the demands for reconstruction raced ahead of aesthetic debates, and a stylistic consistency did not, eventually, emerge. The architects were Associated Architects of Napier, comprising C. T. Natusch & Sons, Finch & Westerholm, J. A. Louis Hay and E. A. Williams. For some projects, the architects worked as a collective. Much of their inspiration for the rebuilding came from the United States and North American influences on the rebuilding included Spanish Mission, favoured for 'its multifarious advantages, notably economy, simplicity and safety'.[22] Another influence was the Chicago school; Hay was an admirer of Frank Lloyd Wright and owned portfolios of his early Chicago buildings.

The Napier architects also drew on the decorative forms and elements of the international Art Deco style

– geometrical forms, smooth stucco surfaces, moulded angular relief decoration – sometimes combining these with regional references. Two buildings featured significant use of Maori motifs, since the angular lines of some Maori art, like some Australian Aboriginal art, were ideally suited to the angular vocabulary of Art Deco decoration. The ASB building on the corner of Hastings and Emerson streets, originally built as the Bank of New Zealand by the Wellington firm of Crichton, McKay & Haughton in 1932, has been described as 'tattooed – a veritable Bank of Aotearoa' (plate 38.12).[23] Maori designs decorate cornices and panels around the coffered ceiling, and a mask from the head of a *taiaha* is used in the main corners. The other building containing Maori motifs is the former Ross & Glendinning building, whose exterior frieze derived from a rafter pattern drawn from fern fronds, painted red and black.

Deco forms and decoration lingered in some areas of architecture and the decorative arts in Australia until the 1950s. Late manifestations of the style include the Maritime Services Board building (now the Museum of Contemporary Art) in Sydney, designed in 1936 but not completed until 1952. Nevertheless, in general, the end of the 1930s marked the decline of Art Deco in Australia and New Zealand as the influence of Modernism, focusing on 'form without ornament', began to be felt throughout the region.

38.12 Crichton, McKay & Haughton, exterior of the ASB Bank at night, Napier, New Zealand. 1932. Photo: Rufus Wood.

39 Art Deco in South Africa

Dipti Bhagat

In 1936, South Africa hosted a momentous *Empire Exhibition* in Johannesburg, the British Dominion's industrial capital. The spectacular Art Deco styling of the exhibition's built form and decorative programme was an exemplary expression of an Empire Dominion that asserted during the 1920s and 1930s a young, white nationhood of multi-layered hybridities; of dual belongings, both international and national, and of a modernity emerging from traditions past and poised on the brink of future progress. In its internationalism, South Africa shed its peripheral identity and extended its metropolitan reach into British Africa as the economic hub and cultural centre of the continent, seeking also to maintain Empire-wide connections and forge cultural links with such American cities as New York. Within this network of international belonging, the Dominion of South Africa became less 'colonial' and increasingly 'national'. Emerging from an imperial Europe and its own traditions of a colonial frontier settlement, South Africa aspired to a future as a capitalist, urban and exceptionally white nation on the African subcontinent. South Africa's white hegemony had been secured through the removal of any vestiges of black sovereignty in 1910, when the former South African colonies – British and Boer/Afrikaner in origin – formed the Union of South Africa under the aegis of the British Empire. The exclusive position of the white population was reinforced during the inter-war years by the forced removal of urban black populations, by the racial zoning of urban areas and by the institution of urban pass laws. These measures created a controlled space for South Africa's black people, in which they were seen not as citizens but as charges of a modern government, as exotic aspects of South Africa's landscape and, more typically, as the resources of an economically powerful white nation. And indeed, South Africa's remarkable recovery from the Depression was founded upon the riches of the gold mines below Johannesburg worked by a wealth of black labour. In this young nation, eclectic Deco-inspired form, style and motifs framed Africa's white Dominion as culturally sophisticated and racially distinct. For, while architectural, artistic and design practice had been inherited and adapted from its source in Europe, South Africa in the 1930s – in particular at the *Empire Exhibition* – presented it as successfully domesticated, special to the South African environment.

By the 1930s, South Africa's urban environment was characterized by architecture and design of remarkable eclecticism: Art Deco flourished amid an existing Beaux-Arts classicism and an emerging International Style. Not until the latter years of the 1930s and in the 1940s did South Africa's Deco architecture become more closely aligned with its small but internationally recognized Modern Movement under the influence of Rex Martienssen and his commitment to Corbusian principles. Indeed, the support among the public, developers and much of the architectural profession for Art Deco styling, with its decorative yet geometrical play of forms, facilitated the popular acceptance of Modernism after the Second World War. However, during the 1930s the accelerated modernization of South Africa's urban locations resulted in an intangible stylistic evolution that was reflected in a hybrid architecture. For example, Herbert Baker's Barclays Bank in Cape Town (1933) utilized almost interchangeable classical and Art Deco motifs, while elsewhere Deco motifs were regularly applied as a stylistic additive to buildings fundamentally Modernist in principle.[1] The iconic Escom House in Johannesburg, as designed by P. Rogers-Cooke in 1935, had an ornate Art Deco façade combined with a Beaux-Arts axial plan (plate 39.2). When the building was finally adapted and built by Pearse & Fassler in 1937, the flamboyant Deco embellishments of the rounded edges and arched entrance were refined for an austere Deco of starker, more accentuated verticality. This suggests the influence of G. E. Pearse, whose Professorship of Architecture at the University of Witwatersrand (and tutelage of Martienssen) gave impetus to a South African Modernism. Escom House remained

39.1 Irma Stern, *The Hunt*. Oil on canvas. South African, 1926. Irma Stern Museum, University of Cape Town. Courtesy of the Trustees of the Irma Stern Estate.

Johannesburg's Deco monument until its demolition in the 1980s.

Underpinning this diversity were contemporary debates about what might constitute an appropriate style for South Africa's public building. The initial rejection of Modernism in the early 1930s by public and practitioners, vocalized through the popular and the professional press, resulted in a retreat from radical design to a more conservative, decorative style that responded to the aspirations of corporate clients. While at the turn of the 1930s the architectural avant-garde launched South African architecture – at least ideologically – into a 'heroic' Modern Movement phase, the more conservative, established architects, and the general public, remained deeply sceptical about Modernism. For them, notions of 'modernity' and 'modern design' were equated with Art Deco. The *South African Architectural Record* in particular provided a forum for public and professional debate, mainly in response to its Martienssen-led Modernist viewpoint: 'Corbusier [figures] too largely in its pages and ... the work of his disciples in this country [is] given too much prominence.'[2] This kind of critique is revealing of a pervasive anxiety among South African artists, designers, architects and ideologues about the young nation's need to develop a truly patriotic style. In this context, Herbert Baker's 'Edwardian Cape' aesthetics based on Arts and Crafts historicism were venerated; notwithstanding his Britishness, his work with the Cape Dutch style was seen to have established a South African vernacular. Artist Hendrick Pierneef strongly articulated a desire for a national style: 'We must stop looking through European glasses when we are painting and designing ... Each country and each period has its own style, why cannot we create a truly South African one?'[3] Nevertheless, Pearse in particular saw the importation of modern styles from the centres of America, Britain and Europe to South African cities as appropriate for a fully internationalized young nation.[4] Indeed, in 1921 he had founded South Africa's first school of architecture at the University of the Witwatersrand, Johannesburg, from which southern Africa's most influential architects graduated. The University of Cape Town followed with a parallel architectural school. By 1930 both came fully within the associative remit of the Royal Institute of British Architects, and study abroad was deemed general practice. The Wits school was also the editorial base from which the *South African Architectural Record* was run. Of both professional and popular appeal, it regularly published authoritative essays on European and American design developments that were highly influential.

In 1936, Johannesburg was the South African locus for this internationalism. Celebrating the Jubilee of its foundation as a mine camp in 1886, and hosting an *Empire Exhibition*, Johannesburg was seen as an African metropolis, not on the peripheries of the Empire but dynamically situated on the circuit of an international Modernism. The Jubilee's lavish souvenir photo album flaunted its 50-year architectural trajectory from the corrugated iron

39.2 P. Rogers-Cooke, Escom House, Johannesburg. 1935. MuseuMAfricA, Johannesburg.

shanty to the high-rise flat and the skyscraper. The ever-ascending iconography of the skyscraper crystallized South Africa's 'national progress', its 'greater future'[5] and its capitalist success. This imagery was effectively exemplified on the cover of the *Jubilee Souvenir* (plate 39.3). Rendered in brilliant silver and gold, the graphics present Johannesburg as gold itself. On the cover of the *Souvenir* the mine camp provides a swell of gold from which literally rises the lithe and efficient skyscraper, epitomizing the unambiguous affluence and rational advance of city and nation. Perspectively enhanced, the verticalism of the skyscraper – an Art Deco leitmotif and a representation of the Escom House design – at once places Johannesburg and South Africa ascending on an axis, from the depths of the mine camps to the heights of national success and international recognition. Immensely popular, the *Souvenir* was a lasting record of civic, national and indeed international Art Deco, but also itself a luxury artefact.

Although South Africa's internationalism was generally a form of Eurocentrism, a new cultural factor came to disrupt the traditional London–periphery relationship: the growing New York–Johannesburg axis.[6] So successful was the imagining of Johannesburg as an American city that the South African Eric Rosenthal likened his view of New York in 1939 to 'an immensely magnified version of central Johannesburg'.[7] Of course, these newly received forms were not without local inflections, many of them the result of the Depression. South Africa's Deco high-rises were modest in height and eschewed the 'cult of weightlessness' that was becoming apparent in American structures. The Dominion's building industry was essentially craft-based. Its unskilled labour and local materials were adequate for the carcass of the building, but all else, from mechanical equipment to plumbing accessories and wood products, was imported.[8]

Urban South Africa boasted an impressive range of Art Deco styling, from fully sculpted architectural form to embellished façades and lavishly decorated interiors. Cinema design – prolific after 1922 – significantly popularized Art Deco. The Colosseum in Johannesburg, by Rogers-Cooke, was characteristic of this 'cinema-style' Deco. It exhibited an Egyptian iconography of columns with papyrus capitals surrounded by a chevron border and framed by enormous stylized figures resembling mummy sarcophagi. The foyer continued this geometric design in the structure – the columns and stairs – and in the decoration, with its quintessentially Deco sunburst pattern (plate 39.4). An austere

39.3 Cover of the *Souvenir of the Golden City's Golden Jubilee*. Johannesburg, 1936. Africana Library, Johannesburg.

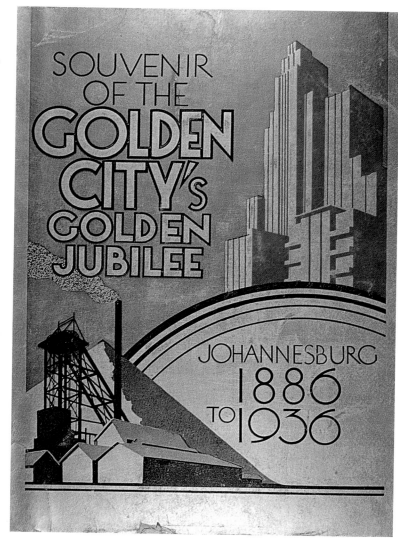

39.4 P. Rogers-Cooke, foyer of the Colosseum theatre, Johannesburg. 1936. Reproduced with kind permission of Piet de Beer.

39.5 Old Mutual Building. Cape Town, 1940.
Courtesy of the Cape Art Deco Society.

Deco was exemplified by the ladies' powder room, with its black velvet walls and silver papyrus pilasters, the small fountain, sycamore fittings and silver carpet adding luxury to the pleasurable experience of cinema entertainment. The auditorium décor, however, was of unbridled fantasy, a fairy city of castles and weirdly fecund vegetation surrounded by a realistic representation of the South African sky.

International Deco style was most successfully made local through the integrated use of a South African vocabulary. The Old Mutual building in Cape Town (1940)[9] offers spectacular displays of national imagery in its stylized motifs of indigenous wildlife, while a sculptural frieze around the exterior depicts the success of European supremacy and 'civilization' over the African subcontinent. This is reinforced by stylized 'native' busts on the façade representing South Africa's racial types.[10] Furthermore, the building itself was clad in the granite of Paarl Mountain: this was an Art Deco constructed literally and metaphorically from local sources (plate 39.5). Interior decoration elaborated this South Africanism: the lift doors are etched with designs of local flora and fauna and mural scenes of Afrikaner nationalist history. Reminiscent of exotic decoration at the Paris 1931 *Exposition coloniale*, in South Africa such decorative schemes assuredly combined corporate and a new *localised*, colonial interest, for while the

39.6 Poster for the 1936 *Empire Exhibition*, Johannesburg. Colour lithograph. South African, 1936. Africana Library, Johannesburg.

white Dominion was keen to differentiate itself from Britain, it was still colonial itself in terms of its own culture of racial hegemony.[11]

This marrying of national history and the peculiarities of a local landscape with corporate design, a recurrent theme in South Africa's commercial Art Deco, was explicitly visible in the displays of the *Empire Exhibition* of 1936.[12] It is this determining feature of Art Deco that, in turn, fully internationalized the South African Deco style. Closely associated with Johannesburg's own history of commercial prowess – and hosted by the African metropolis – the exhibition was a demonstration of South Africa's 'march of art and artisanry, industry and culture',[13] but it was also intended to boost South Africa's image abroad, encourage tourism and call attention to the country's artistic vitality.

Accordingly, the South African Railways and Harbours (SAR&H) pavilion, for instance, employed a decorative scheme with a stylized historical mural that depicted the development of transport as a metaphor for the civilization of the African subcontinent under European patronage. Thus, the traditional African message carrier and the eighteenth-century wagon gave way to modern and streamlined air, rail and sea transport. This type of finely executed mural, with motifs of South African scenery, flora, fauna and 'indigenous African' life, was a regular feature of the exhibition. Designed by the South African artist Phyllis Gardner – who trained at the Royal College of Art in London – and critically acclaimed, the SAR&H mural represented a culturally sophisticated nation, one that was embodied in the aesthetic excellence of the murals themselves. This image was reinforced by the design of the exhibition itself, which displayed South Africa's modernity and internationalism: the architectural styling of Johannesburg's Empire town was praised both in South Africa and abroad for its 'gay modernism'.[14] A design competition had invited national students registered with the Institute of South African Architects to submit proposals for the façades of prominent commercial buildings required for the event. Out of this it was a late Art Deco, with a 'noble aspect' of 'simple, square modern outlines' and 'a treatment of large plane surfaces terminating at the ends with graceful horizontal features' that came to distinguish South Africa's Empire gala.[15] The *South African Architectural Record* hailed the designs as unique and appropriately national: for

39.7 Victoria Falls pavilion at the 1936 *Empire Exhibition*, Johannesburg. *The Golden City's Golden Jubilee*, Johannesburg, 1936. Africana Library, Johannesburg.

their large planar surfaces which provided a canvas for the play of Johannesburg's high-veld sunshine, and for their non-adherence to overseas exhibition conventions as displayed at Chicago (1933) and other, European, exhibitions.

Nevertheless, these designs were part of the Deco-inspired international vocabulary of exhibition styling. They influenced the exuberant design of Glasgow's 1938 *Empire Exhibition* but in turn were reminiscent of European models. The central Tower of Light in Johannesburg that illuminated both the city and the exhibition recalled the electric moons envisioned by the Italian Futurists, as well as Rob

Mallet-Stevens's 'study in concrete' for the tourist pavilion at the Paris 1925 Exhibition (plate 39.6 and see plate 22.1). In Johannesburg, the cuboid Tower with horizontal ribbing became a motif across the exhibition, seen in street lighting and flag masts with modernistic ferrules. Other pavilions featured large, blank surfaces of horizontal projection, identified by modern typographic architecture: blocked, three-dimensional, sans-serif lettering, excellent canvases for South African sunlight (plate 39.7). The striking Deco imagery of the exhibition's architecture was also present in the official graphics and in the publicity for many of the pavilions that represented South Africa's leading industries. It thus aligned industry with the civic, national and Empire festivities and presented the nation as both an illustrious centre of Africa and a member of the international community (plate 39.8).

39.8 Publicity issued for the 1936 *Empire Exhibition*, Johannesburg. *Painter's Pie Magazine*, 1936. Africana Library, Johannesburg.

The exhibition's chief architect, J. A. Hoogterp, himself exemplified this internationalism. Johannesburg-born and trained with Herbert Baker, Hoogterp had overseen the building of New Delhi, several government buildings in Kenya and the layout of the city of Lusaka. And through Hoogterp, the exhibition's Deco styling retained an aspect of historicism. Government pavilions also kept inflections of traditional styling: the British pavilion rendered the classical motifs of colonnade and column as modern geometrical shafts; while South Africa's government pavilion referred back to the eighteenth-century Cape style with its rich overmantels over classical doorways, which recalled early frontier settlement and embodied a national vernacular. While acutely aware of avoiding 'an old world atmosphere', Hoogterp's recourse to historical vernacular for the permanent government pavilion expressed a desire to articulate both a vivid South Africanism and a traditionalism that would 'not be subject to the caprices of fashions in architecture', which would render 'present-day ideas out of date in a comparatively short while'.[16] It was thus a faith in continued and rapid future progress that informed a reliance on enduring historical motifs. The historically located government pavilion reiterated how South Africa's eclectic Art Deco utilized national history as a complement to the modernity of internationally directed industry.

The duality of South Africa's celebratory Modernism – an impetus at once national and cosmopolitan – was seen at its most complex in the exhibition's representation of South Africa's black populations as primitive and exotic. In many of South Africa's public buildings, decorative programmes demonstrated Art Deco's fascination with the 'primitive', exoticizing the black body through highly stylized images that relied upon racial stereotypes. The 'native' busts on the façade of Cape Town's Old Mutual, described above, provide a good example of this tendency, as does the elegant motif of a black female figure in the stained glass façade by Jan Juta in the Anglo-American building in Johannesburg. While these motifs show a general affinity with primitivism in European art and design, they also reveal a less direct process of exoticization through aesthetic appropriation. Modified by European primitivism, and informed by specifically national racial ideology, these South African images of black bodies constituted a powerful metaphor for white wealth and civilized sophistication. As in Europe, the use of black African imagery in the decorative arts was also a means of suggesting the 'spontaneous' and the vernacular without resorting to inherited

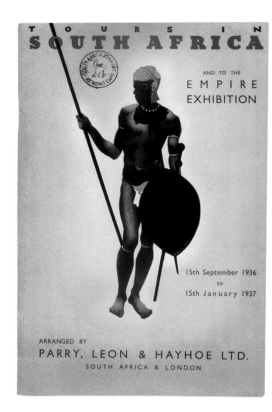

European traditions: this primitivism distinguished white 'South Africa' as modern, while also distinct from Europe. In a country where racial segregation was implemented to ensure white supremacy, the use of the black body as a motif – with all its attendant European primitivist meanings of heightened sexuality and physical power – provided a means of representing a dominated race. The cover of a 1936 tour guide to South Africa, on which the stylized form of a 'Zulu warrior' cuts a powerful image of exotic South Africa, is an example of this complexity (plate 39.9). The blackness of the warrior's skin is emphasized by the sharp highlights of his jewellery, his loincloth and the effect of overhead sunshine on his head, shoulders, thigh and feet. He stands as a metaphor for the sun-drenched landscapes of South Africa, his quiescent pose embodying the leisured tourism possible through a once threatening Zulu nation. Here the South African 'primitive' serves a dual function: as a tourist attraction for the international consumer, and a decorative motif on an explicitly modern book design.

However, South African primitivism oscillated between the avant-garde and the popular, between exoticization and familiarity. The paintings of Irma Stern exemplify this dichotomy. Her 'primitivist' portrayals of South Africa's 'natives' suggest in their vibrant, expressionist colour the influence of the European avant-garde, notably Max Pechstein and Die Brücke (plate 39.1). Yet the sitters are also seen as locals and rendered with true subjectivity. In this fashion, they proclaim the importance of

the individual when European primitivism preferred to consign the 'native' to anonymity or to see him as part of the landscape.[17] While European primitivism articulated a degree of estrangement, the motif of the Zulu warrior, described above, expressed a local relationship with a specified 'primitive' culture – whether 'Zulu' or 'Bushman' – thereby confirming white belonging and supremacy. Unlike the paintings of Stern, this imagery – like that utilized for the Old Mutual building – depicted a racial type. In this context, indigenous African motifs were used in support of settler nationalism. Furthermore, South Africa's primitivism was stimulated by the proximity of 'the native'. This presence demanded a 'solution', which was zdelivered through the distancing exoticization of primitivist imagery: thus the presence of a Zulu warrior becomes 'contained' in a decorative motif.

This rhetoric also determined the display of 'indigenous African' arts and crafts, some traditional and others transfigured by the white South African taste for contemporary Deco styling. Whether of ethnographic interest, collected nationally and classified by university anthropology departments, or the hybridized work of 'modern Native artists interpreting *their* conception of things in a futuristic manner',[18] these objects were seen to exemplify the slower development of South Africa's black races. At the same time, they were also valued by white designers and craftspeople for their 'refined simplicity' (see Chapter 7). The most popular indigenous motif adapted in this way was the chevron design. In use, the chevron evoked patterns found on the ruins of Great Zimbabwe (especially when executed in local granite), while also complementing the internationally popular Deco 'zigzag' motifs. It embellished such diverse South African Deco designs as the exterior of Astor Mansions in Johannesburg and Market House in Cape Town, as well as the mirrored lobby of the 'jazz style' interior of McManus Printers in Cape Town.

The perceived instinct of black craftspeople for 'abstraction' also gave rise to a reciprocal process in which South African educationists encouraged Africans to assimilate European motifs. And unsurprisingly, the chevron motif reappeared as 'typical' decoration on modern, hybrid arts and crafts produced for white consumption. Nevertheless, these crafts were rarely displayed at international exhibitions – the Johannesburg event was an exception – for more favourable, in international terms, were the 'traditional' crafts or 'exotica' that demonstrated the authentic attributes of 'primitive' life. The 1936 exhibition did, however, feature 'modern native artists'. They emerged from the Native Training Schools where crafts had been introduced in 1921 to sustain the indigenous skills of pottery, basketry and weaving and to initiate new practices. Particularly influential among the Native educationists was John Adams, who had trained in ceramics at the Royal College of Art and was head of the Technical College School of Art in Durban for the duration of his stay between 1914 and 1921. His promotion of pottery in schools in the Natal region resulted in several local exhibitions of 'modern native ceramics', which became popular with Natal's white populace keen to acquire indigenous African crafts. Adams's commitment to his pottery teaching in Durban and to the promotion of a South African craftsmanship led him to investigate the clays in Natal and to use a dark local terracotta for all his South African work. His departure in 1921 took him to Poole Potteries where he designed, in collaboration with O. J. P. Oxley of Durban, the dramatic Art Deco war memorial at St Mary's Greyville, Durban. The memorial employs angular stylized figures framed by a triumphant sunburst, its use of yellow and turquoise strongly reflecting the jewel-like sarcophagi found in Tutankhamun's tomb. Indeed, it is this very reference that provoked a rejection of the memorial among Durbanites, who considered the vivid 'orientalism' to be blasphemous.[19]

Craft education at the Durban school, particularly in pottery, also established for the young white nation its first, highly successful studio-ceramic production. Named the Ceramic Studio, it supplied the South African market with luxury Deco ware locally designed and made. The Studio was founded in 1925, in Olifantsfontein in the Transvaal, by Marjorie Johnstone and Gladys Short, students of John Adams who had also trained at the Royal College. Producing painted tiles, architectural faience, monumental ceramic sculpture, vases and tableware, it flourished at a time when wealthy South African consumers only supported luxury manufactured goods from Britain and Europe – whether purchased through local department stores or through travel abroad. The Studio struggled to compete, using impure local clays that were too ferrous for porcelain and finally resorting to importing china clay from Wenger's of Stoke-on-Trent. Despite healthy orders for the standardized tableware (known as 'Linn Ware'), the Studio's greatest profits were from its 'artistic', Deco ceramics, which were bought by an elite consumer group deeply concerned to promote South African design.

Adams's flamboyant use of colour filtered significantly into the work of the Ceramic Studio. The most popular domestic Deco wares were those decorated with bright colours, the shade most in demand being a deep sea green. Such glazes and colour recall the popular vases by Keith Murray for Wedgwood; indeed, the prominence of British-made ceramics in South Africa in the 1920s and 1930s is likely to have shaped public taste significantly.[20] The Studio's founders, Johnstone and Short, were in fact ardent admirers of Bernard Leach and Shoji Hamada – as evidenced by their few studio pieces with subtle earthen glazes decorated with simple brushstrokes. However, the South African public was less discerning in its taste and the demand for Art Deco colour won out.

In its architectural work the Studio was committed to faience, in the manner of Della Robbia ware, with nationalist, symbolic imagery. This was due in part to the profound influence of John Adams, but also to the study visits that Short, Johnstone and the other designers had made to London. There they saw the V&A's collections of Italian majolica and Islamic ceramics, which inspired the production of 'museum studies' that were then exhibited in Durban. The Studio's decorative tilework was very popular and included the Addington Children's Hospital in Durban, 11,000 painted tiles for the new Johannesburg Railway Station and work for domestic flats such as Ritchie McKinlay's Quadrant House in Durban (1927).

The Studio was widely appreciated by South African architects and designers and drew many local artists into its design workshops. It was also strongly supported by the local and national press, especially the South African Woman's Weekly (supplement to the Natal Mercury), which ensured publicity for its work. Exhibition stalls guaranteed direct buyers, while most of its domestic wares were sold through the Studio or through department stores such as Shepherd & Barker or Garlick's.

That a South African Art Deco prospered alongside British and European imports is shown by an exhibition held in Cape Town in 1990, Decorative Arts of the West, 1900-1940. The Art Deco objects displayed were of the finest, most luxurious examples, from a silver cake plate to exquisite jewellery. Yet, virtually all the objects had been made overseas. All the objects had been drawn from private ownership in South Africa, which suggests that South Africa's Eurocentrism during the 1920s and 1930s operated at a very domestic level. Indeed, the South African press, from the weekend newspapers to such specialist journals as the South African Builder and the South African Architectural Review, promoted a South African Art Deco to match if not rival that of Europe and America, commenting that the wealthy South African housewife boasted a 'luxury home ... like an advertisement from an American magazine'.[21] This posture conveyed the idea of modernity to rival that of Europe and America, but was also conceived, in a local context, as a means of asserting white South Africa's cultural difference from 'the native' and its supremacy over him. Thus, while Art Deco here integrated national inflections, it refused real assimilation with the locality. In South Africa, Deco was peculiarly expressive of a delimited nationhood. The beam cast by the Empire Exhibition's Tower of Light reached only a privileged population in modern houses serried on the horizon. With the black population forcibly removed and Johannesburg declared a white city, the Tower's dazzling light did little to brighten the black townships that existed then as now. In this sense, South Africa's internationalism was about escaping the local.

40 Decline and Revival

Charlotte Benton and Tim Benton

'Art Deco ... is historically interesting as a search for design capable of relating to the modern world, not with the technological purity of more earnest expressions of modernity, but with an abandon calculated to stimulate popular fantasy.'[1]

Situated between traditionalist and radical – historical revival styles and Modernism – past and future, Art Deco 'bridged antagonistic realms'.[2] It provided a popular 'other' to Modernism and a modern stimulus to traditionalism, from around 1910 until the outbreak of the Second World War. Its playful qualities, glamour, mastery of metaphor and allusion, and synthesizing impulses catered to a wide range of aspirations. It expressed the ambitions of new classes of entrepreneurs and designers in the period of reconstruction following the First World War, but it also captured the imagination of Middle America in the Depression era. It proved capable of carrying messages of national identity, allowing the authority of classical conventions of design to be adapted to a variety of specific cultural iconographies.[3] This, together with its associations with metropolitan glamour and chic, allowed it to became a global style, crossing regional and national boundaries like a bush fire, carried largely on the winds of commercial promotion and fashion. It was the style of leisure and entertainment, of travel, romance, sexual and personal liberation, youth and adventure. Yet, in the service of capitalism, it also worked to limit individual ambition, by stimulating consumption through the creation of desires for new goods. In America, it became the style of anti-totalitarian democracy and free trade.[4] Above all, it was a 'modern' style, new in spirit and detail, saturated with allusions to modern technology and progress – an expression of optimism in the future.

Nothing is as explanatory of a style as the circumstances of its passing and rediscovery. Art Deco was definitively killed off by the Second World War, or rather by the mentality of service, sacrifice and social reform engendered by that war. In the years of austerity that followed, especially in Europe,

architects and designers applied themselves to the task of physical and social reconstruction. The New Town and housing estate came to occupy centre stage in many architects' imaginations, and satisfying the demand for new household equipment became a central task for designers. The demise of Art Deco was gradual rather than abrupt, however. In Europe it had begun to lose favour soon after its first flowering at the Paris 1925 Exhibition, as the attraction of stripped classicism for official architecture was increasingly matched by a fashion for simplified vernacular or regional styles, particularly for the domestic environment.[5] The spread and consolidation of Modernism in the late 1920s and early 1930s also affected the later course of Art Deco. In Scandinavia, for example, a commitment to notions of the greater social good, which had tempered earlier expressions of Art Deco in the region, tended to favour the spread of Modernism in the late 1920s and early 1930s.[6] And in Britain, Modernism – whose social agenda could be readily assimilated to lingering Arts and Crafts philosophies – was given a boost by the arrival of refugee architects and designers from continental Europe.

Art Deco survived, however, in much of Europe in the 1930s, among these competing styles, though the decorative exuberance of the 1920s was often tamed[7] and the style's associations with luxury production made it vulnerable to the effects of the Depression. In Austria, the Wiener Werkstätte closed in 1931 following financial difficulties; and in France, several leading practitioners were reduced to penury by the early 1930s.[8] Yet Art Deco flourished in the design of buildings for entertainment, retail and transportation. And, through a process of filtering down, neo-cubistic ceramics, glass and textiles, derived from the fashionable prototypes of the 1920s, began to saturate the high street. Thus, by the end of the decade, Art Deco decorative motifs had become popular but démodé. When the young Nikolaus Pevsner, recently arrived in England, wrote his *Enquiry* into British industrial design, he saw Deco as a vulgar debasement of 'the aesthetic laws'

40.1 The Perisphere and the Trylon at the 1939 New York World Fair. *L'Illustration*, 10 June 1939. NAL. Photo: René Bras.

40.2 Marco Zanini, 'Colorado', teapot. Earthenware. Italian, 1983. Made by Ceramiche Flavia for Memphis. V&A: C.207-1985.

of industrial design, 'dishonest' and evidencing a 'universal and irresistible longing to escape'.[9]

There were also more insistent challenges to Art Deco's legitimacy. The rise of virulently nationalist and anti-Modernist sentiments was accompanied by determinedly conservative reinterpretations of national vernaculars and the classical, as well as an emphasis on 'local' handcraft traditions in opposition to industrial production. Although most marked in Nazi Germany, these tendencies were echoed elsewhere in Europe. At the same time, however, the exodus of refugee architects and designers contributed to the spread of the 'modern' ideologies and sensibilities of both Art Deco and Modernism to the further fringes of Europe,[10] as well as to America and the countries of Latin America, Australasia, Africa and the Middle and Far East, giving new or renewed impetus to the concept of 'modernity' in these regions.

For a style characterized by the 'unrest and impatience of the age',[11] Art Deco had a surprisingly long life, spanning three decades. But, by the eve of the Second World War, it was largely played out. The New York World Fair of 1939 marked the last full expression of the American form of the style and was a portent of things to come (plate 40.1). Talbot Hamlin, writing in 1938, voiced the view of many American critics when he stated that: 'Formal relationships ... are more important in a republic than anywhere else ... an architecture based primarily on a sense of form, an architecture seeking the expression of permanence and monumentality as a symbol of republican idealism, is the natural architecture of a republic.'[12]

In line with such views, the design of the fair was marked by Modernized Classical buildings representing governmental functions.[13] Yet the official exhibits of the totalitarian regimes of the Soviet Union, Nazi Germany and Fascist Italy also employed variants of Modernized Classicism.[14] Accordingly, the organizers of the fair also sought to represent the ideology of democracy in a quite different way, by emphasizing the practice of consumerism as evidence of the play of free choice in a democratic society. Pavilions would compete freely to promote their wares, and the whole fair would operate like a giant shopping mall.[15]

Here the specialists who had sprung up, by the early 1930s, to generate desire for new products and services, had a key role. These were the industrial designers and stylists, who included Henry Dreyfuss, Raymond Loewy, Egmont Arens, Donald Deskey, Gilbert Rohde, Russel Wright and Walter Dorwin Teague.[16] Supported by the new sciences of

consumer psychology, advertising and opinion polls, they were seen to understand – better than architects – how visually to represent democratic capitalism. They were 'men believed to be in touch with the realities of the machine yet capable of speaking the public's language, of expressing a new concept of beauty and design'.[17] It was their job to 'demonstrate the American way of living' and American democracy in the face of the totalitarian regimes of Europe, the USSR and Asia.

And yet, the increasing sophistication of design and salesmanship had begun to provoke a reaction. An Advisory Committee on Consumer Interests was established during the planning of the fair but, in February 1939, 21 members resigned, protesting that the rights and interests of consumers had not been protected. The exhibition underlined the tensions between the rights of citizens to have accurate information and fair prices and the pressures from industry and commerce to maximize production by boosting consumption by all possible means. Although the producers won on this occasion, it was not without opposition. Frederick Gutheim saw the fair's commercial buildings as revealing 'a licentious liaison between architecture and big business for the blatant purpose of advertising and sales. If a single style had been generated, it should be called the "Corporation Style".'[18]

The ability of Art Deco to act effectively as a 'Corporation Style' was one of its great strengths, but it also provided the basis for a new and critical analysis of capitalism: 'The Fair's pejoratively called Corporation Style – in which colors, lighting and bold, sometimes delightfully bizarre forms, were employed to mythologize business's and industry's role in the shaping of America's future – offers an excellent perspective from which to begin.'[19]

The pavilions of the great automobile manufacturers, such as Ford and General Motors, and the producers of energy and communications, such as Edison, AT&T and RCA, presented an overwhelmingly seductive view of a future liberated by the motor car, electrification and new materials. It encompassed every aspect of urban planning and domestic life. The General Motors pavilion, with its Futurama exhibit – in which visitors seated on a belt of armchairs were moved across a model of Democricity, with its motorways, tower blocks and green belts – was voted the most popular exhibit in a Gallup survey.[20] But this kind of corporate styling and explicit celebration of consumerism would be severely affected by the Second World War, when even the large corporations had to bend to the war effort.

Subsequently, post-war austerity, together with the need for rapid reconstruction – particularly in occupied Europe and the Far East – created strong pressures for increased rationalization and functionalism.

Furthermore, the New York World Fair never strayed far from the lessons of Coney Island. From the start, an Amusement Zone was planned alongside, and it did better business than the more serious parts of the fair. The giant National Cash Register till overlooking the entrance to the Amusement Zone symbolized very effectively the straightforward American approach to taking money for pleasure. Like Coney Island – which for decades had lit up Manhattan's eastern horizon at night – and like other Deco sites and buildings, the fair promoted itself and its pleasures with the spectacle of light:

> Visible for miles around, a flood of multi-colored light drenches the sky above the glowing spectacle that is the *Fair* at night. Light, fire, color, water and sound have been ingeniously and subtly blended to create a dazzling scene that embraces every band of the spectrum ... The city of magic, it might well be called, an enchanting vision hinting at the future in artificial illumination.[21]

The outbreak of war eventually put out the lights, and the spirit of uninhibited self-expression and display that they had expressed. Many of the architects and designers who planned and built the New York World Fair paid lip service to Modernist axioms,[22] though – as most critics noted – the fair's buildings were highly decorative in intention and form.[23] Efforts were made to control ornament and individualistic expression through the regulation of sound levels, lighting, colour and signage. Combined with the fair's Beaux-Arts layout, these tempered the exuberance of many of the initial designs for individual pavilions. This spirit of restraint and rational planning was given a further boost during the war, when the standardization imposed by wartime conditions prepared the ground for Modernism to sweep the board after the peace. The New York World Fair prefigured both these standardizing tendencies and the social programmes that would follow.

The fair's theme was 'building the World of Tomorrow with the tools of today'. The power of science and technology to liberate men and women from the slavery of manual labour was a constant leitmotif. Gilbert Rohde was given the task of representing this in the 'Community Interests' exhibit. It showed five sets, from the 'Work, Work, Work' display representing a village green in 1789 to Set 4, which represented 'Mrs Modern' – the American housewife ordering her shopping by telephone. Set 5 showed American men and women moving beyond individual consumerist interests. 'Freed in time and place' they would have 'time for interest in government, in community, in the group. Time to plan for our community'.[24] Science and consumerism were presented as leading to a utopia of democratic rationalism and collective idealism. This dream did not long survive the war; but in America – as in many other countries – there was a shift of emphasis for a time, from individual consumerism to social organization and planning, and to more restrained representations of corporate capitalism. Thus many of the themes that we have seen throughout this book as staples of Art Deco (individualism, fashion and glamour, fantasy and fun, display and promotion, the decorative as an essential ingredient of consumerism, and a modern style associated with new materials and technologies) were turned on their head in the 1950s and 1960s. Though some notable expressions of decorative exuberance inspired by Art Deco practices survived,[25] the style's characteristic decorative repertoire and cheerfully commercial traits were widely abandoned in favour of design languages redolent of the larger social good – whether Modernist or modernized Scandinavian vernacular.[26]

In several countries, too, the early post-war period saw an explicit association of Modernism – condemned as 'degenerate' and 'Jewish-Bolshevik' in Nazi Germany and as 'bourgeois formalism' in Stalin's USSR – with specifically democratic values. With the advent of the Cold War, Modernist visual culture – albeit shorn of much of its social programme and with an emphasis on its formal values – was promoted by many 'western' countries as a symbol of freedom of expression. Modernism's post-war spread was also underwritten by influential publications enshrining the history and values of its 'pioneers' in the 1920s and 1930s, and underlining its ethical and ideological dimensions.[27] In this context, a view of Art Deco as lightweight, commercial and manipulative became established orthodoxy and the style languished neglected until the 1960s. In the Soviet 'bloc', where Modernism continued to be regarded as 'bourgeois formalism', Art Deco was ignored because of its explicit associations with capitalist values; but, following the collapse of Communism, it began to be re-evaluated.[28]

The rediscovery of Art Deco in the West coincided with the growth of a new market for modish and individualistic design and a growing interest in architectural conservation. The context for the first was the economic boom evoked by British Prime Minister Harold Macmillan's boast that 'You've never had it so good'; that of the second by growing evidence of the social and economic consequences of wholesale city centre redevelopments and the building of vast, monotonous housing estates. Widespread disillusion with the results of social planning encouraged the wealthy to flaunt economic difference and others to seek 'alternative' means of self-expression. The new interest in Deco was fuelled by the rise of the counter-culture, with its celebration of individualism, youth and liberated sexuality, alongside that of popular culture. The latter included American commercial culture, memorably defined by the British Pop artist Richard Hamilton as 'popular, expendable, low cost, mass produced, young, witty, sexy, glamorous and big business'.[29] In this context, the very virtues that had enabled Modernism to supplant Art Deco – its seriousness, social purpose, ethical pretensions, rationalism and austerity – now counted against it.

The Deco revival was encouraged by exhibitions and publications and – just like the original style – by its associations with fashion, a booming retail culture, film stars and youthful glamour. In a survey of 1969, the fashion commentator Janet Street-Porter – also a collector – and the fashion designer Ossie Clark both picked Art Deco buildings as their 'magic places'.[30] In London, Biba, the youth-oriented fashion boutique, employed neo-Deco graphics and restored the 1930s Deco Rainbow Room restaurant in the Derry & Toms department store. In New York, stores such as Macy's and Bloomingdales commissioned Deco makeovers. Deco-inspired – and repro Deco – lines were introduced.[31] Deco sites, such as Miami Beach, and key Deco buildings and interiors – including the spectacular Rainbow Room in the RCA building in the Rockefeller Center complex – were stylishly refurbished.[32] There was renewed interest in Hollywood itself.[33] Stars, such as Barbra Streisand, were among early collectors; and new films – including *Bonnie and Clyde* (1967), *The Sting* (1973) and *Mommie Dearest* (1981; based on the life of Joan Crawford) – exploited a wave of curiosity about and nostalgia for the period, as did re-presentations of period plays and musicals with Deco revival or neo-Deco sets and costumes.[34]

The style's original address to both luxury and popular markets now made it accessible to a wide range of new enthusiasts. As Janet Street-Porter wrote, in a somewhat acerbic review of Bevis Hillier's book, *Art Deco*, 'The number of fans of the thirties and all its visual goodies (not just the work of famous exponents of the style, but the anonymous everyday objects that are now being collected) has been growing for some time.' She also made a heart-felt plea for the characteristic qualities of the style to be taken seriously by contemporary designers: 'The *real* revival is not in the revamping of graphics or fashion but in realizing once again the best aims of Art Deco – to unite the artist and mass production techniques to produce objects that are not only well designed and functional yet possess specific, individual, human quality'.[35]

In practice, Art Deco was rediscovered at precisely the moment that a negative judgement on Modernism became general and a desire for the expression of fantasy widespread. For three decades or so – mirroring its original lifespan – Art Deco offered a resource to be mined for the expression of symbolic and decorative values, as well as glamour and wit. It encouraged Post-modern architects and designers, including Philip Johnson, Robert Venturi, Ettore Sottsass and others,[36] across the spectrum of design practice, to employ a richer iconography, to be playful and to take risks with materials, colours, surfaces, shapes and visual references (plate 40.2).

The rise, fall and rediscovery of Art Deco provide useful lessons in the history of style, the place of theory and the role of the arts in society. Designers stray too far from human appetites at their peril. The Deco revival and the development of a more critical and human view of Modernism, informed by feminism and post-Structuralism, has created the space to replace an 'either-or' approach to Modernism and its decorative 'other', Art Deco, by 'both-and'. Art Deco can now better be understood neither as a 'false' Modernism nor as debased classicism but as a different response to the same pressures of the contemporary world.

Notes

Chapter 1: The Style and the Age

1. Throughout this book, the words 'modern' and 'modernity' are used to refer to the general attributes of the changing world as perceived by contemporaries (whether technical – such as new materials, sources of power and new means of communication and transportation, or social – such as the changing status and role of women). 'Modernism', which was contemporary with Art Deco, is used, in the context of fine art, to describe tendencies towards abstraction, a criticism based on formal analysis and the assumption that fine art is, and should be, disinterested. 'Modernism' applied to architecture and design designates a rational, analytical – and often socially engaged – approach, which prioritizes the search for design solutions to society's collective needs and largely rejects ornament.
2. Examples of such visions in film of the period include Fritz Lang's *Metropolis* (1926), Abel Gance's *End of the World* (1930) and *Things to Come* (1936), produced by Alexander Korda and directed by William Cameron Menzies.
3. Francis Scott Fitzgerald, *The Great Gatsby* (New York, 1925; reprinted many times since). Widely seen as the defining novel of the Jazz Age, the book portrays the shallowness and decadence of the era.
4. Ruth Vassos, 'Advertising', in John Vassos and Ruth Vassos, *Contempo: This American Tempo* (New York, 1929), n.p.
5. Edwin Avery Park, *New Backgrounds for a New Age* (New York, 1927), p. 161.
6. See Rossana Bossaglia, *L'Art Déco* (Bari, 1984), p. 3. Bossaglia later accepted that an Art Deco style might be identified in certain formal elements and typologies.
7. Bevis Hillier, *Art Deco of the 20s and 30s* (London, 1968) p. 9. Alastair Duncan, a prolific writer on the style, claims 'Art Deco is now seen as the first universal style based on legitimate principles of design to have emerged in 125 years'; see Alastair Duncan, *Modernism: Modernist Design, 1880-1940. The Norwest Collection, Norwest Corporation, Minneapolis* (Woodbridge, 1998), p. 178.
8. A search on titles containing the words 'Art Deco' in the on-line catalogue of the Library of Congress gives an indication of the extent of the literature, as do the articles cumulatively listed in the *Art Index*. Other indications of the wide interest in the style are the many Art Deco societies worldwide, the World Congress on Art Deco, which takes place every other year (its first congress held in Miami Beach in 1991), and numerous Art Deco websites. An international list of Art Deco societies and related groups can be found in Barbara Capitman, Michael D. Kinerk and Dennis W. Wilhelm, *Rediscovering Art Deco* (New York, 1994), pp. 219-20.
9. Martin Greif, 'Defining Art Deco', Art Deco Society of New York *News*, vol. 2, no. 1 (January-February 1982), p. 2.
10. Ibid.
11. Rosemarie Haag Bletter, 'Introduction', in Carla Breeze, *New York and Art Deco* (New York, 1993), p. 8.
12. Richard Guy Wilson, 'Defining Art Deco', Art Deco Society of New York *News*, vol. 3, no. 3 (Fall 1983), p. 2.
13. Ludwig Wittgenstein, *Philosophical Investigations* (Oxford, 1953).
14. Ibid, p. 66.
15. Ralph Ströhle makes this kind of contrast in his book *Faszination Art Deco* (Berlin, 1993), p. 16.
16. Paul Gaultier, 'A l'Exposition des arts décoratifs', *Revue bleue* (January-December 1925), pp. 633-6; quote from p. 634. Other critics made similar observations.
17. Later published in Le Corbusier, *L'Art décoratif d'aujourd'hui* (Paris, 1925); English edition, *The Decorative Art of Today* (London, 1987).
18. *Les Années '25': Art Déco/Bauhaus/Stijl/Esprit Nouveau* (Paris, 1966). Here François Mathey wrote, 'Comment les "Années folles" succèdent à la "Belle Epoque", l'Art Déco au Modern Style (Art Nouveau), comment aussi à travers cette apparente continuité apparaissent et s'imposent les symptômes d'un art mondial impatient de surgir'; p. 10.
19. Hillier (1968).
20. Ibid, pp. 12-13. Hillier used the term in preference to alternatives such as 'style 1925' or 'jazz modern' because it was not associated only with the 1920s. He indicates that it was already used by dealers, and cites an article in *The Times* of 2 November 1966 and an issue of *Elle* magazine (November 1967), which devoted 22 pages to 'Les Arts déco', as examples of its wider use.
21. Bevis Hillier, *The World of Art Deco* (New York and London, 1971), p. 45.
22. Confusingly, Battersby used the term 'modernism' for Art Deco after 1925; see Martin Battersby, *The Decorative Twenties* (London, 1969), p. 7 and the chapter entitled 'The New Modernism', pp. 52ff. As a collector, Battersby had something of a vested interest in identifying the style with elite production. Hillier notes, in his introduction to Bevis Hillier and Stephen Escritt, *Art Deco Style* (London, 1997), that his 1968 book provoked criticisms for associating luxury production and the 'camp' or kitsch.
23. An early example is Alain Lesieutre, whose text begins 'This is not a book for people who are embarrassed by splendour or put off by luxury'; see Alain Lesieutre, *Art Deco* (New York and London, 1974), p. 7. See also Pierre Kjellberg, *Art Déco: Les Maîtres du mobilier, le décor des paquebots* (Paris, 1998). Such authors include both 'modernized traditional' and 'decorative Modernist' work of the 1920s, and many include the more attenuated version of 'modernized traditional' that appeared in France from the late 1920s.
24. Patricia Bayer, *Art Deco Interiors: Decoration and Design Classics of the 1920s and 1930s* (New York and London, 1990) p. 7. See also Patricia Bayer, *Art Deco Architecture: Design, Decoration and Detail from the Twenties and Thirties* (New York, 1998). Alastair Duncan has also promoted an inclusive definition of Art Deco; see Alastair Duncan, *Art Deco* (London, 1988) and *American Art Deco* (London, 1986). However, many authors do not clarify the relationship between the early French 'pure, high-style' and later popular manifestations of Art Deco.
25. This neglect resulted from the dominance of Modernist orthodoxies among practising architects, critics and historians; see David Gebhard's comments on this issue, quoted later on p. 19 and see note 35 below.
26. One of the first Art Deco preservation societies, the Miami Design Preservation League, was founded by Barbara Baer Capitman in 1973. The Art Deco Society of New York, which produced a newsletter from 1981, exerted a formidable influence on the New York City Landmarks Preservation Commission (founded in 1965); its vigorous lobbying contributed to the listing of most Art Deco skyscrapers and cinemas in New York City, beginning with Raymond Hood's American Radiator building (1924) in 1974.
27. See, for example, Howard Mandelbaum and Eric Myers, *Screen Deco* (New York and Bromley, c.1985); Michel Collomb, *La Littérature art déco: Sur le style d'époque* (Paris, 1987); Edward Lucie-Smith, *Art Deco Painting* (London, 1990). Studies of Art Deco in individual countries or cities include Judith Singer Cohen, *Cowtown Moderne: Art Deco Architecture of Fort Worth, Texas* (College Station, TX. c.1988); Anna Sieradzka, *Art déco w Europie i w Polsce* (Warsaw, 1996); Rossana Bossaglia and Valerio Terraroli, *Milano déco: La fisionomia della città negli anni venti* (Milan, 1999). In addition there are books about the Art Deco ranges of manufacturers. These include Paula Ockner and Leslie Piña, *Art Deco Aluminum: Kensington* (Atglen, PA, 1997), on Lurelle Guild's work for Kensington Ware; Richard J. Kilbride, *Art Deco Chrome: The Chase Era* (Stamford, CT, 1998), on Art Deco wares produced by the Chase Brass & Copper Company.
28. See Giovanna Franci and others, *In viaggio attraverso il deco americano* (Florence, 1997), p. 11: 'The term Deco is a universal label attached to the most varied manifestations of the "modern" in America, linked to the birth of industrial design, the laws of the marketplace and the desire to explore the new possibilities opened up by the so-called machine age ... Deco in the USA manages to incorporate diverse styles within a common taste'.
29. The 1966 exhibition at the Musée des Arts Décoratifs in Paris drew on its large collection of work, acquired from the Paris 1925 Exhibition onwards. The Metropolitan Museum of Art in New York also obtained a number of Art Deco works in the 1920s; see Penelope Hunter, 'Art Deco and the Metropolitan Museum of Art', *Connoisseur*, vol. 179 (April 1972), pp. 273-81. In England, Martin Battersby was the inspiration behind *The Jazz Age* exhibition shown at Brighton Museum and Art Gallery in 1969, which began an active policy of collecting Art Deco thereafter; see Jessica Rutherford, *Art Nouveau, Art Deco and the Thirties: The Furniture Collections at Brighton Museum* (Brighton, 1983).
30. The most notable example of the latter was the sale of Jacques Doucet's extensive collection in November 1972; see Hôtel Drouot sales catalogue, *Ancienne Collection Jacques Doucet. Mobilier Art Déco provenant du Studio Saint-James à Neuilly* (Paris, 1972).
31. The adjective was used retrospectively by Bevis Hillier, the exhibition's curator. For the catalogue, see Hillier (1971). The book jacket was designed by Bentley, Farrell, Burnett.
32. See, for example, Martin Greif, *Depression Modern: The Thirties Style in America* (New York, 1975), p. 14. Greif was partisan in wanting to recover much of what Hillier had classed as Deco for a serious tradition of American Modernism, as have several other American writers since; see, for example, J. Stewart Johnson, *American Modern, 1925-1940: Design for a New Age* (New York, 2000). Greif was also critical of the exploitation of nostalgia for the Thirties in films such as *Bonnie and Clyde* (1967) and *The Sting* (1973).
33. The concept of 'Post-modernism' is associated with the writings, from the 1970s onwards, of French and other cultural theorists such as Michel Foucault, François Lyotard and Frederic Jameson. These authors challenge the notion that Western rationalist traditions of thought, as developed from the Renaissance to the early twentieth century, can still provide useful signposts to understanding the world. Broadly speaking, Post-modernists are sceptical of 'grand narratives' or universal truths, stress the plural, fragmentary and subjective nature of reality, and the relativity of values. In general, they see no distinction between high and low culture and, in respect of visual culture, stress that the image is the reality. For some titles – from a vast literature – see Marshall Berman, *All that is Solid melts into Air: The Experience of Modernity* (London, 1983); Perry Anderson, *The Origins of Postmodernity* (London, 1998); David Harvey, *The Condition of Postmodernity: An Enquiry into the Origins of Cultural Change* (Oxford, 1990). For Post-modernism in architecture, see the many publications of Charles Jencks.
34. Venturi and Scott Brown have been seen as originating Post-modernism in architecture, through their publications and buildings of the late 1960s and early 1970s. In his *Complexity and Contradiction in Architecture* (Garden City, NY, 1966) Robert Venturi challenged the doctrinaire tenets of architectural Modernism; he argued that instead of *either/or* (function *or* meaning, etc.), architects could have *both/and*. Robert Venturi, Denise Scott Brown and Steven Izenour's *Learning from Las Vegas* (Cambridge, MA, 1972) suggested that architects should be more receptive to the tastes and values of ordinary people and drew attention to the symbolic content and vitality of the commercial vernacular. Venturi and Scott Brown deny that they are Post-modernists or originated Post-modernism in architecture (see 'A bas Postmodernism of course', on their website at http://www.vsba.com/home/essay.html), but it is easy to see both why they have been attributed this role and why they have been enthusiasts for Deco. The rise of Post-modernism in architecture and design also encouraged re-readings of Modernism as a more diverse phenomenon than had been assumed previously.
35. David Gebhard, *Tulsa Art Deco* (Tulsa, 1980), p.17.
36. For reasons of its socially 'progressive' programme, Modernism was often espoused by and associated with the Left in the years before the Second World War and those that immediately followed. With the advent of the Cold War, the apparent co-option of Modernism by the 'West' for anti-Communist propaganda and the frequent association of Modernism with elite audiences, many on the Left distanced themselves from the phenomenon. The Marxist philosopher Ernst Bloch was an early 'objector' to Modernism; see his essay 'On Fine Arts in the Machine Age' (1964), in Ernst Bloch, *The Utopian Function of Art and Literature* (Cambridge, MA, and London, 1988), pp. 200-7.
37. Neither discipline was specifically concerned with design or inter-war popular culture, but both provided useful perspectives for their study. Studies of America as a consumer society developed from the 1950s; a significant early publication was David M. Potter, *People of Plenty: Economic Abundance and the American Character* (Chicago, 1954). Of particular interest, in the context of Art Deco's acceptance in America, is Neil Harris, 'Museums, Merchandising and Popular Taste: The Struggle for Influence', in Ian M. G. Quimby (ed.), *Material Culture and the Study of American Life* (New York, 1978), pp. 140-74, which indicates the formative influence of the department store on American taste in the early twentieth century; see Jeffrey L. Meikle, 'American Design History: A Bibliography of Sources and Interpretations', *American Studies International*, vol. xxiii, no. 1 (April 1985), pp. 3-40.
38. One reason for this was that the reaction against Modernism, and Modernist historiography, was expressed in a plurality of new approaches (feminism, semiotics, etc.) which challenged the use of stylistic categories as meaningful or appropriate ways to approach and interpret visual culture. Another was the reluctance of many academics, particularly non-American ones, to deal with such an avowedly commercial phenomenon as Art Deco – an unease that has been dissipated by the widespread growth of consumption studies.
39. David Gebhard, 'Moderne Architecture', *Journal of the Society of Architectural Historians*, vol. 31, no. 3 (October 1972), pp. 230-1.
40. The latter including Rudolf Schindler, Richard Neutra and Gregory Ain.
41. David Gebhard and Harriette Von Breton, *Los Angeles in the Thirties, 1931-1941* (Layton, UT, 1975; revised and enlarged edition, Los Angeles, 1989). The WPA (Works Progress Administration) was established by the Roosevelt government to execute a public works programme to mitigate the effects of the Depression.
42. The terminology was not always consistently applied, however. 'Moderne' (from the French word), a term in use during the Deco period, came to be widely employed by Anglo-Saxon authors both to denote the influence of the French decorative arts and to designate works that corrupted the principles of Modernism. Elayne H. Varian used 'style moderne' as a synonym for Art Deco in her *American Art Deco Architecture* (New York, 1975), p. 1. Confusingly, the French themselves have no term to designate the type of work to which Anglo-Saxon authors have applied 'Moderne'. 'Modernistic', another term in use during the inter-war years, also came to designate novel, or 'modern', work that differed in intention from Modernism However, even those who use these terms in a positive sense have also used them to designate work that is somehow not 'genuinely modern', either by the measure of Modernism or by some other measure.
43. See also note 1.
44. On Lubetkin, see Peter Coe and Malcolm Reading, *Lubetkin and Tecton: Architecture and Social Commitment* (London, 1981); John Allan, *Berthold Lubetkin: Architecture and the Tradition of Progress* (London, 1992), Chapter 7. Inspector Poirot, the creation of Agatha Christie, has more than once passed through this space in dramatizations of Christie's detective novels for British television.
45. See Sarah M. Morgan, *Art Deco: The European Style* (New York, 1990), p. 42, in which the gallery of Le Corbusier's La Roche house as remodelled in 1928 is claimed as 'a significant influence on modernistic Art Deco'.
46. Eckart Muthesius's interiors for the Maharaja of Indore's palace, Manik Bagh (1930-1), for example, incorporated works by both Deco and Modernist artists and designers; see Reto Niggl, *Eckart Muthesius: International Style, 1930: The Maharaja's Palace in Indore: Architecture and Interior* (Stuttgart, 1997). In the early 1930s, as Art Deco increasingly abandoned surface ornament, there was a degree of formal convergence between Art Deco and Modernism.
47. These debates have themselves come about as a result of the influence of Post-modernism on academic discourse.
48. Among Viennese influences were the works of Josef Hoffmann and Dagobert Peche, c.1900-6; both designers subsequently embraced a form of 'modernized tradition'. Other influences included the work of the Scottish designer Charles Rennie Mackintosh.
49. Striking examples of French Art Deco stylized naturalism can be seen in the work of Edouard Bénédictus and Paul Poiret's Atelier Martine.
50. Reino Liefkes draws attention to some of the direct links between Dutch Art Nouveau and Art Deco; see Chapter 15.
51. See Paul Greenhalgh, 'The Style and the Age', in Paul Greenhalgh (ed.), *Art Nouveau, 1890-1914* (London, 2000), p. 18.
52. As Tag Gronberg observes, here film was emphasized as a French invention; see Chapter 13.
53. Such mannequins were first employed in up-market Parisian boutiques. As Jeremy Aynsley notes, these ambiguous figures became a trope in fine and graphic art, as well as photography, during the 1910s and 1920s; see Chapter 26.
54. Including women's magazines and specialist architecture and interior

design journals.
55. Notably the albums published by Charles Moreau in Paris.
56. See note 46. Following the Maharaja's death in 1956, the palace became an official administrative building. The furnishings were auctioned in Monte Carlo in 1980, when some pieces were acquired by museums.

Chapter 2: The Great War, Mass Society and 'Modernity'

1. The cartoon is reproduced in Arthur Marwick, *Britain in Our Century: Images and Controversies* (London, 1984), p. 77.
2. The term was widely used; the term 'common woman' less so. Official terminology was a little more sophisticated during and after the Second World War.
3. Thomas C. Reeves, *Twentieth Century America: A Brief History* (New York and Oxford, 2000), p. 84.
4. Robert Sobel, *The Age of Giant Corporations: A Microeconomic History of American Business, 1914-1984* (Westport, Conn., and London, 1984), p. 57.
5. Reeves (2000), p. 95.
6. Ibid, p. 84.
7. Ibid, p. 87.
8. James F. McMillan, *Twentieth Century France: Politics and Society, 1898-1991* (London and New York, 1992), p. 78.

Chapter 3: Egyptomania

1. *Encyclopédie des arts décoratifs et industriels modernes*, vol. i (Paris, 1925), pp. 11, 16.
2. See Bevis Hillier and Stephen Escritt, *Art Deco Style* (London, 1997), pp. 27-32.
3. *Encyclopédie* (1925), vol. iv, p. 52.
4. See, for example, *Encyclopédie* (1925), vol. i, pls xxxvi, lxxx (*Le luxe*); vol. x, pl. xx (*Vision d'Orient*).
5. Department of Overseas Trade, *Reports on the Present Position and Tendencies of the Industrial Arts as indicated at the International Exhibition of Modern Decorative and Industrial Arts, Paris, 1925* (London, 1925), pp. 11-26; introductory survey by Sir Hubert Llewellyn Smith, Chairman of the editorial committee, which included Sir Reginald Blomfield, Eric Maclagan and Sir Frank Warner.
6. Department of Overseas Trade (1925), pp. 27-9, 120-22, 128.
7. For two excellent, detailed accounts of the discovery, see H. V. F. Winstone, *Howard Carter and the Discovery of the Tomb of Tutankhamun* (London, 1993), pp. 139-59; and T. G. H. James, *Howard Carter: The Path to Tutankhamun* (London, 1992), pp. 191-246. In the mid-1920s, the preferred English spelling was 'Tutankamen' or 'Tutankhamen'; today 'Tutankhamun'. For more extensive treatments of the cultural impact of the discovery, see Christopher Frayling, *The Face of Tutankhamun* (London, 1992), especially pp. 10-60; Bob Brier, *Egyptomania* (Brookville, NY, 1992), pp. 16-36.
8. Photographs to illustrate this theme were exhibited in *The Pharaoh's Photographer: Harry Burton, Tutankhamun and the Metropolitan's Egyptian Exhibition*, at the Metropolitan Museum, New York, 11 September-30 December 2001. On the cinematic metaphor, see Antonia Lant, 'The Curse of the Pharaoh, or How Cinema Contracted Egyptomania', *October* (Spring 1992), pp. 87-112. Some of the finest contemporary reproductions of Burton's work appeared in the 'Egypt Number' of the *Illustrated London News*, 3 February 1923.
9. Edmé-François Jomard (ed.), *Déscription de l'Egypte ou Recueil des observations et des recherches qui ont été faites en Egypte pendant l'expédition de l'armée française*, book A, vol. iii (Paris, 1808-28; reprint, Cologne, c.1994), pl. 51.
10. See Hans Nadelhoffer, *Cartier, Jewellers Extraordinary* (London, 1984), pp. 149-55, and *Egyptian Influences on Cartier's Creations*, Cartier Archive leaflet (London, n.d.). The *Illustrated London News* ran an article on 'The "Tutankhamen" Influence in Modern Jewellery' on 26 January 1924. The temple gate clock was sold by Christie's, New York on 24 April 1991 with a special catalogue. The prediction, by Pierre Cartier, was printed in the *New York Times*, 8 February 1923.
11. See Frayling (1992), pp. 10-12. The accompanying BBC documentary series, *Chronicle*, programme 3, featured archive footage of 'Pleasures of the Nile' and other examples of Tutmania.
12. *New York Times*, 1, 7, 8, 18, 21, 25 February 1923.
13. See American *Vogue*, 1 April 1923, editorial; also 15 April 1923, pp. 51, 57, 115; 1 May 1923, pp. 63-4, 135; 15 July 1923; 1 August 1923, p. 40; 1 September 1923.
14. Micki Forman, 'Tutmania', *Dress*, vol. 4 (1978), pp. 7-14.
15. For coverage of British Tutmania in fashion, see *The Times*, 23 January 1923; *Daily Express*, 9, 13, 21 March 1923; *Daily Mail*, 10, 16 April 1923; *Morning Post*, 16 April 1923; 'Royal Wedding Number' of the *Illustrated London News*, 28 April and 5 May 1923. *Punch* satirized the craze throughout February and April 1923, then again in January and March 1924.
16. See Martin Battersby, James Stevens Curl, *The Egyptian Revival* (London, 1982), Chapter X, also, *The Decorative Twenties* (London, 1969), pp. 140-41.
17. See Hillier and Escritt (1997), pp. 116-21.
18. See Frayling (1992), p. 21.
19. See Frayling (1992), pp. 21-3. Wyndham Lewis's most celebrated essay on this, 'The Dithyrambic Spectator – The Origins and Survival of Art', first appeared in *The Calendar of Modern Letters*, vol. 2 (April 1925).
20. Robert Graves and Alan Hodge, *The Long Weekend, 1918-1939* (London, 1940; reprint, London, 1991), pp. 125-7.
21. Extract from Evelyn Waugh, *Labels: A Mediterranean Journal* (London, 1930; reprints, 1985 and 1991), cited in *New York Times*, 20 December 1978.
22. See Frayling (1992), pp. 24-5; also, Charles Higham, *Cecil B. De Mille* (New York, 1973), pp. 92-5.
23. See James (1992), p. 401.
24. See Hillier and Escritt (1997), pp. 167-8; also, Frayling (1992), pp. 60-66; and Curl (1982), pp. 205-8.
25. Frayling, ibid. Philologist Dr Alan Gardiner and the craftsmanlike Howard Carter did not always see eye to eye (see, for example, James (1992), pp. 180-87, 385-6). Gardiner thought Carter 'a difficult man', and Carter thought Gardiner a 'meddler'. But both became involved with the Victoria and Albert Museum – in their different ways – following the discovery. Gardiner arranged an exhibition of copies of 84 Theban wall paintings, in July and August 1923. The Director of the Museum introduced the slim catalogue by writing, 'At the present moment recent discoveries have invested the Theban Tombs with a particular interest'. Carter gave a lecture at the Museum on 'Colour', 17 October 1934, with special reference to Sir Joshua Reynolds, Richard Redgrave and John Ruskin. Neither the exhibition nor the lecture made any mention of Tutmania, or indeed of Tut's tomb. The Museum's definition of decoration and design at that time could not quite bring itself to encompass either.

Chapter 4: Deco Sculpture and Archaism

1. The period between 1870 and 1914 has been described as the 'age of the great excavations'. However, much of the material uncovered then would only filter through into the popular consciousness in the succeeding years, and further important archeological discoveries were still to come, notably the Etruscan and Egyptian finds (see Chapter 3 for the latter).
2. Isadora Duncan is specially well known for her influence on French artists, but there were many other contemporary exponents of 'free dance', including Mary Wigman in Germany and Margaret Morris in Britain, who returned to a notional pre-Hellenic classicism. Other sources were more exotic, including the Cambodian dancers who inspired Rodin, and Diaghilev's Ballets Russes. Dancers from the Russian troupe inspired many sculptures that often combined portrait-homage with life-study.
3. This was commissioned by Philip Sassoon for his country home at Hite.
4. Friedrich Goldscheider (established in Paris in 1892) presented its own pavilion in 1925 and represented sculptors such as Max Blondat, Pierre le Faguys, Raoul Lamourdedieu, Charles Malfray, Pierre Traverse and Jan and Joël Martel. In Berlin, Ferdinand Preiss set up Preiss-Kassler, which dominated chryselephantine production and was employing ten sculptors by the 1920s. Other *maisons d'édition* included Edmond Etling & Cie, Friedlander Co. and Phillips & MacConnel.
5. And must be seen in the light of Ponti's sustained campaign for a modern understanding of classicism, promulgated most notably through the magazine *Domus*; see Chapter 19.
6. Jagger received some casebook Art Deco commissions from notable English patrons. *Scandal* was commissioned by Lord Melchett for his London home and another version, *Nymph and Satyr*, by Sir Stephen Courtauld. Both bronze reliefs used a similar 'cut-out' composition, but while the sinuous silhouette of the former was left free, the other was mounted on oak.
7. The Monument to Svatopluk Čech, 1918-23, in which the newly founded Czechoslovakia echoes the commemorative style of the French Third Republic.
8. See Chapter 14 of Michele H. Bogart's excellent *Public Sculpture and the Civic Ideal in New York City, 1890-1930* (Chicago, 1989) for her discussion of the Rockefeller artists' attempts to depict 'modern progress'.

Chapter 5: Ancient Mexican Sources of Art Deco

1. *Q: The Winged Serpent* (1982), director Larry Cohen, Arkoff International and Larco Productions, starring Michael Moriarty and David Carradine.
2. Designed by William Van Alen, the Chrysler building was completed in 1930 and, for a short period, was the highest building in New York; see Chapter 22.
3. *New York Herald Tribune*, 14 November 1931.
4. For a detailed account of the development of such issues, see Paul Greenhalgh, *Ephemeral Vistas: Expositions Universelles, Great Exhibitions and World Fairs, 1851-1939* (Manchester, 1988).
5. Antonio Peñafiel, *Explication de l'edifice mexicaine à l'Exposition international de Paris en 1889* (Barcelona, 1889).
6. I am indebted to the interesting account of the Mexican presence at the World Fairs by Mauricio Tenorio-Trillo, *Mexico at the World's Fairs: Crafting a Modern Nation* (Berkeley and Los Angeles, 1996); pp. 64-80 are particularly relevant to the 'Aztec Palace'.
7. The function of this section of the Chicago exhibition is discussed in James Gilbert, *Perfect Cities: Chicago's Utopias of 1893* (Chicago, 1991), p. 109.
8. See Dimitri Tselos, 'Exotic Influences in the Architecture of Frank Lloyd Wright', *Magazine of Art* (April 1953), p. 163.
9. See David Gebhard, *Robert Stacy-Judd: Maya Architecture and the Creation of a New Style* (Santa Barbara, 1993) and Marjorie I. Ingle, *The Mayan Revival Style: Art Deco Mayan Fantasy* (Salt Lake City, 1990).
10. To some extent, local variations became the hook on which to hang a series of indigenous decorative references. Elements of Maya, Inca or Navajo style could co-exist in the same schema; see, for example, Carla Breeze, *Pueblo Deco* (New York, 1990).
11. The use of a generic rather than specific Indian past could be seen as a logical product of the desire to escape from the negative characterization of the Native American in the anthropological writings of late nineteenth-century American authors such as Lewis Henry Morgan; see Benjamin Keen, *The Aztec Image in Western Thought* (New Brunswick, NJ, 1971), pp. 380-410.
12. Maya architecture remained popular at US shows and exhibitions, appearing at the *Pan American Exposition* in Buffalo (1900), the *Louisiana Purchase Exhibition* in St Louis (1904), the *Panama California Exposition* in San Diego in 1915 and again at the 1933 Chicago *Centennial Exhibition*. Sylvanus G. Morley (see note 15) published regular features on the topic in the *National Geographic* throughout the first decades of the twentieth century, and in 1926 George Oakley Totten produced his widely read *Maya Architecture* (Washington, DC, c.1926; reprint, New York, 1973).
13. John L. Stephens, *Incidents of Travel in Central America, Chiapas and Yucatan*, with illustrations by Frederick Catherwood (New York, 1841).
14. Herbert J. Spinden, *A Study of Maya Art* (Cambridge, MA, 1913), p. 15.
15. Sylvanus Griswold Morley (1883-1948) was responsible for a series of publications that popularized Maya culture in the first half of the twentieth century, probably most clearly evidenced by his later compilation of findings, *The Ancient Maya* (Stanford and London, 1946). Between 1914 and 1929 he oversaw the Carnegie Institute work at Chichen Itza, which included the reconstruction of its main pyramid temple, the 'Castillo'.
16. In the early 1920s, the *New York Times* funded an archeological expedition to the Yucatan, led by Gregory Mason and Herbert Spinden (then an assistant curator at the Peabody Museum). The expedition was reported in the paper at various intervals and formed the basis of Mason's book, *Silver Cities of Yucatan* (New York and London, 1927).
17. Manuel Gamio (ed.), *La Problación del Valle de Teotihuacán* (Mexico City, 1922).
18. The interest generated by the cultural debates of the post-revolutionary period in Mexico made it a popular destination for the avant-garde traveller. Rivera, Kahlo and their circle were keen to introduce visitors to the wonders of the Aztec past. 'Tourists' of this type in the 1920s included Edward Weston, Tina Modotti, D. H. Lawrence and Sergei Eisenstein. Lawrence's *The Plumed Serpent*, dealing with his perceptions of the Mexican debates, was published in 1926. See also Nancy Newhall (ed.), *The Daybooks of Edward Weston* (New York, 1990).
19. For an introduction to the various issues within this complex subject, see Ignacio Bernal, *A History of Mexican Archaeology: The Vanished Civilizations of Middle America* (London, 1980) and Robert Wauchope, *They Found the Buried Cities* (Chicago and London, 1965).
20. Bertram Wolfe, *The Fabulous Life of Diego Rivera* (New York, 1963), particularly 'The Art of a Continent', pp. 277-96.
21. Tenorio-Trillo (1996), pp. 227-32.

Chapter 6: Inspiration from the East

1. Bengt de Törne, 'Letter from Paris', *Apollo*, vol. 1, no. 1 (June 1925), pp. 363-4.
2. From the 1640s Japan operated a 'closed country' policy and the Dutch were the only westerners permitted to trade with the country. National isolation was brought to an end in 1853 when an American squadron arrived off Japan's coast demanding that it open its ports to foreign powers. After diplomatic and trading treaties were signed with the West, Japanese goods flooded into Europe and America leading to a craze for all things Japanese.
3. See Anna Jackson, 'Orient and Occident', in Paul Greenhalgh (ed.), *Art Nouveau, 1890-1914* (London, 2000), pp. 100-113.
4. C. T. Loo built his famous pagoda in 1926-8 in collaboration with the French architect Fernand Bloch. Loo had begun dealing in Chinese art in 1902 and was one of the first to respond to the changing tastes and increased availability of older works. Yamanaka & Co. was a Japanese company that had started to sell Asian art in the West in the 1890s. Interestingly, by the 1930s 90% of the objects it sold were Chinese.
5. Quoted in LeRoy C. Breunig (ed.), *Apollinaire on Art: Essays and Reviews, 1902-1918* (New York, 1972; reprint, 1988), pp. 128-9.
6. There were significant publications on Chinese art by authors such as Edouard Chavannes, Paul Pelliot, Osvald Sirén and Robert Lockhart Hobson.
7. For example the excavation from 1927 of the site of the Shang dynasty (c.1700-1050 BC) capital near Anyang.
8. *Catalogue of a Collection of Chinese Art* (exh. cat. Burlington Fine Art Club; London, 1915), p. ix.
9. The dates of these dynasties are: Shang (c.1700-1050 BC), Zhou (1050-221 BC), Song (960-1127), Yuan (1127-1368), Ming (1368-1644) and Qing (1644-1911).
10. See H. J. Kim and M. R. DeLong, 'Sino-Japanism in Western Women's Fashionable Dress in *Harper's Bazar*, 1890-1927', *Clothing and Textiles Research Journal*, vol. 11, no. 1 (1992), pp. 24-30.
11. *Inrō* are small, segmented containers designed to carry medicines or seals. For examples of Cartier's cigarette and vanity cases, see Judy Rudoe, *Cartier, 1900-1939* (London, 1997), pp. 126-8.
12. It is possible that some of the inlaid lacquer came from the Ryūkyūan Islands or Japan, though it was still very much in the Chinese style.
13. *Illustrated London News*, 2 December 1922, p. 897.
14. Jade pieces are generally described as being 'carved', but jade is actually too hard to be worked in this way so abrasive sands are used with grinding and cutting tools to wear away the stone.
15. Quoted in Jessica Rawson, *Chinese Jade from the Neolithic to the Qing* (London, 1995), p. 15.
16. Such pieces can be distinguished from earlier ones as they have no function in traditional Chinese costume. Some pieces for Deco jewellery were also cut in Japan.
17. I am grateful to Edmund Chin for this information.
18. For illustrations, see *La Renaissance de l'art français et des industries de luxe* (December 1921), p. 627 and *L'Art et les artistes*, vol. ix (1924), p. 281.
19. I am grateful to Judith Green for alerting me to this interior.

20. Other notable films include Frank Capra's *The Bitter Tea of General Yen* (1933) and Josef Von Sternberg's *The Shanghai Gesture* (1941).
21. This character was created as the Japanese were encroaching on China, so it has been suggested that Ming the Merciless represented a Japanese, rather than a Chinese, threat. The name, however, was very clearly Chinese. The comic strip originated in 1934 and the film series dates to 1936-40.
22. Sax Rohmer, *The Mystery of Dr Fu Manchu* (London, 1913; reprint, Bath, 1992); republished in *The Fu Manchu Omnibus*, vol. i (London, 2000), p. 15. There were ten Fu Manchu novels published between 1913 and 1939 and a further four after the war. The novels are awash with stereotypical images of eastern dacoits, thugs and dusky-skinned damsels. There are also references to Japanese samurai and Egyptian mummies. Sax Rohmer was the pseudonym of Arthur Sarsfield Ward.
23. *Illustrated London News*, 11 July 1925, p. 59, reporting on the theories of anthropologist Aimé-François Legendre.
24. Alexander Iacovleff, 'Preface' to Chu-Chia-Chein and Alexander Iacovleff, *The Chinese Theatre* (London, 1922), pp. 5-6.
25. Raymond Koechlin, 'Les Bronzes chinois', *Art et décoration*, vol. 47 (1925), p. 44.
26. Craig Clunas, 'Oriental Antiquities/Far Eastern Art', *Positions: East Asia Cultures Critique*, vol. 2, no. 2 (1994), p. 335.
27. Roger Fry (ed.), *Chinese Art* (London, 1925).
28. Quoted in Christopher Green (ed.), *Art Made Modern: Roger Fry's Vision of Art* (London, 1999), p. 150.
29. The objects that can be identified from the 1930 illustration include: on the left-hand side, a Chinese Buddhist painting and, on top of the cabinets, a Kangxi period (1662-1722) blue and white jar and a late Ming jar of the type exported to south-east Asia; on the cabinet to the right on the back wall, a seventeenth- or eighteenth-century jar from South China (or possibly Korea); on the table a late Ming dynasty bronze, or possibly wood, figure; under the table, a pillar carpet and a late Ming dynasty (or possible Vietnamese) jar. My thanks to my colleague Rose Kerr for this information.
30. This panel is sometimes titled *Le magicien de la nuit*.
31. Asian lacquerwork had always been much admired in the West and there had been various attempts to replicate it with pigments and resins, but until the twentieth century no one had learned the methods of its production.
32. Lacquer can be drawn from various trees, but the most commonly used for artistic purposes are *Rhus verniciflua* in Japan and *Rhus succedanea* in China.
33. Japanese names are given in Japanese order, family name first followed by given name.
34. The lacquer gave Gray a skin complaint, a common problem experienced when handling the material. She therefore concentrated purely on the design of pieces, leaving the lacquering to Sugawara and his assistants.
35. *La Renaissance de l'art française et des industries de luxe* (July 1925), quoted in Félix Marcilhac, *Jean Dunand: His Life and Works* (London, 1991), pp. 69-70.
36. *Lacque arrachée* (literally 'pulled up') involves applying a wooden spatula to a freshly lacquered (wet) surface, pressing it down and then raising it quickly to produce an effect of wavy granulation. The surface is then polished smooth.
37. *Daily Mail*, 10 June 1922, quoted in Caroline Constant, *Eileen Gray* (London, 2000), p. 37.
38. 'Lacquer Walls and Furniture Displace Old Gods in Paris and London', *Harper's Bazar* (September 1920), p. 130.

Chapter 7: Collecting and Constructing Africa

1. Guillaume Apollinaire, 'Les Arts à Paris', 15 July 1918, quoted in LeRoy C. Breunig (ed.), *Apollinaire on Art: Essays and Reviews, 1902-1918* (New York, 1972; reprint, 1988), p. 470.
2. Quoted by David A. Bailey in *Rhapsodies in Black: Art of the Harlem Renaissance* (London, 1977), p. 20.
3. Guillaume Apollinaire, 'Exoticism and Ethnography', *Paris Journal*, 12 September 1912, quoted in Breunig (1988), p. 244.
4. André Malraux, *La Tête d'obsidienne* (Paris, 1974), pp. 10-11, quoted in Sieglinde Lemke, *Primitivist Modernism: Black Culture and the Origins of Transatlantic Modernism* (Oxford, 1998), p. 36.
5. Guillaume Apollinaire, 'Exoticism and Ethnography', *Paris Journal*, 12 September 1912, quoted in Breunig (1988), p. 246.
6. Vlastislav Hofman, 'Nový principy v architecktuře' (New principles in architecture), *Styl*, vol. 5 (1913), pp. 13-24, quoted in Alexander von Vegesack, *Czech Cubism* (Weil am Rhein, 1991), p. 69.
7. Henri Clouzot and André Level, *Première Exposition d'art nègre et d'Océanie organisée par Paul Guillaume du 10 au 31 mai 1919* (Galerie Devambez, Paris, 1919), p. 1.
8. André Level, quoted in Jean-Louis Paudrat, 'From Africa', in William Rubin (ed.), *'Primitivism' in 20th Century Art: Affinity of the Tribal and the Modern*, vol. i (New York, 1984), p. 159.
9. Ibid.
10. Franz Boas, *Primitive Art* (Oslo, 1927), p. 1.
11. Quoted in Lemke (1998), p. 7.
12. Telegram from Vicomte de Noailles to Legrain, quoted in Philippe Garner, 'Pierre Legrain – Décorateur', *Connoisseur*, vol. 189, no. 760 (1975), p. 134.
13. Quoted in Jody Blake, *Le Tumulte Noir* (University Park, PA, 1999), p. 1.
14. W. E. B. Du Bois, *Dark Princess* (New York, 1928; reprints, Millwood, NY, 1974 and Jackson, MS, c.1995), p. 20.

Chapter 8: National Traditions

1. *L'Atelier Primavera et la décoration moderne, 1913-1923* (Paris, 1923), p. 20.
2. See *Die Ausstellung München 1908* (Munich, 1908).
3. G. V., 'La Course à l'abîme', *Art et industrie* (July 1909), n. p.; referring to the defeat in 1870 of the French imperial army in Sedan.
4. M. P. Verneuil, 'Le Salon d'automne', *Art et décoration* (1910), p. 132.
5. Frédéric Masson, 'Nos Leaders: L'Art munichois et ses apôtres', *L'Excelsior*, 30 March 1915, p. 31.
6. 'Réglement du VIIème Salon', *Catalogue du septième salon de la Société des artistes décorateurs* (1912), p. 39.
7. André Vera, 'Le Nouveau Style', *L'Art décoratif*, vol. xxvii (January 1912), p. 29.
8. André Vera, 'Modernité et tradition', *Les Arts français*, vol. 3 (1919), pp. 95-6.
9. The *Salons d'automne* and the *Salons de la société des artistes décorateurs*.
10. Guillaume Janneau, 'Introduction à l'Exposition des arts décoratifs, considérations sur l'esprit moderne', *Art et décoration*, vol. lxvii (May 1925), pp. 151-2.
11. Jean Laran, 'Notre Enquête sur le mobilier moderne: Ruhlmann', *Art et décoration*, vol. xxxvii (January 1920), p. 6.
12. Musée des Arts Décoratifs, Paris. The table was made by Félix Rémond in 1823.
13. Château de Fontainebleau, for the Salon de l'Impératrice, by Jacob Desmalter, c.1808.
14. *La Demeure française*, vol. 1 (1925), p. 49.
15. 1907 and 1908; both in the collections of the Union Française des Arts du Costume (UFAC), Paris.
16. André Vera, 'Le Nouveau Style', *L'Art décoratif*, vol. xxvii (January 1912), pp. 31-2.
17. Léon Moussinac, *Étoffes imprimées et papiers peints* (Paris, 1924), p. 231.
18. Quoted in Werner Schweiger, *Wiener Werkstätte: Design in Vienna, 1903-1932* (London, 1984), p. 30.
19. Victoria and Albert Museum, W.26-1990. The chair was exhibited at the third German *Kunstgewerbe Ausstellung* in Dresden in 1906.
20. *Deutsche Kunstgewerbeausstellung*.
21. *Deutscher Werkbund Austellung*, Cologne, 1914.
22. Paul Schulze-Naumburg, 'Biedermeier Stil?', *Die Kunstwart*, vol. 19 (1905-6), pp. 131-7.
23. Musée des Arts Décoratifs, Paris.
24. Raymond Cogniat, *Dufy décorateur* (Geneva, 1957), p. 20.
25. First published in 1942; see Victor Lhuer, *Les Costumes bretons* and *Le Costume auvergnat et bourbonnais* (Barbentane, 2001).
26. Luc Benoist, 'Victor Lhuer, dessinateur et tisserand', *Art et décoration*, vol. liii (1928), p. 115-21.
27. M. P. Verneuil, 'L'Enseignement de l'art décoratif en Pologne', *Art et décoration*, vol. xlix (1926), p. 39.
28. Paul Greenhalgh, 'Alternative Histories', in Paul Greenhalgh (ed.), *Art Nouveau, 1890-1914* (London, 2000), pp. 36-53.

Chapter 9: Avant-Garde Sources

1. Helen Appleton Read, 'The Exposition in Paris', part 1, *International Studio*, vol. 82 (November 1925), pp. 94-7 (pp. 93, 95, 96).
2. See Christopher Green, *Cubism and its Enemies: Modern Movements and Reaction in French Art, 1916-1928* (New Haven and London, 1987); David Cottington, *Cubism in the Shadow of War: The Avant Garde and Politics in Paris, 1905-1914* (New Haven and London, 1998).
3. See, for example, L'Herbier's *Vertige* and René Le Somptier's *Le P'tit Parigot* (both 1926), and Conway's *Our Blushing Brides* (1929, art director Cedric Gibbons).
4. For Gray, see J. Stewart Johnson, *Eileen Gray, Designer* (London, 1979); Peter Adam, *Eileen Gray: Architect/Designer: A Biography* (London, 1987); Philippe Garner, *Eileen Gray: Design and Architecture, 1878-1976* (Cologne, 1993); Caroline Constant, *Eileen Gray* (London, 2000). For Legrain, see Léon Rosenthal, 'Pierre Legrain, relieur', *Art et décoration*, vol. xliii (1923), pp. 172-85; Rose Adler, *Reliures* (Paris, n.d. [1929]), pl. 23; Jacques-Anthoine Legrain/Société de la Reliure Originale, *Pierre Legrain, relieur* (Paris, 1965). For Likarz, see Angela Völker, *Textiles of the Wiener Werkstätte, 1910-1932* (New York, 1994).
5. For Doucet, see André Joubin, 'Jacques Doucet', *Gazette des Beaux-Arts*, 6th series, vol. iii (February 1930), pp. 69-82; Hôtel Drouot sales catalogue, *Ancienne Collection Jacques Doucet. Mobilier Art Déco provenant du Studio Saint-James à Neuilly* (Paris, 1972); François Chapon, *Mystère et splendeurs de Jacques Doucet, 1853-1929* (Paris, 1984); Claire Brisby, 'Jacques Doucet and the Patronage of Art Deco', *Apollo*, vol. cxlix, no. 447 (May 1999), pp. 31-9.
6. See Pierre Legrain, *Objets d'art* (Paris, 1929), which includes designs by the lacquerer and metalsmith Jean Dunand, the jewellers and silversmiths Jean Fouquet, Jean Goulden and Gérard Sandoz, the glassmaker Maurice Marinot and the bookbinder Geneviève de Léotard.
7. Hagenauer's 'Buste de jeune fille', 1930 (private collection), was based on Constantin Brancusi's *Mlle Pogany* heads. Others associated with avant-garde circles also contributed to this popularization. For example, the German architectural critic Adolf Behne designed lamps in glass and mixed materials, derived directly from Bauhaus *Vorkurs* exercises. Illustrated in contemporary publications, such as *Le Luminaire*, these encouraged other designers, including those of the Desny firm in France, to employ similarly bold abstractions.
8. This is evident in the work of some American architects and designers, several of whom – including Norman Bel Geddes, Raymond Hood, Ely Jacques Kahn and French-born Raymond Loewy – were familiar at first-hand with European avant-garde art and new design tendencies in France and Germany.
9. See Richard Martin, *Cubism and Fashion* (New York, 1998), p. 91.
10. Albert Gleizes and Jean Metzinger, *Du Cubisme* (Paris, 1912); here quoted from Charles Harrison and Paul Wood (eds), *Art in Theory, 1900-1990* (Cambridge, MA and Oxford, 1992), p. 189.
11. Now in the collection of the Musée des Années Trente in Boulogne-Billancourt.
12. Including Giacomo Balla and Fortunato Depero; see Chapter 19.
13. The phrase 'From the easel to the machine', signifying the move from autonomous to engaged artistic practice, derives from the title of a text by Nikolai Taraburkin, *Ot molberta k mashine* (Moscow, 1923); reprinted in French in Andrei Nakov, *Nikolai Taraboukine: Le Dernier Tableau* (Paris, 1972), pp. 27-84. Russian Constructivist stage designs, in particular those by Liubov Popova for *The Magnificent Cuckold* and Varvara Stepanova for *The Death of Tarelkin*, had a considerable impact in avant-garde circles outside Russia by the early 1920s.
14. See Nancy Troy, *The De Stijl Environment* (Cambridge, MA and London, 1983).
15. The Bauhaus was formed on the basis of the Weimar Kunstgewerbeschule (directed until the First World War by the Belgian architect – and former Art Nouveau practitioner – Henry van de Velde). Gropius transformed the institution by encouraging cross-fertilization between fine art, craft and industrial design.
16. Such correspondences can be seen in paintings by Paul Klee and textile designs by Gunta Stölzl, or in abstract sculptures by Laszlo Moholy-Nagy and Marianne Brandt's designs for teapots and lamps.
17. Quoted in Cottington (1998), p. 170.
18. For Dufy, see Raymond Cogniat, *Dufy, décorateur* (Geneva, 1957); David Guillon/Galerie Fanny Guillon-Lafaille, *Dufy-Poiret modèles* (Paris, 1998); Anne Tourlonias and Jack Vidal, *Raoul Dufy: L'Oeuvre en soie: Logique d'un oeuvre ornemental industriel* (Avignon, c.1998); Christian Briend and Jacqueline Munck, *Raoul Dufy* (Paris, 1999).
19. For Sonia and Robert Delaunay, see Sonia Delaunay, *Compositions, couleurs, idées* (Paris, n.d. [c.1930]); Jacques Damase, *Sonia Delaunay: 1925* (Brussels, c.1974); Paulo Ferreira, *Correspondence de quatre artistes portugais: Almada-Negreiros, José Pacheco, Souza-Cardoso, Eduardo Vianna avec Robert et Sonia Delaunay* (Paris, 1972); Bibliothèque Nationale, *Sonia & Robert Delaunay* (Paris, 1977); MAM (Musée d'Art Moderne de la Ville de Paris), *Robert et Sonia Delaunay* (Paris, 1985); Jacques Damase, *Sonia Delaunay: Fashion and Fabrics* (London, 1991); Stanley Baron, *Sonia Delaunay: The Life of an Artist* (London, 1995).
20. The Delaunays used the words 'simultaneous' and 'simultaneity' to denote their interest in colour contrasts, influenced by the ideas of Michel Eugène Chevreul which, published in his book *De la loi du contraste simultanée des couleurs, et de l'assortiment des objets colorés considéré d'après cette loi* (Paris, 1839), were an important source for Modernist artists.
21. A poem by Blaise Cendrars, *La Prose du Transsibérien* (Paris, 1913). For examples of Delaunay's designs for book covers, see Bibliothèque Nationale (1977); MAM (1985).
22. When the Russian Revolution cut off the financial support she had formerly received from her family.
23. Contemporary photographs suggest that she not only made 'simultaneous' designs but also applied her characteristic decorative motifs to regional vernacular objects; see the illustrations in Ferreira (1972).
24. To replace Bakst's designs for Diaghilev's 1909 production, lost during a tour in South America. Diaghilev also invited the Delaunays to form a more permanent relationship with his company.
25. Baron (1995), p. 75.
26. Robert was not actively involved in the business, but collaborated on some interior designs. His simple cubic furniture provided a sympathetic foil to Sonia's textile and other designs. For examples, see Bibliothèque Nationale (1977); MAM (1985).
27. See André Salmon, *John Storrs and Modern Sculpture* (New York, 1923); Noel Frackman, *John Storrs* (New York, 1987).
28. Similar techniques were selectively used by other fashion illustrators, including Lucien Boucher, Giron and Alexandre Iacovleff. And Richard Martin notes that the art directors of American *Vogue* and *Harper's Bazaar* in the late 1920s, themselves graphic designers, were well aware of such work; see Martin (1998), p. 128. Thayaht also made Futurist designs for male clothing.
29. For Productivist design, see *Art into Production: Soviet Textiles, Fashion and Ceramics, 1917-1935* (Oxford and London, 1984); Vladimir Tolstoy, *Russian Decorative Arts, 1917-1937* (New York, 1990).
30. At the Erste Deutsche Herbstsalon in Berlin and Arturo Ciacelli's art gallery in Stockholm.
31. See Margaret L. Davis, *Bullocks Wilshire* (Los Angeles, c.1996). The store rapidly became a favourite of some of Hollywood's biggest stars. Later taken over by Macy's, the building was damaged in the Los Angeles race riots of 1992 and closed in 1993. Renovated, it is now the Law Library of Southwestern University's School of Law.
32. Without Cubism, De Stijl and Constructivism, the ingenious, spatially complex designs for lamps, furniture or textiles by Pierre Chareau, Jacques Le Chevallier, or Eileen Gray would have been unthinkable. Furniture designs by Félix del Marle, bookbindings by Pierre Legrain and buildings by Rob Mallet-Stevens also interpreted the formal vocabulary of De Stijl in overtly decorative ways. For del Marle, see Andrei Nakov, *Félix del Marle, 1889-1952* (Paris, 1973); Domitille d'Orgeval, *Félix del Marle* (Grenoble, 2000). The De Stijl influence on Mallet-Stevens is clear in his designs for the 'Pavillon du Tourisme' and the 'Ambassade Française' at the Paris 1925 Exhibition. By contrast, his concrete trees – designed with the Martel brothers – gave visitors to the exhibition a glimpse of the principles of

Cubist sculpture developed by Picasso over a decade earlier. For Mallet-Stevens, see Léon Moussinac, *Mallet-Stevens* (Paris, 1931); Dominique Deshoulières, *Rob Mallet-Stevens, architecte* (Brussels, 1980); Jean-François Pinchon, *Rob Mallet-Stevens: Architecture, Furniture, Interior Design* (Cambridge, MA, 1990).
33. From an article by Louis Vauxcelles, 'Les Idées du décorateur Louis Süe', published in 1918; quoted in Suzanne Tise, *Between Art and Industry: Design Reform in France, 1851-1939* (Ann Arbor, 1991), p. 273.
34. The name was given to the exhibit by contemporary critics.
35. This negative criticism continues; see Yves-Alain Bois, 'Cubistic, Cubic, and Cubist', in Eve Blau and Nancy Troy (eds), *Architecture and Cubism* (Montreal and Cambridge, MA, 1997), pp. 187-92.
36. Quoted in Cottington (1998), p. 173; see also note 35. For other readings of the exhibit, see Marie-Noëlle Pradel, 'La Maison cubiste en 1912', *L'Art de France*, vol. 1 (1961), pp. 177-86; David Cottington, 'The Maison Cubiste and the Meaning of Modernism in pre-1914 France', in Blau and Troy (1997), pp. 17-40; Tise (1991), pp. 160-7; Nancy Troy, *Modernism and the Decorative Arts in France: Art Nouveau to Le Corbusier* (New Haven and London, 1991), pp. 79-89; Nancy Troy, 'Domesticity, Decoration and Consumer Culture: Selling Art and Design in pre-World War I France', in Christopher Reed (ed.), *Not at Home: The Suppression of Domesticity in Modern Art and Architecture* (London, 1996), pp. 113-29.
37. Contemporary and more recent commentators have also noted the references to regional traditions; see Cottington in Blau and Troy (1997).
38. For Czech Cubist architecture and design, see Ivan Margolius, *Cubism in Architecture and the Applied Arts: Bohemia and France, 1910-1914* (Newton Abbott, c.1979); Alexander von Vegesack (ed.), *Czech Cubism: Architecture, Furniture and Decorative Arts, 1910-1925* (London, 1992); Vera J. Běhal, 'Czech Cubism in Arts and Crafts: "Artěl – Studio for the Plastic Arts in Prague " and the "Prague Art Workshop"', *Kosmas: Journal of Czechoslovak and Central European Studies*, vol. 7, nos 1-2 (1988), pp. 155-73.
39. Lise-Léon Blum, 'Le Goût au théâtre: Les Ballets Russes', *Gazette du bon ton*, vol. ii (1914), pp. 253-6 (p. 253). Diaghilev later commissioned other avant-garde artists to design sets and costumes; see note 24.
40. For Poiret, see Paul Poiret, *En habillant l'époque* (Paris, 1930; reprint, Paris, 1986) and *My First Fifty Years* (London, 1930); Palmer White, *Poiret* (London, 1973); Yvonne Deslandres and Dorothée Lalanne, *Paul Poiret, 1879-1944* (London, 1987). White reproduces a photograph of Poiret and his wife in oriental costume for a 'Persian Celebration' in 1911. Richard Martin has observed that Poiret saw that 'fashion required creative and artistic partnerships and seized the vocabulary of art when possible to describe his ideas'; Martin (1998), p. 109.
41. The term was often used indiscriminately to denote avant-garde art in general; see note 1.
42. Read (1925), p. 95. The so-called 'Cubist rose' was a frequently cited example of such simplified naturalistic decoration; the motif can be found in a number of drawings by Louis Süe and André Mare held by the Institut Français d'Architecture (IFA), in Paris.
43. Changing social conditions and tastes brought demands for a more relaxed and manageable domestic environment. The development of new materials and techniques – like blockboard, which could be moulded in large sheets and bonded by new adhesives with the thin veneers of fine woods made possible by new techniques of cutting – contributed to the simplification and 'streamlining' even of 'modernized traditional' practice. For examples of this tendency in Jacques-Emile Ruhlmann's work, see Florence Camard, *Ruhlmann: Master of Art Deco* (London, 1984) and *Ruhlmann: Un Génie de l'art déco* (Paris and Montreal, 2001).
44. Notable examples of surprising combinations of materials can be found in designs by Jean Dunand, in which eggshell fragments, delicately tinted and decoratively arranged, are fixed by a final coat of clear lacquer.
45. As the American critic Clement Greenberg observed in a 1954 essay 'Abstract, Representational and So Forth'; Clement Greenberg, *Art and Culture: Critical Essays* (Boston, 1961), pp. 133-8 (p. 136).
46. Originally a PhD thesis; first published in German as *Abstraktion und Einfühlung* (Neuwied, 1907; later published in English).
47. See Sheldon Cheney and Martha Candler Cheney, *Art and the Machine: An Account of Industrial Design in 20th Century America* (New York, 1936; reprint, 1992).
48. Ibid, p. 38.
49. See Museum of Modern Art, *Machine Art* (New York, 1934; reprints, 1969 and 1994).
50. Herbert Read, *Art and Industry* (London, 1934), p. 7.
51. For English translations of Loos's essay 'Ornament and Crime', see Arts Council, *The Architecture of Adolf Loos* (London, 1985) and *Ornament and Crime: Selected Essays/Adolf Loos* (Riverside, CA, c.1998).
52. See, for example, J. Stewart Johnson, *American Modern, 1925-1940: Design for a New Age* (New York, 2000).
53. E. L. Bird, 'The Architectural Association Excursion to Paris', *Architectural Association Journal*, vol. liii (December 1937), pp. 265-83 (p. 268).
54. See Cottington (1998), p. 169; he refers to the period around the First World War, but the same holds true for the 1920s and beyond.

Chapter 10: From Pattern to Abstraction

1. André Vera, 'Le Nouveau Style', *L'Art décoratif*, vol. xxvii (January 1912), p. 32.
2. See, for example, *Les Années '25': Art Déco/Bauhaus/Stijl/Esprit Nouveau*, 2 vols (Paris, 1966); Yvonne Brunhammer and Suzanne Tise, *The Decorative Arts in France, 1900-1942: La Société des Artistes Décorateurs* (New York, 1990); Nancy Troy, *Modernism and the Decorative Arts in France: Art Nouveau to Le Corbusier* (New Haven and London, 1991).
3. Among a number of Austrian precedents were the decorative floral panels by Carl Otto Czescha for the Hochsreith hunting lodge of c.1906.
4. Such as Girault's perfume and hairdressing salon in the Boulevard des Capucines, Paris, by Azéma, Edrei & Hardy.
5. As in the floor of his Post Office Savings Bank in Vienna (1904-6).
6. As in Henri Belloc's Paris Gaumont of 1931.
7. Cheney Brothers was a forward-looking textile company that had launched a series of prints based on Brandt's metalwork designs of 1924.
8. The triumph of fashion over function was seen in the solid, triangular shapes of the teacup handles. Difficult to hold, they were later replaced with perforated versions.
9. The Atelier Martine was a commercial success, with orders from many countries including the United States; a London branch was established in 1924.
10. Of particular note was the massive *British Empire Exhibition* at Wembley of 1924 and 1925. For a focused discussion on particular aspects, see Jonathan Woodham, 'Images of Africa and Design at the British Empire Exhibitions between the Wars', *Journal of Design History*, vol. 2, no. 1 (1989), pp. 15-33.
11. A. Defries, 'Craftsmen of the Empire: A Comparative Study of Decoration and the Industrial Arts', *Architectural Review*, vol. lv, no. 331 (June 1924), p. 262.
12. This was also seen in the Stehli Silks Corporation's 'Americana' textile series of 1927 with titles like 'Gentlemen Prefer Blondes', 'Hollywood' and 'Manhattan'; see Chapters 31 and 34.
13. Reeves studied with Fernand Léger in Paris during the seven years she was away from the United States (1920-27).
14. Frankl discussed American alternatives to European models in his books *New Dimensions* (New York, 1928) and *Form and Reform* (New York, 1930).
15. Such as Edward J. Wimmer's marquetry mother-of-pearl and boxwood cabinet of 1910-14.
16. It sold more than 56,000 units in the first 18 months on the market.
17. H. Morley, 'A House Full of Horrors', *Household Words*, vol. vi (4 December 1852), quoted in Stephen Bayley, *Taste* (London, 1983), p. 40.
18. Georg Muche, 'Bildende Kunst und Industrieform' [Fine art and industrial form], *Bauhaus*, vol. 1, no. 1 (Dessau, 1926), pp. 5-6.
19. In *Les Cahiers d'aujourd'hui*, vol. 5 (June 1913), pp. 247-57.
20. Le Corbusier, *L'Art décoratif d'aujourd'hui* (Paris, 1925); for the English edition, see *The Decorative Art of Today*, translated and introduced by James I. Dunnett (London, 1987). Le Corbusier's uncompromisingly stark 'Pavillon de L'Esprit Nouveau' at the Paris 1925 Exhibition stood in fierce opposition to the decorative opulence of Ruhlmann's 'Hôtel d'un Collectionneur'.
21. In cities like Frankfurt, Stuttgart and Dessau.
22. Philip Johnson, 'History of Machine Art', *Machine Art* (1934; reprinted for MOMA, New York, 1969), n.p.
23. As quoted in M. Greif, *Depression Modern: The Thirties Style in America* (New York, 1975), p. 43.
24. Dorothy Todd and Raymond Mortimer, *The New Interior Decoration: An Introduction to Its Principles, and International Survey of Its Methods* (London, 1929), p. 23.
25. Nikolaus Pevsner, in his seminal text *Pioneers of the Modern Movement* (London, 1936), assumed a moral stance in line with the thinking of the 'Pioneers' about whom he was writing.
26. Evelyn Waugh, *A Handful of Dust* (London, 1934; Harmondsworth, 1979), p. 79.
27. H. S. Goodhart-Rendel, 'The Fitness of Ornament', in John de la Valette (ed.), *The Conquest of Ugliness: A Collection of Contemporary Views on the Place of Art in Industry* (London, 1935), p. 42.

Chapter 11: The Exotic

1. G. Bauer, 'Le Théâtre; Une Nègre', *Annales*, 18 October 1925.
2. See Edward Said, *Orientalism* (New York, 1978).
3. Frances Toor, *Mexican Popular Arts* (Mexico, 1939), p. 11.
4. Ibid, p. 10.
5. Guillaume Apollinaire in an article on African and oceanic sculptures in *Les Arts à Paris*, 15 July 1918, quoted in LeRoy C. Breunig (ed.), *Apollinaire on Art: Essays and Reviews, 1902-1918* (New York, 1972; reprint, 1988), p. 470.
6. There was increasing concern over the financial viability and growing independence movements in various colonies. See Romy Golan, *Modernity and Nostalgia: Art and Politics in France between the Wars* (New Haven and London, 1995); Herman Lebovics, *True France: The Wars over Cultural Identity, 1900-1945* (Ithaca, 1992); Patricia A. Morton, *Hybrid Modernities: Architecture and Representation at the 1931 Colonial Exhibition, Paris* (Cambridge, MA, 2000).
7. *Exposition coloniale internationale à Paris en 1931*, p. 68, quoted in Lebovics (1992), p. 39.
8. Lebovics (1992), p. 57.
9. Léandre Vaillat, 'Le Décor de la vie: L'Exposition coloniale en 1931', *Le Temps*, 71 (13 March 1931), quoted in Morton (2000), p. 277.
10. Morton (2000), pp. 281-2.
11. Janniot had previously been commissioned to produce sculptural programmes for Ruhlmann's 'Hôtel d'un Collectionneur', designed by Pierre Patout at the Paris 1925 Exhibition, and for the ocean liner *Ile de France*. He went on to design the programme for the Palais de Tokyo at the Paris World Fair of 1937.
12. Laprade, quoted in Morton (2000), p. 280.
13. Jacques-Emile Ruhlmann executed the office of Paul Reynaud, the new Minister of the Colonies, dedicated to Africa, and Eugène Printz provided the designs for the office of Maréchal Lyautey, representing Asia. The furnishings of the two offices were made of exotic woods from the colonies, ebony and palmwood respectively.
14. Germany had been stripped of its colonies at the end of the First World War. Following the scale and expenditure on the *British Empire Exhibition* held at Wembley in 1924, Britain had decided not to exhibit.
15. Belgium organized the Exposition internationale de Bruxelles at Tervueren in 1897 to promote colonial enterprise.
16. The exhibition displayed plants, animals, minerals, artefacts, film, photography and painting brought back from the expedition.
17. Pierre Trévières, *Vogue* (May 1926).
18. Jean Gallotti, *Vogue* (December 1927), p. 48.
19. Ibid.
20. Elisabeth de Gramont, Duchess of Clermont-Tonnerre, 'The Lacquer Work of Miss Eileen Gray', *Living Arts*, no. 3 (March 1922), p. 148.
21. Gray later dismissed such Symbolist and decorative designs, particularly those she created for Jacques Doucet, as her style gradually shifted towards Modernism. The trajectory of her career is similar to that of a number of other designers whose path to Modernism was via exotic decoration.
22. Quoted in Caroline Constant, *Eileen Gray* (London, 2000), p. 34.
23. Interview with Sargent Johnson, *San Francisco Chronicle*, October 1935, quoted in Lizzetta LeFalle-Collins and Judith Wilson, *Sargent Johnson: African American Modernist* (San Francisco, 1998), p. 15.
24. Alain Locke, 'The Legacy of the Ancestral Arts', *Survey Graphic* (March 1925).
25. An ancient-Egyptian/African lineage became a common theme in the period and was explored by many black American artists and writers.
26. Aaron Douglas, untitled essay, Aaron Douglas papers, quoted in Donna M. Cassidy, *Painting the Musical City: Jazz and the Cultural Identity in American Art, 1910-1940* (Washington, DC, 1997), p. 119.
27. André Schaeffner, 'La Découverte de la musique noire', *La Présence africaine*, 8-9 (March 1950), p. 218, quoted in Jody Blake, *Le Tumulte Noir: Modernist Art and Popular Entertainment in Jazz-Age Paris, 1900-1930* (University Park, PA, 1999), p. 6.
28. Anne Shaw Faulkner, 'Does Jazz put Sin into Syncopation?', *Ladies Home Journal*, 38 (August 1921), p. 16.
29. Janet Flanner, *Paris was Yesterday, 1925-1939* (New York, 1934; reprint, 1972), p. xx.
30. André Levinson, *L'Art vivant* (February 1925), quoted in Petrine Archer Straw, *Negrophilia: Avant-Garde and Black Culture in the 1920s* (New York and London, 2000), p. 118.
31. Sieglinde Lemke, *Primitivist Modernism: Black Culture and the Origins of Transatlantic Modernism* (Oxford, 1998), p. 6.
32. Publication of *L'Art précolombien: L'Amérique avant Christophe Colomb* by Jean Babelon, Georges Bataille and Alfred Métraux (Paris, 1930). The first major exhibition, *L'Art de l'Amérique*, was held in the Pavillon de Marsan, Paris, in 1928; in the same year, Adolphe Basler and Ernest Brummer published *L'Art précolombien* (Paris, 1928). And in 1931 André Breton and Paul Eluard published their own collections in *Sculptures d'Afrique, d'Amérique, d'Océanie* (Paris, 1931). The book included Alaskan Eskimo, British Columbian, pre-Columbian and Nazca works.
33. Quoted in Rosalind Krauss, *The Originality of the Avant-Garde and other Modernist Myths* (Cambridge, MA, 1987), p. 230.

Chapter 12: The International Exhibition

1. Frank Warner and A. F. Kendrick, 'Textiles', in Department of Overseas Trade, *Reports on the Present Position and Tendencies of the Industrial Arts as indicated at the International Exhibition of Modern Decorative and Industrial Arts, Paris, 1925* (London, 1925), pp. 67-115; quote from p. 75.
2. See note 1. More recently, Paul Greenhalgh has written of the 1925 Exhibition as 'a unique instance, where an exhibition gave birth to and then publicized a style'; see Paul Greenhalgh, *Ephemeral Vistas: The Expositions Universelles, Great Exhibitions and World's Fairs, 1851-1939* (Manchester, 1998), p. 165.
3. *Prima esposizione internazionale d'arte decorative*; see Chapter 19.
4. Quoted in Nancy Troy, *Modernism and the Decorative Arts in France: Art Nouveau to Le Corbusier* (New Haven and London, 1991), p. 163. Couyba was a senator with a longstanding specialist interest in the decorative arts who, after the First World War, became Director of the Ecole des Arts Décoratifs in Paris. For the earlier background, see Suzanne Tise, *Between Art and Industry: Design Reform in France, 1851-1939* (Ann Arbor, 1991); Debora L. Silverman, *Art Nouveau in Fin-de-Siècle France: Politics, Psychology and Style* (Berkeley and Los Angeles, 1989); Leora Auslander, *Taste and Power: Furnishing Modern France* (Berkeley, Los Angeles and London, 1996).
5. Quoted in Troy (1991), p. 163.
6. These included the foundation of museums of decorative art in major German cities, the reform of design education, the encouragement of productive links between artists and designers, industry and commerce, and support for exhibits of decorative arts in Germany and abroad. See John Heskett, *Design in Germany, 1870-1918* (London, 1986) and Joan Campbell, *The German Werkbund: The Politics of Reform in the Applied Arts* (Princeton, 1978).
7. Quoted in Troy (1991), p. 49, from an article by Genuys in the *Revue des arts décoratifs* (1909).
8. Quoted in Heskett (1986), p. 65, from an article in *Deutsche Kunst und Dekoration* (1904-5).
9. See, for example, Maud Oliver, 'German Arts and Crafts at the St. Louis Exhibition', *Studio*, vols xxxiii-xxxiv (1905), pp. 233-8. Muthesius, now well known for his study of English freestyle architecture, *Das englische Haus* (Berlin, 1904/5), was a civil servant in the Prussian Ministry of Trade and Commerce with responsibility for art education.

10. French critics frequently failed to distinguish between German and Austrian firms. The art critic André Salmon noted that several 'German' workshops existed even in the heart of the French furniture industry, the Faubourg Saint-Antoine, before the First World War; see Pascal Forthuny, 'Les Décorateurs allemands à Paris en 1924?', *L'Amour de l'art*, vol. iii (1922), pp. 53-64. Léandre Vaillat quoted the export figures from the French Department of Overseas Trade in his book *La Cité renaissante* (Paris, 1913). The respective values of German and French exports to the USA were 126,922,680 francs and 39, 938, 870 francs; see also Vaillat's article on the exhibition in *L'Illustration*, 18 November 1922, pp. 481-3. The significance of such figures for France's economy and self-esteem seems obvious, given its loss of major industrial resources with the annexation of Alsace-Lorraine following the Franco-Prussian War of 1870-1.
11. Siegfried Bing, *La Culture artistique en Amérique* (Paris, 1895) for the Director of Fine Arts, Henri Roujon.
12. This last was reflected both in the search for a 'modern' French style (see Chapter 8) and in the foundation, in 1912, of Primavera at Au Printemps, the first of the decorative art studios – dedicated to the design and production of quality 'modern' furnishings for a bourgeois clientele – which were established by the leading department stores in the run up to the 1925 Exhibition (see Chapter 14).
13. Quoted in Troy (1991), p. 163.
14. The 'art social' movement, which emerged in France in the 1880s, attracted support from both the Left and Centre of the political spectrum. It supported initiatives for popular education and promoted the arts as a means to social emancipation. The movement was associated with contemporary initiatives in housing reform, which gained impetus, from 1889, with the creation of the Société Française des Habitations à Bon Marché and with the institution of state subsidies for low-cost housing in 1894. The decorative (or 'useful') arts were seen to be central to palliating 'social problems', because they could enhance both domestic and public environments. 'Art social' ideas remained topical in the early twentieth century in the context of debates about the use of the sites made available by the demolition of the fortifications of Paris and about the 'îlôts insalubres' of central Paris, also with the expansion of social housing programmes in the years following the First World War.
15. Quoted in Troy (1991), p. 164. Marx was Inspector General of the Museums of France.
16. What would disappear in the intervening years was the 'art social' dimension of the project; as realized, the exhibition would be one of articles *de luxe*.
17. Guilleré was an adviser to Primavera and his wife, Charlotte Chauchet-Guilleré, was its artistic director until the late 1920s. For Guilleré's role in the SAD, see Chapter 14. See also Yvonne Brunhammer and Suzanne Tise, *The Decorative Arts in France, 1900-1942: La Société des Artistes Décorateurs* (New York, 1990) and Suzanne Tise, 'Les Grands Magasins', in Catherine Arminjon and others, *'L'Art de vivre': Decorative Arts and Design in France, 1789-1989* (London, 1989), pp. 73-105.
18. See M. Roblin (Député), *Rapport fait au nom de la Commission du commerce et de l'industrie chargée d'examiner la proposition du loi tendant à organiser en 1915 à Paris une Exposition internationale des arts décoratifs modernes*, Chambre des Députés, 10e Legislature, Session de 1912 (Paris, 1912).
19. Tise (1991), p. 182.
20. Henri Magne, 'Vue d'ensemble sur l'Exposition internationale des arts décoratifs et industriels, Paris, avril-octobre 1925'; text of a lecture given on 18 January 1925 (copy in the library of the Musée des Arts Décoratifs, Paris).
21. As M. Sibille, Député for Maine et Loire, asserted in the Assemblée Nationale on 4 June 1914; quoted in Tise (1991), p. 222.
22. See Tise (1991), pp. 233-7, 245-6.
23. The Germans had systematically destroyed steel and textile factories when they evacuated occupied territories; see Tise (1991), pp. 245-6.
24. The project could be presented as one worthy of national consensus because of the urgent need to increase exports and the relevance to all of 'modern' design; the 'politics of prestige' had a long tradition in France; see Tise (1991), p. 316.
25. Quoted in Joan Kahr, *Edgar Brandt: Master of Art Deco Ironwork* (New York, 1999), p. 119.
26. Among notable markers of this shift of direction was the launch of the journal *La Renaissance de l'art français et des industries de luxe* in 1918.
27. The tightening up of the regulations was partly intended to deter the participation of the type of manufacturer who would treat the project as a 'foire d'échantillons'. In 1922, the Chambre Syndicale des Artistes Décorateurs Modernes set out principles for collaboration between manufacturers and decorative artists; see 'Chronique', *Art et décoration* (May 1922), pp. 11-12.
28. Figures given by contemporary and more recent authors vary from 21 to 26.
29. Helen Appleton Read, 'The Exposition in Paris', part 1, *International Studio*, vol. 82 (November 1925), pp. 93-7; quote from p. 93. Hubert Llewellyn Smith noted the 'huge disproportion' between the French and other exhibits, Department of Overseas Trade (1925), pp. 9-50; quote from p. 11.
30. See Campbell (1978) and Heskett (1986). Germany's war-time propaganda and the Deutsche Gewerbeschau held in Munich in 1922 to demonstrate German superiority in the applied arts particularly fuelled French fears.
31. Forthuny (1922); his article includes responses to surveys he carried out in 1919 and 1922.
32. Ibid, p. 61.
33. Ibid, pp. 61-2.
34. Construction had begun on the exhibition site in March 1924; the invitation was issued by the French Ambassador in Berlin towards the end of 1924; see 'Chronique', *Art et décoration* (December 1924), p. 5. Tise (1991), p. 323, notes that a privately sponsored exhibition of German design was organized by Bruno Paul and shown at a location on the Champs-Elysées during the exhibition.
35. Llewellyn Smith, Department of Overseas Trade (1925), p. 11.
36. See J. Stewart Johnson, *American Modern, 1925-1940: Design for a New Age* (New York, 2000), p. 8.
37. Llewellyn Smith, Department of Overseas Trade (1925), p. 11.
38. Their displays determined by the interests of the 'mother' country.
39. Interestingly, in view of the contemporary interest in things African (see Chapters 7 and 11), Edouard Michel commented, about exhibits in the Belgian pavilion inspired by work from the Congo, that 'The use of geometric patterns which blend seamlessly with one another, the association of wood, ivory and bone and the use of plaited straw, show clearly what the colonies, in a re-established order [un juste retour des choses], could offer twentieth-century Europe for its new style'. See Edouard Michel, 'La Section belge', *Art et décoration* (July 1925), pp. 75-88; quote from p. 78.
40. Llewellyn Smith, Department of Overseas Trade (1925), p. 11.
41. These included the site of the former fortifications of Paris (the 'ceinture'), which was re-developed in the late 1920s, largely with low-cost housing.
42. According to an official document published in 1922. The site included part of that previously occupied by the 1900 Exhibition.
43. The exhibition organizers adopted three main modes of display, allowing objects to be shown in different kinds of milieux: individual pavilions, 'galeries' and groups organized by media (shown in the Grand Palais).
44. Tise (1991), p. 313.
45. Llewellyn Smith, Department of Overseas Trade (1925), p. 25.
46. H. C. Bradshaw, 'Architecture', Department of Overseas Trade (1925), pp. 39-50; quote from p. 41.
47. Read (1925), part I, p. 96. Read was not alone in her characterization of the exhibition as a 'dream city'. Paul Gaultier noted that 'In the evening, all this whiteness which is lit by a diffuse light, takes on the allure of a dream city thrown up by the darkness of the night'; see Paul Gaultier, 'A l'Exposition des arts décoratifs', *Revue bleue* (January-December 1925), pp. 633-6; quote from p. 633.
48. Ellow H. Hostache, 'Reflections on the Exposition des Arts Décoratifs', *Architectural Forum*, vol. xliv, no. 1 (January 1926), pp. 11-16; quote from p. 13.
49. W. Francklyn Paris, 'The International Exposition of Modern Industrial and Decorative Art in Paris', part 2, *Architectural Record*, vol. 58 (October 1925), pp. 365-85; quote from p. 375.
50. The celebration of consumption, surface and spectacle is a defining feature of Art Deco. It links the otherwise distinctly different visual *partis* of Maurice Dufrène's boutiques on the Pont Alexandre III, Raymond Hood's American Radiator building in New York and Hollywood film sets and dance routines of the 1930s.
51. Paris (1925), part 2, p. 383.
52. Bradshaw, Department of Overseas Trade (1925), p. 50. Metalwork was a *métier* that saw a significant revival in this period, and decorative metalwork is often an identifying feature of Art Deco architecture.
53. Gabriel Mourey, 'The Paris International Exhibition, 1925: The French Buildings', *Studio*, vol. xc (1925), pp. 16-21; quotes from pp. 16, 19.
54. Helen Appleton Read, 'The Exposition in Paris', part 2, *International Studio*, vol. 82 (December 1925), pp. 160-5; quote from p. 160.
55. W. Francklyn Paris, 'The International Exposition of Modern Industrial and Decorative Art in Paris', part 1, *Architectural Record*, vol. lviii (July-December 1925), pp. 265-77; quote from p. 265.
56. These included the introduction of large sheet plywood and new adhesives, which allowed fine wood veneers to be applied over large, unbroken surfaces.
57. 'Cubism' was often used to connote avant-garde art more generally.
58. H. P. Shapland, 'Furniture', Department of Overseas Trade (1925), pp. 61-6; quote from p. 61. The official American report on the exhibition also noted the presence of several exhibitors from the Faubourg St Antoine who had previously devoted themselves entirely to the reproduction of period furniture. See *Report of a Commission appointed by the Secretary of Commerce to Visit and Report upon the International Exposition of Modern Decorative and Industrial Art in Paris, 1925* (Washington, 1926).
59. Partly because of its opposition to the dominance of economic (rather than artistic) considerations, as the project developed; see Tise (1991), p. 340.
60. Paris (1925), part 1, p. 275.
61. Gaston Varenne, 'L'Exposition des arts décoratifs: Le Mobilier français', *Art et décoration* (July 1925), pp. 1-44; quote from p. 4.
62. The device allowed natural and artificial lighting effects to be adjusted at will.
63. René Chavance, introduction to *Une Ambassade française* (Paris, c.1925), p. 24.
64. On the instructions of the Minister of Fine Arts, Paul Léon; the panels were later reinstated.
65. Members of the UAM included architects, bookbinders, furniture, graphic and textile designers, silversmiths and the new profession of *ingénieur-éclairiste*; see Tise (1991), pp. 364-5. See also René Herbst, *25 Années UAM* (Paris, 1956); Arlette Barré-Despond, *Union des artistes modernes* (Paris, 1986); Yvonne Brunhammer and others, *Les Années UAM, 1929-1958* (Paris, 1988). The group was not initially, as is often assumed, united by a common social programme or 'functionalist' aesthetic, though it later moved in this direction.
66. He has often been compared to the historic luminaries of French cabinetmaking.
67. Quoted in Florence Camard, *Ruhlmann: Master of Art Deco* (London, 1984), p. 10, from an article by Ruhlmann in *L'Illustration*, 30 June 1930.
68. Quoted in Tise (1991), p. 274, from an article by Ruhlmann in *Les Arts français*, no. 9 (1917).
69. In addition to the *pièce de résistance* designed by Ruhlmann himself – the cabinet lacquered by Jean Dunand with a decorative design by Jean Lambert-Rucki – the Grand Salon alone included ambitious figurative painting by Jean Dupas, metalwork by Edgar Brandt, wall-hangings by Stéphany, Aubusson tapestry upholstery by Gaudissart and sculptures by Antoine Bourdelle and Pompon.
70. Varenne (1925), p. 5.
71. Read (1925), part 1, p. 97.
72. Including the use of lacquer and autogenous welding.
73. As Suzanne Tise has characterized it; see Tise (1991), p. 326.
74. Frequently backed by the opportunity to place orders.
75. La Maîtrise at Galeries Lafayette, Pomone at Au Bon Marché, Primavera at Au Printemps and Studium Louvre at Magasins du Louvre. The symbolic significance accorded these pavilions by their siting is not surprising, given that the department stores had played a leading role – through their establishment of modern decorative art studios led by such well known designers as Maurice Dufrène and Paul Follot – in advancing the aims of the exhibition through promoting the design and production of 'modern', well made goods suited to contemporary bourgeois tastes and lifestyles (see Chapter 14).
76. C. Z[ervos], 'La Leçon de l'Exposition des arts décoratifs et industriels de 1925', *Les Arts de la maison*, vol. 3 (Autumn-Winter 1925), p. 27; quoted in Troy (1991), p. 185.
77. Varenne (1925), p. 6. Some more recent commentators have assumed that the stores reached a wide market. Kenneth Silver, for example, suggests that they presented 'mass-produced goods ... to a fairly large audience'; see Kenneth Silver, *Esprit de Corps: The Art of the Parisian Avant-Garde and the First World War, 1914-1925* (London, 1989), p. 366. However, contemporary evidence suggests that this was not the case.
78. Warner and Kendrick, Department of Overseas Trade (1925), p. 75.
79. Emily Genauer, *Modern Interiors Today and Tomorrow* (New York, 1939), p. 18. The official American report on the exhibition also acknowledged the importance of department stores in disseminating contemporary work; see note 58.
80. Llewellyn Smith, Department of Overseas Trade (1925), pp. 20-21.
81. René Chavance, 'La Section autrichienne', *Art et décoration* (September 1925), pp. 120-32 (pp. 120, 125).
82. Gabriel Mourey, 'The Paris International Exhibition: Interior Decoration and Furnishing' and 'The Paris International Exhibition: Regional Art', *Studio*, vol. xc (1925), pp. 154-7 and 239-45.
83. Llewellyn Smith, Department of Overseas Trade (1925), p. 18.
84. See note 82 above; quote from p. 154.
85. Llewellyn Smith, Department of Overseas Trade (1925), p. 12. In the following decade, the USA would emerge as the major producer in this field.
86. Shapland, Department of Overseas Trade (1925), p. 61.
87. Llewellyn Smith, Department of Overseas Trade (1925), p. 15.
88. These were composed of a statutory seven French members and of foreign members in proportion to the numerical importance of each of the exhibition classes.
89. Llewellyn Smith, Department of Overseas Trade (1925), p. 15.
90. See Anna Sieradzka, *Art Déco w Europie i w Polsce* (Warsaw, 1996), part 2, chapter 3.
91. Hostache (1926), p. 16.
92. Waldemar George, 'L'Exposition des arts décoratifs et industriels modernes de 1925', *L'Art vivant* (1925), pp. 285-8.
93. Llewellyn Smith, Department of Overseas Trade (1925), p. 23.
94. Ibid.
95. See Le Corbusier, *L'Art décoratif d'aujourd'hui* (Paris, 1925; reprint, 1959). The influence of Modernist historiography has ensured that this and other writings by Le Corbusier, together with the 'Esprit Nouveau' pavilion, have played a prominent role – perhaps unwarrantedly – in accounts of French design in the early twentieth century and the 1925 Exhibition, such as that by Troy.
96. See Johnson (2000) and *Report of a Commission* (1926).
97. Its longer-term legacy to French design is indicated by Stéphane Laurent in Chapter 14.
98. Including Ruhlmann, the fashion designer Lucien Lelong and the graphic designer A. M. Cassandre; see also Chapter 31.
99. Rudolph Rosenthal and Helena L. Ratzka, *The Story of Modern Applied Art* (New York, 1948), p. 180; see also *Les Echos d'art* (October 1932).
100. Shapland, Department of Overseas Trade (1925), p. 61.
101. Magne (1925).
102. See *Report of a Commission* (1926).
103. Ibid.

Chapter 13: Paris 1925: Consuming Modernity

1. 'En guise de préface à une visite de l'Exposition', *Catalogue général officiel: Exposition internationale des arts décoratifs* (Paris, 1925), n.p.; Department of Overseas Trade, *Reports on the Present Position and Tendencies of the Industrial Arts as indicated at the International Exhibition of Modern Decorative and Industrial Arts, Paris, 1925* (London, 1925), p. 11. On the 1925 Paris Exhibition, see Nancy J. Troy, 'Reconstructing Art Deco: Purism, the Department Store, and the Exposition of 1925', in Nancy Troy, *Modernism and the Decorative Arts in France: Art Nouveau to Le Corbusier* (New Haven and London, 1991), pp. 159-226.
2. Georges Le Fève, 'L'Exposition internationale des arts décoratifs et industriels modernes: L'Architecture', *L'Art vivant*, vol. 19 (1 October 1925), pp.18-29.

3. For an extended discussion of the significance of the boutique in 1925, see Tag Gronberg, *Designs on Modernity: Exhibiting the City in 1920s Paris* (Manchester and New York, 1998).
4. For a photograph of the 'Vieux Paris' exhibit at the 1900 Paris *Exposition universelle*, see Philippe Bouin and Christian-Philippe Chanut, *Histoire française des folies et des expositions universelles* (Paris, 1980), p. 154. The 'Vieux Paris' exhibit needs to be considered in relation to the turn-of-the-century preoccupation with 'historic' Paris; for an account of this, see Molly Nesbit, *Atget's Seven Albums* (New Haven and London, 1992), pp. 16, 20, 21, 24-6, 62-73.
5. See the official catalogue *Salon d'automne 1924, du 1er novembre au 14 décembre, 17e exposition* (Paris, 1924), pp. 363-7. The 'Art Urbain' section of the Salon was organized by Marcel Temporal.
6. Luc Benoist, 'Les Arts de la rue', *Beaux-Arts: Revue d'information artistique* (August 1925), p. 260.
7. See, for example, Henri Clouzot's comment on the boutiques on show at the 1924 *Salon d'automne*: 'Since the war, Parisian commerce has produced a lively and charming face'; see 'Les arts appliqués au Salon d'automne', *La Renaissance de l'art français et des industries de luxe* (January 1925), p. 16. Post-war luxury consumerism can be related to the growth of the 'nouveaux riches' in France and the United States.
8. Raymond Bouyer, 'Les Devantures parisiennes', *La Renaissance de l'art français et des industries de luxe* (December 1919), p. 534. *La Renaissance* was one of several journals promoting 'les arts décoratifs' in the period following the First World War. As Kenneth Silver has argued, the title of this journal indicates 'the extent to which the decorative arts, together with painting, were understood as being part of a national post-war program to reassert French culture' in the face of German competition; see Kenneth Silver, 'Matisse's Retour à l'Ordre', *Art in America*, vol. 75, no. 6 (June 1987), p. 117.
9. Robert Forrest Wilson, *Paris on Parade* (Indianapolis, 1924-5), p. 27; Darcy Braddell, 'Little Shops of Paris', *Architectural Review*, vol. lxiii, no. 356 (July 1926), pp. 3-9.
10. Wilson (1924-5), p. 113. For more recent discussions of the idea of Paris as a woman's (or feminized) city, see Elizabeth Wilson, *The Sphinx in the City: Urban Life, the Control of Disorder, and Women* (London, 1991); Andrea Weiss, *Paris as a Woman: Portraits from the Left Bank* (London and San Francisco, 1995).
11. 'Groupe de la parure', *Encyclopédie des arts décoratifs et industriels modernes*, vol. ix (Paris, 1925), p. 9. On women's shopping in relation to French nineteenth-century exhibitions, see Shane Adler Davis, '"Fine Cloths on the Altar": The Commodification of Late Nineteenth-Century France', *Art Journal* (Spring 1989), pp. 85-9; Abigail Solomon-Godeau, 'The Other Side of Venus: The Visual Economy of Feminine Display', in Victoria De Grazia and Ellen Furlough, *The Sex of Things: Gender and Consumption in Historical Perspective* (Berkeley, Los Angeles and London, 1996), pp. 113-50.
12. According to the official report on the 1925 Exhibition published by the British Department of Overseas Trade, 'Of the women's costumes, especially in the French Section, it is observed that "very many of them appeared to be exceptional pieces which were certainly not to be seen anywhere in the daily life of the people of Paris"'; see Hubert Llewellyn Smith, 'Introductory Survey: 2. Representative Character', Department of Overseas Trade (1925), p. 13. See also 'Vêtement – section française', *Encyclopédie*, vol. ix (1925), p. 21.
13. 'Model by Pack-Ann' (a wordplay on Paquin), Wilson (1924-5), p. 24.
14. Henri Clouzot, 'La Parure', in *Paris Arts Décoratifs: Guide de l'Exposition* (Paris, 1925), p. 224.
15. 'Le principe ... de la mode est de faire toujours du nouveau', 'Parfumerie – section française', *Encyclopédie*, vol. ix (1925), p. 73.
16. 'Parure', *Encyclopédie*, vol. i (1925), p. 65.
17. Henri Clouzot, 'La Rue de la Paix – la place Vendôme – la Rue de Castiglione', *La Renaissance de l'art français et des industries de luxe* (June 1923), p. 300.
18. For discussion of a 'cinematic' shop display at the 1924 *Salon d'automne*, see Gronberg (1998), pp. 86-91.
19. Richard Abel, *French Cinema: The First Wave, 1915-1929* (Princeton, 1984), pp. 252, 255.
20. On Marcel L'Herbier's *L'Inhumaine* (1924), see Abel (1984), p. 385: 'From the production's inception in the summer of 1923, as a French showcase for the American market, L'Herbier and his colleagues at Cinégraphic planned to make it a sort of "summary, a provisional summary, of all that was artistically advanced in France two years before the famous Exposition des Arts Décoratifs." This included the work of (besides Pierre MacOrlan) the painter Fernand Léger, the architect Rob Mallet-Stevens, the composer Darius Milhaud, the furniture designer Pierre Chareau, the fashion designer Paul Poiret'; see also Abel (1984), pp. 143, 207.
21. *Encyclopédie*, vol. ix (1925), p. 10.
22. Guillaume Janneau, 'Le Visage de la rue moderne', *Bulletin de la vie artistique* (November 1924), p. 498. For a history of advertising in France, see Marc Martin, *Trois Siècles de publicité en France* (Paris, 1992).
23. On 1920s Parisian shop window display, see Tag Gronberg, 'Beware Beautiful Women: The 1920s Shop Window Mannequin and a Physiognomy of Effacement', *Art History* (September 1997), pp. 375-96.
24. From Fernand Léger, 'A Critical Essay on the Plastic Quality of Abel Gance's Film *The Wheel*', originally published 1922 in *Comœdia*; see Fernand Léger, Les Fonctions de la peinture (Paris, 1965), p. 22. Léger made the connection between film and shop display; in his essay (unpublished, c.1924) on his own film *Ballet mécanique*, he wrote: 'we are living through the advent of the object that is thrust on us in all those shops that decorate the streets' (ibid, p. 50).
25. For a Post-modern interpretation of the relationship between cinema viewing and shopping, see Anne Friedberg, *Window Shopping: Cinema and the Postmodern* (Berkeley, Los Angeles and Oxford, 1993).
26. The title of Loos's novel (first published in 1925), as well as its 'diary' format, is a kind of parody of John Cleland's *Memoirs of a Woman of Pleasure* (c.1749), often referred to as *Fanny Hill*.
27. Anita Loos, *Gentlemen Prefer Blondes: The Illuminating Diary of a Professional Lady* (1925; reprinted London, 1982), p. 78.
28. Ibid, p. 87.
29. In reality, the 'education' of Americans in Parisian luxury shopping began even before their departure for France. Nineteenth-century entrepreneurs such as John Wanamaker organized Paris fashion shows for their customers. Wanamaker also built a life-size replica of the Rue de la Paix in his Philadelphia department store. See Richard Abel, 'The Perils of Pathé or the Americanization of the American Cinema', in Leo Charney and Vanessa R. Schwartz (eds), *Cinema and the Invention of Modern Life* (Berkeley, Los Angeles and London, 1995), p. 197 and Friedberg (1993), p. 80.
   Tourist-shoppers could avail themselves of a range of shopping guides to the French capital, such as Thérèse Bonney and Louise Bonney, *A Shopping Guide to Paris* (New York, 1929), written particularly for American visitors, or the trilingual (French, English, Spanish) *Livre d'adresse de madame (Annuaire de la parisienne): Répertoire des principaux spécialistes et fournisseurs parisiens ainsi que de multiples adresses d'ordre pratique; Pour tout ce qui intéresse la femme et la maîtresse de maison* (Paris, 1922).
30. Charles Dana Gibson, *The Education of Mr. Pipp* (New York and London, 1899), n.p. The Mr Pipp illustrations (originally published in *Life* magazine) depict an American ironmaster who at the prompting of his domineering wife and two attractive daughters undertakes a family voyage to Europe.
31. Mary Louise Roberts, *Civilization without Sexes: Reconstructing Gender in Postwar France, 1917-27* (Chicago and London, 1994).
32. On 1920s women's fashion, see for example: Valerie Steele, *Paris Fashion: A Cultural History* (New York and Oxford, 1988), Chapters 11 and 12; Madeleine Ginsburg, *Paris Fashions: The Art Deco Style of the 1920s* (London, 1989); Valerie Steele, 'Chanel in Context', in Juliet Ash and Elisabeth Wilson (eds), *Chic Thrills: A Fashion Reader* (London, 1992), pp. 118-26.
33. It is important to point out, however, that (as revealed by commercial initiatives such as those of Wanamaker, see note 29 above) the marketing of Paris as 'a woman's city' involved interests other than those of women (or indeed, those of the French). The promotion of Paris as a feminized city of high fashion was fundamental to economic concerns of other countries. In the case of the United States, an identification with this version of 'Paris' was vital to the sale of goods, both American and French, the mass-produced as well as the luxurious. See Abel (1995), p. 197; Gronberg (1998), pp. 26-7, 155-6.
34. For a discussion of the imagery of the woman motorist in relation to that of the 1920s feminine toilette, see Tag Gronberg, 'Making up the Modern City: Modernity on Display at the 1925 International Exposition', in Carol S. Eliel, *L'Esprit Nouveau: Purism in Paris, 1918-1925* (Los Angeles, 2001), pp. 101-28.
35. On women practitioners in the arts at this period, see for example: Isabelle Anscombe, *A Woman's Touch: Women in Design from 1860 to the Present Day* (London, 1984); Shari Benstock, *Women of the Left Bank: Paris, 1900-1940* (London, 1987); Bridget Elliott and Jo-Ann Wallace, *Women Artists and Writers: Modernist (im)positionings* (New York and London, 1994); Gill Perry, *Women Artists and the Parisian Avant-Garde: Modernism and 'Feminine' Art, 1900 to the late 1920s* (Manchester and New York, 1995).
36. On Gloria Swanson as an American (but internationally recognized) 'modern woman', see Donald Albrecht, *Designing Dreams: Modern Architecture in the Movies* (New York, 1986), p. xiv. Delaunay's embroidered wool coat for Swanson is illustrated and dated 1923 in Jacques Damase, *Sonia Delaunay: Fashion and Fabrics* (Paris and London, 1991); see pp. 84-5 and 169. According to Elisabeth Morano: 'A coat decorated with rectilinear motifs ... was particularly popular, and brought commissions from the architects Gropius and Breuer; Gloria Swanson's version was completely embroidered. Other film actresses and theater actresses, like Paulette Pax, Gabrielle Dorziat, and Lucienne Bogaert, bought from Delaunay', Elisabeth Morano (introduction), *Sonia Delaunay: Art into Fashion* (New York, 1986), p. 21. For a photograph (dated 'late 1920s') of the designer Eyre de Lanux wearing a similar coat, see Anscombe (1984), p. 126.
37. Sonia Delaunay's fashions and textiles were used in Marcel L'Herbier's highly successful film *Le Vertige* (1926) and René Le Somptier's *Le P'tit Parigot* (1926). The sets included paintings by Delaunay's husband (Robert Delaunay) and the stylish modern designs were by the architect Rob Mallet-Stevens. These films are characterized as 'modern studio spectaculars' by Abel (1984), pp. 212-13. See also Monique Schneider-Maunoury, 'Les Delaunay flirtent avec le cinéma', in Emmanuelle Toulet (ed.), *Le Cinéma au rendez-vous des arts: France, années 20 et 30* (Paris, 1995), pp. 84-93.
38. On Sonia Delaunay in relation to issues of female artistic identity, see Tag Gronberg, 'Working in Tandem', *Art History* (June 1996), pp. 313-16 and Tag Gronberg, 'Deco Venus', in Caroline Arscott and Katie Scott, *Manifestations of Venus: Art and Sexuality* (Manchester and New York, 2000), pp. 142-55, 214-18.

Chapter 14: The Artist-Decorator

1. Nancy Troy, *Modernism and the Decorative Arts in France: Art Nouveau to Le Corbusier* (New Haven and London, 1991); Stéphane Laurent, 'Le Style Déco', *Anjia Magazine* (August 2000), pp. 66-72.
2. Stéphane Laurent, *Les Arts appliqués en France: Genèse d'un enseignement, 1851-1940* (Paris, 1999).
3. Stéphane Laurent, 'Les Industries du meuble de 1830 à 1950', in Jean-Baptiste Minnaert, *Le Faubourg Saint-Antoine: Architecture et métiers d'art* (Paris, 1998), pp. 118-24.
4. Such an exhibition was first suggested by the radical Socialist deputy C.-M. Couyba in 1906, as part of his annual budget proposal for the Ministry of Fine Arts; see Chapter 12.
5. Paul Greenhalgh, *Ephemeral Vistas: The Expositions Universelles, Great Exhibitions and World's Fairs, 1851-1939* (Manchester, 1988).
6. The Union was renamed the Union Centrale des Arts Décoratifs (UCAD) in 1882. See Yvonne Brunhammer, *Le Beau dans l'utile: Un Musée pour les arts décoratifs* (Paris, 1992).
7. Marius Vachon, *Les Musées et les écoles d'art industrielle en Europe* (Paris, 1890). See also, Marius Vachon, *Nos Industries d'art en péril* (Paris, 1882); Marius Vachon, *Pour la défense de nos industries d'art: L'Instruction artistique des ouvriers en Allemagne, Angleterre, et en Autriche: Missions officielles d'enquête* (Paris, 1899).
8. For Carabin, see *L'Art et les métiers*, no. 5 (January-February 1912), pp. 6-13. Charles-Edouard Jeanneret's report was commissioned and published by the school of art in his native town: *Etude sur le mouvement d'art décoratif en Allemagne* (La Chaux-de-Fonds, 1912; reprinted New York, 1968).
9. During the war many artist-decorators had been employed in the Camouflage Service, where some had enough free time to continue practising their profession. They won the confidence of the government and received the commission to design the Victory Celebration in Paris in 1919, for which Louis Süe, André Mare and Paul Vera designed the centrepiece – a cenotaph to the war dead
10. See, however, Suzanne Tise, 'Les Grands Magasins', in Catherine Arminjon and others,*'L'Art de Vivre': Decorative Arts and Design in France, 1789-1989* (London, 1989), pp. 73-105.
11. Guilleré's wife, Charlotte Chauchat-Guilleré, became its director.
12. Although the stripped modernistic gained ground in the 1920s, as did an increasingly simplified form of modernized tradition.
13. For the campaign led by Léandre Vaillat, see Jean-Claude Vigato, *Architecture régionaliste: France, 1890-1950* (Paris, 1995).
14. See Florence Camard, *Michel Dufet, architecte-décorateur* (Paris, 1988).
15. For an account of the SAM, see Jacques Rouaud, *Soixante Ans d'arts ménagers*, 2 vols (Paris, 1989 and 1993).

Chapter 15: Germany, Austria and the Netherlands

1. Suzanne Tise, *Between Art and Industry: Design Reform in France, 1851-1939* (Ann Arbor, 1991), p. 323.
2. For Richard Riemerschmid, see Winfried Nerdinger, *Riemerschmid: Vom Jugendstil zum Werkbund: Werke und Dokumente* (Munich, 1982), pp. 194-6 and Frederic J. Schwartz, *The Werkbund: Design Theory and Mass Culture before the First World War* (New Haven and London, 1996), pp. 123-5. For Bruno Paul, see Thomas Drebusch and others, *Bruno Paul: Deutsche Raumkunst und Architektur zwischen Jugendstil und Moderne* (Munich, 1992), pp. 148-9, 156-7.
3. Nancy Troy, *Modernism and the Decorative Arts in France: Art Nouveau to Le Corbusier* (New Haven and London, 1991), pp. 58-61.
4. John Heskett, 'Design in Inter-War Germany', in Wendy Kaplan (ed.), *Designing Modernity: The Arts of Reform and Persuasion, 1885-1945: Selections from the Wolfsonian* (Miami Beach and London, 1995), pp. 257-9.
5. From 1906 onwards, both Bruno Paul and Richard Riemerschmid had pioneered standardized – part machine made – furniture.
6. Ingeborg Becker and Dieter Högermann, *Bröhan-Museum: Berliner Porzellan vom Jugendstil zum Functionalismus, 1889-1939* (Berlin, 1987), pp. 151-3; Petra Werner, *Die zwanziger Jahre: Deutsches Porzellan zwischen Inflation und Depression: die Zeit des Art Deco?!* (Hohenberg an der Eger, 1992), p. 61. The sculptor Joseph Wackerle also modelled porcelain figures for the KPM and Nymphenburg factories.
7. Drebusch and others (1992), pp. 239-40. The room was designed in 1925 but some of the furnishings, such as the carpet, were older 'standard' designs.
8. Werner (1992), pp. 66-9; Bröhan-Museum, *Kunst der Jahrhundertwende und der zwanziger Jahre Bröhan*, vol. i of *Sammlung Karl H. Bröhan Berlin* (Berlin, 1985), cat. 405-6.
9. Becker and Högermann (1987), pp. 161-3.
10. Victor Arwas, *Art Deco* (London, 1980; New York, 1992; reprint, New York, 2000), pp. 140-63.
11. Karl H. Bröhan, *Bröhan Museum Berlin: Berlin State Museum for Art Nouveau. Art Deco and Functionalism, 1889-1939: Arts, Crafts, Industrial Design, Picture Gallery* (Berlin, 1998), pp. 180-1.
12. Ibid, pp. 182-3.
13. Ibid, pp. 198-9.
14. Tilmann Buddensieg, *Keramik in der Weimarer Republik, 1919-1933: Die Sammlung Tilmann Buddensieg im Germanischen Nationalmuseum* (Nuremberg, 1985).
15. Bröhan-Museum, *Kunst der 20er und 30er Jahre*, vol. iii of *Sammlung Karl H. Bröhan Berlin* (1985) pp. 507-15.
16. Rolf-Peter Baacke, *Lichtspielhausarchitectur in Deutschland: Von der Schaubude bis zum Kinopalast* (Berlin, 1982), pp. 108-29.
17. Volker Duvigneau, *Plakate in München, 1840-1940* (Munich, 1978); Volker Duvigneau and Norbert Götz, *Ludwig Hohlwein, 1874-1949* (Munich, 1996), pp. 214-43.
18. *L'Autriche à l'Exposition internationale des arts décoratifs et industriels modernes* (Paris, 1925), pp. 39-49, lists literally hundreds of participants: firms, workshops and individual artists.
19. Elisabeth Schmuttermeier, 'Wiener Werkstätte', in John Sillevis and others, *Wiener Werkstätte: Keuze uit Weense collecties* (The Hague, 1998), pp. 18-19; Hoffmann collected folk embroideries himself. See also, Angela

Völker and Roberta Pichler, *Textiles of the Wiener Werkstätte, 1910-1932* (London, 1994; original German edition, 1990).
20. Peter Noever, *Die Überwindung der Utilität: Dagobert Peche und die Wiener Werkstätte* (Vienna, 1998); *Beyond Utility: Dagobert Peche and the Wiener Werkstätte* (New Haven, 2002).
21. Gabriele Fabiankowitsch, 'Dagobert Peches Rolle in der Wiener Werkstätte', in Noever (1998), pp. 59-60.
22. For Ehrlich's silver designs for Begeer, see Annalies Krekel-Aalberse, *Carel J. A. Begeer, 1883-1956* (Zwolle, 2001), pp. 118-22. See also Gabriele Fahr-Becker, *Wiener Werkstätte, 1903-1932* (Cologne, 1995), pp. 89-94; Ehrlich designed the plasterwork for the Sonia Knips House by Hoffmann in 1924-5.
23. Peter Rath, *Lobmeyr: Helles Glas und klares Licht* (Vienna, Cologne and Weimar, 1998), pp. 74-5, fig. 33; *L'Autriche à l'Exposition internationale* (1925). Lobmeyr presented a large selection of engraved glass at the Paris 1925 Exhibition.
24. Völker (1994), p. 119, note 38, quotes the architect Armand Weiser in *Neues Wiener Tagblatt.*
25. Schmuttemeier, in Sillevis and others (1998), p. 22.
26. Bröhan (1998), pp. 152-3; Waltraud Neuwirth, *Bimini-Wiener Glaskunst des Art Deco*, vol. ii of *Lampengeblasenes Glas aus Wien* (Vienna, 1992), pp. 139-45.
27. Ibid.
28. Frans van Burkom, 'Kunstvormgeving in Nederland', in Adriaan Venema and others, *Amsterdamse School: Nederlandse architectuur, 1910-1930* (Amsterdam, 1975), p. 84. For the Amsterdam School, see also Wim de Wit (ed.), *The Amsterdam School: Dutch Expressionist Architecture, 1915-1930* (Cambridge, MA and London, 1983).
29. Adriaan Venema, 'Sociaal-economische aspecten van de Amsterdamse School', in de Wit (1983), pp. 3-14.
30. Martijn F. le Coultre, *Wendingen, 1918-1932: Architectuur en vormgeving* (Blaricum, 2001). *Wendingen* was a hugely influential magazine with many institutional subscribers.
31. This style, which was strongly influenced by the graphic work of Lauweriks, became known as 'Wijdeveld (or Wendingen) typography' or 'Linear School'.
32. T. M. Eliëns, M. Groot and F. Leidelmeijer, *Avant-Garde Design: Dutch Decorative Arts, 1880-1940* (London, 1997), p. 130.
33. Although the three special Frank Lloyd-Wright issues of *Wendingen* did not appear until late 1925 and early 1926, his influence was substantial from about 1910 onwards.
34. E. Bergvelt, F. van Burkom and K. Gaillard, *Van neorenaissance tot postmodernisme: Honderdvijfentwintig jaar Nederlandse interieurs, 1870-1995/From Neo-Renaissance to Post-Modernism: A Hundred and Twenty-Five Years of Dutch Interiors, 1870-1995* (Rotterdam, 1996), pp.135-41. The building that is generally recognized as the first example of this new aesthetic is the Scheepvaarthuis in Amsterdam, an office building housing six shipping companies, designed by J. M. van der Mey, M. de Klerk and P. Kramer in 1912-16.
35. For architectural sculpture, see Ype Koopmans, *Muurvast en gebeiteld: Beeldhouwkunst in de bouw, 1840-1940/Fixed & Chiselled: Sculpture in Architecture, 1840-1940*, 2 vols (Rotterdam, 1994 and 1997); *L'Art hollandais à l'Exposition internationale des arts décoratifs et industriels modernes* (Paris, 1925), pp. 20-22, 26-8, 75.
36. Ibid, pp. 72, 77, 28; the urn is just visible on the interior photograph, above the stairs on the right. Van den Eijnde established his reputation with his work on the façade of the Scheepvaarthuis in Amsterdam, which was represented in 1925 with a photograph. See note 34 for the Scheepvaarthuis.
37. Ibid, pp. 74, 112 respectively.
38. Mechteld de Bois, *C. A. Lion Cachet, 1864-1945* (Assen and Rotterdam, 1994). Lion Cachet, himself part of the selection committee, was particularly renowned for the lush and luxurious interiors he designed for a small group of wealthy patrons around 1900.
39. *L'Art hollandais à l'Exposition internationale* (1925), pp. 61-2, 86, 102. Several of these interiors were represented in Paris through photographs, furniture and fabrics. There was also a carpet (p. 101) and a decorative book cover in batik on parchment by Lion Cachet (p. 128).
40. De Bois (1994), p. 202, fig. 256; *L'Art hollandais à l'Exposition internationale* (1925), pp. 57, 59, 102.
41. For Colenbrander's pottery, see Titus M. Eliëns, *T. A. C. Colenbrander (1841-1930): Ontwerper van de Haagse Plateelbakkerij Rozenburg* (Zwolle and The Hague, 1999); R. Mills, 'Kleurnuancen: T. A. C. Colenbrander als tapijtontwerper', *Jong Holland*, vol. 10, no. 2 (1994), pp. 6-31, is devoted to his designs for carpets.
42. *L'Art hollandais à l'Exposition internationale* (1925), pp. 100, 110-11.
43. Annalies Krekel-Aalberse and others, *Jan Eisenloeffel, 1876-1957* (Zwolle, 1996). His designs for metal tableware and other utensils in base metal were meant for a relatively wide public, while he also designed more exclusive silver products for the Begeer factory. Some of his designs proved extremely popular and remained in production until the late 1920s.
44. Eliëns, Groot and Leidelmeijer (1997), pp. 102, 240.
45. For the designs for furniture and interiors by the Amsterdam School designers, see Bergvelt, Burkom and Gaillard (1996), pp. 141-60.
46. De Klerk had no special interest in the construction, which he hid beneath a layer of dark veneer and brightly coloured, thick velvet upholstery. The tassels on the armchairs and their ski-shaped gliders all contribute to this luxuriously clad, exotic fantasy.
47. The exhibition display included two types of armchair, a table and a sideboard, wall panelling and a fire surround and hearth. The exhibits were previously used in a showroom for 't Woonhuys.
48. Kramer continued to build a large number of bridges in this style in Amsterdam.
49. *L'Art hollandais à l'Exposition internationale* (1925), p. 71.
50. The interior was stripped of much of its original panelling and stained glass in the 1960s. Parts are still in situ, while much of the removed panelling is now in the Centraal Museum, Utrecht. The main two balusters have recently resurfaced and are now in a private collection. Recently a rolling programme has started to restore and reinstall the stained glass windows of the staircase.
51. Ellie Adriaansz, 'Fragmenten uit een kleurijk oeuvre. Drie biocoopinterieurs van Jaap Gidding', *Jong Holland*, vol. 2, no. 2 (1995), pp. 6-21.
52. Renny Ramakers, *Tussen kunstnijverheid en industriële vormgeving: De Nederlandse Bond voor Kunst in Industrie* (Utrecht, 1985). Berlage was a member of the Deutscher Werkbund and was involved in attempts – from 1914 onwards – to establish a similar society in the Netherlands, something that only succeeded much later in 1924 with the creation of the Bond voor Kunst in Industrie (BKI, the Association for Art in Industry).
53. Emy Hoogenboezem, *Jac. Jongert, 1883-1942: Graficus tussen kunst en reclame* (The Hague, 1982).
54. Ingeborg De Roode and Marjan Groot, *Amsterdamse School: Textiel, 1915-1930* (Bussum and Tilburg, 1999).
55. For Metz & Co., see Petra Timmer, *Metz & Co.: De creatieve jaren* (Rotterdam, 1995).
56. Ibid, p. 64.
57. E. van Straaten, 'Theo van Doesburg', in Carel Blotkamp (ed.), *De vervolgjaren van de Stijl, 1922-1932* (Amsterdam and Antwerp, 1996), pp. 53-5.
58. Oud had defected from De Stijl in 1922 because he found it too theoretical and restrictive.
59. Van Ravesteyn's stark, rectangular bedroom suite in plain wood, painted black and white, was conceived as three-dimensional compositions entirely built up from square and rectangular shapes, with no added decoration.
60. Erik de Jong and Hoos Blotkamp, *S. van Ravesteyn: Nederlandse architectuur* (Amsterdam, 1977).
61. E. Teverne, C. Wagenaar and M. de Vletter, *J. J. P. Oud: Poetic Functionalist: The Complete Works, 1890-1963* (Rotterdam, 2001), pp. 411-21.

Chapter 16: Art Deco in Central Europe

1. François Burkhardt, 'Czech Cubism Today', in Alexander von Vegesack (ed.), *Czech Cubism* (London, 1992), p. 98.
2. Karol Homolacs, *L'Ornamentation suivant la méthode de Charles Homolacs* (Kraków, 1925).
3. Gaston Varenne, 'L'Exposition des arts décoratifs: La Section polonaise', *Art et décoration*, vol. xlviii, special exhibition issue (September 1925), p. 90.
4. Jerzy Warchałowski, 'Jak Sen', *Ster*, no. 11 (1926).
5. Mieczys¢aw Szczuka, 'Czy sztuka decoracyjna?', *Blok*, no. 10 (1925), p. 1.
6. Steven A. Mansbach, *Modern Art in Eastern Europe: From the Baltic to the Balkans, c.1890-1939* (Cambridge, 1999), p. 312.
7. Gyula Szekfü, *Három nemzedék és ami utana következik* (Budapest, 1935).
8. Éva Kiss, 'La Formation et les sources de l'Art Déco hongrois', in Martine Caeymaex, *Art Deco en Europe* (Brussels, 1989), pp. 215-6.
9. András Ferkai, 'Art Deco in Hungarian Architecture', *Interpress Graphic*, no. 9 (1986), pp. 28-9.

Chapter 17: 'Lovely Neoclassical Byways': Art Deco in Scandinavia

1. See Paul Greenhalgh (ed.), *Art Nouveau, 1890-1914* (London, 2000) for the symbolism of radical Art Nouveau and the arguments for the inclusion of hitherto unrecognized new art movements in Finland, Hungary and Russia.
2. See Michael Snodin and Elisabet Stavenow-Hidemark (eds), *Carl and Karin Larsson: Creators of the Swedish Style* (London, 1997), pp. 66-8. The Larssons' importance in combining folk tradition with late classicism was crucially influential in the invention of the 1890s Swedish Gustavian style, which was 'based on the legacy of Gustav III who reigned from 1771-1792 [and] brought into vogue a new simplicity, rural yet elegant'.
3. Eva Eriksson, 'Rationalism and Classicism, 1915-1930', in Claes Caldenby and others (eds), *Twentieth Century Architecture: Sweden* (Munich and New York, 1998), p. 52.
4. See the interior of the Faaborg Museum illustrated, for instance, in David McFadden (ed.), *Scandinavian Modern Design: 1880-1980* (New York, 1980), p. 102, no. 93, from the Faaborg Museum Archive.
5. Eva Eriksson, in Caldenby and others (1998), p. 52.
6. See Jennifer Hawkins Opie, 'Helsinki: Saarinen and Finnish Jugend', in Greenhalgh (2000), pp. 374-87.
7. Paul David Pearson, *Alvar Aalto and the International Style* (New York, 1978); see pp. 33-4 for a persuasive case for Aino and Alvar Aalto's formative education and early influences.
8. Gunilla Frick has explored this period in 'Furniture Art or a Machine to Sit on? Swedish Furniture Design and Radical Reforms', *Scandinavian Journal of Design History*, vol. i (1991), pp. 102-3.
9. The tiny studies done around 1912 by Auguste Rodin of Cambodian dancers and Vaslav Nijinsky of the Ballets Russes as they visited Paris were possibly familiar to sculptors like Jean Gauguin.
10. Department of Overseas Trade, *Reports on the Present Position and Tendencies of the Industrial Arts as indicated at the International Exhibition of Modern Decorative and Industrial Arts, Paris, 1925* (London, 1925), p. 135.
11. These vases were designed in 1919 and had been shown previously in Gothenburg in 1923, at the tri-centenary exhibition, where the displays were intended to celebrate the grandest and most luxuriously elaborate production. The reliefs of the *Four Winds* by Ivor Johnsson were also shown at Gothenburg.
12. Philip Morton Shand, 'Stockholm, 1930', *Architectural Review*, vol. 68, no. 405 (1930), p. 67.
13. Ibid, p. 69.
14. Ibid, p. 70.
15. Ibid, p. 69.
16. Ibid, p. 70.
17. Dag Widman, 'Pioneers, Breakthrough, Triumph', in Kerstin Wickman (ed.), *Orrefors: A Century of Glassmaking* (Stockholm, 1998), p. 243, footnote 47. See also Per G. Råberg, *Funktionlistiskt genombrott* (Stockholm, 1972), p. 224. The change was marked by a manifesto, 'Acceptera' (1931), to which the emerging Modernists subscribed.
18. Eric de Maré, *Gunnar Asplund, A Great Modern Architect*, Architectural Biographies, vol. 5 (London, 1955), p. 13.
19. Arvi Ilonen, *Helsinki: An Architectural Guide* (Keurru, 1990), p. 104, no. 68. The building contains 87 apartments, consisting of one room and a kitchen, and four shops.
20. Ibid, p. 88, no. 32.
21. For an account of the *ryijy* revival, see J. Hawkins Opie, 'Helsinki: Saarinen and Finnish Jugend', in Greenhalgh (2000), pp. 374-87.
22. Ellen Key, *Skönhet för alla* (Stockholm, 1899).

Chapter 19: Italian Architecture and Design

1. Described in Vittorio Pica, 'L'arte decorativa all'Esposizione di Torino', *Emporium*, fasc. iv (1903) and welcomed in 'Cronaca. L'inaugurazione della I esposizione internazionale d'arte decorative moderna', *L'arte decorativa moderna*, vol. i, no. 3 (1902) as 'the bravest and most daring effort attempted in our country'.
2. See Carlo Enrico Rava, 'Spirito latino', *Domus*, vol. 11 (February 1931), pp. 24-9.
3. Raffaello Giolli, 'L'artigiano al bivio', *Colosseo*, vol. iii (October 1933), pp. 190-4. The Ente Nazionale per l'Artigianato e le Piccole Industrie (ENAPI) was the product of a law of 19 May 1922 that set up regional committees to support local trades. It promoted exhibitions and commissioned artists and architects to provide designs for local craftsmen. The official attitude on how to improve the standard of craftsmanship can be gauged from a statement in the official Fascist journal, in 1927: 'Let an artist, selected by competition organized by a special jury, be fascistically imposed on them and give them models to follow'; see Vittorio Gregotti (ed.), *Il disegno del prodotto industriale: Italia, 1860-1980* (Milan, 1986), p. 133.
4. Mazzucotelli taught at the Umanitaria from 1903 to 1924. The Quartis, father and son, taught at both the Umanitaria and ISIA. Guido Balsamo Stella was a regular teacher, and even the Roman Duilio Cambellotti held classes in 1919.
5. A predecessor was the *Esposizione Regionale Lombarda*, 1919, held in the building of the Società Umanitaria in Milan and promoted by Augusto Osimo, director of the Umanitaria, and Guido Marangoni, art critic and publisher, who went on to found the very important journal *La Casa Bella* (renamed *Casabella* in 1929).
6. Described by Agnoldomenico Pica as a set of 'cabalistic hieroglyphs from an unknown and marvellous world'; see *Casabella*, vol. 29 (May 1930). For the cultural environment of Milan in the Art Deco period, see Rossana Bossaglia and Valerio Terraroli, *Milano Déco: La fisionomia della città negli anni venti* (Milan, 1999). Bossaglia prefers to group the Art Deco of the 1930s with the Novecento style.
7. Schools of architecture in Venice, Turin, Florence and Naples soon followed, while in Milan a department of architecture was developed in the Engineering Faculty of the Polytechnic; see Andrea Nulli, '1919-1945', in Gregotti (1986), p. 128.
8. Richard-Ginori was itself an amalgamation in 1896 of Giulio Richard's factories in Milan and Florence and the Doccia works of the Marchesi Ginori Lisci. Richard-Ginori produced a very wide range of goods, from sanitary ware to electrical insulators. Its production of luxury goods formed part of a calculated strategy to promote its range.
9. Guido Andlovitz was born in Trieste but took his inspiration from traditional Venetian ceramics and earthenware, modernizing it by reference to Viennese and French fashions. The Studio Ars Labor Industrie Riunite was founded in 1923 by Luigi Toso, Guglielmo Barbini, Giuseppe d'Alpaos and Gino Francesconi. Guido Balsamo Stella was its artistic director for a while, and the firm commissioned work from the best Venetian designers, including Vittorio Zecchin and Atte Gasparetto. Guido Balsamo Stella was born in Turin but came from a Murano family. From 1905 he spent several years in Munich, working with Albert Welti and exhibiting with the Bavarian Secessionists. In 1914, he was in Sweden, learning the engraving techniques that had made Orrefors famous. His education was completed by visits to Prague, from whence he brought Franz Pelzel to work with him in Italy. Pelzel remained artistic director at SALIR until his death. Marcello Nizzoli was trained at the art school in Parma; he began as a designer, working with his sister Matilde who specialized in embroidered silk. After winning a gold medal in the Paris 1925 Exhibition for his Piatti shawls, he turned increasingly to graphic work, designing posters for Campari bitters and cordials, and exhibition design; see Arturo Carlo Quintavalle, *Marcello Nizzoli* (Milan, 1989).
10. Margherita Sarfatti, *L'Italie à l'Exposition internationale des arts décoratifs et industriels modernes, Paris 1925* (Paris, 1925), p. 7.
11. Ibid.
12. Gio Ponti, 'Le ragioni dello stile moderno', *L'Italia all' esposizione internazionale di arti decorative e industriali moderne* (Paris and Milan, 1925), pp. 69-72. See also Lisa Licitra Ponti, *Gio Ponti: The Complete Work, 1923-1978* (London, 1990) and Ugo La Pietra, *Gio Ponti* (Milan, 1988).

13. Ibid.
14. Marinetti had written to Mussolini in 1924 urging him to include the Futurists in the Paris 1925 Exhibition.
15. A letter (27 Sept V 1927), from Croce, commander of the 156 Centuria of the Opera Nazionale Balilla, the 'Tenacissima', thanking Depero for the pennant. Croce hopes to give the Centuria 'an exquisitely Futurist tone'. He concludes 'Futurism and Fascism know no obstacles'; see MART Depero archive.
16. Two gold medals for his tapestries, a Diploma of Honour in the 'Art of Living' category, a silver medal for wood art and industry and a bronze for his toys. On 5 December 1925, Depero wrote to his wife saying, 'the next time I come to Paris, I must load up with stuff'. He had been successful with Pavlova and was going to visit Poiret; see MART, Depero archive, 1004/1. He also participated in Frederick Kiesler's *International Theatre Exhibition*, Steinway Hall, New York, in 1926.
17. I. de Guttry, M. P. Maino and G. Raimondi, *Duilio Cambellotti: Arredi e decorazioni* (Bari, 1999)
18. They designed the furniture for the Palazzo di Giustizia, Milan (1931-41) and the Palazzo del INPS (Istituto Nazionale Fascista per la Prevadenza Sociale), Milan (1931), designed by Marcello Piacentini. They also made the furniture, to Gio Ponti's design, for a prize-winning ship's cabin for the fourth *Biennale* in Monza, 1930; see *Eugenio e Mario Quarti: Dall'ebenisteria Liberty all'arredamento moderno* (Milan, 1980), p. 21 and Mario Lupano, *Marcello Piacentini* (Bari, 1991).
19. Roberto Papini, 'Dagli architetti ai pastori', *Emporium*, no. 369 (September 1925), pp. 138-60.
20. The Novecento began as a group of painters in 1923 with an exhibition at the Galleria Pesaro in Milan. This group included Mario Sironi and Achille Funi, both dedicated to developing a new style of monumental mural. Sironi worked closely with Muzio, but also with members of the Rationalist group of modern architects, including Pietro Lingeri and Giuseppe Terragni. As Luciano Patetta points out, Picasso, Stravinsky and Hindemith all toyed with classicism during the 1920s; see Luciano Patetta, *L'architettura in Italia, 1919-1943: Le polemiche* (Milan, 1972), p. 19.
21. Giovanni Muzio, 'L'architettura a Milano intorno all'Ottocento', *Emporium*, no. 317 (May 1921), pp. 241-58.
22. Fulvio Irace, *Giovanni Muzio, 1893-1982* (Milan, 1994), pp. 61-80. The first project was submitted on 24 December 1919 by the builders and their engineer, Pierfausto Barelli. Muzio's revised scheme, which allowed the company to exploit the site more effectively, was sent in on 16 June 1920.
23. '... la scelta di Muzio è di accostare ai frammenti di una tradizione classica, e in particolare Palladiana, secondo un ordine e una logica nuovi: *objets trouvés* in un repertorio disperso dal tempo nella città'; see Giorgio Ciucci, *Gli architetti e il Fascismo: Architettura italiana, 1922-1944* (Turin, 1989), p. 63.
24. The original seven were Sebastiano Larco, Guido Frette, Luigi Figini, Carlo Enrico Rava, Gino Pollini, Giuseppe Terragni and Adalberto Libera, who joined in 1927. The group published four theoretical articles in *La rassegna italiana* between December 1926 and May 1927. A larger and more ambitious organization, the MIAR, launched an exhibition in 1928, claiming sympathy with the practical essence of Imperial Rome. This was followed by a second exhibition, in Rome in 1931, which included a 'Report on Architecture' dedicated to Mussolini and written by the new publicist of the group Pietro Maria Bardi. Pressured to reorganize as a professional group within the Sindacato Nazionale di Architettura Fascista, the Modernists formed the RAMI (Raggrupamento Architetti Moderni Italiani) in 1931 and broadened its base to include more architects from Rome. The high point of Rationalism in Italy was the *Triennale* of 1933, from which point the group's fortunes declined.
25. For the history of the Italian Rationalists, see Patetta (1972): the Venice Biennale exhibition catalogue Silvio Danesi and Luciano Patetta, *Il Razionalismo e l'architettura in Italia durante il Fascismo* (Venice, 1976); Franco Brunetti, *Architetti e fascismo* (Florence, 1993); Ciucci (1989); Dennis Doordan, *Building Modern Italy: Italian Architecture, 1914-1936* (Princeton, 1988); Richard Etlin, *Modernism in Italian Architecture, 1890-1940* (Cambridge, MA and London, 1991).
26. See Giuseppe Pagano, 'Tre anni di architettura in Italia', *Casabella*, vol. x, no. 110 (February 1937), pp. 2-5. Pagano compares the Casa Rustici by Lingeri and Terragni, with its grid of exposed concrete structural elements, with the work of Muzio, claiming that both 'betray a need for decoration'.
27. Prampolini and the art critic Mario Recchi founded the Casa d'Arte Italiana in March 1919, and this was followed in October by Depero's Casa d'Arte Depero in Rovereto. In 1921, the Casa d'Arte Bragaglia and the Experimental Theatre in the Baths of Septimus Severus in Rome were installed by Virgilio Marchi, an eccentric follower of Sant'Elia; these were among his few constructed works.
28. Fortunato Depero, 'Manifesto of Advertising', *Futurismo*, vol. i, no. 2 (15-30 June 1932).
29. Ibid, cited in Gabriella Belli, *Depero Futurista: Rome, Paris, New York, 1915-1932 and More* (Turin, 1999), p. 137.
30. Reconstructed models in MART (based on the original drawing, MD 2508-A) and photographs of the models made at various scales in the 1920s.
31. See Steven Heller and Louise Fili, *Italian Art Deco Graphic Design between the Wars* (San Francisco, 1993).
32. Among his best known exhibition displays were the 'Sala delle Medaglie d'Oro' at the Mostra dell'Aeronautica, Milan, 1934; the 'Salone d'Onore' at the sixth Milan *Triennale*, 1936 (both with Edoardo Persico); the 'Padiglione dei Coloranti Nazionali del Tessile' in Rome, 1937; and the displays for the aluminium manufacturer Montecatini at the *Fiera di Milano* in 1937; see Quintavalle (1989), pp. 270-73.
33. The *Manifesto dell'aeropittura futurista* was published on 22 September 1929 and signed by Filippo Tommaso Marinetti, Giacomo Balla, Fortunato Depero, Ernesto Prampolini, Gerardo Dottori and others. 'Aeropittura', a style of painting evoking a pilot's view of the world, was one of the main manifestations of what Enrico Crispolti dubbed the 'second Futurism', which was heavily implicated in the militaristic triumphalism of Fascism. See Enrico Crispolti, 'Svolgimento del Futurismo', in Renato Barilli and others, *Gli Anni Trenta* (Milan, 1982), pp. 175-200 and Enrico Crispolti, *Il secondo futurismo, Torino, 1923-38: Cinque pittori più uno scultore* (Turin, 1962). See also Enrico Crispolti, *Architettura futurista: Antonio Sant'Elia* (Modena, 1984), pp. 11-85.
34. 'Manifesto dell'architettura aerea', *Sant'Elia*, vol. ii, no. 3 (Rome, 1 February 1934); Anna Marai Matteucci Armandi and others, *Angiolo Mazzoni: 1894-1979: Architetto nell'Italia tra le due guerre* (Casalecchio di Reno, 1984).
35. For example, the frescoes of Benedetta Marinetti in the Palazzo delle Poste, Palermo, 1931-4; stained glass windows by Tato and Depero in the Direzione Generale delle Poste e Telegrafi in Trento, 1929-33; and the frescoes by Prampolini and Luigi Colombo Fillia in the Palazzo Postale, La Spezia, 1930-1.
36. Roberto Papini, *Le arti d'oggi: Architettura e arti decorative in Europa* (Milan and Rome, 1930). The introduction to this book is reprinted in Bossaglia and Terraroli (1999).
37. The point of this utopia is clarified by the dedication, to 'Benito Mussolini, honorary citizen of Universa'.
38. This tactic of stylistic stigmatization reminds us not only of the 'Degenerate Art' exhibitions in Germany, but also of the Modernist architect P. M. Bardi's *Tavola degli orrori* (1931), a collage of precisely the kind of modernizing classicism that Papini supported.
39. Dante Baldelli became artistic director of his uncle's ceramics firm, Ceramica Rometti, in 1928, after graduating as a sculptor in the Roman Academy. The militaristic theme of archers appears in many of his designs; see Silvia Barisione, Matteo Fochessati and Gianni Franzone, *La visione del prisma: La collezione Wolfson* (Milan, 1999), p. 185.
40. The Palazzo Gualino (Turin, 1928-9), by Pagano and Levi Montalcini, includes coloured linoleum compositions in most of the spaces, and Pagano made a number of designs for such floors; see Alberto Bassi and Laura Castagno, *Il designer Giuseppe Pagano* (Bari, 1994), pp. 45-56 and figs 40-41.
41. For example, Raffaello Giolli, 'Pubblicità', *Casabella-Costruzioni*, vol. 132 (December 1938), p. 25, cited in Carlo de Seta (ed.), *Giolli: L'architettura razionale* (Bari, 1972), p. 399.
42. In fact, the Balilla model shown here was the first version, which was restyled in 1935 to match the 1500. The Vatican objected to the poster on sexual grounds; see Gerald Silk, *Automobile and Culture* (Los Angeles, 1984), p. 113.
43. See Gregotti (1986), p. 213.

Chapter 20: Conscience and Consumption: Art Deco in Britain

1. Donald R. Knight and Alan D. Sabey, *The Lion Roars at Wembley: British Empire Exhibition, 60th Anniversary, 1924-1925* (New Barnet, 1984), p. 113.
2. Department of Overseas Trade, *Reports on the Present Position and Tendencies of the Industrial Arts as indicated at the International Exhibition of Modern Decorative and Industrial Arts, Paris, 1925* (London, 1925), p. 9.
3. Ibid, pp. 37 and 31.
4. Ibid, p. 94.
5. The Design and Industries Association was launched in 1915, with the aim of improving standards of manufactured (as opposed to handcrafted) products. Early members included William Richard Lethaby, Hubert Llewellyn Smith, Ambrose Heal and Harold Stabler.
6. Department of Overseas Trade (1925), p. 141.
7. Ibid, p. 23.
8. Ibid, p. 23.
9. Ibid, p. 61.
10. Ibid, p. 63.
11. John C. Rogers, 'Modern Decoration at Waring's', *DIA Quarterly* [Journal of the Design and Industries Association], vol. 6 (December 1928), pp. 4, 6.
12. Barbara Tilson, 'The Modern Art Department, Waring and Gillow, 1928-1931', *Journal of the Decorative Arts Society*, no. 8 (1983), pp. 40-49; Nancy Troy, *Modernism and the Decorative Arts in France: Art Nouveau to Le Corbusier* (New Haven and London, 1991), pp. 177, 180-81, 187 and passim; Alan Powers, *Serge Chermayeff: Designer, Architect, Teacher* (London, 2001), pp. 15-22 and passim.
13. Tilson (1983), p. 40.
14. See Bevis Hillier and Stephen Escritt, *Art Deco Style* (London, 1997), pp. 157-8.
15. The short-lived Twentieth Century Group (1930-33) was based in Cambridge and members included Wells Coates, Raymond McGrath, Frederick Etchells, Maxwell Fry and Chermayeff. The MARS (Modern Architecture Research) Group (1933-57) aimed to research and communicate the needs of modern architecture.
16. Plan furniture, designed by Walter Knoll & Co. of Stuttgart; see Barbara Tilson, 'Plan Furniture, 1932-1938: The German Connection', *Journal of Design History*, vol. 3, nos 2 and 3 (1990), pp. 145-55.
17. The Deutscher Werkbund was founded in Munich in 1907 in order to improve standards of design and manufacture.
18. Nikolaus Pevsner, *An Enquiry into Industrial Art in Britain* (Cambridge, 1937), p. 12.
19. Ibid, pp. 10, 112.
20. Ibid, pp. 19, 28, 81, 94, and 112.
21. Osbert Lancaster, *Homes Sweet Homes* (enlarged edition, London, 1953), pp. 72 and 76.
22. J. Leslie Martin, Ben Nicholson and Naum Gabo (eds), *Circle: International Survey of Constructive Art* (London, 1937).
23. Ibid, p. 215.
24. Bevis Hillier, *Art Deco of the Twenties and Thirties* (London, 1968).
25. Ibid, p. 9.
26. Nikolaus Pevsner, *Victorian and After*, vol. 2 of *Studies in Art, Architecture and Design* (London, 1968), p. 193.
27. Ibid, p. 230. Pevsner is referring to an article in *Trend*, 1936.
28. Ibid, p. 231.
29. See Peter Rose, '"It must be done now": The Arts and Crafts Exhibition at Burlington House, 1916', *Decorative Arts Society Journal*, no. 17 (1993), pp. 6-7.
30. See Alan Powers, *Modern Block Printed Textiles* (London, 1992), pp. 26-8.
31. See Cheryl Buckley, *Potters and Paintresses: Women Designers in the Pottery Industry, 1870-1955* (London, 1990).
32. Eva Weber, *Art Deco* (London, 1989), p. 132.
33. Buckley (1990), p. 119.
34. Pevsner (1937), p. 105.
35. Department of Overseas Trade (1925), p. 117. Autogenous soldering, or welding, was a recently introduced technique that allowed different types of metal to be more effectively combined together in a single design, as was frequently the case in Brandt's work.
36. Ibid, p. 122.
37. See David Dean, *The Thirties: Recalling the English Architectural Scene* (London, 1983), pp. 131-2. The controller of the London, Midland and Scottish Railway Hotel services agreed in correspondence with Oliver Hill that the hotel should be 'very modern', and that 'we must walk with kings in the hotel, but not lose the common touch in the bar'.

Chapter 21: British Art Deco Ceramics

1. See Jennifer Hawkins Opie, 'Art and Deco: The Problems of British Ceramics in the International Exhibition, Paris 1925', *The V&A Album*, vol. 4 (London, 1985), p. 341.
2. Nikolaus Pevsner, *An Enquiry into Industrial Art in Britain* (Cambridge, 1937), p. 74.

Chapter 22: Art Deco Architecture

1. Rossana Bossaglia, *L'Art Déco* (Bari, 1984), p. 1.
2. This is the view taken by Alastair Duncan: 'the subject "Art Deco architecture" does not relate to a specific style of 1920s /30s architecture *per se*, but to the distinctive style of modern ornamentation applied to new American buildings at the time'; see Alastair Duncan, *American Art Deco* (London, 1986), p. 146.
3. For example, Henry Russell Hitchcock and Philip Johnson included a whole chapter in their book, *The International Style*, entitled 'The Avoidance of Applied Decoration'. 'The supposedly novel ornament from which architecture is now freeing itself has put us on our guard against innovations which are merely decorative. The force of all self-conscious theory tends to deny the necessity of ornament as such'; see Henry Russell Hitchcock and Philip Johnson, *The International Style* (New York, 1932; reprinted 1966), p. 74.
4. A bewildering array of different buildings is included in the literature of Art Deco; see, for example, Patricia Bayer, *Art Deco Architecture: Design, Decoration and Detail from the Twenties and Thirties* (New York, 1992); Jean-Paul Bouillon, *Journal de l'Art déco* (Geneva, 1988); B. Capitman, M. D. Kinerk and D. W. Wilhelm, *Rediscovering Art Deco USA* (New York, 1994); Bevis Hillier, *The Style of the Century* (London, 1983; revised edition, 1998); David Gebhard and Harriette Von Breton, *LA in the Thirties* (Los Angeles, 1975); David Gebhard, *The National Trust Guide to Art Deco in America* (New York, 1996); Stewart Morgan, *Art Deco the European Style* (London, 1990); Cervin Robinson and Rosemarie Haag Bletter, *Skyscraper Style: Art Deco in New York* (New York, 1975); Elayne H. Varian, *American Art Deco Architecture* (New York, 1975).
5. Nancy Troy has shown how far Le Corbusier and other Modern Movement architects were engaged in the decorative arts community. Le Corbusier had excellent relations with André Groult and Paul Poiret and used fashionable firms, such as Selmersheim and Ruhlmann, in specifying furnishings and fittings for his clients; see Nancy Troy, *Modernism and the Decorative Arts in France: Art Nouveau to Le Corbusier* (New Haven and London, 1991) and Tim Benton, *The Villas of Le Corbusier, 1920-1930* (New Haven and London, 1987).
6. For a contemporary survey, see P. M. Hooper, 'Modern Architectural Decoration', *Architectural Forum*, vol. xlviii (February 1928), pp. 152-61.
7. Kahn's unpublished autobiography, Avery Architecture Library, Columbia University; cited in Françoise Bollack and Tom Killian, *Ely Jacques Kahn: New York Architect* (New York, 1995), p. xi.
8. Ely Jacques Kahn, 'On Decoration and Ornament' (1929), in his book *Ely Jacques Kahn* (New York and London, 1931), p. 21.
9. Prost was the official architect and urbanist of Morocco (1915-20).
10. He returned to classicism for most of his 1930s work.
11. Such as the Ford building in the Boulevard des Italiens, Paris, 1931.
12. 'As a fashion, it (Art Deco) lacks neither taste nor charm; it has its arbitrary side which is pleasant in a fanciful way but which cannot be considered as a style. Style and fashion are too easily confused ... all these decorative motifs are in vogue like a hat or a foxtrot, but they have the disadvantage of dating, therefore ageing'; see Rob Mallet-Stevens, 'Evolution ou mort de l'ornement', *L'Architecture d'aujourd'hui*, no. 6 (1933), p. 96.
13. Mallet-Stevens's first article, 'L'Art contemporain', appeared in the Belgian journal *Le Home* in 1911, and in the same year he began writing a regular column in another Belgian journal, *Tekhné*. He had first-hand knowledge of Hoffmann's Palais Stoclet, designed for his uncle, which he visited regularly as a child.

14. Including Francis Jourdain, Pierre Chareau and Edouard-Joseph Bourgeois (usually known as Djo-Bourgeois), Fernand Léger, the Delaunays and the Martel brothers.
15. These included *L'Inhumaine* (1924) and *Le Vertige* (1926), with sets and costumes by Robert and Sonia Delaunay. In all, Mallet-Stevens worked on ten films between 1920 and 1930; see L. Wouters, 'Cinéma et architecture', in Jean-François Pinchon, *Rob. Mallet-Stevens: Architecture, mobilier, decoration* (Paris, 1986), pp. 98-115.
16. The villa for Doucet remained on paper; that for Poiret was nearly complete when the couturier went bankrupt; but de Lempicka's apartment was completed.
17. For example, the Art Deco villa for the Comte de Noailles at Hyères, 1923-8. The film about the Villa Noailles, *Les Mystères du Château du Dé*, celebrates a luxurious and decadent avant-garde world; see G. Monnier, C. Briolle and A. Fuzibet, *Rob Mallet-Stevens: La Villa Noailles* (Paris, 1990) for the full building history.
18. This scheme was well publicized in Europe and in North America; see, for example, P. M. Hooper, 'The Rue Mallet-Stevens Paris', *Architectural Forum*, vol. xlviii, no. 3 (March 1928), pp. 505-8.
19. See Gustav Adolf Platz, *Die Baukunst der neuesten Zeit* (Berlin, 1927).
20. Henry Russell Hitchcock, 'Two Chicago Fairs', *The New Republic*, vol. v (21 January 1931), p. 271.
21. John Burchard, *The Architecture of America* (New York, 1961), paraphrased by Norbert Messler in *The Art Deco Skyscraper in New York* (New York and Berne, 1986), p. 25. More favourable assessments of New York skyscrapers of the period include Edwin Avery Park, *New Background for a New Age* (New York, 1927) and Randolph William Sexton, *The Logic of Modern Architecture* (New York, 1929).
22. Raymond Hood, in an article entitled 'Architecture of the Night', May 1930, cited in a paper by Tim Rub, 'Lighting up the Town', at the 1986 Art Deco Week symposium, extracted in the Art Deco Society of New York *News*, vol. 6, no. 1 (Spring 1986), p. 24.
23. Harvey Wiley Corbett, 'The American Radiator Building, New York City', *Architectural Record*, vol. 55, no. 5 (May 1924), p. 476. Yet the architectural qualities of the building were much admired, and this was the first of the skyscrapers to achieve Landmark status.
24. Contemporaries understood the creative implications of the Zoning Laws: 'The effect of the zoning law is the most interesting single phenomenon in American architecture today ... A skyscraper must depend for its effect upon its mass and silhouette'; see George Harold Edgell, *The American Architecture of To-day* (New York, 1928), p. 356.
25. Walter Kilham describes coming across Raymond Hood one afternoon, with a scalpel in his hand, cutting slices off the clay model of the Daily News building prepared by Rene Chambellan: '"Do you mind", he said, "if I do a little zoning myself?" ... I could hardly believe my eyes. After all that had been said of the value of rental space in the tower, this chiselling was throwing away pure gold. We backed off to take a look. Somehow, arbitrary or not, the building now had a tapering effect: it began to look the way a modern skyscraper should in the new day of set-backs and towers ... The scheme, as architects say, had "arrived"'; see Walter H. Kilham, *Raymond Hood, Architect* (New York, 1973), p. 23. See also Raymond M. Hood and Arthur T. North, *Raymond Hood* (New York and London, 1931), where Hood is quoted as saying: 'Form or mass, determined by the plan, is the dominant element of outward appearance.'
26. For example, R. W. Sexton, 'Unifying Architecture in America', *International Studio*, no. 83 (February 1926), pp. 41-5. Rosemary Haag Bletter defines Art Deco skyscraper architecture in terms of decoration that, though essentially eclectic, employs crystalline-faceted forms originating in German Expressionism and Constructivism; see Haag Bletter (1975), pp. 39-40.
27. For a modern interpretation of Ferriss's thunderous drawings, which tries to associate his work with the European avant-garde; see Eduardo Subirats, *La Transfiguración de la noce: La utopia arquitectonica de Hugh Ferriss* (Malaga, 1992).
28. The British architect Howard Robertson wrote about Ferriss: 'He has the gift of communicating to even the least promising composition the poetic breath of his perspective ... The best way of using his talent was to give him the plans, go to bed and come back next day to see the whole composition finished. He is the perfect "*automatic pilot*"'; quoted from Rem Koolhaas, *Delirious New York* (New York, 1994), p. 95.
29. See Dan Klein, 'The Chanin Building, New York', *Connoisseur*, vol. 1, no. 186 (July 1974), pp. 162-9. Searchlights located on the 53rd floor transformed the crown of the building into a beacon at night.
30. The 56-metre (185-foot) terminal spire was built in secret, hidden in the building's fire shaft, to be hoisted into place only when the Lincoln building, by H. Craig Severance, had been topped out at 282 metres high (927 feet). In a 'blaze of publicity', Van Alen hoisted his 'vertex' into place, to make the Chrysler building the tallest in the world, until in turn it was outdone by the Empire State building; see R. A. M. Stern, G. Gilmartin and T. Mellins, *New York 1930: Architecture and Urbanism between the two World Wars* (New York, 1987), p. 605.
31. See Carol Willis, 'Form follows Finance: The Empire State Building', in David Ward and Olivier Zunz (eds), *The Landscape of Modernity: New York City, 1900-1940* (Baltimore and London, 1997), pp. 160-90.
32. Koolhaas (1994), p. 115.
33. The building was completed just as the Depression began to bite. Most of the office space remained unlet throughout the 1930s; only a little over 25% of the space was let by 1932.
34. For example in Edie Nadelman's limestone relief of 'construction workers' leaning against stylized New York skyscrapers on the Fuller building (Walker & Gillette, 1938) and the marble mosaic roundels in its lobby pavement. See also 60 Wall Tower, by Clinton & Russell, Holton & George (associated architects), 1932, where a model of the building in stone decorates the entrance. See also Rosemarie Haag Bletter and Carla Breeze, *New York Deco* (New York, 1993), pp. 8-17, where a number of sculptural and two-dimensional decorative representations of skyscrapers are illustrated.
35. The frozen fountain was an archetype of Art Deco iconography; see Chapter 10.
36. Claude Bragdon, *The Frozen Fountain* (New York, 1932), p. 11.
37. Ibid, p. 6.
38. Ralph T. Walker, writing in *Pencil Points* in 1938, cited in Messler (1986), p. 62. Walker designed a number of buildings for the New York Telephone Company, including one of the first Art Deco buildings in New York, the Barclay-Vesey building, 1923-6.
39. Cited in Paul Goldberger, *The Skyscraper* (New York, 1981; London, 1982), p. 80.
40. Alfred H. Barr, 'Preface' in Hitchcock and Johnson (1932), p. 14. See also Ada Louise Huxtable, *The Tall Building artistically Considered* (New York, 1982).
41. Koolhaas (1994), p. 105, note 26.
42. Like Hood, Kahn had a degree from the Beaux-Arts in Paris and was also a member of the German professional association, the Bund Deutscher Architekten.
43. Walter Kilham records his first meeting with Raymond Hood in 1927, discussing Le Corbusier's *Vers une architecture* (1923) and *Urbanisme* (1925); see Kilham (1973), p. 23.
44. 'The lightness, simplicity and lack of applied verticalism mark this skyscraper as an advance over other New York skyscrapers and bring it within the limits of the International Style'; see Hitchcock and Johnson (1932), p. 156.
45. For the Rockefeller Center, see Carol H. Krinsky, *Rockefeller Center* (New York, 1978); for the RCA building, see Stern, Gilmartin and Mellins (1987), pp. 617-71; Kilham (1973), pp. 158-9.
46. Hood was almost certainly aware of the idea of the 'Stadkrone' ('city crown') which the German Expressionist architect Bruno Taut developed in the years immediately following the First World War.
47. Eugene Clute, 'Glass: A New Sculptural Medium', *Pencil Points* (August 1933), pp. 206-7.
48. See, for example, Friedrich Sieburg, 'Le Rôle économique de Casablanca vu par un écrivain allemand', *Bulletin économique de Maroc* (July 1938), pp. 205-7. Some of this work is now being studied and re-evaluated in social, functional and decorative terms: see Jean-Louis Cohen and Monique Eleb, *Casablanca: Mythes et figures d'une aventure urbaine* (Paris, 1998); Jean-François Lejeune and Allan T. Shulman, *The Making of Miami Beach: The Architecture of Lawrence Murray Dixon* (Miami Beach, 2000); Peter Shaw and Peter Hallett, *Art Deco Napier: Styles of the Thirties* (Napier, 1990; reprint, Nelson, 1994); P. Goldman and others, *Tel Aviv Modern Architecture, 1930-1939* (Berlin, 1994).
49. James Weber Linn, *The Official Pictures of A Century of Progress Exhibition Chicago 1933*, Reuben H. Donnelly Corporation Chicago, 1933 (in the Larry Zim Collection, Cooper-Hewitt Museum, New York). The rays from the star Arcturus, taking 40 years to reach the earth, began their journey in the year of the Chicago *Colombian World Fair* of 1893.
50. R. F. C. Dawes, *A Century of Progress Exhibition: Official View Book* (Chicago, 1933).
51. For an account of the special effects of colour and lighting at the exhibition, see 'The Story of Neon Light and its Brothers', *World's Fair Weekly* (4th week, ending 24 June 1933), pp. 16 ff.
52. Helen A. Harrison, *Dawn of a New Day: The New York World's Fair, 1939/40* (New York, 1980).
53. Warren Irving Susman, 'The People's Fair: Cultural Contradictions of a Consumer Society', in Harrison (1980), p. 19.
54. These buildings illustrated the seven themes devised by the Theme Committee to represent the 'major functional divisions of modern living': Production and Distribution, Transportation, Communication and Business Systems, Food, Medicine and Public Health, Science and Education and Community Interests.
55. Walter Dorwin Teague, who was on the Design Board from the start, invited Norman Bel Geddes, Henry Dreyfuss, Raymond Loewy, Egmont Arens, Donald Deskey, Russel Wright and Gilbert Rhode to take part.
56. Hubert Worthington, address to RIBA students, reported in *Pencil Points* (April 1927), p. 197.
57. A. Trystram Edwards, 'The Clash of Colour or the Moor of Argyll Street', *Architectural Review*, vol. lxv (June 1929), pp. 289-98. The 'Moor' reference is explained by the black surface of Hood's building which, he explains, was meant to stand out from the white façades in Argyll Street: 'If you had been black, I would have been white'.
58. Ibid.
59. Raymond McGrath, '"Light Opera", Savoy Theatre by Frank Tugwell Architect and Basil Ionides (Interior)', *Architectural Review*, vol. lxvii (1930), p. 21.
60. J. J. Snowdon and R. W. Platts, 'Great West Road Style', *Architectural Review*, vol. mlvi (July 1974), pp. 21-7. The American architect Gilbert was part of the deal, but he never moved to England, and Wallis worked with Thomas Cox and his own son Douglas Wallis.
61. Samuel Lionel Rothafel, known as Roxy, the patron of the RCA Music Hall, claimed to have had a vision of the effect of the interior while watching a sunset on his return to New York by sea in 1931.
62. Chester H. Liebs, *Main Street to Miracle Mile: American Roadside Architecture* (Baltimore, 1985); John A. Jakle and Keith A. Sculle, *The Gas Station in America* (Baltimore, 1994); Richard J. S. Gutman and Elliott Kaufman, *American Diner* (New York, 1979).
63. Two well illustrated German examples are Hans Poelzig's Grosses Schauspielhaus, Berlin, 1919, and Erich Mendelsohn's Universum Cinema, Berlin, 1929-30.
64. See Robert Venturi, *Complexity and Contradiction in Architecture* (New York, 1966) and R. Venturi, D. Scott Brown and S. Izenour, *Learning from Las Vegas* (Cambridge, MA, 1972).
65. See Jean Baudrillard, *America* (New York, 1988): 'The irresistible rise of the simulacrum is something you can simply feel here without the slightest effort' (p. 104).
66. Edwin Avery Park, *New Backgrounds for a New Age* (New York, 1927), cited in Messler (1986), p. 27.

Chapter 23: Art Deco Fashion

1 Evelyn Waugh, *Vile Bodies* (London, 1930; reprinted Harmondsworth, 1953), p. 48.
2 Ibid, p. 51.
3 Francis Scott Fitzgerald, *The Great Gatsby* (New York, 1925; reprinted London, 1993), p. 112.
4 Richard Martin, *Cubism and Fashion* (New York, 1999).
5 Cecil Beaton, *The Glass of Fashion* (London, 1954).
6 Thérèse Bonney and Louise Bonney, *A Shopping Guide to Paris* (New York, 1929).
7 Flamboyant garments with the Myrbor label in the Victoria and Albert Museum came from the wardrobe of society hostess Emilie Grisby, who cultivated a taste for the exotic.
8 Yvonne Brunhammer, *1925* (Paris, 1976).
9 In articles in *Forum* (1922) and *L'Art et la mode* (Paris, 1927).
10 In the archives of the Musée de la Mode et du Textile, Paris.
11 *Country Life*, 18 March 1933.
12 Given to the V&A in 1960.
13 One rare and prime example, 'arguably the dress of the century' (Martin (1999)), is in the collection of the Metropolitan Museum of Art, New York.
14 *Vogue*, 1 October 1926.
15 Amy de la Haye and Valerie Mendes, *Twentieth Century Fashion* (London, 1999).
16 Meredith Etherington-Smith, *Patou* (London, 1983).
17 Bettina Ballard, *In My Fashion* (London, 1960).
18 Doris Langley Moore, *Pandora's Letter Box* (London, 1929).
19 Beverley Nichols, *The Sweet and Twenties* (London, 1958).
20 Micki Forman, 'Tutmania', *Dress*, vol. 4 (1978), pp. 7-14.
21 *Queen* (London, 1924).
22 Pattern books in the Musée Historique des Tissus, Lyon.
23 Elsie de Wolfe, *After All* (London, 1935).
24 Cecil Beaton, *The Book of Beauty* (London, 1930).
25 *Vogue*, 5 March 1967.

Chapter 24: Art Deco Jewellery

1. Hubert Llewellyn Smith, 'Introductory survey', in Department of Overseas Trade, *Reports on the Present Position and Tendencies of the Industrial Arts as indicated at the International Exhibition of Modern Decorative and Industrial Arts, Paris, 1925* (London, 1925), p. 9.
2. Henry Wilson, 'Metalwork', in Department of Overseas Trade (1925), p. 122.
3. Henry Wilson, 'Metalwork', in Department of Overseas Trade (1925), p. 124.
4. *Fémina* (1926).
5. *Queen*, 17 June 1925, p. 13.
6. *Goldsmiths' Journal* (October 1926), p. 82.
7. *Illustrated London News*, 26 September 1925, p. 592.
8. *Queen*, 22 November 1919, p. 680.
9. Loelia, Duchess of Westminster, *Grace and Favour* (London, 1961), p. 97.
10. *Queen*, 11 March 1925, p. 20.
11. *The Watchmaker & Jeweller, Silversmith & Optician* (January 1934).
12. *Goldsmiths' Journal* (May 1928), p. 245, article originally published in the National Jewelers' Publicity Association, Newark, NJ.
13. *Goldsmiths' Journal* (February 1930), p. 656.
14. French *Vogue* (September 1934); Judy Rudoe, *Cartier: 1900-1939* (London, 1998), p. 19.
15. Loelia, Duchess of Westminster (1961), p. 97.
16. *Queen*, 22 November 1919, pp. 680, 676.
17. Loelia, Duchess of Westminster (1961), p. 95.
18. *Queen*, 15 April 1925, p. 9.
19. Georgina Howell, *In Vogue* (London, 1975), p. 105.
20. Henry Wilson, 'Metalwork', in Department of Overseas Trade (1925), p. 123.
21. Gilles Néret, *Boucheron: Four Generations of a World-Renowned Jeweler* (New York, 1988), p. 112.
22. Georges Fouquet, 'Jewellery and Goldsmiths' Work in France', *Studio*, vol. 99 (1930), pp. 327-9.
23. Ibid.
24. *Goldsmiths' Journal* (September 1927), pp. 893-4.
25. Shena Mason, *Jewellery Making in Birmingham, 1750-1995* (Chichester, 1998), p. 125.
26. *Goldsmiths' Journal* (September 1930), p. 703.
27. Sylvie Raulet, *Art Deco Jewellery* (London, 1985), p. 255.
28. *The Jeweller and Metalworker*, 1 July 1925, p. 948.
29. Mason (1998), p. 117. There were, however, slight upsurges in 1923, 1925 and 1928.
30. *Goldsmiths' Journal* (January 1928).
31. *Goldsmiths' Journal* (May 1928), p. 256.
32. *Queen*, 22 April 1925, p. 3.
33. *Goldsmiths' Journal* (September 1928), p. 826, article originally published in the National Jewelers Publicity Association, Newark, NJ.
34. Ibid.
35. *Goldsmiths' Journal* (May 1928), p. 242, article originally published in the National Jewelers Publicity Association, Newark, NJ.

36. *The Jeweller and Metalworker*, 15 February 1934, p. 188.
37. Henry Wilson, 'Metalwork', in Department of Overseas Trade (1925), p. 117.

Chapter 25: Photography and the New Vision

1. Yvonne Deslandres, *Paul Poiret* (London, 1987), p. 130; Martin Harrison, *Shots of Style: Great Fashion Photographs Chosen by David Bailey* (London, 1985), pp. 15-16.
2. Anne Ehrenkranz, *A Singular Elegance: The Photographs of Baron Adolf de Meyer* (San Francisco, 1994), p. 35.
3. John Szarkowski, *Photography until Now* (New York, 1989), p. 189.
4. Reissued as *Encyclopédie des arts décoratifs et industriels modernes au XXème siècle*, 12 vols (New York, 1977).
5. See Jean-Christophe Molinier and others, *Jardins de ville privés, 1890-1930* (Paris, 1991), front jacket flap. For Kahn's project more generally, see Jeanne Beausoleil, *Albert Kahn, 1860-1940: Réalités d'une utopie* (Boulogne sur Seine, 1995).
6. *Rapport général: Exposition des arts décoratifs et industriels modernes*, vol. ix (Paris, 1929), p. 53.
7. Vladimir Birgus, *The Photographer František Drtikol* (Prague, 2000), p. 29.
8. Ibid, p. 30.
9. Ibid, p. 42.
10. Mark Haworth-Booth and Brian Coe, *A Guide to Early Photographic Processes* (London, 1983), pp. 23, 92.
11. Birgus (2000), p. 42.
12. Ibid, p. 48.
13. Edward Steichen, *A Life in Photography* (Garden City, NY, and London, 1963), n.p., Chapter 7.
14. Quoted in Ronald J. Gedrim (ed.), *Edward Steichen: Selected Texts and Bibliography* (Oxford, 1996), p. 81.
15. Ibid.
16. Patricia Johnston, *Real Fantasies: Edward Steichen's Advertising Photography* (Berkeley, 1997), p. 113.
17. Ibid.
18. Ibid, p. 107.
19. Steichen (1963), Chapter 7.
20. Johnston (1997), p. 128.
21. Steichen (1963), plate 190.
22. Ehrenkranz (1994), pp. 122-33.
23. Ibid, p. 116.
24. Vicki Goldberg, *Margaret Bourke-White: A Biography* (New York, 1986), plate 28.
25. Jonathan Silverman, *The Life of Margaret Bourke-White* (New York, 1983), p. 12.
26. Goldberg (1983), pp. 143-4, plate 27.
27. Emmanuelle de l'Ecotais and Alain Sayag, *Man Ray: Photography and its Double* (Paris and London, 1998), pp. 60-61.
28. Personal communication from Man Ray to the author.
29. John Esten, Willis Hartshorn and Merry Foresta, *Man Ray in Fashion* (New York, 1990), p. 18.
30. Ibid, p. 16.
31. *Art et décoration*, vol. xlix (January – June 1926), pp. 53-60.
32. Virginia Zabriskie, letter to the present writer (8 December 1994): 'Michael Fresson remembers his father working on the screens that were commissioned for the *Normandie*. I was told that these screens were for the children's playroom and that she also designed the furniture'. Albin-Guillot file, Photography Collection, Department of Prints, Drawings and Paintings, V&A. Albin-Guillot's own copy of *Micrographie décorative* is in the National Art Library at the V&A.
33. See especially Christian Bouqueret, *Des Années folles aux Années noires: La Nouvelle Vision photographique en France, 1920-1940* (Paris, 1997); Dominique Baqué, 'Le Premier Grand Illustré français, *Vu*' in Dominique Bacqué (ed.) *Les Documents de la modernité: Anthologies de textes sur la photographie de 1919 à 1939* (Paris, 1993); Sandra Phillips, David Travis and Weston J. Naef, *André Kertész of Paris and New York* (London, 1985); Kim Sichel, *Germaine Krull: Photographer of Modernity* (Cambridge, MA, and London, 1999).
34. Many of the photographers referred to here are represented in the extraordinary Ford Motor Company Collection, assembled by John C. Waddell, at the Metropolitan Museum of Art, New York; see Maria Morris Hambourg and Christopher Phillips, *The New Vision: Photography between the World Wars: Ford Motor Company Collection at the Metropolitan Museum of Art, New York* (New York, 1989).
35. I am indebted to Lisa Kolosek, who wrote the first book on Bonney, for kindly sharing her research with me; see Lisa Kolosek, *The Invention of Chic: Thérèse Bonney and Paris Moderne* (New York and London, 2002). There are major Bonney archives at the Bancroft Library, University of California, Berkeley; the Cooper-Hewitt, National Design Museum, New York; the Bibliothèque Historique de la Ville de Paris and the Caisse Nationale des Monuments Historiques et des Sites, Paris. An intriguing glimpse of Bonney is offered by R. Becherer, 'Picturing Architecture Otherwise: The Voguing of the Maison Mallet-Stevens', *Art History*, vol. 23, no. 4 (November 2000), pp. 559-98.
36. I am indebted to the as-yet-unpublished doctoral research into the history and aesthetics of *Vu* by Penelope Rook, post-graduate student at the Courtauld Institute of Art, London.
37. An exhibition and publication on Hoppé are in preparation by Graham Howe, director of the E. O. Hoppé Archive at Curatorial Assistance, Inc., Pasadena, California.
38. See David Mellor, *Modern British Photography, 1919-1939* (London, 1980).
39. See James Enyeart, *Bruguière: His Photographs and his Life* (New York, 1977).
40. Cecil Beaton, *Photobiography* (London, 1951), p. 26.
41. Ibid, p. 43.
42. For generously sharing his insights into the subject of this essay, I offer sincere thanks to Philippe Garner.

Chapter 26: Art Deco Graphic Design and Typography

1. Gaston Quénioux, *Les Arts décoratifs modernes (France)* (Paris, 1925).
2. Thorstein Veblen, *Theory of the Leisure Class* (New York, 1899; reprinted with an introduction by Robert Lekachman, New York and London, 1994); Adolf Loos, 'Ornament and Crime' (1908) in *Ornament and Crime: Selected Essays/ Adolf Loos* (Riverside, CA, 1998).
3. C. H. St John Hornby in Department of Overseas Trade, *Reports on the Present Position and Tendencies of the Industrial Arts as indicated at the International Exhibition of Modern Decorative and Industrial Arts, Paris, 1925* (London, 1925).
4. For a contemporary review of bookbindings, see Rose Adler, *Reliures*, (Paris, 1931).
5. See Chapter 13. Books such as Frederick Kiesler, *Contemporary Art Applied to the Store* (London, 1930) and René Herbst, *Modern French Shops and the Interior* (London, 1927) were important for the dissemination of these ideas.
6. Steven Heller and Louise Fili, *French Modern: Art Deco Graphic Design* (San Francisco, 1997), p. 31.
7. Patricia Frantz Kery, *Art Deco Graphics* (London, 1986). See Chapter 10 for a full consideration of the origins of Art Deco ornament.
8. See Chapter 16, in particular.
9. On the French situation, see Nancy Troy, *Modernism and the Decorative Arts in France: Art Nouveau to Le Corbusier* (New Haven and London, 1991); for the Werkbund, see Frederic J. Schwartz, *The Werkbund: Design Theory and Mass Culture before the First World War* (New Haven and London, 1996).
10. For the full range of the exhibition display, see 'L'Art du Livre', in *Encyclopédie des arts décoratifs et industriels modernes au XXème siècle*, 12 vols (Paris, 1925; reprinted New York, 1977).
11. See Chapter 25.
12. Erté, *Things I Remember: An Autobiography* (London, 1975).
13. Arlette Barré-Despond, *UAM: Union des artistes modernes* (Paris, 1986).
14. Henri Mouron, *Cassandre: Posters, Typography, Stage Designs* (London, 1985).
15. On Modernism in the United States, see James Sloan Allen, *The Romance of Commerce and Culture: Capitalism, Modernism, and the Chicago–Aspen Crusade for Cultural Reform* (Chicago and London, 1983).
16. André Thérive, 'Paul Colin: Peintre de décors et d'affiches', *Arts et métiers graphiques*, no. 10 (March 1929), pp. 615-20; Henry Louis Gates Jr and Karen C. C. Dalton, *Josephine Baker and La Revue Nègre: Paul Colin's Lithographs of Le Tumulte Noir in Paris 1927* (New York, 1997).
17. Fernand Léger, 'Notes on Contemporary Plastic Life' (1923), in Edward F. Fry (ed.), *Functions of Painting by Fernand Léger* (London, 1973).
18. Christopher Green, 'Léger and L'Esprit Nouveau', in Tate Gallery, *Léger and Purist Paris* (London, 1970).
19. Blaise Cendrars and Fernand Léger, *La Fin du monde (filmée par l'ange)* (Paris, 1919).
20. Mark Haworth-Booth, *E. McKnight Kauffer: A Designer and his Public* (London, 1979).
21. Heinz Waibl, *The Roots of Italian Visual Communication* (Castellarano, 1998). See also, Germano Celant, *Marcello Nizzoli* (Milan, 1968) and Gabriella Belli, *Depero Futurista: Rome – Paris – New York, 1915-1932* (Milan, 1999).
22. Kery (1986), p. 29.
23. Jeremy Aynsley, *Graphic Design in Germany, 1890-1945* (London, 2000).
24. For new typefaces and aspects of the typographic industry in the inter-war years, see Christopher Burke, *Paul Renner: The Art of Typography* (London, 1998). In France, Charles Peignot (1897-1983) oversaw the creation of new typeface designs for Deberny et Peignot from 1923 until c.1960. In the 1950s the firm made fonts for the new Lumitype phototypesetting machines; however, the extent of Peignot's investment in Lumitype cost him the control of Deberny et Peignot.
25. Cassandre [Adolphe Mouron], 'Bifur, caractère de publicité dessiné par A. M. Cassandre', *Arts et métiers graphiques*, no. 9 (January 1929), p. 578.
26. Raymond M. Hood and Arthur T. North, *Raymond Hood* (New York and London, 1931).
27. For Walter Benjamin, see Susan Buck-Morss, *The Dialectics of Seeing: Walter Benjamin and the Arcades Project* (Cambridge, MA, 1991) and Walter Benjamin, *The Arcades Project* (Cambridge, MA and London, 1999). For Siegfried Kracauer, see the essays 'The Mass Ornament', 'Boredom' and 'Farewell to the Linden Arcade' in Siegfried Kracauer, *The Mass Ornament: Weimar Essays* (Frankfurt am Main, c. 1963; translated and edited by Thomas Y. Levin, Cambridge, MA and London, 1995). For a recent commentary on critical theory and urban display, see Janet Ward, *Weimar Surfaces: Urban Visual Culture in 1920s Germany* (Berkeley and London, 2001).
28. For the work of Bauhaus graphic and typographic designers, see Ute Brüning (ed.), *Das A und O des Bauhauses* (Leipzig, 1995).
29. For this point of view, see Jan Tschichold, *The New Typography: A Handbook for Modern Designers* (Berlin, 1928; translated by R. McLean with an introduction by Robin Kinross, Berkeley, c. 1995).
30. The Deutscher Werkbund exhibition of that name, *Form ohne Ornament*, was held in Stuttgart in 1924.
31. The most famous was by the American Walter Dill Scott, *The Theory of Advertising* (London, 1909), which was available in French by 1911 as *Commerce et industrie: Les Procédes modernes de vente* (Paris, 1911). For a commentary on American approaches to advertising at this time, see Roland Marchand, *Advertising the American Dream: Making Way for Modernity, 1920-1940* (Berkeley, 1985).
32. Douglas McMurtrie, *Modern Typography and Layout* (Chicago, 1929) and Alfred Tolmer, *Mis en Page: The Theory and Practice of Lay-out* (London, 1931). Traditionally, these texts have been interpreted as falling outside pedigree Modernism.
33. Heller and Fili (1995).
34. See Chapter 34 in this volume. Jeffrey L. Meikle, *Twentieth Century Limited: Industrial Design in America, 1925-1939* (Philadelphia, 1979).
35. For his own account of this, see Raymond Loewy, *Never Leave Well Enough Alone* (New York, 1951).

Chapter 27: Art Deco Bindings

1. See J. Léautaud, 'Modern Bindings for Modern Books', *International Studio*, vol. 84 (June 1926), pp. 70-73.
2. Société de la Reliure Originale (Jacques-Anthoine Legrain and others), *Pierre Legrain, relieur: Répertoire descriptif et bibliographique de mille deux cent trente-six reliures* (Paris, 1965), p. xix.
3. Ibid.
4. Renée Moutard-Uldry, 'Paul Bonet', *L'Art et les artistes*, vol. 34 (March 1937), p. 203.
5. Léautaud (1926), p. 70. He credited Doucet with encouraging, more or less single-handedly, 'the development of the new renaissance in bookbinding'.

Chapter 30: Art Deco and Hollywood Film

1. John Vassos, 'The Movies', in John Vassos and Ruth Vassos, *Contempo: This American Tempo* (New York, 1929), n.p.
2. From Commission on Educational and Cultural Films, *The Film in National Life* (London, 1932), p. 78; quoted in Jeffery Richards, *The Age of the Dream Palace* (London, 1984), p. 11.
3. Marcel L'Herbier, *Cinéma d'aujourd'hui*, no. 78, p. 84; quoted in Jean-François Pinchon, *Rob. Mallet Stevens: Architecture, Furniture and Interior Design* (Cambridge, MA, 1990), p. 95.
4. The Club des Amis du Septième Art (CASA) was established in 1921 by Louis Delluc. Members included Marcel L'Herbier, Jean Epstein, Germaine Dulac, Abel Gance, Rob Mallet-Stevens, Fernand Léger, Blaise Cendrars and Jean Cocteau. Its aim was to raise cinema to the level of other arts.
5. Paul Rotha, *Celluloid: The Film Today* (London, 1933), p. 46.
6. See Neal Gabler, *An Empire of their Own: How the Jews Invented Hollywood* (New York, 1988); Lary May, *Screening out the Past: The Birth of Mass Culture and the Motion Picture Industry* (Oxford, 1980).
7. See Robert Sklar, *Movie-Made America: A Cultural History of American Movies* (New York, 1975).
8. Howard S. Cullman, quoted in Allardyce Nicoll, *Film and Theatre* (London, 1936), p. 7.
9. Hortense Powdermaker coined the phrase in her book *Hollywood: The Dream Factory* (London, 1951).
10. These techniques committed exhibitors to programmes of films, sight unseen, and with often only a title to go on.
11. By 1925, for example, 95% of screen time in Britain was dedicated to showing American films, and similar inroads were made elsewhere.
12. Sir Philip Cunliffe Lester, President of the Board of Trade, quoted in Richards (1984), p. 62.
13. Lt Col. R. V. K. Applin, quoted in the House of Commons by the *Daily Express*, 18 March 1927; quoted in Richards (1984), p. 63.
14. John Bird, *Cinema Parade: Fifty Years of Film Shows* (Birmingham, 1947), p. 15.
15. Quoted in Roger Manvell, *Film* (London, 1944), p. 131.
16. Nicoll (1936), p. 177.
17. Quoted in Beverly Heisner, *The Art of Hollywood* (London, 1990), p. 76.
18. May (1980), p. 205.
19. Quoted in Donald Albrecht, *Designing Dreams: Modern Architecture in the Movies* (London, 1986), p. 40.
20. Quoted in Howard Mandelbaum and Eric Myers, *Screen Deco: A Celebration of High Style in Hollywood* (Santa Monica and Bromley, 1985), p. 140.
21. Rotha (1933), pp. 50-51.
22. See Howard Gutner, *Gowns by Adrian: The MGM Years, 1928-1941* (New York and London, 2001).
23. F. Scott Fitzgerald, *The Jazz Age* (New York, 1931), p. 9.
24. H. Llewellyn Smith and others, *The New Survey of London Life and Labour*, vol. 9 (London, 1935), p. 47.
25. J. P. Mayer, *British Cinemas and their Audiences* (London, 1948), p. 43.
26. Margaret Farrand Thorp, *America at the Movies* (New Haven, 1939; reprints, London, 1946, New York, 1970).
27. Siegfried Kracauer, *The Mass Ornament* (Frankfurt am Main, c.1963; translated and edited by Thomas Y. Levin, Cambridge, MA and London, 1995).
28. Quoted in Michael Minden and Holger Brachman (eds), *Fritz Lang's Metropolis: Cinematic Visions of Technology and Fear* (Rochester, 2000), p. 4.
29. Fitzgerald (1931), p. 5.

Chapter 31: 'The Filter of American Taste': Design in the USA in the 1920s

Grateful thanks are due to Jewel Stern, whose pioneering research yielded some of the best sources quoted in this essay. Thanks also to Dr Joel Hoffman, who gave this text his customary insightful editing.

1. Gilbert Seldes, 'Profiles: The Long Road to Roxy', *New Yorker*, vol. 9 (February 25, 1933), p. 24.
2. C. Adolph Glassgold, 'Some Modern Furniture Designers', *The House Beautiful*, vol. 67 (February 1930), p. 165.
3. *Report of a Commission appointed by the Secretary of Commerce to Visit and Report upon the International Exposition of Modern Decorative and Industrial Art in Paris, 1925* (Washington, 1926), p. 16.
4. Quoted in Janet Kardon (ed.), *Craft in the Machine Age: The History of Twentieth-Century American Craft, 1920-1945* (New York, 1996), p. 253.
5. In 1929, Bach presented *The Architect and Industrial Arts: An Exhibition of Contemporary American Design*, which displayed room settings by nine different architects. The exhibition was so popular that its original six-week run was extended to over six months. The Metropolitan Museum of Art library has a full run of these catalogues.
6. Ella Burns Meyers, 'Trends in Decoration', *Good Furniture Magazine* (September 1928), p. 128. This article clearly demonstrates that the vocabulary for describing the new style was interchangeable in 1930s America. On page 128 alone, the terms 'modern', 'moderne', 'modernistic' and 'modernism' are all used equally to describe these 'trends in decoration'.
7. Samuel Reyburn, *An Exposition of Modern French Decorative Art: Lord & Taylor, New York* (New York, 1928), introduction (n.p.).
8. Quoted in Gordon Eliot Sands, 'The Osborn Furniture: Modern Decorative Arts and the Department Store', *The Decorative Arts Society Newsletter*, vol. 9 (September 1983), p. 2. See Sands' article for a detailed account of the way Mrs Osborn achieved a French Art Deco look on an American middle-class budget. Her letters, now in the Beinecke Rare Book and Manuscript Library at Yale University, discuss ordering bedroom furniture from Lord & Taylor.
9. Nellie Sanford, 'An Architect-Designer of Modern Furniture', *Good Furniture Magazine*, vol. 30 (March 1928), pp. 116-17.
10. Ibid, p. 118.
11. See, for example, Glassgold (1930), p. 166. He compares Schoen with the émigré designers, writing, 'for while Schoen shows French influence, the others, excepting Miss Karasz, evidence an artistic heritage culled from German or Austrian sources'.
12. Seldes (1933), p. 24.
13. See exhibition catalogue, *Contempora Exposition of Arts and Industry* (New York, 1929).
14. Seldes (1933), p. 24.
15. Paul T. Frankl, *Form and Re-form: A Practical Handbook of Modern Interiors* (New York, 1930), p. 51.
16. 1925: Les Tendances générales', *L'Amour de l'art*, vol. 6 (1925), p. 288-9; quoted in Kathryn B. Hiesinger and George H. Marcus, *Landmarks of Twentieth-Century Design* (New York, 1993), p. 77.
17. C. Adolph Glassgold, 'The Decorative Arts', *Arts*, vol. 14 (December 1928), p. 341.
18. Mary Fanton Roberts, 'Beauty Combined with Convenience in Some Modernistic Rooms', *Arts & Decoration*, vol. 30 (February 1929), p. 72; quoted in Ashley Brown, 'Ilonka Karasz: Rediscovering a Modernist Pioneer', *Studies in the Decorative Arts*, vol. 8 (Fall-Winter 2000-2001), p. 80.
19. Helen Appleton Read, 'Twentieth-Century Decoration: The Filter of American Taste', *Vogue*, vol. 71 (June 1928), p. 116.
20. Frankl (1930), p. 3.
21. 'American Modernist Furniture Inspired by Sky-Scraper Architecture', *Good Furniture*, vol. 29 (September 1927), p. 119.
22. 'Metals that Lend Harmony to the Home', *New York Times*, 11 December 1927, p. 116.
23. Henry Adams, *Viktor Schreckengost and 20th-Century Design* (Cleveland, 2000), p. 15.
24. *New York Times*, 11 December 1927, p. 115.
25. 'Skyscraper Age in Silver', *Boston Evening Transcript*, 13 January 1928. From Shreve Company archives, Black Scrapbook, Courtesy the Rhode Island School of Design.
26. As quoted in Glassgold (1928), p. 229; quoted in Richard Guy Wilson, Dianne H. Pilgrim and Dickran Tashjian, *The Machine Age in America, 1918-1941* (New York, 1986), p. 294.
27. Glassgold (1930), p. 166.
28. Jeffrey L. Meikle, 'Domesticating Modernity: Ambivalence and Appropriation, 1920-1940', in Wendy Kaplan (ed.), *Designing Modernity: The Arts of Reform and Persuasion, 1885-1945: Selections from the Wolfsonian* (London, 1995), pp. 143-68.

Chapter 32: American Metalwork between the Wars

1. Charles Venable, *Silver in America, 1840-1940: A Century of Splendor* (Dallas, 1995), p. 248.
2. For more on chromium, see Richard Guy Wilson, Dianne H. Pilgrim and Dickran Tashjian, *The Machine Age in America, 1918-1941* (New York, 1986), p. 314; Donald-Brian Johnson, *Chase Complete: Deco Specialties of the Chase Brass & Copper Co.* (Atglen, PA, 1999). For aluminium, see Sarah Nichols, *Aluminum by Design* (Pittsburgh, PA, 2000).
3. The persistence of Arts and Crafts styles, especially the colonial revival, is evident as late as 1937, when the Brooklyn Museum's exhibition on contemporary silver included Scandinavian-inspired silver by Smed, a Federal-style tea urn by Gebelein and simple, lobed bowls by Arthur Stone; see Brooklyn Museum, *Contemporary Industrial and Handwrought Silver* (Brooklyn, 1937).
4. For Bowles and Zimmermann, see Wendy Kaplan (ed.), *'The Art That is Life': The Arts & Crafts Movement in America, 1875-1920* (Boston, 1987), pp. 268-9, cat. 130; pp. 270-72, cat. 132. For Brigham, see Marilee Boyd Meyer and others, *Inspiring Reform: Boston's Arts and Crafts Movement* (New York, 1997), p. 207.
5. Robert Judson Clark and others, *Design in America: The Cranbrook Vision, 1925-1950* (New York, 1983), pp. 164-7.
6. Jeannine Falino, 'Women Metalsmiths', in Pat Kirkham (ed.), *Women Designers in the USA: 1900-2000* (New York, 2000), pp. 234-5.
7. Martin Eidelberg (ed.), *Design 1935-1965: What Modern Was* (New York, 1991), p. 81, fig. 94.
8. Claire Selkurt, 'New Classicism: Design of the 1920s in Denmark', *The Journal of Decorative and Propaganda Arts*, vol. 4 (Spring 1987), pp. 16-29.
9. Karen Davies, *At Home in Manhattan: Modern Decorative Arts, 1925 to the Depression* (New Haven, 1983), p. 114, cat. 80; Falino (2000), figs 9-11; Annelies Krekel-Aalberse, *Art Nouveau and Art Deco Silver* (New York, 1989), p. 125.
10. Venable (1995), p. 278.
11. Alastair Duncan, *Modernism: Modernist Design, 1880-1940. The Norwest Collection, Norwest Corporation, Minneapolis* (Woodbridge, 1998), p. 235; Falino (2000), p. 233.
12. Davies (1983), p. 76, cat. 54. A similar service in silver was made by Tiffany & Co. (private collection).
13. J. Stewart Johnson, *American Modern, 1925-1940: Design for a New Age* (New York, 2000), p. 85.
14. Gift catalogue, 1936 Revere Copper & Brass Incorporated, catalogue item no. 7044. Designer Frederick Preiss created candlesticks (not illustrated) in 1937 to match the tray. Information on the Bel Geddes service was provided by former Revere employee Michael T. Hoke.
15. For a survey of all the industrial design exhibitions at the Metropolitan Museum of Art, see R. Craig Miller, 'Modern Design at the Metropolitan Museum of Art', *Modern Design in the Metropolitan Museum of Art, 1890-1990* (New York, 1990), pp. 1-45. The International Silver Company produced Saarinen's urn in silver; their Wilcox division produced a version in silver plate; see Johnson (2000), pp. 106, 173. For the Von Nessen design, see Johnson (1999) p. 217.

Chapter 33: New Materials and Technologies

1. Paul T. Frankl, *New Dimensions: The Decorative Arts of Today in Words & Pictures* (New York, 1928), p. 61.
2. Robert R. Updegraff, *The New American Tempo: And the Stream of Life* (Chicago, 1929).
3. Paul T. Frankl, *Form and Re-Form: A Practical Handbook of Modern Interiors* (New York, 1930), pp. 1633.
4. Douglas B. Hobbs, 'Aluminum – A Decorative Metal', *Good Furniture and Decoration*, vol.35 (August 1930), p. 94.
5. Walter Dorwin Teague, 'Structural and Decorative Trends in Glass', *American Architect*, vol. 141 (May 1932), p. 110.
6. Harold Eberlein and Cortlandt Hubbard, *Glass in Modern Construction: Its Place in Architectural Design and Decoration* (New York, 1937), p. 22.
7. Libby-Owens-Ford Glass Company, *52 Designs to Modernize Main Street with Glass* (Toledo, 1935), p. 1.
8. Teague (1932), p. 112.
9. Nathan George Horwitt, 'Plans for Tomorrow: A Seminar in Creative Design', *Advertising Arts* (July 1934), p. 29.
10. 'What Man Has Joined Together…', *Fortune*, vol. 13 (March 1936), p. 69.
11. Guild quoted in E. F. Lougee, 'From Old to New with Lurelle Guild', *Modern Plastics*, vol. 12 (March 1935), p. 14.
12. Teague quoted in 'Designers' Task Defined', *New York Times*, 13 December 1939, p. 42.
13. Peter Müller-Munk, 'The Future of Product Design', *Modern Plastics*, vol. 20 (June 1943), p. 77.
14. Franklin E. Brill, 'What Shapes for Phenolics', *Modern Plastics*, vol. 13 (September 1935), p. 21.
15. Peter Müller-Munk, 'Vending Machine Glamour', *Modern Plastics*, vol. 17 (February 1940), p. 66.
16. Richard Guy Wilson, Dianne H. Pilgrim and Dickran Tashjian, *The Machine Age in America, 1918-1941* (New York, 1986), p. 147.

Chapter 34: The Search for an American Design Aesthetic: From Art Deco to Streamlining

1. Constance Rourke, 'American Art: A Possible Future', *American Magazine of Art*, vol. xxvii, no. 7 (July 1935), pp. 390-404; quotes from pp. 395, 392.
2. Paul Frankl, 'Just What is this Modernistic Movement', *Arts & Decoration*, vol. xxix, no. 1 (May 1928), pp. 56-7, 108, 117; quote from p. 56.
3. Ibid, p. 56.
4. 'Editorial: Designers – European and American', *Good Furniture Magazine*, vol. xxxii, no. 4 (April 1929), pp. 167, 172; quote from p. 167.
5. Between 1925 and 1927 Stehli produced textile patterns by well known American artists. These included Edward Steichen's abstractions of ordinary objects such as matches, sugar cubes and mothballs (see Chapter 25), and the cheerful John Held Jr designs of cartoonish jazz bands and jitterbugging college boys.
6. As note 4.
7. Nellie C. Sanford, 'Modern Furniture Designed in America: It Must Meet American Living Conditions', *Good Furniture Magazine* (April 1929), pp. 184-92; quotes from pp. 184, 186.
8. Ibid, pp. 184, 186.
9. Matlack Price, 'Contempora', *Good Furniture Magazine* (May 1929), pp. 71-6; quotes from pp. 71, 76.
10. Ibid, pp. 71, 76. By 1940 63% of America's foreign-born population had become naturalized, an increase above the 55% figure in 1930. Likewise, immigration to the USA dropped substantially between the 1920s and the 1930s.
11. Paul Frankl, *Form and Re-Form: A Practical Handbook for Modern Interiors* (New York, 1930), p. 13.
12. The former including Frederick Kiesler, Kem Weber, Winold Reiss, Ilonka Karasz, Joseph Urban, William Lescaze and Walter Von Nessen; the latter including Frank Lloyd Wright, Donald Deskey, Ruth Reeves, Gilbert Rohde and Eugene Schoen.
13. See C. Adolph Glassgold, 'Modern American Industrial Design', *Arts & Decoration*, vol. xxxv, no. 3 (July 1931), pp. 30-31, 87; quotes from p. 30. AUDAC's members included Lucian Bernhard, Donald Deskey, Frederick Kiesler, Robert Leonard, Lee Simonson, Kem Weber and Paul Frankl. See Mel Byars, 'Introduction: What Makes American Design American?', in Richard Lawrence Leonard and C. Adolph Glassgold (eds), *Modern American Design: By the American Union of Decorative Artists and Craftsmen* (New York, 1930; reprinted New York, 1992), pp. v-xix.
14. Frankl (1930), pp. 18-19.
15. Charles R. Richards, 'Sane and Insane Modernism in Furniture', *Good Furniture Magazine* (January 1929), pp. 8-14: quotes from pp. 8, 11, 10, 13.
16. See 'Are We Different?', *Arts & Decoration*, vol. xl, no. 11 (December 1933), p. 18. For Frankl's evolving views, see Paul Frankl, *New Dimensions: The Decorative Arts of Today in Words and Pictures* (New York, 1928), pp. 16-17.
17. Elizabeth M. Boykin, 'The Grace of Modern Glass Design', *Arts & Decoration*, vol. xxxvii, no. 5 (September 1932), pp. 15, 59; quotes from pp. 15, 59.
18. Wilhelm Lotz, 'Industrial Art in Germany', *American Magazine of Art*, vol. xxii, no. 2 (February 1931), p. 103-8.
19. Norman Bel Geddes, *Horizons* (Boston, 1932), p. 222.
20. Earnest Elmo Calkins, 'Advertising, Builder of Taste', *American Magazine of Art*, vol. xxi, no. 9 (September 1930), pp. 497-502 (quote from p. 499.)
21. Roy Sheldon and Egmont Arens, *Consumer Engineering: A New Technique for Prosperity* (New York, 1932), p. 2.
22. 'Modern Growing Up?', *Arts & Decoration*, vol. xlii, no. 2 (December 1934), p. 2.
23. Harold Van Doren, *Industrial Design: A Practical Guide to Product Design and Development* (New York, 1940; reprinted New York, 1954), p. 180.
24. This success helped to secure a role for the industrial design profession.
25. 'Consumer Engineering', *Product Engineering*, vol. 2, no. 5 (May 1931), p. 221.
26. Jeffrey L. Meikle, *Twentieth Century Limited: Industrial Design in America, 1925-1939* (Philadelphia, 1979), pp. 48, 36, 49. Bel Geddes had befriended Mendelsohn in 1924.
27. 'AE-79, Chapter 75', autobiography, stamped 1955; memorandum, 26 October 1933, from Norman Bel Geddes to Earl Newsom regarding Chrysler 'Secret Account'; NBG Archive, Harry Ransom Humanities Research Center, University of Texas, Austin. See also Nicolas P. Maffei, 'Designing the Image of the Practical Visionary: Norman Bel Geddes, 1893-1958', unpublished PhD thesis, Royal College of Art, London, 2001.
28. 'I salute Walter P. Chrysler and Fred Zeder FOR BUILDING THIS AUTHENTIC AIRFLOW CAR'; advertisement, *Saturday Evening Post*, 16 December 1933. Chrysler Corporation, Q account, 271, O/S7, advertisement announcing arrival of Airflow. NBG Archive, Harry Ransom Humanities Research Center, University of Texas, Austin.
29. Jeffrey L. Meikle, 'Domesticating Modernity: Ambivalence and Appropriation, 1920-1940', in Wendy Kaplan (ed.), *Designing Modernity: The Arts of Reform and Persuasion, 1885-1945* (London, 1995). Contemporaries, including Frankl, spoke of 'domesticating' the machine.
30. Franklin E. Brill, 'Designing for the Eye', *Product Engineering*, vol. 4, no. 1 (January 1933), pp. 16, 17.
31. Arthur Pulos, 'Nothing Succeeds like Success: Raymond Loewy, the Thirties and Forties', in Angela Schönberger (ed.), *Raymond Loewy: Pioneer of American Industrial Design* (Munich, 1990), pp. 80-81.
32. It also domesticated the transatlantic passage that changed the lives of so many émigrés.
33. See Richard F. Bach, 'Machanalia', *American Magazine of Art*, vol. xxii, no. 2 (February 1931), p. 101; John McAndrew, '"Modernistic" and "Streamlined"', *Bulletin of the Museum of Modern Art*, vol. 6, no. 5 (December 1938), pp. 2-3.
34. Philip Johnson 'History of Machine Art: Machine Art and Handicraft', Museum of Modern Art, *Machine Art* (New York, 1934; reprints 1969, 1994), n.p.
35. Alfred H. Barr Jr, 'Machine Art and Geometrical Beauty', in Museum of Modern Art (1934; 1969, 1994), n.p.
36. Sheldon Cheney and Martha Candler Cheney, *Art and the Machine: An Account of Industrial Design in 20th-Century America* (New York, 1936), pp. 98, 102.
37. Van Doren (1940/1954), pp. 179, 189, 196, 187.
38. Russel Wright, in H. G. T., 'Outlines for Living', *Arts & Decoration*, vol. xxxix, no. 7 (November 1933), pp. 6-9; quotes from p. 8.
39. E. H., 'Fashion and Furniture', *Arts & Decoration*, vol. xl, no. 3 (January 1934), pp. 21-5; quotes from pp. 21, 23.
40. The Futurama emphasized streamlined living, where science, technology and urban planning would make for more efficient travel, increased health and a superior standard of living. In a simulated aeroplane flight the miniature world was viewed from moving seats by 27,500 people a day for nearly two years.
41. Sigfried Giedion, *Mechanization Takes Command: A Contribution to Anonymous History* (Oxford, 1948), p. 608.
42. Ibid, p. 611.
43. 'Does American Have a Design Heritage?', *Product Engineering*, vol. 30, no. 20 (18 May 1959), pp. 36-43; Dreyfuss quotes from pp. 36, 37.
44. Rourke (1935), pp. 390-404; quotes from p. 392.

Chapter 35: Art Deco in East Asia

1. *All About Shanghai* (Shanghai, 1934; reprinted Oxford, 1983), pp. 43-4.
2. Akimoto Shunkichi, *The Lure of Japan* (Tokyo, 1934), pp. 51-2.
3. *Catalogue illustré de la Section japonaise à l'Exposition internationale des arts décoratifs et industriels modernes* (Paris, 1925), p. 10.
4. Department of Overseas Trade, *Reports on the Present Position and Tendencies of the Industrial Arts as indicated at the International Exhibition of Modern Decorative and Industrial Arts, Paris, 1925* (London, 1925), p. 56.
5. Both groups sought to create a new style of art, though the latter aimed to do so within the framework of Chinese traditions. The troubled political situation in China (see page 37) meant that the Chinese Government was not in a position to participate directly in the exhibition. Nor did it provide the organizers with any financial support.
6. *La Chine à l'Exposition internationale des arts décoratifs et industriels modernes à Paris 1925* (Paris, 1925), p. 21.
7. Department of Overseas Trade (1925), p. 114.
8. See Craig Clunas, 'Chinese Art and Chinese Artists in France, 1924-1925', *Arts asiatiques: Annales du museé Guimet et du musée Cernuschi*, vol. 44 (1989), pp. 100-106.
9. The period takes it name and dates from the reign of the Emperor Taishō. Compared to his dynamic father, Emperor Meiji, Taishō was an insubstantial figure. He was plagued by a mental illness that was to lead to his own son, Hirohito, being declared Regent in 1920.
10. You could live in a 'cultural house', buy a 'cultural rice cooker', etc.
11. This term is an abbreviation of Ginza and *burabura*, an adverb that indicates wandering with little aim other than the chance encounter of pleasures along the way.
12. Men had begun to wear western style clothes in the Meiji period, but in the 1920s most Japanese women, even in urban areas, continued to wear kimono. Long hair had always been a symbol of feminine beauty in Japan.
13. The first Imperial Hotel had been built in Neo-Renaissance style in 1890. By 1910 it was decided that a larger, more up-to-date hotel was needed.
14. Frank Lloyd Wright, *The Future of Architecture* (New York, 1953); quoted in Kevin Nute, *Frank Lloyd Wright and Japan: The Role of Traditional Japanese Art and Architecture in the Work of Frank Lloyd Wright* (New York and London, 1993), p. 154.
15. For an analysis of the buildings and its relationship to Japanese architecture, see Margo Stipe, 'Wright and Japan', in Anthony Alofsin (ed.), *Frank Lloyd Wright: Europe and Beyond* (Berkeley and London, 1999), pp. 31-42.
16. The earthquake struck on the opening day of the new hotel. Its survival owed more to luck than to Wright's 'floating' foundations. The Imperial Hotel also survived the Second World War, but in 1965 it was demolished. The entrance hall, lobby and reflecting pool were saved and re-erected at the Meiji Mura, a huge outdoor architectural museum near Nagoya. A new high-rise Imperial Hotel now stands in its place.
17. Japanese and Chinese names are given throughout in Asian order, family name first followed by given name.
18. In 1922 Ishimoto had become the first Japanese architect to study with Walter Gropius.
19. In 1926 Emperor Taishō died and was succeeded by Hirohito who became Emperor Shōwa.
20. Now the National Museum of Art.
21. See Elise K. Tipton, 'The Café: Contested Space of Modernity in Inter-war Japan', in Elise K. Tipton and John Clark (eds), *Being Modern in Japan: Culture and Society from the 1910s to the 1930s* (Honolulu, 2000), pp. 119-20.
22. Quoted in Edward Seidensticker, *Tokyo Rising: The City since the Great Earthquake* (New York, 1990), p. 27.
23. Now preserved as the Tokyo Metropolitan Teien Art Museum.
24. The Imperial Household Department (or Agency as it is now known) is a branch of the Japanese government that deals with affairs relating to the Imperial family.
25. *Shinsa gairon; Paris bankoku sōshoku bijitsu kogei hakurankai seifu sando jinmu hokoku* [Overview of the jury selection; government-supported administrative report of the Paris International Exposition of Decorative Arts and Crafts], 1925.
26. These groups lobbied for the inclusion of crafts in the government's prestigious *Teiten* exhibition. Their eventual success, in 1927, symbolized the re-evaluation of hierarchies, adopted from the West, that privileged painting and sculpture above other art forms.
27. Quoted in Chiaki Ajioka, *Early Mingei and the Development of Japanese Crafts, 1920s-1940s*, unpublished PhD thesis, Australian National University, 1995, p. 171.
28. In 1936 they, and a number of other Mukei members, formed Jitsuzai Kōgei Bijutsukai (Actuality Craft Movement), which put more emphasis on utility.
29. See Ryūichi Matsubara and others, *Kyoto no kōgei: Dentō to henkaku no hazaman ni* [Crafts reform in Kyoto, 1910-1940: A struggle between tradition and renovation] (Kyoto, 1998).
30. The name of this society is not usually translated. *Sōjun* means 'verdant and moist'.
31. Kimono were still worn by the majority of women in Japan, but their design also reflected modern styles. Those worn in urban areas often had Art Deco patterns.
32. Mikimoto sold cultured pearls to the West in enormous quantities after 1925, but it was not until after the Second World War that he started to sell pearls actually strung in Japan.
33. 'Manchuria's Super-Express *Asia*', *Contemporary Manchuria*, vol. ii, no. 1 (January 1938), p. 45. This journal, published in English, aimed to bring 'knowledge of the unprecedented changes' in Manchuria 'to the western world'.
34. The Japanese called their territory Manshūkoku, though it is usually referred to today by the Chinese term Manchukuo.
35. Louise Young, *Japan's Total Empire: Manchuria and the Culture of Wartime Imperialism* (Berkeley and London, 1998), pp. 241-59.
36. Ri Ko-ran in Japanese, Li Xianglan in Chinese. After the war the actress went to Hollywood and established a career as Shirley Yamaguchi. After a career as a television reporter, she became a politician in Japan.
37. Well known names such as Sun Yat-sen and Chiang Kai-shek are given in the older, Wade Giles system of transliteration; other names are given in the modern Pinyin system. The Qing dynasty fell in 1911 and a Republic was declared on 1 January 1912, with Sun Yat-sen as provisional president. Northern warlords subsequently declared independence and, from 1921, were at war with the Nationalist Government. Sun Yat-Sen died in 1925, and in 1926 Chiang Kai-shek assumed control of the Guomintang. The first congress of the Chinese Communist Party was held in Shanghai in 1921. In 1927 the Guomintang and Communists fought together against the warlords, but Chiang Kai-shek then betrayed his allies, executing over 12,000 people. The Communists were forced to regroup in isolated rural areas, but support for them continued to grow. In 1934 the Japanese installed the last Qing emperor, Puyi, as puppet leader of Manchukuo.
38. *All about Shanghai* (1934/1983), p. 43.
39. W. H. Auden and Christopher Isherwood, *Journey to War* (London, 1939), p. 237. Auden and Isherwood also went to factories and workshops, making them two of the very few visitors to the city who saw its darker side.
40. See Leo Ou-fan Lee, *Shanghai Modern: The Flowering of a New Urban Culture in China, 1930-1945* (Cambridge and London, 1999), pp. 9-11. Shanghai was the home of Art Deco in China, but the style was also found in other treaty ports such as Tsingtao (Qingdao) and Tientsin (Tianjin) and in British-owned Hong Kong.
41. Now the Peace Hotel.
42. The company was founded in Hong Kong in 1868 by English architect William Salway. In the 1920s it opened offices in Shanghai. The P&T Group is still a thriving architectural practice in East Asia.
43. Now the Shanghai Mansions.
44. In 1916 Hudec was taken prisoner by Russia and sent to Siberia, but in 1918 he managed to escape. He made his way to Shanghai, where he worked for an American company in the city before opening his own offices in 1925. In 1927-8 he made a sketching trip to the United States. His first name is sometimes given as 'Ladislaus'.
45. Now part of the Jin Jiang Hotel complex.
46. Now part of the Garden Hotel.
47. Tess Johnston and Deke Erh, *A Last Look: Western Architecture in Old Shanghai* (Hong Kong, 1998), p. 72.
48. Now the Dong Hu Hotel.
49. In Pinyin the name would be Gu Huilan, but she is always known as Madame Koo.
50. Madame Wellington Koo with Isabella Taves, *No Feast Lasts Forever* (New York, 1975), p. 182.
51. 'Shanghai Boom', *Fortune*, January 1935; quoted in Andrew Field, 'Selling Souls in Sin City: Shanghai Singing and Dancing Hostesses in Print, Film and Politics, 1920-1949', in Zhang Yingjin (ed.), *Cinema and Urban Culture in Shanghai, 1922-1943* (Stanford, 1999), p. 105.
52. See illustration in Lee (1999), fig. 13, following p. 150.
53. *Qipao* is Mandarin, *cheongsam* Cantonese.
54. These posters were traditionally printed with calendars and given by companies to clients in the New Year.
55. See Francesca Dal Lago, 'Crossed Legs in 1930s Shanghai: How "Modern" is the Modern Woman?', *East Asian History*, no. 19 (June 2000), pp. 103-44.
56. Japan had a strong presence in Shanghai. Having gained treaty rights in 1895, the Japanese were, by 1915, the largest foreign contingent in the city.
57. Lu Xun, the father of modern Chinese literature, was one of the leading intellectuals of the May Fourth movement, a major cultural body that begun as a political protest on 4 May 1919 following the transfer to Japan of rights to Shandong Province (previously held by Germany) at the Versailles Peace Conference. Lu Xun was one of many artists and writers who sought intellectual refuge from the repressive Chinese authorities in the foreign settlements of Shanghai in the 1920s and 1930s. Many thousands of Jews and White Russians also fled there.

Chapter 36: Indo-Deco

1. Sharada Dwivedi and Rahul Mehrotra, *Bombay: The Cities Within* (Bombay, 1995), p. 201.
2. Ibid, p. 270.
3. Norma Evenson, *The Indian Metropolis: A View toward the West* (New Haven and London, 1989), p. 165.
4. See the comments of Claude Batley, Principal of the J. J. School of Arts from 1923 to 1943, in the *Journal of the Indian Institute of Architects*, vol. i, no. 3 (January 1935), p. 103.
5. *Journal of the Indian Institute of Architects*, vol. iv, no. 3 (January 1938), p. 116.
6. Ibid, p. 115.
7. *Journal of the Indian Institute of Architects*, vol. iii, no. 3 (January 1937), back jacket.
8. *Journal of the Indian Institute of Architects*, vol. i, no. 1 (April 1934), p. viii.
9. *Journal of the Indian Institute of Architects*, vol. iv, no. 3 (January 1938), pp. 319-23.
10. Dwivedi and Mehrotra (1995), p. 247; Jon Alff, 'Temples of Light: Bombay's Art Deco Cinemas and the Birth of Modern Myth', in Pauline Rohatgi and others, *Bombay to Mumbai: Changing Perspectives* (Mumbai, 1997), p. 251.
11. Alff (1997), p. 253.
12. Ibid, p. 254.
13. Dwivedi and Mehrotra (1995), p. 249.
14. Ibid, p. 253.
15. *Journal of the Indian Institute of Architects*, vol. i, no. 3 (January 1935), p. xvi; Dwivedi and Mehrotra (1995), p. 253.
16. *Journal of the Indian Institute of Architects*, vol. i, no. 4 (April 1935), pp. 120-2.
17. Iyer, Kamu (ed.), *Buildings that Shaped Bombay: Works of G. B. Mhatre, FRIBA, 1902-1973* (Mumbai, 2001), p. 19.
18. Amin Jaffer, *Furniture from British India and Ceylon* (London, 2001), pp. 109-13.
19. Ibid, p. 113.
20. Jon Lang, Madhavi Desai and Miki Desai, *Architecture* and *Independence: The Search for Identity: India, 1880-1980* (Delhi, 1997), pp. 106-9.
21. Giles H. R. Tillotson, *The Tradition of Indian Architecture: Continuity, Controversy and Change since 1850* (Delhi, 1989), pp. 46-56.
22. Hans Nadelhoffer, *Cartier: Jewellers Extraordinary* (London, 1984), p. 159.
23. Reto Niggl, *Eckart Muthesius: International Style, 1930. The Maharaja's Palace in Indore: Architecture and Interior* (Stuttgart, 1996), p. 18.
24. Ibid, pp. 17-18.
25. Ibid, pp. 18-19, 93.
26. Ibid, pp. 38-9, 41-2, 74-6.
27. Ibid, pp. 60, 74, fig. 6.
28. Ibid, pp. 124-45.
29. George Michell, *The Royal Palaces of India* (London, 1994), p. 223.
30. Michell (1994), p. 222.
31. Fred Holmes and Ann Newton Holmes, *Bridging Traditions: The Making of Umaid Bhawan Palace* (Delhi, 1995), pp. 7-8.
32. Holmes and Holmes (1995), p. 9.
33. Ibid, pp. 9-10.
34. Ibid, pp. 17-44.
35. Ibid, p. 46.
36. Indian subjects that received a similar sculptural treatment may be seen in the carved elephants at the Viceroy's House, New Delhi and in the friezes of peasants on the New India Assurance building and the Mutual Insurance building, Bombay.
37. Holmes and Holmes (1995), p. 82.
38. Ibid, p. 96.
39. Ibid, pp. 101-2.
40. Ibid, p. 102.
41. Jessica Rutherford, 'Alistair Maynard, MBE (1903-1976)', *Journal of the Decorative Arts Society, 1890-1940*, vol. 3 (1979), p. 26.
42. OIOC, D1219.
43. OIOC, D1219, pp. 1-5.
44. OIOC, D1219, letter of 10 October 1934.
45. Evenson (1989), p. 169.
46. Ibid.
47. *Journal of the Indian Institute of Architects*, vol. vi, no. 2 (October 1939), p. 33.
48. Anne Watson (ed.), *Beyond Architecture: Marion Mahony and Walter Burley Griffin: America, Australia, India* (Sydney, 1998), p. 152.

Chapter 37: Ambiguously Modern: Art Deco in Latin America

1. Landowski never went to Brazil, and his design was based on a preliminary study by the Italian Lelio Landucci. The difficult task of building the monument was undertaken by a team of Brazilian engineers led by Heitor da Silva Costa, Pedro Viana da Silva and Heitor Levy. See Lucia Grinberg, 'República Católica – Cristo Redentor', in Paulo Knauss (ed.), *Cidade vaidosa: Imagens urbanas do Rio de Janeiro* (Rio de Janeiro, 1999), pp. 64-7; Affonso Fontainha, *História dos monumentos do Distrito Federal* (Rio de Janeiro, 1954), pp. 213-14.
2. Grinberg (1999), pp. 61-4; Fontainha (1954), p. 213. Other, more conventional, designs for the monument were proposed and rejected.
3. As famously articulated by Herwin Schaefer, and Sigfried Giedion and Nikolaus Pevsner before him.
4. For examples, see Luiz Paulo Conde and others, 'Proto-modernismo em Copacabana', *Arquitetura revista*, vol. 3 (1985/6), pp. 40-49; Luiz Paulo Conde, *'Art Déco*: Modernidade antes do movimento moderno', *Art Déco na América Latina: 1º Seminário internacional* (Rio de Janeiro, 1997), pp. 69-70.
5. Jorge Ramos, 'Buenos Aires *déco*: A outra modernidade', *Art Déco na América Latina* (1997), pp. 60-64. On the idea of 'modernity resistant to the Modernist cliché', see Luiz Fernando Franco, 'Francisco Bologna, ou modernidade resistente ao clichê modernista', *Arquitetura revista*, vol. 6 (1988), pp. 15-16.
6. Ramos (1997), p. 63; Enrique X. de Anda Alanis, 'A arquitetura *déco* no México: Uma proposta de vanguarda em tempos de modernidade', *Art Déco na América Latina* (1997), pp. 29-35.
7. See Thomas E. Skidmore and Peter H. Smith, *Modern Latin America* (Oxford, 1989), pp. 340-48; David Bushnell and Neill Macauley, *The Emergence of Latin America in the Nineteenth Century* (Oxford, 1994); D. C. M. Platt (ed.), *Business Imperialism, 1840-1930: An Enquiry based on British Experience in Latin America* (Oxford, 1977). On the development of republicanism in Brazil, see José Murilo de Carvalho, *A formação das almas: O imaginário da República no Brasil* (São Paulo, 1990), Chapter 5.
8. See Jaime Larry Benchimol, *Pereira Passos: Um Haussmann tropical* (Rio de Janeiro, 1990), especially Chapters 12 and 13.
9. For a broader discussion of the relations between design and national style, see Jeremy Aynsley, *Nationalism and Internationalism: Design in the*

Twentieth Century (London, 1993), especially pp. 31-42.
10. See Humberto Eliash Diaz, 'O *Art Déco* no Chile: Último estilo acadêmico e primeiro estilo moderno', *Art Déco na América Latina* (1997), pp. 56-7; Rachel Sisson, 'Rio de Janeiro, 1875-1945: The Shaping of a New Urban Order', *Journal of Decorative and Propaganda Arts*, vol. 21 (1995), pp. 146-7.
11. Anda Alanis (1997), pp. 29-30.
12. Ibid, p. 30; Eliash Diaz (1997), pp. 56-7; Ramos (1997), p. 62.
13. On the dissemination of Art Deco as a popular building style in Argentina, see Ramos (1997), p. 61.
14. See also Roberto Segre, 'Havana *déco*: Alquimia urbana da primeira modernidade', *Art Déco na América Latina* (1997), pp. 41-2.
15. At this point, the focus of this essay shifts even more narrowly to the case of Brazil since, despite a common historical experience, Latin America is only a homogeneous cultural unit when viewed from an external vantage point. The observations derived from the Brazilian experience, more familiar to the author, may or may not be applicable to other Latin American contexts.
16. Though the avenue was inaugurated in 1944, it is still arguable whether it was ever 'completed', since large tracts of the urban fabric then destroyed remain essentially undeveloped to this day.
17. For a detailed account, see Evelyn Furquim Werneck Lima, *Avenida Presidente Vargas: Uma drástica cirurgia* (Rio de Janeiro, 1990).
18. On the broader ideological project in the fields of education and culture, spearheaded by education minister Gustavo Capanema, see Simon Schwartzman, Helena Maria Bousquet Bomeny and Vanda Maria Ribeiro Costa, *Tempos de Capanema* (São Paulo, 2000), especially Chapters 3 and 9.
19. See Monica Pimenta Velloso, *Modernismo no Rio de Janeiro: Turunas e Quixotes* (Rio de Janeiro, 1996), pp. 31-4; Tadeu Chiarelli, *Um jeca nos vernissages* (São Paulo, 1995), pp. 53, 64-65; Annateresa Fabris (ed.), *Modernidade e modernismo no Brasil* (Campinas, 1994), especially pp. 46-9, 57-65, 114-17; Flora Süssekind, *Cinematógrafo de letras: Literatura, técnica e modernização no Brasil* (São Paulo, 1987), pp. 12-16. For a politically aligned critique, see also Antonio Arnoni Prado, *1922 – Intinerário de uma falsa vanguarda: Os dissidentes, a Semana e o Integralismo* (São Paulo, 1983).
20. Irma Arrestizábal, 'John Graz and the Graz-Gomide Family', *Journal of Decorative and Propaganda Arts*, vol. 21 (1995), pp. 181-95.
21. José E. Mindlin, 'Illustrated Books and Periodicals in Brazil, 1875-1945', *Journal of Decorative and Propaganda Arts*, vol. 21 (1995), p. 64.
22. See ibid, pp. 68-9; see also Nelson Werneck Sodré, *A história da imprensa no Brasil* (Rio de Janeiro, 1966), pp. 341-7, 399-400, 427-8; Velloso (1996), pp. 56-74; Beatriz Resende, 'Melindrosa e Almofadinha, *Cock-tail* e arranha-céu: Imagens de uma literatura *Art Déco*', *Art Déco na América Latina* (1997), p. 87.
23. A fuller analysis of the magazine's evolution and design is undertaken in Aline Haluch, *A Maçã: Manifestações de design no inicio do século XX*, unpublished MA thesis, Pontifícia Universidade Católica, Rio de Janeiro, 2002.
24. See Velloso (1996), pp. 12-14.
25. The Portuguese text reads: 'Esses macacos africanos não resistem ao nosso clima. Por que? Aqui eles dão o prego.' The phrase *dar o prego* (to wear out) is a pun on *macaco-prego*, a species of monkey native to Brazil. In one sense, the African monkey gives in (or gives out) to its Brazilian counterpart.

Chapter 38: 'A Growing Enthusiasm for Modernity': Art Deco in Australia

1. Ernest Wunderlich, *All my Yesterdays: A Mosaic of Music and Manufacturing* (Sydney, 1945), pp. 93-4.
2. Alleyne Zander, 'The Exhibition of British Art in Industry at the Royal Academy', *Art in Australia*, series 3, vol. 59 (May 1935), pp. 36-43.
3. *Art in Australia*, series 3, vol. 60 (August 1935), p. 49. One set, purchased in Australia by the Wirth Circus family, is now in the collection of the Art Gallery of South Australia, Adelaide.
4. 'Australian Furniture', *Art in Australia*, series 3, vol. 65 (November 1936), p. 81.
5. Margaret Preston, 'The Indigenous Art of Australia', *Art in Australia*, series 3, vol. 11 (March 1925), p. 34.
6. Deborah Edwards, *'This Vital Flesh': The Sculpture of Rayner Hoff and his School* (Sydney, 1999), p. 13.
7. A proposal for an Anzac Memorial in Sydney stemmed from the first anniversary of the disastrous Gallipoli landing in 1916. The final monument was intended to commemorate all those from New South Wales who fought in the First World War.
8. C. Bruce Dellit, 'Modern Movement in Design', *Art in Australia*, series 3, vol. 56 (August 1934), p. 68
9. Wunderlich (1945), pp. 93-4.
10. The Wilson Hall was destroyed by fire in 1945. Fortunately, Waller's window survived and, after conservation in 1997, is now dramatically installed in the Ian Potter Museum of Art, Melbourne.
11. Now in the collection of the Art Gallery of South Australia, Adelaide.
12. *The Burdekin House Exhibition: Catalogue* (1929), n.p.
13. Ibid.
14. Ibid.
15. 'Australian Furniture', *Art in Australia*, series 3, vol. 65 (November 1936), p. 81.
16. Ibid, p. 84.
17. Kenneth Wilkinson, 'Michael O'Connell's Fabrics', *Art in Australia*, series 3, vol. 67 (15 May 1937), p. 50.
18. 'The Department of Art at the East Sydney Technical Museum', *Art in Australia*, series 3, vol. 58 (February 1935), pp. 43-4.
19. Quoted in Ross Thorne, *Cinemas of Australia via USA* (Sydney, 1981), p. 96.
20. Peter Shaw and Peter Hallett, *Art Deco Napier: Styles of the Thirties* (Napier, 1990; reprint, Nelson, 1994), p. 12.
21. Quoted in Shaw and Hallett (1994), pp. 14-5.
22. Ibid.
23. Ibid, p. 20.

Chapter 39: Art Deco in South Africa

1. For example, the decorative details of Johannesburg's Stanhope Mansions of 1935.
2. 'The Year in Review', *South African Architectural Record* (December 1934), p. 310.
3. Hendrick Pierneef, *Natal Advertiser* (Durban), 13 July 1926, p. 7.
4. Geoffrey Eastcott Pearse, 'Epochs in Building History', *The Star* (Johannesburg), 22 September 1936, p. 24.
5. Jan Smuts, *Rand Daily Mail* (Johannesburg), 23 September 1936, and p.7.
6. See Daniel Herwitz, 'Modernism at the Margins', in Hilton Judin and Ivan Vladislavic (eds), *Blank – Architecture: Apartheid and After* (Rotterdam, 1999), p. 412. The American high-rise had extended Johannesburg's skyline by 1902, earlier than it had in London.
7. W. H. Howie, 'Contemporary Architecture', *Lantern*, vol. vii (4 June 1958), p. 336.
8. E. Rosenthal, cited in Marilyn Martin, 'Art Deco Architecture in South Africa', *Journal of Decorative and Propaganda Arts*, vol. 20 (1994), p. 20.
9. The Colonial Mutual Life Society similarly established itself in Johannesburg and across the Empire in Australia (Hobart, Brisbane, Adelaide), displaying its corporate image in these locations through a confident, corporate Art Deco style. See also Patrick van Daele and Roy Lumby, *A Spirit of Progress: Art Deco Architecture in Australia* (Sydney, 1997).
10. See also Federico Freschi, 'Big Business Beautility: The Old Mutual Building, Cape Town, South Africa', *Journal of Decorative and Propaganda Arts*, vol. 20 (1994), pp. 39-57.
11. Freschi (see note 10) suggests that the decorative iconography serves commerce 'rather than' Empire.
12. This type of decorative mural was also common to a number of Art Deco public buildings of the 1930s, including the General Post Office buildings in Johannesburg (1935) and Cape Town (1941). Both mythologized their corporate identity with murals of unfolding historical narratives.
13. *The Star* (Johannesburg), 14 September 1936.
14. This was the universal descriptor for the exhibition's style in the national and international press.
15. *The Star* (Johannesburg), 29 September 1936.
16. *The Star* (Johannesburg), 12 October 1936.
17. Neville Dubow (ed.), *Paradise: The Journals and Letters of Irma Stern, 1917-1933* (Diep River, 1991), introduction.
18. *Daily Dispatch* (East London), 29 September 1936 (author's emphasis).
19. Melanie Hillebrand, *Art and Architecture in Natal, 1910-1940* (Durban, 1986), p. 218.
20. Melanie Hillebrand, *The Women of Olifantsfontein: South African Studio Ceramics* (Cape Town, 1991), p. 7.
21. 'The Lovely Homes of Johannesburg', *Cape Times Supplement*, 18 August 1936.

Chapter 40: Art Deco: Decline and Revival

1 William H. Jordy, *American Buildings and their Architects: The Impact of European Modernism in the mid-Twentieth Century* (Garden City, NY, 1976), p. 79.
2. The phrase was used by Richard Striner in 'Art Deco: Polemics and Synthesis', *Winterthur Portfolio*, vol. 21, no. 5 (Spring 1990), pp. 21-34.
3. For example, native American or Australian motifs, or representations of national myths and symbols.
4. As was demonstrated by the international exhibitions at Chicago (1933-4), San Francisco (1939) and New York (1939).
5. This trend was partly encouraged by the perceived threat of cultural homogenization as a result of the worldwide appeal of Hollywood films.
6. In practice Art Deco continued to find expression in the work of several designers.
7. In France, for example, some designers who had experimented with decorative Modernism, like Jean-Charles Moreux, turned towards a sophisticated neo-Rococo and a graceful classicism in the 1930s.
8. Early casualties were luxury bindings; the bookbinder François-Louis Schmied was one of those who went bankrupt at this time. Some official financial support was made available, in an effort to preserve luxury industry and high-quality craft skills, and several leading Deco artists were commissioned to make designs for the interiors of the luxury ocean liner *Normandie*. However, by the time she was launched, in the mid-1930s, her elaborate interiors seemed incompatible with the increasing taste for simplified forms, streamlining and more discreet means of expressing luxury.
9. Nikolaus Pevsner, *An Enquiry into Industrial Art in England* (Cambridge, 1937), pp. 9, 10 and passim. Some of the results of the commercializing impulses condemned by Pevsner can now be seen in a more positive light. Furthermore, increasing commercial realism was often associated with considerable technical ingenuity, as in the work of the Italian designer Marcello Nizzoli, who skilfully combined avant-garde forms with new materials and lighting technologies to create spectacular exhibition and shop window displays.
10. Notably to Turkey.
11. A phrase used by a contemporary critic commenting on the Paris 1925 Exhibition.
12. Talbot Hamlin, 'A Contemporary American Style', *Pencil Points*, vol. 19, no. 2 (February 1938), p. 101. Hamlin saw a 'demand' for monumentality as deriving from 'the people' who, 'in the long run, hold the purse strings'.
13. For example, the Court of States, the United States (Federal) building and the City of New York Administration building.
14. In these respects the New York World Fair was like other major international exhibitions of the late 1930s, such as that held in Paris in 1937.
15. The Theme Committee even structured the fair along the lines of production, distribution and exchange, but added a social dimension by including the themes of Medicine and Public Health, Science and Education and Community Interests.
16. All of whom were involved in the fair's design.
17. Helen A. Harrison, *Dawn of a New Day: The New York World's Fair, 1939-40* (New York, 1980), p. 6.
18. Frederick Gutheim, 'Buildings at the Fair', *Magazine of Art*, vol. 32 (May 1939), pp. 286-9.
19. Eugene A. Santomasso, 'The Design of Reason', in Harrison (1980), p. 40.
20. The rise of Gallup during the 1930s marked the closing of the loop from production to consumption, ensuring that producers could obtain 'scientific' information about the popularity of their products from selected population samples.
21. From the official guidebook to the New York World Fair, cited in Harrison (1980), p. 46.
22. See the chapter headings, which include 'Fitness to Function', 'Fitness to Materials', 'Fitness to Techniques', 'Unity' and 'Simplicity', in Walter Dorwin Teague's book *Design this Day: The Technique of Order in the Machine Age* (New York, 1940).
23. Talbot Hamlin, for example, was critical of the 'spurious Modernist detailing' in the project designs; see Talbot Hamlin, 'The Architectural League Exhibition', *Pencil Points*, vol. 19 (June 1938), pp. 342-56.
24. Cited in Harrison (1980), p. 8.
25. Particularly in America, in such examples as Paul Fuller's designs for Wurlitzer jukeboxes and Detroit automobile styling.
26. The latter was much admired as an adaptable, moderate style.
27. Including Sigfried Giedion, *Space, Time and Architecture* (Cambridge, MA and London, 1941; reprinted 1949, 1954); Nikolaus Pevsner, *Pioneers of Modern Design* (first published as *Pioneers of the Modern Movement*, London, 1936; 2nd edition, New York and London, 1949; reprinted several times since); Reyner Banham, *Theory and Design in the First Machine Age* (London, 1960; New York, 1967; reprinted several times since).
28. Renewed interest in the style was encouraged by its commercial currency as well as interest in its earlier role in the expression of national and regional identities.
29. Richard Hamilton, in a letter to the architect Peter Smithson in 1957. The celebration of American commercial culture was a central feature of the work of a number of American Pop artists, including Roy Lichtenstein and Andy Warhol. In Britain such interests were evident amongst the members of the Independent Group (founded 1952), who included Hamilton, the art critic Lawrence Alloway, the architects Peter and Alison Smithson and the architectural critic and historian Reyner Banham.
30. See 'Treasure Island', *Architectural Design*, vol. 39, no. 6 (1969), pp. 310 and 316 for Street-Porter and Clark's responses. The former chose the Rainbow Room in Derry & Toms; the latter chose the Ideal Standard building by Raymond Hood and Gordon Jeeves.
31. Sometimes by firms active in the original development and promotion of the style, such as Cartier, the jewellers.
32. Some non-Deco buildings of the period were also refurbished in a Deco-influenced manner. A notable example was Theo Crosby/Pentagram's revamping of the interior of Burnet, Tait & Lorne's Unilever House in London.
33. By the 1980s, several Art Deco buildings there had been refurbished and neo-Deco designs built; and two exhibitions at the Los Angeles County Museum of Art at this time highlighted 1930s Hollywood film costume design and the work of Hollywood photographers.
34. These included revivals of Noel Coward's *Design for Living* (1933) and Earl Carroll's *Vanities* (1932), as well as films made for television – such as those based on Agatha Christie's novels – which used real period interiors as backdrops.
35. Janet Street-Porter, 'Where has all the Fun gone?', *Architectural Design*, vol. 39, no. 5 (1969), p. 242.
36. Including such groups as the Italian collaborative Studio Alchymia (and later Memphis) and, in graphic design, the Pushpin Studios.

Bibliography

General art, architecture and design

Primary materials

Boykin, Elizabeth M., 'The Grace of Modern Glass Design', *Arts & Decoration*, vol. xxxvii (September 1932)

Brill, Franklin E., 'Designing for the Eye', *Product Engineering*, vol. 4 (January 1933)

Brill, Franklin E., 'What Shapes for Phenolics?', *Modern Plastics*, vol. 13 (September 1935)

Calkins, Earnest Elmo, 'Advertising, Builder of Taste', *American Magazine of Art*, vol. xxi, no. 9 (September 1930)

Cheney, Sheldon, *The New World Architecture* (London and New York, 1930)

Editorial, 'Designers – European and American', *Good Furniture Magazine*, vol. xxxii, no. 4 (April 1929)

Department of Overseas Trade, *Reports on the Present Position and Tendencies of the Industrial Arts as Indicated at the International Exhibition of Modern Decorative and Industrial Art, Paris, 1925* (London, 1925)

Encyclopédie des Arts décoratifs et industriels modernes, 12 vols (Paris, 1925; reprint, New York, 1977)

Farkas, E. and Durach, Felix, *Architektur innerraume film* (Stuttgart, 1927)

Fearon, K. O., 'The Book-Jacket as a Sales Aid', *Commercial Art and Industry*, vol. 7, no. 39 (September 1929), pp. 89-97

Frankl, Paul, *Form and Re-form: A Practical Handbook of Modern Interiors* (New York, 1930)

Frankl, Paul, *New Dimensions: The Decorative Arts of Today in Words & Pictures* (New York, 1928)

Genauer, Emily, *Modern Interiors Today and Tomorrow* (New York, 1939)

H., E., 'Fashion and Furniture', *Arts & Decoration* vol. xl, no. 3 (January 1934), pp. 21-5

Hitchcock, Henry Russell and Johnson, Philip, *The International Style* (New York, 1932; reprint, New York, 1966 and 1996)

Hobbs, Douglas B., 'Aluminum – A Decorative Metal', *Good Furniture and Decoration*, vol. 35 (August 1930)

Hodgkin, Eliot, *Fashion Drawing* (London, 1932)

Horwitt, Nathan George, 'Plans for Tomorrow: A Seminar in Creative Design', *Advertising Arts* (July 1934)

Kiesler, Frederick, *Contemporary Art Applied to the Store* (London, 1930)

Léautaud, J., 'Modern Bindings for Modern Books', *International Studio*, vol. 84 (June 1926)

Magne, Henri-Marcel (ed.), *Rapport général: Exposition des arts décoratifs et industriels modernes*, 12 vols (Paris, 1925-31)

McAndrew, John, '"Modernistic" and "Streamlined"', *Bulletin of the Museum of Modern Art*, vol. 6, no. 5 (December 1938)

McMurtrie, Douglas, *Modern Typography and Layout* (Chicago, 1929)

Muche, Georg, 'Bildende Kunst und Industrieform', *Bauhaus*, vol. 1, no. 1 (Dessau, 1926)

Museum of Modern Art, *Machine Art* (New York, 1934; reprints, New York, 1969 and 1994)

Sexton, Randolph William, *The Logic of Modern Architecture* (New York, 1929)

Todd, Dorothy and Mortimer, Raymond, *The New Interior Decoration: An Introduction to its Principles and International Survey of its Methods* (London, 1929)

Tolmer, Alfred, *Mise en Page: The Theory and Practice of Layout* (London, 1931)

Tschichold, Jan, *Die neue Typographie* (Berlin, 1928); translated as, *The New Typography: A Handbook for Modern Designers* (Berkeley, 1995)

Van Doren, Harold, *Industrial Design: A Practical Guide to Product Design and Development* (New York, 1940)

Secondary sources

Arwas, Victor, *Art Deco* (London, 1980; New York, 1992; reprint, New York, 2000)

Arwas, Victor, *Art Deco Sculpture* (London, 1992)

Arwas, Victor, *Art Deco Sculpture: Chryselephantine Statuettes of the Twenties and Thirties* (London, 1975)

Arwas, Victor, *Glass: Art Nouveau to Art Deco* (London, 1977; reprint, 1987)

Atterbury, Paul, *Art Deco Patterns: A Design Source Book* (London, 1990)

Aynsley, Jeremy, *Nationalism and Internationalism: Design in the Twentieth Century* (London, 1993)

Battersby, Martin, *The Decorative Thirties* (London, 1971)

Battersby, Martin, *The Decorative Twenties* (London, 1969)

Bayer, Patricia, *Art Deco Architecture: Design, Decoration and Detail from the Twenties and Thirties* (London, 1992)

Bayer, Patricia, *Art Deco Interiors: Decoration and Design Classics of the 1920s and 1930s* (New York and London, 1990)

Blau, Eve and Troy, Nancy, *Architecture and Cubism* (Montreal and Cambridge, MA, 1997)

Bossaglia, Rossana, *L'Art Déco* (Bari, 1984)

Bouillon, Jean-Paul, *Art Déco, 1903-1940* (Geneva and New York, 1989)

Brunhammer, Yvonne, *1925* (Paris, 1976)

Brunhammer, Yvonne, *The Art Deco Style* (London, 1983)

Brunhammer, Yvonne, *The Nineteen Twenties Style* (London and New York, 1969)

Bush, Donald J., *The Streamlined Decade* (New York, 1975)

Caeymaex, Martine and Lambrechts, Marc (eds), *L'Art Déco en Europe: Tendances décoratives dans les arts appliqués vers 1925* (Brussels, 1989)

Chenoune, Farid, *A History of Men's Fashions* (London, 1996)

Constantino, Maria, *Fashion of a Decade: The 1930s* (London, 1991)

Curl, James Stevens, *The Egyptian Revival* (London, 1982)

Curtis, Penelope, *Sculpture, 1900-1945: After Rodin* (Oxford, 1999)

Dars, Celestine, *A Fashion Parade: The Seeberger Collection* (London, 1977)

Deslandres, Yvonne and Müller, Florence, *Histoire de la mode au XXème siècle* (Paris, 1986)

Dorner, Jane, *Fashion in the Twenties and Thirties* (London, 1973)

Duncan, Alastair, *American Art Deco* (London, 1986)

Duncan, Alastair, *Art Deco* (London, 1988)

Duncan, Alastair, *Art Deco Furniture* (London, 1997)

Duncan, Alastair, *Modernism: Modernist Design, 1880-1940. The Norwest Collection, Norwest Corporation, Minneapolis* (Woodbridge, 1998)

Eidelberg, Martin (ed.), *Design, 1935-1965: What Modern Was* (Montreal and New York, 1991)

Gabardi, Melissa, *Art Deco Jewellery, 1920-1949* (Woodbridge, 1989)

Gebhard, David, 'About Style, not Ideology', *AIA Architecture*, vol. 72, no. 12 (December 1983)

Gebhard, David, 'Moderne Architecture', *Journal of the Society of Architectural Historians*, vol. 31, no. 3 (October 1972)

Giedion, Sigfried, *Mechanization Takes Command: A Contribution to Anonymous History* (Oxford, 1948; reprint, New York, 1969)

Green, Christopher (ed.), *Art Made Modern: Roger Fry's Vision of Art* (London, 1999)

Greif, Martin, 'Defining Art Deco', *Art Deco Society of New York News*, vol. 2, no. 1 (January-February 1982)

Guillaume, Valérie, *Europe, 1910-1939: Quand l'art habillait le vêtement* (Paris, 1997)

Haedrich, Marcel, *Coco Chanel: Her Life, Her Secrets* (New York, 1971)

Hall-Duncan, Nancy, *The History of Fashion Photography* (New York, 1979)

Harrison, Martin, *Shots of Style: Great Fashion Photographs Chosen by David Bailey* (London, 1985)

Haworth-Booth, Mark and Coe, Brian, *A Guide to Early Photographic Processes* (London and Westerham, 1983)

Heller, Steven and Chwast, Seymour, *Jackets Required* (San Francisco, 1995)

Herald, Jacqueline, *Fashions of a Decade: The 1920s* (London, 1991)

Hiesinger, Kathryn B. and Marcus, George H, *Landmarks of Twentieth-Century Design* (New York, 1993)

Hillier, Bevis and Escritt, Stephen, *Art Deco Style* (London, 1997)

Hillier, Bevis, *Art Deco of the Twenties and Thirties* (London, 1968)

Hillier, Bevis, *The Style of the Century* (London, 1983; revised, 1998)

Hillier, Bevis, *The World of Art Deco* (London, 1971)

Howell, Georgina, *In Vogue: Six Decades of Fashion* (London, 1975)

Kaplan, Wendy (ed.), *Designing Modernity: The Arts of Reform and Persuasion, 1885-1945* (London, 1995)

Kery, Patricia Frantz, *Art Deco Graphics* (London, 1986)

Kjellberg, Pierre, *Art Déco: Les Maîtres du mobilier: Le Décor des paquebots* (Paris, 1988)

Klein, Dan, McClelland, Nancy and Haslam, Malcolm, *In the Deco Style* (London, 1987)

Komanecky, Michael and Fabbri Butera, Virginia, *The Folding Image: Screens by Western Artists of the Nineteenth and Twentieth Centuries* (New Haven, 1984)

Krauss, Rosalind E., *The Originality of the Avant-Garde and Other Modernist Myths* (Cambridge, MA, 1987)

Krekel-Aalberse, Annelies, *Silver, 1880-1940: Art Nouveau, Art Deco* (Stuttgart, 2001)

La Vine, W. Robert, *In a Glamorous Fashion* (London, 1981)

Lambrechts, Marc (ed.), *L'Art Déco en Europe: Tendances décoratives dans les arts appliqués vers 1925* (Brussels, 1989)

Laver, James, *Women's Dress in the Jazz Age* (London, 1975)

Lesieutre, Alain, *Art Déco* (New York and London, 1974)

Lichtenstein, Claude and Engler, Franz (eds), *The Aesthetics of Minimized Drag: Streamlined, A Metaphor for Progress* (Zurich, 1994)

Lucie-Smith, Edward, *Art Deco Painting* (London, 1990)

Margolius, Ivan, *Cubism in Architecture and the Applied Arts: Bohemia and France, 1910-1914* (Newton Abbott, c.1979)

Martin, Richard, *Cubism and Fashion* (New York, 1998)

Martin, Richard, *Fashion and Surrealism* (New York, 1987)

Milbank, Caroline Rennolds, *Couture: The Great Fashion Designers* (London, 1985)

Miller, R. Craig, *Modern Design in the Metropolitan Museum of Art, 1890-1990* (New York, 1990)

Miller, John, 'The Book Jacket – Its Later Development and Design', *Antiquarian Book Monthly Review*, vol. 15, no. 12 (December 1988), pp. 452-61

Morgan, Sarah, *Art Deco: The European Style* (New York, 1990)

Mulvagh, Jane and Mendes, Valerie, *Vogue History of 20th Century Fashion* (London, 1988)

Musée des Arts Décoratifs, *Les Années 25: Art Déco/Bauhaus/de Stijl/Esprit Nouveau* (Paris, 1966)

Néret, Gilles, *L'Art des années trente: Sculpture, architecture, design, décor, graphisme, photographie, cinéma* (Paris, 1987)

Nichols, Sarah (ed.), *Aluminum by Design* (Pittsburgh, 2000)

Packer, William, *Fashion Drawings in Vogue* (Camberley, 1988)

Packer, William, *The Art of Vogue Covers* (London, 1980)

Powers, Alan, *Front Cover: Great Book Jacket and Cover Design* (London, 2001)

Powers, Alan, *Modern Block Printed Textiles* (London, 1992)

Raulet, Sylvie, *Art Deco Jewellery* (New York and London, 1985; reprint, London, 2002)

Remaury, Bruno, *Dictionnaire de la mode au XXème siècle* (Paris, 1994)

Robinson, Julian, *Fashion in the 30s* (London, 1978)

Rosenthal, Rudolph and Ratzka, Helena L. Williams, *The Story of Modern Applied Art* (New York, 1948)

Rosner, Charles, *The Growth of the Book Jacket* (London, 1954)

Rothstein, Natalie (ed.), *Four Hundred Years of Fashion* (London, 1984)

Rutherford, Jessica, *Art Nouveau, Art Deco and the Thirties: The Furniture Collections at Brighton Museum* (Brighton, 1983)

Ryersson, Scot D. and Yaccarino, Michael Orlando, *Infinite Variety, The Life and Legend of the Marchesa Casati* (New York, 1999)

Scarisbrick, Diana, *Ancestral Jewels* (London, 1989)

Scarlett, Frank and Townley, Marjorie, *Arts Décoratifs 1925* (London and New York, 1975)

Sparke, Penny, *The Plastics Age: From Modernity to Post-Modernity* (London, 1990)

Steele, Valerie, *Women in Fashion: Twentieth Century Designers* (New York, 1991)

Ströhle, Ralph, *Faszination Art Deco* (Berlin, 1993)

Vassiliev, Alexandre, *Beauty in Exile: The Artists, Models, and Nobility who Fled the Russian Revolution and Influenced the World of Fashion* (New York, 2000)

Venturi, Robert, *Complexity and Contradiction in Architecture* (Garden City, NY, 1966)

Venturi, Robert, Scott Brown, Denise and Izenour, Steven, *Learning from Las Vegas* (Cambridge, MA, 1972)

Wilson, Richard Guy, 'Defining Art Deco', *Art Deco Society of New York News*, vol. 3, no. 3 (Fall 1983)

Worsley, Harriet, *The Hulton Getty Picture Collection: Decades of Fashion* (London, 2000)

General culture, history, society, technology and theory

Primary materials

Allardyce, Nicoll, *Film and Theatre* (London, 1936)

Apollinaire, Guillaume, 'Exoticisme et ethnographie', *Paris Journal*, 12 September 1912

Boas, Franz, *Primitive Art* (Oslo and Cambridge, MA, 1927)

Chavance, René 'Chez un cinéaste', *Art et décoration*, vol. 52 (August 1927)

'Consumer Engineering', *Product Engineering*, vol. 2, no. 5 (May 1931)

Cooke, Alistair A., *Garbo and the Night Watchman: A Selection of British and American Film Critics* (London, 1937)

Covarrubias, Miguel, *Negro Drawings* (London and Paris, 1927)

Cunard, Nancy, *Negro: An Anthology* (London, 1934)

Davy, Charles (ed.), *Footnotes to the Film* (London, 1937)

De Wolfe, Elsie, *After All* (London, 1935)

De Zayas, Marius, *African Negro Art and its Influence on Modern Art* (New York, 1916)

Du Bois, W. E. B., *Dark Princess: A Romance* (New York, 1928; reprints, Millwood, NY, 1974, Jackson, MS, 1995)

Einstein, Carl and Westheim, Paul, *Europa Almanach: Malerei, Literatur, Architektur, Plastik, Bühne, Film, Mode* (Potsdam, 1924)

Einstein, Carl, *Negerplastik* (Munich, 1920)

Fescourt, Henri, *Le Cinéma des origines à nos jours* (Paris, 1932)

Gain, André, 'Le Cinéma et les arts décoratifs', *L'Amour de l'art*, vol. 9, no. 9 (September 1928)

Gibbons, Cedric, 'The Art Director', in Stephen Watts (ed.), *Behind the Screen: How Films are Made* (London, 1938)

Graves, Robert and Hodge, Alan, *The Long Weekend, 1918-1939* (London, 1940; reprint, London, 1991)

Greer, Howard, *Designing Male* (New York, 1949)

Guillaume, Paul and Apollinaire, Guillaume, *Sculptures nègres* (Paris, 1917)

Guillaume, Paul and Munro, Thomas, *La Sculpture nègre primitive* (Paris, 1929)

Hunter, William and Nash, Paul, *Scrutiny of Cinema* (London, 1932)

James, Thomas Garnet Henry, *Howard Carter: The Path to Tutankhamun* (London, 1922)

Lachenbruch, Jerome, 'Interior Decoration for the Movies: Studies from the Work of Cedric Gibbons and Gilbert White', *Arts & Decoration* (January 1921)

Laing, A. B., 'Designing Motion Picture Sets', *Architectural Record*, vol. 74, no. 1 (July 1933), pp. 59-64

Langley Moore, Doris, *Pandora's Letter Box: A Discourse on Fashionable Life* (London, 1929)

Lewis, Wyndham, *Paleface* (London, 1929)

Loewy, Raymond, *The Locomotive: Its Aesthetic* (London and New York, 1937)

Mallet-Stevens, Robert, *Le Décor moderne au cinema* (Paris, 1928)

Manvell, Roger, *Film* (London, 1944)

Moussinac, Léon, 'Le Décor et le costume', *Art et décoration*, vol. 51 (1926)

Rotha, Paul, *Celluloid: The Film Today* (London and New York, 1933)

Sheldon, Roy and Arens, Egmont, *Consumer Engineering: A New Technique for Prosperity* (New York, 1932; reprint, New York, 1976)

Thorp, Margaret Farrand, *America at the Movies* (London, 1946)

Veblen, Thorstein, *Theory of the Leisure Class* (New York, 1899; reprints, London and New York, 1994, New York, 2001)

Vechten, Carl van, *Nigger Heaven* (New York, 1926; reprint, New York, 1951)
Waugh, Evelyn, *A Handful of Dust* (London, 1934)
Waugh, Evelyn, *Labels: A Mediterranean Journal* (London, 1930; reprints, 1985 and 1991)
Waugh, Evelyn, *Vile Bodies* (London, 1930)

Secondary sources

Abel, Richard, *French Cinema: The First Wave, 1915-1929* (Princeton, 1984)
Albrecht, Donald, *Designing Dreams: Modern Architecture in the Movies* (New York, 1986)
Anderson, Perry, *The Origins of Postmodernity* (London, 1998)
Anscombe, Isabelle, *A Woman's Touch: Women in Design from 1860 to the Present Day* (London, 1984)
Antonova, Irina Aleksandrovna and Merkert, Jörn, *Berlin Moskau, 1900-1950* (Munich and New York, 1995)
Arscott, Caroline and Scott, Katie, *Manifestations of Venus: Art and Sexuality* (Manchester and New York, 2000)
Ash, Juliet and Wilson, Elisabeth (eds), *Chic Thrills: A Fashion Reader* (London, 1992)
Baláz, Béla, *Theory of the Film: Character and Growth of New Art* (London, 1952)
Balio, Tino, *Grand Design: Hollywood as a Modern Business Enterprise, 1900-1930* (New York, 1993)
Ballard, Bettina, *In my Fashion* (London, 1960)
Barrios, Richard, *A Song in the Dark: The Birth of the Musical Film* (Oxford, 1995)
Basinger, Jeanine, *A Woman's View: How Hollywood Spoke to Women, 1930-1960* (New York and London, 1994)
Bayley, Stephen, *Taste* (London, 1983)
Becker, Vivienne, *Fabulous Fakes* (London, 1988)
Behrend, George, *Grand European Expresses: The Story of the Wagons-Lits* (London, 1962)
Behrend, George, *The History of the Wagon-Lits* (London, 1959)
Bergala, Alain, *Magnum Cinema: Photographs from the Last 50 Years of Movie-Making* (London, 1995)
Berman, Marshall, *All that is Solid Melts into Air: The Experience of Modernity* (London, 1983)
Bernstein, Gail Lee, *Recreating Chinese Women, 1600-1945* (Berkeley and Oxford, 1991)
Bhabha, Homi K., 'The Other Question: The Stereotype and the Colonial Discourse', *Screen*, vol. 24, no. 6 (1983)
Biennale di Firenze, 2nd, *Moda/Cinema* (Milan, 1998)
Bilski, Emily D. (ed.), *Berlin Metropolis: Jews and the New Culture, 1890-1918* (New York and Berkeley, 1999)
Bird, John H., *Cinema Parade: Fifty Years of Film Shows* (Birmingham, 1947)
Bloch, Ernst, 'On Fine Arts in the Machine Age', in Ernst Bloch, *The Utopian Function of Art and Literature* (Cambridge, MA and London, 1988)
Bloom, Lisa, *With Other Eyes: Looking at Race and Gender in Visual Culture* (Minneapolis, 1999)
Bordwell, David, Staiger, Janet and Thompson, Kristen, *The Classical Hollywood Cinema: Film Style and Mode of Production to 1960* (London, 1985)
Bruzzi, Stella, *Undressing Cinema: Clothing and Identity in the Movies* (London, 1997)
Carter, Randolph and Cole, Robert, *Joseph Urban: Architecture, Theatre, Opera, Film* (New York and London, 1992)
Charney, Leo and Schwartz, Vanessa R. (eds), *Cinema and the Invention of Modern Life* (Berkeley, Los Angeles and London, 1995)
Clair, Jean, *The 1920s: The Age of the Metropolis* (Montreal, 1991)
Clifford, James, *The Predicament of Culture: Twentieth Century Ethnography, Literature and Art* (Cambridge, MA, 1988)
Collomb, Michel, *La Littérature Art Déco: Sur le style d'époque* (Paris, 1987)
Davis, Margaret L., *Bullocks Wilshire* (Los Angeles, c.1996)
De Grazia, Victoria and Furlough, Ellen, *The Sex of Things: Gender and Consumption in Historical Perspective* (Berkeley, Los Angeles and London, 1996)
Deepwell, Katy (ed.), *Women Artists and Modernism* (Manchester, 1998)
Dyer, Richard and Vincendeau, Ginette, *Popular European Cinema* (London, 1992)
Elliot, Bridget and Wallace, Jo-Ann, *Women Artists and Writers: Modernist (im)positionings* (London and New York, 1994)
Engelmeier, Regine and Engelmeier, Peter W., *Fashion in Film* (Munich, 1990)
Fiske, John, *Reading the Popular* (Boston and London, 1989)
Forissier, Béatrix, *Les Belles Années du cinéma à travers la carte postale: 1895-1935* (Paris, 1979)
Forman, Micki, 'Tutmania', *Dress*, vol. 4 (1978), pp. 7-14
Frayling, Christopher, *The Face of Tutankhamun* (London, 1992)
French, Philip, *The Movie Moguls: An Informal History of the Hollywood Tycoons* (London, 1969)
Friedberg, Anne, *Window Shopping: Cinema and the Postmodern* (Berkeley, Los Angeles and Oxford, 1993)
Garland, Madge, *Fashion, 1900-1939* (London, 1975)
Garland, Madge, *The Changing Face of Beauty: Four Thousand Years of Beautiful Women* (London, 1957)
Garland, Madge, *The Indecisive Decade: The World of Fashion and Entertainment in the Thirties* (London, 1968)
Goldwater, Robert, *Primitivism in Modern Art* (Cambridge, MA, 1986)
Greenhalgh, Paul (ed.), *Art Nouveau, 1890-1914* (London, 2000)
Greenhalgh, Paul, *Ephemeral Vistas: The Expositions Universelles, Great Exhibitions and World's Fairs, 1851-1939* (Manchester, 1988)
Hansen, Miriam Bratu, 'The Mass Production of the Senses: Classical Cinema as Vernacular', *Modernism/Modernity*, vol. 6, no. 2 (April 1999)
Harvey, David, *The Condition of Postmodernity: An Enquiry into the Origins of Cultural Change* (Oxford, 1990)
Hayne, Donald, *The Autobiography of Cecil B. De Mille* (New Jersey, 1959)
Heisner, Beverly, *Hollywood Art: Art Direction in the Days of the Great Studio* (New York and London, 1990)
Hiller, Susan (ed.), *The Myth of Primitivism: Perspectives on Art* (London, 1991)
Horst, Hoyningen-Huene, George and others, *Salute to the Thirties* (London, 1971)
Jarvie, Ian, *Hollywood's Overseas Campaign: The North Atlantic Movie Trade, 1920-1950* (Cambridge, 1992)
Kanin, Garson, *Hollywood Stars and Starlets, Tycoons and Flesh-Pebblers, Movie-Makers and Money-Makers, Frauds and Geniuses, Hopefuls and Has-Beens, Great Lovers and Sex Symbols* (London, 1975)
Keenan, Brigid, *The Women We Wanted to Look Like* (London, 1977)
Kendall, Elizabeth, *The Runaway Bride: Hollywood Romantic Comedy of the 1930s* (New York, 1990)
Lant, Antonia, 'The Curse of the Pharaoh, or How Cinema Contracted Egyptomania', *October* (Spring 1992), pp. 87-112
Laude, Jean, *Les Arts de l'Afrique noire* (Poitiers, 1966)
Lemke, Sieglinde, *Primitivist Modernism: Black Culture and the Origins of Transatlantic Modernism* (Oxford, 1998)
Loos, Adolf, *Ornament and Crime: Selected Essays/Adolf Loos* (Riverside, CA, 1998)
Loos, Anita, *A Girl like I* (London, 1967)
Loos, Anita, *Gentlemen Prefer Blondes: The Illuminating Diary of a Professional Lady* (London, 1982)
Lu Hsiao Peng, *Transnational Chinese Cinemas: Identity, Nationhood, Gender* (Honolulu, 1997)
Maeder, Edward (ed.), *Hollywood and History: Costume Design in Film* (London, 1987)
Malraux, André, *La Tête d'obsidienne* (Paris, 1974)
Marchetti, Gina, *Romance and the 'Yellow Peril': Race, Sex and Discursive Strategies in Hollywood Fiction* (Berkeley and London, 1993)
Margetson, Stella, *The Long Party: High Society in the 20s and 30s* (London, 1974)
Maxwell, Anne, *Colonial Photography and Exhibitions: Representations of the 'Native' and the Making of European Identities* (London and New York, 1999)
May, Lary, *Screening out the Past: The Birth of Mass Culture and the Motion Picture Industry* (Oxford, 1980)
McAuley, Rob, *The Liners* (London, 1997)
McConathy, Dale and Vreeland, Diana, *Hollywood Costume: Glamour, Glitter, Romance* (New York, 1976)
Nellmann, Dietrich (ed.), *Film Architecture: Set Designs from Metropolis to Bladerunner* (Munich, 1996)
Nichols, Beverley, *The Sweet and Twenties* (London, 1958)
Passek, Jean-Loup, *Twenty Years of German Cinema, 1913-1933* (Paris, 1978)
Poague, Leland A., *The Cinema of Ernst Lubitsch* (London, 1978)
Potter, David M., *People of Plenty: Economic Abundance and the American Character* (Chicago, 1954)
Reed, Christopher (ed.), *Not at Home: The Suppression of Domesticity in Modern Art and Architecture* (London, 1996)
Richards, Jeffrey, *The Age of the Dream Palace: Cinema and Society in Britain, 1930-1939* (London and New York, 1984)
Roberts, Mary Louise, *Civilization without Sexes: Reconstructing Gender in Postwar France, 1917-27* (Chicago and London, 1994)
Robinson, Julian, *The Golden Age of Style* (London, 1976)
Rotha, Paul, *Movie Parade, 1888-1949* (London and New York, 1950)
Rotha, Paul, *The Film till Now: A Survey of the Cinema* (London, 1949)
Rubin, Martin, *Showstoppers: Busby Berkeley and the Tradition of Spectacles* (Chichester, NY, 1993)
Rubin, William, *'Primitivism' in 20th Century Art: Affinity of the Tribal and the Modern*, 2 vols (New York, 1984)
Said, Edward W., *Orientalism* (London, 1978)
Schreier, Sandy, *Hollywood Dressed and Undressed: A Century of Cinema* (New York, 1998)
Sklar, Robert, *Movie Made Cinema: A Cultural History of American Movies* (New York, 1975)
Sklar, Robert, *Silent Screens: The Decline and Transformation of the American Movie Theatre* (Baltimore and London, 2000)
Sparke, Penny (ed.), *One Off: A Collection of Essays by Students on the Victoria and Albert/Royal College of Art Course in the History of Design* (London, 1997)
Spencer, Charles, *Cecil Beaton: Stage and Film Designs* (London, 1994)
Swanson, Gloria, *Swanson on Swanson* (Feltham, 1980)
Taylor, John Russell and Jackson, Arthur, *The Hollywood Musical* (London, 1971)
Torgovnick, Marianna, *Gone Primitive: Savage Intellects, Modern Lives* (Chicago, 1990)
Toy, Maggie, *Architecture and Film* (London, 1994)
Turner, George, 'Behind the Mask of Fu Man Chu', *American Cinematographer*, vol. 7 (January 1995)
Tzara, Tristan, 'Notes on Negro Art', in *Seven Dada Manifestoes and Lampisteries* (London, 1977)
Vallance, Tom, *The American Musical* (London and New York, 1970)
Vescovo, Marisa, *Arte e cinema: Torino, 1930-1945* (Milan, 1997)
Vollard, Ambroise and Macdonald, Violet M., *Recollections of a Picture Dealer* (New York, 1978)
Waugh, Evelyn, *A Handful of Dust* (London, 1934)
Waugh, Evelyn, *Labels: A Mediterranean Journal* (London, 1930; reprints, 1985 and 1991)
Westminster, Loelia Duchess of, *Grace and Favour* (London, 1961)
Whitworth Art Gallery, *Hollywood Film Costume* (Manchester, 1977)
Wollenberger, Hans H., Sigler, Ernst and Wood, Michael, *America in the Movies* (London, 1975)

Europe

AUSTRIA

Journals

Kunst und Kunsthandwerk (Vienna, 1898-1924)

Primary materials

Austrian Commission, *L'Autriche à l'Exposition des arts décoratifs et industriels modernes* (Paris, 1925)
Chavance, René, 'La Section autrichienne', *Art et décoration*, vol. xlviii (September 1925), pp. 120-32

Secondary sources

Fahr-Becker, Gabriele, *Wiener Werkstätte, 1903-1932* (Cologne, 1995)
Neuwirth, Waltraud, *Bimini-Wiener Glaskunst des Art Deco*, vol. ii of *Lampengeblasenes Glas aus Wien* (Vienna, 1992)
Neuwirth, Waltraud, *Die Keramik der Wiener Werkstätte*, vol. i of *Originalkeramiken, 1920-1931* (Vienna, 1981)
Noever, Peter, *Beyond Utility: Dagobert Peche and the Wiener Werkstätte* (New Haven, CT, 2002)
Rath, Peter, *Lobmeyr: Helles Glass und klares Licht* (Vienna, 1998)
Schweiger, Werner, *Wiener Werkstätte: Design in Vienna, 1903-1932* (London, 1984)
Sillevis, John and others, *Wiener Werkstätte: Keuze uit Weense collecties* (The Hague, 1998)
Völker, Angela and Pichler, Rupert, *Textiles of the Wiener Werkstätte* (Vienna, 1990; English translation, London, 1994)
Völker, Angela, *Wiener Mode und Modefotografie: Modeabteilung der Wiener Werkstätte, 1911-1932* (Munich, 1984)

BELGIUM AND THE NETHERLANDS

Primary materials

De Bijenkorf's-Gravenhage, *Uitgegeven ter herinnering aan de opening op 25 maart 1926* (Amsterdam, 1926)
De Jong, J., *De nieuwe richting in de Kunstnijverheid in Nederland: Schets eener gescheidenis der nederlandsche kunstnijverheidsbeweging* (Rotterdam, 1929)
Hack-Wijsmuller, K., *Vernieuwing in onze dagelijksche omgeving* (Rotterdam, 1927)
L'Art hollandais à l'Exposition internationale des arts décoratifs et industriels modernes (Paris and Amsterdam, 1925)
Michel, Edouard, 'La Section belge', *Art et décoration*, vol. lxviii (July 1925), pp. 75-88
Van Ravesteyn, Sybold, *De Sierkunst op Nederlansche passagierschepen* (Rotterdam, 1924)

Secondary sources

Adriaansz, Ellie, 'Fragmenten uit een kleurijk oeuvre. Drie biocoopinterieurs van Jaap Gidding', *Jong Holland*, vol. 2, no. 2 (1995), pp. 6-21
Bergvelt, Ellinoor and others, *Stichting Architectuur Museum: De Amsterdamse School* (Amsterdam, 1975)
Blotkamp, Carel (ed.), *De vervolgjaren van de stijl: 1922-1932* (Amsterdam and Antwerp, 1996)
Broos, Kees and Hefting, Paul, *Grafische vormgeving in Nederland* (Naarden, 1995)
Crouwel, Wim and Engelse, Bram, *Nederlandse architectuur, 1910-1930: Amsterdamse School* (Amsterdam, 1975)
De Boer, S., 'Wijdeveld en het theater', *Jong Holland*, vol. 8 (1992), pp. 25-35
De Bois, M., *C. A. Lion Cachet, 1864-1945* (Assen and Rotterdam, 1994)
De Bois, Mechteld, *Chris Lebeau, 1878-1945* (Assen and Haarlem, 1987)
De Roode, Ingeborg and Groot, Marjan, *Amsterdamse School: Textiel, 1915-1930* (Tilburg, 1999)
De Wit, Wim (ed.), *The Amsterdam School: Dutch Expressionist Architecture, 1915-1930* (Cambridge, MA and London, 1983)
Eliëns, Titus M., Groot, Marjan and Leidelmeijer, Frans, *Avant Garde Design: Dutch Decorative Arts, 1880-1940* (London, 1997)
Eliëns, Titus M., *T. A. C. Colenbrander, 1841-1930: Ontwerper van de Haagse Plateelbakkerij Rozenburg* (Zwolle, 1999)
Fanelli, Giovanni, *Moderne architectuur in Nederland, 1900-1940* ('s-Gravenhage, 1981)
Fraenkel, F., 'The Tuschinski Theatre', *Architectural Review*, vol. 153, no. 915 (May 1973), pp. 323-8
Gaillard, Karin (ed.), *From Neo-Renaissance to Postmodernism: A Hundred and Twenty Years of Dutch Interiors, 1870-1995* (Rotterdam, 1996)
Gaillard, Karin, Spitzen, Wim and Verschuuren, Antoine, *Vormen uit vuur: ESKAF: Eerste Steenwijker Kunst-Aarewerk Fabriek, 1919-1924* (Amsterdam, 2001)
Heller, Steven and Fili, Louise, *Dutch Modern: Graphic Design from De Stijl to Deco* (San Francisco, 1994)
Hoogenboezem, Emy, *Jac. Jongert, 1883-1942: Graficus tussen kunst en reclame* (The Hague, 1982)
Koopmans, Ype, *Muurvast & gebeiteld: Beeldwouwkunst in de bouw, 1840-1940* (Rotterdam, 1994)
Krekel-Aalberse, Annalies and others, *Jan Eisenloeffel, 1876-1957* (Zwolle, 1996)
Krekel-Aalberse, Annelies, *Carel J. A. Begeer, 1883-1956* (Assen and Zwolle, 2001)
Le Coultre, Martijn F., *Wendingen, 1918-1932: Architectuur en vormgeving* (Blaricum, 2001)
Leidelmeijer, Frans and Van der Cingel, Daan, *Art Nouveau en Art Deco in Nederland* (The Netherlands, 1983)
Leidelmeijer, Frans, Eliëns, Titus M. and Groot, Marjan, *Kunstnijverheid in Nederland, 1880-1940* (Bussum, 1999)

Mills, R., 'Kleurnuancen T. A. C. Colenbrander als tapijtontwerper', *Jong Holland*, vol. 10, no. 2 (1994), pp. 6-31
Ramakers, Renny, *Tussen kunstnijverheid en industriële vormgeving: De Nederlandsche Bond voor Kunst en Industrie* (Utrecht, 1985)
Stedelijk Museum, *Industrie & Vormgeving in Nederland, 1850-1950* (Amsterdam, 1985)
Taverne, Ed, Wagenaar, Cor and De Vletter, Martien, *J. J. P. Oud: Poetic Functionalist: The Complete Works, 1890-1963* (Rotterdam, 2001)
Timmer, Petra, *Metz & Co: De creatieve jaren* (Rotterdam, 1995)
Troy, Nancy, *The De Stijl Environment* (Cambridge, MA and London, 1983)
Vandenbreeden, Jos and Vanlaethem, France, *Art Déco et Modernisme en Belgique: Architecture de l'entre-deux-guerres* (Brussels, 1996)

BRITAIN

Journals

Commercial Art, continued as *Commercial Art and Industry* until 1936, then as *Art and Industry* (New York and London, 1922-58)
Country Life (London, 1897-)
Goldsmith's Journal (London, 1915-)
Illustrated London News (London, 1842-)
Jeweller and the Metalworker (London, 1894-1965)
Journal of the Decorative Arts Society (Brighton, 1985-)
Journal of the Design and Industries Association, continued as *DIA Quarterly* (London, 1917-32)
Queen (London, 1863-1970)
Studio (London, 1893-1964)
Studio Yearbook of Decorative Art, continued as *Decorative Art in Modern Interiors* (London and New York, 1906-1973/4)
Watchmaker and Jeweller, Silversmith and Optician (London, 1875-1949)

Primary materials

Beaton, Cecil, *The Book of Beauty* (London, 1930)
De la Valette, John (ed.), *The Conquest of Ugliness: A Collection of Contemporary Views on the Place of Art in Industry* (London, 1935)
Defries, Amelia, 'Craftsmen of the Empire: A Comparative Study of Decoration and the Industrial Arts', *Architectural Review*, vol. lv, no. 331 (June 1924), pp. 262-71
Ionides, Basil, *Colour and Interior Decoration* (London, 1926)
Lancaster, Osbert, *Homes Sweet Homes* (London, 1939)
Miller, Duncan, *Interior Decorating*, 'How to Do It' series (London, 1937)
Morley, H., 'A House full of Horrors', *Household Words* (December 1852)
Patmore, Derek, *Colour Schemes and Modern Furnishing* (London, 1947)
Pevsner, Nikolaus, *An Enquiry into Industrial Art in Britain* (Cambridge, 1937)
Pevsner, Nikolaus, *Pioneers of Modern Design* (London, 1949); first published as Pevsner, Nikolaus, *Pioneers of the Modern Movement from William Morris to Walter Gropius* (London, 1936)
Read, Herbert, *Art and Industry* (London, 1937)
Todd, Dorothy and Mortimer, Raymond, *The New Interior Decoration: An Introduction to its Principles, and International Survey of its Methods* (London and New York, 1929)
Yerbury, Francis Rowland, *Modern Homes Illustrated* (London, 1947)

Secondary sources

Allan, John, *Berthold Lubetkin: Architecture and the Tradition of Progress* (London, 1992)
Battersby, Martin, *The Decorative Thirties* (London, 1971)
Battersby, Martin, *The Decorative Twenties* (London, 1969)
Beaton, Cecil, *Fashion: An Anthology* (London, 1971)
Beaton, Cecil, *Photobiography* (London, 1951)
Beaton, Cecil, *The Glass of Fashion* (London, 1954)
Beaton, Cecil, *The Wandering Years: Diaries, 1922-1939* (London, 1961)
Buckle, Richard, *Self Portrait with Friends: The Selected Diary of Cecil Beaton, 1926-1974* (London, 1979)
Buckley, Cheryl, *Potters and Paintresses: Women Designers in the Pottery Industry, 1870-1951* (London, 1990)
Carrington, Noel, *Design and Decoration in the Home* (London, 1952)
Cartland, Barbara and others, *Norman Hartnell* (London, 1985)
Cartland, Barbara, *We Danced all Night* (London, 1971)
Casey, Andrew and Eatwell, Ann (eds), *Susie Cooper: A Pioneer of Modern Design* (London, 2002)
Casey, Andrew, *20th Century Ceramic Designers in Britain* (Woodbridge, 2001)
Chase, Edna Woolman and Chase, Ilka, *Always in Vogue* (London, 1954)
Coe, Peter and Reading, Malcolm, *Lubetkin and Tecton: Architecture and Social Commitment* (London and Bristol, 1981)
Coleman, Elizabeth A., *The Genius of Charles James* (New York, 1982)
Cooper, Diana, *The Light of Common Day* (London, 1959)
Dean, David, *The Thirties: Recalling the English Architectural Scene* (London, 1983)
Devlin, Polly, *Vogue Book of Photography* (London, 1979)
Eatwell, Ann, *Susie Cooper Productions* (London, 1987)
Ehrenkranz, Anne, *A Singular Elegance: The Photographs of Baron Adolf de Meyer* (San Francisco, 1994)
Garner, Philippe and Mellor, David Alan, *Cecil Beaton* (London, 1994)
Goodden, Susanna, *A History of Heal's: At the Sign of the Four-Poster* (London, 1984)
Griffin, Leonard, *Clarice Cliff: The Art of Bizarre* (London, 1999)
Haworth-Booth, Mark, *E. McKnight Kauffer: A Designer and his Public* (London, 1979)
Hitchmough, Wendy, *The Hoover Factory* (London, 1991)
Joel, David, *The Adventure of British Furniture, 1851-1951* (London, 1953)
Knight, Donald R. and Sabey, Alan D., *The Lion Roars at Wembley: British Empire Exhibition, 60th Anniversary, 1924-1925* (New Barnet, 1984)
Little, Alan, *Suzanne Lenglen: Tennis Idol of the Twenties* (London, 1988)
Marwick, Arthur, *A History of the Modern British Isles, 1914-1999: Circumstances, Events and Outcomes* (Oxford, 2000)
Marwick, Arthur, *Britain in Our Century: Images and Controversies* (London, 1984)
Mason, Shena, *Jewellery Making in Birmingham, 1750-1995* (Chichester, 1998)
Mellor, David, *Modern British Photography, 1919-1939* (London, 1980)
Mendes, Valerie, *British Textiles from 1900 to 1937* (London, 1992)
Menkes, Suzy, *Windsor Style* (London, 1987)
Oliver, Paul, Davis, Ian and Bentley, Ian, *Dunroamin: The Suburban Semi and its Enemies* (London, 1981)
Opie, Jennifer Hawkins and Hollis, Marianne, *Thirties: British Art and Design before the War* (London, 1979)
Pevsner, Nikolaus, *Victorian and After*, vol. 2 in *Studies in Art, Architecture and Design* (London, 1968)
Powers, Alan (ed.), *Modern Britain, 1929-39* (London, 1999)
Powers, Alan, *Serge Chermayeff: Designer, Architect Teacher* (London, 2001)
Snowdon, J. J. and Platts, R. W, 'Great West Road Style', *Architectural Review*, vol. 156, no. 929 (July 1974), pp. 21-7
Storey, Walter Rendell, *Furnishing with Colour* (London and New York, 1945)
Tilson, Barbara, 'The Modern Art Department, Waring and Gillow, 1929-1931', *Journal of the Decorative Arts Society*, no. 8 (1983)
Wilk, Christopher, 'Who was Betty Joel? British Furniture Design between the Wars', *Apollo*, vol. cxlii, no. 401 (July 1995), pp. 7-11
Woodham, Jonathan, 'Images of Africa and Design at the British Empire Exhibitions between the Wars', *Journal of Design History*, vol. 2, no. 1 (1989), pp. 15ff

CENTRAL AND EASTERN EUROPE

Journals

Czechoslovakia

Styl (1908-)
Umělecký měsíčnik (1911-)
Červen (1918-)

Hungary

Magyar iparművészet (1897-)

Poland

Arkady (1935-)
Rzeczy piękne (1918-)

Primary materials

David, Fernand and Léon, Paul, *Exposition internationale des arts décoratifs et industriels modernes: Union des républiques sovietiques socialistes: Catalogue* (Paris, 1925)
Hofman, Vlastislav, 'Nový principy v architecktuře', *Styl*, vol. 5 (1913), pp. 13-24
Homolacs, Karol, *L'Ornementation suivant la méthode de Charles Homolacs* (Kraków, 1925)
Szcuka, Mieczyscaw, 'Czy sztuka decoacyjna?', *Blok*, vol. 10 (1925)
Szekfü, Gyula, *Három nemzedék és ami utana következik* (Budapest, 1935)
Varenne, Gaston, 'L'Exposition des arts décoratifs: La Section polonaise', *Art et décoration*, vol. xlviii (September 1925), pp. 89-99
Verneuil, Maurice Pillard, 'L'Enseignement de l'art décoratif en Pologne', *Art et décoration*, vol. xlix (1926), pp. 33-44
Warchałowski, Jerzy, 'Jak Sen', *Ster*, no. 11 (1926)

Secondary sources

Běhal, Vera J., 'Czech Cubism in Arts and Crafts: "Artěl Studio for the Plastic Arts in Prague" and the "Prague Art Workshop"', *Kosmas: Journal of Czechoslovak and Central European Studies*, vol. 7, nos 1-2 (1988)
Birgus, Vladimir and Brany Antonín, *František Drtikol* (Prague, 1988)
Birgus, Vladimir, *The Photographer František Drtikol* (Prague, 2000)
Crowley, David, *National Style and Nation-State: Design in Poland from the Vernacular Revival* (Manchester, 1992)
Elliott, David and others, *Art into Production: Soviet Textiles, Fashion and Ceramics, 1917-1935* (London, 1984)
Fárová, Anna and Mrázková, Daniela, *František Drtikol* (Cologne and New York, 1983)
Fárová, Anna, *František Drtikol: Photographs des Art Deco* (Munich, 1986)
Ferkai, András, 'Art Deco in Hungarian Architecture', *Interpress Graphic*, no. 9 (1986)
Hornékova, Jana (ed.), *Art deco: Boemia, 1918-1938* (Milan, 1996)
Huml, Irena, 'Polish Art Deco: The Style of Regained Independence (the 1920s)', *Niedzica Seminars*, Association of Polish Art Historians (Warsaw, 1991)
Iparművészeti Múzeum, *Lajos Kozma: Az iparművész, 1884-1948* (Budapest, 1994)
Iparművészeti Múzeum, *Magyar Art Deco* (Budapest, 1985)
Kiss, Éva, 'La Formation et les sources de l'Art Déco hongrois', in Martine Caeymaex and Marc Lambrechts (eds), *Art Déco en Europe: Tendances décoratives dans les arts appliqués vers 1925* (Brussels, 1989)
Klaricová, Katerina, *František Drtikol* (Prague, 1989)
Mansbach, Steven A., *Modern Art in Eastern Europe: From the Baltic to the Balkans, c.1890-1939* (Cambridge, 1999)
Muzeum Narodowe w Krakøwie, *Art Deco w Polsce* (Krakøw, 1993)
Phillips, Sandra S., Travis, David and Naef, Weston J., *André Kertész of Paris and New York* (London, 1985)
Sieradzka, Anna, *Art Déco w Europie i w Polsce* (Warsaw, 1996)
Stritzhenova, Tatiana, *Soviet Costume and Textiles, 1917-1945* (Paris, 1991)
Umlěckoprůmyslové Muzeum v Praze, *Czech Art Deco, 1918-1938* (Milan, 1993; Prague, 1998)
Von Vegesack, Alexander (ed.), *Czech Cubism: Architecture, Furniture and Decorative Arts* (London, 1992)
Yasinskaya, Irina Mikhailovna, *Soviet Textile Design of the Revolutionary Period* (London, 1983)
Zaletova, Lidya and others, *Costume Revolution: Textiles, Clothing and Costume of the Soviet Union in the Twenties* (London, 1989)

FRANCE

Journals

Art et décoration: Revue mensuelle d'art moderne (Paris, 1897-1938)
Art et industrie (Paris, 1909-14, then 1925-54)
Art, goût et beauté (Paris, 1921-33)
Arts et métiers graphiques (Paris, 1927-48)
Fémina (Paris, 1901-38)
Gazette des beaux arts (Paris, 1929)
L'Art décoratif (Paris, 1898-1914)
L'Art et la mode (Paris, 1883-1969)
L'Art vivant (Paris, 1925-39)
L'Officiel de la couture et de la mode (Paris, 1920-)
La Gazette du bon ton (Paris, 1912-25)
La Renaissance de l'art français et des industries de luxe (Paris, 1918-28)
La Revue de l'art ancien et moderne (Paris, 1897-1937)
Le Jardin des modes (Paris, 1922-71)
Modes et manières d'aujourd'hui (Paris, 1912-22)
Revue de l'art (Paris, 1897-1937)
Vogue (Paris, 1920-)

Primary materials

Adler, Rose, *Reliures* (Paris, 1929)
Bénédictus, Edouard, *Variations: Quatre-vingt-six motifs décoratifs en vingt planches* (Paris, 1924)
Bénédictus, Edouard, *Nouvelles variations: Soixante-quinze motifs décoratifs en vingt planches* (Paris, 1929)
Bénédictus, Edouard, *Relais: Quinze planches donnant quarante-deux motifs décoratifs* (Paris, 1930)
Benoist, Luc, 'Les Arts de la rue', *Gazette des beaux arts* (August 1925)
Benoist, Luc, 'Victor Lhuer, dessinateur et tisserand', *Art et décoration*, vol. liii (1928), pp. 115-21
Blanche, Jacques-Emile, *Propos de peintres de Gauguin à la Revue nègre* (Paris, 1928)
Bonney, Thérèse and Bonney, Louise, *A Shopping Guide to Paris* (New York, 1929)
Bouyer, Raymond, 'Les Devantures parisiennes', *La Renaissance de l'art français et des industries de luxe* (December 1919)
Cassandre [Adolphe Mouron], 'Bifur, caractère de publicité dessiné par A. M. Cassandre', *Arts et métiers graphiques*, no. 9 (January 1929)
Catalogue du septième salon de la Société des artistes décorateurs (Paris, 1912)
Catalogue général officiel: Exposition internationale des arts décoratifs (Paris, 1925)
Cendrars, Blaise and Léger, Fernand, *La Fin du monde (filmée par l'ange)* (Paris, 1919)
Chavance, René, *Une Ambassade française: Exposition internationale de 1925* (Paris, 1925)
Clouzot, Henri, *La Ferronnerie moderne: Exposition internationale de 1925* (Paris, 1925-9)
Clouzot, Henri, *Le Style moderne dans la décoration intérieure* (Paris, 1921)
Clouzot, Henri and Level, André, *L'Art d'Afrique et l'art d'Océanie* (Paris, 1919)
Clouzot, Henri and Level, André, *Première Exposition d'art nègre et d'Océanie organisée par Paul Guillaume du 10 au 31 mai 1919* (Paris, 1919)
Cogniat, Raymond, *Dufy, décorateur* (Geneva, 1957)
Colin, Paul, *Le Tumulte noir* (Paris, 1927)
Delaunay, Sonia, *Compositions, couleurs, idées* (Paris, c.1930)
Department of Overseas Trade, *Reports on the Present Position and Tendencies of the Industrial Arts as Indicated at the International Exhibition of Modern Decorative and Industrial Art, Paris, 1925* (London, 1925)
Dervaux, Adolphe, *Les Pavillons étrangers: Exposition internationale de 1925* (Paris, 1925)
Dufrène, Maurice, *Ensembles mobiliers: Exposition internationale de 1925*, 3 vols (Paris, 1925)
Fouquet, Jean, *Bijoux et orfèvrerie* (Paris, 1931)
Gallotti, Jean, 'Le Cabinet de travail d'un grand voyageur', *Vogue* (December 1927), pp. 30-32
Gallotti, Jean, 'Les Arts indigènes à l'Exposition coloniale', *Art et décoration*, vol. lx (September 1931), pp. 69-100
Gramont, Elisabeth de, Duchess of Clermont-Tonnerre, 'The Lacquer Work of Miss Eileen Gray', *Living Arts* (March 1922)
Haardt, Georges-Marie and Audouin-Dubreuil, Louis, *The Black Journey Across Africa with the Citroën Expedition* (London, 1928)
Herbst, René, *Les Devantures, vitrines, installations de magasins: Exposition internationale de 1925* (Paris, 1925; London, 1927)
Hostache, Ellow H., 'Reflections on the Exposition des arts décoratifs', *Architectural Forum*, vol. xliv, no. 1 (January 1926), pp. 11-16
Iribe, Paul, *Les Robes de Paul Poiret racontées par Paul Iribe* (Paris, 1908)
Janneau, Guillaume, 'Introduction à l'Exposition des arts décoratifs, considérations sur l'esprit moderne', *Art et décoration*, vol. lxvii (May 1925), pp. 129-76
Janneau, Guillaume, *Le Luminaire et les procédés d'éclairage nouveaux:*

Exposition internationale de 1925 (Paris, 1929)
Joubin, André, 'Le Studio de Jacques Doucet', *L'Illustration*, 3 May 1930, pp. 17-21
L'Atelier Primavera et la décoration moderne, 1913-1923 (Paris, 1923)
Laran, Jean, 'Notre Enquête sur le mobilier moderne: Ruhlmann', *Art et décoration*, vol. xxxvii (January 1920), pp. 1-12
Le Corbusier, *L'Art décoratif d'aujourd'hui* (Paris, 1925; English translation, London, 1987)
Legrain, Pierre, *Objets d'art* (Paris, 1929)
Lepape, Georges, *Les Choses vues de Paul Poiret* (Paris, 1911)
Livre d'adresse de madame (Annuaire de la parisienne): Répertoire des principaux spécialistes et fournisseurs parisiens ainsi que de multiples adresses d'ordre pratique: Pour tout ce qui intéresse la femme et la maîtresse de maison (Paris, 1922)
Lord & Taylor, *An Exposition of Modern French Decorative Art* (New York, 1928)
Mallet-Stevens, Rob, 'Evolution ou mort de l'ornement', *L'Architecture d'aujourd'hui*, vol. 6 (1933)
Masson, Frédéric, 'Nos Leaders: L'Art munichois et ses apôtres', *L'Excelsior*, 30 March 1915
Mourey, Gabriel, 'The Paris International Exhibition, 1925: The French Buildings', *Studio*, vol. xc (1925), pp. 16-19
Moussinac, Léon, *Etoffes imprimées et papiers peints* (Paris, 1924)
Moutard-Uldry, Renée, 'Paul Bonet', *L'Art et les artistes*, vol. 34 (March 1937)
Paris, W. Francklyn, 'The International Exposition of Modern Industrial and Decorative Art in Paris', part 1, *Architectural Record*, vol. lviii (July-December 1925), pp. 265-77
Paris, W. Francklyn, 'The International Exposition of Modern Industrial and Decorative Art in Paris', part 2, *Architectural Record*, vol. lviii (October 1925), pp. 365-85
Patout, Pierre, *L'Architecture officielle et les pavillons: Exposition internationale de 1925* (Paris, 1925)
Poiret, Paul, *En habillant l'époque* (Paris 1930; reprint, Paris, 1986)
Poiret, Paul, *My First Fifty Years* (London, 1931)
Quénioux, Gaston, *Les Arts décoratifs modernes* (Paris, 1925)
Rambosson, Yvanhoé, *Les Batiks de Madame Pangon* (Paris, 1925)
Rapin, Henri, *La Sculpture décorative moderne: Exposition internationale de 1925* (Paris, 1925)
Read, Helen Appleton, 'The Exposition in Paris', part 1, *International Studio*, vol. 82 (November 1925), pp. 94-7
Read, Helen Appleton, 'The Exposition in Paris', part 2, *International Studio*, vol. 82 (December 1925), pp. 160-5
Report of a Commission Appointed by the Secretary of Commerce to Visit and Report upon the International Exposition of Modern Decorative and Industrial Arts in Paris, 1925 (Washington, 1926)
Roblin, M., *Rapport fait au nom de la Commission du commerce et de l'industrie chargé d'examiner la proposition de loi tendant à organiser en 1915 à Paris une exposition internationale des arts décoratifs modernes*, Chambre des Députés, 10e Legislature, Session de 1912 (Paris, 1912)
Sauvage, Marcel and Baker, Joséphine, *Mémoires de Joséphine Baker* (Paris, 1927)
Séguy, E.-A., *Bouquets et frondaisons: 60 motifs en couleurs* (Paris, 1926?)
Séguy, E.-A., *Suggestions pour étoffes et tapis* (Paris, 1923)
Thérive, André, 'Paul Colin, "Peintres et décors d'affiches"', *Arts et métiers graphiques*, vol. 10 (1929), pp. 615-20
V. G., 'La Course à l'abîme', *Art et industrie* (July 1909), n. p.
Vachon, Marius, *Les Musées et les écoles d'art industriel en Europe* (Paris, 1890)
Vaillat, Léandre, 'Le Décor de la vie: l'Exposition coloniale en 1931', *Le Temps*, vol. 71 (13 March 1931)
Varenne, Gaston, 'L'Architecture à l'Exposition coloniale', *Art et décoration* (1928)
Varenne, Gaston, 'L'Exposition des arts décoratifs: Le Mobilier français', *Art et décoration*, vol. xlviii (July 1925), pp. 1-44
Vauxcelles, Louis, 'Le Salon d'automne de 1910', *L'Art décoratif* (October 1910), pp. 113-45
Vera, André, 'Le Nouveau Style', *L'Art décoratif*, vol. xxvii (January 1912), pp. 21-32
Verne, Henri and Chavance, Réne, *Pour comprendre l'art décoratif moderne en France* (Paris, 1925)
Verneuil, Maurice Pillard, 'Le Salon d'automne', *Art et décoration*, vol. xxviii (November 1910)
Wilson, Robert Forrest, *Paris on Parade* (Indianapolis, 1924-5)

Secondary sources

Abel, Richard, *French Cinema: The First Wave, 1915-1929* (Princeton, 1984)
Addade, Stéphane-Jacques, *Bernard Boutet de Monvel* (Paris, 2001)
Archer Straw, Petrine, *Negrophilia: Avant Garde Paris and Black Culture in the 1920s* (New York, 2000)
Auslander, Leora, *Taste and Power: Furnishing Modern France* (Berkeley, Los Angeles and London, 1996)
Bachollet, Raymond, Bordet, Daniel and Lelieur, Anne-Claude, *Paul Iribe* (Paris, 1982)
Baillen, Claude, *Chanel solitaire* (Paris, 1971)
Ballard, Bettina, *In My Fashion* (London, 1960)
Baqué, Dominique, 'Le Premier Grand Illustré français, *Vu*', in Dominique Bacqué (ed.), *Les Documents de la modernité: Anthologies de textes sur la photographie de 1919 à 1939* (Paris, 1993)
Baron, Stanley, *Sonia Delaunay: The Life of an Artist* (London, 1995)
Barré-Despond, Arlette, *Dictionnaire des arts appliqués et du design* (Paris, 1996)
Barré-Despond, Arlette, *UAM: Union des artistes modernes* (Paris, 1986)
Battersby, Martin, *Art Deco Fashion* (London, 1974)
Baudot, François, *Eileen Gray* (London, 1998)
Becherer, R., 'Picturing Architecture Otherwise: The Voguing of the Maison Mallet-Stevens', *Art History*, vol. 23, no. 4 (November 2000), pp. 559-98
Benstock, Shari, *Women of the Left Bank: Paris, 1900-1940* (London, 1987)
Benton, Tim, *The Villas of Le Corbusier, 1920-1930* (New Haven and London, 1987)
Blake, Jody, *Le Tumulte Noir: Modernist Art and Popular Entertainment in Jazz-Age Paris, 1900-1930* (University Park, PA, 1999)
Bonneville, Françoise de, *Jean Puiforcat* (Paris, 1986)
Bouillon, Jean-Paul, *Art Deco, 1910-1940* (Geneva and New York, 1988)
Bouin, Philippe and Chanut, Christian-Philippe, *Histoire française des folies et des expositions universelles* (Paris, 1980)
Bouqueret, C. and Chavanne, Blandine, *La Nouvelle Photographie en France, 1919-1939* (Poitiers, 1986)
Bouqueret, C., *Laure Albin ou la volonté d'art* (Paris, 1997)
Bouqueret, C., *Les Femmes photographes de la Nouvelle vision en France, 1920-1940* (Paris, 1998)
Bouqueret, Christian, *Des Années folles aux Années noires: La nouvelle vision photographique en France, 1920-1940* (Paris, 1997)
Bouqueret, Christian, *Jean Miral: L'Oeil capteur* (Paris, 1999)
Bréon, Emmanuel (ed.), *Jacques-Emile Ruhlmann: Génie de l'Art déco* (Paris, 2001)
Bréon, Emmanuel and Pepall, Rosalind, *L'Art des années trente* (Paris, 1996)
Breunig, LeRoy C. (ed.), *Apollinaire on Art: Essays and Reviews, 1902-1918* (New York and London, 1972; reprint, 1988)
Brisby, Claire, 'Jacques Doucet and the Patronage of Art Deco', *Apollo*, vol. 149, no. 447 (May 1999), pp. 31-9
Brunhammer, Yvonne and Granet, Amélie, *Les Salons de l'automobile et de l'aviation, 1900-1960* (Paris, 1993)
Brunhammer, Yvonne and Tise, Suzanne, *The Decorative Arts in France, 1900-1942: La Société des Artistes Décorateurs* (New York, 1990)
Brunhammer, Yvonne, *1925* (Paris, 1976)
Brunhammer, Yvonne, *Les Années 25* (Paris, 1966)
Bucaille, Max and Laude, Jean, *Temps noir* (Paris, 1949)
Cain, Julien and Bonet, Paul, *Bibliothèque reliée par Paul Bonet: Relieures mosaïquées sur très beaux livres illustrés, éditions originales et de luxe, grands textes classiques* (Paris, 1963)
Cain, Julien and others, *Poiret le magnifique* (Paris, 1974)
Callu, Florence and others, *Sonia et Robert Delaunay: Le Centenaire* (Paris, 1985)
Camard, Florence, *Michel Dufet, architecte décorateur* (Paris, 1988)
Camard, Florence, *Ruhlmann, Master of Art Deco* (London, 1984)
Camard, Florence, *Süe et Mare* (Paris, 1993)
Chapon, François, *Mystère et splendeur de Jacques Doucet, 1853-1929* (Paris, 1984)
Charles-Roux, Edmonde, *Chanel* (London, 1976)
Charles-Roux, Edmonde, *Chanel and her World* (London, 1981)
Cohen, Jean-Louis and Eleb-Vidal, Monique, *Casablanca: Mythes et figures d'une aventure urbaine* (Paris, 1998)
Colin, Paul, *Le Tumulte noir* (Paris, 1927); reprinted as *Josephine Baker and La Revue Nègre: Paul Colin's Lithographs of Le Tumulte Noir in Paris, 1927*, with introduction by Karen C. C. Dalton and Henry Louis Gates (New York, 1998)
Constant, Caroline, *Eileen Gray* (London, 2000)
Cottington, David, *Cubism in the Shadow of the War: The Avant Garde and Politics in Paris, 1905-1914* (New Haven and London, 1998)
Damase, Jacques, *Sonia Delaunay: Fashion and Fabrics* (Paris and London, 1991)
De la Haye, Amy and Mendes, Valerie, *20th Century Fashion* (London, 1999)
De la Haye, Amy and Tobin, Shelley, *Chanel: The Couturière at Work* (London, 1994)
Delpierre, Madeleine, *Le Costume de 1914 aux Années folles* (Paris, 1990)
Demornex, Jacqueline, *Madeleine Vionnet* (London, 1991)
Deslandres, Yvonne, *Paul Poiret* (London, 1987)
Devauchelle, Roger, *La Reliure en France: Des origines à nos jours*, vol. iii (Paris, 1961)
Drouot, *Ancienne Collection Jacques Doucet* (sale cat., Paris, Drouot, 8 November 1972)
Ducharne, François, *Les Folles Années de la soie* (Lyon, 1975)
Duncan, Alastair and Bartha, Georges de, *Art Nouveau and Art Deco Bookbinding: The French Masterpieces, 1880-1940* (London, 1989)
Eliel, Carol S., *L'Esprit Nouveau: Purism in Paris, 1918-1925* (Los Angeles, 2001)
Erté (Romain Tirtoff), *Things I Remember: An Autobiography* (London, 1975)
Esten, John, Hartshorn, Willis and Foresta, Merry, *Man Ray in Fashion* (New York, 1990)
Etherington-Smith, Meredith, *Patou* (London, 1983)
Garner, Philippe, *Eileen Gray: Designer and Architect* (Cologne, 1993)
Garnier, Guillaume, *Paris Couture, Années trente* (Paris, 1987)
Garnier, Guillaume and others, *Paul Poiret et Nicole Groult* (Paris, 1986)
Gary, Marie-Noël de (ed.), *Les Fouquet: Bijoutiers et joailliers à Paris, 1860-1960* (Paris, 1983)
Gaudriault, Raymond, *La Gravure de mode féminine en France* (Paris, 1983)
Ginsburg, Madeleine, *Paris Fashions: The Art Deco Style of the 1920s* (London, 1989)
Giraudon, Colette, *Les Arts à Paris chez Paul Guillaume, 1918-1935* (Paris, 1993)
Golan, Romy, *Modernity and Nostalgia: French Art and Politics between the Wars* (New Haven and London, 1995)
Golding, John, *Cubism: A History and an Analysis, 1907-1914* (London, 1988)
Goulden, Bernard, *Jean Goulden* (Paris, 1989)
Green, Christopher, *Cubism and its Enemies: Modern Movements and Reactions in French Art, 1916-1928* (New Haven and London, 1987)
Gronberg, Tag, *Designs on Modernity: Exhibiting the City in 1920s Paris* (Manchester and New York, 1998)
Guillon, David, *Dufy-Poiret modèles* (Paris, 1998)
Heller, Steven and Fili, Louise, *French Modern: Art Deco Graphic Design* (San Francisco, 1997)
Herbst, René, *25 Années UAM* (Paris, 1956)
Hergott, Abramovic, *Fernand Léger et l'art africain* (Geneva, 2000)
Kahr, Joan, *Edgar Brandt: Master of Art Deco Ironwork* (New York, 1999)
Kirke, Betty, *Madeleine Vionnet* (San Francisco, 1998)
Kolosek, Lisa, *Thérèse Bonney* (London and New York, 2002)
L'Ecotais, Emmanuelle de and Sayag, Alain, *Man Ray: Photography and its Double* (Paris and London, 1998)
Laurent, Stéphane, *Chronologie du design* (Paris, 1999)
Laurent, Stéphane, *Les Arts appliqués en France: Genèse d'un enseignement, 1851-1940* (Paris, 1999)
Lebovics, Herman, *True France: The Wars over Cultural Identity, 1900-1945* (Ithaca, 1992)
Léger, Fernand, *Functions of Painting* (London and New York, 1973)
Leong, Roger and others, *From Russia with Love: Costumes for the Ballets Russes, 1909-1933* (Canberra, 1999)
Leymarie, Jean, *Chanel* (New York, 1987)
Madsen, Axel, *Coco Chanel: A Biography* (London, 1990)
Marcilhac, Félix, *Jean Dunand: His Life and Works* (London, 1991)
Martin, Marc, *Trois Siècles de publicité en France* (Paris, 1992)
McMillan, James F., *Twentieth Century France: Politics and Society, 1898-1991* (London, 1992)
Morand, Paul, *L'Allure de Chanel* (Paris, 1976)
Morano, Elisabeth (introduction), *Sonia Delaunay: Art into Fashion* (New York, 1986)
Morel, Juliette, *Lingerie Parisienne* (London, 1976)
Morton, Patricia A., *Hybrid Modernities: Architecture and Representation at the 1931 Colonial Exposition, Paris* (Cambridge, MA, 2000)
Mouron, Henri, *Cassandre: Posters, Typography, Stage Designs* (London, 1985)
Nadelhoffer, Hans, *Cartier: Jewellers Extraordinary* (London, 1984)
Néret, Gilles, *Boucheron: Four Generations of a World-Renowned Jeweller* (New York, 1988)
Nesbit, Molly, *Atget's Seven Albums* (New Haven and London, 1992)
Osma, Guillermo, *Fortuny: His Life and his Work* (London, 1980)
Parrot, Nicole, *Mannequins* (Paris, London and New York, 1981)
Penn, Irving and Vreeland, Diana, *Inventive Paris Clothes, 1900-1939* (London, 1977)
Perry, Gill, *Women Artists and the Parisian Avant-Garde: Modernism and 'Feminine' Art, 1900 to the late 1920s* (Manchester and New York, 1995)
Possémé, Evelyne, *1910-1930: Les Années 1925* (Paris, 1999)
Pradel, Marie-Noëlle, 'La Maison cubiste en 1912', *L'Art de France*, vol. i (1961), pp. 177-86
Ritchie, Ward, *Art Deco: The Books of François-Louis Schmied, Artist, Engraver, Printer: With Recollections and Descriptive Commentaries on the Books* (San Francisco, 1987)
Robertson, Bryan and others, *Raoul Dufy, 1877-1953* (London, 1983)
Roegiers, Patrick and Baque, Dominique, *François Kollar* (Paris, 1989)
Rouaud, Jacques, *Soixante Ans d'arts ménagers*, 2 vols (Paris, 1989 and 1993)
Rudoe, Judy, 'Cartier', *Jewellery Studies*, vol. 9 (2001). (Papers of the Symposium held jointly by the British Museum and the Society of Jewellery Historians at the British Museum, 1997)
Rudoe, Judy, *Cartier, 1900-1939* (London, 1997)
Schiaparelli, Elsa, *Shocking Life* (London, 1954)
Sherringham, Michael (ed.), *Parisian Fields* (London, 1996)
Silver, Kenneth, *Esprit de Corps: The Art of the Parisian Avant-Garde and the First World War, 1914-1925* (London, 1989)
Silvermann, Debora L., *L'Art Nouveau in Fin-de-Siècle France: Politics, Psychology and Style* (Los Angeles and Berkeley, 1989)
Sirop, Dominique and others, *Paquin* (Lyon, 1989)
Société de la Reliure Originale (Jacques-Antoine Legrain and others), *Pierre Legrain, relieur: Répertoire déscriptif et bibliographique de mille cent trente-six reliures* (Paris, 1965)
Sougez, Marie-Loup and Rochard, Sophie, *Emmanuel Sougez: L'Eminence grise* (Paris, 1993)
Steele, Valerie, *Paris Fashion: A Cultural History* (Oxford and New York, 1988)
Tate Gallery, *Léger and Purist Paris* (London, 1970)
Thornton, Lynne, 'Negro Art and the Furniture of Pierre Emile Legrain', *Connoisseur*, vol. 181, no. 729 (November 1972), pp. 166-9
Tise, Suzanne, 'Les Grands Magasins', in Catherine Arminjon and others, *'L'Art de Vivre': Decorative Arts and Design in France, 1789-1989* (London, 1989)
Tise, Suzanne, *Between Art and Industry: Design Reform in France, 1851-1939* (Ann Arbor, 1991)
Toulet, Emmanuelle (ed.), *Le Cinéma au*

rendez-vous des arts: France, années 20 et 30 (Paris, 1995)
Troy, Nancy, 'Towards a Redefinition of Tradition in French Design, 1895-1914', *Design Issues*, vol. i (Fall 1984), pp. 53-69
Troy, Nancy, *Modernism and the Decorative Arts in France: Art Nouveau to Le Corbusier* (New Haven and London, 1991)
Tuchscherer, J.-M. and others, *Raoul Dufy: Créateur d'étoffes* (Mulhouse, 1973)
Vassiliev, Alexandre, *Beauty in Exile: The Artists, Models and Nobility who Fled the Russian Revolution and Influenced the World of Fashion* (New York, 2000)
Weiss, Andrea, *Paris as a Woman: Portraits from the Left Bank* (London and San Francisco, 1995)
White, Palmer, *Elsa Schiaparelli* (London, 1986)
White, Palmer, *Haute Couture Embroidery: The Art of Lesage* (Paris, 1987)
White, Palmer, *Paul Poiret* (London, 1973)
Zervos, Christian, 'La Leçon de l'Exposition des arts décoratifs et industriels de 1925', *Les Arts de la maison*, vol. 3 (Autumn-Winter 1925)

GERMANY

Journals

Bauhaus (Dessau, 1926-31)
Dekorative Kunst (Munich, 1897-1929)
Deutsche Kunst und Dekoration (Darmstadt, 1897-1932)
Die Kunst (Munich, 1899-1940)

Primary materials

Bredt, Ernst Wilhelm, 'Bruno Paul – Biedermeier – Empire', *Dekorative Kunst*, vol. 13 (March 1905), pp. 217-28
Forthuny, Pascal, 'Les Décorateurs allemands à Paris en 1924', *L'Amour de l'art*, vol. iii (1922), pp. 53-64
Muche, Georg, 'Bildende Kunst und Industrieform', *Bauhaus*, vol. 1, no. 1 (Dessau, 1926)
Platz, Gustav Adolf, *Die Baukunst der Neuesten Zeit* (Berlin, 1927)
Schultze-Naumburg, Paul, 'Biedermeier Stil?', *Die Kunstwart*, vol. 19 (1905-6), pp. 131-7

Secondary sources

Aynsley, Jeremy, *Graphic Design in Germany, 1890-1945* (London, 2000)
Baacke, Rolf-Peter, *Lichtspielhausarchitectur in Deutschland: Von der Schaubude bis zum Kinopalast* (Berlin, 1982)
Becker, Ingeborg and Högermann, Dieter, *Bröhan-Museum: Berliner Porzellan vom Jugendstil zum Functionalismus, 1889-1939* (Berlin, 1987)
Berghahn, Volker Rolf, *Modern Germany: Society, Economy and Politics in the Twentieth Century* (Cambridge, 1987)
Bröhan, Karl H., *Bröhan-Museum Berlin: Berlin State Museum for Art Nouveau. Art Deco and Functionalism, 1889-1939: Arts, Crafts, Industrial Design, Picture Gallery* (Berlin, 1998)
Bröhan-Museum, *Kunst der 20er und 30er Jahre*, vol. iii of *Sammlung Karl H. Bröhan Berlin* (Berlin, 1985)
Bröhan-Museum, *Kunst des Jahrhundertwende und der Zwanziger Jahre*, vol. i of *Sammlung Karl H. Bröhan Berlin* (Berlin, 1985)
Brüning, Ute (ed.), *Das A und das O des Bauhauses* (Leipzig, 1995)
Buddensieg, Tilmann, *Keramik in der Weimarer Republik, 1919-1933: Die Sammlung Tilmann Buddensieg im Germanischen Nationalmuseum* (Nuremberg, 1985)
Burke, Christopher, *Paul Renner: The Art of Typography* (London, 1988)
Campbell, Joan, *The German Werkbund: The Politics of Reform in the Applied Arts* (Princeton, 1978)
Duvigneau, Volker, *Plakate in München, 1840-1940* (Munich, 1978)
Duvigneau, Volker and Götz, Norbert, *Ludwig Hohlwein, 1874-1949* (Munich, 1996)
Günther, Sonja, *Das deutsche Heim: Luxusinterieurs und Arbeitermöbel von der Gründerzeit bis zum 'Dritten Reich'* (Giessen, 1984)
Heskett, John, '*Design in Inter-War Germany*', in Wendy Kaplan (ed.), *Designing Modernity: The Arts of Reform and Persuasion, 1885-1945* (London, 1995)
Heskett, John, *Design in Germany, 1870-1918* (London, 1986)
Nerdinger, Winfried, *Riemerschmid: Von Jugendstil zum Werkbund: Werke und Dokumente* (Munich, 1982)
Schwartz, Frederic, J., *The Werkbund: Design Theory and Mass Culture before the First World War* (New Haven and London, 1996)
Sichel, Kim, *Germaine Krull: Photographer of Modernity* (Cambridge, MA and London, 1999)
Tilson, Barbara, 'Plan Furniture, 1932-1938: The German Connection', *Journal of Design History*, vol. 3, nos 2 and 3 (1990)
Volmerstein, Tina, *Der Stil der Zwanziger: Art Deco–Bauhaus–De Stijl* (Munich, 1966)
Ward, Janet, *Weimar Surfaces: Urban Visual Culture in 1920s Germany* (Los Angeles and London, 2001)
Werner, Petra, *Die zwanziger Jahre: Deutsches Porzellan zwischen Inflation und Depression: Die Zeit des Art Deco?!* (Berlin, 1992)
Wichmann, Hans, *Design contra Art Déco, 1927-1932: Jahrfünft der Wende* (Munich, 1993)
Ziffer, Alfred, Drebusch, Thomas and others, *Bruno Paul: Deutsche Raumkunst und Architektur zwischen Jugendstil und Moderne* (Munich, 1992)

NORDIC COUNTRIES (DENMARK, NORWAY, FINLAND, SWEDEN)

Journals

Ord och bild (Stockholm, 1892-?)
Scandinavian Journal of Design History (Copenhagen, 1991-)
Skønvirke: Meddelser fra forening for kunsthaandverk (Copenhagen, 1914-27)
Suomen aikakauskirja – (Tidskrift) (Helsinki, 1874-)
Svenska slöjdföreningens tidskrift (Stockholm, 1876-1904)

Primary materials

Key, Ellen, *Skönhet för alla* (Stockholm, 1899)
Shand, Philip Morton, 'Stockholm 1930', *Architectural Review*, vol. 68, no. 405 (1930)
Wettergren, Erik, *The Modern Decorative Arts of Sweden* (London, 1927); first published as *L'Art décoratif moderne en Suède* (Malmö, 1925) to accompany the Paris 1925 Exhibition
Wollin, Nils G., *Modern Swedish Decorative Art* (London, 1931)

Secondary sources

Caldenby, Claes (ed.), *20th Century Architecture: Sweden* (Munich and New York, 1998)
De Maré, Eric, *Gunnar Asplund: A Great Modern Architect* (London, 1955)
Iionen, Arvi, *Helsinki: An Architectural Guide* (Otava, 1990)
McFadden, David (ed.), *Scandinavian Modern Design, 1880-1980* (New York, 1982)
Pearson, Paul David, *Alvar Aalto and the International Style* (New York, 1978)
Selkurt, Claire, 'New Classicism: Design of the 1920s in Denmark', *Journal of Decorative and Propaganda Arts*, vol. 4 (Spring 1987), pp. 16-29
St John Wilson, Colin: *Gunnar Asplund (1885-1940): The Dilemma of Classicism* (London, 1988)

SOUTHERN EUROPE

Journals

Casabella
Domus
Emporium

Primary materials

Giolli, Raffaello, 'L'artigiano al bivio', *Colosseo*, vol. iii (October 1933)
Muzio, Giovanni, 'L'architettura a Milano intorno all'Ottocento', *Emporium*, no. 317 (May 1921), pp. 241-58
Pagano, Giuseppe, 'Tre anni di architettura in Italia', *Casabella*, vol. x, no. 110 (February 1937)
Papini, Roberto, 'Dagli architetti ai pastori', *Emporium*, no. 369 (September 1925), pp. 138-60
Papini, Roberto, *Le arti d'oggi: Architettura e arti decorative in Europa* (Milan and Rome, 1930)
Pica, Vittorio, 'L'arte decorativa all'Esposizione di Torino', *Emporium*, fasc.iv (1903)
Ponti, Gio, 'Le ragioni dello stile moderno', *L'Italia all' Esposizione internazionale di arti decorative e industriali moderne* (Paris and Milan, 1925)
Rava, Carlo Enrico, 'Spirito latino', *Domus*, vol. 11 (February 1931), pp. 24-9
Sarfatti, Margherita, *L'Italie à l'Exposition internationale des arts décoratifs et industriels modernes, Paris 1925* (Paris, 1925)

Secondary sources

Altea, Giuliana and Magnani, Marco, *Pittura e scultura del primo'900* (Nuoro, 1995)
Barilli, Renato and others, *Gli anni trenta* (Milan, 1982)
Barisione, Silvia, Fochessati, Matteo and Franzone, Gianni, *La visione del prisma: La collezione Wolfson* (Milan, 1999)
Bossaglia, Rossana and Terraroli,Valerio, *Milano déco: La fisionomia della città negli anni venti* (Milan, 1999)
Bossaglia, Rossana, *Il Deco italiano: Fisionomia dello stile 1925 in Italia* (Milan, 1997)
Brunetti, Fabrizio, *Architetti e fascismo* (Florence, 1993)
Castagno, Laura, *Il designer Giuseppe Pagano* (Bari, 1994)
Ciucci, Giorgio, *Gli architetti e il Fascismo* (Turin, 1989)
Danesi, Silvia and Patetta, Luciano, *Il Razionalismo e l'architettura in Italia durante il Fascismo* (Venice, 1976)
De Guttry, Irene, Maino, Maria Paola and Raimondi, Gloria, *Duilio Cambellotti: Arredi e decorazioni* (Bari, 1999)
Doordan, Dennis D., *Building Modern Italy: Italian Architecture, 1914-1936* (New York, 1988)
Etlin, Richard, *Modernism in Italian Architecture, 1890-1940* (Cambridge, MA and London, 1991)
Giolli, Raffaello, 'Pubblicità', *Casabella-Costruzioni*, vol. 132 (December 1938)
Gregotti,Vittorio (ed.), *Il disegno del prodotto industriale: Italia, 1860-1980* (Milan, 1986)
Heller, Steven and Fili, Louise, *Deco España: Graphic Design of the Twenties and Thirties* (San Francisco, 1997)
Heller, Steven and Fili, Louise, *Italian Art Deco Graphic Design between the Wars* (San Francisco, 1993)
Irace, Fulvio, *Giovanni Muzio, 1893-1982: Opere* (Milan, 1994)
La Pietra, Ugo (ed.), *Gio Ponti* (Milan, 1988)
Lupano, Mario, *Marcello Piacentini* (Rome, 1991)
Matteucci Armandi, Anna Maria and others, *Angiolo Mazzoni, 1894-1979: Architetto nell'Italia tra le due guerre* (Casalecchio di Reno, 1984)
Patetta, Luciano, *L'architettura in Italia, 1919-1943: Le polemiche* (Milan, 1972)
Pérez Rojas, J., *Art Déco en España* (Madrid, 1990)
Ponti, Lisa Licitra, *Gio Ponti: The Complete Work, 1923-1978* (London, 1990)
Quintavalle, Arturo Carlo, *Marcello Nizzoli* (Milan, 1989)
Stone, Marla Susan, *The Patron State: Culture and Politics in Fascist Italy* (Princeton and Chichester, 1998)
Waibl, Heinz, *The Roots of Italian Visual Communication* (Castellarano, 1998)

United States of America

Journals

Architectural Record (New York, 1891-)
Arts & Decoration (New York, 1919-32)
Fortune (New York, 1930-)
Good Furniture Magazine (Grand Rapids, Mich., 1925-9)
Harper's Bazar, later known as *Harper's Bazaar* (New York, 1867-)
International Studio (New York, 1897-1931)
New Yorker (New York, 1925-)

Primary materials

'American Modernist Furniture Inspired by Sky-Scraper Architecture', *Good Furniture Magazine*, vol. 29 (September 1927)
Bel Geddes, Norman, *Horizons* (New York, 1932; reprint, 1977)
Brooklyn Museum, *Contemporary Industrial and Handwrought Silver* (Brooklyn, 1937)
Cheney, Sheldon and Cheney, Martha Candler, *Art and the Machine: An Account of Industrial Design in 20th Century America* (New York, 1936; reprint, 1992)
Corbett, Harvey Wiley, 'The American Radiator Building, New York City', *Architectural Record*, vol. 55, no. 5 (May 1924)
Dawes, R. F. C., *A Century of Progress Exhibition: Official View Book* (Chicago, 1933)
'Designers' Task Defined', *New York Times*, 13 December 1939
Eberlein, Hubbard, *Glass in Modern Construction: Its Place in Architectural Design and Decoration* (New York, 1937)
Enyeart, James, *Bruguière: His Photographs and his Life* (New York, 1977)
Flanner, Janet, *An American Profile of an Interlude between Two Wars* (Paris and New York, 1940)
Frankl, Paul, 'Just what is this Modernistic Movement', *Arts & Decoration* (May 1928)
Glassgold, C. Adolph, 'The Modern Note in Decorative Arts', *Arts*, vol. 13 (April 1928)
Hitchcock, Henry Russell, 'Two Chicago Fairs', *New Republic*, 21 January 1931
Hood, Raymond and North, Arthur, *Raymond Hood* (London and New York, 1931)
Hooper, P. M., 'Modern Architectural Decoration', *Architectural Forum*, vol. xlviii (February 1928)
Horwitt, Nathan G., 'Plans for Tomorrow: A Seminar in Creative Design', *Advertising Arts* (July 1934)
Kahn, Ely Jacques, *Ely Jacques Kahn* (New York and London, 1931)
Leonard, Richard Lawrence and Glassgold, C. Adolph (eds), *Modern American Design: By the American Union of Decorative Artists and Craftsmen* (New York, 1930; reprint, 1992)
Libby-Owens-Ford Glass Company, *52 Designs to Modernize Main Street with Glass* (Toledo, 1935)
Linn, James Weber, *The Official Pictures of A Century of Progress Exhibition, Chicago 1933* (Chicago, 1933)
Lougee, Earl F., 'From Old to New with Lurelle Guild', *Modern Plastics*, vol. 12 (March 1935)
Meyers, Ella Burns, 'Trends in Decoration', *Good Furniture Magazine* (September 1928)
'Metals that Lend Harmony to the Home', *New York Times*, 11 December 1927
Müller-Munk, Peter, 'The Future of Product Design', *Modern Plastics*, vol. 20 (June 1943)
Müller-Munk, Peter, 'Vending Machine Glamour', *Modern Plastics*, vol. 17 (February 1940)
Park, Edwin Avery, *New Backgrounds for a New Age* (New York, 1927)
Price, Matlack, 'Contempora', *Good Furniture Magazine* (May 1929)
Read, Helen Appleton, 'Twentieth-Century Decoration: The Filter of American Taste', *Vogue*, vol. 71 (June 1928)
Richards, Charles R., 'Sane and Insane Modernism in Furniture', *Good Furniture Magazine* (January 1929)
Rourke, Constance, 'American Art: A Possible Future', *American Magazine of Art*, vol. xxvii, no. 7 (July 1935), pp. 390-404
Salmon, André, *John Storrs and Modern Sculpture* (New York, 1923)
Sanford, Nellie, 'An Architect-Designer of Modern Furniture', *Good Furniture Magazine*, vol. 30 (March 1928)
Sanford, Nellie, 'Modern Furniture Designed in America: It Must Meet American Living Conditions', *Good Furniture Magazine* (April 1929), pp. 184-92
Teague, Walter Dorwin, 'Structural and Decorative Trends in Glass', *American Architect*, vol. 141 (May 1932)
Updegraff, Robert R., *The New American Tempo and the Stream of Life* (Chicago, 1929)
Vassos, John and Vassos, Ruth, *Contempo: This American Tempo* (New York, 1929)
Wright, Russel, 'Outlines for Living', *Arts & Decoration*, vol. xxxix, no. 7 (November 1933)

Secondary sources

Adams, Henry, *Viktor Schreckengost and 20th Century Design* (Cleveland, OH, 2000)
Allen, James Sloan, *The Romance of Commerce and Culture: Capitalism, Modernism, and the Chicago–Aspen Crusade for Cultural Reform* (Chicago and London, 1983)
Baker, A. Houston, *Modernism and the Harlem Renaissance* (Chicago, 1987)
Baudrillard, Jean, *America* (London, 1988)
Bearden, Romare and Henderson, Harry, *A History of African American Artists: From 1792 to the Present* (New York, 1993)
Bollack, François Astorg and Killian, Tom, *Ely Jacques Kahn: New York Architect* (New York, 1995)
Bourke-White, Margaret, *Portrait of Myself* (London, 1964)
Boyd Meyer, Marylee and others, *Inspiring Reform: Boston's Arts and Crafts Movement* (Wellesley, MA and New York, 1997)
Brebner, John Bartlett, *Canada: A Modern History* (Ann Arbor, 1970)
Breeze, Carla, *New York Deco* (New York, 1993)
Breeze, Carla, *Pueblo Deco* (New York, 1990)
Brown, Ashley, 'Ilonka Karasz: Rediscovering a Modernist Pioneer', *Studies in the*

Decorative Arts, vol. 8, (Fall-Winter 2000-2001)
Callahan, Sean, *Margaret Bourke-White: Photographer* (Boston and London, 1998)
Callahan, Sean, *The Photographs of Margaret Bourke-White* (London, 1973)
Capitman, Barbara Baer, Kinerk, Michael D. and Wilhelm, Dennis W., *Rediscovering Art Deco USA* (New York and London, 1994)
Cassidy, Donna M., *Painting the Musical City: Jazz and Cultural Identity in American Art, 1910-1940* (Washington, 1997)
Chierichetti, David, *Hollywood Costume Design* (London, 1976)
Clark, Robert Judson and others, *Design in America: The Cranbrook Vision, 1925-1950* (New York, 1983)
Davidson, Abraham, *Early American Modernist Painting: 1910-1935* (New York, 1981)
Davies, Karen, *At Home in Manhattan: Modern Decorative Arts, 1925 to the Depression* (New Haven, 1983)
'Does America Have a Design Heritage?', *Product Engineering*, vol. 30, no. 20 (18 May 1959), pp. 36-43
Douglas, Ann, *Terrible Honesty: Mongrel Manhattan in the 1920s* (New York, 1995)
Duncan, Alastair, *American Art Deco* (London, 1986)
Falino, Jeannine, 'Women Metalsmiths', in Pat Kirkham (ed.), *Women Designers in the USA, 1900-2000* (New York, 2000), pp. 223-45
Frackman, Noel, *John Storrs* (New York, 1987)
Franci, Giovanna and others, *In viaggio attraverso il deco americano* (Florence, 1997)
Gebhard, D. and Von Breton, Harriette, *LA in the Thirties: 1931-1941* (Layton, UT 1975; revised as *Los Angeles in the Thirties: 1931-1941*, Los Angeles, 1989)
Gebhard, David, *Robert Stacy-Judd: Maya Architecture and the Creation of a New Style* (Santa Barbara, 1993)
Gebhard, David, *The National Trust Guide to Art Deco in America* (New York, 1996)
Gebhard, David, *Tulsa Art Deco* (Tulsa, 1988)
Gilbert, James, *Perfect Cities: Chicago's Utopias of 1893* (Chicago, 1991)
Gilroy, Paul, *The Black Atlantic: Modernity and Double Consciousness* (London, 1993)
Goldberg, Vicki, *Margaret Bourke-White: A Biography* (New York, 1986)
Greif, Martin, *Depression Modern: The Thirties Style in America* (New York, 1975)
Gutman, Richard J. S. and Kaufman, Elliott, *American Diner* (New York, 1979)
Gutner, Howard, *Gowns by Adrian: The MGM Years, 1928-1941* (New York, 2001)
Hall, Lee, *Common Threads: A Parade of American Clothing* (Boston, 1992)
Hambourg, Maria Morris and Phillips, Christopher, *The New Vision: Photography between the World Wars: Ford Motor Company Collection at the Metropolitan Museum of Art, New York* (New York, 1989)
Harris, Neil, 'Museums, Merchandising and Popular Taste: The Struggle for Influence', in Ian M. G. Quimby (ed.), *Material Culture and the Study of American Life* (New York, 1977), pp. 140-74
Harrison, Helen A., *Dawn of a New Day: The New York World's Fair, 1939/40* (Flushing, NY, 1980)
Harrison, Robert, *State and Society in Twentieth Century America* (London and New York, 1997)
Heller, Steven and Fili, Louise, *American Art Deco Graphic Design* (San Francisco, 1995)
Ingle, Marjorie I., *The Mayan Revival Style: Art Deco Mayan Fantasy* (Salt Lake City, 1984)
Jakle, John A. and Sculle, Keith A., *The Gas Station in America* (Baltimore, 1994)
Johnson, Donald-Brian, *Chase Complete: Deco Specialities of the Chase Brass & Copper Co.* (Atglen, PA, 1999)
Johnson, J. Stewart, *American Modern, 1925-1940: Design for a New Age* (New York, 2000)
Johnston, Patricia, *Real Fantasies: Edward Steichen's Advertising Photography* (Berkeley and London, 1997)
Kaplan, Wendy (ed.), *'The Art that is Life': The Arts & Crafts Movement in America, 1875-1920* (New York, 1987)
Kardon, Janet (ed.), *Craft in the Machine Age: The History of Twentieth-Century American Craft, 1920-1945* (New York, 1995)
Kilbride, Richard J., *Art Deco Chrome: The Chase Era* (Stamford, CT, 1998)
Kilham, Walter Harrington, *Raymond Hood, Architect* (New York, 1973)
Klein, Dan, 'The Chanin Building, New York', *Connoisseur*, vol. 1, no. 186 (July 1974), pp. 162-9
Koolhaas, Rem, *Delirious New York* (New York, 1973; reprint, Rotterdam, 1994)
Lejeune, Jean-François and Schulman, Allan T., *The Making of Miami Beach: The Architecture of Lawrence Murray Dixon* (New York, 2000)
Lemke, Sieglinde, *Primitivist Modernism: Black Culture and the Origins of Transatlantic Modernism* (Oxford, 1998)
Liebs, Chester H., *Main Street to Miracle Mile: American Roadside Architecture* (Boston, 1985)
Maffei, Nicolas P., 'Designing the Image of the Practical Visionary: Norman Bel Geddes, 1893-1958', unpublished PhD thesis, Royal College of Art, London, 2001
Mandelbaum, Howard and Myers, Eric, *Screen Deco: A Celebration of High Style in Hollywood* (New York and Bromley, 1985)
Marchand, Roland, *Advertising the American Dream: Making Way for Modernity, 1920-1940* (Berkeley, 1985)
McEuen, Melissa A., *Seeing America: Women Photographers between the Wars* (Lexington, VA, 2000)
Meikle, Jeffrey L., *American Plastic: A Cultural History* (New Brunswick, 1995)
Meikle, Jeffrey L., *Twentieth Century Limited: Industrial Design in America: 1925-1939* (Philadelphia, 1979)
Messler, Norbert, *The Art Deco Skyscraper in New York* (New York, 1986)
Milbank, Caroline Rennolds, *New York Fashion: The Evolution of American Style* (New York, 1989)
Niven, Penelope, *Steichen: A Biography* (New York, 1989)
Ockner, Paula and Pina, Leslie, *Art Deco Aluminum: Kensington* (Atglen, PA, 1997)
Powell, Richard J. and Bailey, David A., *Rhapsodies in Black: Art of the Harlem Renaissance* (London, 1997)
Proddow, Penny and Healy, Debra, *American Jewelry: Glamour and Tradition* (New York, 1987)
Raulet, Sylvie, *Van Cleef and Arpels* (New York, 1987)
Reeves, Thomas C., *Twentieth Century America: A Brief History* (New York and Oxford, 2000)
Robinson, Cervin and Haag Bletter, Rosemarie, *Skyscraper Style: Art Deco in New York* (New York, 1975)
Sands, Gordon Eliot, 'The Osborn Furniture: Modern Decorative Arts and the Department Store', *Decorative Arts Society Newsletter*, vol. 9 (September 1983)
Schönberger, Angela (ed.), *Raymond Loewy: Pioneer of American Industrial Design* (Munich, 1990)
Silverman, Jonathan, *The Life of Margaret Bourke-White* (New York, 1983)
Smith, Terry, *The Making of the Modern: Industry, Art and Design in America* (Chicago, 1993)
Sobel, Robert, *The Age of Giant Corporations: A Microeconomic History of American Business, 1914-1984* (Westport, CT and London, 1984)
Steichen, Edward, *A Life in Photography* (London, 1963)
Steichen, Joanna, *Steichen's Legacy: Photographs, 1895-1973* (New York, 2000)
Stern, Robert A. M., Gilmartin, Gregory and Mellins, Thomas, *New York 1930: Architecture and Urbanism between the Two World Wars* (New York, 1987)
Subirats, Eduardo, *La transfiguración de la noce: La utopia arquitectonica de Hugh Ferriss* (Malaga, 1992)
Susman, Warren Irving, 'The People's Fair: Cultural Contradictions of a Consumer Society', in Helen A. Harrison, *Dawn of a New Day: The New York World's Fair, 1939/1940* (Flushing, NY, 1980)
Szarkowski, John, *Photography until Now* (New York, 1989)
Tselos, Dimitri, 'Exotic Influences in the Architecture of Frank Lloyd Wright', *Magazine of Art* (April 1953)
Turner, Gordon, *The Empress of Britain: Canadian Pacific's Greatest Ship* (Toronto, 1992)
Varian, Elayne H., *American Art Deco Architecture* (New York, 1975)
Venable, Charles, *Silver in America, 1840-1940: A Century of Splendour* (Dallas, 1995)
Venturi, Robert, Scott Brown, Denise and Izenour, Steven, *Learning from Las Vegas* (Cambridge, MA, 1972)
Williams, Elisabeth A., 'Art and Artefact at the Trocadéro: Ars America and the Primitivist Revolution in European Identities', in George W. Stocking (ed.), *Objects and Others: Essays on Museums and Material Culture* (Madison, Wisc., 1985), pp. 146-66
Wilson, Richard Guy, Pilgrim, Dianne H. and Tashjian, Dickran, *The Machine Age in America, 1918-1941* (New York, 1986)

Asia: China, Japan, India

Journals

Gofujin Techō [Lady's handbook] (Tokyo, Shiseido)
Josei [Woman] (Tokyo)
Journal of the Indian Institute of Architects (Bombay, 1934-)
Ku-Raku [Joys and sorrows] (Tokyo)
Liangyou Huabao [Young companion's pictorial] (Shanghai)
Shanghai Huabao [Shanghai pictorial] (Shanghai)
Shinseinen [New youth] (Tokyo)
Shirabaka [White birch] (Tokyo)

Primary materials

Acton, Harold, *Memoirs of an Aesthete* (London, 1948)
Akimoto Shunkichi, *The Lure of Japan* (Tokyo, 1934)
Auden, W. H. and Isherwood, Christopher, *Journey to War* (London, 1939)
Burlington Fine Art Club, *Catalogue of a Collection of Chinese Art* (London, 1915)
Catalogue des ouvrages modernes de peinture, sculpture, arts décoratifs et des oeuvres anciennes: Exposition d'art japonais au Salon de la société nationale des beaux-arts (Paris, 1922)
Catalogue illustré de la section japonaise à l'Exposition internationale des arts décoratifs et industriels modernes (Paris, 1925)
Chu Chia-Chein and Iacovleff, Alexandre, *The Chinese Theatre* (London, 1922)
Exposition d'Art japonais (École classique contemporaine) (Paris, 1929)
Fréchet, André, 'Notre Enquête sur le mobilier moderne: La Lacque', *Art et décoration*, vol. 37 (1920), pp. 41-8
Fry, Roger (ed.), *Chinese Art* (London, 1925)
Koechlin, Raymond, 'Les Bronzes chinois', *Art et décoration*, vol. 47 (1925), pp. 44-56
La Chine à l'Exposition internationale des arts décoratifs et industriels modernes à Paris, 1925 (Paris, 1925)
Liberty & Co., *Jade Amulets* (London, 1919)
Nott, Sydney Charles, *Chinese Jade throughout the Ages* (London, 1936)
Royal Academy of Arts, *Catalogue of the International Exhibition of Chinese Art, 1935-6* (London, 1935)
Ruan Lingyu, no. 2 of *Dian Ying Nu Ming Xing Zhao Xiang Ji* [Albums of Chinese movie stars] (Shanghai, 1934)

Secondary sources

Ajioka, Chiaki, *Early Mingei and the Development of Japanese Crafts, 1920s-1940s*, unpublished PhD thesis, Australian National University, Canberra, 1995
Alff, Jon, 'Art Deco, Gateway to Indian Modernism', *Architecture + Design* (November-December 1991), pp. 57-63
Alff, Jon, 'Temples of Light: Bombay's Art Deco Cinemas and the Birth of Modern Myth', in Pauline Rohatgi and others, *Bombay to Mumbai: Changing Perspectives* (Mumbai, 1997), pp. 250-57
All about Shanghai (Shanghai, 1934; reprinted Oxford, 1983)
Andrews, Julia F. and Shen, Kuiyi, *A Century in Crisis: Modernity and Tradition in the Art of Twentieth Century China* (New York, 1998)
Baker, Barbara (ed.), *Shanghai: Electric and Lurid City* (Oxford, New York and Hong Kong, 1998)
Bognar, Botond, *Nikken Sekkei: Building Future Japan, 1900-2000* (New York, 2000)
Brandon, Reiko Mochinaga, *Bright and Daring: Japanese Kimono in the Taisho Mode* (Honolulu, 1996)
Clark, Hazel, *The Cheongsam* (Oxford and New York, 2000)
Clunas, Craig 'Chinese Art and Chinese Artists in France, 1924-25', *Arts Asiatiques: Annales du Museé Guimet et du Museé Cernuschi*, vol. 44 (1989), pp. 100-106
Clunas, Craig, 'Oriental Antiquities/Far Eastern Art', *Positions: East Asia Cultures Critique*, vol. 2, no. 2 (1994), pp. 318-55
Dal Lago, Francesca, 'Crossed Legs in 1930s Shanghai: How "Modern" is the Modern Woman?', *East Asian History*, no. 19 (June 2000), pp. 103-44
Duus, P., *The Twentieth Century*, vol. 6 of *The Cambridge History of Japan* (Cambridge, 1988)
Dwivedi, Sharada and Mehrotra, Rahul, *Bombay: The Cities Within* (Bombay, 1995)
Evenson, Norma, *The Indian Metropolis: A View toward the West* (New Haven and London, 1989)
Faulkner, Rupert, *Japanese Studio Crafts: Tradition and the Avant-Garde* (London, 1995)
Fraser, James and others, *Japanese Modern: Graphic Design between the Wars* (San Francisco, 1996)
Gumpert, Lynn (ed.), *Face to Face: Shiseido and the Manufacture of Beauty, 1900-2000* (New York, 2000)
Hansford, S. Howard, *Jade: Essence of Hills and Streams* (Cape Town, Johannesburg and London, 1969)
Hida Toyojirō, *Modernism no Kōgeikatachi* [Modernism and craftsmen: The 1920s and the 1930s] (Tokyo, 1983)
Hokkaido Museum of Modern Art (ed.), *Nihon Kōgei no Seishunki, 1920-1945* [Craft movements in Japan, 1920-1945] (Tokyo, 1996)
Holmes, Fred and Newton Holmes, Ann, *Bridging Traditions: The Making of Umaid Bhawan Palace* (Delhi, 1995)
Huebner, Jon W., 'Architecture on the Shanghai Bund', *Papers on Far Eastern History*, vol. 39 (1989), pp. 127-65
Inax Corporation, *Kenchiku no Terracotta* [Terracotta in architecture] (Tokyo, 1983)
Iyer, Kamu (ed.), *Buildings that Shaped Bombay: Works of G. B. Mhatre, FRIBA, 1902-1973* (Mumbai, 2001)
Jaffer, Amin, *Furniture from British India and Ceylon* (London, 2001)
Johnston, Tess, *A Last Look: Western Architecture in Old Shanghai* (Hong Kong, 1998)
Kaneko, Kenji and Imai, Yōko, *Sugiura Hisui Ten: Toshi Seikatsu no Designer* [Hisui Sugiura: A retrospective] (Tokyo, 2000)
Kim, H. J. and DeLong, M. R., 'Sino-Japanism in Western Women's Fashionable Dress in *Harper's Bazar*, 1890-1927', *Clothing and Textiles Research Journal*, vol. 11, no. 1 (1992), pp. 24-30
Kirihara, Donald, *Patterns of Time: Mizoguchi and the 1930s* (Madison, 1992)
Koo, Madame Wellington with Taves, Isabella, *No Feast Lasts Forever* (New York, 1975)
Kyoto Costume Institute (ed.), *Mōdo no Japonism* [Japonism in fashion] (Kyoto, 1994)
Lang, Jon, Desai, Madhavi and Desai, Miki, *Architecture & Independence: The Search for Identity: India, 1880-1980* (Delhi, 1997)
Lee, Leo Ou-fan, *Shanghai Modern: The Flowering of a New Urban Culture in China, 1930-1945* (Cambridge, MA and London, 1999)
Levy, Adrian and Scott-Clark, Cathy, *The Stone of Heaven: The Secret History of Imperial Green Jade* (London, 2001)
Ling, Pan, *In Search of Old Shanghai* (Hong Kong, 1982)
Martin, Richard and Koda, Howard, *Orientalism: Visions of the East in Western Dress* (New York, 1994)
Matsubara, Ryūichi and others, *Kyoto no Kōgei: Dentō to Henkaku no Hazaman ni* [Crafts reform in Kyoto, 1910-1940: A struggle between tradition and renovation] (Kyoto, 1998)
Meech, Julia, *Frank Lloyd Wright and the Art of Japan: The Architect's other Passion* (New York, 2001)
Menzies, Jackie (ed.), *Modern Boy, Modern Girl: Modernity in Japanese Art, 1910-1935* (Sydney, 1998)
Michell, George, *The Royal Palaces of India* (London, 1994)
Mie Prefectural Museum (ed.), *1910s*, vol. i of *Nijū-seiki Nihon Bijitsu Saiken* [A retrospective view of the art of the twentieth century] (Tsu, 1995)
Mie Prefectural Museum (ed.), *1920s*, vol. ii of *Nijū-seiki Nihon Bijitsu Saiken* [A retrospective view of the art of the twentieth century] (Tsu, 1996)
Mie Prefectural Museum (ed.), *1930s*, vol. iii of *Nijū-seiki Nihon Bijitsu Saiken* [A retrospective view of the art of the twentieth century] (Tsu, 1999)
Mikimoto Pearl Island Co. Ltd (ed.), *Kajayaki no Seiki: Mikimoto Shinjū Hatsmei 100 Shūnen Kinen* [A century of glistening: Commemorating 100 years since the

discovery of Mikimoto pearls] (Toba, 1993)
Minick, Scott and Ping, Jiao, *Chinese Graphic Design in the Twentieth Century* (London, 1990)
Ng Chun Bong and others (eds), *Chinese Woman and Modernity: Calendar Posters of the 1910s-1930s* (Hong Kong, 1996)
Niggl, Reto, *Eckart Muthesius: International Style, 1930: The Maharaja's Palace in Indore: Architecture and Interior* (Stuttgart, 1996)
Nute, Kevin, *Frank Lloyd Wright and Japan: The Role of Traditional Japanese Art and Architecture in the Work of Frank Lloyd Wright* (London and New York, 1993)
P&T Group, *P&T Group: 130 Years of Architecture in Asia* (Hong Kong, 1998)
Rawson, Jessica, *Chinese Jade from the Neolithic to the Qing* (London, 1995)
Reischauer, Edwin O. and Craig, Albert M., *Japan: Tradition and Transformation* (Sydney, London and Boston, 1979)
Reynolds, Jonathan M., 'The Bunriha and the Problem of "Tradition" for Modernist Architecture in Japan, 1920-1928', in Sharon A. Minichiello (ed.), *Japan's Competing Modernities: Issues in Culture and Democracy, 1900-1930* (Honolulu, 1998)
Rohmer, Sax, *The Fu Manchu Omnibus*, vol. 1 (London, 2000)
Seidensticker, E., *Tokyo Rising: The City since the Great Earthquake* (New York, 1990)
Seidensticker, Edward, *Low City, High City: Tokyo from Edo to the Earthquake* (London, 1983; reprint, Cambridge, MA, 1991)
Sergeant, Harriet, *Shanghai* (London, 1991)
Silverberg, M., 'The Café Waitress Serving Modern Japan', in Stephen Vlastos (ed.), *Mirror of Modernity: Invented Traditions of Modern Japan* (Berkeley, Los Angeles and London, 1998)
Silverberg, Miriam, 'Remembering Pearl Harbour, Forgetting Charlie Chaplin and the Case of the Disappearing Western Woman: A Picture Story', in Tani E. Barlow (ed.), *Formations of Colonial Modernity* (Durham and London, 1997), pp. 249-94
Spence, Jonathan, *The Search for Modern China* (London, Sydney, Auckland and Johannesburg, 1990)
Steele, Valerie and Major, John S., *China Chic: East meets West* (New Haven and London, 1999)
Stewart, David B., *The Making of a Modern Japanese Architecture: 1868 to the Present* (Tokyo and New York, 1987)
Stipe, Margo, 'Wright and Japan', in Anthony Alofsin (ed.), *Frank Lloyd Wright: Europe and Beyond* (Berkeley, Los Angeles and London, 1999)
Suetsugu, Takashi, *Nihon no Art Deco* [Japanese Art Deco] (Tokyo, 1999)
Tanigawa Masami, *Measured Drawing: Frank Lloyd Wright in Japan* (Tokyo, 1980)
Thornton, Richard S., *Japanese Graphic Design* (London, 1991)
Tillotson, Giles H. R., *The Tradition of Indian Architecture: Continuity, Controversy and Change since 1850* (Delhi, 1989)
Tipton, Elise K. and Clark, John (eds), *Being Modern in Japan: Culture and Society from the 1910s to the 1930s* (Honolulu, 2000)
Tokyo Jin [Tokyo people], no. 152 (April 2000)
Tokyo Metropolitan Teien Art Museum (ed.), *Art Deco to Tōyō 1920-30 nendai: Paris o Yume Mita Jidai* [Art Deco and the Orient, 1920s-1930s: Longing for Paris] (Tokyo, 2000)
Tokyo Metropolitan Teien Art Museum (Tokyo, 1987)
Waring & Gillow, *Estimate Sketches for Furnishing Hyderabad House*, Oriental and India Office Collections, British Library, D1219 (New Delhi)
Watson, Anne (ed.), *Beyond Architecture: Marion Mahony and Walter Burley Griffin: America, Australia, India* (Sydney, 1998)
Wood, Frances, *No Dogs and not many Chinese: Treaty Port Life in China, 1843-1943* (London, 1998)
Yamamoto Taketoshi and Nishizawa Tamotsu (eds), *Hyakkaten no Bunka-shi: Nihon no Shōhi Kakumei* [The cultural history of the department store: A revolution of consumption in Japan] (Tokyo, 1999)
Young, Louise, *Japan's Total Empire: Manchuria and the Culture of Wartime Imperialism* (Berkeley and London, 1998)
Zhang Yingjin (ed.), *Cinema and Urban Culture in Shanghai, 1922-1943* (Stanford, 1999)
Zhang, Yenfeng, *Lao Yue Fen Pai Guang Gao Hua* [Old calendar advertisements] (Taipei, 1994)

South America

Primary materials

Gamio, Manuel (ed.), *La problación del Valle de Teotihuacan* (Mexico, 1922)
Museum of Modern Art, *Twenty Centuries of Mexican Art* (New York, 1940)
Peñafiel, Antonio, *Explication de l'Edifice mexicain à l'Exposition internationale de Paris en 1889* (Barcelona, 1889)
Spinden, Herbert J., *A Study of Maya Art* (Cambridge, MA, 1913)
Stephens, John, *Incidents of Travel in Central America: Chiapas and Yucatan* (New York, 1841)

Secondary sources

Anda Alanís, Enrique X. de, 'A arquitetura déco no México: Uma proposta de vanguarda em tempos de modernidade', *Art Déco na América Latina 1º Seminário Internacional* (Rio de Janeiro, 1997), pp. 29-35
Anda Alanís, Enrique X. de, *Art Déco: Un país nacionalista, un Mexico cosmopolita* (Mexico, 1997)
Arrestizábal, Irma, 'John Graz and the Graz-Gomide Family', *Journal of Decorative and Propaganda Arts*, vol. 21 (1995), pp. 181-95
Art Déco na América Latina: 1º Seminário Internacional (Rio de Janeiro, 1997)
Benchimol, Jaime Larry, *Pereira Passos: Um Haussmann tropical* (Rio de Janeiro, 1990)
Bernal, Ignacio, *A History of Mexican Archaeology* (London, 1980)
Bushnell, David and Macauley, Neil, *The Emergence of Latin America in the Nineteenth Century* (Oxford, 1994)
Carvalho, José Murilo de, *A formação das almas: O imaginário da república no Brasil* (São Paulo, 1990)
Chiarelli, Tadeu, *Um jeca nos vernissages* (São Paulo, 1995)
Eliash, Humberto, 'O *Art Déco* no Chile: Último estilo acadêmico e primeiro estilo moderno', *Art Déco na América Latina: 1º Seminário internacional* (Rio de Janeiro, 1997)
Fabris, Annateresa (ed.), *Modernidade e modernismo no Brasil* (Campinas, 1994)
Fontainha, Affonso, *História dos monumentos do Distrito Federa* (Rio de Janeiro, 1954)
Franco, Luiz Fernando, 'Francisco Bologna, ou modernidade resistente ao cliché modernista', *Arquitetura revista*, vol. 6 (1988)
Grinberg, Lucia, 'República Católica-Cristo Redentor', in Paulo Knauss (ed.), *Cidade vaidosa: Imagens urbanas do Rio de Janeiro* (Rio de Janeiro, 1999)
Keen, Benjamin, *The Aztec Image in Western Thought* (New Brunswick, NJ, 1971)
Lima, Evelyn and Furquim, Werneck, *Avenida Presidente Vargas: Uma drástica cirurgia* (Rio de Janeiro, 1990)
Luiz, Paulo Conde and others, 'Proto-modernism em Copacabana', *Arquitetura revista*, vol. 3 (1985/6), pp. 40-49
Luiz, Paulo Conde, 'Art Déco: Modernidade antes do movimento moderno', *Art Déco na América Latina: 1º Seminário internacional* (Rio de Janeiro, 1997)
Mindlin, José E., 'Illustrated Books and Periodicals in Brazil, 1875-1945', *Journal of Decorative and Propaganda Arts*, vol. 21 (1995)
Platt, Desmond (ed.), *Business Imperialism, 1840-1930: An Enquiry based on British Experience in Latin America* (Oxford, 1977)
Prado, Antonio Arnoni, *1922: Itinerário de uma falsa vanguarda: Os dissidentes, a Semana e o integralismo* (São Paulo, 1983)
Ramos, Jorge, 'Buenos Aires déco: A outra modernidade', *Art Déco na América Latina: 1º Seminário internacional* (Rio de Janeiro, 1997), pp. 60-64
Resende, Beatriz, 'Melindrosa e Almofadinha, Cock-tail e arranha-céu: Imagens de uma literatura Art Déco', *Art Déco na América Latina: 1º Seminário internacional* (Rio de Janeiro, 1997)
Schwartzman, Simon, Bomeny, Helena Maria Bousquet and Costa, Vanda Maria Ribeiro, *Tempos de Capanema* (São Paulo, 2000)
Segre, Roberto, 'Havana déco: Alquimia urbana da primeira modernidade', *Art Déco na América Latina: 1º Seminário internacional* (Rio de Janeiro, 1997)
Sisson, Rachel, 'Rio De Janeiro, 1875-1945: The Shaping of a New Urban Order', *Journal of Decorative and Propaganda Arts*, vol. 21 (1995), pp. 146-7
Skidmore, Thomas E. and Smith, Peter H., *Modern Latin America* (Oxford, 1989)
Sodré, Nelson Werneck, *A história da imprensa no Brasil* (Rio de Janeiro, 1966)
Süssekind, Flora, *Cinematógrafo de letras: Literatura, técnica e modernização no Brasil* (São Paulo, 1987)
Tenorio-Trillo, Mauricio, *Mexico at the World's Fairs: Crafting a Modern Nation* (Chicago, 1991)
Velloso, Mônica Pimenta, *Modernismo no Rio de Janeiro: Turunas e Quixotes* (Rio de Janeiro, 1996)
Wolfe, Bertram, *The Fabulous Life of Diego Rivera* (New York, 1963)

Australasia

Architecture (Sydney, 1917-55)
Art in Australia (Sydney, 1916-?)
The Home (Sydney, 1920-40)

Primary materials

The Burdekin House Exhibition: Catalogue (Sydney, 1929)
Wilkinson, Kenneth, 'Michael O'Connell's Fabrics', *Art in Australia*, series 3, vol. 67 (15 May 1937), pp. 50-53
Wunderlich, Ernest, *All my Yesterdays: A Mosaic of Music and Manufacturing* (Sydney, 1945)

Secondary sources

Bogle, Michael, *Design in Australia, 1880-1970* (Sydney, 1998)
Cochrane, Grace, *The Crafts Movement in Australia: A History* (Sydney, 1992)
Draffin, Nicholas, *The Art of M. Napier Waller* (Melbourne, 1978)
Edwards, Deborah, *'This Vital Flesh': The Sculpture of Rayner Hoff and his School* (Sydney, 1999)
Fahy, Kevin and Simpson, Andrew, *Australian Furniture: Pictorial History and Dictionary, 1788-1938* (Sydney, 1998)
Ferson, Mark and Nilsson, Mary (eds), *Art Deco in Australia: Sunrise over the Pacific* (Sydney, 2001)
Graham, Marjorie, *Australian Glass of the 19th and early 20th Century* (Sydney, 1981)
Graham, Marjorie, *Australian Pottery of the 19th and early 20th Century* (Sydney, 1979)
Ives, Heather, *The Art Deco Architecture of Napier* (New Zealand, 1982)
Lumby, Roy and van Daele, Patrick, *A Spirit of Progress: Art Deco Architecture in Australia* (Sydney, 1997)
McPhee, John, 'Simple Modern Furniture of the 1930s', *Art in Australia*, vol. 37, no. 1 (1999), pp. 82-7
McPhee, John, *Australian Decorative Arts in the Australian National Gallery* (Canberra, 1982)
Menz, Christopher, *Australian Decorative Arts: 1820s-1990s: Art Gallery of South Australia* (Adelaide, 1996)
Museum of Sydney, *Art Deco: Exhibition Guide* (Sydney, 1999)
Schofield, Anne and Fahy, Kevin, *Australian Jewellery: 19th and early 20th Century* (Sydney, 1990)
Shaw, Peter and Hallett, Peter, *Art Deco Napier: Styles of the Thirties* (Napier, 1990; reprint, Nelson, 1994)
Thomas, Daniel, 'Art Deco in Australia', *Art in Australia*, vol. 9, no. 4 (1972), pp. 338-51
Thomas, David, *The Art of Christian Waller* (Bendigo, Victoria, 1992)
Thorne, Ross, *Cinemas of Australia via USA* (Sydney, 1981)
Timms, Peter, *Australian Studio Pottery and China Painting* (Melbourne, 1986)
Watson, Anne (ed.), *Beyond Architecture: Marion Mahony and Walter Burley Griffin: America, Australia, India* (Sydney, 1998)

South Africa

Primary materials

Battiss, Walter, *The South African Paint Pot* (Pretoria, 1942)
Daily Dispatch, 29 September 1936 (East London)
Pearse, Geoffrey Eastcott, 'Epochs in Building History', *Star*, 22 September 1936 (Johannesburg)
Pierneef, Hendrik, *Natal Advertiser*, 13 July 1926 (Durban)
Smuts, Jan, *Rand Daily Mail*, 22 September 1936 (Johannesburg)
'The Lovely Homes of Johannesburg', *Cape Times Supplement*, 18 August 1936
'The Year in Review', *South African Architectural Record* (December 1934), p. 310

Secondary sources

Bell, Brendan and Calder, Ian (eds), *Ubumba: Aspects of Indigenous Ceramics in KwaZulu-Natal* (Pietermaritzburg, 1998)
Berman, Esmé, *Art and Artists of South Africa* (Rotterdam, Cape Town, 1983)
Chipkin, Clive, *Johannesburg Style: Architecture and Society, 1880s-1960* (Cape Town, 1993)
Crump, Alan, Niekerk, Raymund van and Grundlingh, Geoffrey, *Public Sculpture and Reliefs: Cape Town* (Woodstock, 1988)
Dubow, Neville (ed.), *Paradise: The Journals and Letters of Irma Stern, 1917-1933* (Diep River, 1991)
Fransen, Hans, *Three Centuries of South African Art* (Pietermaritzburg, 1982)
Freschi, Federico, 'Big Business Beautility: The Old Mutual Building, Cape Town, South Africa', *Journal of Decorative and Propaganda Arts*, vol. 20 (1994), pp. 39-57
Greig, Doreen, *A Guide to Architecture in South Africa* (Cape Town, 1971)
Hillebrand, Melanie, *Art and Architecture in Natal, 1910-1940* (Durban, 1986)
Hillebrand, Melanie, *The Women of Olifantsfontein: South African Studio Ceramics* (Cape Town, 1991)
Hilton, Judin and Vladislavic, Ivan (eds), *Blank – Architecture: Apartheid and After* (Rotterdam, 1999)
Howie, W. D., 'Contemporary Architecture', *Lantern*, vol. vii (4 June 1958)
Howie, W. D., *Contemporary Architecture in South Africa* (Pretoria, 1958)
Louw, Teresa and others, *The Buildings of Central Cape Town*, 3 vols (Cape Town, 1978-84)
Martin, Marilyn, 'Art Deco Architecture in South Africa', *Journal of Decorative and Propaganda Arts*, vol. 20 (1994), pp. 9-37
Mount, Marshall W., *African Art: The Years Since 1920* (Bloomington, Ind., 1973)
Oxley, John, *Stained Glass in South Africa* (Rivonia, 1994)

Object List

Art Deco 1910-1939 V&A 27 March – 20 July 2003

Note: the object list was correct at the time of going to press.
Dimensions: height x width x depth.

Introduction

THE STYLE AND THE AGE

Jacques-Emile Ruhlmann: dressing table.
Oak with amaranth and mahogany veneer; ebony and ivory inlays; silver-bronze mirror frame and fittings; mirrored glass. 119 x 76 x 52.5 cm. French, 1925. V&A: W.14-1980. Plate 8.6.

Tamara de Lempicka (born in Poland): *Jeune fille en vert*.
Oil on panel. 61.5 x 45.5 cm. Around 1927. Centre Georges Pompidou, Paris. MNAM: JP 557 P. Plate 1.1.

Enoch Boulton: 'Jazz', ginger jar.
Earthenware, painted in enamels and gilt. 26 x 23 cm (diameter). British, *c*.1928-30. 'Carlton Ware' made by Wiltshaw & Robinson Ltd. V&A: Circ.526-1974. Plate 21.3.

Jeanne Paquin: 'Chimère', evening gown.
Embroidered and beaded silk. 122 x 120 cm (circumference of the hem). French, 1925. V&A: T.50-1948. Plate 6.5.

Franz Hagenauer: mirror with woman's head.
Brass and mirrored glass. Height: 64.5 cm. Hagenauer workshops, Vienna. Austrian, *c*.1925. Bröhan-Museum, Berlin: inv. no. 95.909.

Yamazaki Kakutarō: jewellery box.
Lacquer on wood. 17 x 25.5 x 10.5 cm. Japanese, 1934. Kyoto Municipal Museum. Plate 6.16.

Erik Magnussen (born in Denmark): 'Cubic', coffee service, or 'The Lights and Shadows of Manhattan'.
Silver, silver gilt and oxidized silver. Coffee pot height: 24.1 cm. American, 1927. Made by Gorham Manufacturing Company. Museum of Art, Rhode Island School of Design, Providence: 1991.126.488.1-4. Gift of Textron Inc. Plate 32.2.

John R. Morgan: Waterwitch outboard motor.
Steel, aluminium and rubber. 94 x 40.6 x 61 cm. American, 1936. Made by Sears, Roebuck. Gift of John C. Waddell, 1998. The Metropolitan Museum of Art, New York: 1998.537.28. Plate 33.10.

Cassandre (Adolphe Mouron): *Etoile du Nord*, poster.
Colour lithograph. 105.4 x 76.2 cm. French, 1927. V&A: E.224-1935. Plate 2.4.

Sources

ANCIENT AND EXOTIC

Egypt

Reproduction of the vulture pectoral of Tutankhamun.
Imitation of gold inlaid with lapis lazuli and coloured glass. Original is ancient Egyptian, from a tomb at Biban el-Moluk, 18th Dynasty. National Museums of Scotland: A.1976.113.

Reproduction of the pectoral of Princess Sit-Hathor.
Gold inlaid with imitation cornelian, lapis lazuli and turquoise. Original is ancient Egyptian, from Dashur, 12th Dynasty. National Museums of Scotland: A.1976.114.

Winged scarab.
Faience. 5 x 17.8 cm. Egyptian, Late Period, 790-332 BC. Museum of Fine Arts, Boston: 72.3019a-c.

Inlay in the form of a lotus.
Faience. 4.8 x 4.6 cm. Egyptian, New Kingdom, Dynasty 18, 1539-1295/1292 BC. Museum of Fine Arts, Boston: 27.1438.

Pectoral.
Bright blue faience with black details. Height: 9.1 cm. Egyptian, Third Intermediate Period, Dynasty 21, 1075-945 BC. Museum of Fine Arts, Boston: 56.315.

Cartier: Egyptian sarcophagus vanity case.
Gold, platinum, carved bone, sapphires, emeralds, diamonds, onyxes and enamel. 3.3 x 4 x 15 cm. French, 1925. Cartier Collection, Geneva: VC 70 A25. Plate 3.1.

Cartier: Egyptian *nécessaire*.
Enamelled gold, coral, lapis lazuli, emeralds, diamonds, platinum and Egyptian calcite plaque. 2.1 x 5.2 x 9.8 cm. French, 1927. Cartier Collection, Geneva: VC 65 A27.

Cartier: Egyptian *nécessaire*.
Gold, mother-of-pearl, coral, lapis lazuli, onyx, diamonds and blue-glazed Egyptian faience figure. 9.2 x 44 x 20 cm (with ring and thongs). French, 1924. Cartier Collection, Geneva: VC 64 A 24.

Cartier: Flying scarab brooch.
Gold, platinum, rubies, emeralds, diamonds, citrine, onyx and faience. 12.43 x 5.51 x 1.90 cm. French, 1925. Cartier Collection, Geneva: CL 264 A25.

Sequin jacket with Egyptian motifs.
Hand-beaded lurex. 67 x 53 cm. Probably French, *c*.1922-9. V&A: T.91-1999. Plate 3.5.

Classical Art

Vase.
Earthenware. Red figure technique. 34.29 x 17.78 cm. Greek, c.450-440 BC. V&A: 738-1864.

Raoul Dufy: *Cortège d'Orphée*, design for a textile.
Pencil and bodycolour on point paper. 123 x 86 cm. French, *c*.1927. V&A: E.1401-2001.

Paul Manship: *The Flight of Europa*.
Bronze. 53 x 79.3 x 21.9 cm. American, 1925. Collection Lionel and Geraldine Sterling. Plate 1.4.

Jaroslav Horejc: *Pallas Athena*.
Painted and gilded carved wood. Height: 38 cm. Czech, 1920. UPM – Decorative Arts Museum, Prague: 59.583.

Carl Milles: *Dancing Maenad*.
Carved limestone. 160 x 102 x 60 cm. Swedish, 1912. Carl Milles Museum, Stockholm. See Plate 4.1 for bronze version.

Ancient Mexican Art

Auguste Lazo (Mexican): tiles with Mayan motifs.
Glazed stoneware. Framed: 124.2 x 95.55 x 10.2 cm; tile: 30 x 20.32 cm. Made by American Encaustic Tiling Company, 1928. Collection John P. Axelrod on loan to the Museum of Fine Arts, Boston. Plate 5.8.

Lydia Bush-Brown Head: 'Temple of the Mayan Indians', furnishing fabric. Silk. 77.5 x 125 cm. American, 1926. Gift of Mrs Francis Head. Cooper-Hewitt, National Design Museum, Smithsonian Institution: 1977-77-7. Plate 5.3.

Inspiration from the Far East

Lacquer panels from a shrine.
Lacquer on wood. 153.5 x 34.5 cm; 153.5 x 35 cm; 148.5 x 37.5 cm; 148.5 x 36.8 cm. Japanese, 19th century. V&A: W.1A/9-1913, W.1A/10-1913, W.1A/11-1913 and W.1A/12-1913. Plate 6.13.

Lacquer samples.
Lacquer on wood. 18.3 x 7.3 x 1.1 cm. Japanese, *c*.1850-75. Acquired from Siegfried Bing in 1875. V&A: 1100-1875 (part numbers: 9; 21; 22; 23; 26; 45; 46; 59; 62; 65; 68; 69; 74; 75; 82; 84). Plate Part 1 opener.

Gift cover (*fukusa*), 'Cranes'.
Satin silk, with embroidery in silk and metallic thread. 84 x 67 cm. Japanese, mid 19th century. V&A: T.20-1923.

Box and lid.
Jade. 3.2 x 8.5 cm (diameter). Chinese, 18th century. V&A: C.1929&A-1910. Plate 6.6.

Marriage token.
Jade. 10.5 x 6 x 2.5 cm. Chinese, 18th century. V&A: C.1913-1910. Plate 6.6.

Snuff bottle.
Lapis lazuli, with a stopper of coral set in gilded metal. 6 x 4.8 x 2.5 cm. Chinese, second half of the 19th century. V&A: C.1594-1910.

Mauboussin: two bracelets.
Gold, set with carved jade, lapis lazuli or coral. Both 21 x 2 cm. French, *c*.1927. Collection Victor and Gretha Arwas, London. Plate 6.7.

Bracelet.
Carved jade, with coral set with diamonds on platinum. 19.4 x 2.7 cm. French, *c*.1925. Collection Victor and Gretha Arwas, London. Plate 6.7.

Boucheron: circular brooch.
Jade, carved lapis lazuli and platinum. 9.3 cm (max. diameter). French, *c*.1925. Collection Victor and Gretha Arwas, London. Plate 6.7.

Boucheron: Corsage ornament.
Lapis, coral, jade and onyx set with diamanté and gold; pendant in turquoise, diamond and platinum. 9 x 14.8 cm. French, 1925. Designed by Hirtz for the Paris 1925 Exhibition. The pendant remade in 1988. Collection Boucheron, Paris. Plate 24.5.

Edgar Brandt: 'Les cigognes d'Alsace', panels for a lift cage.
Lacquer and metal on wood. Main panel: 194.5 x 126 cm. French, 1928. For Selfridges, London. V&A: Circ.719-1971. Plate 20.11.

Africa

Bird mask.
Patinated wood and brass. 40 x 19 cm. Yaouré, Baoulé, Ivory Coast, early 20th century. Formerly in the collection of Paul Guillaume. Musée des Arts d'Afrique et d'Océanie, Paris: MNAM 65.9.2. Plate 7.1.

Stool.
Wood and brass. 39 x 26 x 46 cm. Bondjos, Democratic Republic of Congo (formerly Zaire), 20th century. Musée des Arts d'Afrique et d'Océanie, Paris: AF 8850. Plate 7.11.

Textile.
Raffia. 76 x 69 cm. Kuba, Democratic Republic of the Congo (formerly Zaire), early 20th century. Musée des Arts d'Afrique et d'Océanie, Paris: AP 88.1.7. Plate 7.2.

Jean Lambert-Rucki: *Tête cubiste*.
Black lacquered wood with silver inlays and mosaic. Height: 67.5 cm. French, 1920. Bröhan-Museum, Berlin: inv. no. 84.088.

Sargent Johnson: mask.
Copper with ceramic inlay. 30.5 x 26.7 x 6.4 cm. American, *c*.1934. Collection John P. Axelrod, Boston, MA. Plate 11.12.

Pierre Legrain: stool.
Lacquered wood, horn, gilding. 52 x 64.1 x 26.6 cm. French, *c*.1923. Commissioned for Jacques Doucet's apartment at 46 Avenue du Bois, Paris. Virginia Museum of Fine Arts, Richmond: 92.5. Plate 7.10.

Jean Dunand and Jean Lambert-Rucki: chair. Carved and lacquered wood. 95.5 x 49.5 x 50 cm. French, 1924. Private collection, Paris. Plate 7.9.

THE AVANT-GARDE

Pablo Picasso (Spanish): costume for the Chinese conjurer in *Parade*, choreographed by Léonide Massine for the Ballets Russes. Satin and silver cloth. Trousers: 94 x 71 cm; jacket: 149.8 x 91.4 cm. Around 1917. Theatre Museum, London: S.84B-1985. Plate 9.16.

Léon Bakst (Russian): stage design for the Ballets Russes *Schéhérazade*. Gouache and watercolour with gold highlights on paper. 54.5 x 76 cm. 1911. Musée des Arts Décoratifs, Paris: MIN B.A. ss n° (41). Plate 9.15.

Albert Gleizes: *Brooklyn Bridge*.
Oil and sand on cardboard. 148.1 x 120.4 cm. French, 1915. Collection Mr and Mrs David Mirvish, Toronto.

Jean Metzinger: *Fruit and Jug on a Table*.
Oil on canvas. 116 x 80.5 cm. French, 1916. Fanny P. Mason Fund. Museum of Fine Arts, Boston: 57.3.

Raymond Duchamp-Villon: model for the façade of the Maison Cubiste.
Replica 48 x 60 x 10 cm. Private collection, Paris. See Plate 9.14 for original.

Josef Csaky (born in Hungary): *Cônes et sphères*.
Bronze. Height: 70 cm. Around 1919. Bröhan-Museum, Berlin: inv. no. 80-037.

Alvin Langdon Coburn: *Vortograph*. Gelatin silver print. American, 1917. Royal Photographic Society, Bath: RPS488. Plate 25.3.

Sonia Delaunay (Russian): illustration for Blaise Cendrars, *La Prose du Transibérien et la petite Jehanne de France*, Paris, Editions des Hommes Nouveaux, 1913. Edition n.111. Pochoir (watercolour) on imitation Japanese paper with parchment cover. 199.1 x 35.5 cm. NAL: AM 1984-581. Plate 9.12.

Robert Delaunay: *Air, fer et eau*.
Oil on canvas. 97.4 x 151.4 cm. French, 1937. Art Gallery of Ontario.

Fernand Léger: *Nature morte à la chope*.
Oil on canvas. 92.1 x 60 cm. French, 1921-2. Tate Modern, London: T02035.

Fernand Léger: *Nature morte*.
Oil on canvas. 119.3 x 87.5 cm. French, 1919. Art Gallery of Ontario.

Constantin Brancusi (born in Romania): *Bird in Space*.
Bronze. 1935. Private collection

Fortunato Depero: 'Skyscrapers and Tunnel'. Coloured tempera panel. Italian. Museo di Arte Moderna e Contemporanea di Trento e Rovereto: MD 86-B.

Fortunato Depero: design for the advertising hall for the House of Futurist Art. Italian, 1927-8. Museo di Arte Moderna e Contemporanea di Trento e Rovereto: MD 426-A.

Cuthbert Hamilton: Vorticist plate.
Stoneware. Diameter: 17.8 cm. British, *c*.1915. V&A: C.120-1984.

Kasimir Malevich: cup and tea pot.
Porcelain. Tea pot height: 16.3 cm. Russian, 1923. Made by the Lomonosov State porcelain factory, Leningrad. Bröhan-Museum, Berlin: inv. no. 92-035.

Nikolai M. Suetin: writing set with inkpot.
Porcelain, painted in enamels. 12.4 x 14.6 cm. Russian, *c*.1925. Made by the Lomonosov State porcelain factory, Leningrad. Bröhan-Museum, Berlin: inv. no. 92-019. Plate 9.9.

Pavel Janák: coffee service.
Earthenware, painted in enamels. Coffee pot height: 22 cm; creamer height: 14 cm; sugar bowl height: 11.5 cm; cup height: 6.8 cm. Czech, 1911. UPM – Decorative Arts Museum, Prague: 30.846/1ab; 73.520.ab; 73.521.ab; 52.190.ab.

Vlastislav Hofman: coffee set.
Earthenware, painted in enamels. Coffee pot height: 17.5 cm; creamer height: 11 cm; sugar bowl height: 6.5 cm; cup height: 5 cm. Czech, 1913-14. UPM – Decorative Arts Museum, Prague: 30.850/1ab, 2, 3-5ab. Plate 16.3.

Josef Gocár: vitrine.
Black-stained oak with mahogany veneer. 165.5 x 88 x 40 cm. Czech, 1913. UPM – Decorative Arts Museum, Prague: 1388/4. Plate 16.2.

Pavel Janák: design for a monumental interior.
Ink on paper. 39.5 x 42.5 cm. Czech, 1912. NTM, Prague.

Pavel Janák: *Vision of Architecture*.
Paper. 40 x 56 cm. Czech, 1906. NTM, Prague.

Theo van Doesburg (Christian Emil Kuepper): a floor plan for the Café Aubette, Strasbourg. Paper with ink, gouache and pencil. 52.9 x 98.7 cm. Dutch, 1926. Centre Georges Pompidou, Paris. MNAM: AM 1987-1067. Plate 9.10.

ART NOUVEAU

Josef Hoffmann: fruit basket.
Silver. 27 x 23 x 23 cm. Austrian, 1904. Made by the Wiener Werkstätte. V&A: M.40-1972.

Charles Rennie Mackintosh: smoker's cabinet.
Ebonized wood with cedar wood veneer, inlaid with Erinoid. 59 x 33 x 58.4 cm. British, 1916. From Derngate, Northampton. V&A: Circ.856-1956. Plate 10.2.

Paul Follot: tea pot and creamer.
Silver. Tea pot: 16.2 x 13 cm; creamer: 10 x 14.5 cm. French, *c*.1904. V&A: M.105&A-1978.

Frank Lloyd Wright: window triptych.
Stained glass and lead. 102.7 x 165 cm. American, c.1912. Designed for the Avery Coonley Playhouse, Riverside, Illinois. V&A: C.115-1992.

NATIONAL TRADITIONS

Rob Mallet-Stevens: *Magasins de nouveautés, Cité moderne*.
Ink and pencil on paper. 48.2 x 33.5 cm. French, 1921. Centre Georges Pompidou, Paris. MNAM: AM 1987-613.

Atelier Martine: dress fabric (three samples). Block-printed satin. 43 x 84 cm; 40.5 x 84 cm; 42 x 84 cm. French, 1919. For Paul Poiret. V&A: T.539, 540, 541-1919. Plate 10.9.

Georges Lepape: plate 2 from *Les Choses de Paul Poiret vues par Georges Lepape*, Paris, 1911.
Hand-coloured pochoir. 28.6 x 29 cm. V&A: Circ.262-1976.

Paul Follot: dressing table and chair.
Carved, gilt and lacquered wood with portor marble, silk damask upholstery. Table: 132 x 120 x 48 cm; chair: 85 x 46.5 x 56 cm. French, 1919-20. Musée d'Art Moderne de la Ville de Paris: AMOA 440 & 441. Plate 8.4.

Paul Follot: carpet.
Wool. 200 x 150 cm. French, 1919-29. Made by D.I.M. V&A: T.77-1982. Plate 8.3.

René Lalique: *Deux paons*, lamp.
Glass, with moulded and cut decoration, on a Bakelite base. Height: 45.1 cm. French, *c*.1925. Made at the Lalique glassworks (Verreries d'Alsace). V&A: C.73-1972. Plate 18.1.

Otto Prutscher: tea and coffee service.
Silver and ivory. Tea pot, coffee pot, tea urn, burner, sugar bowl and tongs, tea strainer, two jugs and a tray. Tray: 58.9 x 48.1 cm; tea kettle: 25.5 x 16.6 cm; stand: 17 x 22.3 cm; tea pot: 20.9 x 14 cm; coffee pot: 21.7 x 11.2 cm; jug: 13.8 x 10.9 cm. Austrian, c.1920. V&A: M.38-1970. Plate 8.11.

Waldemar Raemisch: silver candlestick.
Silver. Height: 52 cm. German, c.1927. Bröhan-Museum, Berlin: inv. nos 91-055, 93-907.

Melkiorre Melis: vase.
Earthenware, painted in enamels. 35.6 x 21.6 cm. Italian, c.1923. The Mitchell Wolfson Jr Collection. The Wolfsonian-Florida International University, Miami Beach, Florida: 84.7.17. Plate 8.13.

Einar Forseth: tapestry sample.
Linen, wool and gold thread. 160 x 187 cm. Swedish, 1924. Woven by Elsa Gullberg at the Konserthuset textile studio, Stockholm. Donated by Anders Tengbom, Yvonne Wetterholm and Ann-Mari von Bismarck. National Museum, Stockholm: 136/1972. Plate 17.11.

The Paris 1925 Exhibition

Robert Bonfils: poster for the Paris 1925 *Exposition internationale des arts décoratifs et industriels modernes*. Colour woodblock. 60 x 39.7 cm. French, 1925. Printed by Imprimerie Vaugirard, Paris. V&A: E.1200-1925. Plate 10.1.

Pierre Turin: medal.
Struck bronze. 0.5 x 8.3 cm (diameter). French, 1925. Made by Paris Mint, for the Paris 1925 Exhibition. V&A: Circ.1-1973.

'GRAND SALON', 'HÔTEL DU COLLECTIONNEUR'

Stéphany for Jacques-Emile Ruhlmann: wall covering.
Woven silk and cotton. 204 x 130 cm. French, 1925. Made by Cornille Frères. Musée de la Mode et du Textile, Union Centrale des Arts Décoratifs, Paris: inv. no. 25168. See Plate 12.13 for the sample in the Musée Historique des Tissus, Lyon.

Jacques-Emile Ruhlmann, Jean Dunand, Jean Lambert- Rucki and Jean Goulden: cabinet.
Black lacquer with incised silver decoration. 195.5 x 248.9 x 73.6 cm. French, 1925. De Lorenzo, New York. Plate 12.9.

Jacques-Emile Ruhlmann: 'Table araignée'.
Macassar ebony veneer. 85 x 60 x 60 cm. French, 1918-19. V&A: Circ.328-1967. Plate 12.12.

Jean Dupas: *Les Perruches*.
Oil on canvas. French, 1925. Xavier Roberts Collection. Plate 12.14.

Antoine Bourdelle: *Héraklès archer*.
Bronze. 60 x 57 x 30 cm. French, cast 1909. Exhibited in the 'Grand Salon' of the 'Hôtel du Collectionneur' at the 1925 Paris exhibition. Fourth study, first composition, with head of the Commandant Doyen Parigot. Cast by Rudier. Musée Bourdelle, Paris: MB BR 1243. Plate 12.10.

François Pompon: *Ours blanc*.
White marble. 30.5 x 44.5 x 10.16 cm. French, designed in 1920. Private collection, New York.

Jacques-Emile Ruhlmann: pair of armchairs.
Macassar ebony veneer and bronze, with Aubusson tapestry by Emile Gaudissart. French, c.1925. Private collection, New York. Plate 12.15.

Jacques-Emile Ruhlmann: Banquette.
Macassar ebony veneer and bronze, with Aubusson tapestry by Emile Gaudissart. French, c.1925. Private collection, New York. Plate 12.15.

'PAVILLON D'UNE AMBASSADE FRANÇAISE'

André Groult: chiffonnier.
Mahogany, ivory and sharkskin. 150 x 77 x 32 cm. French, 1925. Musée des Arts Décoratifs, Paris: inv. no. 998.257.1. Plate 12.7.

Marie Laurencin: *Portrait of a Woman (L'ambassadrice)*.
Oil on canvas. 98 x 67 cm. French, 1925. Signed *'A Nicole Groult, ton amie, Marie'*. Private collection. Plate 12.6.

Pierre Chareau: desk.
Oak and mahogany with rosewood veneer. 77.5 x 139.7 x 77.5 cm. French, 1925. Primavera Gallery, New York.

BOUTIQUES

Mannequin head.
Hand-painted metal. 79 x 31 x 22 cm. Probably French, c.1925. V&A: T.3-2002. Plate 23.1.

Cloche hat.
Pink straw with appliqué trim. 17 x 22.6 cm (diameter). British, c.1925. Made by Kilpin Ltd. V&A: T.442-1977. Plate 23.1.

Sonia Delaunay (Russian): jacket.
Cotton, wool and silk. Height: 70 cm. 1924. Musée de la Mode et du Textile, Paris. Collection of the Union Française des Arts du Costume: UF 65-10-2. Plate 13.10.

Natalia Goncharova (Russian): dress.
Silk appliqué. 122 x 58 cm. French, 1924-6. Made by Myrbor. V&A: Circ.329-1968. Plate 23.4.

ENGLISH PAVILION

Sir Edward Maufe: writing desk.
Mahogany, camphor wood and ebony, gessoed and gilded with white gold; ivory and rock crystal; silk handles. 107 x 134.3 x 53 cm. British, 1925. V&A: Circ.898-1968. Plate 20.1.

Harold and Phoebe Stabler: 'The Bull'.
Press-moulded stoneware. 33.5 x 33.5 x 14 cm. British, designed 1914. Made c.1921-4 by Carter, Stabler & Adams (Poole Pottery, Dorset). V&A: C.113-1977. Plate 20.1.

Minnie McLeish (attr.): furnishing fabric.
Roller-printed cotton. 132 x 71 cm. British, 1920-25. Made by William Foxton, London. V&A: Circ.667-1966.

Gregory Brown: furnishing fabric.
Roller-printed cotton. 274.3 x 132 cm. British, 1922. Made by William Foxton, London. V&A: T.325-1934. Plate 20.8.

AUSTRIAN PAVILION

Josef Hoffmann: bowl.
Gilded metal. 18 x 29 cm. Austrian, c.1924. V&A: M.41-1972. Plate 1.11.

DUTCH PAVILION

Michel De Klerk: sideboard.
Mahogany, mahogany veneer, plywood and brass hardware. 75.6 x 81.9 x 49.5 cm. Dutch, c.1917. Commissioned by F.J. Zeegers for 't Woonhuys. Made by 't Woonhuys. The Mitchell Wolfson Jr Collection. The Wolfsonian-Florida International University, Miami Beach, Florida: 1989.328.4.

Michel De Klerk: armchair.
Mahogany, mohair velvet upholstery, leather straps and brass. Dutch, c.1915-16. 99.7 x 83.8 x 82.3 cm. Commissioned by F. J. Zeegers for 't Woonhuys. Made by 't Woonhuys. The Mitchell Wolfson Jr Collection. The Wolfsonian-Florida International University, Miami Beach, Florida: TD1989.328.2a-b.

Jaap Gidding: carpet.
Wool. 310 x 224 cm. Dutch, 1920. Rijksmuseum, Amsterdam: BK-1979-36. Plate 15.15.

Carel Adolph Lion Cachet: 'Mermaid', furnishing fabric.
Velvet. 136 x 93 cm. Dutch, 1918. Made by Schellens en Marto. Rijksmuseum, Amsterdam: BK-1971-194.

Jan Eisenloeffel: clock.
Bronze, partly gilded, and enamel. 62 x 70 x 16 cm. Dutch, 1925. Stedelijk Museum, Amsterdam: KNA 286. Plate 15.12.

Johannes Steltman: tea service.
Silver and cornelian. Tea pot: 10.5 cm; sugar bowl: 7.2 cm; creamer: 6.2 cm. Dutch, 1925. Haags Gemeentemuseum, The Hague: mme 1980 0008, 0009, 0010. Plate 15.13.

H. A. van den Eijnde: urn.
Silver. 60.3 x 21.5 x 21.5 cm. Dutch, 1918. Made by J. M. Van Kempen & Zn. Museum Boijmans Van Beuningen, Rotterdam: MBZ 348.

CZECH PAVILION

Frantisek Kysela: *Pottery*.
Wool tapestry. 270 x 241 cm. Czech, 1925. Made by Marie Teinitzerová at Jindrichův Hradec tapestry workshops. UPM – Museum of Decorative Arts, Prague: inv. no. 97.187. Plate 16.4.

Frantisek Drtikol: *Composition 1925*.
Bromoil print. 28.1 x 22.3 cm. Czech, 1925. UPM – Museum of Decorative Arts, Prague: GF40296. Plate 25.4.

Frantisek Drtikol: *Reclining Form*.
Bromoil print. 29 x 23.5 cm. Czech, 1925. UPM – Museum of Decorative Arts, Prague: GF 40380.

Jaroslav Horejc (Czech): *Abundance of Nature*, vase.
Cut and engraved glass. Height: 17.3 cm. 1922-3. Made by Lobmeyr. UPM – Museum of Decorative Arts, Prague: 65 908. Plate 18.6.

Jaroslav Horejc (Czech): *Three Goddesses*, vase.
Cut and engraved glass. Height: 20.8 cm. 1922-3. Made by Lobmeyr. UPM – Museum of Decorative Arts, Prague: d-1072/1.

ITALIAN PAVILION

Fortunato Depero: *Serrada*.
Wool tapestry. 313 x 272 cm. Italian, 1920. Museo di Arte Moderna e Contemporanea di Trento e Rovereto: PAT 002642. Plate 19.1.

Gio Ponti and Libero Andreotti: 'La conversazione classica'.
Porcelain. 57 x 31.5 cm. Italian, 1927. Made by Manufattura di Doccia, Richard-Ginori. Museo Poldi Pezzoli, Milan: inv. no. 3358. Plate 19.2.

SWEDISH AND DANISH PAVILIONS

Arthur Carlsson Percy: tureen.
Earthenware, painted in enamels. Height: 36 cm. Swedish, 1930. Made by Gefle Porslinsfabrik, Gävle. Similar to the tureen displayed in the Paris 1925 Exhibition. National Museum, Stockholm: NMK 174/1930. Plate 17.10.

Eric Grate: 'Bergslagsurnan' (Metallurgy), urn.
Cast iron. 106 x 80 cm. Swedish, 1919. Made by Näfveovarns Bruk. National Museum, Stockholm: NMK57/1923.

Simon Gate: 'Parispokallen' ('Paris cup'), vase with cover.
Engraved glass. 75 x 47 cm. Swedish, 1922. Made by Orrefors. Given to the City of Paris. Musée d'Art Moderne de la Ville de Paris: AMOA 476. Plate 17.6.

Edvard Hald: *Fireworks*, vase and stand.
Blown and engraved glass. Stand: 2 x 20.2 cm (diameter); vase: 20.5 x 26.6 cm (diameter). Swedish, 1921-30. Made by Orrefors. V&A: Circ.52&a-1931. Plate 18.5.

Edvard Hald: *Negro Hut*, vase with cover.
Blown and engraved glass. Height: 25.7cm. Swedish, designed in 1918. Made by Orrefors. Bröhan-Museum, Berlin: inv. no. 83-014.

Erik Gunnar Asplund: 'Senna', chair.
Mahogany, leather and ivory. 112 x 92 x 115 cm. Swedish, 1925. Made by David Blomberg. Nordiska Museet, Stockholm: 280.237. Plate 17.9.

The Spread of Deco

THE EXOTIC

René Buthaud: vase. Stoneware. 23.5 x 24 cm (diameter). French, c.1920. V&A: C.292-1987. Plate 7.7.

Eileen Gray (Irish): screen.
Lacquer on wood, with silver leaf veneer. 207 x 435 x 1.7 cm (each panel: 207 x 54 x 1.7 cm). French, 1928. V&A: W.40-1977. Plate 6.12.

Eileen Gray (Irish): 'Pirogue', day bed.
Lacquered wood with silver leaf. 72 x 270 x 64.9 cm. Around 1919-20. Virginia Museum of Fine Arts, Richmond: 85.112. Plate 11.10.

John Raedecker: *Personification of Amersterdam, Amstel and IJ*.
Carved wood. 200 x 120 x 30 cm; base: 8 x 120 x 35 cm. Dutch, 1927-8. In the former Council Hall of the Town Hall, now Amsterdam Grand Hotel. Stedelijk Museum, Amsterdam: VBA 786.

Jean Dunand: pair of vases.
Lacquered brass and wrought iron. Both 152 x 44 cm (diameter). French, c.1931. Musée d'Art Moderne de la Ville de Paris: AMOA 1. Plate 11.4.

Jean Dunand: *Les peuples d'Asie, Indochine* and *Les peuples d'Afrique, Cameroun*, pair of decorative panels.
Lacquer on aluminium. Each panel: 348 x 180 cm. French, 1930. From the Bibliothèque du Musée des Colonies. Musée des Arts d'Afrique et d'Océanie, Paris: AF3889-4; AF3889-2. Plate 11.3.

André Granet and Roger-Henri Expert: *Fontaine de la belle fleur* at the 1931 *Exposition coloniale internationale* in Paris. Gouache and pastel on paper. 61.5 x 38.5 cm. French, c.1930-31. Institut Français d'Architecture, Paris. Fonds Granet.

André Granet and Roger-Henri Expert: *Fontaine du théâtre d'eau* at the 1931 *Exposition coloniale internationale* in Paris. Gouache on paper. 51 x 70 cm. French, 1931. Institut Français d'Architecture, Paris. Fonds Granet.

Armand Rateau: torchère.
Patinated bronze and marble. 185 x 54.5 cm. French, c.1920-22. For Jeanne Lanvin. Musée des Arts Décoratifs, Paris: inv. no. 39908 A, B.

Armand Rateau: chaise-longue.
Patinated bronze. 64 x 153 x 60 cm. French, 1920-22. For Jeanne Lanvin. Musée des Arts Décoratifs, Paris: inv. no. 39902. Plate 11.9.

Edgar Brandt: wall-light.
Wrought iron. 59.5 x 57.5 x 22 cm. French, c.1922. V&A: Circ.264-1971.

Raoul Dufy: *La danse*. Furnishing fabric.
Printed linen. 182 x 127 cm. French, c.1925. Made by Bianchini-Férier. V&A: Circ.113-1939. Plate 8.14.

Raoul Dufy: furnishing fabric.
Printed linen. 119 x 127 cm. French, c.1920. Made by Bianchini-Férier. V&A: Misc.2:30-1934. Plate 10.7.

Raoul Dufy: *Les conques*, furnishing fabric.
Printed linen. 118 x 171.5 cm. French, c.1924. Made by Bianchini-Férier. V&A: Circ. 112-1939.

René Buthaud: vase.
Earthenware painted in enamels. 28.5 x 21 cm (diameter). French, c.1926. Musée des Arts Décoratifs: inv. no. MIN B.A. 8935.

Gustav Miklos (Hungarian): carpet.
Wool. 156 x 85 cm. Around 1921. For the apartment of Jacques Doucet in Neuilly. Musée des Arts Décoratifs, Paris: inv. no. 38161.

Pierre Legrain: chair.
Palm wood veneer, lacquer and parchment. 78 x 45 x 45 cm. French, c.1924. For the apartment of Jacques Doucet in Neuilly. Musée des Arts Décoratifs, Paris: inv. no. 38139.

Marcel Coard: armchair.
86 x 66 x 78.5 cm. French, c.1920-25. For the apartment of Jacques Doucet in Neuilly. Musée des Arts Décoratifs, Paris: inv. no. 38156.

Josef Csaky (born in Hungary): sculpture of a head.
Crystal and onyx. 33.8 x 10.5 x 10 cm. Around 1930. Private collection, Paris. Plate 9.8.

Jacques Lipchitz (born in Lithuania): fire surround.
Limestone. 46.5 x 150.5 x 32.7 cm. French, c.1929. For the apartment of Jacques Doucet in Neuilly. Museum of Fine Arts, Boston: 1986-4. Plate 9.7.

Jacques Lipchitz (born in Lithuania): pair of andirons.
Gilt bronze and iron. 37 x 37 x 58 cm. French, c.1928. For the apartment of Jacques Doucet in Neuilly. Museum of Fine Arts, Boston: 1984.5-6.

Etienne Cournault: pair of glass panels.
Verre églomisé. Height of each panel: 6.35 cm. French, c.1931. For the apartment of Jacques Doucet in Neuilly. Primavera Gallery, New York.

Jean Fouquet: necklace and bracelet.
Ebony, chrome-plated metal and gold. Necklace diameter: 15.5 cm; bracelet diameter: 181.1 cm. French, 1931. Private collection, New York. Plate 24.19.

Van Cleef & Arpels: bracelet.
Ivory, coral and gold. Diameter: 21.6 cm. American, 1931. Private collection, New York. Plate 24.12.

Jean Dunand: bracelet.
Silver and enamel. 9.5 x 5.7 to 6.7 cm (diameter). French, 1927. Formerly in the collection of Mme Agnès. Collection Zoya Gerhath. Plate 7.6.

Georges Fouquet: brooch.
White gold, blue enamel, diamonds. 8 x 9.2 cm. French, c.1931. Private collection. Plate 24.4.

Man Ray (American): model wearing a necklace by Jean Fouquet.
Gelatin silver print. 22.86 x 17.78 cm. Around 1931. Private collection, New York. Plate 24.18.

Man Ray (American): *Noire et blanche*.
Gelatin silver print, positive. 17.7 x 23.6 cm. 1926. Private collection. Plate 25.9.

Man Ray (American): *Noire et blanche*.
Gelatin silver print, negative. 17.7 x 23.6 cm. 1926. Private collection. Plate 25.10.

Paul Colin: plates from *Le Tumulte noir*, Paris, Editions d'Art Succès, 1927.
Colour pochoir. 47.3 x 31.8 cm. NAL: L.1228-1983.

Tamara de Lempicka (born in Poland): *La Belle Rafaëla*.
Oil on Canvas. 64 x 91 cm. 1927. Private collection, London

THE MODERNE

Walter Gilbert: frieze panel.
Cast and painted aluminium. 43.5 x 192.2 x 2.5 cm. British, 1933. Made by Bromsgrove Guild for Derry & Toms, Kensington High Street, London. V&A: M.262-1984. Plate 1.6.

Raymond Hood: door surround.
Enamelled iron. 60 x 124 cm. British, c.1928. For Ideal House, National Radiator Company building, Regent Street, London. V&A: M.75-1982.

Maurice Marinot: vase.
Blown and engraved glass. Height: 31.8 cm. French, 1923. V&A: C.3&a-1964. Plate 18.3.

Camile Fauré: vase.
Silvered and enamelled copper. 29.3 x 31.6 cm (diameter). French, c.1925. V&A: C.57-1978.

Liqueur set.
Dark, smoke-coloured glass. Decanter height: 25.5 cm. Czech, c.1930. Made by Moser, Karlovy Vary-Dvory. UPM – Museum of Decorative Arts, Prague: 92895ab, 92901. Plate 18.7.

Aristide-Michel Colotte: vase.
Polished glass. Height: 21 cm. German, 1927. Bröhan-Museum, Berlin: inv. no.75-001.

Jean Goulden: clock.
Silvered bronze with enamel. 36.2 x 25.7 x 12.4 cm. French, 1928. Collection Stephen E. Kelly. Plate 9.1.

Jean Puiforcat: clock.
Nickel-plated bronze with white marble. 19 x 19 x 3.8 cm. French, 1932. Primavera Gallery, New York. Plate 1.7.

Tétard Frères: 'Eclipse', tea and coffee service.
Silver. Coffee pot height: 12.5 cm. French, 1931. Bröhan-Museum, Berlin: inv. no. 91-048.

Luciano Baldessari: 'Luminator', standing lamp.
Chrome-plated steel. 184 x 80 x 65 cm. Italian, 1929. Museo di Arte Moderna e Contemporanea di Trento e Rovereto: MART 101. Plate 19.9.

Jean-Jacques Adnet: chandelier.
104.1 x 83.8 cm. French, c.1929. Primavera Gallery, New York. Plate 14.9.

Robert Block: dressing table.
Black lacquered wood, mirror and clear plastic. 132 x 153 x 44 cm. Swiss, c.1935. V&A: W.36-1987.

Syrie Maugham: mirrored screen.
Silvered wood and mirrored glass. Each panel: 203 x 50 x 3.3 cm. British, 1935. V&A: W.146-1978. Plate 20.4.

Denham Maclaren: chair.
Glass, metal fixings and zebra skin upholstery. 68 x 57 x 85 cm. British, 1931. V&A: W.26-1979. Plate 33.5.

Christian Barman: electric fan heater.
Chrome-plated metal. 30.5 x 41.5 x 31 cm. British, 1938. Made by HMV. V&A: W.71-1978.

Betty Joel: carpet.
Wool. 180.5 x 105 cm. British, 1935-7. V&A: T.296-1977. Plate 20.6.

Edward McKnight Kauffer: *Soaring to Success! Daily Herald - The Early Bird*. Poster. Colour lithograph. 299 x 152.2 cm. American, 1918-19. V&A: E.35-1973. Plate 20.7.

Raymond McGrath: Fischer's restaurant, exterior perspective.
Pencil and coloured chalks on paper. 22 x 34.2 cm. British, 1932. V&A: Circ.565-1974.

Raymond McGrath: Fischer's restaurant, interior perspective.
Watercolour. 64 x 69 cm. British, 1922. V&A: Circ.566-1974.

Auguste Bonaz: necklace.
Galalith. 22.9 x 15.2 cm. French, 1930s. Primavera Gallery, New York. Plate 24.20.

René Lalique: box and cover.
Bakelite. 2.4 x 7.5 (diameter) cm. French, c.1935. V&A: C.15-1981. Plate 1.5.

Dressing-table box and cover.
Bakelite. 10.2 x 10.2 x 7.6 cm. British, 1930s. Made by Halex Ltd. V&A: W.55-1983.

Ashtray.
Bakelite. 8.4 x 8.9 cm. British, c.1935. Made by Roanoid Ltd. V&A: C.54-1984.

Ashtray.
Bakelite. 8.4 x 8.9 cm. British, c.1935. Made by Roanoid Ltd. Collection John Jesse.

Clarice Cliff: 'Inspiration', jug.
Earthenware painted in enamels. 25 x 17 cm. British, c.1930. V&A: C.76-1976.

Clarice Cliff: 'Sunray', vase.
Earthenware, painted in enamels. 13.3 x 15.4 cm. British, c.1929-30. Made by Arthur J. Wilkinson Ltd. V&A: C.74-1976. Plate 21.4.

Chris van der Hoef: tea service.
Earthenware painted in enamels. Pot and cover: 27.5 x 11.2 cm (diameter); teapot: 19 x 10.5 cm (diameter); sugar bowl: 16 x 8.5 cm (diameter); creamer: 11.2 cm (height); tea cup and saucer: 5 x 8.5 cm (diameter); bowl: 8 x 16 cm (diameter). Dutch, 1926. Made by N. V. Plateelbakkerij Zuid Holland, Gouda. Museum Boijmans Van Beuningen, Rotterdam: V 971 (V974 a,b) (Kn&V); V 972 a-f (KN&V).

Nora Guldbrandsen: coffee set.
Porcelain. Coffee pot: 20.4 x 20.2 x 12.9 cm; creamer: 8.8 x 11.7 x 8.2 cm; sugar bowl: 10.5 x 13.9 x 10.1 cm. Norwegian, 1929-31. Made by Porsgrund Porselaensfabrik. V&A: C.144-1987. Plate 17.12.

Eva Stricker: tea service.
Stoneware. Tea pot: 13.5 x 25 cm. German, c.1930. Made by Schramberg faience factory. Bröhan-Museum, Berlin: inv. no. 81-500. Plate 15.4.

Ludwig Gies: 'Jazzkapelle'.
Porcelain. Height: 36 cm. German, 1925. Made by Staatliche Porzellan-Manufaktur, Berlin. Bröhan-Museum, Berlin: inv. no. 82-083. Plate 15.3.

Charlotte Calm-Wierink: head of a girl.
Earthenware, painted in enamels. Height: 22.6 cm. Austrian, 1920-25. Made by the Wiener Werkstätte. V&A: C.185-1986. Plate 15.8.

Jean Luce: two plates.
French. Cooper-Hewitt, National Design Museum, Smithsonian Institution.

Figure.
Porcelain, painted in enamels. 37.7 x 20.1 cm. Austrian, 1920-35. Made by Goldscheider. V&A: C.52-1985.

Percy Metcalf: 'Lion'.
Glazed earthenware. 38.1 x 30.5 cm. British, 1924. Made by Ashtead Potters. V&A: C.20-1925.

Susie Cooper: ginger jar.
Earthenware, painted in enamels. 34.3 x 30.5 (diameter) cm. British, c.1926-7. Made by Susie Cooper Pottery. V&A: C.193-1977. Plate 21.5.

John Skeaping: 'A Group of Axis Deer'.
Earthenware. Height: 18.1 cm. British, 1927. Made by Josiah Wedgwood & Sons Ltd. V&A: C.426-1934. Plate 21.7.

Raoul-Eugène Lamourdedieu: lamp stand.
Silver-plated bronze, marble and glass. 42.8 x 35 x 13 cm. French, c.1930. V&A: Circ.197-1972. Plate 4.4.

Demêtre Chiparus (Romanian): *Les Girls*.
Bronze and ivory. 54 x 65 x 20 cm. Around 1930. Private collection, New York. Plate 4.8.

Oliver Bernard: partial reconstruction of the foyer of the Strand Palace Hotel, London. Glass, marble, metallic mounts and fixtures. 1930-1. V&A: Circ.758-1969. Plate 20.13.

Elsa Schiaparelli (Italian): evening coat.
Scarlet taffeta. 200 x 128 cm (arms outstretched). 1939. V&A: T.52-1965. Plate 23.12.

Jeanne Lanvin: evening dress.
Purple satin. 146 x 112 cm (circumference of the hem). French, winter 1935. V&A: T.340-1965. Plate 23.9.

Chanel: evening dress.
Sequins on chiffon. 152 x 156 cm (circumference of the hem). French, 1932. V&A: T.339-1960. Plate 23.6.

Madeleine Vionnet: evening dress.
Pink satin, with diamanté buckle. 152 x 140 cm (circumference of the hem). French, 1933. V&A: T.203-1973. Plate 23.10.

Jean Patou: evening dress.
Beaded crêpe. 146 x 84 cm (circumference of the hem). French, 1937. V&A: T.336-1974. Plate 23.8.

Charles James: evening gown.
Black satin. 152 x 79 cm (circumference of the hem). British, 1936-7. V&A: T.290-1978. Plate 23.13.

Gérard Sandoz: cigarette case.
Silver, enamel, lacquer and eggshell. 8.3 x 10.4 x 0.7 cm. French, c.1929. V&A: Circ.329-1972.

Lacloche Frères: vanity case.
Jade, diamonds and onyx. 8.3 x 4.8 cm. French, c.1925. V&A: M.24-1976. Plate 24.7.

Cigarette case
Enamel. 8.25 x 6.35 cm. British, 1931. Hallmarked London 1931 and stamped R & R (Ramsden & Roed). Collection John Jesse.

Handbag.
Aluminium and plastic. 15 x 22.5 x 2 cm. French, c.1925. V&A: T.238-1982.

René Lalique: set of glasses.
Pre-moulded transparent glass. Madeira glass: 18.4 x 11.8 cm (diameter); burgundy glass: 18.2 x 7.8 cm (diameter); champagne glass: 17.7 x 6.8 cm (diameter); liqueur glass: 16.2 x 6.2 cm (diameter). French, c.1925. Made at the Lalique glassworks (Verreries d'Alsace). V&A: Circ.34-1970 A-C. Plate 18.2.

Cigarette box.
Silver and ivory. 13.8 x 8.6 cm. British, 1938-9. Made by H. Murphy. V&A: Circ.228&a-1938.

Cigarette lighter.
Chromium plated steel and white plastic. 5.6 x 9.2 x 11.1 cm. American, c.1925. Made by the Art Metal Works Inc. for Ronson, Newark. V&A: Circ.266-1971. Plate 1.16.

Cocktail shaker.
Electroplated nickel silver, with chrome finish. 25 x 7.2 (diameter) cm. British, c.1930. Made by Mappin & Webb. V&A: M.226-1984.

Cigarette holder.
Silver. Height: 18 cm (35 cm open). Around 1925. V&A: Circ.40-1972.

Florence Henri: advertisement for 'Parfums Jeanne Lanvin'.
Gelatin silver print. 25.2 x 19.6 cm. French, 1929. V&A: PH.272-1982. Plate 25.12.

Cecil Beaton: *Miss Nancy Beaton as a Shooting Star*.
Gelatin silver print. 50.5 x 39.3 cm. British, 1929. V&A: PH.965-1978. Plate 25.13.

Edward Steichen: Art Deco clothing design, photographed in the apartment of Nina Price. Gelatin silver print. 34.3 x 27.2 cm. Published in American *Vogue*, 1 June 1925. Condé Nast, New York. Plate 25.5.

Man Ray (American): *Study for Anatomies*.
Gelatin silver print. 23.5 x 17.5 cm. French, c.1930. Centre Georges Pompidou, Paris. MNAM: AM 1995-281 (389).

Man Ray (American): *Electricité*.
Photogravure. 26 x 20.5 cm. French, 1931. From the *Electricité* portfolio published by the Compagnie Parisienne de Distribution de l'Electricité. V&A: E.1653-2001. Plate 25.11.

Cartier: vanity case with greyhounds.
Enamelled black on gold, with diamonds, emeralds and ruby. 9.5 x 7.7 x 2 cm. French, 1920. The Pierre Cartier Foundation: FPC11.

Cartier: vanity case with panther.
Gold, rubies, emerald, sapphire, diamonds, turquoise, mother-of-pearl and enamel. 10.2 x 4.3 x 1.5 cm. French, 1925. Private collection, Switzerland. Plate 24.6.

Cartier: pylon pendant.
Diamonds and onyx in open-back platinum setting. 7.75 x 4.9 cm. French, 1913. Cartier Collection, Geneva: NE 01 A13. Plate 24.1.

Cartier: brooch.
Carved ruby and onyx, drop-shaped pearl, briolette-cut pink tourmaline, diamonds and onyx. 15.2 x 3.5 cm. French, 1914. Private collection. Plate 24.3.

Cartier: 'tree' tiara.
Platinum, diamonds, onyx and natural pearls. 4 x 15 cm. French, 1914. Private collection.

Cartier: 'Persian style' fringe necklace.
Platinum, emerald and diamonds. 16 x 23 cm. French, 1932. Cartier Collection, Geneva: NE25 A32.

Georges Fouquet: tassel necklace.
Frosted rock crystal, nylon, onyx and enamel. Pendant: 19 x 4.5 cm. French, 1925. Private collection, New York. Plate 24.16.

Jean Fouquet: bracelet and ring.
Crystal, amethysts, moonstone and platinum. Bracelet diameter: 8.2 cm; ring: 2.8 cm. French, c.1930. Primavera Gallery, New York. Plate 24.11.

Jean Fouquet: bracelet.
White and yellow gold with onyx. 19 x 3.2 cm. French, c.1930. Primavera Gallery, New York. Plate 24.14.

Jean Fouquet: bracelet.
White gold with diamonds and aquamarines. Diameter: 58 cm. French, c.1930. Private collection, Landsbro, Inc. Plate 24.10.

Raymond Templier: brooch.
Diamonds set in platinum. 3 x 2 cm. French, 1928. Collection Victor and Gretha Arwas, London. Plate 24.15.

Raymond Templier: bracelet with brooch.
Silver, platinum, gold, onyx and diamonds. 5.3 x 5.8 x 6.4 cm. French, c.1925-30. Gift of the Sydney and Frances Lewis Foundation. Virginia Museum of Fine Arts, Richmond: 85.257a/b. Plate 24.13.

Gérard Sandoz: 'Guitar', pendant.
Frosted crystal, labradorite, lacquer, pink and white gold and black silk. Pendant: 12.7 x 5 cm. French, c.1928. Private collection, New York. Plate 24.17.

Rose Adler: binding for Sidonie-Gabrielle Colette, *Chéri*, Paris, Editions de la Roseraie, 1925. Edition number 48/100. Morocco leather, stamped and foiled. 28 x 22.9 x 4.8 cm. French, 1925. Gift of Sydney and Francis Lewis. Virginia Museum of Fine Arts, Richmond: 85.37 a/b. Plate 27.5.

Paul Bonet: binding for André Marty, *La Petite Ville*, Paris, 1927.
30.5 x 20.3 x 3.2 cm. French, 1927. Private collection, New York. Plate 27.3.

Robert Bonfils: binding for Abbé A. F. Prévost, *Manon Lescaut*, Paris, 1931.
Red morocco with gilt tooling, black onlays and watered silk doublures. 24 x 19.5 x 5.7 cm. French, 1931. Collection Victor and Gretha Arwas, London. Plate 27.1.

Madeleine Kohn: binding for Paul Morand, *Tendres stocks*, Paris, Emile-Paul Frères, 1924.
Morocco, with inlays and gold tooling. 25.6 x 18.5 x 2.5 cm. French, c.1924. NAL: L.3518-1958.

Sybil Pye: binding for *The Apocrypha*, London, New York, Nonesuch Press, Dial Press, 1924.
Black morocco, with orange onlays and gold tooling. 31.6 x 21 x 2.6 cm. British, 1924. NAL: L.494-1938. Plate 27.4.

Pierre Legrain: binding for Franz Toussaint, *Le Jardin des caresses*, Paris, H. Piazza, 1914. Calf inlaid with morocco, gilt tooling. 31 x 23.9 x 3.5 cm. French, c.1914 . NAL: Circ.663-1972. Plate 27.6.

Pierre Legrain: binding for Charles Nodier, *Histoire du chien Brisquet*, Paris, Pelletan, 1900.
Dark blue morocco, with fawn onlays, gold and blind tooling, gilt edges. 29.9 x 23.8 x 2.8 cm. French, c.1950. Made by Jacques-Anthoine Legrain after an earlier design by Pierre Legrain. NAL: L.800-1951.

Louis Creuzevault: binding and inside covers for a *de luxe* edition of *Le Cantique des cantiques*, translated by Ernest Renan, Paris, François-Louis Schmied, 1925.
Black calf with gold-tooled lettering; inlaid leather on inside covers. 25.3 x 19 x 2.8 cm. French, 1925. NAL: L.2564-1983. Plate 27.7.

Binding for Anatole France, *Balthasar*, Paris, Ferroud, 1926.
Dark red calf with inlay of calf and niger of various colours; gilt and blind tooling. 19 x 13.8 x 2.1 cm. French, 1926. NAL: L.6240-1982. Plate 3.3.

The Deco World

TRAVEL AND TRANSPORTATION

Jan and Joel Martel: 'Locomotive in Motion' train model.
Sheet aluminium and lacquered wood. 40 x 100 x 20 cm. French, 1931. Collection Stewart Johnson, on loan to the Metropolitan Museum of Art, New York.

Cassandre (Adolphe Mouron): *Nord Express*, poster.
Colour lithograph. 105.4 x 75 cm. French, 1927. V&A: E.223-1935. Plate 29.1.

J. R. Tooby: *Empress of Britain, Canadian Pacific Railways*, poster.
Colour lithograph. 101.6 x 63.5 cm. British, c.1931-40. Printed by Sanders, Phillips & Co. V&A: E.2215-1931. Plate 29.7.

Roger Broders: *Marseille: Porte de l'Afrique du Nord*, poster.
Colour lithograph. 101.6 x 63.5 cm. French, 1920-32. Printed by Lucien Serre & Co. V&A: E.3642-1932.

Horace Taylor: *The Royal Mail Line to New York*, poster.
Colour lithograph. 101.6 x 63.5 cm. British, 1920-25. Printed by Sanders, Phillips & Co. V&A: E.516-1925.

Roger Broders: *Le tour du Mont Blanc. Paris-Lyon-Méditerranée*, poster.
Colour lithograph. 101.6 x 63.5 cm. French, 1927. Printed by Lucien Serre & Co. V&A: E.519-1929. Plate 29.2.

A. E. Mason: *Johannesburg: The Metropolis of South Africa*, poster.
Colour lithograph. 101.6 x 63.5 cm. South African, c.1930. The Mitchell Wolfson Jr Collection. The Wolfsonian-Florida International University, Miami Beach, Florida: TD1989.5.12.

Mexico, poster.
Colour lithograph. 99.44 x 68.6 cm. Mexican, c.1935. The Mitchell Wolfson Jr Collection. The Wolfsonian-Florida International University, Miami Beach, Florida: XX1992.224.

Satomi: *Japan, Japanese Government Railways*, poster.
Colour lithograph. 103.3 x 63.2 cm. Japanese, 1937. Printed by Seihan Printing Company. V&A: E.2043-1938. Plate 29.5.

Poster for Soviet Armenia.
Colour lithograph. 101.6 x 63.5 cm. Russian, c.1936. Issued by Intourist. V&A: E.2666-1938.

Sugiura Hisui: *The Only Subway in the East: Service between Ueno and Asakusa is Started*, poster.
Colour lithograph. 91.8 x 82 cm. Japanese, 1927. National Museum of Modern Art, Tokyo. Plate 35.8.

Cassandre (Adolphe Mouron): *Normandie, Le Havre–Southampton–New York*, poster.
Colour lithograph. 100 x 64 cm. French, 1935. Collection William W. Crouse.

Jupp Wiertz: 'A pleasant trip to Germany', poster. Colour lithograph. 100 x 64 cm. German, 1936-7. Probably German National Railways. Collection David Benrimon.

Louis Vuitton: travel case or *nécessaire Marthe Chenal*.
29 x 52 x 15 cm (closed). French, 1925. Musée Louis Vuitton, Asnières. Plate 14.2.

INDIA

Canopy bed.
Silver-covered wood. 206 x 154 x 216 cm. Indian, 1922. Attributed to craftsmen from the princely state of Udaipur, Orissa. Made for the Maharajah of Surguja. Talisman, Dorset, UK. Plate 36.1.

Narotamdas Bhau: tea service.
Silver and celluloid. Tea pot: 15.9 x 19.1 x 5.4 cm; creamer: 12.7 x 13.3 x 4.1 cm; sugar bowl: 7.6 x 10.5 x 5.1 cm; sugar tongs: 11.4 x 1.9 cm. Indian, c.1920-29. The Mitchell Wolfson Jr Collection. The Wolfsonian-Florida International University, Miami Beach, Florida: 85.9.24.1, 2, 3a-b, 4. Plate 36.15.

Bernard Boutet de Monvel: *The Mahajara of Indore in Occidental Dress*.
Oil on canvas. 210 x 110 cm. French, 1929. Private collection. Plate 36.5.

Bernard Boutet de Monvel: *The Mahajara of Indore in Maratha Dress*.
Oil on canvas. 180 x 180 cm. French, 1934. Private collection. Plate 36.6.

Eckart Muthesius: chair.
Leather, frosted glass and silver-plated nickel. 94 x 89 x 110 cm. German, c.1930. Made for the library of the Maharajah of Indore. Private collection, London.

JAPAN

Hyōsaku Suzuki II: lacquer cabinet.
Lacquer on wood. 83.5 x 112.5 x 30.5 cm. Japanese, 1937. Kyoto Municipal Museum.

Haruji Naitō: wall clock.
Cast bronze. Japanese, 1927. National Museum of Modern Art, Tokyo. Plate 35.6.

Shinobu Tsuda: *Fighting Cock*.
Cast bronze. 55 x 16 x 27 cm. Japanese, 1934. Kyoto Municipal Museum.

Katsuaki Toyoda: vase.
Bronze. 40 x 35 cm (diameter). Japanese, 1937. National Museum of Modern Art, Kyoto.

Robukei Kyomizu VI: vase.
Earthenware, painted in enamels. 45.5 x 31.6 cm (diameter). Japanese, 1933. Kyoto Municipal Museum.

Frank Lloyd-Wright: dinner set.
Porcelain. Cup: 5.7 x 10.9 cm; bowl: 4.5 x 19 cm; plate 27.1 cm (diameter). Japanese, designed c.1922. Made in 1984 by Noritake-Heinz & Co. for the Imperial Hotel, Tokyo. V&A: C.223 A to C-1984.

CHINA

Jacket for a woman.
Silk and sequins. 105 x 49 x 5 cm (collar depth). Chinese, c.1922. V&A: FE.61-1995.

Qipao (*cheong sam*)
Silk. Chinese, 1930s. Private collection.

AUSTRALIA

Fisk Radiolette, model 33.
Black and green phenolic. 33 x 29.8 x 22.8 cm. Australian, c.1936. Collection Jeffrey S. Salmon, London. Plate 33.7 (left)

Michael O'Connell: 'Bacchantes', furnishing fabric.
Printed cotton. 159 x 119 cm. British, 1937. Made by Edinburgh Weavers. V&A: Circ.472-1939. Plate 38.10.

AMERICA

Manhattan Modern and the Skyscraper Aesthetic

Charles Turzak: *Man with Drill*.
Woodcut on paper. 43.2 x 35.6 cm. American, c.1937. Collection John P. Axelrod on loan to the Museum of Fine Arts, Boston.

John Storrs: *Forms in Space, Number 1*.
Stainless steel and copper. 72.4 x 14.3 x 13.5 cm. American, c.1924. M. Francis Lathrop Fund, 1967. The Metropolitan Museum of Art, New York: 67.238. Plate 9.13.

Ruth Reeves: 'Manhattan', furnishing fabric.
Block-printed cotton. 254 x 94 cm. American, 1930. Made by W. & J. Sloane, New York. V&A: T.57-1932. Plate 31.8.

Owen H. Ramsburg: Rockefeller Center architectural model, RCA building.
Basswood. Model base: 106.7 x 304 cm. Around 1935. Museum of the City of New York: 98.128.1.

Hugh Ferris: *Manhattan Bank Company Building*.
Charcoal and pencil on paper. 96 x 18.1 cm. American, c.1929 Museum of the City of New York: 39.468.

Margaret Bourke-White: *Top of the Chrysler Building, New York*.
Gelatin silver print. 13.6 x 9.5 cm. American, 1931. Ford Motor Company Collection. Gift of Ford Motor Company and John C. Waddell, 1987. The Metropolitan Museum of Art, New York: 1987.110.338. Plate 5.1.

Rene Paul Chambellan: entrance gates to the executive suite, 52nd floor, Chanin building, New York.
Wrought iron and bronze. American,1928. Gift of Mr Marcy Chanin. Cooper-Hewitt, National Design Museum, Smithsonian Institution. Plate 31.3.

Paul T. Frankl (born in Austria): desk and bookcase.
Walnut, paint and brass handles. 210.8 x 124 x 54 cm. American, c.1928. For Frankl Galleries, New York City. Collection John P. Axelrod on loan to the Museum of Fine Arts, Boston. Plate 31.7.

Walter von Nessen: table lamp.
Silvered brass. 78.7 x 46.4 cm. American, 1928. Made by Nessen Studio, Inc. Gift of John C. Waddell, 1998. The Metropolitan Museum of Art, New York: 1998.537.41a-d.

Norman Bel Geddes: 'Manhattan', cocktail set.
Chrome-plated brass. Shaker: 33 x 8.3 cm; tray: 36.8 x 29.2 cm; each cup: 11.4 x 6.4 cm. American, 1937. Made by Revere Copper & Brass Company, Rome, NY. Gift of John C. Waddell, 1998. The Metropolitan Museum of Art, New York: 1998.537.11ab-18. Plate 32.5.

Louis W. Rice: 'Skyscraper', cocktail shaker.
Electroplated nickel silver. 28.3 x 18.4 x 10.5 cm. American, 1928. Made by Bernard Rice's Sons, Inc., New York. John C. Waddell Collection. Promised gift of John C. Waddell. The Metropolitan Museum of Art, New York. Plate 32.3.

Jan Matulka (born in Czechoslovakia): *Musical Instruments*.
Oil on canvas. 108 x 90.2 cm. Collection John P. Axelrod on loan to the Museum of Fine Arts, Boston. Plate 2.8.

Ralph Barton: 'Gentlemen Prefer Blondes', dress fabric.
Crêpe de Chine. 50 x 47.5 cm. American, 1927. Stehli Silks Corporation. V&A: T.87L-1930.

Viktor Schreckengost: punch bowl from the 'Jazz Bowl' series.
Glazed porcelain with sgrafitto decoration. 22.9 x 42.9 cm (diameter). American, 1931. Made by the Cowan Pottery Studio, Rocky River, Ohio. Gift of Susan Morse Hilles in memory of Paul Hellmuth. Museum of Fine Arts, Boston: 1990.507. Plate 31.9.

Maija Grotell: vase.
Earthenware. 32.1 x 18.4 cm. American, 1938-45. Museum of Fine Arts, Boston: 1985.812.

American Deco

John Gutmann (born in Germany): *Elevator Garage, Chicago*.
Gelatin silver print. 23.6 x 17.8 cm. American, 1936. Ford Motor Company Collection. Gift of Ford Motor Company and John C. Waddell, 1987. The Metropolitan Museum of Art, New York: 1987.1100.122. Plate 2.1.

Paul Strand: *Akeley Motion Picture Camera*.
Gelatin silver print. 24.5 x 19.5 cm. American, 1922. The Metropolitan Museum of Art, New York: 1987.1100.3.

Ralph Steiner: *Power Switches*.
Gelatin silver print. 19 x 24.2 cm. American, c.1930. The Metropolitan Museum of Art. New York: 1987.1100.277.

Sturtevant Lincoln: *Bank Interior*.
Gelatin silver print. 24 x 19 cm. American, 1938. The Metropolitan Museum of Art, New York: 1987.1100.447.

Edward Steichen: *Spectacles*.
Gelatin silver print. 27.2 x 34.3 cm. American, 1927. Fabric design for Stehli Silks Corporation. V&A: Circ.970-1967. Plate 25.6.

Donald Deskey: screen.
Wood, canvas, paint and metal fittings. 148.6 x 194.4 cm. American, c.1930. Collection John P. Axelrod, Boston, MA, on loan to the Museum of Fine Arts, Boston. Plate 31.1.

Donald Deskey: 'Lysistrata', screen.
Lacquer on wood and chrome. 135.2 x 212.7 cm. American, c.1930. Designed for the dining room of Gilbert Seldes' apartment. Xavier Roberts Collection.

Paul Frankl: hair brush, comb and mirror.
Celluloid and mirrored glass. Mirror: 28 x 15 cm; brush: 17.2 x 10.2 x 3.4 cm; comb: 19 x 5.1 x 0.7 cm. American, 1930. Collection John P. Axelrod on loan to the Museum of Fine Arts, Boston.

Paul T. Frankl (born in Austria): dressing table.
Lacquered wood, brass and mirrored glass. 172.7 x 221 x 48.3 cm. Mirror: 150 cm (diameter). American, c.1930. Collection John P. Axelrod, Boston, MA. Plate 34.2.

Eugene Schoen: étagère.
Bakelite, bronze and chestnut wood. 118.7 x 129.5 x 36.2 cm. American, 1929. Purchase, Robert and Meryl Feltzer Fund Gift, 1984. Gift of Robert and Meryl Feltzer Fund. The Metropolitan Museum of Art, New York: 1984.320. Plate 33.2.

Peter Müller-Munk (born in Germany): tea service.
Silver and ivory. Tea pot: 25.7 x 23.5 x 18.5 cm; water pot: 20.3 x 24.4 x 7 cm; sugar bowl: 12.7 x 19.7 x 8.3 cm; creamer: 11.4 x 15.9 x 5.7 cm; tray: 1.5 x 62.9 x 34.9 cm. American, 1931. Gift of Mr and Mrs Herbert R. Isenburger, 1978. The Metropolitan Museum of Art, New York: 1978.439.1-5. Plate 32.1.

Walter Von Nessen: 'Coronet', coffee urn.
Chrome-plated metal, plastic and glass. 31.8 x 28 x 25.4 cm. American, 1929. Made by Chase Brass & Copper Company. Museum of Fine Arts, Boston: 41.1987.

Tiffany & Co.: mirror set.
Silver, mahogany and velvet. 42.2 x 39.7 x 33.3 cm. American, 1935. Collection John P. Axelrod, Boston, MA, on loan to the Museum of Fine Arts, Boston.

Donald Deskey: table lamp.
Chrome-plated metal and glass. 31.1 x 11.1 x 14.3 cm. American, c.1927. Made by Deskey-Vollmer. Collection John P. Axelrod, Boston, MA, on loan to the Museum of Fine Arts, Boston. Plate 31.5.

Sidney Biehler Waugh: 'Gazelle', bowl.
Glass. 18.4 x 16.5 (diameter) cm. American, 1935. Made by Steuben Glassworks. Purchase, Edward C. Moore, Jr, Gift, 1935. The Metropolitan Museum of Art, New York: 35.94.1ab.

Pavel Tchelitchew: 'Acrobats', vase.
Engraved glass. 31.6 x 28 cm. American, 1939. Made by Steuben Glassworks. V&A: Circ.86-1952.

Sidney Biehler Waugh: 'Zodiac', plate.
Wheel-engraved glass. Diameter: 40.5 cm. American, 1935. Made by Steuben Glassworks. V&A: C.112-1935.

Industrial Design, Styling and Streamlining in America

Boris Lovett-Lorski: *Venus*.
Bronze. 238 x 98 x 55.5 cm (base: 12 x 57.5 x 51.5 cm). American, cast in Paris by Alexis Rudier, c.1932. Musée d'Art Moderne de la Ville de Paris: AMS353.

High-Voltage Railway Electrification, mosaic panel.
Aluminium and Micarta laminate. 124.5 x 246.4 cm. American, 1933. From the Westinghouse pavilion at the 1933 *Century of Progress Exposition*. The Mitchell Wolfson Jr Collection. The Wolfsonian-Florida International University, Miami Beach, Florida: 83.6.11a-c. Plate 33.6.

Kem Weber (born in Germany): 'Zephyr' electric clock.
Brass and Bakelite. 8.3 x 20.3 x 7.9 cm. American, c.1934. Made by Lawson Time Inc. Gift of David A. Hanks, 1986. The Metropolitan Museum of Art, New York: 1986.418.2. Plate 10.13.

Walter Dorwin Teague: Kodak Bantam Special, camera.
Painted brass, glass and leather. 8.3 x 11 x 4.5 cm. American, designed 1933-6. Made by Kodak Company, Rochester, New York. Royal Photographic Society, Bath.

Walter Dorwin Teague: three Beau Brownie cameras in blue, black and brown. American, 1930-33. Made by Eastman Kodak. Royal Photographic Society, Bath. Plate 9.2.

Russel Wright: pitcher, from 'American Modern' dinnerware.
Earthenware. 27 x 21.6 x 16.8 cm. American, designed in 1937. Made by Steubenville Pottery Company. V&A: Gift of Charles Zemaitis.

Frederick Hurten Rhead: 'Fiestaware'. Earthenware. American, 1936. Designed for Laughlin China Company. Cooper-Hewitt, National Design Museum, Smithsonian Institution: large plate: 1991-68-2; small plate: 1991-68-4; pitcher: 1991-68-14; tumbler: 1991-68-13; cup and saucer: 1991-68-10; demi-tasse and saucer: 1991-68-12; bowl: 1991-68-5.

J. Palin Thorley: refrigerator pitcher with tray.
Earthenware. 19.4 x 9 x 23.5 cm. American, 1940. Designed for Westinghouse Electric Company. Gift of David A. Hanks, 1981. The Metropolitan Museum of Art, New York: 1998.537.3ab.

Norman Bel Geddes and Worthen Paxton: 'Soda King' syphon bottles.
Chrome-plated metal, brass, paint and rubber. Each bottle: 24.8 x 11.1 cm. American, 1938. John C. Waddell Collection. Promised gift to the Metropolitan Museum of Art, New York: L.2000.600.6-8.

Peter Müller-Munk (born in Germany): 'Normandie', water pitcher.
Chrome-plated brass. 30.5 x 7.6 23.8. American, 1935. Made by Revere Copper and Brass Company. Anonymous gift, 1989. The Metropolitan Museum of Art, New York: 1989.394. Plate 34.7.

Norman Bel Geddes: 'Patriot', radio, model 400.
Catalin. 18.5 x 26.5 x 13.6 cm. American, 1940. Made by Emerson Radio and Phonograph Corporation. V&A: W.31-1992. Plate 10.3.

Harold Van Doren and John Gordon Rideout: Air-King radio.
Plaskon urea formaldehyde. 29.2 x 22.2 x 19 cm. American, c.1934. Made by Air-King Products Company. Collection Jeffrey S. Salmon, London. Plate 33.7 (right).

Gilbert Rohde: electric clock.
Chrome-plated and enamelled metal and glass. 16.5 x 29.2 x 12.7 cm. American, c.1933. Made by Herman Miller Clock Company. John C. Waddell Collection. Promised gift to the Metropolitan Museum of Art, New York: L.2001.1.31.1.

Gilbert Rohde: desk lamp.
Chrome-plated steel and brass. 17.8 x 35.6 x 5.78. American, 1933. Made by Mutual-Sunset Lamp Manufacturing Company, Inc. John C. Waddell Collection. Promised gift to the Metropolitan Museum of Art, New York: L.2000.600.16.

Kem Weber (born in Germany): airline chair.
Wood and Naugahyde. 80.7 x 64.1 x 93.5 cm. American, 1934. Collection John P. Axelrod, Boston, MA. Plate 34.1.

Walter Dorwin Teague: 'Nocturne', radio, model 1186. Glass, metal and wood. 115.6 x 110.5 x 39.4 cm. American, c.1936. Made by Sparton Corporation, Jackson, MI. The Mitchell Wolfson Jr Collection. The Wolfsonian-Florida International University, Miami Beach, Florida: XX1990.168.

Ice gun.
Enameled and chrome-plated steel. 16.5 x 27.9 x 7 cm. American, c.1935. Made by Opco Company, Los Angeles. John C. Waddell Collection. Promised gift of Mark A. McDonald to the Metropolitan Museum of Art, New York: L.2001.2.

John Vassos (born in Romania): portable phonograph, model RCA Victor Special. Aluminium, chrome-plated steel, plastic and velvet. 20 (54.5 open) x 42 x 43 cm. American, c.1930. Made by RCA. V&A: W.1-1997. Plate 33.12.

Egmont Arens and Theodore C. Brookhart: 'Streamliner', meat slicer.
Aluminium, steel and rubber. 34.3 x 53.3 x 38.1 cm. American, designed in 1940, manufactured from 1944. Made by Hobart Manufacturing Company. Gift of John C. Waddell, 2002. The Metropolitan Museum of Art, New York: 2000.600.1. Plate 34.4.

Paul Fuller: jukebox, model 700.
Metal and glass. Manufactured by Wurlitzer. 143 x 84 x 64 cm. American, 1940. Norman Terry Jukeboxes, Norfolk.

Gordon Miller Buehrig, Auburn 851 'Boat Tail' Speedster. South African Grand Prix, 1936. American, 1935. Private collection.

Name Index

Note: The following includes artists, architects, decorative artists, designers, photographers, film-makers and designers, 'stars', and others who contributed to the Deco phenomenon or its contemporary interpretation.

Illustration plate numbers are in *italic*, and listed after the page numbers. Page numbers in **bold** indicate chapters.

Subject Index

Note: Illustration plate numbers are in *italic*, and listed after the page numbers. Page numbers in **bold** indicate chapters, or an extended treatment.